UNEQUAL LIVES

GENDER, RACE AND CLASS IN THE WESTERN PACIFIC

UNEQUAL LIVES

GENDER, RACE AND CLASS IN THE WESTERN PACIFIC

EDITED BY NICHOLAS BAINTON, DEBRA MCDOUGALL,
KALISSA ALEXEYEFF AND JOHN COX

Australian
National
University

PRESS

PACIFIC SERIES

ANU
PRESS

Published by ANU Press
The Australian National University
Acton ACT 2601, Australia
Email: anupress@anu.edu.au

Available to download for free at press.anu.edu.au

ISBN (print): 9781760464103
ISBN (online): 9781760464110

WorldCat (print): 1231438133
WorldCat (online): 1231438255

DOI: 10.22459/UE.2020

Cover design and layout by ANU Press

Cover artwork: John Siune, Papua New Guinea, 1965–2016.
*Boi pren na girl Pren Tupela I stap long Port Morsbi city. Tupela lusim pasin bilong ples na
kisim pasin bilong wait man (Boyfriend and girlfriend live in Port Moresby city. They leave
traditional ways behind and take on whiteman style)* 1999.
Synthetic polymer paint on yellow medium weight cardboard, 90 x 65cm.
Purchased 2017, Queensland Art Gallery | Gallery of Modern Art Foundation.
Collection: Queensland Art Gallery | Gallery of Modern Art.
© Estate of John Siune
Photograph: Natasha Harth, QAGOMA

Contents

Preface: Scholar, Teacher, Mentor, Friend: Essays in Honour
of Martha Macintyre vii

Prologue: Pragmatism, Prescience and Principle xi
Neil Maclean

1. Unequal Lives in the Western Pacific 1
    Nicholas Bainton and Debra McDougall

2. 'I Will Be Travelling to Kavieng!': Work, Labour and Inequality
    in New Ireland, Papua New Guinea 47
    Paige West and John Aini

3. The Unequal Place of Anthropology in Cross-Disciplinary
    Research on Environmental Management in the Pacific and
    What to Do About It 77
    Simon Foale

4. The Problem of the Semi-Alienable Anthropologist 109
    Melissa Demian

5. Global Health, Tuberculosis and Local Health Campaigns:
    Reinforcing and Reshaping Health and Gender Inequalities
    in Lihir, Papua New Guinea. 131
    Susan R. Hemer

6. The Missionary's Dilemma: A Short History of Christian Marriage
    and its Impact upon Gender Equality in Maisin Society. 157
    John Barker

7. Gendered Ambition and Disappointment: Women and Men
    in a Vernacular Language Education Movement in Melanesia 183
    Debra McDougall

8. Stingy Egalitarianism: Precarity and Jealousy at the
    Sisiak Settlement, Madang, Papua New Guinea. 213
    Deborah Gewertz and Frederick Errington

9. Inequalities of Aspiration: Class, Cargo and the Moral Economy
    of Development in Papua New Guinea 237
    John Cox

10. Exiles and Empty Houses: Contingent Events and Their Aftermath
    in the Ok Tedi Hinterland 267
    Dan Jorgensen

11. Transforming Inequalities and Uncertainty: Gender, Generational
    and Class Dimensions in the Gende's *Longue Durée* 305
    Laura Zimmer-Tamakoshi

12. From Donation to Handout: Resource Wealth and Transformations
    of Leadership in Huli Politics. 335
    Michael Main

13. Measuring Mobilities and Inequalities in Papua New Guinea's
    Mining Workforce 359
    Colin Filer

14. Menacing the Mine: Double Asymmetry and Mutual
    Incomprehension in Lihir. 401
    Nicholas Bainton

15. Intersecting Inequalities, Moving Positionalities: An Interlude 439
    Margaret Jolly

Coda: A Legacy of Engaged Anthropology

Encountering Anthropology: An Interview with Martha Macintyre 471
Martha Macintyre and Alex Golub

Personal Reflections and Tributes to Martha Macintyre

First Contact with Martha 505
Chris Gregory

Martha and Me in the 1990s. 509
Bronwen Douglas

Humour, Homes and Gardens: Martha, Feminism and Anthropology . . .521
Kalissa Alexeyeff

I First Met Martha Macintyre Twice: Or How I Became
an Anthropologist 527
John Cox

What Would Martha Do? Confessions of a Hypochondriac in the Field . . .531
Michael Main

Martha, My Mentor 537
Sarah Richards-Hewat

Martha: My Friend, My Role Model 541
Dora Kuir-Ayius

The Work of Martha Macintyre, So Far 545

Contributors 555

Preface: Scholar, Teacher, Mentor, Friend: Essays in Honour of Martha Macintyre

This volume emerges from a two-day gathering in February 2019 at the University of Melbourne to celebrate the work of Martha Macintyre, whose four decades of groundbreaking scholarship exemplify the contributions that anthropologists make to grappling with the challenges of inequality. The first day involved the presentation of tributes and celebratory papers by close colleagues, friends and former students, some of which can be found at the end of this volume. The day concluded with a celebratory dinner that featured somewhat raucous (and largely unpublishable) informal speeches by Colin Filer, Margaret Jolly, Mary Patterson and Deborah Gewertz. The second day comprised a scholarly workshop titled 'The persistence of inequality in the Pacific', in reference to Martha's seminal 1998 paper on the persistence of gender inequality in Papua New Guinea (PNG) and her enduring ethnographic attention to the issue of inequality in its many guises.

Crossing the boundaries between academic and applied work, Martha's research has focused on some of the most pressing problems that have been faced by Papua New Guineans: poverty, ill health, criminal violence and police violence, environmental destruction and the impacts of resource extraction. Throughout her corpus, she has tracked the effects of unequal power relationships between men and women. Whether writing of classic anthropological subjects such as Massim exchange and mortuary ritual or gender relations, masculinity, health and medicine, human rights, law and order, mining and development or political ecology, Martha has investigated the ways that unequal social relationships within and beyond indigenous societies generate physical, structural and symbolic violence. Her work highlights distinctively Melanesian understandings of personhood but also always analyses cultural difference as emerging within a broader context of historical change.

In an era when anthropology, generally, and Melanesian anthropology, in particular, has tended towards abstractions—grand theorisations of the nature of the person, the cosmos or social relations—and where ethnographic detail is sometimes valued only for the ways it serves theory, Martha has given primacy to these wicked real-world problems of unequal social relations. She cuts through assumptions that are often taken for granted and prevailing ideologies to grasp better the experiences, frustrations and perspectives of those people that she writes about and collaborates with. Indeed, the force of her writing often comes from her indignation at the injustice of a world in which some lives are valued more than others, and access to resources and opportunities flow from these valuations.

Martha has continued to return to PNG, which is by no means an easy place to conduct research. Her sustained on-the-ground engagement with her ethnographic interlocutors, Papua New Guinean colleagues and co-researchers is evident in her writing, which is incisive and sophisticated but always written with a broader audience in mind. Martha is a former president of the Australian Anthropological Society, and she was editor of its flagship journal, *The Australian Journal of Anthropology*, from 2008 to 2015. In 2012, she was elected a Fellow of the Academy of Social Sciences in Australia and she is a Life Fellow of the Australian Anthropological Society and the Association for Social Anthropology in Oceania. She has inspired several generations of anthropologists with a remarkable legacy of teaching and mentoring. Moreover, she has been instrumental in laying down the foundations for a future generation of anthropologists to find new ways of making anthropology relevant and useful in the lives of others.

Here, we have merely sketched the contours of this remarkable career—we can do no better than to point readers to Neil Maclean's perceptive Prologue to discover Martha's multifaceted scholarship. The first chapter of this collection then orientates readers to the question of inequality in the Western Pacific, past and present, to situate the substance of this volume and the focus of Martha's research. The longer chapters that comprise this book take issues that have been at the core of her work as a starting point for exploring multiple dynamics and scales of inequality as we enter the third decade of the twenty-first century. Margaret Jolly's characteristically cogent Interlude provides a moment to reflect upon the connecting themes throughout the volume, followed by a coda comprising an edited interview with Martha that charts her experiences and encounters with anthropology and a bibliography of her work to date. This provides the setting—or the *mise en scène*—for a series of personal tributes to Martha as scholar, teacher, mentor and friend.

Nick Bainton, Debra McDougall, Kalissa Alexeyeff, and John Cox
December 2020

Note: January 2021
It is with deep sorrow we acknowledge one of our contributors who died in the days before this volume went to press. Fred Errington was a great friend to all of us and, together with the love of his life Deborah Gewertz, produced foundational studies of class and social change in Melanesia. Fred was a towering figure in anthropology and worked to encourage others and nurture their ideas. This volume carries the imprint of his collegiality and scholarship.

Prologue: Pragmatism, Prescience and Principle

Neil Maclean

The advantage of reflecting on a good career is that one also reflects on the value of academia and the diverse strands that make it up. Martha's has been an excellent career to reflect upon. In her tribute to Martha (included at the end of this volume), Dora Kuir-Ayius has given us the metaphor of the *bilum* (a woven string bag) to describe this. In this volume, her colleagues, students and collaborators celebrate Martha as writer, researcher, teacher and supervisor, editor, policy activist and participant observer. The *bilum* metaphor asks us to consider the way those strands feed off each other to motivate a career that demonstrates both strength and form. Here, I will concentrate on the intellectual, ethical and political form of Martha's work. However, I also want to acknowledge Martha's sustained contributions to anthropology in Australia, including her work as editor of *The Australian Journal of Anthropology* and the work involved in supporting anthropology through the Australian Research Council process.

What struck me, both as I revisited Martha's work and listened to the speakers at the workshop that formed the genesis for this volume, was the coherence of intellectual, ethical and political underpinnings; the intellectual conceptualisation of methods, problems and concepts; the ethical obligation to register inequality and injustice and also to pay attention to people's own goals and the political imperative to get things done.

Martha and I both first visited Papua New Guinea (PNG) in 1979. This was a time when the perspective on anthropology was both historical and material, and the context, of course, was postcolonial. Martha came to that context not only with a historical consciousness but also well and truly steeped in a century of the historiography, archaeology and ethnography of the *kula* ring (a regional trading network in PNG). What is remarkable in one of Martha's first papers, 'Warfare and the changing context of "kune" on Tubetube' (1983), is the piecing together of evidence from different points in the regional space of the Massim and different points in time and the situation of interpretations of both warfare and the *kula* in their regional and historical specificity. The article sets the stage for Martha's sustained critical scepticism of the assumption of 'culture'.

Her empirical attitude is pre-cultural in the sense that it values the regional sense of material flows and political dynamics, rather than privileging the perspective of supposedly distinctive cultural positions within those regions—part of that 'translocal microregionalism' identified by Lederman (1998, p. 440) as a through line of the literature on Melanesia. Martha's empirical attitude is also post-cultural, in the sense that she views the politics of these regions as integral to Melanesians' responses to both the violence and possibilities of colonial and postcolonial contexts. It is from the point of view of the convergence of pre-cultural and post-cultural perspectives that Martha mounts her rejection of the closure or equilibrium model of the *kula* ring (a similar convergence forms a key point of Lederman's take on the 'culture area').

From my reading, this rejection is key to Martha's work, because it brings into play the connection between historical perspective and questions of agency that runs through her work. It envisions the Massim as a set of interconnections—where the horizon of a politics lies elsewhere, with people who may or may not be persons.

This brings me to the next major strand in her work. I remember a 1994 conversation with Martha about the implications of Marilyn Strathern's *Gender of the gift* (1988), particularly the configuration of agency, individuality and personhood. Martha was particularly concerned with what she understood to be the exclusion of objectification as an integral aspect of the treatment of socially significant human others in Melanesian social systems—in other words, that these social systems might, at critical moments, depend on the denial of personhood to others. The result of this concern was her 1995 paper, 'Violent bodies and vicious exchanges: Personification and objectification in the Massim'. She rejected the mapping of the following oppositions onto one another: commodity logic/gift logic, reification/personification and Western/Melanesian.

She critiqued this as a 'benign' view that elides specifically Melanesian connections between violence and reification and the integral role these play in the dynamics of exchange (Macintyre, 1995, p. 34).

In the Massim context, 'partibility encompasses ideas of dismemberment, destruction and violence' (Macintyre, 1995, p. 34) and also depersonalisation (1995, p. 32). The classification of captives in war as *gum* is telling:

> We called them 'our meat'. We called them *gum*. *Gum*, this word is old. It means a payment of flesh. Before, that man or child or woman was somebody. But we call them *gum*. Not a person, just our thing. We address the captive as *gum*. (Macintyre, 1995, p. 35)

The point of Martha's analysis was not the cultural dominance of either personification or objectification, but rather that both were integral moments of a dialectics of exchange and violence. Her informant Pansi 'explains quite clearly that the personification of a group of people in the captive is necessary for the objectification of the *gum* to have force and meaning' (1995, p. 38).

This dialectic of objectification and personification is made particularly clear in an account of the reclaiming of a female captive by her kin group. Martha showed that:

> she as a person is first objectified, then given a social identity within a group, then bargained for in terms of her substitutability, then personified as a mother within Tubetube social space, and finally reconstituted within her natal group by virtue of her exchangeability for pigs and valuables. (1995, p. 38)

This series of moves were based on the capacity for the 'abstraction' of the woman's reproductive capacity; therefore, Martha's implication is that these dialectics are intrinsic to exchanges surrounding marriage. It is telling that the violence of that abstraction is noted in the account itself: 'our daughter is not a pig, we do not want pigs. You cannot substitute for her with mwali or bagi' (1995, p. 38).

For Strathern, the pivot (or elbow) is the key to her conception of an agent who acts with 'another in mind' (1988, p. 272). For Martha, it is the exploitation of this dialectic of personification and objectification, the figure of the *gum* that opens up the possibilities of agency. Over time, her work has developed in such a way as to allow the discussion to exist in parallel to distinctive contemporary forms of male and female agency. Three strands of discussion have been particularly salient: violence and the intersections of Christianity and domesticity, on the one hand, and of work and money, on the other.

Martha's work has been integral to the development of the literature on the intersection of gender and modernity and of the specific problem of masculinity within that framework. The three key ways in which a critique of culture has had formative impacts on anthropology are also key to her work: a genuinely historical anthropology, fundamental concern with the way that anthropology as practice and as a body of data has been embedded in colonialism and its legacy, and gender as a generative and foundational form of difference. She has been particularly concerned with the intersection of masculinity and violence (Macintyre, 2008). Martha renewed her critique of Strathern's emphasis on partibility and of the dominant role it had assumed in accounts of Melanesian social reproduction. In her view, this account obscures the significance of 'relations of conflict and exclusion', and by extension from previous work of objectification, that are 'manifest in situations of contestation and rivalry' (Macintyre, 2008, p. 180) and integral to the historical dynamics of Melanesian societies. In Martha's view, it is only by recognising these historical continuities that we can understand the ways in which such capacities for violence have intersected with the forms of violence and alienation that are peculiar to modernity. One side of this argument concerns how the 'view that "strangers were enemies" and the parochial dimensions of conflict in the past continue to be expressed in settings where conflict arises' (2008, p. 187). In this way, new sources of violence may be folded back into a distinctively segmentary political dynamics. However, Martha has also argued that what is at stake here are not only tactical and strategic understandings of male agency but also 'continuities in masculine embodiment and self-presentation, as both beautiful and dangerous' (2008, p. 181)—the figure of the Melanesian Rambo is key in this context. Most tellingly, it is only if we recognise these continuities that we can understand the ways in which young Melanesian men turn against their own relational social contexts in embracing forms of hyper-masculinised autonomy. In Martha's view, the only adequate approach is to ground both dynamics in forms of historical continuity.

A similar kind of argument for a historically specific understanding of Melanesian engagements with modernity is to be found in Martha's work with Margaret Jolly (1989) on domesticity, family and gender in the Pacific. In their Introduction, they emphasise the convergence of three factors or processes:

1. the *longue durée* of the impact of Christianity, colonialism and trade on these systems
2. the enormous variability of Melanesian domestic and household relationships and their articulation within a wider politics
3. the considerable variations in European takes on domesticity, sexuality and gender that were engaged in this history.

In part, this model speaks to the feedback dynamics of this history, in which local transformations in Christianity in one part of the Pacific inform later missionising processes in other parts. Equally important, however, are the very active two-way processes through which mission models find their fit with local domestic and gender relationships: 'the link between missionary desires, actual mission models, and perceived changes in Pacific domesticity is not a direct chain of causation' (Jolly & Macintyre, 1989, p. 11). It is in the undetermined nature of that chain that Martha finds agency.

To describe what I understand Martha to envision in these histories, I return to what is conventionally represented as the opposition between gift and commodity forms and reinstate them as forms of historical continuum, consistent with Mauss' account. When these two meet in Martha's imagination, they do not do so in mutual antagonism and incomprehension, but rather as a kind of exploratory finding of fit— potentially exploitative, but also liberating, forms of fit. In this idea, the potential for the commodified and objectified form of exchange is always inherent in the concealed interest of the gift. Further, what meets is not only the gift and its politics but forms of work and forms of violence. Martha's work invites questions not only of logical histories of money, but also logical histories of the gift and of violence. All three are grasped as exhibiting internal dynamics of objectification and abstraction, even as they exist in tension with relationality and partibility. In this, we find the internal connection between Martha's anthropology and her engagement with development studies and a range of consultancy projects with gender, work and resource politics at their heart.

I have already emphasised that Martha's historical perspective disposes her to critique closed, or simply self-sustaining, models of culture. This is equally a function of her ethical bent. This raises not only the imperative to understand but also questions about wellbeing and rights and of their intimate companions, violence and power—about the future, about capabilities and their denial and the morality of labour. Martha has always discussed the way women remain prisoners of certain kinds of social dynamic, but she has also placed emphasis on the moments at which they, often suddenly and surprisingly, walk away from them, as indeed may men (Biersack, Jolly & Macintyre, 2016; Macintyre, 2011, 2017). She identifies women who move into the wage economy as a way of gaining direct control of wealth and who then move back into the gift economy of kinship as transactors in their own right (Macintyre, 2011). As I read Martha, it is not only the commodifying power of money—reciprocal independence, in Gregory's terms (1982, pp. 100–101)—that allowed women such mobility, but also the potential within the gift economy itself for an objectifying perspective. I believe her view to be that, unless we work to understand what enables people to walk away from such dynamics, and what futures they see in those contexts, our broader social theory will remain impoverished. The dynamics of fit that I discussed above form part of the way in which Martha approaches this. Equally important are feminist critiques of masculine models of individuality and autonomy, such as possessive individualism, and a recognition of the importance of care and the way it is religiously mediated in PNG, as a continuity in Melanesian modernity.

However, I believe there to be a kind of transhistorical understanding of capability, and of key human processes such as labour, that enables Martha to see and work with a critique of culture in both understanding these contexts and in approaching them as policy and local political issues. In this, we see the quite radical nature of her divergences from Strathern's more Dumontian take on difference. At the same time, she clearly wants to avoid being trapped into the Nussbaum (2000) and Sen (1999) ethnocentrism of tradition as (by definition) 'unfreedom' and of agency as an idealised civic without inherent potentialities for violence. She is equally concerned to avoid the faux universalism of human rights regimes in her engagement with Merry and the 'vernacularisation' of rights (cited in Biersack & Macintyre, 2016, pp. 10–12).

There are two keys to the way Martha steers a course between the Scylla and Charybdis of the assumptions of cultural coherence, on the one hand, and of the abstractions of rights and capabilities, on the other. One is her career-long commitment to research based on participant observation: the understanding of people and their actions in the real context of their lives and the sustained tracking of people and contexts over time. In this way, culture reappears not as the assumption of coherence, but rather as the concrete specificities of context and the carefully recorded and analysed meaning-based forms of agency through which people build lives and imagine futures in those contexts. The other lies in the sustained character of her writing over time: a commitment to writing complexity as an understanding of the complex of relationships and interests that converge in a situation. Three features of Martha's writing struck me: her insistence that readers pay attention to detail and find the argument within it; a commitment to clear writing, accompanied by a refusal to allow readers to evade complexity, and an ever-present awareness of the past and its diversity, which informs a writing problem firmly embedded in the 'what is' of the present.

A 2006 article Martha wrote for the *Development Bulletin* on indicators of violence against women brought much of this into focus. Her overall points were clear—there is no point in collecting numbers if they are not used, and you cannot use the numbers if you do not understand how and why they were collected. Her description of her own practice is salutary in its detail:

> In my own work, monitoring crime in an area where there is a large mining project, I note the reports that are recorded in the occurrence book, noting every person who comes and speaks to the police officer at the desk. I also note whether any action was taken, any investigation or charges laid. Does she withdraw the charges? Does this lead to a court case? Does the victim of the crime turn up to court? Is the person convicted? Depending on which dataset I chose to go with, I could have a prevalence rate of 0.5 per cent or 15 per cent. I know that under-reporting is a problem in all countries, but how do I decide what to multiply it by to estimate actual prevalence? (Macintyre, 2006, p. 61)

In sum, Martha writes against closed systems and de-contextualised abstractions. She methodologically works to understand people in their context; however, she does not write to trap them in it. She names the interests that actors bring to specific contexts and insists on giving those interests explanatory power and ethical force, whether negative or positive. Martha's work is pragmatic in the very best sense that William James gave to the term:

> [she] turns away from abstraction and insufficiency, from verbal solutions, from bad *a priori* reasons, from fixed principles, closed systems and pretended absolutes and origins. [She] turns towards concreteness and adequacy, towards facts, towards action and towards power (James, 1904).

References

Biersack, A. & Macintyre, M. (2016). Introduction: Gender violence and human rights in the Western Pacific. In A. Biersack, M. Jolly & M. Macintyre (Eds), *Gender violence and human rights: Seeking justice in Fiji, Papua New Guinea and Vanuatu* (pp. 1–46). Canberra, ACT: ANU Press. doi.org/10.22459/GVHR.12.2016

Biersack, A., Jolly, M. & Macintyre, M. (Eds). (2016). *Gender violence and human rights: Seeking justice in Fiji, Papua New Guinea and Vanuatu*. Canberra, ACT: ANU Press. doi.org/10.22459/GVHR.12.2016

Gregory, C. (1982). *Gifts and commodities*. London, England: Academic Press.

James, W. (1904). What is pragmatism. In *William James, Writings 1902–1920*. The Library of America. Retrieved from www.marxists.org/reference/subject/philosophy/works/us/james.htm

Jolly, M. & Macintyre, M. (1989). Introduction. In M. Jolly & M. Macintyre (Eds), *Family and gender in the Pacific: Domestic contradictions and the colonial impact* (pp. 1–18). Cambridge, England: Cambridge University Press.

Lederman, R. (1998). Globalisation and the future of culture areas: Melanesianist anthropology in transition. *Annual Review of Anthropology, 27*(1), 427–449. annualreviews.org/doi/full/10.1146/annurev.anthro.27.1.427

Macintyre, M. (1983). Warfare and the changing context of 'Kune' on Tubetube. *The Journal of Pacific History, 18*(1), 11–34. doi.org/10.1080/00223348308572456

Macintyre, M. (1989). Better homes and gardens. In M. Jolly & M. Macintyre (Eds), *Family and gender in the Pacific: Domestic contradictions and the colonial impact* (pp. 156–169). Cambridge, England: Cambridge University Press.

Macintyre, M. (1995). Violent bodies and vicious exchanges: Personification and objectification in the Massim. *Social Analysis: The International Journal of Social and Cultural Practice, 37*, 29–43.

Macintyre, M. (2006). Indicators of violence against women. *Development Bulletin, 71*, 61–63.

Macintyre, M. (2008). Police and thieves, gunmen and drunks: Problems with men and problems with society in Papua New Guinea. *The Australian Journal of Anthropology, 19*(2), 179–193. doi.org/10.1111/j.1835-9310.2008.tb00121.x

Macintyre, M. (2011). Money changes everything: Papua New Guinean women in the modern economy. In M. Patterson & M. Macintyre (Eds), *Managing modernity in the Western Pacific* (pp. 90–120). Brisbane, Qld: University of Queensland Press.

Macintyre, M. (2017). Women working in the mining industry in Papua New Guinea: A case study from Lihir. In K. Lahiri-Dutt & M. Macintyre (Eds), *Women miners in developing countries* (pp. 131–144). London, England: Routledge.

Nussbaum, M. (2000). *Women and human development: The capabilities approach.* Cambridge, England: Cambridge University Press.

Sen, A. (1999). *Development as freedom.* Oxford, England: Oxford University Press.

Strathern, M. (1988). *The gender of the gift: Problems with women and problems with society in Melanesia.* Berkeley, CA: University of California Press.

1

Unequal Lives in the Western Pacific

Nicholas Bainton and Debra McDougall

In October 2018, as Papua New Guinea (PNG) prepared to host the Asia-Pacific Economic Cooperation (APEC) meeting in Port Moresby, journalists reported on stark disparities that were drawing the ire of the nation. News headlines announced that the national government had just splurged on 40 Maseratis for APEC leaders (Beldi, 2018). Photos showed cargo planes unloading carefully sheathed luxury cars, each one valued at more than 100 times PNG's per capita gross domestic product (GDP). Government officials claimed these were needed to transport visiting dignitaries in 'comfort and safety' (if not style). In a nation where most roads are in disrepair and four-wheel-drives are a transport necessity, rather than a luxury, many people were outraged by the purchase. Meanwhile, in Enga Province, hundreds of kilometres from the APEC hype, a young child died of polio, more than 20 years after the last polio death and 18 years after the country was declared free of polio. His death was not an isolated case; approximately 140 other Papuan New Guineans were reportedly suffering from severe polio symptoms (Murray-Atfield, 2018). The outbreak of this once-vanquished disease, contrasted with such ostentatious displays of wealth in the nation's capital, was a vivid manifestation of a failing health system, entrenched inequalities and perverse political priorities.

The following year, the small atoll nation of Tuvalu hosted the Pacific Islands Forum. Regional inequalities once again reached the headlines. This time, attention focused on the threat posed by climate change to people in the Pacific and Australia's refusal to acknowledge a climate crisis and take meaningful action on this issue. Regional leaders could barely disguise their anger at Australia's failure to recognise its moral responsibilities to its 'Pacific family' (Kabutaulaka & Teaiwa, 2019; Regenvanu, 2019). Back in Australia, the deputy prime minister blithely dismissed these concerns, stating that Pacific Islanders 'will continue to survive … because many of their workers come here and pick our fruit' (McCormack, 2019). Referring to the Seasonal Worker Program, his comments evoked a colonial arrogance that highlighted the deep inequalities structuring relations between Australia and the Pacific. Parallels were quickly drawn with the history of indentured labour, where Pacific Islanders were 'blackbirded' throughout the nineteenth century to work in Australian cane fields (Banivanua-Mar, 2006; Stead & Altman, 2019). As this volume goes to press, the COVID-19 pandemic is also highlighting dramatic differences in life chances across and within national borders. The medical systems of the Western Pacific are ill-equipped to deal with existing health challenges, let alone this new virus (Aqarau, 2020; Wood, 2020). Aside from the risks of the virus itself, the pandemic threatens to trigger fear and social unrest, including anti-sorcery violence (Cox & Phillips, 2015; Hukula, Forsyth & Gibbs, 2020). And in Australia, temporary Pacific workers are not being provided with the same substantial social support that other workers are now receiving from the government (Stead, 2020).

These events reflect the radically divergent effects of globalised capitalism on the lives of people who call the Western Pacific home. Wherever we look, the powerful are siphoning life-giving resources away from the poor with impunity—sometimes with their support at the ballot box. Lavish consumption by the powerful few is combined with declining living standards for the majority. This scenario is unfolding across the world; however, as the chapters in this volume show, the abomination of growing inequality takes a distinctive form in the western corner of the Pacific. The region came under colonial rule from the late nineteenth century, but indigenous inhabitants were not displaced from their land by settlers in the way that the peoples of Australia, Hawai'i or Aotearoa New Zealand were. The almost-continent-sized island of New Guinea and the large volcanic islands to its east are rich in soil, minerals, water, forests and people. Yet this remains the poorest region of the Pacific, with the lowest GDP per capita and the lowest human development index scores (United Nations Development Programme, 2018).

Our focus in this volume is primarily PNG, with a chapter on Solomon Islands and reflections on Vanuatu. These three countries are often identified as part of the geocultural region of 'Melanesia'—a term that emerged from the racialised sciences of nineteenth-century Europe and remains important as a marker of sub-regional identity among both independent and colonised states of the Western Pacific (Jolly, 2001; Kabutaulaka, 2015; Lawson, 2013; Thomas, 1989). PNG, Solomon Islands and Vanuatu are all linguistically and culturally diverse nations with small immigrant populations. These features set them apart from Fiji, also identified as 'Melanesian', where discussions of inequality pivot on the racialised tensions between citizens with indigenous and migrant backgrounds (Bryant-Tokalau, 2012; Trnka, 2008). In contrast to West Papua and New Caledonia, PNG, Solomon Islands and Vanuatu are politically independent, no longer subject to racialised colonial rule. Although independence ended some of the most overt forms of racial inequality, the region remains beholden to foreign donors who use their military and economic power to undermine the priorities of Pacific peoples and their visions of the future. Simply put, race remains important in local understandings of inequality. The regions' struggling middle or working classes resent the exponential differences between their own paltry wages and those of handsomely paid (and mostly white) consultants from former colonial powers and other metropolitan nations. Meanwhile, the rising economic and political power of China has led to new and disturbing expressions of anti-Chinese violence.

This volume teases out particular dilemmas of inequality in the Western Pacific. Through close ethnographic inquiry, the authors show that current inequalities cannot be disentangled from deep colonial legacies and neo-colonial discrimination; they argue that contemporary inequalities are multidimensional and multiscale. In the remainder of this introductory chapter, we reflect upon the significance of global inequality, its particularities in the Western Pacific and chart the contribution that anthropologists have made towards understanding one of the most pressing issues of the region and our time. We sketch an intersectional approach to inequality in the Western Pacific (as both an approach and a point of commonality between the chapters) and then provide an overview of the major threads running through the volume.

A Global Epidemic of Inequality

As we move further into the twenty-first century, we are witnessing both the global extensification and local intensification of inequality. The statistics are stupendous; over the past three decades, income and wealth inequality have grown exponentially, and the gap between the mega-rich and the rest has grown deeper and wider.[1] Scholars and public intellectuals, politicians and the public and multilateral institutions like the United Nations (UN) are increasingly concerned with inequality as a powerfully malign feature of contemporary life. Inequality is not only terrible for those at the bottom but also terrible for those at the top, not least of all because it fuels social and political instability (Wilkinson & Pickett, 2009). This manifests in multiple and mutable ways and is especially so in the Western Pacific.

To be sure, considerable improvements have been observed in global quality of life. In the Global North, the years that followed World War II produced great economic prosperity and optimism, and many governments were committed to some form of wealth distribution, including to former colonies in the Global South. Economic modernisation and development programs provided technical assistance and capital injection to help the global poor 'catch up'. Development aid was deeply tied to Cold War politics. It was also grounded in an ideology of progress within the booming economies of Europe and the United States that promised a path for the future in the poorer countries of the world. In more recent decades, global levels of absolute poverty, illiteracy, child malnutrition and child labour have fallen at some of the fastest rates in human history and life expectancy has increased for many people. The proportion of the global population living in servitude has fallen dramatically, and many people who were formally persecuted due to their gender, race, sexuality or disability now enjoy a wider range of rights and freedoms. Likewise, a smaller proportion of the global population lives under authoritarian, tyrannical or dictatorial regimes and, despite the global rise of authoritarian politics, a larger proportion of people live within some form of moderately accountable democracy.

---

1   By 2018, the global top 1 per cent of earners had captured twice as much of global growth in income as the poorest bottom 50 per cent of the population (Alvaredo et al., 2018).

Arguably, however, these measures of rising wellbeing say little about whether people feel that their lives are improving. If globalisation has brought people closer together, this real or virtual proximity has also highlighted the vast differences in standards of living across different classes and countries. Moreover, while gains have occurred in some places, absolute levels of poverty have increased in other places, especially Sub-Saharan Africa (World Bank, 2018). The grim effects of neoliberal political and economic reforms in the 1970s have been profound, often unravelling previous improvements and hard-fought gains made during the so-called era of 'embedded liberalism'. As the World Bank and the International Monetary Fund enforced their structural adjustment programs and other forms of 'shock therapy' (Klein, 2007), the economies of many smaller and poorer nations were crushed in ways that immiserated the lives of their inhabitants, while the economies of many Western nations (and the accounts of specific corporations) prospered at their expense. The global spread of neoliberal policies and projects has undermined the capacity of nation states to buffer the vagaries of market forces and ensure the wellbeing of all their people. The relentless privatisation of public goods and services, the reduction of social assistance programs and the removal of government regulations on big corporations (or the failure to apply these rules consistently) has helped to entrench massive socioeconomic inequalities.

Privatisation has also meant that the contract between labour and capital has been torn apart; workers in this new economy are forced to adapt to the logic of the temporary and insecurity has been normalised under the guise of flexibility. In a world that seems to be developing a contemptuous attitude towards the poor and working classes, the ideal subject is the responsible 'self-managing entrepreneur', who is expected to believe that the path to freedom and wellbeing can be found in greater levels of self-exploitation—or plain hard work. At the same time, reliance upon the extraction of non-renewable resources has unleashed new forms of inequality linked to environmental destruction and forced dislocation, the privatisation and enclosure of common property and modern forms of wage slavery. Old forms of 'primitive accumulation' that transferred labour and raw resources from the colonies to the core through bloody raids and violent seizures have been supplanted by more insidious and enduring forms of 'accumulation by dispossession' that redistribute wealth upwards and across capitalist economies (Harvey, 2005). A sizeable portion of this wealth is now concentrated in the hands of an emerging global oligarchy that, according to Thomas Piketty (2014), reflects a global return to 'patrimonial capitalism', which we could summarise as a form of 'accumulation by inheritance'. A proliferation of tax breaks and tax havens have further redefined the geography of accumulation, as dis-embedded and unencumbered capital flows freely between global cities and their once-remote tax haven entrepôts (Shaxson, 2011).

Feelings of abject disconnection and pervasive expressions of resentment have emerged among some low-income populations in the spaces left by the decline in traditional working-class forms of social and political solidarity. Identity- and place-based politics have flourished, as cultural interests trump economic interests and political leaders exploit the fears and aspirations of those who long for the supposed security of times gone by. In some industrialised democracies, these political and economic changes have engendered feelings of anxiety and helplessness, which partly aid in explaining the rise of populist politicians, the revival of older political forms and the re-emergence of paranoid politics and authoritarian responses.

Against this global backdrop, we believe that a focus on inequality is important due to the ways that inequality consistently undermines individual and collective wellbeing. Beyond an inability to enjoy the things that money can buy, the poor of the world are more vulnerable in almost every imaginable way, perhaps most frighteningly by climate change–induced catastrophes and other environmental and viral hazards that the world's wealthy have caused but are able to escape (Jolly, 2019; Robbins, 2017). As we noted at the outset, this asymmetry has become an urgent issue in the Pacific. The consequences of such uneven development are profound, and these processes might be understood as another form of 'slow violence' that is imposed upon disadvantaged groups of people in distant places.

Capitalism(s) and the State in the Western Pacific

Serious socioeconomic and political inequality has a relatively shallow history in the Western Pacific. In the pre-colonial era, status hierarchies were relatively modest—nowhere did the socio-genealogical distance between chiefs and commoners approach those of the great kingdoms of Tonga or

Hawai'i. Moreover, unlike the islands of eastern Indonesia, Western Pacific societies were not incorporated into ancient Hindu–Buddhist polities or Muslim trading networks. Until the advent of European colonialism in the late nineteenth century, no imperial languages were superimposed, no tributes were exacted, and no overarching power claimed sovereignty over local communities. Political authority was grounded in relationships with ancestors, living kinsfolk and allies. Even where status was inherited genealogically, there was little intergenerational accumulation of material wealth or rights to mobilise labour. Inequalities certainly existed— everywhere, men exercised power over women, and elders exercised power over youth. However, until the last generation or two, there were no classes or castes, no landless peasants and no aristocrats.

The history of contemporary inequality in the Western Pacific begins with colonial expropriation of land, labour and resources in the nineteenth century. The presence of European traders and whalers transformed indigenous social worlds through new infectious diseases, tobacco, trade goods and steel tools. Local leaders with access to Europeans were able to dominate those without such access—the beginning of new kinds of internal inequalities.[2] Perhaps the most momentous development in the islands of Melanesia was the labour trade. Early recruiters used violence and trickery; later, the need for money and trade goods induced tens of thousands of recruits to sign up with limited awareness of the harsh conditions and high mortality rates they would face on the plantations of Queensland and Fiji (Banivanua-Mar, 2006; Siegel, 1985). In the early twentieth century, Australia's racist immigration legislation ended the Queensland labour trade but indenture continued within the boundaries of newly established colonial administrations. This internal labour mobility helped to consolidate the differentiation between 'haves' and 'have-nots' within the territories that would become Vanuatu, Solomon Islands and PNG.

These emergent inequalities had powerful effects when PNG gained independence from Australia in 1975, Solomon Islands from the United Kingdom in 1978 and Vanuatu from the condominium government of France and the United Kingdom in 1980. Colonial administrations sought to create an indigenous elite, as quickly as possible, to staff government offices and fill other roles that had hitherto been reserved for white men.

2   See, for example, Martha Macintyre (1994) on the importance of colonial relations in the dominance of Trobriand Islanders in the *kula* exchange network in Papua New Guinea.

Class inequalities began to take the place of racial hierarchies. Regional differences in experiences of colonialism also produced ethnic arrogance, as some groups considered themselves more civilised, Christianised and modern than others, by virtue of longer and more intense engagement with commerce, colonial government and Christianity (Errington & Gewertz, 1994). Others harboured simmering resentments over exploitation of land and labour by the national government or by fellow citizens (Allen, 2013; Bennett, 2002).

Political independence coincided with a transition from labour-intensive plantation economies to resource extraction. These changes in the social organisation of labour created large-scale disruption and, as Matthew Allen observed, 'one would be hard-pressed to name a single extractive project in Melanesia that has not produced violence of some form' (2018, p. 6). Inequality lies at the heart of all such conflict—rage that some individuals and groups are benefiting, while others are not, and frustration at the unfulfilled promises of states and corporations. After PNG obtained independence, the mining sector steadily expanded through a succession of large-scale projects (Bainton, 2010; Jacka, 2015; Kirsch, 2014). As holes were being dug and mineral wealth was being exported, international capital fuelled the expansion of the logging industry in PNG and Solomon Islands from the early 1980s, leaving a trail of environmental destruction and dashed hopes for development (Allen, 2011; Bennett, 2000; Filer & Sekhran, 1998). With a growing number of multinational resource companies operating in the region, and as thousands of international labourers and companies find employment and business opportunities in these industries (Bainton & Jackson, 2020), contemporary resource extraction resembles a second wave of colonial expansion. Paternalistic colonial states may have been replaced by politically independent states; over time, however, these have become 'contractual states' or 'corporate states' (Kapferer, 2005) that have outsourced their development responsibilities to foreign corporations while wealth is accrued in distant lands or tax havens such as those found in Vanuatu (Rawlings, 2011).

Other forms of dispossession are at play in Vanuatu, whose independent government refused commercial logging. A strong reliance upon tourism and construction as alternative 'roads' to development has allowed international investors and local collaborators to seize large tracts of rural and urban land for tourist resorts and residential properties, dispossessing many customary landowners (McDonnell, 2017). The various land transformations unfolding in Vanuatu can be understood as forms of 'land grabbing' or very specific examples of the 'processes of exclusion' found by Derek Hall and his colleagues in the South-East Asian context (Hall, Hirsch & Li, 2011; McDonnell, Allen & Filer, 2017). Although tourism provides opportunities to celebrate cultural traditions, it simultaneously exacerbates existing forms of dispossession—these 'exotic encounters' overwhelmingly shape the ways that global others regard the people of Vanuatu and the broader region as a whole (Alexeyeff & Taylor, 2016; West, 2016).

Such transactions and extractions have created a new class of people who are both displaced and 'dis-emplaced' or, simply, 'out of place'. Now, more than ever, human migration is a pressing development issue—it is also an issue of justice, human rights and social imaginaries. Throughout the Western Pacific, people are relocating in increasing numbers in search of economic opportunities and services, safer environments or a better existence (Lindstrom & Jourdan, 2017). Although much of this migration follows a 'rural to urban' path, some movement is also 'rural to rural', particularly to agricultural and resource frontier zones (Bainton & Banks, 2018). In these contexts, where customary forms of landownership typically prevail, land-poor migrants enter into a broad range of formal and informal arrangements to access land for residence and subsistence, which in turn generates complex social relations (and sometimes bloody conflicts) between 'insiders' and 'outsiders' or 'landowners' and 'tenants'. The scale and speed of this in-migration, particularly to frontier zones, stresses local environments, local identities and the social and political fabric of local 'landowning' communities in ways that are often not anticipated, desirable or reversible (Bennett, 2002; Koczberski, Curry & Anien, 2015).

Some migrants find the better life they were seeking; they may obtain jobs or access to money, improved health and education for their children or a status that they could not have achieved by staying at home. Many face enormous pressure, living in entrenched conditions of unacceptable poverty, with no access to land, no real prospects and no real escape (Bainton, 2017). For a long time, it was widely held that homelessness was a not a problem in the Western Pacific—that it was structurally and socially impossible in these countries where everyone could either claim some customary connection to a 'place' or rely upon social relations for support or the so-called '*wantok* system'. While anthropologists have long documented the challenges faced by rural migrants in urban centres (Levine & Levine, 1979; Morauta & Ryan, 1982; Strathern, 1975) and the social relations of informal urban 'settlements' (Goddard, 2005; Hukula, 2015; Rooney, 2017; Zimmer-Tamakoshi, 1998), the issue of homelessness has evaded sustained anthropological attention and generally only been observed in passing. However, rising homelessness in cities such as Port Moresby must be understood as a critical index of extreme inequality and broader socioeconomic shifts.

Resentment about the way wealth is being generated from local land but not shared with local people is compounded by a situation in which foreign states are seen to be engaging with the people and governments of the region in fundamentally self-interested ways. Development aid has always been tied to post–World War II geopolitical alliances and, thus, the self-interest of the donor nations. However, this aid—so important in supporting many of the projects that do make a difference in ordinary lives—is increasingly tied to political projects. Panicked about China's rising influence in the region, Western powers are seeking to entrench their status as preferred allies and development partners of Pacific Island nations. However, Australia's intransigence on the threat of climate change means that many people across the region are questioning established allegiances and looking elsewhere for support (Morgan, 2019; Teaiwa, 2019).

Perhaps the most distressing manifestation of geopolitical inequality is the implementation of Australia's offshore detention policies, which resulted in hundreds of asylum seekers being incarcerated on Manus Island in PNG and the small island nation of Nauru (Boochani, 2018). These policies contravene international human rights conventions; they also reflect broader geopolitical inequalities, as the Australian government imposes its political and economic will upon its former colonies who remain dependent upon Australian aid. The refugee-industrial complex reproduces multiple levels of antagonism between Australia and PNG, guards and detainees or 'clients service officers' and their 'clients' (Coetzee, 2019), prisoners and landowners or, supposedly, 'genuine asylum seekers' and 'illegal cue jumpers' (or the *sans-papiers*), to name but a few. Old and new tropes of savagery coalesce in Manus through forms of mutual mischaracterisation, as local residents and foreign prisoners adopt the white Australian fear of Muslims and ideas of racial superiority to describe each other as 'cannibals' and 'terrorists' (Rooney, 2020; Salyer, 2018)—depictions that ultimately deny human dignity.

Let us be clear, then—these postcolonial states are not suffering from 'underdevelopment'. Rather, they are suffering from the overdevelopment of inequality-maximising and profit-maximising forms of capitalism, which transform land and resources into commodities without opportunities for meaningful labour. They are suffering from a lack of government capacity to mitigate the environmental and social harms of resource capitalism and harness and distribute its windfall profits to all citizens of the state. Finally, they are suffering the consequences of struggling to be truly self-determined in the face of conflicting pressures from the larger states surrounding them.

Inequality Lived Locally: Anthropological Perspectives

Anthropology's most lasting contribution to the study of inequality has come from its empirical focus on those who bear the brunt of capitalist expansion, those who are on the resource frontiers, those whose stories are rarely the focus of global news and those who are often not even counted in statistics. Since Malinowski's famous research in the Trobriands, ethnographic research in the Western Pacific has also inspired some of the discipline's most ambitious challenges to Western assumptions about society, economy, personhood and social relationships. The work collected in this volume engages with a range of these scholarly discussions. However, these chapters also evince unease with grand social theory that reduces complexity and overlooks social change—a reflection of the intellectual orientation of anthropologist Martha Macintyre, whose work has inspired this volume. This frustration with theoretical abstraction also reflects the pragmatics and politics of research practice. Several contributors have worked across academic and applied settings, many have done fieldwork in diverse sites across the region, and almost all have done fieldwork across decades rather than in one intensive visit. The editors are all based in Australia, a nation whose foreign policy and aid programs have direct effects on the lives of Western Pacific people. Therefore, we approach anthropological theory not as an end in and of itself, but as a means to better apprehend the lives of ordinary people. Here, we focus on five intersecting issues that have attracted anthropological attention to the lived experience of inequality: egalitarianism and hierarchy, capitalism and class, gender relations, racial inequality and local responses to inequality.

11

Egalitarianism and Hierarchy

The small-scale and fluid structures of Western Pacific polities have long been a focus of anthropological analysis. Much of this analysis is orientated around typological models of political structures or cultural ideologies. Another important strand of analysis has focused less on these typological contrasts and more on historical transformations of hierarchy and egalitarianism.

In 1963, Marshall Sahlins famously contrasted the 'chiefs' of the large Polynesian kingdoms of eastern Oceania with the 'big men' of the small-scale Melanesian polities of western Oceania. In Polynesia, he suggested, a chief's power was determined by his place in an overarching political hierarchy: a nested structure of authority into which a leader was born. In contrast, power in Melanesia was personal—grounded in a leader's ability to build factions, rally allies, demonstrate generosity, call in debts and amass resources through energetic action. Sahlins later admitted that his schema was an oversimplification; more problematically, the essay suggests that Polynesians had 'advanced' more than Melanesians, an implication that Epeli Hauʻofa (1975) saw as affirming centuries of colonial racism. Sahlins' provocation is nevertheless useful in highlighting the extent to which leadership in the Western Pacific has been grounded in social relationships rather than overarching institutions.

This big man/chief model is only one of the frameworks anthropologists have used to understand political status in the Western Pacific. Roger Keesing (1985) argued that a troika of 'priest, chief and warrior' was appropriate to seaboard Melanesia, rather than the 'big man' of the New Guinea Highlands. Some anthropologists have focused on common features of Austronesian societies that stretch from Madagascar to Hawaiʻi: founder ideologies, an emphasis on precedence and a sense of hereditary leadership (Jolly & Mosko, 1994; more recently, see Ku & Gibson, 2019; cf. Barker, 2019). Maurice Godelier distinguished between the Melanesian 'big men', whose authority came through control of wealth, and the 'great men', whose power came through ritual or esoteric knowledge (Godelier, 1986; Godelier & Strathern, 1991). Scholars have used these models to understand colonial transformations of leadership; John Barker, for example, called indigenous pastors the 'new great men' of the region (2012), whereas others have documented the proliferation of modern paths to power through education, business and government, the reification of customary exchange activities or the combination of all of these (Bainton, 2008).

Another influential strand of scholarship on egalitarianism in Melanesia has taken inspiration from Louis Dumont. Dumont aimed to understand the configuration of values within whole societies; he depicted India as orientated around holism and hierarchy, whereas the modern West was orientated around individualism and egalitarianism. In a paper that applied Dumontian analysis to the ethnography of Melanesia, Joel Robbins (1994) argued that Dumont conflated individualism and egalitarianism and overlooked the degree to which these value orientations conflict. Robbins argued that equality is a far more central value in Melanesian societies than those of the West and that this value is realised through relationality, rather than the holism or individualism identified by Dumont. Although Dumont has been widely criticised for his ahistoricism, Robbins adopted Dumont's approach in his now-classic ethnography of Urapmin Christianity to theorise the clash of moral values in a situation of dramatic cultural change (Robbins, 2004). This Dumontian approach also animated Mark Mosko's critiques of Robbins' claim that evangelical Christianity is 'unrelentingly individualist' (Mosko, 2015) and has been influential in other work on ideologies of hierarchy and egalitarianism (Rio & Smedal, 2008). However, as one of us argued more than a decade ago (McDougall, 2009), such Dumontian-inspired analyses of ideologies of individualism reveal little about the lived experience of individualism, particularly in an era of rapidly increasing socioeconomic inequality.

In contrast to approaches that focus on typologies and essentialist contrasts across cultures or civilisations, Martha Macintyre is among scholars who have insisted on understanding indigenous leadership, exchange, personhood and individualism in Melanesia in the historical context of colonialism, which had reorganised regional relationships, established a monopoly on violence and enforced a colonial peace that enabled an efflorescence of exchange networks (Macintyre, 1983, 1995; see also Douglas, 1979). In the context of broader interest in the 'invention of tradition' (Hobsbawm & Ranger, 1983; Jolly, 1992; Keesing & Tonkinson, 1982), anthropologists also turned their attention to the ways that colonial missions and administrations sought out and sometimes helped to create the office of 'chief'. In some situations, these neo-traditional roles have had profound and lasting effects, particularly when authority is grounded in the church and, more ambivalently, the state (see e.g. Keesing, 1969; McDougall, 2015; White, 1991). Whether they were colonial inventions or not, chiefs were proliferating all over the region in the decades following political independence, combining traditional and novel forms of power (Main, this volume; White, 1992; White & Lindstrom, 1997).

One aspect of this transformation is institutionalisation. Post–World War II and postcolonial male leaders tended to emerge with the support of kin groups; however, their authority was also derived from the translocal structures of government administration and translocal missions. This incipient bureaucratisation or depersonalisation of authority was short-lived—power was still very personalised. For our purposes, the more important transformation is the disarticulation of power from generative relationships with kin and land. This dynamic is evident in Keir Martin's (2013) discussion of new forms of social stratification in post-disaster East New Britain. Whereas older big men accumulated and then distributed wealth, new 'big shots' mobilise relational ties to build power and access wealth (often under the name of 'tradition'); however, they are typically seen as failing to adequately redistribute the benefits (see also Zimmer-Tamakoshi, 1997). They are accused of forgetting about their kin, keeping everything for themselves and cutting off their relational networks to live as selfish individuals. Such laments resonate in almost every community in the Western Pacific (Bainton, 2009).

Nowhere is the alienation of power from local relationships more evident than in large-scale resource extraction projects (Filer & Le Meur, 2017). The 'ideology of landownership' (Filer, 1997) appears to 'ground' power in localised kin groups, whereas in fact, the constitution of corporate landowning groups has served to concentrate power in the hands of individual brokers whose power is derived from companies and the state. These new 'tribal' leaders of the extractive industries are rarely accountable to the people whose interests they may claim to represent, generating the kinds of impasses that often lead to violent conflict. For the female members of these 'resource communities', the absence of male accountability is particularly stark. Although earlier forms of personalised politics were always dominated by males, kin relations and lineage structures often gave women a degree of power, particularly (but certainly not exclusively) in those matrilineally oriented islands of the Western Pacific. As Macintyre has shown in her work on gender and mining in Melanesia, the rise of extractive economies has routinely excluded women from the benefits of extraction in a more thoroughgoing and distinctly non-traditional way. Across Melanesia and beyond, men gain more jobs than women and have greater access to project-related wealth (Beer, 2018; Lahiri-Dutt & Macintyre, 2006). Despite recent attempts to address the role of 'women in mining' and related industries, their employers often implicitly (and sometimes explicitly) reinforce values of male economic privilege that affect familial relations and marginalise women (Macintyre, 2017, p. 11).

Capitalism and Class

Discussions of changing political authority—the unequal distribution of power over persons within a society—are intrinsically linked to changing economic relations. Although class distinction, like racial distinction, is a form of inequality previously exogenous to the Western Pacific, class consciousness has evidently emerged across the region with some very Melanesian characteristics. As such, we use the term 'class' in both analytical and descriptive senses to describe the historically particular relationship between labour and capital that is central to political economy and, more generally, to economic inequality of various sorts, including gradations of personal and household income and wealth, distinctions between 'landowners' and 'non-landowners', 'big shots' and 'grassroots' and so forth. In this section, we chart the ways in which anthropologists have invoked class analysis and focused on the social relations of accumulation.

Anthropologists have asked how 'pre-colonial' distinctions have been altered, enhanced or erased as these societies have engaged with cash economies and state-based political systems. Pioneering fieldwork conducted in the highlands of PNG between the 1950s and 1970s sought to understand and theorise historical forms of inequality and the transitions that were occurring in the late colonial period (Strathern, 1982). This work focused on then current topics of enquiry, including relations of production (Josephides, 1985; Kelly, 1993; Modjeska, 1982), systems of exchange (Sillitoe, 1979; Strathern, 1971) and the question of whether some groups were seemingly 'pre-adapted' to the competition of market economies (Finney, 1973), all of which provided opportunities for further theorising ideas of inequality. Much of the anthropology that followed has been concerned with the twin issues of change and inequality.

The introduction of cash currencies and market economies did not completely undermine existing sociopolitical structures. Cash and trade goods were often easily absorbed into forms of ceremonial exchange and put to good use for social and political purposes. These changes illustrated the capacity of some ceremonial economies to absorb new objects and forms of wealth, while resisting the absorption of values and practices associated with them in the global capitalist economy. Sahlins called this process 'develop*man*', which he contrasted with 'development', whereby introduced items are used in ways that enable people to become 'more like themselves' on a grander scale (1992). These inflationary dynamics of traditional exchange are evident in many places. As some people harness newfound wealth for customary purposes, existing sociopolitical hierarchies and systems of value are redefined (Bainton & Macintyre, 2016) and others are pushed out of regional economies altogether (Zimmer-Tamakoshi, this volume). These changes have created new forms of distinction between what can and cannot be sold for cash (Akin & Robbins, 1999), eclipsing any allegedly hard division between gifts and commodities (Foster, 2008; Gregory, 1982).

More epochal than the creation of new markets for foreign goods has been the transformation of land and labour into commodities. In the plantation era, some late colonial village leaders of coastal and island Melanesia were able to tap into the wealth produced; they expanded cooperative societies, bought ships, built wharfs and sometimes used the infrastructure of missions to connect to broader trading economies. The shift to extractivism reconfigured regional socioeconomic dynamics, with little accumulated wealth remaining in local hands or invested in local lands. Consequently, most people of the Pacific have now concluded that capital accumulation is happening, very clearly, elsewhere.

Many rural communities hope that resource extraction will bring 'development'. Some extractive ventures have improved the lives of some communities in the absence of the state, even if only temporarily (Jorgensen, this volume). Yet the impoverishment of many 'host communities' and the degradation and pollution of their environments expose the corporate rhetoric of 'shared value' and 'social responsibility' as self-serving constructs designed to further corporate interests. These outcomes are not simply the result of rapacious and unaccountable corporations. Political elites and dominant landowners also redirect the flow of wealth by whisking money away in offshore investments and real estate, or they consume this wealth through conspicuous forms of largesse to ensure political power and support (see Main, this volume). The extractive relations that characterise these enclaves are underpinned by unequal ownership of the means of production (land and capital), use of capital and land to generate profits under competitive conditions, uneven distribution of the burdens and benefits of extraction, groups of customary landowners who expect privileged access to the mineral wealth generated from their lands (and the jobs and business contracts created by these projects) and groups of people who are compelled to sell their labour to subsist (Bainton, this volume). To the extent that different actors succeed in their different endeavours, their accumulation squeezes others out or suppresses their rights and interests, reinforcing and sometimes deepening the inequalities from which it all began.

By the 1990s, anthropological research was exploring how class ties were overtaking the ties of family, clan or even regional identities, as elites and the new urban middle class sought ways to distinguish themselves from their rural relatives (Gewertz & Errington, 1999). While the gap between the grassroots and the big shots continues to grow unabated, the waged and salaried working class or middle class also continues to expand its ranks (Cox, 2018, this volume). This growth has created additional forms of labour stratification—some people working for resource companies and other multinational companies form a kind of 'labour aristocracy', while public sector employees survive on more modest or meagre wages with fewer cheques and perquisites (Filer, this volume; Golub & Rhee, 2013). The overall growth in educational opportunities also means that the number of people leaving school and university has outstripped the opportunities for meaningful employment, producing a disillusioned and disaffected generation of educated citizens with fewer prospects for the future (McDougall, this volume). The rising cost of urban life and the insecurity and instability of employment and other livelihood opportunities (Sharp et al., 2015) has created previously unknown levels of precarity among town and city dwellers as the myth of subsistence affluence is replaced by the reality of urban poverty.

Gender Relations

Scholars and popular commentators who characterise the Western Pacific as 'egalitarian' tend to focus exclusively on relationships among men (Jolly, 1987). Like other feminist anthropologists all around the world (see especially Reiter, 1975; Rosaldo, Lamphere & Bamberger, 1974), scholars of the Western Pacific were interested in how one could understand the apparent universality of male political dominance in ways that did not smuggle in distinctly Euro-American or Western cultural models. Feminist historians and anthropologists sought to retrieve women's voices from historical archives and to understand the ways that indigenous forms of patriarchy were transformed by the patriarchal structures of colonialism, capitalism and Christianity (Barker, this volume; Douglas, 2003; Jolly & Macintyre, 1989; Ram & Jolly, 1998).

The quest to understand apparently universal gender inequalities without reproducing the culture-bound assumptions of Western social theory lies at the centre of Marilyn Strathern's influential *Gender of the gift* (1988). Strathern suggested that gender inequality can be explained in terms of the degree to which a person can constitute themselves as an individual or a member of neatly bounded social groups. Due to their reproductive capacity (women's ability to birth others from their own bodies), women were far less able to 'cut' the relationships that bound them to others. Men, she argued, could (at least sometimes) emerge from these networks of relationships to stand as autonomous, agentive and self-contained bodies. Crucially, these entities could be the individual person or a collective clan group—both were social forms that denied connections to the others that made them. Strathern was not uninterested in historical change (see e.g. Strathern, 1987); however, by mobilising 'fictional' binaries of 'Us/Them', 'West/Melanesia' and 'Gift/Commodity', she pushed any analysis of colonial transformations to the background. This caused an apparent schism between the so-called 'new Melanesian anthropology' and the 'new Melanesian history' (see Foster, 1995; Josephides, 1991; Keesing & Jolly, 1992; Scott, 2007).

Macintyre was among those who most powerfully bridged the polarities of this era, drawing on her deeply historical understanding of exchange relationships and gendered personhood in the Massim to challenge both the romanticism and presentism of the emerging orthodoxies of 'Melanesian personhood'. She argued that the efflorescence of exchange systems, which were so central to the constitution of persons in the region, was profoundly shaped by forcible colonial pacification (Macintyre, 1983). Macintyre urged theorists of Melanesian personhood to attend to the ways that these ideologies and practices were manifest through not only the constructive constitution of persons through exchange but also the violent destruction of bodies through warfare (Macintyre, 1995). Macintyre's clear-eyed attention to colonial transformations and the darker side of indigenous cultural ideologies and practices informed her ongoing focus on gender—not only as a principle of social organisation but also as an axis of discrimination that truncated the lives of women and girls in PNG and beyond.

Scholars committed to understanding contemporary gender inequality in the Pacific turned attention to both colonial political economies and Christianity. The landmark *Family and gender in the Pacific*, edited by Margaret Jolly and Martha Macintyre (1989), showed that current gender inequality is not a simple continuation of supposedly traditional customs, as is too often suggested by so much contemporary commentary on high rates of gender-based violence in the Pacific. In many cases, introduced forms of male domination have both overlaid and exacerbated indigenous patriarchy and opened new possibilities for contestation. European Christian missions and contemporary indigenous Christianity have been particularly paradoxical in this regard (Choi & Jolly, 2014; Tomlinson & McDougall, 2013). Victorian-era missions glorified the domestic role of women, viewing their proper place as in the home rather than in the agricultural work that is the very definition of productive femininity in most of the Western Pacific. Yet Christianity also opened new spaces for socialisation, particularly the critically important women's fellowship groups that emerged (along with non–church affiliated women's cooperatives) throughout the 1960s and 1970s in most Christian churches in Melanesia. Sometimes moving from localised concerns to broader forms of activism and peace movements, these church groups were the 'missing rib of indigenous feminism' according to Anne Dickson-Waiko (2003; see also Barker, this volume).

The commodification of traditional forms of exchange has sometimes had deleterious effects on gender relations. This is especially the case where 'bridewealth' payments—understood by anthropologists as an acknowledgement of relations of indebtedness across kin or lineage groups and opening the way for lifelong exchanges—are reframed around the logics of commodity exchange as the simple purchase of women, or what is commonly called 'bride price' payments (Filer, 1985; Jolly, 2015). Holly Wardlow has shown how Huli women in the highlands of PNG have reacted in rage to this sort of alienation from their own reproductive power (2006). Other work on PNG women in the modern economy suggests a slightly more positive trajectory. Writing of women who have leveraged education and skills for salaried positions in the civil service or mining economy, Macintyre argued that 'money changes everything' (2011). Able to avoid or disengage with marital relations that have become both increasingly important and increasingly oppressive in many pockets of PNG society, these modern women are able to become the heads of their own households, choosing to invest in their own relationships with extended kin (Spark, 2017, 2019; Zimmer-Tamakoshi, 1993, 1998). From this perspective, rather than merely reproductive capacity or biological sex, it is 'position' in a broader political and economic space that shapes experiences of gendered personhood and agency (Cox & Macintyre, 2014; Macintyre & Spark, 2017; Spark, Cox & Corbett, 2019).

Changing gender relations, particularly the new autonomy of salaried urban women, is sometimes experienced as deeply threatening by Melanesian men, particularly in those contexts in which they see their own possibilities narrowed and aspirations squashed. Anthropologists have documented such backlashes, which often embrace romanticised notions of neo-traditional male-dominated *kastom* and reject the idea of human rights (seen here as 'women's rights') (Macintyre, 2012; Taylor, 2008a). To this end, anthropologists are paying greater attention to the ways that Melanesian masculinities are 'changing' (Taylor, 2008b) and 'moving' (Jolly, 2008) as men meet the challenges of rapidly changing environments and societal expectations, blending received modalities of gender, sexuality, economy and authority with exogenous forms. The historical processes of colonialism, Christian conversion, market penetration and urbanisation have upset and displaced once 'hegemonic' forms of masculinity, as the flux and change of Melanesian gender relations has given rise to a plurality of masculinities and 'emergent' expressions of these new masculine ideals (Biersack, 2016; Jolly, 2008; Jolly, Stewart & Brewer, 2012; Munro, 2017; see also McDougall, this volume; Zimmer-Tamakoshi, this volume).

Racial Inequality

The people of the Western Pacific were subject to shocking manifestations of colonial racism. Racist ideologies in the colonial era justified exploitative labour practices; these ideologies were later mobilised in the era of decolonisation to argue that Melanesians were not, and might never be, ready for independence (Banivanua-Mar, 2006, 2016). The region was also among those sites where the early 'science of race' was developed (Douglas, 2008). Euphemised racial attitudes are continuously encountered in the postcolonial era among ex-colonisers, neo-colonial institutions and their agents and in local strategies of identity and resistance. As Tarcisius Kabutaulaka has argued (2015), the legacy of European racism continues to shape how outsiders see and interact with the region; more disturbingly, perhaps, people of the Pacific have themselves taken up some of this racial thinking in their attitudes towards one another.

Racial inequality in postcolonial Melanesia has been transformed as it intersects with other forms of inequality. In some situations, new class inequalities have eclipsed old racial hierarchies. For instance, these patterns are evident in the ways that some urban elites in PNG project a 'cargo cult' or handout mentality on to the rural grassroots (see Cox, this volume). However, the emergence of class differences, and a strong awareness of these distinctions and interests, has not erased the legacies of racist regimes, the persistence of racial discrimination and persecution or forms of racial scapegoating. Ceridwen Spark, for example, has documented the racialised experience and humiliations of professional Melanesian women working in Australian development programs (2020). The misconception that 'racial differences are materially true and determine the physical, intellectual, moral or social qualities of identifiable groups' (Douglas, 2008, p. 3) continues to shape sociopolitical relations within Western Pacific nations and in engagements with other Pacific Islanders, people of European descent and Asian descent. Race, in other words, no longer simply means white supremacism.

Postcolonial racial dynamics continue to pivot around longstanding Euro–Australian distinctions. The legacies of colonial racial categories are most tellingly evidenced in the persistence of terms like 'mixed race' or '*hapkas*' (Goddard, 2017; Winter, 2017) to describe people of 'mixed parentage' (Johnson & McGavin, 2017). Just as racialised negative self-perceptions are produced when colonial attitudes are internalised (Bashkow, 2006), negative attitudes towards Asian migrants have a similar colonial legacy and tend to mirror the ways in which some whites denigrate Asian people. Melanesians of all class status can be found reproducing the racist discourse of colonialism with respect to Asian migrants. In PNG, Asians are frequently imagined as possessing a rapacious culture and an absence of morality, which is then rhetorically contrasted with Melanesian sociality and Christian virtues (Cox, 2015). While many Melanesians enter into advantageous arrangements with Asian migrants, and many people draw a distinction between 'old' and 'new' Asians (Crocombe, 2007), there remains a deep suspicion and resentment towards Asian residents who are accused of buying their way into the region and taking up the few economic opportunities open to poor islanders (Smith, 2013). These sentiments have elicited a kind of 'reactive nationalism' (Barclay, 2012) that has occasionally erupted into large-scale riots targeting Asian businesses in major urban centres. This rising anti-immigrant racism on the part of those who have missed out on the benefits of globalisation again links the dynamics of the Western Pacific to global metropolitan politics, where the victims of neoliberal policies that have gutted the welfare state seem to direct their anger at migrants rather than the leaders responsible for their misery.

Local Responses to Inequality

Studies focusing on the dramatic new forms of inequality emerging in the Western Pacific paint a dire picture. It is difficult to see how local processes of levelling and commitment to community wellbeing could make a dent in the inequality-maximising forms of global capitalism that are inserting themselves in every corner of society. A glimmer of hope may be found in the renewed focus on equality in the UN Sustainable Development Goals and the possibility that these global frameworks will influence policies and priorities on the ground. Inequality is finally being recognised as a universal issue and global crisis; this may signal a long-overdue shift in emphasis from perpetual growth to a more justice-centred future.

Moreover, the history of Melanesia is full of movements in which people have worked together to bring about a vision of a common good. As Tracey Banivanua-Mar observed, 'Indigenous peoples found and practised discrete, and often localised, forms of self-determination that resisted administrative borders of convenience and developed Indigenous alternatives to national sovereignty' (2016, p. 151). However, rather than being recognised as movements for political autonomy, 'almost universally, these were dismissed as cargo cults and the mere incessant talk of custom' (2016, p. 167). The label 'cargo cult' drew attention to only one aspect of such movements: an attempt to access material goods and wealth possessed by whites. Colonial attempts to contain these movements, and anthropological analysis seeking to understand them, have emphasised the millenarian and messianic aspects of these movements and seen them as adjustments to aspects of modern life (Burridge, 1971; Lawrence, 1964; Mead, 1956). More recent work, such as that of Banivanua-Mar, has viewed such movements as responses to colonial inequality and oppression, as expressing a desire for moral equivalence and as embedded in translocal networks (Errington & Gewertz, 2004; Keesing, 1992; Lindstrom, 1993). David Akin (2013) argued that the Maasina Rule movement in Solomon Islands should be viewed as a struggle for civil and political rights in the late colonial British Empire and part of the broader story of civil rights movements throughout the world. In common with other anti-colonial and civil rights movements of the mid-century in every corner of the world, these Melanesian autonomy movements were social and spiritual, rather than technical or bureaucratic. Echoes of these movements can be found throughout the Western Pacific and beyond, where some of these activities have become institutionalised as indigenous churches and regional political organisations, reflecting the persistence of normative modernist desires and the uneven distribution of wealth and opportunity.

In the past decade or so, this sense of hope and the desire for social justice has been most forcibly directed towards the elimination of 'gender violence' or 'family and sexual violence' (as it is commonly termed in PNG) and sorcery accusation–related violence. In response to the apparent upsurge in gender-based violence in all its dreadful manifestations, a variety of 'reformist' movements have emerged at the local and national levels. These movements, and their agents, must navigate a path between their commitment to the ideology of universal human rights and local cultural orders that are often deemed (by outsiders in particular) as obstacles to be overcome. These imposed hierarchies—between the universal and the particular—create specific challenges on the ground for the task of 'translating' and 'transplanting' the international human rights regime. Similar to earlier movements concerned with social transformation, anthropologists have been particularly well placed to undertake historically informed ethnographic analysis of these new rights-based movements to understand the history of a globalising Western Pacific (Biersack, Jolly & Macintyre, 2016; Hildson et al., 2000).

Making Sense of Inequality: Intersectionality in the Western Pacific

A longstanding tension in anthropology between celebrating diverse ways of being and calling out injustice has re-emerged in debates about whether anthropology is overly focused on the 'suffering subject'—those people living in pain and poverty or under conditions of violence and oppression (Knauft, 2019; Ortner, 2016). Robbins (2013), for example, has made a case for an 'anthropology of the good' that seriously engages the aspirational and idealising aspects of people's lives. In contrast, Paige West (2018) has criticised what she sees as a worrying trend in anthropology to find hope in everything; perhaps we must simply learn to sit with suffering more? Anthropologists who continue to work in the Western Pacific cannot escape the increasingly harsh conditions that characterise many rural and urban settings and shape local aspirations and the potential for the future.

Making sense of these conditions is no easy task. While popular attention is often focused on the distribution of wealth and income, inequality has many other dimensions that often intersect with and compound each other, including gender, race, class, age, ethnicity, disability and sexuality, to name but a few. As the chapters in this volume show and the foregoing discussion illustrates, it is critical that we attend to the transformation of inequality, not simply its persistence or expansion. Wardlow (2018) and various others have suggested that we can usefully understand these transformations through the lens of intersectionality, which, in the most basic sense, is a metaphor for the ways that different forms of inequality and discrimination 'intersect' dynamically with each other—picture a person at a junction with different inequalities speeding towards them or, perhaps, to use more island-like imagery, a person caught in a convergence of currents. This is a not a grand theory but instead a prism for observing complexity in the world—the events and conditions of social, economic and political life, and experiences of the self, are rarely shaped by single factors. They are formed and reproduced through an assorted array of factors in mutually influencing ways. These convergences create obstacles and impediments in individual lives that are not always easily understood or identified within conventional modes of thinking about specific inequalities or through single-axis frameworks (e.g. 'class' or 'race').[3] Rather than treating race and gender, or other dimensions and categories, as simple add-ons to an economic base, intersectionality demands a multidimensional and multiscale view of inequality—each of the chapters in this volume tackle this head-on. As has often been noted, capital is intersectional—it intersects with the bodies that produce labour,

---

3   Kimberle Crenshaw (1989) is often credited with coining the term 'intersectionality' (although the core ideas of intersectionality emerged earlier in various texts and in practice). See also Jolly's Interlude (this volume).

the places where resources are extracted and the racialised, gendered and class-based structures that produce and enhance the accumulation of wealth.

By focusing on intersections and transformations, we are forced to attend to the temporal and spatial dimensions of specific kinds of inequality in this region. Attention to historical dimensions assists in identifying forms of change and continuity that unfold over time—allowing us to simultaneously 'look back' and critically re-assess received assumptions about past practices and contemporary conditions and to 'look forward' to future prospects. That is, we can begin to understand how forms of inequality between people are historically produced. We are also forced to move beyond simple rural–urban binaries and dispel myths that underpin regional imageries of land-connected subsistence farmers (or images of 'rural affluence') to attend to the disparities that exist among rural families, or what can be understood as 'relative rural poverty' (Burton, 2018; Wardlow, 2018). Quite simply, some rural families are poorer and more vulnerable than others. The diversity of this region militates against broad generalisations, highlighting the need to consider unique intersections or conjunctures in different times and places. Likewise, by considering the geographical dimensions of inequality, our attention is directed to the uneven flow of things—capital, power, ideas and materials—across the ocean and the landscape. This allows us to grasp the ways in which some places have benefited historically from relationships of dispossession and the transfer of wealth from elsewhere and how their present condition is partly the result of such inequities (Bebbington & Humphries Bebbington, 2018). These geographies of power and inequality shape place-making processes and the lives of individuals living in the Western Pacific.

The authors in this volume analyse the enduring structures and experiences of inequality in the communities of the Western Pacific and the forms of subordination, dispossession, indignity and humiliation that constitute their unequal lives, in addition to the multiple counter-movements and forms of agency that emerge in response to these transformations. Taken as a whole, this volume presents a broad picture of intersecting inequalities, heterogeneous forms of violence and oppression and diverse kinds of dispossession, in addition to the structures, institutions, beliefs and assumptions that underpin and reproduce them.

The Chapters

The chapters in this volume focus on contemporary transformations of inequality, as gendered, race- and class-based inequalities intersect in novel ways to entrench existing inequities and create new varieties of vulnerability. The authors consider not only multiple dimensions of inequality but also multiple scales: local, national, regional and global/world historical. Through close ethnographic scrutiny, they highlight how relationships between seniors and subalterns, agents and patients, patrons and clients, vary across scales—that is, how different scales of inequality emerge in lived experience. For example, while it might be argued that, from a regional perspective, PNG is subordinate to Australia, from a national perspective, the folks driving around in Maseratis during and after the APEC meeting mentioned at the outset are hardly subaltern. These sorts of multiscale inequalities, found throughout the volume, may also be understood as a kind of intersectionality in the generalised metaphorical sense of the term.

These forms of socioeconomic inequality are also reflected in forms of epistemological inequality; as anthropologists have long observed, some people's knowledge is valued more than others. As Indigenous anthropologists globally and in the Western Pacific have attested (Hukula, 2018; Rooney, 2018), they face multiple barriers to participation in Western-centric institutions, let alone sustained interrogation of alternative values and epistemologies. We recognise that such inequality is evident in this volume: of all contributors, only John Aini and Dora Kuir-Ayius are from the Western Pacific.

Several chapters in the volume provide a frame for thinking about the possibilities and limitations of anthropological research, knowledge production and persistent forms of epistemic inequality. Paige West and John Aini analyse the costs and exploitative relations that often underpin the production of knowledge but are rarely acknowledged or accounted for. In places like PNG, small locally based non-governmental organisations (NGOs) play a critical role in facilitating the production of conservation and environmental knowledge. These local organisations are located within a broader field of patron–client relationships between small NGOs and 'big international NGOs'. But the structural inequalities contained in conservation funding cause material inequalities that create the conditions whereby small NGOs must undertake a great deal of unpaid work

1. UNEQUAL LIVES IN THE WESTERN PACIFIC

and incur a range of social and economic debts to service the requests (and opportunities) presented by large NGOs. The capacity to mobilise networked social relations of obligation and reciprocity is critical in meeting these requests. This work is frequently rendered invisible (and structural inequalities are hidden) when outsiders naively interpret these activities as expressions of 'island hospitality'—and this forms yet another manifestation of the casual and insouciant expression of white privilege. Anthropologists are reminded that much of their work, and the knowledge they produce, is underpinned by debts that can never be repaid.

In a similar vein, Simon Foale exposes the epistemological injustice that arises from the false hierarchy between the so-called 'soft' and 'harder' sciences. Within metropolitan centres of knowledge production, different kinds of knowledge are valued differently. Whose knowledge production is recognised, and why, matters a great deal. Charting his own disciplinary journey from marine biology to anthropology, settling on a form of critical political ecology, Foale argues against the undeserved hegemony of natural scientists in cross-disciplinary projects on environmental problems in the Pacific. He exposes the ways in which natural scientists reinvent an 'anti-politics machine' of reductionist, managerial and deeply neo-colonial social science, which studiously ignores so much of what anthropology has contributed, and can continue to contribute, to understanding and addressing the complex nexus between environmental problems and inequality in the Pacific.

Taking up ideas of attachment and partibility that have been so central to theories of Melanesian personhood, Melissa Demian suggests that anthropologists—like pigs (Macintyre, 1984)—are 'semi-alienable'. Having worked first in Suau in Milne Bay, Demian finds herself thinking through the categories of Suau language and being identified by Papua New Guineans not only as a European but also as being from Suau, as the PNG place from which she 'comes from'. Tracking back and forth between her experience in Suau and the urban contexts where she has later undertaken applied research on gender and family violence, her chapter analyses the awkward but productive relationship between anthropologists and the communities with whom they work and the sort of knowledge that emerges through these collaborations.

Susan Hemer approaches the question of knowledge production from a rather different angle by considering the multiple scales of inequality that support the spread of tuberculosis (TB) in the Lihir Islands in

PNG, which are also host to a large-scale gold mining operation. Global health policies and guidelines may acknowledge the socioeconomic and political contexts of diseases like TB; in practice, though, these treatment regimens are singular, vertical and context-free. As these global policies are translated into national and local contexts, important inequalities are often obfuscated and compounded because treatment programs focus on individual failures and responsibilities rather than the relationship between this disease and structural factors such as poverty and uneven development. The mining operation has given many Lihirians better access to health services than other Papua New Guineans, but TB is nevertheless flourishing in Lihir. Hemer argues that this is partly the result of health programs that highlight individual or cultural failures and suppress the specific social and gendered inequalities that influence the extent to which some people will seek diagnosis and continue with their treatment. By ignoring inequality, these programs only help to intensify it.

Several chapters deal with the transformation of gendered inequalities, including changing notions of masculinity. In a historical analysis of marriage practices in Maisin society, John Barker upends stereotypes of indigenous patriarchy and missionary impacts to demonstrate how gender relations were intensely transformed through more than a century of engagement with Christianity. As Anglican missionaries waged a long-term campaign to impose sacramental marriage, Maisin communities have navigated a path between customary obligations that are grounded in the traditional ideal of balanced exchange relationships between families and Anglican orthodoxy that regards marriage as a lifelong commitment to one's partner and the church itself. Just as the traditional ideal of 'amity' was better understood as a point of reference for measuring actualities, the Anglican ideal of equality was not necessarily achieved in practice. Inequalities between men and women, and young and old, are brought to the fore as different groups attempt to move between mission rules and customary obligations and as enduring tensions in marriage are transferred to the church. It was the establishment of the Mother's Union, a local women's church group, that has had the most contradictory effects, because it simultaneously provides women with a platform for greater economic autonomy (disrupting male control over economic matters) and enables older women to exert authority over younger women and usurp the power of the clergy.

As is the case with medical care provided by missionaries and miners, the benefits of schooling are unevenly spread across geographical regions, social classes and genders. Global efforts to expand access to schooling have led to children spending longer in school and have reduced gender disparities in schooling; nevertheless, rural and poor students often find that, by the time they achieve a qualification, it is no longer sufficient to obtain a job. Debra McDougall's chapter analyses the experiences of Solomon Islander students who have joined a remarkable vernacular language school. All students and teachers she interviewed were critical of the conventional school curriculum, which begins with English—a language few children understand. Her chapter reminds us that language is a crucial aspect of inequality and explores why some of the contradictions of schooling are experienced differently by men and women. Both young women and men saw how learning the grammar of their own language helped them in formal schooling, but only young men spoke of the shame they experienced in school and feelings of worthlessness when they failed exams or were unable to find work. The frustration and sense of 'lostness' she describes are evident across the collection, particularly in the chapter by Gewertz and Errington. In Ranongga, though, this frustration is being addressed in a positive way.

Deborah Gewertz and Frederick Errington reflect upon Sepik settlement life on the outskirts of Madang, where a form of 'stingy egalitarianism' has emerged as a survival strategy in response to increasing levels of precarity; food and generosity are scarce and unruly gangs of disaffected young men abound. Social relations have descended into a form of pre-emptive levelling, in which individuals refuse to let others get ahead. The insecurity and unpredictability of settlement life offer few opportunities for people to invest in cultural traditions or to be more like themselves, as Marshall Sahlins would have it. Under these conditions, standing out is difficult and unwise. The study of settlement life involves pitfalls for researchers and their subjects and their research presence—although grounded in longstanding and enduring relations of reciprocity with people from the Sepik region—has produced unwanted and unanticipated effects. Their presence provided unique opportunities for some individuals to get ahead, albeit temporarily, exacerbating existing jealousies and contentions with other people. Much like West and Aini's contribution, their confronting experience serves as a timely reminder of the sometimes-unintended consequences of our presence as researchers and the relationships we form.

John Cox examines how the growing gap between PNG's urban middle class and the nation's rural poor, the 'grassroots', is shaped and reproduced. Whereas middle-class aspirations are often framed in terms of global discourses of progression and prosperity, when the grassroots express their desires for development, they are frequently disparaged and dismissed as lazy 'cargo cultists' waiting for 'something for nothing'. Different moral evaluations of desire legitimatise the accumulative practices of elites and render the aspirations and demands of their poorer followers immoral, greedy and superstitious. When a series of 'fast money' schemes swept across the region towards the end of the twentieth century, rural and urban investors alike sought their fortunes in these schemes. Many hopeful investors lost a lot of money—popular accounts characterised middle-class investors as rational and sophisticated (even if the majority failed to make a profit), whereas their grassroots counterparts were cast as gullible and simple. These emerging class distinctions are being further reinforced as the moral economy that binds rural and urban relatives—and ensures some form of wealth redistribution—is being restructured around donor–client models as members of the middle class begin to see their rural kin as subjects who must be mobilised for development.

Dan Jorgensen's chapter links back to the theme of masculinities and economic stratification and forward to the final chapters that discuss inequality and resource extraction. Jorgensen explores the possibilities for conducting a 'remote ethnography' of the present, a kind of 'processual anthropology'. Focusing on two unexpected events that dramatically affected the lives of Telefomin people and others living in the hinterland of the giant Ok Tedi mine in PNG, Jorgensen combines both analysis and a form of 'witnessing' to emphasise the structural inequalities that shape Telefomin futures. In the lead up to 2011, there was an unprecedented outbreak of violent attacks against alleged witches in a rural village. This was later followed by a prolonged period of drought in 2015, which had a devastating effect upon the region. When critical river transport routes became unnavigable due to insufficient water flow, the mining company suspended operations. This also provided the necessary 'shock' to enact another major change and close the mining town, raising critical questions about the future of the mine and, ultimately, the region. Jorgensen demonstrates how historical perspectives demand that the ethnography of the present necessarily points towards the future, which in turn highlights the contingent nature of events. These cases also neatly illustrate how the multiple scales of inequality emerge in daily life. The local beneficiaries of the mine may be perceived as (illegitimate) superiors to the 'lost boys' (or wayward men) in the village. Yet, these same beneficiaries are also subalterns without agency in the face of the company's decision to effectively close the local town.

Laura Zimmer-Tamakoshi charts the long-term engagement with capitalism and the resulting transformations that have given rise to new forms of inequality and uncertainty among the Gende, who reside in the Bismarck Mountains in Madang Province. Gende social relations have been completely reorganised around the political economy of extraction and the promise of instant wealth. The ceremonial exchanges that once constituted a kind of 'moral economy' among the Gende and their neighbours have been transformed beyond recognition, as men compete with huge sums of money to secure their position among an elite set of landowners to lay claim to land and other forms of wealth. The rise of new power brokers has left many young Gende males feeling disempowered, creating intergenerational tensions and troubled masculinities. But the most novel (and potentially destabilising) form of inequality to emerge is among women—not only the widening gap between males or between men and women—as some women have been able to capitalise on new economic opportunities to subvert patriarchal power structures and cut their social ties to assert new forms of autonomy.

Michael Main describes a similar set of generational changes in the context of the massive Papua New Guinea Liquefied Natural Gas (PNG LNG) project that covers vast tracts of Huli territory in Hela Province. Not only has this project failed to meet local expectations for development and change, but it has also reconfigured expressions of male authority, much like other extractive ventures in the region. In the 1950s, Robert Glasse described a system of Huli political authority that drew a distinction between expert knowledge and the ability to accumulate wealth. The PNG LNG project has created the conditions for these two types of leadership to converge, as those who are able to make successful truth claims about land and genealogies are able to secure huge quantities of wealth from the project, which they then convert into more political power. The adoption or 'invention' of the role of 'paramount chief', in what was formerly regarded as a 'chiefless society', has corresponded with increased levels of competition and bloody conflict and the elite capture of wealth.

While much discussion has focused on the relationship between extractive companies and the communities affected by their operations, much less has been written about the Papua New Guineans employed in the extractive industries, some of whom are recruited because they belong to project-affected communities, while others are recruited from further afield. Colin Filer addresses this gap in his chapter on the forms of inequality and mobility that are created, moderated and accentuated through the employment opportunities created by large-scale mining in PNG. The mineral policy framework in PNG creates a series of 'zones of entitlement' around each major project, which entitles different sections of the population to different project-related benefits, including employment and business contracts. There are good reasons to believe that the extractive sector workforce is more mobile, in both a geographical and social sense, than any other sectoral workforce in PNG; elements of this workforce may even be considered as a sort of 'labour aristocracy' within the wage-earning population. The relationship between the social and geographical mobility of these workers, the inequalities within and beyond their ranks and the extent to which they have become detached from the moral economy that binds other Papua New Guineans to networks of kinship and affinity within the so-called '*wantok* system' would suggest that some jobs are better for 'development' than others.

In the final chapter, Nick Bainton considers the unequal social relations that have emerged within and across the different 'zones of entitlement' that surround the Lihir gold mine and the various counter-movements that have arisen in response to the asymmetries of power and wealth between the company and the community. The difference between the expectations of the community for corporate-funded social and economic development in return for access to their land and the ways in which the company has enacted its commitment to the ideology of 'corporate social responsibility' has resulted in a state of mutual incomprehension. Coupled with the impacts from the mine, this has produced a strong sense of indignation; community members frequently accuse the company and the government of reducing them to mere 'spectators on their own land'—an expression that reflects a specific type of subjectivity that accompanies large-scale resource extraction. Local outrage over this situation often manifests in a remarkable expression of negative agency, as the customary landowners of the mine lease areas use a traditional taboo marker (known locally as a *gorgor*) to menace the mine.

Bridging the substantive chapters and the personal reflections on Martha Macintyre's legacy that conclude this volume, Margaret Jolly's 'Interlude' reminds us of the intersecting inequalities of gender, race and class that are foregrounded throughout the preceding chapters and also in so much of Martha's work. Jolly underscores three key characteristics of Martha's scholarship: a sustained critique of class and gender inequality, insistent attention to historical transformation and a strong ethic of ethnographic fidelity. After weaving together themes from each of the papers, Jolly brings us back to the vignette from the Pacific Islands Forum that featured at the outset of this chapter to underscore the urgency and the gravity of the inequalities inherent in our shared climate emergency. In our increasingly overheated world, existing inequalities will only assume more perverse and tragic forms. It is difficult to be optimistic about the future when the fossil fuel industries and Australia's sclerotic political system seem incapable of change. In these troubling times, Jolly reminds us of the best that anthropology can offer, exemplified in Martha's work: the capacity to bring activism and scholarship to bear on the most serious issues of our time, to genuinely engage those who have much to lose and those who have much to contribute.

References

Akin, D. (2013). *Colonialism, Maasina rule and the origins of Malaitan kastom.* Honolulu, HI: University of Hawai'i Press.

Akin, D. & Robbins, J. (1999). *Money and modernity: State and local currencies in Melanesia.* Pittsburgh, PA: University of Pittsburgh Press.

Alexeyeff, K. & Taylor, J. (2016). *Touring Pacific cultures.* Canberra, ACT: ANU Press. doi.org/10.22459/TPC.12.2016

Allen, M. G. (2011). The political economy of logging in Solomon Islands. In R. Duncan (Ed.), *The political economy of economic reform in the Pacific* (pp. 277–301). Manila, Philippines: Asian Development Bank.

Allen, M. G. (2013). Melanesia's violent environments: Towards a political ecology of conflict in the western Pacific. *Geoforum, 44*, 152–161.

Allen, M. G. (2018). *Resource extraction and contentious states: Mining and the politics of scale in the Pacific Islands.* Singapore: Springer Singapore.

Alvaredo, F. et al. (2018). *World Inequality Report 2018.* World Inequality Lab. Retrieved from wid.world/world-inequality-lab/

Aqarau, T. (2020, 9 April). COVID-19 and Solomon Islands: The first casualties and possible ramifications. *DevPolicyBlog.* Retrieved from devpolicy.org/covid-19-and-solomon-islands-the-first-casualties-and-possible-ramifications-20200409/

Bainton, N. A. (2008). Men of kastom and the customs of men: Status, legitimacy and persistent values in Lihir, Papua New Guinea. *The Australian Journal of Anthropology, 19*(2), 195–213.

Bainton, N. A. (2009). Keeping the network out of view: Mining, distinctions and exclusion in Melanesia. *Oceania, 79*(1), 18–33.

Bainton, N. A. (2010). *The Lihir destiny: Cultural responses to mining in Melanesia.* Canberra, ACT: ANU E Press. doi.org/10.22459/LD.10.2010

Bainton, N. A. (2017). Migrants, labourers and landowners at the Lihir gold mine, Papua New Guinea. In C. Filer & P.-Y. Le Meur (Eds), *Large-scale mines and local-level politics: Between New Caledonia and Papua New Guinea* (pp. 313–351). Canberra, ACT: ANU Press. doi.org/10.22459/LMLP.10.2017

Bainton, N. A. & Banks, G. (2018). Land and access: A framework for analysing mining, migration and development in Melanesia. *Sustainable Development, 26*(5), 450–460.

Bainton, N. & Jackson, R. T. (2020). Adding and sustaining benefits: Large-scale mining and landowner business development in Papua New Guinea. *The Extractive Industries and Society, 7*(2), 366–375. doi.org/10.1016/j.exis.2019.10.005

Bainton, N. A. & Macintyre, M. (2016). Mortuary ritual and mining riches in Island Melanesia. In D. Lipset & E. Silverman (Eds), *Mortuary dialogues: Death ritual and the reproduction of moral community in Pacific modernities* (pp. 110–132). New York, NY: Berghahn.

Banivanua-Mar, T. (2006). *Violence and colonial dialogue: The Australian-Pacific indentured labor trade.* Honolulu, HI: University of Hawai'i Press.

Banivanua-Mar, T. (2016). *Decolonisation and the Pacific: Indigenous globalisation and the ends of empire.* Cambridge, England: Cambridge University Press.

Barclay, K. (2012). Development and negative constructions of ethnic identity: Responses to Asian fisheries investment in the Pacific. *The Contemporary Pacific, 24*(1), 31–64.

Barker, J. (2012). The enigma of Christian conversion: Exchange and the emergence of new great men among the Maisin of Papua New Guinea. In L. Dousset & S. Tcherke´zoff (Eds), *The scope of anthropology: Maurice Godelier's work in context* (pp. 46–66). Oxford, England: Berghahn.

Barker, J. (2019). Mixed grammars and tangled hierarchies: An Austronesian-Papuan contact zone in Papua New Guinea. *Anthropological Forum, 29*(3), 284–301.

Bashkow, I. (2006). *The meaning of whitemen: Race and modernity in the Orokaiva cultural world*. Chicago, IL: University of Chicago Press.

Bebbington, A. & Humphreys Bebbington, D. (2018). Mining, movements and sustainable development: Concepts for a framework. *Sustainable Development*, *26*(5), 441–449. doi.org/10.1002/sd.1888

Beer, B. (2018). Gender and inequality in a postcolonial context of large-scale capitalist projects in the Markham Valley, Papua New Guinea. *The Australian Journal of Anthropology*, *29*(3), 348–364.

Beldi, L. (2018, 17 October). PNG government splurges on 40 Maseratis for APEC leaders as polio returns to the country. *Australian Broadcasting Corporation*. Retrieved from www.abc.net.au/news/2018-10-12/png-splurges-on-40-custom-maseratis-as-polio-returns/10366734

Bennett, J. A. (2000). *Pacific forest: A history of resource control and contest in Solomon Islands, c. 1800–1997*. Cambridge, England: White Horse Press.

Bennett, J. A. (2002). *Roots of conflict in Solomon Islands. Though much is taken much abides: legacies of tradition and colonialism* (SSGM Discussion Paper 2005/5). Retrieved from dpa.bellschool.anu.edu.au/experts-publications/publications/1541/roots-conflict-solomon-islands-though-much-taken-much-abides

Biersack, A. (2016). Introduction: Emergent masculinities in the Pacific. *The Asia Pacific Journal of Anthropology*, *17*(3–4), 197–212. doi.org/10.1080/144422 13.2016.1186215

Biersack, A., Jolly, M. & Macintyre, M. (Eds). (2016). *Gender violence and human rights: Seeking justice in Fiji, Papua New Guinea and Vanuatu*. Canberra, ACT: ANU Press. doi.org/10.22459/GVHR.12.2016

Boochani, B. (2018). *No friend but the mountains: Writing from Manus prison*. Sydney, NSW: Pan Macmillan Australia Pty Ltd.

Bryant-Tokalau, J. (2012). Twenty years on: Poverty and hardship in urban Fiji. *Bijdragen tot de Taal-, Land- en Volkenkunde, 168*(2/3), 195–218.

Burridge, K. (1971). *New heaven, new earth: A study of millenarian activities*. Oxford, England: Basil Blackwell.

Burton, J. (2018). Are the people of Manda in Middle Fly poor? A development assessment using the Oxford Multidimensional Poverty Index. *Contemporary PNG Studies: DWU Research Journal, 28*, 85–98.

Choi, H & Jolly, M. (Eds). (2014). *Divine domesticities: Christian paradoxes in Asia and the Pacific*. Canberra, ACT: ANU Press. doi.org/10.22459/DD.10.2014

Coetzee, J. M. (2019, 26 September). Australia's shame. *The New York Review of Books*. Retrieved from www.nybooks.com/articles/2019/09/26/australias-shame/

Cox, J. (2015). Israeli technicians and the post-colonial racial triangle in Papua New Guinea. *Oceania, 85*(3), 342–358.

Cox, J. (2018). *Fast money schemes: Hope and deception in Papua New Guinea.* Bloomington and Indianapolis, IN: Indiana University Press.

Cox, J. & Macintyre, M. (2014). Christian marriage, money scams and Melanesian social imaginaries. *Oceania, 84*(2), 138–157.

Cox, J. & Phillips, G. (2015). Sorcery, Christianity and the decline of medical services in Melanesia. In M. Forsyth & R. Eves (Eds), *Talking it through: Responses to sorcery and witchcraft beliefs and practices in Melanesia* (pp. 37–54). Canberra, ACT: ANU Press. doi.org/10.22459/TIT.05.2015

Crenshaw, K. (1989). Demarginalising the intersection of race and sex: A black feminist critique of antidiscrimination doctrine, feminist theory and antiracist politics. *University of Chicago Legal Forum, 1989*(1), 139–168.

Crocombe, R. (2007). *Asia in the Pacific: Replacing the West*. Suva, Fiji: IPS Publications.

Dickson-Waiko, A. (2003). The missing rib: Mobilising church women for change in Papua New Guinea. *Oceania, 74*(1–2), 98–119.

Douglas, B. (1979). Rank, power, authority: A reassessment of traditional leadership in South Pacific societies. *The Journal of Pacific History, 14*(1), 2–27. doi.org/10.1080/00223347908572362

Douglas, B. (2003). Christianity, tradition and every modernity: Towards an anatomy of women's groupings in Melanesia. *Oceania, 64*(1), 6–23.

Douglas, B. (2008). Foreign bodies in Oceania. In Douglas, B. & C. Ballard (Eds), *Foreign bodies: Oceania and the science of race 1750–1940* (pp. 3–30). Canberra, ACT: ANU E Press. doi.org/10.22459/FB.11.2008

Errington, F. & Gewertz, D. (1994). From darkness to light in the George Brown Jubilee: The invention of nontradition and the inscription of a national history in East New Britain. *American Ethnologist, 21*(1), 104–122.

Errington, F. & Gewertz, D. (2004). *Yali's question: Sugar, culture and history.* Chicago, IL: University of Chicago Press.

Filer, C. (1985). What is this thing called brideprice? *Mankind, 15*(2), 163–183.

Filer, C. (1997). Compensation, rent and power in Papua New Guinea. In S. Toft (Ed.), *Compensation for resource development in Papua New Guinea* (pp. 156–189). Canberra, ACT: The Australian National University.

Filer, C. & Le Meur, P. Y. (2017). *Large-scale mines and local-level politics: Between New Caledonia and Papua New Guinea*. Canberra, ACT: ANU Press. doi.org/10.22459/LMLP.10.2017

Filer, C. & Sekhran, N. (1998). *Loggers, donors and resource owners*. London, England: International Institute for Environment and Development.

Finney, B. (1973). *Big-men and business: Entrepreneurship and economic growth in the New Guinea Highlands*. Canberra, ACT: Australian National University Press.

Foster, R. J. (1995). *Social reproduction and history in Melanesia: Mortuary ritual, gift exchange and custom in the Tanga Islands*. Cambridge, England: Cambridge University Press.

Foster, R. J. (2008). *Coca-globalisation: Following soft drinks from New York to New Guinea*. New York, NY: Palgrave Macmillan.

Gewertz, D. & Errington, F. (1999). *Emerging class in Papua New Guinea: The telling of difference*. Cambridge, England: Cambridge University Press.

Goddard, M. (2005). *The unseen city: Anthropological perspectives on Port Moresby, Papua New Guinea*. Canberra, ACT: Pandanus Books.

Goddard, M. (2017). A categorical failure: 'Mixed race' in colonial Papua New Guinea. In F. Fozdar & K. McGavin (Eds), *Mixed race identities in Australia, New Zealand and the Pacific Islands* (pp. 133–146). New York, NY: Routledge.

Godelier, M. (1986). *The making of great men: Male domination and power among the New Guinea Baruya*. Cambridge, England: Cambridge University Press.

Godelier, M. & Strathern, M. (Eds). (1991). *Big men and great men: Personifications of power in Melanesia*. New York, NY: Cambridge University Press.

Golub, A. & Rhee, M. (2013). Traction: The role of executives in localising global mining and petroleum industries in Papua New Guinea. *Paideuma, 59*, 215–235.

Gregory, C. A. (1982). *Gifts and commodities*. London, England: Academic Press.

Hall, D., Hirsch, P. & Li, T. M. (2011). *Powers of exclusion: Land dilemmas in Southeast Asia*. Singapore: National University of Singapore Press.

Harvey, D. (2005). *A brief history of neoliberalism*. Oxford, England: Oxford University Press.

Hauʻofa, E. (1975). Anthropology and Pacific Islanders. *Oceania*, 45(4), 283–289. doi.org/10.1002/j.1834-4461.1975.tb01871.x

Hildson, A. M., Macintyre, M., Mackie, V. & Stivens, M. (Eds). (2000). *Human rights and gender politics: Perspectives on the Asia Pacific region*. London, England: Routledge.

Hobsbawm, E. & Ranger, T. (Eds). (1983). *The invention of tradition*. Cambridge, England: Cambridge University Press.

Hukula, F. (2015). *Blok laif: An ethnography of a Mosbi settlement* (Doctoral thesis). University of St Andrews, Scotland. Retrieved from hdl.handle.net/10023/11367

Hukula, F. (2018, 26 September). Melanesian anthropology em nem nating. *Society for Cultural Anthropology*. Retrieved from culanth.org/fieldsights/melanesian-anthropology-em-nem-nating

Hukula, F., Forsyth, M. & Gibbs, P. (2020). The importance of messaging for COVID-19. What can we learn from messaging against sorcery accusation related violence? *National Research Institute Papua New Guinea*. Retrieved from pngnri.org/index.php/blog/159-the-importance-of-messaging-for-covid-19-what-can-we-learn-from-messaging-against-sorcery-accusation-related-violence-2

Jacka, J. (2015). *Alchemy in the rain forest: Politics, ecology and resilience in a New Guinea mining area*. Durham, NC: Duke University Press.

Johnson, H. & McGavin, K. (2017). Constructing and interpreting 'mixed race' and 'mixed parentage' in Papua New Guinea. In F. Fozdar & K. McGavin (Eds), *Mixed race identities in Australia, New Zealand and the Pacific Islands*. New York, NY: Routledge.

Jolly, M. (1987). The chimera of equality in Melanesia. *Mankind*, 17(2), 168–183.

Jolly, M. (1992). Specters of inauthenticity. *The Contemporary Pacific*, 4(1), 49–72.

Jolly, M. (2001). Imagining Oceania: Indigenous and foreign representations of a sea of islands. In D. Yui & Y. Endo (Eds), *Framing the Pacific in the 21st century: Coexistence and friction* (pp. 29–48). Tokyo, Japan: Center for Pacific and American Studies, University of Tokyo.

Jolly, M. (2008). Moving masculinities: Memories and bodies across Oceania. *The Contemporary Pacific*, 20(1), 1–24.

Jolly, M. (2015). Braed praes in Vanuatu: Both gifts and commodities. *Oceania*, *85*(1), 63–78.

Jolly, M. (2019). Engendering the anthropocene in Oceania: Fatalism, resilience, resistance. *Cultural Studies Review*, *25*(2), 172–195.

Jolly, M. & Macintyre, M. (Eds). (1989). *Family and gender in the Pacific: Domestic contradictions and the colonial impact*. Cambridge, England: Cambridge University Press.

Jolly, M. & Mosko, M. (1994). Transformations of hierarchy: Structure, history and horizon in the Austronesian world. *History and Anthropology*, *7*(1–4), 1–18.

Jolly, M., Stewart, C. & Brewer, C. (Eds). (2012). *Engendering violence in Papua New Guinea*. Canberra, ACT: ANU E Press. doi.org/10.22459/EVPNG. 07.2012

Josephides, L. (1985). *The production of inequality: Gender and exchange among the Kewa*. London, England: Tavistock.

Josephides, L. (1991). Metaphors, metathemes and the construction of sociality: A critique of the new Melanesian ethnography. *Man*, *26*(1), 145–161.

Kabutaulaka, T. (2015). Representing Melanesia: Ignoble savages and Melanesian alternatives. *The Contemporary Pacific*, *27*(1), 74–145.

Kabutaulaka, T. & Teaiwa, K. (2019). *Climate, coal, kinship and security in Australia-Pacific relations*. Retrieved from www.internationalaffairs.org.au/australian outlook/climate-coal-kinship-and-security-in-australia-pacific-relations/

Kapferer, B. (2005). New formations of power, the oligarchic-corporate state and anthropological ideological discourse. *Anthropological Theory*, *5*(3), 285–299.

Keesing, R. (1969). Chiefs in a chiefless society: The ideology of modern Kwaio Politics. *Oceania*, *38*(4), 278–280.

Keesing, R. (1985). Killers, big men and priests on Malaita: Reflections on a Melanesian troika system. *Ethnology*, *24*(4), 237–252. doi.org/10.2307/ 3773736.

Keesing, R. (1992). *Custom and confrontation: The Kwaio struggle for cultural autonomy*. Chicago, IL: University of Chicago Press.

Keesing, R. & Jolly, M. (1992). Epilogue. In J. G. Carrier (Ed.), *History and tradition in Melanesian anthropology*. Berkeley, CA: University of California Press.

Keesing, R. & Tonkinson, R. (Eds). (1982). Reinventing traditional culture: The politics of kastom in island Melanesia [Special issue]. *Mankind*, *13*(4).

Kelly, R. (1993). *Constructing inequality: The fabrication of a hierarchy of virtue among the Etoro*. Ann Arbor, MI: University of Michigan Press.

Kirsch, S. (2014). *Mining capitalism: The relationship between corporations and their critics*. Oakland, CA: University of California Press.

Klein, N. (2007). *The shock doctrine: The rise of disaster capitalism*. New York, NY: Metropolitan Books.

Knauft, B. (2019). Good anthropology in dark times: Critical appraisal and ethnographic application. *The Australian Journal of Anthropology*, *30*(1), 3–17.

Koczberski, G., Curry, G. N. & Anjen, J. (2015). Changing land tenure and informal land markets in the oil palm frontier regions of Papua New Guinea: The challenge for land reform. In G. Curry, G. Koczberski & J. Connell (Eds), *Migration, land and livelihoods: Creating alternative modernities in the Pacific* (pp. 67–82). Abingdon, England: Routledge.

Ku, K. H. & Gibson, T. (2019). Hierarchy and egalitarianism in Austronesia. *Anthropological Forum*, *29*(3), 201–215. doi.org/10.1080/00664677.2019.1626216

Lahiri-Dutt, K. & Macintyre, M. (2006). *Women miners in developing countries: Pit women and others*. Aldershot, England: Ashgate.

Lawrence, P. (1964). *Road belong cargo: A study of the cargo movement in the Southern Madang District New Guinea*. Melbourne, Vic.: Melbourne University Press.

Lawson, S. (2013). Melanesia: The history and politics of an idea. *The Journal of Pacific History*, *48*(1), 1–22.

Levine, H., B. & Levine, M. (1979). *Urbanisation in Papua New Guinea: A study of ambivalent townsmen*. Cambridge, England: Cambridge University Press.

Lindstrom, L. (1993). *Cargo cult: Strange stories of desire from Melanesia and beyond*. Honolulu, HI: University of Hawai'i Press.

Lindstrom, L. & Jourdan, C. (2017). Urban Melanesia. *Journal de la Société des Océanistes*, *144–145*(1), 5a–22a.

Macintyre, M. (1983). Warfare and the changing context of Kune on Tubetube. *The Journal of Pacific History*, *18*(1–2), 11–34.

Macintyre, M. (1984). The problem of the semi-alienable pig. *Canberra Anthropology*, *7*(1–2), 109–122.

Macintyre, M. (1994). Too many chiefs? Leadership in the Massim in the colonial era. *History and Anthropology*, 7(1–4), 241–262.

Macintyre, M. (1995). Violent bodies and vicious exchanges: Personification and objectification in the Massim. *Social Analysis*, 37, 29–43.

Macintyre, M. (2011). Modernity, gender and mining: Experiences from Papua New Guinea. In K. Lahiri-Dutt (Ed.), *Gendering the field: Towards sustainable livelihoods for mining communities* (pp. 21–32). Canberra, ACT: ANU E Press, doi.org/10.22459/GF.03.2011.02

Macintyre, M. (2012). Gender violence in Melanesia and the problem of millennium development goal No. 3. In M. Jolly, C. Stewart & C. Brewer (Eds), *Engendering violence in Papua New Guinea* (pp. 239–266). Canberra, ACT: ANU E Press. doi.org/10.22459/EVPNG.07.2012

Macintyre, M. (2017). Flux and change in Melanesian gender relations. In Macintyre, M. & C. Spark (Eds), *Transformations of gender in Melanesia* (pp. 1–22). Canberra, ACT: ANU Press. doi.org/10.22459/TGM.02.2017

Macintyre, M. & Spark, C. (Eds). (2017). *Transformations of gender in Melanesia*. Acton, ACT: ANU Press. doi.org/10.22459/TGM.02.2017

Martin, K. (2013). *The death of the big men and the rise of the big shots: Custom and conflict in East New Britain*. New York, NY: Berghahn.

McCormack, M. (2019, 16 August). Pacific islands will survive climate crisis because they 'pick our fruit', Australia's deputy PM says. *The Guardian*. Retrieved from www.theguardian.com/australia-news/2019/aug/16/pacific-islands-will-survive-climate-crisis-because-they-can-pick-our-fruit-australias-deputy-pm-says

McDonnell, S. (2017). Urban land grabbing by political elites: Exploring the political economy of land and the challenges of regulations. In S. McDonnell, M. G. Allen & C. Filer (Eds), *Kastom, property and ideology: Land transformations in Melanesia* (pp. 283–304). Canberra, ACT: ANU Press. doi.org/10.22459/KPI.03.2017

McDonnell, S., Allen, M. & Filer, C. (Eds). (2017). *Kastom, property and ideology: Land transformations in Melanesia*. Canberra, ACT: ANU Press. doi.org/10.22459/KPI.03.2017

McDougall, D. (2009). Christianity, relationality and the material limits of individualism: Reflections on Robbins's becoming sinners. *The Asia Pacific Journal of Anthropology*, 10(1), 1–19.

McDougall, D. (2015). Customary authority and state withdrawal in Solomon Islands: Resilience or tenacity? *The Journal of Pacific History*, *50*(4), 450–472.

Mead, M. (1956). *New lives for old: Cultural transformation - Manus, 1928–1953*. New York, NY: William Morrow and Company.

Modjeska, N. (1982). Production and inequality: Perspectives from central New Guinea. In A. Strathern (Ed.), *Inequality in New Guinea Highlands societies* (pp. 50–108). Cambridge, England: Cambridge University Press.

Morauta, L. & Ryan, D. (1982). From temporary to permanent townsmen: Migrants from the Malalaua district, Papua New Guinea. *Oceania*, *53*(1), 39–55.

Morgan, M. (2019). *Winds of change: Pacific islands and the shifting balance of power in the Pacific Ocean* (SGDIA Working Paper No 10). Retrieved from University of the South Pacific website: apo.org.au/node/262801

Mosko, M. (2015). Unbecoming individuals: The partible character of the Christian person. *HAU: Journal of Ethnographic Theory*, *5*(1), 361–393.

Munro, J. (2017). Gender struggles of educated men in the Papuan highlands. In M. Macintyre & C. Spark (Eds), *Transformations of gender in Melanesia* (pp. 45–68). Canberra, ACT: ANU Press. doi.org/10.22459/TGM.02.2017

Murray-Atfield, Y. (2018, 3 October). 'Polio came back': Fears for hundreds of children after first PNG death in 20 years. *Australian Broadcasting Corporation*. Retrieved from www.abc.net.au/news/2018-10-03/polio-death-recorded-in-png-for-first-time-in-more-than-20-years/10328594

Ortner, S. B. (2016). Dark anthropology and its others: Theory since the eighties. *HAU: Journal of Ethnographic Theory*, *6*(1), 47–73. doi.org/10.14318/hau6.1.004

Piketty, T. (2014). *Capital in the twenty-first century*. Cambridge, England: The Belknap Press of Harvard University Press.

Ram, K. & Jolly, M. (1998). *Maternities and modernities*. Cambridge, England: Cambridge University Press.

Rawlings, G. (2011). Relative trust: The Vanuatu tax haven and the management of elite family fortunes. In M. Patterson & Macintyre, M. (Eds), *Managing modernity in the Western Pacific* (pp. 260–305). St Lucia, Qld: University of Queensland Press.

Regenvanu, R. (2019, 19 August). Vanuatu will host the next Pacific Islands Forum. We want to know if Australia really wants a seat at the table. *The Guardian*. Retrieved from www.theguardian.com/world/2019/aug/20/vanuatu-will-host-the-next-pacific-islands-forum-we-want-to-know-if-australia-really-wants-a-seat-at-the-table

Reiter, R. R. (1975). *Toward an anthropology of women*. New York, NY: Monthly Review Press.

Rio, K. & Smedal, O. H. (2008). *Hierarchy: Persistence and transformation in social formations*. New York, NY: Berghahn Books.

Robbins, B. (2017). *The beneficiary*. Durham, NC: Duke University Press.

Robbins, J. (1994). Equality as value: Ideology in Dumont, Melanesia and the West. *Social Analysis, 36*, 21–70.

Robbins, J. (2004). *Becoming sinners: Christianity and moral torment in a Papua New Guinea society*. Berkeley, CA: University of California Press.

Robbins, J. (2013). Beyond the suffering subject: Toward an anthropology of the good. *Journal of the Royal Anthropological Institute, 19*(3), 447–462. doi.org/10.1111/1467-9655.12044

Rooney, M. N. (2017). 'There's nothing better than land': A migrant group's strategies for accessing informal settlement land in Port Moresby. In S. McDonnell, M. G. Allen & C. Filer (Eds), *Kastom, property and ideology: Land transformations in Melanesia* (pp. 111–143). Canberra, ACT: ANU Press. doi.org/10.22459/KPI.03.2017

Rooney, M. N. (2018, 26 September). Hotspot: From reciprocity to relationality: Anthropological possibilities. *Society for Cultural Anthropology*. Retrieved from culanth.org/fieldsights/other

Rooney, M. N. (2020, 11 March). Behrouz Boochani's *No Friend but the Mountains*: An Oceanian lens. *DevPolicyBlog*. Retrieved from devpolicy.org/behrouz-boochanis-no-friend-but-the-mountain-an-oceanian-lens-20200311/

Rosaldo, M. Z., Lamphere, L. & Bamberger, J. (1974). *Woman, culture and society*. Stanford, CA: Stanford University Press.

Sahlins, M. (1963). Poor man, rich man, big-man, chief: Political types in Melanesia and Polynesia. *Comparative Studies in Society and History, 5*(3), 285–303.

Sahlins, M. (1992). The economics of develop-man in the Pacific. *Res: Anthropology and Aesthetics, 21*(Spring), 13–25.

Salyer, J. C. (2018, December). *Old savage, new savage: The denial of human dignity in the age of human rights*. Paper presented at the European Society for Oceanists, Cambridge, England.

Scott, M. W. (2007). Neither 'new Melanesian history' nor 'new Melanesian ethnography': Recovering emplaced matrilineages in Southeast Solomon Islands. *Oceania, 77*(3), 337–354. doi.org/10.1002/j.1834-4461.2007. tb00020.x

Sharp, T., Cox, J. Spark, C., Lusby, S. & Rooney, M. (2015). *The formal, the informal and the precarious: Making a living in urban Papua New Guinea* (SSGM Discussion Paper 2015/2). Canberra, ACT: The Australian National University.

Shaxson, N. (2011). *Treasure islands: Tax havens and the men who stole the world*. London, England: Palgrave Macmillan.

Siegel, J. (1985). Origins of Pacific Islands labourers in Fiji. *Journal of Pacific History, 20*(1), 42–54.

Sillitoe, P. (1979). *Give and take: Exchange in Wola society*. Canberra, ACT: Australian National University Press.

Smith, G. (2013). Nupela masta? Local and expatriate labour in a Chinese-run nickel mine in Papua New Guinea. *Asia Studies Review, 37*(2), 178–195.

Spark, C. (2017). Getting comfortable: Gender, class and belonging in the 'new' Port Moresby. *Journal of the Société des Océanistes, 144–145*(1), 147–158.

Spark, C. (2019). At home in the city: Educated women, housing and belonging in Port Moresby. In S. Pinto et al. (Eds), *Interdisciplinary unsettlings of place and space: Conversations, investigations and research* (pp. 183–195). Singapore: Springer.

Spark, C. (2020). 'Two different worlds': Papua New Guinean women working in development in Port Moresby. *Asia Pacific Viewpoint*. doi.org/10.1111/apv.12271

Spark, C., Cox, J. & Corbett, J. (2019). Gender, political representation and symbolic capital: How some women politicians succeed. *Third World Quarterly, 40*(7), 1227–1245.

Stead, V. (2020, 24 March). Australia's food supply relies on migrant workers who are facing coronavirus limbo. *The Guardian*. Retrieved from www.theguardian.com/world/commentisfree/2020/mar/24/australias-food-supply-relies-on-migrant-workers-who-are-facing-coronavirus-limbo

Stead, V. & Altman, J. (Eds). (2019). *Labour lines and colonial power: Indigenous and Pacific Islander labour mobility in Australia*. Canberra, ACT: ANU Press. doi.org/10.22459/LLCP.2019

Strathern, A. (1971). *The rope of Moka: Big-men and ceremonial exchange in Mount Hagen, New Guinea*. Cambridge, England: Cambridge University Press.

Strathern, A. (1982). *Inequality in New Guinea Highlands societies*. Cambridge, England: Cambridge University Press.

Strathern, M. (1975). *No money on our skins: Hagen migrants in Port Moresby*. Port Moresby, Papua New Guinea: The Australian National University.

Strathern, M. (1987). *Dealing with inequality: Analysing gender relations in Melanesia and beyond*. Cambridge, England: Cambridge University Press.

Strathern, M. (1988). *The gender of the gift*. Berkeley, CA: University of California Press.

Taylor, J. (2008a). The social life of rights: 'Gender antagonism', modernity and raets in Vanuatu. *The Australian Journal of Anthropology, 19*(2), 165–178.

Taylor, J. (2008b). Changing Pacific masculinities: The 'problem' of men. *The Australian Journal of Anthropology, 19*(2), 125–135.

Teaiwa, K. (2019). No distant future: Climate change as an existential threat. *Australian Foreign Affairs, 6*, 51–70.

Thomas, N. (1989). The force of ethnology: Origins and significance of the Melanesia/Polynesia division. *Current Anthropology, 30*(1), 27–41.

Tomlinson, M. & McDougall, D. (2013). *Christian politics in Oceania*. New York, NY: Berghahn.

Trnka, S. (2008). *State of suffering political violence and community survival in Fiji*. Ithaca, NY: Cornell University Press.

United Nations Development Programme. (2018). *United Nations Development Programme annual report 2018*. Retrieved from annualreport.undp.org/

Wardlow, H. (2006). *Wayward women: Sexuality and agency in a New Guinea society*. Berkeley, CA: University of California Press.

Wardlow, H. (2018, December). *Thinking through intersectionality and gender inequality in Papua New Guinea*. Paper presented at the European Society for Oceanists, Cambridge, England.

West, P. (2016). *Dispossession and the environment: Rhetoric and inequality in Papua New Guinea*. La Vergne, TN: Columbia University Press.

West, P. (2018, December). *Dispossession and disappearance in the post sovereign Pacific: The regional resettlement agreement between Australia and Papua New Guinea, an ethnography of loss*. Paper presented at the European Society for Oceanists, Cambridge, England.

White, G. M. (1991). *Identity through history: Living stories in a Solomon Islands society*. Cambridge, England: Cambridge University Press.

White, G. M. (1992). The discourse of chiefs: Notes on a Melanesian society. *The Contemporary Pacific, 4*(1), 73–108.

White, G., M. & Lindstrom, L. (Eds). (1997). *Chiefs today: Traditional Pacific leadership and the postcolonial state*. Stanford, CA: Stanford University Press.

Wilkinson, R. G. & Pickett, K. (2009). *The spirit level: Why more equal societies almost always do better*. London, England: Allen Lane.

Winter, C. (2017). Lingering legacies of German colonialism: The 'mixed race' identities in Oceania. In F. Fozdar & K. McGavin, *Mixed race identities in Australia, New Zealand and the Pacific Islands* (pp. 147–161). New York, NY: Routledge.

Wood, T. (2020, 30 March). What will COVID-19 mean for the Pacific: A problem in four parts. *DevPolicyBlog*. Retrieved from devpolicy.org/what-will-covid-19-mean-for-the-pacific-a-problem-in-four-parts-20200330/

World Bank. (2018). Poverty and shared prosperity 2018: Piecing together the poverty puzzle. Washington, DC: World Bank.

Zimmer-Tamakoshi, L. (1993). Nationalism and sexuality in Papua New Guinea. *Pacific Studies, 16*(4), 20–48.

Zimmer-Tamakoshi, L. (1997). The last big man: Development and men's discontents in the Papua New Guinea Highlands. *Oceania, 68*(2), 107–122.

Zimmer-Tamakoshi, L. (1998). Women in town: Housewives, homemakers and household managers. In L. Zimmer-Tamakoshi (Ed.), *Modern Papua New Guinea* (pp. 195–210). Kirksville, MO: Thomas Jefferson University Press.

2

'I Will Be Travelling to Kavieng!': Work, Labour and Inequality in New Ireland, Papua New Guinea

Paige West and John Aini

Introduction

Date: 9 June
Subject: Introduction and Arrival in Kavieng 1st of July
To: Ailan Awareness

Dear John,

My name is Mary[1] and I am a Master's student in Human Rights at [a big famous university in Europe]. I'm also an aspiring filmmaker. Next month, I will be travelling to Kavieng to study local forms of resistance to [a very controversial topic] in Papua New Guinea.

Mr Martin Simpson [a staff member of a big international non-governmental organisation (BINGO)] has notified me that you will be my contact person for accommodation in Kavieng. I have

---

1   We use pseudonyms throughout this paper.

therefore attached my travel itinerary and will be arriving in Kavieng on the 1st of July at 3:00 pm. He has provided me with this address for my stay: C/- P. O. Box 329, Kavieng, NIP.

I am writing to you to introduce myself and to hear if there are any things that I should plan for when I arrive – taxi, etc? My tickets are attached.

I look forward to hearing from you and meeting you very soon!

Best regards,
Mary

The emails almost always follow the above format. After the signature, the sender has attached their flight details, including their ticket receipt and itinerary. The reader of the email, the director of Ailan Awareness, a small New Ireland–based Papua New Guinea (PNG) non-governmental organisation (NGO), and one of the co-authors of this chapter, usually rereads the email several times, worries about it for two to three days. Then, they forward it on to their research partner, the other co-author of this chapter, who is a professor at a university in New York City and who now handles much of the initial correspondence between Ailan Awareness and the people whom the two of them have begun to view, over the course of their 13-year collaboration, as 'hard work'.

The sender of the email is, invariably, between the ages of 19 and 30 and from Europe, Australia or the United States (US). They are always white.[2] They are either in a terminal degree program, working as a 'freelance' filmmaker, photographer or activist or travelling with the intent of developing a project to apply for a terminal degree program or make a proposal for some form of future creative work. They wish to come to New Ireland Province, PNG, to 'do work' that is in some way connected to a liberal politics of social and environmental justice, the conservation of biological or cultural diversity or some form of humanitarian-related

---

2   Henry (2019) has called for more a more engaged and robust study of whiteness in the literature concerned with the global movement of cosmopolitan elites. He asked that we engage a critical race theory framework to understand the structural features that uphold white supremacy and the structural inequality faced by non-white actors. Although it is focused on voluntourism, we think his call also fits for the phenomena we are examining. Moore (2019) examined issues of race and racism in her work on sciences as tourism in the Bahamas, to show the asymmetries of power that underpin sciences and that are reinforced by tourism. In an unpublished work (Aini & West, n.d.), drawing on these scholars, we have begun to think through the racial politics of whiteness in conservation in PNG. We do not have the space to rehearse our arguments here; however, we wish to mark that whiteness matters tremendously.

topic. These people want to 'make a difference'. They have almost always been in touch with someone working for a BINGO in PNG who knows about Ailan Awareness and their work and who has, to use a term from American gridiron football, 'punted' their request for help on to the director of Ailan Awareness. The sender, often someone who knows almost nothing about PNG, the politics between big non-governmental organisations (NGOs) and small NGOs or the financial situation of small NGOs, assumes that the PNG NGO is there to help facilitate their project. They assume this because they were told so by whoever connected them to Ailan Awareness.

The sender of the email has rarely done any serious reading of the vast body of anthropological literature concerning their topic of interest, New Ireland Province or PNG more generally. They have often read popular works about the place and its biological and cultural context there (e.g. magazine and newspaper articles). Therefore, they are unlikely to have been exposed to any sustained discussion and analysis of the *in situ* social conventions around exchange, reciprocity, gender relations or the local systems of prestige and honour. The sender never speaks a local language—of which there are 18 in New Ireland Province—and rarely possesses any linguistic ability in Melanesian Tok Pisin, the creole language that is the most widely used language in the country. More often than not, they are travelling to the country on a tourist visa and are paying for their visit with their own funds.

Since the 1980s, scholars have described people like the ones we endeavour to understand in this chapter as 'scientific tourists' (see Laarman & Perdue, 1989). West has argued that scientific tourism is a form of 'alternative tourism' that allows tourists to build prestige and social capital and that it allows for complex identity work that is both self-building and guilt-alleviating (West, 2008, pp. 604–606). She demonstrated that scientific tourism is usually, in the context of PNG, a form of ecotourism and argued that people like some of the ones we describe in this chapter are enacting a form of scientific tourism (West, 2008). More recently, Moore has shown how entire tourism economies develop with 'research' and 'science' as crucial components of their infrastructure (Moore, 2019). Moore, working in the Bahamas, showed how formalised research experiences designed by universities and longstanding research institutions work to structure experience and socioeconomic-ecological life for local people (Moore, 2019). She has argued that, through examining these touristic forms, we can also come to understand something crucial about our current sociopolitical-ecological world—what some have called the 'anthropocene' (Moore, 2019, p. 25).

Other scholars have demonstrated the connection between research tourism and volunteer tourism (Campbell, Gray & Meletis, 2008). While volunteer tourists may have different intentions to ecotourists and research tourists, there are certainly overlaps in intention, desire and outcome in the forms (Campbell, Haalboom & Trow, 2007; Gray & Campbell, 2007). Both ecotourism and volunteer tourism are big business (Conran, 2011) and big sites for scholarly analysis (Butcher & Smith, 2015). Butcher and Smith (2015) argued that volunteer tourism is based on a sense among cosmopolitan elites that travel should be connected to something of political and ethical significance, and that people engaged in it use it as a way to engage in political action. As a form, it allows people to feel that they have shown care and 'made a difference', while at the same time building a kind of self that they see as moral, ethical and connected to a global ethic of responsibility (Butcher & Smith, 2015). Others working in this field of analysis have argued that more analysis is required of the effects of this form of tourism on the localities in which it is enacted and that we must see the people making these trips as agents and not simply as passive, well-meaning individuals caught up in systems of capitalist extraction (Griffiths, 2016). Therefore, we see this chapter as connecting to the tourism literature.

In this chapter, we analyse these kinds of requests and the social and economic interactions and relations that enable them and stem from them, using four different lenses. First, we locate this kind of request within a broader field of structural inequality and patron–client relationships that envelop small NGOs in places like PNG, by describing the history of Ailan Awareness and its relationships with BINGOs. Further, we show how this history creates the conditions of possibility for both the 'punting' of the requests and the practice of saying 'yes' to the requests by Ailan Awareness staff.[3] Second, we describe in detail the form that these requests

---

3   We are highly attuned to the extreme sensitivity that BINGOs experience when scholars and practitioners write about them. We do not write about them lightly and we are not 'blaming' them for anything. Rather, we are focusing on their structural position in systems of inequality in PNG. We could also highlight the structural position of other kinds of institutions (e.g. churches, government offices, universities or businesses) in systems of inequality in the country. This would also not be about 'blame'. We do not intend to hurt the feelings of the BINGOs or their staff with our analysis. Rather, we attempt to illuminate a system that is both inherently unequal and enduring.

manifest through communication, and we expose both the naivety and the privilege behind them. We do this to clarify the structural conditions that allow for the production of inequality that we demonstrate throughout the chapter. Next, we show the forms of work and economic expenditures required to meet these requests and the social and economic debts incurred in meeting them. We contextualise this in a brief discussion of labour and conservation more generally. Alongside this, we examine the mobilisation of networked social relations of obligation and reciprocity required and expended when this sort of request is met. Finally, we tie all of this back to the enduring structural inequality that forms the conditions of work for small NGOs and the continuation of a kind of labour-intensive patron–client relationship between small and large NGOs. We do not analyse the motivations that drive these individuals to come to New Ireland; therefore, this is not an ethnographic study of their touristic desires. Nor do we analyse the identity work that these individuals undertake during and after their visits. Our interest is primarily the inequality that is exacerbated by their visit—inequality that they may well not understand prior to, during or after their visit.

The literature on inequality in PNG has focused on inequality in relation to traditional, yet changing, local sociocultural contexts (Kelly, 1993; Strathern, 1982); in relation to the colonial economy (Fitzpatrick, 1980), in terms of gender relations (Beer, 2018; Josephides, 1985; Zimmer-Tamokoshi, 2016) and in access to education (Johnson, 1993), knowledge (Ryan et al., 2016) and development (Connell, 2005). Gewertz and Errington (1999) have shown how various existing inequalities intersect with the emergence of class position, status and ideology in a postcolonial context. Wardlow (2006) has shown how historic and entrenched sociocultural inequalities, such as those mentioned above, intertwine with new forms of labour and work to produce cultured forms of envy, resentment and desire.[4] More recently, Roberts (2019b) has connected an analysis showing that large-scale logging and agricultural development increase local inequalities and disproportionately negatively affect women and lower-status individuals to an analysis of the structural inequalities that allowed for the issuing of the special agricultural and business leases that resulted in the same logging and agricultural projects. This could be read simply as an enduring anthropological interest in forms of difference

---

4   For a broad overview of the anthropological treatment of inequality in PNG, see Bainton and McDougall (this volume).

and their emergence in PNG.[5] However, Fabinyi, Foale and Macintyre (2015) have shown that concerns about the emergence and entrenchment of inequality are paramount in the minds of Papua New Guineans. They demonstrated that, without a doubt, understanding 'local priorities' regarding inequality and its redress should be a key goal of scholarship, policy making and development priorities (Fabinyi, Foale & Macintyre, 2015, p. 472). Our interest in inequality, conservation organisations and people who are 'hard work' follows this literature and, in particular, the arguments that understanding the relationship between individual inequality, how Papua New Guineans see and understand it and structural inequalities that are underpinned by larger, non-local relations of power, is important to Papua New Guineans.

---

5   This brings us to the question of where anthropologists fit into our analysis. Anthropologists have been coming to what is now New Ireland Province since the German colonial period of the 1880s. They have extracted objects such as Malagan funerary pieces, information such as kinship diagrams and land ownership charts and knowledge such as detailed descriptions concerning ontological propositions about what is, what can be and what will be. Little of this extracted material has ever been adequately repatriated to New Ireland and the anthropologists who have extracted it have benefited tremendously through the acquisition of paid positions as scholars, promotion to tenured positions and esteem notoriety in their field. Some of these anthropologists have maintained deep, enduring and complex social relationships of exchange and reciprocity with the people they have worked with. They return to their field sites frequently, maintain close communication with 'communities' and individuals when they are at home (rather than in PNG), pay for young people from the places they work to go to school or enter trade training programs, write grant proposals for community development projects and, more generally, sit comfortably within longstanding, enduring networks of reciprocity and exchange. Further, some of their anthropological work does 'benefit' the communities and individuals who contributed to it. These anthropologists seem to understand that their accumulation of both financial capital and social capital is tied to their extraction of material from New Ireland; therefore, they understand that their social relations there must be maintained and reciprocated adequately. However, some anthropologists do not seem to understand this point; consequently, their work serves as another form of extraction. Indeed, this is the case for all of what is now PNG. In this chapter, we do not have the space to articulate and examine the complexities of what we conceptualise as 'the debt that can never be paid' that anthropologists incur with their research in PNG. In a longer work, we would tease out the difference between knowledge production, something that we value and believe that anthropologists contribute to in both positive and negative ways (West, 2016), and pure knowledge and labour extraction—what we think happens with requests like the ones we will describe in the rest of this chapter. Suffice it to say, we do not believe anthropologists are innocent; however, we do believe, as our analysis is focused on a different kind of actor (one who visits New Ireland once and often never has anything else to do with the place), that a deep analysis of anthropology is beyond the scope of this particular paper.

Inequality, BINGOs and Ailan Awareness

In 1993, after working in and around international conservation NGOs and the National Fisheries Authority (NFA) as fisheries specialists and developing a critique of their practices, three young men from Lovongai Island (New Hanover) founded Ailan Awareness. Their initial goal was to engineer a new approach to local marine conservation that diverged from the norm of externally generated conservation goals that were developed, implemented and assessed by outsiders to one that grounded all new projects within the context of local sovereignty over resources, conservation initiatives and projects and the potential future of resources (Aini & Nason, 2016; Aini & West, 2018; West & Aini, 2018; see also Foale, this volume). In the 1990s, the founders of Ailan Awareness developed what has come to be known as 'The Road Show'—a process where Ailan Awareness staff go to coastal communities to conduct 'conservation awareness', helping rural and remote people to understand some of the science behind observable changes in coastal and marine biophysical environments and introducing them to scientific management techniques that were thought to help mitigate these changes. Employing men and women from New Ireland who spoke the local languages, understood the local political and social structures and who were, in most cases, socially embedded into the communities through the long tentacles of kinship relations and obligations across the region, the Road Show proved to be a very effective way to convey the goals of the Coastal Fisheries Management and Development Project (CFMDP), a project funded by the PNG government and various ocean conservation–related projects. During the following decade, word of the success that CFMDP was finding through their partnership with Ailan Awareness spread quickly in PNG. To say that there was a frenzied buy-in from BINGOs focused on marine conservation and from the national government for the methodology developed by Ailan Awareness would be an understatement.[6]

---

6   The NGO currently supports environmental conservation efforts in over 20 local communities (projects that were crafted by community residents rather than outside NGOs), supports a project developed by local master carvers focused on revitalising Malagan carving techniques and traditions and passing those traditions on to young people, conducts scholarly research on topics from climate change to Special Agricultural Business Leases (SABLs) and land grabbing and runs a small school focused on teaching at the nexus of local epistemology and ontology and the scientific method. Over the past 25 years, the NGO has been locally successful and has become internationally recognised for both its conservation work and its radical anti-dispossession stance and practice (Gokkon, 2018a, 2018b).

The late 1990s and early 2000s comprised the heyday of Community-Based Resource Management (CBRM) and Integrated Conservation and Development (ICAD) projects (Halvaksz, 2020; Van Helden, 1998; Wagner, 2007; West, 2006). These projects were generated in the Global North, based on conservation goals that had been identified by scientists working for BINGOs and in partnerships between those organisations, multilateral institutions (e.g. the United Nations) and big international lending institutions (e.g. the World Bank). The 'country programs' of the conservation BINGOs then carried out these projects locally. Part of the ideology driving them was the notion that previous conservation project failure, a chronic issue for conservation-related interventions, could be staved off by incorporating 'local people' into the management of biological diversity. Soon, Ailan Awareness had more work than they could manage. Everyone wanted a local team to go out to rural sites and 'teach' people about conservation, in general, and garner 'local participation' in their specific project. Ailan Awareness got swept up in this and performed well in terms of assisting NGOs and others to facilitate their projects. However, their vision—that of an organisation that also worked to educate outsiders regarding the importance of full local sovereignty over biodiversity conservation projects—was not fulfilled.

Throughout the late 1990s and early 2000s, most of the BINGOs working in island PNG wanted to engage Ailan Awareness to do CBRM and ICAD education. However, they were only willing to pay them for services rendered per project; they were unwilling to support them further by funding organisational operating costs such as office rent, computer support or salaries for staff at times when there were no projects to be done (see West, 2016). This put the founders of Ailan Awareness in an awkward position—they needed the work from the BINGOs to continue to do the unpaid project work that Ailan Awareness was undertaking with communities; therefore, they felt that they had to take the work offered to them. Essentially, a 'patron–client' relationship developed between the small NGO and several big organisations—Ailan Awareness became a service provider to the very kinds of projects that John, Miller and Michael, its founders, had initially founded the organisation to counter.

Through their success in undertaking and completing contract work for the BINGOs, Ailan Awareness became a kind of cover for BINGOs, so that they could say to their funders—organisations that were increasingly nervous following several well-publicised critiques of such organisations' lack of local engagement and local partners (see Chapin, 2004)—that they had engaged an indigenous NGO as an equal partner in their work. However, these partnerships were incredibly unequal. Ailan Awareness was only engaged to do waged contract work; they were not consistently funded at a level that allowed for them to adequately maintain an office, a staff, a vehicle or a boat. All of these are required to be a functioning NGO and, at the time, were being paid for through the Gillet Preston and Associates, Asian Development Bank (ADB) and NFA partnership. However, with Ailan Awareness listed on major grant proposals to multilateral organisations and major global conservation funders, the big NGOs were able to garner the vast majority of the money that flowed into the area for marine conservation.[7]

There are three notable exceptions to this pattern. First, the NGO has a longstanding relationship with archaeologists from the University of Papua New Guinea and has collaborated extensively with that work across the province. Second, since 2005, the ADB partnered with the NFA of PNG and hired the fisheries consultancy firm Gillet Preston and Associates to manage CFMDP; they, in turn, contracted John Aini and Ailan Awareness to adapt the Road Show to the needs of their project. They funded full costs of running the NGO for several years and allowed the organisation to take some of the support work offered to them by the BINGOs. They did this because they believed that the work being done in New Ireland by the BINGOs formed a positive contribution to marine resource conservation. This period of funding was the only time in its history that Ailan Awareness has not had to rely on the BINGOs and the structural position that they hold in the world of international conservation. Finally, since 2007, the NGO has partnered with anthropologists, ecologists and lawyers from Barnard College and Columbia University to expand the NGO's focus to include projects that work to maintain local sovereignty over both biological and cultural diversity through revitalisation projects, local awareness projects, research project partnerships and locally generated but internationally supported small-scale conservation initiatives.

During this time, due to their success with this contract work, another form of relationship emerged between Ailan Awareness and outside institutions; they became known as a 'fixer' for others in New Ireland. BINGOs turned to them to help facilitate their projects logistically,

---

7   This also happened across the country simultaneously, in relation to national terrestrial conservation NGOs and projects (West, 2016).

even when they were not engaged to do the Road Show, specifically, or 'awareness', more generally. BINGOs also began to ask Ailan Awareness to provide them with logistical support when they held organisation meetings and workshops and when they brought potential donors, journalists and filmmakers to the area. Multilateral institutions began asking them to assist with organising trips for visiting dignitaries. Diplomatic missions began asking them to organise visits for ambassadors, international diplomatic core visitors and others to rural villages across the region. Media outlets such as the BBC, the *New York Times* and *The Guardian*, unaffiliated film crews from China, France and the United Kingdom (UK) and global justice organisations, such as Global Witness and Canopy Watch, began contacting Ailan Awareness when they wanted to send a group or an individual to the area, to do a story, find a story or gather data about logging, mining or fishing.

These ongoing requests require time, money, networks, work and labour. Sometimes, Ailan Awareness is reimbursed or compensated for the money and labour expended in fulfilling these requests; however, more often than not, this does not occur. They are never compensated—how could they be—for the forms of obligation that they amass across the province when they call on their personal kinship obligations and networks to help meet these requests. They are never compensated for the expertise that they provide regarding local social practices and customs and local marine tenure organisation. Outsiders assume that their requests are minor and do not think through the kinds of expenditures that are involved in setting the conditions of possibility for their work in or visit to New Ireland.

A recent example of this kind of request and the associated labour is as follows: Ailan Awareness was contacted by a large group of researchers through one of the international embassies in Port Moresby and asked to help facilitate a visit to New Ireland by several scholars from an institution that had contacted the embassy for help. They wanted to come to New Ireland to do a pilot study for future possible research. The embassy contacted Ailan Awareness through one of their longstanding research partners, who suggested that Ailan Awareness could help the scholars negotiate prices for transportation and accommodation on the island during their research period. Ailan Awareness agreed to help. In addition to helping to secure transportation and accommodation, they paid to clear access for the scholars to the villages they wanted to visit and paid village elders for their time spent guiding the visitors. Further, upon their arrival in New Ireland, Ailan Awareness provided the scholars with food, beer and a 'traditional hornbill dance', during their brief visit to the Ailan Awareness office in Kaselok Village.

During their time in New Ireland, the scholars asked a crew of local men to assist them with their work. Ailan Awareness staff working on that crew reported that 'we went without lunch in the bush for two days while they ate cans of canned tuna and bully beef'. Eventually, John Aini organised some of his distant relatives to provide the workers with wild cassava harvested on their land. He was able to call on longstanding obligations and debts that people had to him and Ailan Awareness. The people he called on reciprocated in socially appropriate ways and, in doing so, transferred debts of reciprocation back towards John and Ailan Awareness.

Ailan Awareness was never reimbursed for the cash that they spent to facilitate this visit. Nor were they compensated for the labour they provided—neither the physical labour nor the more nuanced labour of mobilising kinship relations to arrange their accommodation, negotiate their transportation to and from their site or the work it took to negotiate access to the site. This kind of work was rendered invisible when it was described as 'island hospitality'; in fact, the seemingly hospitable relations of the Ailan Awareness staff will demand that that hospitality be reciprocated over and over again for the foreseeable future. The relatives will demand that Ailan Awareness and its staff contribute to funeral costs and other cultural demands for years to come because they assume that Ailan Awareness received extensive financial compensation from the group.

Many of the kinds of requests illustrated by the above example are part of what the Ailan Awareness staff have come to view as part of the price of doing work in PNG. Their structural position is such that larger institutions such as BINGOs, government offices, multilateral institutions and diplomatic missions hold sway over many of the resources that the small NGO requires to continue its work. 'Helping' them with these kinds of requests may result in the amassing of both good will and obligation from the requestor to Ailan Awareness. The staff of Ailan Awareness reads and orders these requests through a Melanesian social order of exchange, obligation and kinship relations. They assume that their work will result in strengthening these kinds of ties. They also assume that 'the good will' they will amass with actors and organisations that do not readily participate in Melanesian forms of sociality—what sociologists who do not work in Melanesia might call 'social capital'—has the potential to garner actual financial capital in the form of grants, fellowships and support for the small NGO, its student interns and its national staff.

The group of international researchers mentioned above, for example, built good will between the NGO and the embassy and, given that the embassy had publicised the NGO's work in the past, their expenditure was seen as part of a networked series of social relations. Additionally, similar visits from Global Witness resulted in a series of reports that exposed illegal logging on Lovangai and the relationship between that logging and SABLs, creating the conditions for a parliamentary inquiry into the situation. Further, a visit from the US Navy strengthened partnerships between Ailan Awareness and researchers at the University of Papua New Guinea. Finally, a recent Canopy Watch visit resulted in a beautiful website that focused on the various social and ecological crises currently taking place on Lovangai. We interpret these requests and their costs as providing benefits to local communities and the mission of Ailan Awareness. They are part of the ongoing, enduring sociality of reciprocity in both New Ireland and PNG, more generally.

Requests such as the one we outlined at the beginning of this chapter are different. They come from individuals who will likely come to New Ireland once, who will never return any of their findings (or film or images) to the people or the place and who will usually never contact anyone who facilitated their visit again after that visit. After over a decade of meeting these kinds of requests, Ailan Awareness has come to the conclusion that no one in PNG benefits in any discernible way from the significant work they require; therefore, they are a pernicious element of structures of inequality that keeps the NGO from doing the work they wish to do. Further, we argue that these requests perpetuate a series of deeply troubling, racialised hierarchies of inequality.

Below, we provide one example of the course taken by these kinds of requests and the visits. We wish to stress that this one example is of a type that occurs repeatedly. This type begins with an initial email, moves through a period where Ailan Awareness provides information, then into a period in which they discover that the requestor knows nothing about New Ireland, resulting in a social 'mess' and a host of debts to be paid by Ailan Awareness. What follows will be uncomfortable reading for some. Some may think something along the lines of 'oh, but they meant well, they are just young and naive'. We follow Professor Chelsea Bond, a Munanjahli scholar who recently argued that thinking of, talking about and casting people as 'well-meaning' both covers all manner of historical sins and reinforces contemporary white privilege (Bond & West, 2018). We extend this line of thinking to demonstrate how these kinds of requests reinforce structural inequality.

Visiting New Ireland Province to 'Do Work'

The biophysical environment in which Ailan Awareness works is under threat from a variety of internationally driven processes, from global climate change to illegal logging and fishing, the growth of oil palm plantations and mineral resource extraction through gold mining (Nason, 2018; Roberts, 2019a). New Ireland Province may be thought of as a microcosm of all global threats to biological diversity. Therefore, it draws the attention of liberal subjects who wish to study, document and counter what they perceive as environmental injustice. New Ireland Province also sits squarely in that zone of Euro–American–Australian settler–tourist imagination that might be called 'a tropical paradise' (Foale & Macintyre, 2005). The area is spectacularly beautiful, the people are welcoming and kind, there occurs very little violence or crime, and it is part of PNG, a place that also occupies a particular kind of place in the consciousness of outsiders in terms of how visiting it makes them see, feel about and cast themselves. From the colonial period (Stella, 2007) to the present (West, 2016), visitors have used their visits to PNG to fashion themselves as intrepid explorers. Following their visits, visitors increasingly cast themselves as valiant voices for global equality and environmental justice who are, due to their experiences in the country, more aware of global inequality than others (West, 2012, p. 178). These are the kinds of visitors whose requests we examine in the rest of this chapter.

Each visit begins with the initial email. In the time between the initial email to Ailan Awareness and the person's arrival, numerous other emails are also sent between Ailan Awareness staff, Paige West and the impending visitor. Some of these, if the person is a student, are invariably between West and the student's supervisors. Some involve the project staff person at the BINGO that has suggested Ailan Awareness might help them with their visit. Some readers may wonder why Ailan Awareness do not just ignore the initial email. We stress that the people emailing have always been in touch with someone in a structural position of power (in relation to the small NGO) and that, more often than not, this person works for a BINGO upon which, at some point in time, the small NGO has relied for project funding. Therefore, the director of the NGO feels obligated to answer the email; further, to say 'no' to requests makes him feel both 'ashamed' and that he is not maintaining proper social relationships. This is, for him, an untenable existential crisis—if he is not willing to 'help' and return previous social connections, he begins to question his identity and his role in the world. The anthropologist feels that it is not her place to say 'yes' or 'no' to anyone when it comes to their desire to come to PNG, because she is also a 'visitor' to the country, albeit a longer-term one. Although they have a long-term research partnership and through customary obligations and affects are now 'brother and sister', she also feels strongly that everything that Ailan Awareness does, or does not do, should be the decision of Ailan Awareness; therefore, she always follows her collaborator's lead. Further, if the person emailing is a student, she feels an obligation to help because she knows that people help her PhD students when they begin to develop their projects (although she hopes that they behave in radically different ways to those that we outline below).

In a recent case (that is distinct from the one we described at the beginning of this chapter), in which the sender emailed Ailan Awareness three weeks before he was to arrive (having already purchased his airline tickets), our initial reply, following multiple emails between New Ireland and New York, asked the sender for more information about his proposed 'project', his funding and his adviser, in addition to his plans for accommodation and if he had been in contact with any of the people in the communities that he planned on spending time with during his visit to New Ireland. The sender, a first-year master's student who we will call 'Brian', replied to our initial message, beginning a series of messages in which we worked to discern his expectations, how he aimed to pay for his visit to New Ireland and the level of engagement he had had with the community members that he wanted to come and spend time with. Below, we give further details of our interactions with him and his advisers, because these mirror how the vast majority of these requests and interactions unfold.

Brian, who had contacted Ailan Awareness only three weeks prior to his planned arrival, replied to Paige West's first email, the one that asked the questions given above, five days after it was sent, with a very friendly email that offered more detail about his proposed project (including his research questions), identified his adviser and gave us a link to their research page. He also advised that his project was to be funded 'privately', that he had not booked a hotel because he intended to stay at the Ailan Awareness researcher bungalow, which he had heard about through the BINGO with whom he had been in contact, and that he had not been in touch with any of the communities that he was planning to visit or work with. His project, which will not be described in detail (to protect his anonymity), entailed the examination of an issue that intersects with questions of land ownership, resource extraction, governance and the role of civil society and transnational activists in natural resource–related conflict and environmental conservation.

Paige and John discussed Brian's email on the day of receipt and replied the following day, with a list of five things that they thought he should be aware of before coming to New Ireland—please keep in mind that he had already purchased his airline tickets from the UK to New Ireland before he sent his initial email to Ailan Awareness. Our email to him comprised what we have come to view as 'the provisioning of information'. First, we explained to Brian that the Ailan Awareness bungalow funds the *Solwara Skul*, an Ailan Awareness project, and that the rate is USD 150 or USD 100 per night, depending on whether food and transportation are included; further, the bungalow was, unfortunately, already rented for part of his prospective stay in New Ireland. Second, the bungalow is located 13 km from Kavieng town; therefore, he must be willing to ride local buses to and from town if he decided to stay there without paying the additional USD 50 per night. Third, the area of his planned work is over 80 km from town, and much of the required travel would be via public transportation on very poor quality roads. Therefore, we urged Brian to connect with the BINGO with whom he had already been in contact to form a plan for his transportation to the area. Fourth, we reminded him that people in New Ireland speak 18 different languages, in addition to Melanesian Tok Pisin; although people in town speak English, he would need to engage a translator for the entirety of his work in the more rural parts of the province if he did not speak Tok Pisin (which he did not). Finally, we gave Brian the names of several anthropologists who had worked in the communities he wanted to visit, in the hope that he would contact them to learn more about the local history and custom. We also reminded him that local people have the right to refuse researchers who wish to conduct work in their communities; this had already been the case with some recent attempts to research his topic of interest in the area.

Brian replied the next day with a short email that thanked us for the information we had provided and informed us that he had booked alternative accommodation for those dates that the Ailan Awareness bungalow was unavailable, that he would be contacting the anthropologists we suggested and that he would contact the BINGO that had connected him with Ailan Awareness. Brian did not mention the bungalow fees we had quoted; therefore, we emailed him again to remind him of the costs and request that he inform Ailan Awareness if he intended to book it for the first 15 days of his stay. He replied that he would like to book the bungalow, including the additional transportation and food fee, and asked how he should pay for the accommodation. Paige replied that he must pay in kina, which could be obtained from any ATM in Port Moresby or at the airport on the way into the country, but that the ATMs in Kavieng were both broken; therefore, he must organise the money before he arrived in New Ireland. We also attached an invoice for USD 2,250—the total cost of his stay at the Ailan Awareness bungalow. Four days later, Brian replied, asking if he would have 'streaming internet' in the bungalow. This request marks the moment that such interactions shift to what we now call the 'knowing nothing phase'.

Paige replied to explain the nature of internet access in the country and the best way to obtain a SIM card for his phone at the airport in Port Moresby, including information about the national provider, Digicel, and its fee structures. Four days prior to his scheduled flights to PNG, Brian emailed to tell Paige that he had encountered 'a little predicament' and required some help. He was to be travelling over a bank holiday and would not be able to access a bank in the UK with enough time for that bank to order and prepare the cash. He was worried about being able to obtain enough kina in either Australia or Port Moresby before arriving in Kavieng, because his bank had recently imposed a withdrawal limit on his account. He asked if he could bring US dollars or make a bank transfer to the Ailan Awareness account. Paige immediately replied that he could transfer funds directly to the Ailan Awareness account, including the account details and copying in John Aini and Ailan Awareness. She then told Brian that he must do this prior to his arrival because John had to buy supplies, pay a female relative to come from a village site to serve as the cook, pay another to come to serve as the cleaner, pay for the car he had to hire to transport her (because Ailan Awareness does not have a vehicle) and pay for the boat to bring the driver and one security guard from Lovongai. During this time, Paige and John remained in contact with one another regarding the situation, in addition to Brian's advisers, who were curtly apologetic about his lack of preparation for the visiting but did not provide any promise of support in terms of rectifying the situation.

Brian's final email to Paige prior to his arrival in New Ireland arrived on the evening before his international flight and explained that he would try to obtain the money before arriving in Kavieng. However, that same evening, he also emailed John. Those emails began with a request for the Ailan Awareness bank account details, which had already been supplied by Paige. At 10:14 pm, John provided the account details, followed by the Society for Worldwide Interbank Financial Telecommunication (SWIFT) code (10:19 pm). At 10:23 pm, Brian requested the bank's address. John replied at 10:24 pm; Brian replied immediately with a message saying that the postal code for the bank was required (10:24 pm). At 10:33 pm, Brian sent a message that said, 'Thank you very much. I have now made the transfer and my bank has notified me that the amount will be transferred to you on Tuesday', closing with a pleasant 'sincere apologies'. Over the next seven days, no further emails were received from Brian. In New York, Paige assumed that the bank transfer had been processed and that all was well—unfortunately, it was not.

Brian arrived in Kavieng and was transported from the airport to the Ailan Awareness compound and given access to the bungalow. He was also offered the extraordinary hospitality that is common during a visit to a PNG village. The Ailan Awareness compound is in Kaselok Village, a Tigak-speaking village along the Boluminski highway; the village sits between the highway and the Pacific Ocean on the east coast of New Ireland. Ailan Awareness has been situated on land owned by people from Kaselok since 2001 and has hosted hundreds of NGO-related guests. Residents understand the social conventions that European, American and Australian visitors desire when they first come to a rural (or peri-rural) place in PNG; for example, that visitors do not want children, pigs or curious onlookers hanging around their accommodation or locals dropping by with questions or to share stories or food. Residents also understand the visual iconography of 'paradise' that visitors desire, and they work hard to provide this to them. The bungalow itself is magnificent. It was constructed in the traditional style of Lovongai (New Hanover), sits 5 metres from the beach and looks out over a fringing reef. It has a bedroom, an equal-sized veranda, screens on the windows and access to a private bathroom and shower block.

Brian stayed for only five days at Kaselok, before informing John and his family that he was moving to 'a more comfortable and cheap place'. This departure shamed everyone at Ailan Awareness; they felt terrible that Brian had not found the accommodation acceptable. Additionally, John and others had to spend time discussing this with the residents of Kaselok, who also felt shame due to the early departure. On the day he left Kaselok, John and his family took Brian into Kavieng; John assumed that he would pay for his accommodation, food and transportation for those five days prior to departing because the transferred funds still had not appeared in his bank account. Brian assured John that the transfer had been made and that the bank was just slow. The next day John went to the bank and waited 112 minutes in line to check on the transfer—still, it had not arrived. That same day, while at a hotel in Kavieng, Brian emailed John to say that he required an International Bank Account Number (IBAN) code for the transfer. John replied that this not the case in PNG; rather, banks require a SWIFT code. Once again, he provided all the bank details that Brian would need to complete the transfer.

The following day, Brian emailed Paige to inform her of delays with the payment, saying that he had tried to make the bank transfer twice but had been declined both times. The next day, he emailed John again with an attached screenshot showing that he had entered John's bank details. However, this was not a receipt for money that had been sent—it was simply a screen showing the entered details and text that read 'Hit enter to send funds'. Brian also included an apology to John, assuring him that the bank details had been worked out and the transfer was imminent. This was John's last email from Brian—to date, Ailan Awareness has received no funds from Brian. John finally admitted to Paige that Brian had never paid, saying, 'I felt ashamed to ask for it anymore'. This shame was compounded by the shame that John, his relatives and the residents of Kaselok experienced when Brian departed early for a more 'comfortable' location.

Work, Labour, Expenditure and Inequality

We view 'work' as both the creative somatic refashioning of some materials in the world and creative engagement with others to maintain, enhance and create social networks of obligation and exchange. We see 'labour' as the measure and analysis of 'work' when it is tied to the capitalist system of production. Anthropologists have illustrated the work and labour required to create the idea of a pristine environment in need of conservation (Foale & Macintyre, 2005), the ideological work and labour that contribute to the crafting of conservation agendas (see Carrier & West, 2009), how the work and labour of designing conservation agendas has shifted from the purview of scientists to economists (Cleary, 2018) and the work and labour that are expended in trying to align local, regional and international conservation agendas (Wahlen, 2013). Anthropologists have also discussed the social and economic disparity between local and non-local conservation workers and conservation NGO employees (Hathaway, 2013; Lowe, 2006; Vivanco, 2007; West, 2016). However, very few have examined, in detail, the labour that contributes to the success of conservation interventions on the ground.

Genese Sodikoff provides an exception; she has tracked the labour of manual workers in Madagascan conservation projects (Sodikoff, 2009, 2012). She showed that workers perform a range of duties related to monitoring reserve boundaries, cataloguing species, maintaining infrastructure, working with local communities to help them understand conservation rules and working as guides for tourists and scientists. Without such workers, conservation projects simply could not exist, nor could the scientific 'discoveries' that feed back into the international valuation of internationally funded parks, reserves and conservation areas. Sodikoff examined the creation of value in the forests, the effects of hierarchy and highlighted 'the mundane tasks that have made possible the acquisition of certain types of knowledge and the evolution of certain philosophies of nature' (Sodikoff, 2012, p. 7).

Catherine Wahlen (2013) has argued that we must do more to understand the inequality that both underpins local, national and international conservation staff and employee interactions and the inequality that emerges through the course of conservation projects. We agree with Wahlen, believing that, in the context of PNG, one appropriate starting point is to analyse the 'work' that emerges in the wake of requests such as Brian's. Why, given that Brian's trip to PNG was not part of a broader conservation project, do we connect his trip to this broader field of analysis? We do this because he was 'punted' to Ailan Awareness by a BINGO and because he later wrote a master's thesis that focused on the extremely controversial topic that he initially proposed. In this thesis, he offers conservation and activist solutions to the problems generated by the topic; therefore, his trip fed back into the work of fashioning external conservation agendas for the country and the work of his own self-fashioning as a scholarly voice in conservation.

During the five days that Ailan Awareness staff were responsible for Brian's visit, they undertook a range of activities that we might consider work. However, this work actually began prior to his visit:

> When I receive an email, the cost and the stress start. First, I have to run around looking for a good internet connection to answer the email. Then, I have to pay for the data to send the emails. Every bit of email costs money to send and receive. If I can't find a spot in Kaselok, I have to go into town where the reception is better. This costs money (email costs and fuel) as well as time.

> Then, once I have replied, if we decide to help the person, I start the organising—getting in touch with people, my relatives and the Ailan Awareness contacts to organise for the person to visit the place they want to visit or learn about the topic they want to learn about (e.g. logging, SABLs, shark calling, undersea mining), organising accommodation at *Solwara Skul* bungalows if they are to stay with us in Kaselok or getting quotes from hotels in Kavieng for visitors wanting to stay in town, making calls to organise boats and trustworthy skippers, physically seeing boat owners and making sure that their engines are trustworthy, securing a hire care if I am not going to be their driver, finding the best prices for fuel and then paying deposits for everything or asking for credit all over town to secure the reservations. Then, I have to spread the word with calls and texts or physically going to see and to make the communities aware that they will be visiting. This is before anyone even arrives.

After various details are confirmed, financial expenditures begin. Below, we give a rough estimate for how much a five-day stay, such as Brian's, costs Ailan Awareness:

Fixed Costs (all given in PGK)
Internet service (600 MB): 40
Electricity (fan, lights and refrigerator): 40
Phone service: 50
Ailan Awareness support staff travel:[8] 600

---

8   The cost for Ailan Awareness support staff to travel from Lovangai to Kaselok for the visit is PGK 100 (for one round trip). We use six staff for each visit (two cooks/cleaners, two carriers/general workers, one security guard and one guide), which incurs a total of PGK 600.

Pre-visit cleaning materials and bungalow dry goods: 80
Hire car: 700
Fuel: 300
Food for staff:[9] 330
Total: PGK 2,140 (approximately USD 637)

Salary Costs
Salary for support staff (600 per day): 3,000
Ailan Awareness director salary: 400
Total: PGK 3,400 (approximately USD 1,012)

Prior to Brian's arrival, Ailan Awareness paid the fixed costs of USD 637. Recall that, in our initial communication with Brian, after he had settled on staying with Ailan Awareness for 15 days, we sent him an invoice for USD 2,250. Therefore, over the course of five days, Ailan Awareness spent almost one-third of the amount he agreed to pay but never paid. This amount represents approximately 1.7 per cent of the NGO's total operating budget for 2018.[10] Further, because Brian never paid his bills, none of the Ailan Awareness staff were paid for the work they did during his visit. Therefore, following Brian's visit, Ailan Awareness were USD 637 out of pocket, because he did not pay his fee, in addition to the debts incurred by not paying the support staff salaries. This USD 637 was not part of any approved project budgets for 2018; therefore, John Aini was required to reimburse the NGO for these costs from his own personal funds. This amount represented 4.25 per cent of his total annual salary for 2018.

Further, these calculations do not capture other forms of expenditure mobilised for Brian's visit. For example, that unpaid PGK 3,000 in salary for support staff (that Ailan Awareness was unable to pay because Brian never paid them) created both a financial debt and an enormous social debt. The NGO will pay for this repeatedly, in terms of having to reciprocate the time and work outlaid by these staff members. Ailan Awareness also mobilised kin and broader social networks in the region of New Ireland that Brian wished to visit. Prior to his visit, Ailan Awareness

---

9   We provide three meals per day: approximately six packets of rice (PGK 4 per packet = PGK 24), three cans of canned fish (PGK 5 per can = PGK 15), one packet of sugar (PGK 6), one packet of coffee (PGK 9) and six bundles of greens (PGK 12). The total cost is PGK 66 per person per day.
10   For the 2018 fiscal year, the total Ailan Awareness operating budget (for which they had funding) was USD 37,500. This includes all NGO expenses (including operating costs and salary) and the amount was funded by the Christensen Fund. These are all directed funds, meaning they are project related and not part of a general operating budget.

staff visited those communities and gained permission for him to visit. This entailed the amassing of obligations to people in those communities, which will be repaid in the future via contributions to weddings, funerals, births and political campaigns. Ailan Awareness will also have to host members of those (very remote) communities, if they arrive in Kavieng with no place to stay, and loan money to elders from those communities when they require bus fares back to their villages. They have, in other words, incurred social debts that are impossible to quantify and will be repaid over the coming years.

Of these costs, one Ailan Awareness staff member said:

> Our visitors don't know these costs, how should they know, who would tell them? I am ashamed or they might think I am just another Papua New Guinean trying to rob them or I don't want their stay to be expensive. A lot complain about the airfares, saying it's so expensive travelling in PNG, of which I agree. But they don't … they think sometimes … when I arrive at the airport in a car to pick them up, what do they think that the car runs on? How do they think we pay for that? And they sit on the veranda of our bungalow and they say how beautiful it is and how nice it is to have a fresh and clean bed, cooked food, lights for them at night. Did it just happen? Is it a miracle?

Over the course of any visitor stay, Ailan Awareness staff perform various kinds of work, some of which may be thought of as 'labour' that can easily be tied to and valued through a monetised system of social relations. First, the staff spends time going to places to set the conditions for the visitor's visit. This work can, and should be, valued at an hourly or daily rate. For example, if a staff member spends a day driving to the coast to organise for a visitor to go and shoot footage in a remote village, she or he should be paid for it. Second, staff spend money to prepare for the visitor's arrival—they hire a cleaner to replace the linen and ensure the guesthouse shower and bathroom faculties are clean and in working order. They hire women to come and cook for the guest and purchase staple foods such as rice, cooking oil and salt. They rent a boat or a car to transport the visitor, which must be paid upfront. Each of these aspects is easily monetised. Again, you might ask, 'why doesn't Ailan Awareness just have a rate sheet to give to people?' In answer, we ask the reader to consider Brian, who was provided with this information and still failed to pay. While his is an extreme example, it is often the case that a visitor is unaware of any of the kinds of work discussed in this section, even when it occurs around them. The labour required to make their stay possible is invisible. Visitors tend to assume that everything they observe occurring is part of 'island hospitality' or that it is covered by the rental costs of the Ailan Awareness bungalow. We cannot express this enough—PNG is an extraordinarily expensive country. The daily rental costs of USD 100 (PGK 300) or the USD 150 (PGK 450) only cover the labour costs (cooking, cleaning, power and water) and the transportation (for the higher fee) in and around Kaselok and Kavieng. Everything else that we have outlined, all other easily monetised forms of work, is additional.

Each visitor also generates other forms of work, forms that are less easily monetised. For example, if a visitor wishes to go to a village down the east coast of the island to spend a month collecting footage for a film, Ailan Awareness staff must visit the village at least once (but often more than once) before the visitor arrives to explain who the visitor is, what they will be doing, why they will be doing it, where they wish to do it and how the information gained will be used. The staff must then secure access to the sites the visitor wishes to visit, which almost always entails multiple conversations with multiple family groups and leaders. This work relies on existing social relations between Ailan Awareness and the residents of the village and extensive 'local knowledge' of the social and political factors at play in each locality. This specialised knowledge is immensely valuable— no work can be performed successfully in New Ireland without it. We imagine that it is also possible to monetise this kind of work, although it would be more difficult than in the case of the work outlined in the previous paragraph. The staff can be paid for their time, for the time taken to do the logistical work prior to the visit. However, how could the value of the specialised knowledge required be calculated? How could we do this adequately for each different kind of social situation? Again, a flat or hourly rate of pay might provide a starting point for monetary compensation; however, how could staff expenditure in terms of drawing on their own obligations be repaid? When an obligation is met by people in our imagined village above (an obligation that allows for the visit), how could both the debt that the staff member has relinquished and the newly incurred debt be monetised? How could the long-term engagements that create networks of obligation and exchange be monetised? Finally, and much more importantly, do we want them to be?

Two final forms of work are even more difficult to discuss and, we believe, nearly impossible to monetise or even reciprocate. First, being a 'friendly native' is exhausting work. Over the course of their long collaboration,

Paige West has watched John Aini do what she would call (and he would not) the 'emotional work of being Indigenous'. This comprises the enacting of a particular form of subjectivity for outsiders that, while adjacent to his subject position as a Maimai (cultural leader or chief), keeper of customary knowledge and tradition, researcher and scholar, father, brother, uncle, grandfather and person fully enmeshed in local, regional, national and international networks of obligation and reciprocity, is also different. For outsiders, he becomes their window into and connection to both his culture and the two other indigenous societies in New Ireland. He becomes more than a 'translator', or what some have called a 'cultural broker'—outsiders view him as the voice of his people. They do not understand the social world underpinning his status and subjectivity; therefore, they see him as a single individual who can 'be native' for them and teach them. John takes this very seriously—he has dedicated his whole life to the health and wellbeing of his people and their biophysical surroundings. How could he be compensated in monetary terms for the work of representing three worlds to outsiders?

Second, for over a decade, John Aini has observed Paige West 'worry'. He says, 'you worry about everything. About all that I go through, about our family, about the people here in New Ireland and their fate'. He has also highlighted that she worries constantly about Ailan Awareness funding, because she is the primary grant writer for the organisation. He says, 'I know you worry that I spend our grant money to help these people, and that makes me worry'. Her work in this regard is not invisible to him or to the many partners of Ailan Awareness across the province. He, and others, understand that she has a good job that pays well; however, they worry that she is continually worried about the NGO and its ability to do work and support all the people who depend on it.

Bruce Robbins identified the kind of modern subject that we have discussed in this chapter in *The Beneficiary* (2017). By 'beneficiary', Robbins described the modern 'well-meaning' subject who fails to understand their role in the social and ecological inequality they wish to address with their 'work' (Robbins, 2017). He focused on humanitarian aid workers who do not see how their lives of consumption in the Global North are built upon the very social and environmental injustices that they seek to remedy through their waged labour. He argued that they are unaware of (or unable to see) their own role in the structures that cause global suffering and structural inequality, linking this inability to see with a kind of global cosmopolitanism that has existed for generations.

In this chapter, we have shown how the structural inequality that underpins conservation funding and practice in PNG causes material inequalities that create the conditions in which small NGOs must perform extra work to stay afloat and feel obligated to undertake work and labour that is not strictly part of their organisation's mission. In a structural sense, they are locked into the patron–client relationship with BINGOs and must engage in these if they wish to continue working in PNG. One result of this 'lock in' is that when BINGOs of all kinds (not just conservation-related ones) connect people like Brian to Ailan Awareness, people that we see as beneficiaries, it is nearly impossible for the small NGO to turn them away. To do so would both hurt their relationships with the BINGOs, upon whom they to some extent depend, and cause shame and pain to their staff. This reinforces the already existing structural inequalities discussed at the beginning of this chapter. These well-meaning beneficiaries become a conduit for the ongoing dispossession of Indigenous peoples in PNG, something that we are sure they never meant to be.

Acknowledgements

The authors' collaboration has been funded by the Christensen Fund, the US Ambassador's Fund for Cultural Preservation, Barnard College and Columbia University. We wish to thank these funders. Our work would not be possible without the countless members of the communities we work with in New Ireland. There are too many people to acknowledge individually, but collectively they are the reason we do this work and our lives are richer because of them. We also wish to thank Cathy Hair, Shaun and Shannon Keane, Matthew Leavesley, Catherine Sparks and Hugh Walton for their ongoing support of Ailan Awareness.

References

Aini, J. & Nason, P. (2016, February). *A conversation on climate change in the Papua New Guinea Islands*. Retrieved from www.envirosociety.org/tag/john-aini/

Aini, J. & West, P. (2018, June). *Communities matter: Decolonizing conservation management*. Plenary Lecture presented at the International Marine Conservation Congress, Kuching, Malaysia.

Aini, J. & West, P. (n.d.). Beneficiary moves to innocence: Whiteness, power and history in conservation in Papua New Guinea. Unpublished manuscript.

Beer, B. (2018). Gender and inequality in a postcolonial context of large-scale capitalist projects in the Markham Valley, Papua New Guinea. *The Australian Journal of Anthropology, 29*(3), 348–364.

Bond, C. & West, P. (2018, May 23). *Race, colonialism and the politics of representation.* Retrieved from brisbanefreeuniversity.org/2018/05/14/bfu-presents-race-colonialism-the-politics-of-representation/

Butcher, J. & Smith, P. (2015). *Volunteer tourism: The lifestyle politics of international development.* Abingdon, England: Routledge.

Campbell, L. M., Gray, N. J. & Meletis, Z. A. (2008). Political ecology perspectives on ecotourism to parks and protected areas. In K. S. Hanna, D. A. Clark & D. S. Slocombe (Eds), *Transforming parks and protected areas: Policy and governance in a changing world* (pp. 200–221). Abingdon, England: Routledge.

Campbell, L. M., Haalboom, B. J. & Trow, J. (2007). Sustainability of community-based conservation: Sea turtle egg harvesting in Ostional (Costa Rica) ten years later. *Environmental Conservation, 34*(2), 122–131.

Carrier, J. G. & West, P. (2009). *Virtualism, governance and practice vision and execution in environmental conservation.* New York, NY: Berghahn Books.

Chapin, M. (2004). A challenge to conservationists. *World Watch Magazine, 17*(6), 17–31.

Cleary, D. B. (2018). What are the grounds needed for dialogue? In P. B. Larsen & D. Brockington (Eds), *The anthropology of conservation NGOs* (pp. 251–258). Cham, Switzerland: Palgrave Macmillan.

Connell, J. (2005). *Papua New Guinea: The struggle for development.* London, England: Routledge.

Conran, M. (2011). They really love me!: Intimacy in volunteer tourism. *Annals of Tourism Research, 38*(4), 1454–1473.

Fabinyi, M., Foale, S. & Macintyre, M. (2015). Managing inequality or managing stocks? An ethnographic perspective on the governance of small-scale fisheries. *Fish and Fisheries, 16*(3), 471–485. doi.org/10.1111/faf.12069

Fitzpatrick, P. (1980). *Law and state in Papua New Guinea.* London, England: Academic Press.

Foale, S. & Macintyre, M. (2005). Green fantasies: Photographic representations of biodiversity and ecotourism in the Western Pacific. *Journal of Political Ecology*, *12*(1), 1–22. doi.org/10.2458/v12i1.21671

Gewertz, D. & Errington, F. (1999). *Emerging class in Papua New Guinea*. New York, NY: Cambridge University Press.

Gokkon, B. (2018a, 12 July). 'Decolonising conservation': Q&A with PNG marine activist John Aini. Retrieved from news.mongabay.com/2018/07/decolonizing-conservation-qa-with-png-marine-activist-john-aini/

Gokkon, B. (2018b, 16 July). *Protecting PNG's oceans: Q&A with marine activist John Aini*. Retrieved from news.mongabay.com/2018/07/protecting-pngs-oceans-qa-with-marine-activist-john-aini/

Gray, N. J. & Campbell, L. M. (2007). A decommodified experience? Exploring aesthetic, economic and ethical values for volunteer ecotourism in Costa Rica. *Journal of Sustainable Tourism*, *15*(5), 463–482.

Griffiths, M. (2016). An opinion piece. A response to the special issue on volunteer tourism: The performative absence of volunteers. *Journal of Sustainable Tourism*, *24*(2), 169–176. doi.org/10.1080/09669582.2015.1071382

Halvaksz, J. A. (2020). *Gardens of gold: Place-making in Papua New Guinea*. Seattle, WA: University of Washington Press.

Hathaway, M. J. (2013). *Environmental winds: Making the global in Southwest China*. Berkeley, CA: University of California Press.

Henry, J. (2019). The unspeakable whiteness of volunteer tourism. *Annals of Tourism Research*, *76*, 326–327. doi.org/10.1016/j.annals.2018.09.003

Johnson, P. L. (1993). Education and the 'new' inequality in Papua New Guinea. *Anthropology and Education Quarterly*, *24*(3), 183–204.

Josephides, L. (1985). *The production of inequality: Gender and exchange among the Kewa*. New York, NY: Taylor & Francis.

Kelly, R. C. (1993). *Constructing inequality: The fabrication of a hierarchy of virtue among the Etoro*. Ann Arbor, MI: University of Michigan Press.

Laarman, J. G. & Perdue, R. R. (1989). Science tourism in Costa Rica. *Annals of Tourism Research*, *16*(2), 205–215.

Lowe, C. (2006). *Wild profusion: Biodiversity conservation in an Indonesian archipelago*. Princeton, NJ: Princeton University Press.

Moore, A. (2019). *Destination anthropocene: Science and tourism in the Bahamas.* Durham, NC: Duke University Press. doi.org/10.2307/j.ctvpb3wqz

Nason, P. (2018). Sounding sovereignty: The politics of presence in the Bismarck Archipelago (Unpublished doctoral thesis). Colombia University, New York.

Robbins, B. (2017). *The beneficiary.* Durham, NC: Duke University Press.

Roberts, J. (2019a). 'We stay the same': Life logging and the continuing pursuit of development on New Hanover Island (Lovangai), Papua New Guinea (Unpublished doctoral thesis). Department of Anthropology, University of Texas, San Antonio.

Roberts, J. (2019b). 'We live like this': Local inequalities and disproportionate risk in the context of extractive development and climate change on New Hanover Island, Papua New Guinea. *Oceania, 88*(3), 68–88.

Ryan, S., Curry, G. N., Germis, E., Koczberski, G. & Koia, M. (2016). Challenges to the democratisation of knowledge: Status hierarchies and emerging inequalities in educational opportunities amongst oil palm settlers in Papua New Guinea. In M. Robertson & P. K. E. Tsang (Eds), *Everyday knowledge, education and sustainable futures: Transdisciplinary approaches in the Asia-Pacific Region* (pp. 123–139). Singapore: Springer.

Sodikoff, G. (2009). The low-wage conservationist: Biodiversity and perversities of value in Madagascar. *American Anthropologist, 111*(4), 443–455. doi.org/10.1111/j.1548-1433.2009.01154.x

Sodikoff, G. (2012). *Forest and labour in Madagascar: From colonial concession to global biosphere.* Bloomington, IN: Indiana University Press.

Stella, R. T. (2007). *Imagining the other: The representation of the Papua New Guinean.* Honolulu, HI: University of Hawai'i Press.

Strathern, A. (1982). *Inequality in New Guinea Highlands societies.* Cambridge, England: Cambridge University Press.

Van Helden, F. (1998). *Between cash and conviction: The social context of the Bismarck-Ramu integrated conservation and development project.* Boroko, Papua New Guinea: National Research Institute.

Vivanco, L. A. (2007). *Green encounters: Shaping and contesting environmentalism in rural Costa Rica.* New York, NY: Berghahn Books.

Wagner, J. (2007). Conservation as development in Papua New Guinea: The view from Blue Mountain. *Human Organization, 66*(1), 28–37. doi.org/10.17730/humo.66.1.q21q23v06t374204

Wahlen, C. B. (2013). The anomalous is ubiquitous: Organisations and individuals in Papua New Guinea's conservation efforts (Unpublished doctoral thesis). University of Michigan, Ann Arbor.

Wardlow, H. (2006). *Wayward women: Sexuality and agency in a New Guinea society.* Berkley, CA: University of California Press.

West, P. (2006). *Conservation is our government now: The politics of ecology in Papua New Guinea.* Durham, NC: Duke University Press.

West, P. (2008). Tourism as science and science as tourism: Environment, society, self, and other in Papua New Guinea [with Comments]. *Current Anthropology, 49*(4), 597–625. doi.org/10.2307/20142693

West, P. (2012). *From modern production to imagined primitive: The social world of coffee from Papua New Guinea.* Durham, NC: Duke University Press.

West, P. (2016). *Dispossession and the environment: Rhetoric and inequality in Papua New Guinea.* New York, NY: Columbia University Press.

West, P. & Aini, J. (2018, June). *Critical approaches to dispossession in the Melanesian Pacific: Conservation, voice and Collaboration.* Keynote Lecture, presented at the POLLEN 2018 Political Ecology Network Biennial Conference, Oslo, Norway.

Zimmer-Tamakoshi, L. (2016). Inequality and changing masculinities among the Gende in Papua New Guinea: The 'good', the 'bad' and the 'very bad'. *The Asia Pacific Journal of Anthropology, 17*(3–4), 250–267.

3

The Unequal Place of Anthropology in Cross-Disciplinary Research on Environmental Management in the Pacific and What to Do About It

Simon Foale

Introduction

As someone with undergraduate training in marine science, but whose core intellectual interests in the relationship between environmental knowledge and marine resource management have pulled me towards anthropology over three or so decades now, I have become frustrated by anthropology's marginalisation in interdisciplinary research on environmental problems. My collaborations with Martha Macintyre, commencing with my PhD research in the mid-1990s, convinced me of the power of ethnographic insights to illuminate fundamental social, cultural and political dimensions of environmental challenges. Simultaneously, our collaboration fired an interest in political ecology that has since expanded considerably. My work with World Wildlife Fund in the Solomon Islands (1999–2001) sharpened my focus on the extent to which environmental science (particularly the sub-discipline of conservation biology) is not only concerningly steeped in and shaped by ideology, but also routinely and wantonly oblivious to unequal power/knowledge relations (Clifton & Foale, 2017; Foale & Macintyre, 2005; Foale, Dyer & Kinch, 2016). Subsequent academic positions with anthropologists (The Australian National University), then biologists (James Cook University [JCU]) and anthropologists again (JCU post-2012) have only increased my alarm at the undeserved hegemony of natural scientists within cross-disciplinary projects. Too often, natural scientists reinvent an 'anti-politics machine' (Ferguson, 1990) of reductionist, managerial and deeply neo-colonial 'social science' that studiously ignores much of what anthropology has contributed, and can continue to contribute, to increasingly pressing environmental problems in the Pacific and beyond. This chapter explores the simultaneous appropriation and dumbing-down of social research by contemporary natural scientists, primarily through politically disengaged and often transparently scientistic approaches, which are greatly aided and abetted by the 'metric fixation' (Muller, 2018) of modern universities. I conclude that the only way to combat these politics is through greater collaboration within anthropology and a more strategic approach to publishing, research funding applications and communicating our knowledge to audiences outside the academy.

In this chapter, I critique the system of managerialist politics that sustains the cultural and financial hegemony of a distinct set of Western scientific (i.e. Linnaean/Darwinian/Victorian) values of nature. These values comprise a combination of species-centric intrinsic value and industrial Western aesthetic value (see Foale & Macintyre, 2005; Foale et al., 2016), which ultimately perpetuates the dominance of reductionist approaches, and the disciplines that favour them, in environmental research and advocacy. Environmental anthropologists have long argued that the values underpinning and legitimising much global conservation work—including neo-colonial interventions in the lives of economically marginalised peoples in the name of biodiversity preservation—are fundamentally socially and politically constructed. Further, these values and politics are increasingly imbricated with the same forms of neoliberal ideology that simultaneously privilege the natural and medical sciences, and marginalise the social sciences and humanities, within the academy.

I substantiate this argument with case studies of debates and campaigns about nature conservation, particularly the conservation of tropical marine ecosystems (including coral reefs) and fishery management. The first case concerns environmental functionalism and assumptions about a traditional Pacific fisheries conservation ethic; the second concerns coral reef resilience and the exaggeration of the importance of reef-associated fisheries for food security. These cases underscore the failure by transnational biodiversity conservationists to critically reflect on the extent to which their own brand of 'conservation science' is socially constructed and the apparent inability of many, if not most, of the transnational conservation community to engage seriously with global economic inequality.

Not only are the reductionist-managerialist approaches taken by transnational environmentalists misleading in terms of their erasure of culture, history and politics, but some are now being viewed as downright wrong, in terms of the 'natural science' that they draw on. Some salient examples of this include the exaggeration of the food security importance of coral reefs, which are in fact fundamentally unproductive systems, and a tendency to overemphasise the role of overfishing of herbivorous fish as a key threat to coral reefs and their ecosystem services. More problematically, reductionist-managerialist approaches have for a long time failed to engage with drivers of environmental destruction and poverty on a global scale, particularly (but not exclusively) corporate profit-shifting and capital flight. This occurs despite the fact that poverty alleviation has been a mandate for environmentalists via the Integrated Conservation and Development model since the 1990s.

I argue that the kinds of reductionism favoured and funded by the contemporary academy (and lauded by much of the media) routinely waste time and money and frequently lag far behind the thinking of anthropologists. Anthropologists do not habitually work with large quantitative datasets, nor seek to frame their work as 'hard science'. For this reason, in addition to their penchant for focusing on power relations, including within their own institutions and governments, they have been less successful in influencing governments, the media and research funders. Unfortunately, this has rendered anthropologists more vulnerable to the systematic attacks on the humanities and social sciences that have been observed for several decades across the English-speaking world.

On Method and Mismeasurement

While most anthropologists do not opt for large quantitative surveys, some do, which usually produces very interesting results (see e.g. Burton, 2007; Henrich et al., 2005; Zimmer-Tamakoshi, 2012). However, the majority of ethnographic work involves observation and interviewing of participants, with an emphasis on describing aspects of culture, politics and history that are pertinent to particular questions or fields of inquiry. Since the ascendancy of neoliberal and managerialist ideologies in English-speaking universities, this approach has been steadily devalued; instead, more reductionist and ostentatiously quantitative approaches have found favour and funding, including within the social sciences. The sad reality is that when research results are represented numerically, they tend to be perceived as intrinsically more factual and legitimately 'data'-like. Crucially, 'while we are bound to live in an age of measurement, we live in an age of mismeasurement, over-measurement, misleading measurement and counter-productive measurement' (Muller, 2018, p. 3). Qualitative researchers commonly point out that 'not everything that counts can be counted, and not everything that can be counted counts' (popularly but apparently erroneously attributed to Einstein); however, this trend remains unchanged at the time of writing.

Alan Chalmers' brilliant primer on the history and philosophy of science, *What is this thing called science* (1999), includes an excellent introductory chapter on inductive reasoning and its limitations. Chalmers described just how complex the process of structuring an inquiry based on inductive logic (which underpins a great deal of quantitative, survey-based research) actually is:

> So it would seem that it is a mistake to presume that we must first observe the facts about apples before deriving knowledge about them from those facts, because the appropriate facts, formulated as statements, presuppose quite a lot of knowledge about apples. (Chalmers, 1999, p.11)

This philosophical insight goes right to the heart of what I see as highly problematic in the way that reductionist 'social science' is practised by conservation biologists and like-minded 'social scientists' (see e.g. Cinner et al., 2012, Cinner et al., 2016). It is in the framing of the questions to be tested by the production of quantitative data that things seem to, so often, go wrong.

The most common framing problem in environmental science in the Pacific concerns economic personhood—many studies are based on the assumption that everyone behaves like a 'possessive individual' (Macpherson, 1962; Martin, 2007; Sykes, 2007). Rural coastal economies across the biodiversity-rich parts of the Asia Pacific region are based on the use of natural resources; therefore, economic data is routinely sought in studies focusing on sustainable resource management. Such studies assume that engagements with the environment can be hypothesised by assuming that both individuals and collectives are motivated primarily by a desire to accumulate wealth. Melanesian economic personhood is, in stark contrast to this assumption, strongly oriented around redistribution (Curry et al., 2015; Gregory, 2015)—agricultural surpluses are traditionally shared in a competitive arena (usually at traditional feasts), and those who give the most away tend to achieve increased social status and political power. If all Melanesians were rationally acting, economically self-maximising possessive individuals, there would be no need for Melanesian trade store owners to post notices declaring 'No Credit' (see also Curry, 2005, 1999). We would also observe no sabotaging of fish-aggregating devices (Albert et al., 2014), water supplies, mobile phone towers or airstrips— all economically irrational behaviours that are the product of highly competitive and complex political relationships among mostly kin-based social groups, whose economic worldviews depart fundamentally from that of the possessive individual (Bainton & Macintyre, 2013).

Anthropologists know that economic personhood and behaviour vary dramatically among different cultures, and within cultural groups, and are also constantly changing (Gregory, 1997, 1999, 2015; Sykes, 2007). This knowledge, generated mostly through detailed, long-term ethnographic work, has profound implications for the appropriate design and framing of questions around income expenditure (e.g. how it is consumed, accumulated or redistributed), labour investment (Curry et al., 2015) and discounting behaviour in relation to the impact of current harvesting pressure on the future productivity of a resource (Cohen & Foale, 2013; Foale et al., 2011). Economic investigations must account for the intersection of market economies with subsistence and ceremonial activities (Bainton & Macintyre, 2016) and the cultural and political context of complex and often dynamic negotiations over tenure, in addition to individual and collective benefits from both subsistence and commoditised resources (Macintyre & Foale, 2004, 2007). This canon of deeply socially informed environmental and economic research appears to be either unknown or deemed irrelevant by many conservationist researchers who perform large quantitative social surveys investigating environmental conservation and resource management questions with little or no attention to this sort of detail.

In addition to making ungrounded assumptions about human behaviour, transnational conservation biologists and their allies often perceive humans as simply an obstacle to the ultimate goal of saving 'globally important' biodiversity. Biodiversity conservation goals are frequently framed on a scale that encompasses a number of very different cultural groups of people (e.g. the Coral Triangle); therefore, we observe a common inclination to disregard inconvenient cultural complexity when constructing research studies, particularly for projects that are funded by donors whose worldview is shaped primarily by Western environmental ideals.

Researchers with a predilection for quantification and ignorance of (or even contempt for) relevant social theory will count what is easy to count and simply ignore what is not. They will opt for an impressive-looking sample size that may or may not have any useful statistical meaning in relation to parameters that actually matter. Ultimately, such choices are more concerned with the display of 'doing big science' than producing reliable, relevant and useful 'truths'. The current academic system makes this approach, despite extensive published critiques of it (Cannizzo & Osbaldiston, 2019; Ginsberg, 2011; Muller, 2018), easy to get away with and even easier to sell. Austerity within the academy has also applied significant pressure on researchers to spend less time in the field; this applies pressure to generate data in ways other than participant observation, which requires long periods of getting to know host communities, learning their language and achieving a level of rapport that allows many insights into culture, politics and history that would never be possible with briefer periods of contact.

Managerialism within the academy fosters environmental managerialism. Interdisciplinary journals that concern the environment are predominantly edited by natural scientists, who are typically ignorant of large swathes of social literature relevant to human ecology and cultural institutions pertaining to environmental use and management. An increasingly disturbing problem in this rapidly expanding interdisciplinary arena is that natural science journals tend to have a much higher impact factor than purely anthropological or sociological journals.[1] Most natural scientists, particularly the younger cohorts, are highly likely to judge the worth of a given journal, and the work it showcases, based on its impact factor alone. These same scholars also rarely consult books, including edited books, which continue to communicate a large proportion of anthropological research.

Global-scale crisis narratives, panaceas and 'silver bullets' for environmental management are more likely to find favour with the editors of high-impact journals such as *Nature* and *Science* than nuanced, rigorously theorised and painstakingly crafted case studies made in one or a small number of locations. They can also be made more authoritatively with quantitative survey data that not only routinely erases cultural difference and historical or political complexity, but also forces homogenising assumptions about economic behaviour such as possessive individualism or *homo economicus*. Winning the big prize of a publication in *Nature* or *Science* more or less immediately confers rewards such as large research grants and promotion. Therefore, regardless of whether a researcher believes a global-scale approach is one that will be more likely to produce social data that is reliable and closely represents the truth about questions that are the product of theoretically solid research, the incentive to take this approach is significant.

The conservation biology worldview is one in which scientific expertise about a given component of the natural world (be it particular species, such as turtles or tigers, or entire ecosystems, such as coral reefs or rainforests) confers not only a mandate but a right to intervene in the lives of humans anywhere on the planet if they are seen as presenting a proximate threat to the species or ecosystems in question (Dowie, 2011; Fairhead & Leach, 2000; Fairhead, Leach & Scoones, 2012). Therefore, publications on human–environment topics with global scope (as represented by work that provides analyses of peoples who are identified primarily in terms of their dependence on or association with a global conservation target such as coral reefs or rainforests) will be more likely to attract the attention of editors of high-impact (and high-prestige) scientific journals. However, the global scope of the work necessarily applies pressure to erase difference and complexity, which means that universalising forms of social science,

---

1   At the time of writing, *Conservation Biology* and *Ecology and Society* have impact factors of 5.89 and 4.55, respectively, and *Current Anthropology* and *American Anthropologist* have impact factors of 2.32 and 2.709, respectively.

such as behavioural economics or psychology, are more likely to be adopted than anthropology, with its inconvenient focus on diversity. The one standout exception that comes to mind is Joseph Henrich and colleagues' cross-cultural examination of game theory, in which a series of coordinated experiments were run by a large collaborating group of anthropologists across 15 small-scale societies, specifically to demonstrate cross-cultural differences in economic behaviour via the results of playing games such as Ultimatum. The study ultimately convincingly debunked the popular homogenising trope of *homo economicus* (Henrich et al., 2005).

Case 1: Social-Ecological-Systems Theory as Zombie Neofunctionalism

Social-Ecological-Systems (SES) 'theory' (Folke et al., 2005; Folke et al., 2002; Walker & Salt, 2006; Walker et al., 2004) is little more than a reinvention (and rebadging) of the environmental functionalism, also known as neofunctionalism, that dominated environmental anthropology in the 1960s (Lee, 1969; Rappaport, 1968; Vayda, 1961) and had been widely abandoned by most environmental anthropologists by the late 1970s and 1980s (Orlove, 1980). Neofunctionalism was an offshoot of structural functionalism and hypothesised that pre-industrial societies evolved many cultural institutions, including religious beliefs, as adaptations to environmental limits. Common examples of such institutions include taboos on harvesting supposedly limited resources (Rappaport, 1968) or various measures for constraining human population growth, including ritual adult suicide and warfare (Firth, 1983).

However, the founders and contemporary adherents of SES thinking have almost never bothered to engage with the large and very impressive body of environmental anthropology literature of the 1950s and 1960s, which explored and tested neofunctionalist theories, much less the extensive critiques and debates (among anthropologists) about neofunctionalism following this period (e.g. Orlove, 1980; Rappaport, 1984; Vayda, 1989). Even Roy Rappaport, in his 1984 reply to critics of the functionalist aspects of his famous book *Pigs for the ancestors* (1968), argued that his original analysis was 'guided by criticisms of functionalism, rather than functional doctrine per se' (Rappaport, 1984, p. 345).

Nevertheless, SES thinking and theorising, almost all of which has been conducted by ecologists and economists, has been immensely rewarding for those involved. It powerfully underpinned much of the direction of the Millennium Ecosystem Assessment (many SES heavyweights were part of this lavishly funded project) and remains the core belief system and methodological approach of the Stockholm Resilience Institute—a large, well-funded and prestigious enterprise that researches a wide range of environmental problems on multiple scales.

SES thinking routinely asserts that 'indigenous peoples' pre-historically 'evolved' cultural institutions that allowed them to adapt to the limits of their environment (in the case of my field, customary marine tenure and fishing taboos) and that, where people cannot be observed exhibiting a traditional conservation ethic, this must be due to the corrosive influences of Westernisation (Berkes, 1999; Berkes, Colding & Folke, 2000; Cinner et al., 2006; Johannes, 1978). While this may well be true for some groups in some parts of the world, it certainly has not been the case anywhere I have worked in the Pacific—several of my publications critique the critical tenets of SES (Foale, 1998a, 2006a; Foale, Wini & Fernandes, 2017; Foale et al., 2011). Many other (mostly anthropological) studies have produced analogous criticisms of neofunctionalist and/or SES thinking (Bulmer, 1982; Carrier, 1987; Firth, 1965; Lieber, 1994).

Most notably, I possess unpublished data collected in Tikopia in 2010 that supports observations made by Raymond Firth in the 1920s (Firth, 1965). Firth's research showed that, despite Tikopia being one of the most densely populated high islands in the Pacific, and despite having a very tightly managed and highly intensified farming system, Tikopians exercised no proprietary forms of exclusion (marine tenure) or taboos (fishing bans) over their coastal reefs. If we follow SES neofunctionalist logic, if any group of Pacific Islanders should be using extensive and highly elaborated forms of marine tenure and taboos, it would have to be the Tikopians. However, they are not, nor do Tikopians have other traditional regulations that could credibly be counted as having a fisheries management function, such as restrictions on species or fishing gear types (cf. Carrier, 1981).

Neofunctionalist reasoning permits a form of global environmentalist managerialism that shifts the responsibility for environmental management neatly onto economically marginalised people, by appealing to the desirability of preserving ancient cultural heritage as a means of justifying the imposition of that load. This is a clever sleight of hand that excuses scientific imperialism in the name of both cultural and biodiversity preservation. The annoying question of whether any of those owners of said cultural heritage might also aspire to a modern lifestyle, which might come at the expense of the sustainability of their natural resources, is quietly sidelined. Neofunctionalist tropes remain wildly popular with wealthy globetrotting conservationists, natural scientists and documentary makers to this day (e.g. Conservation International, 2019). There will always be a market for these ideas, because jaded, conservation-minded residents of the urban industrialised global North are clearly comforted by the idea that, somewhere in the world, 'indigenous peoples' are living in harmony with nature.

Case 2: Environmentalism, Values and 'Conservation Science'

Conservation scientists self-identify as objective thinkers, perceiving themselves to be 'better' at objectivity than anthropologists, who many of them believe inhabit a lower position in the disciplinary pecking order (Rose, 1997). However, there has long existed a small number of dissenters. Senior conservation biologist John Lawton is on record arguing that 'conservation is not a scientific activity' (1997, p. 4). There now exists a large canon of critical political ecology writing, mostly by anthropologists, that documents high-handed, unscientific and socially obtuse environmentalism (Dowie, 2011; Fairhead & Leach, 1996; Filer, 2004a; Foale & Macintyre, 2005; West, 2006; West, Igoe & Brockington, 2006). Despite the volume and power of this work, it appears to have made little impact on policy or practice within the contemporary international conservation arena. The stark reality is that the academic publishing system has made it possible for conservation biologists to ignore completely any and all critique from the social sciences and from within their own ranks (Lawton, 1997; Redford, 1991; Soule, 1985).

Moreover, few conservation biologists reflect very carefully on why or how they value nature, a topic about which anthropologists, in addition to sociologists, historians and geographers, have written a great deal (Cronon, 1996, 1995; Foale & Macintyre, 2005; Foale et al., 2016; Ingold, 1993, 2000; Milton, 2002, 1993). This is unfortunate; however, it is again possible to see how a lack of curiosity about ontology and epistemology makes it easier to retain one's conviction about a conservation issue—

contemporary academic and research funding structures do nothing to challenge this lack of curiosity. For example, why are certain species, or groups of species, deemed more deserving of scientific attention and conservation funding than others? Why are coral reefs and rainforests more popular research topics among natural scientists than estuaries or heathlands? The ways in which species and ecosystems are valued have as much to do with their aesthetic qualities (Foale & Macintyre, 2005), in addition to the 'cumulative intrinsic value' of large species counts (the so-called 'hotspot' logic; for a critique of this, see Foale et al., 2016), as any ostensibly 'scientific' logic. When working in another country with rural people who speak a different language, few conservation scientists even bother to learn the local language names for the fish, plants and other species they seek to protect (Cohen et al., 2014; Foale, 1998b; Hviding, 2005). If they did, they would immediately realise that local ways of valuing nature are almost certainly very different from their own. In this intellectual and managerial context, it is easy to raise research grants for the conservation of 'iconic' species such as turtles, cetaceans and large mammals (particularly if they have big eyes), with little attention given to the construction of those species' value in the minds of both scientists and the public, who often provide the political leverage to ensure continued flows of funding (Foale & Macintyre, 2005; Foale et al., 2016).

On Epistemological Entitlement—Some Sciences are More Equal than Others

Given the inequalities within the academic publication and funding systems outlined above, it is impossible to be surprised by the obvious sense of entitlement displayed by academics in some disciplines. The prefixes 'hard' and 'soft' are still code for 'legitimate' and 'flaky', respectively. Apparently, James Watson once said that 'there is only one science, physics; everything else is social work' (Rose, 1997, p. 83). My own long-term interactions with marine scientists at various research institutions[2] have provided a wealth of participant-observation data that attest to the depth of conviction among natural scientists of their intellectual and epistemological superiority over all brands of social

2   These include JCU, Australian Institute for Marine Science, Commonwealth Scientific and Industrial Research Organisation (CSIRO) and the Great Barrier Reef Marine Park Authority. An anthropologist colleague based at JCU once observed that Townsville probably has the highest density of marine scientists per square kilometre in the world.

scientists, but most notably those who do not produce large quantitative datasets that can be subject to elaborate and arcane (the more arcane, the more impressive) analyses of variance (for a scathing critique of this behaviour, see Turner, 2019).

However, a far more pernicious problem than disciplinary snobbery and dismissing or completely ignoring academic contributions is the appropriation of ideas that are initially spurned, without due credit. The process is described perfectly by J. B. S. Haldane's (1963) 'four stages of acceptance':

1. This is worthless nonsense.
2. This is an interesting, but perverse, point of view.
3. This is true, but quite unimportant.
4. I always said so.

Below, I consider ideas about the broader political and economic drivers of environmental degradation that have long been a focus of study in anthropology and related disciplines and have now belatedly been appropriated by natural scientists. The first idea is that capital flight via profit-shifting is the most important contemporary driver of inequality and underdevelopment globally; the second is that coral bleaching, not local overfishing, is the pre-eminent threat to coral reefs.

Capital Flight as Primary Contemporary Driver of Inequality and Underdevelopment

Anthropologists have been writing about inequality for a long time (Beteille, 1969; Dumont, 1970; Fabinyi, Foale, & Macintyre, 2013; Lawrence, 1964; Macintyre, 1998; Mead, 1956). But it has not been until the relatively recent publication of survey-based approaches (Wilkinson, 2005; Wilkinson & Pickett, 2009) that inequality as a driver of social ills has attracted widespread treatment in the media (Wike, 2013).[3] However,

3   Another (perhaps more significant) reason for the upswing in media attention to inequality's role as a driver of social damage is the sheer magnitude of the increase in economic inequality in English-speaking countries since the 1970s, in addition to the Global Financial Crisis and numerous recent exposés of financial fraud and corruption.

many natural scientists appear to remain indifferent to the importance of inequality as a fundamental social problem (Büscher et al., 2017)—this is also the case within university management spheres.[4]

Publications such as Nicholas Shaxson's *Treasure islands* (2011), the impressive string of exposés produced by the International Consortium of Investigative Journalists (e.g. LuxLeaks and the Panama Papers) and groups such as the Tax Justice Network and Global Financial Integrity have done much to draw attention to the importance of capital flight as a driver of poverty, underdevelopment and environmental degradation around the world, particularly in low-income countries where resource extraction by multinational corporations remains the primary source of revenue. A crucial fact emerging from this investigative work has been that capital flight resulting from trade mis-invoicing and other financial fraud by transnational resource extractors (mostly logging, mining and fishing companies) significantly eclipses inflows of development aid (Global Financial Integrity, 2015, 2017).

Anthropologists, political scientists and political ecologists (and also investigative journalists) have been at the cutting edge of analysis and commentary about the significance of capital flight as a driver of poverty and corruption (Mousseau & Lau, 2015; Rawlings, 2006, 2011; Sharman, 2008, 2017; Van Fossen, 2012), in addition to pointing out the problems it poses for the SES paradigm that is so central to the worldview of the Resilience Alliance and many conservation biologists (Clifton & Foale, 2017; Fabinyi, Evans & Foale, 2014; Foale et al., 2013; Foale et al., 2016). The idea that biodiversity conservation and the associated preservation of ecosystem goods and services can somehow be achieved primarily with local-scale interventions that help 'communities' of *homo economicus* to comply with a global managerialist template, such as Ostrom's Eight 'Design Principles'[5] (Ostrom, 1990), seems even more

---

4 A bleakly Orwellian twist on Haldane's abovementioned axiom is the recent announcement by JCU, using a set of global metrics, that it has been judged 'best university in the world in its commitment to the United Nations goal for reducing inequality' (James Cook University, 2019). The fact that JCU's Vice Chancellor earned AUD 982,500 in 2017 (Times Higher Education, 2018), and the disparity in pay between senior management and ordinary employees is already very wide and continuing to widen, clearly has not been factored into these metrics.
5 Ostrom's Eight 'Design Principles' for successful collective management of 'common pool resources' (CPRs) are: 1) Clearly defined boundaries; 2) Congruence between appropriation and provision rules and local conditions; 3) Collective-choice arrangement; 4) Monitoring; 5) Graduated sanctions; 6) Conflict-resolution mechanisms; 7) Minimal recognition (by governments) of rights to organise; and 8) (for CPRs that are part of larger systems) Nested enterprises.

ludicrous in the context of the immense financial haemorrhaging that has been accelerating over the past half-century or so. However, in keeping with Haldane's observation, the Resilience Alliance have finally seen fit to claim expertise on the issue (Galaz et al., 2018) and it will be interesting to see how this work affects (or not) the transparently functionalist thinking that has dominated the group's outputs since their inception.

Coral Bleaching

The magnitude of the moral problem posed by coral bleaching (Hoegh-Guldberg, 1999) has long concerned myself and some of my colleagues (Foale, 2006b; Foale & Macintyre, 2005; Foale & Manele, 2004). Despite the immense injustice evident in the fact that coral bleaching is a form of environmental damage that is experienced disproportionately by people in poor tropical countries[6] but driven primarily by the excessive energy consumption (and associated carbon dioxide emissions) of people in rich countries (and, increasingly, also in Brazil, Russia, India and China), opinion leaders in coral reef science have framed the problem differently. For a long time, they have diluted the importance of bleaching by casting it as just one of 'multiple drivers' of coral reef destruction, along with fishing of herbivorous fish and sediment and nutrient runoff (Hughes & Connell, 1999; Hughes et al., 2010; Hughes et al., 2003; Hughes et al., 2006; Hughes, Barnes et al., 2017).

Attention to the non-carbon-related drivers of reef damage, particularly fishing and, even more particularly, fishing of herbivorous species such as parrotfishes (family Scaridae) and surgeonfishes (family Acanthuridae), has driven a vast global program of austerity measures (Clifton & Foale, 2017; Foale et al., 2013), in the form of no-take marine protected areas (MPAs). Environmentalists and marine scientists correctly argue that MPAs, which prohibit fishing within a defined area of sea territory, allow the recovery of fish populations, including the grazing species that some argue prevent overgrowth of corals by macro-algae (more detail on this is given below). Fish population recovery helps to maintain the ecological integrity and functioning of the coral reef ecosystem (Hughes et al., 2006) and eventually also delivers a fishery 'dividend', via the adult fish and fish eggs and larvae that are 'exported' beyond the boundaries of the MPA to areas open to fishing (Russ et al., 2004). The trouble is that most MPA

---

6   The one clear exception being the Great Barrier Reef in Australia.

programs have not been accompanied by any effective schemes to offset either the immediate economic costs of exclusion from no-take areas suffered by mostly very poor (and often landless) fishers in low-income countries (Clifton & Foale, 2017; Fabinyi, 2018) or the global drivers of poverty and inequality (Hickel, 2017; Li, 2010). Despite a long series of critiques by anthropologists and political ecologists of conservation programs that impose local costs for problems that are often primarily driven by global-scale processes (including but not limited to climate change), the natural science literature has continued to focus on local 'solutions'.

The key crisis narrative underpinning the campaign to use MPAs to 'save coral reef biodiversity', by preventing fishing of grazing reef fish species, stems from the paradigm of the coral-algal 'phase shift', an idea that has its origins in work done in the Caribbean (Hughes, 1994; Knowlton, 1992). Here, the irreversible transformation of coral reefs to stands of *Sargassum* spp. (brown macro-algae) was observed as a consequence of over-harvesting of parrotfishes and other grazing fish species, combined with elevated runoff of nutrients and sediments. It is still possible to find examples of phase-shifted reefs; however, there remain problems with the model, including critiques published by high-profile marine scientists (Bruno, Cote & Toth, 2019; Bruno et al., 2009; Russ et al., 2015). The coral-*Sargassum* phase-shift paradigm has also become a central component in the development of 'resilience theory' (Walker & Salt, 2006), as introduced above. For a long time, the work of the Resilience Alliance has studiously ignored the role of colonialism and global capitalism in driving poverty and environmental destruction in the global economic periphery.

In the wake of the back-to-back bleaching episodes on the Great Barrier Reef in 2015 and 2016, the 'multiple drivers' model now appears to have been discarded (or at least temporarily sidelined) and carbon dioxide has now been pronounced to represent the predominant existential threat to coral reefs (Hughes, Kerry et al., 2017). This necessarily amounts to a paradigmatic shift in the burden of 'blame' for coral reef ecosystem degradation from the local to the global, but it remains to be seen whether this will translate to a slowing or cessation in the imposition of austerity programs on economically marginalised coastal fishers. It is unlikely that we will see much engagement of marine scientists with historical and contemporary drivers of poverty and inequality acting on scales larger than the local; therefore, this highly problematic aspect of the 'multiple drivers' approach may persist. While this change in perspective on the importance of bleaching in reef degradation does not amount to a complete appropriation of the longstanding critiques by anthropologists outlined at the start of this section (in line with Haldane's four stages), it does represent a shift in that direction.

The Ascendancy and Dominance of Conservation Biology within the Natural Sciences

Within marine science, some sub-disciplines have taken a back seat for many years, largely as a consequence of the market dominance of conservation-related paradigms, most notably the branch of ecology linking biodiversity to ecological resilience (Hooper et al., 2005; Mora et al., 2011; Worm et al., 2006) and a related branch of ecological economics relating ecosystem resilience to the delivery of ecological goods and services (Costanza et al., 1997). Research on food webs and nutrient cycling on coral reefs (Johannes et al., 1972) flourished in the 1970s and 1980s and established one of the key (and enduring) paradigms of coral reef ecology, which is that reef corals are remarkably adapted to low-nutrient (read: unproductive) environments. The corollary of this is that coral reefs are lousy producers of that most celebrated of ecosystem services—fish (Birkeland, 1997, 2017). Indeed, the numerous studies that show, from various perspectives and with different types of data, that reef fisheries, while species-rich, can be overharvested very quickly and then take a long time to recover (Russ & Alcala, 2010) run strongly counter to the many pronouncements about the pivotal importance of coral reefs for the food security of millions of people in the tropics (for a detailed discussion, see Foale et al., 2016).

A comparatively small number of species underpin protein security for the most heavily populated parts of South-East Asia today: these are uncharismatic schooling sardines, scads, mackerels and tunas and a small number of aquacultured species. Coral reef fish account for, at most, approximately one-fifth of the fish produced in the Philippines, based on government fishery data (Clifton & Foale, 2017) and rural surveys (Dey et al., 2005; Fabinyi, Dressler & Pido, 2017). These (mostly small) pelagic fish occur in vast numbers in nutrient-rich offshore and coastal waters, largely independent of corals and the biodiversity associated with coral reefs that are so valued by conservationists. Importantly, because they are short-lived and fast-growing, they are far more resilient to heavy fishing pressure and, thus, increasingly important for food security, particularly as coastal populations grow. Small (and large) pelagics are also increasingly important for coastal Papua New Guineans and Solomon Islanders (Albert et al., 2014; Foale & Sullivan, 2013; Roeger, Foale & Sheaves, 2016). Despite these stark facts about the relatively minor importance of corals and coral reefs for food security, Web of Science searches show that the great majority of published scientific research on fish and fisheries in the Coral Triangle countries focuses on coral-associated species (Clifton & Foale, 2017).

Clearly, the production of high-status science on coral reefs and their associated fisheries is largely rooted in affluent Western cultural values and ideologies. The exaggeration by conservation biologists of the numbers of people who allegedly depend on reef fisheries for food security is no doubt to help sell the importance of reef conservation programs (principally the implementation of MPAs) to donors. It is a political ploy used because the 'real' reason coral reefs are valued by Western scientists is for their intrinsic (i.e. high species richness) and aesthetic value. The greater focus of scientific publications on fish and fisheries associated with reefs, rather than the small number of uncharismatic but highly productive species (e.g. scads and sardines) that are so important to the lives of poor people in the Asia Pacific region, is simply because conservation scientists are more interested in biodiversity than they are in food security. Technocratic but politically disengaged (or simply disingenuous) research on coral reefs enjoys a larger market and continues to reward researchers with more lucrative grants than the critical approaches taken by most anthropologists and political ecologists.

Conservation without Development is, still, Imperialism

If we take the ideas of Freire (1973) about the pivotal role of education for critical consciousness seriously, as well as the ideas of Sen (1999) and Nussbaum (2011) about capabilities, then the mandate for adequately funded education and health systems in Papua New Guinea (PNG) and other low-income countries should sit front and centre for all conservationists interested in socially just, locally owned and controlled pathways to sustainable resource management and biodiversity conservation (see especially West & Aini, this volume). How can the grassroots a) mobilise against their corrupt, patriarchal and predatory elites and b) grasp the importance of the burgeoning threats to their natural resources (principally from transnational capitalists, but also from population pressure) if the mean number of years PNG women spend in school is still less than four (United Nations Development Programme, 2019)? Other branches of the aid community attempt to assist with the education sector in countries such as PNG. However, my point is the ongoing emptiness of the supposed 'development' part of the 'conservation-and-development' paradigm, as prosecuted by the big international NGOs and multilateral agencies, despite well over two decades of sustained critique (Filer, 1994, 2004a, 2004b, 2011; Foale, 2001; Van Helden, 2001; West, 2006).

The overwhelming majority of academics critiquing and protesting against the corrosive impacts of managerialism and the gerrymandered metrics system in the academy are from the humanities and social sciences (Cannizzo & Osbaldiston, 2019; Ginsberg, 2011; Muller, 2018; Turner, 2019). At JCU, several natural scientists have engaged in this debate; however, most natural, earth and medical scientists are either mute or actively support the system. The main reason for this is that many of those who are advantaged by the system prefer to interpret that advantage as personal virtue (in a striking parallel with George Lakoff's model of American conservatives' contempt for the poor as moral failures; see Lakoff, 2009). This occurs despite the fact that academic jobs in the natural and medical sciences are becoming just as precarious as those in the social sciences and humanities.

Unfortunately, the extent to which neoliberal logics now control the 'market' for academic knowledge production means that the kinds of inquiry that interrogate and critique neoliberalism will inevitably be marginalised in that market. Stephen Turner has observed that:

> academic markets are not free markets, in which good ideas compete; they are artificial markets, in which the participants compete for real prizes but under rules that constrain them in ways that transform and deform them. They are, in short, the perfect embodiment of neoliberalism: competition to serve a purpose set by others, not competition in which the ends themselves are subject to competition. (2019, p. 239)

Conclusion

Anthropology has opened my eyes to insights into the scientific enterprise and global conservation work that have been transformative, but clearly also burdensome, as epitomised by Arundhati's Roy's famous line: 'the trouble is that once you've seen it, you can't unsee it. And once you've seen it, keeping quiet, saying nothing, becomes as political an act as speaking out' (Roy, 2001, p. 7).

I credit (or perhaps I should blame!) Martha Macintyre, in addition to others in her network, for this change in perspective, which I do not regret, but that has made life and work more complicated for me than I anticipated. While I have not lost any interest in the biology, ecology, evolution and fate of marine life, I can no longer identify as a professional biologist. My adopted discipline of anthropology, however, while enlightening and intellectually empowering, is clearly imperilled by the same neoliberal culture that appears to be advantaging the natural sciences, at least in the institution at which I am currently employed. Having grown up in a colony (the British Solomon Islands), I strongly identify with the powerful perspective on, and critique of, colonialism (both classical and contemporary) that is offered by anthropology and allied disciplines. Colonialism today is manifested in transnational, donor-funded, natural science–dominated conservation work, despite the large canon of (mostly anthropological) work that demonstrates its many problems.

Anthropology, with its persistent focus on the particular, but also an eye on the big picture, will always resist the homogenising demands of the managerialist environmentalism that routinely seeks to find panaceas and 'silver bullets' on a global scale. Anthropologists already view the scientific community's global framing of environmental governance for what it is—just another form of imperialism. Therefore, the challenge for environmental anthropologists is to find ways to convince the scientific community to embrace those powerful anthropological tools of reflexivity and critical political economy to recognise and understand the importance of capitalism and possessive individualism (in addition to population growth) in driving environmental degradation. They must join us in addressing these, rather than routinely scapegoating (albeit in highly politically finessed terms) a homogenised 'Malthusian peasantry', whose economic marginality and consequent heavy dependence on natural resources allows them to be constructed as the primary threat to 'globally important' biodiversity.

Some natural scientists 'get' the arguments I have outlined here, so I do not wish this to be a blanket condemnation. But there remains much work to be done to reach those who remain blind to these issues. Anthropologists must also work more collaboratively and collegially to help their younger scholars win grants and break into the system despite the existing handicaps. Anthropologists do not work in teams nearly as much as natural scientists do and would benefit, both intellectually and financially, from doing so. I will continue to reach out to, and collaborate with, my natural science colleagues, despite persistent cultural and structural barriers to redressing the unequal power relationship between us.

Acknowledgements

I wish to thank Nick Bainton, Debra McDougall, Kalissa Alexeyeff and John Cox for their Herculean efforts to organise this volume. I thank Martha Macintyre for many years of inspiring and mind-expanding collaboration and discussions and for introducing me to so many great minds. Thanks also to Nick Osbaldiston for introducing me to the work of Stephen Turner.

References

Albert, J. A., Beare, D., Schwarz, A.-M., Albert, S., Warren, R., Teri, J., … Andrew, N. L. (2014). The contribution of nearshore fish aggregating devices (FADs) to food security and livelihoods in Solomon Islands. *PLoS ONE*, *9*(12), e115386. doi.org/10.1371/journal.pone.0115386

Bainton, N. A. & Macintyre, M. (2013). 'My Land, My Work': Business development and large-scale mining in Melanesia. In F. McCormack & K. Barclay (Eds), *Engaging with capitalism: Cases from Oceania* (Vol. 33) (pp. 139–165). United Kingdom: Emerald Books.

Bainton, N. A. & Macintyre, M. (2016). Mortuary ritual and mining riches in Island Melanesia. In D. Lipset & E. K. Silverman (Eds), *Mortuary dialogues: Death ritual and the reproduction of moral communities in Pacific Modernities* (pp. 110–132). New York, NY: Berghahn.

Berkes, F. (1999). *Sacred ecology: Traditional ecological knowledge and resource management*. Philadelphia, PA: Taylor & Francis.

Berkes, F., Colding, J. & Folke, C. (2000). Rediscovery of traditional ecological knowledge as adaptive management. *Ecological Applications, 10*(5), 1251–1262.

Beteille, A. (Ed.). (1969). *Social inequality*. Harmondsworth, England: Penguin.

Birkeland, C. (1997). Symbiosis, fisheries and economic development on coral reefs. *Trends in Ecology & Evolution, 12*(9), 364–367.

Birkeland, C. (2017). Working with, not against, coral-reef fisheries. *Coral Reefs, 36*(1), 1–11. doi.org/10.1007/s00338-016-1535-8

Bruno, J. F., Cote, I. M. & Toth, L. T. (2019). Climate change, coral loss and the curious case of the parrotfish paradigm: Why don't marine protected areas improve reef resilience? In C. A. Carlson & S. J. Giovannoni (Eds), *Annual Review of Marine Science* (Vol. 11) (pp. 307–334).

Bruno, J. F., Sweatman, H., Precht, W. F., Selig, E. R. & Schutte, V. G. W. (2009). Assessing evidence of phase shifts from coral to macroalgal dominance on coral reefs. *Ecology, 90*(6), 1478–1484. doi.org/10.1890/08-1781.1

Bulmer, R. N. H. (1982). Traditional conservation practices in Papua New Guinea. In L. Morauta, J. Pernetta & W. Heaney (Eds), *Traditional conservation in Papua New Guinea: Implications for today* (pp. 59–77). Boroko, Papua New Guinea: Institute of Applied Social and Economic Research.

Burton, J. (2007). The anthropology of personal identity: Intellectual property rights issues in Papua New Guinea, West Papua and Australia. *The Australian Journal of Anthropology, 18*(1), 40–55.

Büscher, B., Fletcher, R., Brockington, D., Sandbrook, C., Adams, W. M., Campbell, L., … Shanker, K. (2017). Half-earth or whole earth? Radical ideas for conservation, and their implications. *Oryx, 51*(3), 407–410. doi.org/10.1017/S0030605316001228

Cannizzo, F. & Osbaldiston, N. (Eds). (2019). *The social structures of global academia*. London, England: Routledge.

Carrier, J. (1981). Ownership of productive resources on Ponam Island, Manus Province. *Journal de la Societe des Oceanistes, 37*, 205–217.

Carrier, J. (1987). Marine tenure and conservation in Papua New Guinea. In B. J. McCay & J. M. Acheson (Eds), *The question of the commons: The culture and ecology of communal resources* (pp. 142–167). Tucson, AZ: University of Arizona Press.

Chalmers, A. F. (1999). *What is this thing called science?* (3rd ed.). St Lucia, Qld: University of Queensland Press.

Cinner, J., Marnane, M. J., McClanahan, T. R. & Almany, G. R. (2006). Periodic closures as adaptive coral reef management in the Indo-Pacific. *Ecology and Society*, *11*(1).

Cinner, J. E., Huchery, C., MacNeil, M. A., Graham, N. A. J., McClanahan, T. R., Maina, J., … Mouillot, D. (2016). Bright spots among the world's coral reefs. *Nature (London)*, *535*, 416–419. doi.org/10.1038/nature18607

Cinner, J. E., McClanahan, T. R., MacNeil, M. A., Graham, N. A. J., Daw, T. M., Mukminin, A., … Kuange, J. (2012). Comanagement of coral reef social-ecological systems. *Proceedings of the National Academy of Sciences of the United States of America*, *109*(14), 5219–5222. doi.org/10.1073/pnas.1121215109

Clifton, J. & Foale, S. (2017). Extracting ideology from policy: Analysing the social construction of conservation priorities in the Coral Triangle region. *Marine Policy*, *82*, 189–196. doi.org/10.1016/j.marpol.2017.03.018

Cohen, P. & Foale, S. J. (2013). Sustaining small-scale fisheries with periodic closures. *Marine Policy*, *37*, 278–287. doi.org/10.1016/j.marpol.2012.05.010

Cohen, P., Tapala, S., Rikio, A., Kukiti, E., Sori, F., Hilly, Z., … Foale, S. (2014). Developing a common understanding of taxonomy for fisheries management in north Vella Lavella, Solomon Islands. *SPC Traditional Marine Resource Management and Knowledge Information Bulletin*, *33*, 3–12.

Conservation International. (2019). *Revitalising conservation traditions: The story of Gwala*. Retrieved from www.conservation.org/asia-pacific/stories/gwala-rising

Costanza, R., d'Arge, R., de Groot, R., Farber, S., Grasso, M., Hannon, B., … van den Belt, M. (1997). The value of the world's ecosystem services and natural capital. *Nature (London)*, *387*(6630), 253–260.

Cronon, W. (Ed.). (1995). *Uncommon ground: Toward reinventing nature*. New York, NY: W.W. Norton and Company.

Cronon, W. (1996). The trouble with wilderness: Or, getting back to the wrong nature. *Environmental History*, *1*(1), 7–28.

Curry, G. (1999). Markets, social embeddedness and precapitalist societies: The case of village trade stores in Papua New Guinea. *Geoforum*, *30*, 285–298.

Curry, G. (2005). Doing 'business' in Papua New Guinea: The social embeddedness of small business enterprises. *Journal of Small Business and Entrepreneurship*, *18*(2), 231–246.

Curry, G., Koczberski, G., Lummani, J., Nailina, R., Peter, E., McNally, G. & Kuaimba, O. (2015). A bridge too far? The influence of socio-cultural values on the adaptation responses of smallholders to a devastating pest outbreak in cocoa. *Global Environmental Change*, *35*, 1–11. doi.org/10.1016/j.gloenvcha. 2015.07.012

Dey, M. M., Rab, M. A., Paraguas, F. J., Piumsombun, S., Bhatta, R., Alam, M. F. & Ahmed, M. (2005). Fish consumption and food security: A disaggregated analysis by types of fish and classes of consumers in selected Asian countries. *Aquaculture Economics & Management*, *9*(1–2), 89–111. doi.org/10.1080/ 13657300590961537

Dowie, M. (2011). *Conservation refugees: The hundred-year conflict between global conservation and native peoples*. Cambridge, MA: The MIT Press.

Dumont, L. (1970). *Homo hierarchicus: The caste system and its implications*. Oxford, England: Oxford University Press.

Fabinyi, M. (2018). Environmental fixes and historical trajectories of marine resource use in Southeast Asia. *Geoforum*, *91*, 87–96. doi.org/10.1016/ j.geoforum.2018.02.033

Fabinyi, M., Dressler, W. H. & Pido, M. (2017). Fish, trade and food security: Moving beyond 'availability' discourse in marine conservation. *Human Ecology*, *45*, 177–188. doi.org/10.1007/s10745-016-9874-1

Fabinyi, M., Evans, L. & Foale, S. J. (2014). Social-ecological systems, social diversity and power: Insights from anthropology and political ecology. *Ecology and Society*, *19*(4). doi.org/10.5751/ES-07029-190428

Fabinyi, M., Foale, S. & Macintyre, M. (2013). Managing inequality or managing stocks? An ethnographic perspective on the governance of small-scale fisheries. *Fish and Fisheries*, *16*(3), 471–485.

Fairhead, J. & Leach, M. (1996). *Misreading the African landscape: Society and ecology in a forest-savanna mosaic*. Cambridge, England: Cambridge University Press.

Fairhead, J. & Leach, M. (2000, 5 May). The nature lords. *Times Literary Supplement*, pp. 3–4.

Fairhead, J., Leach, M. & Scoones, I. (2012). Green grabbing: A new appropriation of nature? *Journal of Peasant Studies*, *39*(2), 237–261. doi.org/10.1080/ 03066150.2012.671770

Ferguson, J. (1990). *The anti-politics machine: Development, depoliticization, and bureaucratic power in Lesotho.* Minneapolis, MN: University of Minnesota Press.

Filer, C. (1994). The nature of the human threat to Papua New Guinea's biodiversity endowment. In N. Sekhran & S. Miller (Eds), *Papua New Guinea biodiversity country study: The costs and benefits of conserving Papua New Guinea's biodiversity* (pp. 187–199). Port Moresby, Papua New Guinea: Papua New Guinea Department of Environment and Conservation, Conservation Resource Centre.

Filer, C. (2004a, March). *Hotspots and handouts: Illusions of conservation and development in Papua New Guinea.* Paper presented at the Bridging Scales and Epistemologies Conference, Alexandria, Egypt.

Filer, C. (2004b). The knowledge of indigenous desire: Disintegrating conservation and development in Papua New Guinea. In A. Bicker, P. Sillitoe & J. Pottier (Eds), *Development and local knowledge: New approaches to issues in natural resources management, conservation and agriculture* (pp. 64–92). London, England: Routledge.

Filer, C. (2011). Interdisciplinary perspectives on historical ecology and environmental policy in Papua New Guinea. *Environmental Conservation, 38*(2), 256–269. doi.org/10.1017/s0376892910000913

Firth, R. (1965). *Primitive Polynesian economy* (2nd ed.). London, England: Routledge and Kegan Paul.

Firth, R. (1983). *We, the Tikopia: A sociological study of kinship in primitive Polynesia.* Stanford, CA: Stanford University Press. (Original work published 1936.)

Foale, S. (1998a). Assessment and management of the trochus fishery at West Nggela, Solomon Islands: An interdisciplinary approach. *Ocean and Coastal Management, 40,* 187–205.

Foale, S. (1998b). What's in a name? An analysis of the West Nggela (Solomon Islands) fish taxonomy. *SPC Traditional Marine Resource Management and Knowledge Information Bulletin, 9,* 2–19.

Foale, S. (2001). 'Where's our development?' Landowner aspirations and environmentalist agendas in Western Solomon Islands. *The Asia Pacific Journal of Anthropology, 2*(2), 44–67.

Foale, S. (2006a). The intersection of scientific and indigenous ecological knowledge in coastal Melanesia: Implications for contemporary marine resource management. *International Social Science Journal, 58*(187), 129–137.

Foale, S. (2006b, March, 2004). *The scale and epistemology of coral bleaching in Papua New Guinea.* Paper presented at the Bridging Scales and Epistemologies, Alexandria.

Foale, S. & Macintyre, M. A. (2005). Green fantasies: Photographic representations of biodiversity and ecotourism in the Western Pacific. *Journal of Political Ecology, 13*, 1–22.

Foale, S. & Manele, B. (2004). Social and political barriers to the use of Marine Protected Areas for conservation and fishery management in Melanesia. *Asia Pacific Viewpoint, 45*(3), 373–386.

Foale, S. & Sullivan, N. (2013). *Improving livelihoods of coastal artisanal fishing communities in Madang Province, Papua New Guinea, through piloting alternative fishing methods* (WWF Project Number WMPO 006). Retrieved from Townsville and Port Moresby: researchonline.jcu.edu.au/31884/

Foale, S., Dyer, M. & Kinch, J. (2016). The value of tropical biodiversity in rural Melanesia. *Valuation Studies, 4*(1), 11–39. doi.org/10.3384/VS.2001-5992.164111

Foale, S., Wini, L. & Fernandes, L. (2017). *The Arnavon community marine conservation area: A review of successes, ongoing challenges and lessons learned. A report to the MACBIO project.* Retrieved from Suva: macbio-pacific.info/wp-content/uploads/2017/11/Arnavon-Is-Review-digital-091117.pdf

Foale, S., Cohen, P., Januchowski, S., Wenger, A. & Macintyre, M. (2011). Tenure and taboos: Origins and implications for fisheries in the Pacific. *Fish and Fisheries, 12*(4), 357–369. doi.org/10.1111/j.1467-2979.2010.00395.x

Foale, S., Adhuri, D., Aliño, P., Allison, E. H., Andrew, N., Cohen, P., … Weeratunge, N. (2013). Food security and the Coral Triangle Initiative. *Marine Policy, 38*, 174–183. doi.org/10.1016/j.marpol.2012.05.033

Folke, C., Hahn, T., Olsson, P. & Norberg, J. (2005). Adaptive governance of social-ecological systems. *Annual Review of Environment and Resources, 30*, 441–473.

Folke, C., Carpenter, S., Elmqvist, T., Gunderson, L., Holling, C. S. & Walker, B. (2002). Resilience and sustainable development: Building adaptive capacity in a world of transformations. *Ambio, 31*(5), 437–440.

Freire, P. (1973). *Education for critical consciousness.* New York, NY: The Seabury Press.

Galaz, V., Crona, B., Dauriach, A., Jouffray, J.-B., Österblom, H. & Fichtner, J. (2018). Tax havens and global environmental degradation. *Nature Ecology & Evolution, 2,* 1352–1357. doi.org/10.1038/s41559-018-0497-3

Ginsberg, B. (2011). *The fall of the faculty: The rise of the all-administrative university and why it matters.* Oxford, England: Oxford University Press.

Global Financial Integrity. (2015). *Financial flows and tax havens: Combining to limit the lives of billions of people.* Retrieved from www.gfintegrity.org/report/ financial-flows-and-tax-havens-combining-to-limit-the-lives-of-billions-of- people/

Global Financial Integrity. (2017). *Illicit financial flows to and from developing countries: 2005–2014.* Retrieved from www.gfintegrity.org/wp-content/ uploads/2017/05/GFI-IFF-Report-2017_final.pdf

Gregory, C. A. (1997). *Savage money: The anthropology and politics of commodity exchange.* Amsterdam, The Netherlands: Harwood.

Gregory, C. A. (1999). South Asian economic models for the Pacific? The case of microfinance. *Pacific Economic Bulletin, 14*(2), 82–92.

Gregory, C. A. (2015). *Gifts and commodities* (2nd ed.). Chicago, IL: HAU Books.

Haldane, J. (1963). Review of the truth about death. *Journal of Genetics, 58,* 463–464.

Henrich, J., Boyd, R., Bowles, S., Camerer, C., Fehr, E., Gintis, H., … Tracer, D. (2005). 'Economic man' in cross-cultural perspective: Behavioral experiments in 15 small-scale societies. *Behavioral and Brain Sciences, 28*(6), 795–855.

Hickel, J. (2017). Is global inequality getting better or worse? A critique of the World Bank's convergence narrative. *Third World Quarterly, 38*(10), 2208– 2222. doi.org/10.1080/01436597.2017.1333414

Hoegh-Guldberg, O. (1999). Climate change, coral bleaching and the future of the world's coral reefs [Review]. *Marine & Freshwater Research, 50*(8), 839–866.

Hooper, D. U., Chapin, F. S., Ewel, J. J., Hector, A., Inchausti, P., Lavorel, S., … Wardle, D. A. (2005). Effects of biodiversity on ecosystem functioning: A consensus of current knowledge. *Ecological Monographs, 75*(1), 3–35.

Hughes, T. P. (1994). Catastrophes, phase-shifts, and large-scale degradation of a Caribbean coral-reef. *Science, 265*(5178), 1547–1551.

Hughes, T. P. & Connell, J. H. (1999). Multiple stressors on coral reefs: A long-term perspective. *Limnology & Oceanography, 44*(3), 932–940.

Hughes, T. P., Bellwood, D. R., Folke, C. S., McCook, L. J. & Pandolfi, J. M. (2006). No-take areas, herbivory and coral reef resilience. *Trends in Ecology & Evolution*, *22*(1), 1–3. doi.org/10.1016/j.tree.2006.10.009

Hughes, T. P., Graham, N. A. J., Jackson, J. B. C., Mumby, P. J. & Steneck, R. S. (2010). Rising to the challenge of sustaining coral reef resilience. *Trends in Ecology & Evolution*, *25*(11), 633–642. doi.org/10.1016/j.tree.2010.07.011

Hughes, T. P., Baird, A. H., Bellwood, D. R., Card, M., Connolly, S. R., Folke, C., … Roughgarden, J. (2003). Climate change, human impacts, and the resilience of coral reefs. *Science*, *301*(5635), 929–933.

Hughes, T. P., Barnes, M. L., Bellwood, D. R., Cinner, J. E., Cumming, G. S., Jackson, J. B. C., … Scheffer, M. (2017). Coral reefs in the Anthropocene. *Nature (London)*, *546*(7656), 82–90. doi.org/10.1038/nature22901

Hughes, T. P., Kerry, J. T., Alvarez-Noriega, M., Alvarez-Romero, J. G., Anderson, K. D., Baird, A. H., … Wilson, S. K. (2017). Global warming and recurrent mass bleaching of corals. *Nature (London)*, *543*(7645), 373–377. doi.org/10.1038/nature21707

Hviding, E. (2005). *Reef and rainforest: An environmental encyclopedia of Marovo Lagoon, Solomon Islands / Kiladi oro vivineidi ria tingitonga pa idere oro pa goana pa Marovo* (2nd ed.). Paris, France: UNESCO-LINKS.

Ingold, T. (1993). Globes and spheres: The topology of environmentalism. In K. Milton (Ed.), *Environmentalism: The view from anthropology* (pp. 30–43). London, England: Routledge.

Ingold, T. (2000). *The perception of the environment: Essays on livelihood, dwelling and skill*. London, England: Routledge.

James Cook University. (2019). *JCU rated best in the world against UN goal*. Retrieved from web.archive.org/web/20190622034704/https://www.jcu.edu.au/news/releases/2019/april/jcu-rated-best-in-the-world-against-un-goal

Johannes, R. E. (1978). Traditional marine conservation methods in Oceania and their demise. *Annual Review of Ecology and Systematics*, *9*, 349–364.

Johannes, R. E., McCloske. L. R., Marsh, J. A., Marshall, N., Maragos, J., Alberts, J., … Kinzie, R. A. (1972). Metabolism of some coral reef communities: Team study of nutrient and energy flux at Eniwetok. *Bioscience*, *22*(9), 541–543.

Knowlton, N. (1992). Thresholds and multiple stable states in coral reef community dynamics. *American Zoologist*, *32*, 674–682.

Lakoff, G. (2009). *The political mind: A cognitive scientist's guide to your brain and its politics* (Vol. 292). New York, NY: Penguin.

Lawrence, P. (1964). *Road belong cargo: A study of the cargo movement in the Southern Madang District New Guinea*. Melbourne, Vic.: Melbourne University Press.

Lawton, J. H. (1997). The science and non-science of conservation biology. *Oikos, 79*(1), 3–5. doi.org/10.2307/3546084

Lee, R. B. (1969). Eating Christmas in the Kalahari. *Natural History, 78*(10), 60–63.

Li, T. M. (2010). To make live or let die? Rural dispossession and the protection of surplus populations. *Antipode, 41*, 66–93. doi.org/10.1111/j.1467-8330.2009.00717.x

Lieber, M. D. (1994). *More than a living: Fishing and the social order on a Polynesian atoll*. Boulder, CO: Westview Press.

Macintyre, M. A. (1998). The persistence of inequality: Women in Papua New Guinea since independence. In L. Zimmer-Tamakoshi (Ed.), *Modern Papua New Guinea* (pp. 211–231). Kirksville, MO: Thomas Jefferson University Press.

Macintyre, M. A. & Foale, S. J. (2004). Global imperatives and local desires: Competing economic and environmental interests in Melanesian communities. In V. Lockwood (Ed.), *Globalisation and culture change in the Pacific Islands* (pp. 149–164). Upper Saddle River, NJ: Pearson Prentice-Hall.

Macintyre, M. A. & Foale, S. J. (2007). Land and marine tenure, ownership and new forms of entitlement on Lihir: Changing notions of property in the context of a goldmining project. *Human Organization, 66*(1), 49–59.

Macpherson, C. B. (1962). *The political theory of possessive individualism*. Oxford, England: Clarendon Press.

Martin, K. (2007). Your own buai you must buy: The ideology of possessive individualism in Papua New Guinea. *Anthropological Forum, 17*(3), 285–298.

Mead, M. (1956). *New lives for old: Cultural transformation: Manus, 1928–1953*. New York, NY: Mentor.

Milton, K. (2002). *Loving nature: Towards an ecology of emotion*. London, England: Routledge.

Milton, K. (Ed.). (1993). *Environmentalism: The view from anthropology*. London, England; New York, NY: Routledge.

Mora, C., Aburto-Oropeza, O., Ayala Bocos, A., Ayotte, P. M., Banks, S., Bauman, A. G., … Zapata, F. A. (2011). Global human footprint on the linkage between biodiversity and ecosystem functioning in reef fishes. *PLoS Biol*, *9*(4), e1000606. doi.org/10.1371/journal.pbio.1000606

Mousseau, F. & Lau, P. (2015). *The great timber heist: The logging industry in Papua New Guinea*. Retrieved from www.oaklandinstitute.org/great-timber-heist-logging-industry-papua-new-guinea

Muller, J. Z. (2018). *The tyranny of metrics*. Princeton, NJ: Princeton University Press.

Nussbaum, M. (2011). *Creating capabilities: The human development approach*. Cambridge, MA: The Bleknap Press of Harvard University Press.

Orlove, B. S. (1980). Ecological anthropology. *Annual Review of Anthropology*, *9*, 235–263.

Ostrom, E. (1990). *Governing the commons: The evolution of institutions for collective action*. Cambridge, England: Cambridge University Press.

Rappaport, R. A. (1968). *Pigs for the ancestors: Ritual ecology of a New Guinea People*. New Haven, CT: Yale University Press.

Rappaport, R. A. (1984). *Pigs for the ancestors* (Rev. ed.). New Haven, CT: Yale University Press. (Original work published 1968.)

Rawlings, G. (2006). Regulating responsively for oversight agencies in the Pacific. *State, Society and Governance in Melanesia Targeted Discussion Papers* (February), 29.

Rawlings, G. (2011). Relative trust: The Vanuatu tax haven and the management of elite family fortunes. In M. Patterson & M. Macintyre (Eds), *Managing modernity in the Western Pacific* (pp. 260–305). St Lucia, Qld: University of Queensland Press.

Redford, K. H. (1991). The ecologically noble savage. *Cultural Survival Quarterly*, *15*(1), 46–48.

Roeger, J., Foale, S. & Sheaves, M. (2016). When 'fishing down the food chain' results in improved food security: Evidence from a small pelagic fishery in Solomon Islands. *Fisheries Research*, *174*, 250–259. doi.org/10.1016/j.fishres.2015.10.016

Rose, S. (1997). *Lifelines: Biology beyond determinism*. Oxford, England: Oxford University Press.

Roy, A. (2001). *Power politics*. Cambridge, MA: South End Press.

Russ, G. R. & Alcala, A. C. (2010). Decadal-scale rebuilding of predator biomass in Philippine marine reserves. *Oecologia, 163*(4), 1103–1106. doi.org/10.1007/s00442-010-1692-3

Russ, G. R., Alcala, A. C., Maypa, A. P., Calumpong, H. P. & White, A. T. (2004). Marine reserve benefits local fisheries. *Ecological Applications, 14*(2), 597–606.

Russ, G. R., Questel, S. L. A., Rizzari, J. R. & Alcala, A. C. (2015). The parrotfish-coral relationship: Refuting the ubiquity of a prevailing paradigm. *Marine Biology, 162*(10), 2029–2045. doi.org/10.1007/s00227-015-2728-3

Sen, A. (1999). *Development as freedom*. New York, NY: Anchor Books.

Sharman, J. (2008). Power and discourse in policy diffusion: Anti-money laundering in developing states. *International Studies Quarterly, 52*(3), 635–656. doi.org/10.1111/j.1468-2478.2008.00518.x

Sharman, J. (2017). *The despot's guide to wealth management: On the international campaign against grand corruption*. Ithaca, NY; London, England: Cornell University Press.

Shaxson, N. (2011). *Treasure islands: Tax havens and the men who stole the world*. London, England: The Bodley Head.

Soule, M. (1985). What is conservation biology. *Bioscience, 35*(11), 727–734.

Sykes, K. (2007). Interrogating individuals: The theory of possessive individualism in the Western Pacific. *Anthropological Forum, 17*(3), 213–224.

Times Higher Education. (2018). *Average Australian vice-chancellor's pay tips towards A$1million*. Retrieved from www.timeshighereducation.com/news/average-australian-vice-chancellors-pay-tips-towards-a1-million

Turner, S. (2019). The road from 'vocation': Weber and Veblen on the purposelessness of scholarship. *Journal of Classical Sociology, 19*(3), 229–253.

United Nations Development Programme. (2019). *Human Development Data: Education*. Retrieved from hdr.undp.org/en/data#

Van Fossen, A. (2012). *Tax havens and sovereignty in the Pacific Islands*. St Lucia, Qld: University of Queensland Press.

Van Helden, F. (2001). Through the thicket: Disentangling the social dynamics of an integrated conservation and development project on mainland Papua New Guinea (Unpublished doctoral thesis). Wageningen University, Wageningen, The Netherlands.

Vayda, A. P. (1961). Expansion and warfare among swidden agriculturalists. *American Anthropologist, 63*(21), 346–358.

Vayda, A. P. (1989). Explaining why Marings fought. *Journal of Anthropological Research, 45*(2), 159–177.

Walker, B. & Salt, D. (2006). *Resilience thinking: Sustaining ecosystems and people in a changing world.* Washington DC: Island Press.

Walker, B., Holling, C. S., Carpenter, S. R. & Kinzig, A. (2004). Resilience, adaptability and transformability in social–ecological systems. *Ecology and Society, 9*(2), 5. Retrieved from www.ecologyandsociety.org/vol9/iss2/art5

West, P. (2006). *Conservation is our government now: The politics of ecology in Papua New Guinea.* Durham, NC: Duke University Press.

West, P., Igoe, J. & Brockington, D. (2006). Parks and peoples: The social impact of protected areas. *Annual Review of Anthropology, 35*(1), 251–277. doi.org/10.1146/annurev.anthro.35.081705.123308

Wike, R. (2013). *The global consensus: Inequality is a major problem.* Retrieved from www.pewresearch.org/fact-tank/2013/11/15/the-global-consensus-inequality-is-a-major-problem/

Wilkinson, R. (2005). *The impact of inequality: How to make sick societies healthier.* London, England: Routledge.

Wilkinson, R. & Pickett, K. (2009). *The spirit level: Why equality is better for everyone.* London, England: Penguin.

Worm, B., Barbier, E. B., Beaumont, N., Duffy, J. E., Folke, C., Halpern, B. S., … Watson, R. (2006). Impacts of biodiversity loss on ocean ecosystem services. *Science, 314*(5800), 787–790. doi.org/10.1126/science.1132294

Zimmer-Tamakoshi, L. (2012). Troubled masculinities and gender violence in Melanesia. In M. Jolly, C. Stewart & C. Brewer (Eds), *Engendering violence in Papua New Guinea* (pp. 73–105). Canberra, ACT: ANU E Press, doi.org/10.22459/EVPNG.07.2012

4

The Problem of the Semi-Alienable Anthropologist

Melissa Demian

One sweltering afternoon in the small office of a local non-governmental organisation (NGO) in Lae, the second city and economic engine room of Papua New Guinea (PNG), the discussion had turned from the NGO's activities to more philosophical issues of why urban women faced so many obstacles, including family violence, and how difficult it was for women to find a satisfactory means of redress for it—my topic of research from 2016 to 2017.

'I know you used to work in Milne Bay', said one of the staff members. She was referring to the southeasternmost province of PNG, one of the corners of the country included in its matrilineal fringe. 'But, you know, in most of PNG, it's the men who own the land.' She went on to note that it is men's direct connection to land (*graun* in Tok Pisin) that grants them particular privileges and entitlements and, ultimately, is what differentiates them from women as a category of persons. 'The men are the only source of support and the men are isolating the women from the connections of the Melanesian way', she said. 'The vine needs the tree to grow upwards; the sister needs the support of the brother to flourish.' Echoing the more prosaic observations of my other interlocutors in poetic, and also very Melanesian, terms by means of the gardening metaphor, she was explaining why there were problems with what women were trying to achieve because their menfolk were blocking them from their fundamental source of spiritual power: the land.

She also invoked these concepts as part of a wider philosophy articulated and popularised by Narokobi (1983) as 'The Melanesian Way'. This philosophy was both a charter for the good life, according to the late PNG jurist's positioning of his own nation in the aftermath of independence, and an effort to speak back to the European regimes of knowledge in which he had been educated, with their legal and social scientific grasp of how human beings ought to treat each other—but in a PNG, rather than colonial, register. This meant, among other things, taking seriously the differentiation of persons and the rights and obligations attendant upon persons depending on the way they were so differentiated. This was precisely what the NGO staffer referred to when she reminded me that Papua New Guineans are primarily differentiated by their relationship to land, and that I could not hope to grasp issues such as gender-based violence without starting from that very particular first principle. Talking about violence as a form of inequality—the starting point for most foreign NGOs and national agencies indoctrinated in the language of foreign NGOs—skips over and occludes many of the other proximate causes that Papua New Guineans might regard as contributing to violence. Even where these proximate causes are describable as forms of inequality, they are often located in relationships and systems that are not those upon which the NGOs and other agencies focus, or perhaps even have a political interest in ignoring (Rooney, 2014).

After a century of offering their engagement and hospitality, Melanesian people have become adept at calling the attention of anthropologists to social organisation. This is not quite the 'cultural appropriateness' that has become a mainstay of development discourses (Macintyre, 2001, p. 108), but rather an invitation to attend to those questions that are actually pressing for people who choose to take seriously the assertions of social researchers that our job is, above all, to listen. If non-Melanesian anthropologists have spent most of the history of our relationship with Melanesian peoples insisting that social organisation—the differentiation of persons by means of their relationships—was one of our fundamental areas of interest, Melanesians have responded accordingly by framing their own interests in terms that are intelligible to their foreign interlocutors.

Often, the first aspect that becomes foreclosed in this effort is the possibility of Melanesian people having a say in how they themselves want the social research to look, or whom its primary audience will be (Hukula, 2018).

This is particularly critical in circumstances in which anthropologists have been contracted directly by development projects, either commercial or humanitarian in nature, to do our listening with the ultimate aim of rendering the project more effective. Such were the conditions of my recent work in Lae, as a contract researcher for a major international development organisation. Under these conditions, a researcher enters into a relationship with a research community and occupies two subject positions simultaneously: that of the professional listener, and that of the professional reporter back to the organisation or company for whom they work. For a researcher who has origins in the research community, or a closely related community, a third subject position is added to these first two: that of the 'insider' who must act temporarily like an 'outsider' (Narayan, 1993; Ryang, 2005). These two or three positions may become blurred in a scholarly publication such as this one, which is rather the point of the exercise; in our speaking to a world of academic interlocutors, we must necessarily obscure the multiple positions we occupy and our own differentiation at any given time as researchers, contractors, students, teachers and friends.

Each of these positions also contains its own inequities, generated both by the global structures of inequality and exploitation in which much social research takes place (West & Aini, this volume) and distinctions drawn on a more immediate scale. This chapter is offered as a meditation on how some anthropologists have become exemplars for how to occupy these multiple positions, and of the attachments and detachments they demand at various points in the ethnographic endeavour. Martha Macintyre has been one such exemplar, particularly as I have found myself following a research trajectory that looks very much like hers, seemingly by accident. Did this in fact occur by accident or, as our respective original research communities in Milne Bay Province might argue, was I following a road she had opened up, which was then maintained and extended by the multiple interests in which our lives as researchers are entangled?

On Semi-Alienability

PNG is renowned, among social scientists at least, for its kaleidoscopic internal diversity. While much attention is given to its 800 or so languages, the focus of anthropologists on social organisation, and the other political forms that may proceed from the way societies are understood to reproduce themselves over time, has had certain key effects. I refer both to effects on the way anthropologists have taught ourselves to think about PNG, and the way Papua New Guineans have taught themselves to think about anthropologists. There is a convergence of interests, to be sure, but one of the hallmarks of well-conducted ethnographic work is that the point of convergence is seldom where anthropologists think it will be.

I will return to this point shortly, but first, let us return to that linguistic diversity for a moment. My own apprenticeship as an ethnographer involved, among other things, learning Suau, an Austronesian language spoken by roughly 7,000 people on the south-eastern coast of Milne Bay Province. Once I had come to grips with the possessive system used in this and other Milne Bay languages, I enjoyed playing the following game. Some men would walk by, or perhaps paddle close to the shoreline in a canoe, carrying an indignantly trussed-up pig. I would then ask them the same question three times—except that it was not the same question. In English, it would be 'Whose pig is that?' every time. Not so in Suau, where the shifting of the possessive form in each iteration turned it into a set of differentiated questions. *Hai ena salai*: 'Who owns that pig?' *Hai ana salai*: 'Who are you giving that pig to, so they can eat it?' *Hai salaina*: 'Whose funeral feast are you taking that pig to?'

At that point, the pig-carrying men might laugh or give me a stern look, or both, because the last question is quite intrusive in nature. However, they understood what I was doing and so did not give me a hard time about it; better for their resident *dimdim* (white-skinned foreigner, also the place that such people come from) to learn how to speak properly. 'Speaking properly' in this case also meant thinking properly about pigs, the pre-eminent wealth item in the part of the world where I was working, and their attachment to, detachment from and re-attachment to different people for different socially significant purposes.

I had been primed to do this by one of the most important articles I read in preparation for embarking on fieldwork in Milne Bay all those years ago. The article was 'The problem of the semi-alienable pig' (Macintyre, 1984), and it gave me the required tools for thinking about pigs, specifically, and value, more generally. In her original work on the island of Tubetube in the Engineer Group of Milne Bay's many archipelagos, Macintyre not only learned to play comparable linguistic tricks with the way pigs are spoken about, but showed more significantly that pigs are one of the ways in which Milne Bay people think about relations between human beings. Pigs, as pre-eminent valuables with the heroic capacity to reproduce themselves and the tragic counter-capacity of being killed and eaten at significant points in the human life cycle, shift in and out of their identification with people. In Tubetube and Suau mythology alike, they are identified as having been the replacement exchange item for humans in a deep cannibalistic history. In the languages of both societies, they may be imagined as part of a person or an object of their consumption, depending on who is giving, receiving or eating—hence my question game regarding a pig in mid-transaction. 'Things that a person creates or produces', Macintyre wrote:

> can only effect transformations that bring renown when they are extended beyond the socially defined self and are enchained in serial, semi-alienable relationships with people outside one's immediate relatives. People are invariably friend or foe, affine or consanguine, neighbour or stranger. Pigs are neighbourly food or placatory gifts from enemies. They are flexible objects of exchange and their status in any particular transaction is variable and open to interpretation. (1984, p. 120)

Pigs (and their transaction) assist Milne Bay peoples to resolve, in other words, a conundrum that exists in Milne Bay societies. Pigs and persons are sometimes regarded as inalienable components of one another, as if they were kin or body parts. At other times, they are regarded as separate, so that one may be substituted for the other or even consumed by the other. What changes the status of either the person or the pig vis-à-vis each other is not their inherent identity or alienability. The movement of pigs between persons is itself the process that determines both who the people are in relation to each other, and what kind of entities the pigs are within the terms of a given relationship.

This process can be scaled up. By 'up', I am using the conventional spatial metaphor for indicating that a perspective taken on social relationships is something other than intimate or face-to-face in nature, so that one might be presumed to be talking about an entire society, rather than details such as people and their pigs. But I have in mind Strathern's (2004) observations about detail remaining constant, regardless of where the presumed observer imagines themselves to be standing on an observational scale. For Strathern, any shift in perspective retains the same degree or amount of informational detail regardless of how far 'up' or 'down' the scale of social relationships one moves. She notes that:

> Scale switching not only creates a multiplier effect, it also creates information 'loss'. Different types of data may appear to substitute for one another—a generalisation about socialisation, say, in lieu of a description of a puberty rite. Information loss appears as the eclipse of detail or of scope by whatever is the present focus of enquiry. It can occur equally through domaining as through magnification or telescoping. (2004, p. xv).

What appears to be informational loss with a shift in scale, Strathern argued, also entails information gain—as, for my purposes, when talking about pigs by means of people enables anthropologists to talk about people by means of other people. There are also questions to ask regarding whether any scale of observation can be presumed, particularly when people arrive at their domaining decisions by means of triangulation through pigs, through other valuables or through other persons. This is now a classic issue in anthropology, but one that always bears repeating. One of the things that Papua New Guineans delight in pointing out to visitors who have expressed an interest in social organisation is the way that their systems of value allocation are a critical mode of distinction between their own regional, ethnic or language group and some other group or groups. The scaling of such identifiers is nearly immaterial to the ways in which comparisons are drawn. My Suau friends, for example, made much of the fact that they expected such modest payments in pigs and cash for everything from brideprice exchanges to compensation orders following a court case. This, I was told on numerous occasions, showed how different Milne Bay people were from, say, Motu-speakers from Central Province or people from any of the highlands provinces, where (as my friends had heard or even witnessed) payments in the hundreds of pigs or many thousands of kina might change hands. There was a certain moralistic chauvinism at work in these statements, whereby Milne Bay people could be held up as exemplars of Christian humility and frugality. Beyond this, they were remarking on differences in social organisation and its ramifications, whatever the scale or axis of comparison. 'In the highlands you need two hundred, three hundred pigs to get married,' I heard on several occasions, 'but for we people, four or five pigs is enough!' This would be followed by uproarious laughter, in amazement at the implied avarice of Highlanders, but also with the faintly self-deprecating implication that a person in Milne Bay could simply go and get married on the cheap.

These distinctions matter, both when they are the object of humour and when they are an earnest means of trying to locate a person according to their regional or ethnic parameters, so that you have some ground for explaining something to them they may not understand once they have relocated: 'I know you used to work in Milne Bay, but …'. In this moment, the anthropologist was located in an unanticipated way. I had been prepared, throughout my fieldwork in Lae, to have to re-inscribe my identity among my new interlocutors as a white foreigner—one who originated from the United States, if I could manage to add that qualifier, since it would place me in a politically different relationship to PNG, as compared to being Australian. This choice, as I rapidly learned, was not mine to make. My co-researcher Zuabe Tinning, from Morobe Province herself, introduced me consistently as a Milne Bay woman; this framing would shape many of the conversations that followed. The framing Zuabe chose was a fictional one, as neither my whiteness nor my origin in a wealthy country could be erased by her strategy. The strategy functioned nonetheless to identify me as belonging to a slightly different category of white person: one who did not just drop in and then leave forever, but rather returned consistently enough to acquire a regionally more symmetrical identifier alongside the structurally asymmetrical one. This category also suggested a white person who was perhaps interested in following similar rural-to-urban pathways to those navigated by many Papua New Guineans. By the time I left Lae, at the conclusion of the project, Zuabe and others were saying proudly, 'You're a Morobe woman now, and you have family here now! Come back to rainy Lae!' I had been located, detached and re-attached; the geopolitical scale movement in whose terms I had planned to present myself was backgrounded entirely.

This process can be disorienting for the anthropologist who must learn to think about the social and political relationships in one place in terms of those they learned in another (Macintyre, 2003, p. 122). The process is particularly salient for an intellectual tradition in which the background to any comparative method has nearly always been European and North American societies. A reorientation is required to draw comparisons that are not between a non-European context and those of Europe and its settler-colonial extensions, but rather between one research site and another. Further, when people in one place locate an anthropologist as originally attached to a different part of their own country, the critical question becomes not so much 'What are you doing here', but rather, 'What are you doing here, and not *there*?' A merely institutional account of the researcher's relocation—I was funded to come here, I was hired to come here, there was a new project I wanted to do here, and so forth—will not suffice. The relationship between Papua New Guineans and foreign anthropologists is, again, both a longstanding one, and one that has never only been about institutions and their expectations. It has also been about hospitality and its effects. The reasoning goes something like this: if you have come here, it must be because you want to be with us, rather than those other people, or perhaps in addition to them. In a country characterised by increasing internal mobility and rural–urban migration, this kind of move makes perfectly good sense; however, a question remains for the new host community to answer—what was it about us that drew you here? Often the explanation offered is that it is precisely the same things that cause Papua New Guineans themselves to move around the country and to experiment with the panoply of social and economic forms sometimes associated with concepts such as 'modernity' or 'cosmopolitanism' (Cox, 2018). These terms do not refer to historic periods in the PNG social imagination, but rather to the way certain details of contemporary social life are used as comparators for other details.

Periphery to Metropole and Back Again

Milne Bay Province is in a corner of PNG. This is not a straightforward geographical statement, any more than talking about scaling particular social forms 'up' was a straightforward spatial one. Although the province does encompass the southeasternmost extremity of the Papuan mainland and its adjacent island groups, its fortunes have waxed and waned throughout the colonial and post-independence history of the country. Once a destination of choice for the missionaries, copra planters, bêche-de-mer and pearl traders, and anthropologists who formed the colonial vanguard, it became economically and politically isolated following the conclusion of World War II. To some degree, this isolation has been deliberate, as Milne Bay and European-descended elites alike have resisted infrastructural connections to the rest of the country that represent a threat to the cultural homogeneity and colonial history upon which their influence is founded. And some of it relates to the inevitable movement of capital and its accompanying political interests to more lucrative resource extraction projects elsewhere in the country.

For a brief time, Milne Bay hosted one such project: a gold mine on the island of Misima. Gold has been documented in the Louisiade Archipelago of Milne Bay since the earliest trading exploits of Europeans in the region, but it was not until the late twentieth century that a large open-cast mine was developed. By this time, the practice of mining companies bringing in social researchers to monitor the 'impact' of the mine was well established, in response to lessons learned from the humanitarian disaster on Bougainville and the environmental one at Ok Tedi, both sites of major independence-era gold and copper mines.

Enter the anthropologist. Martha Macintyre was among the first wave of anthropologists hired by mining companies in PNG to undertake what they called 'social impact assessment' and what the anthropologists—crucially—still regarded as ethnography. Misima lies roughly 100 kilometres due east from Tubetube, where Macintyre had established her expertise as a Milne Bay ethnographer; as such, one might have expected there to be a seamless ethnographic transition from one Milne Bay society to another.

This was not to be the case. Notwithstanding any pre-existing differences between Misiman and Tubetube society, the economic and social worlds of Misima were on the verge of transformation. As Macintyre later noted (2007, p. 50), all mines in PNG are located in remote rural parts of the country; therefore, they must create an entire physical and civic infrastructure in lieu of any government investment in the same, let alone the kind of 'organic' cosmopolitanism imagined to emerge in towns and cities whose existence is unrelated to the existence of a mine. With these physical infrastructures also come new social infrastructures of differentiation, as land acquires both monetary value that it never had before, and a potential for alienability that it also never had before, in a country where some 85 per cent of land is held under customary tenure. New distinctions in the qualities of land gave rise to distinctions in the qualities of people, a phenomenon first observed by Macintyre on Misima and later on Lihir, in New Ireland Province. In both cases, she argued, debates over who had the authority to consent to a mine underlined, deepened and, in some cases, outright created any number of social divisions: between young people and their seniors, between men and women, between those holding customary title and those actually living on the land, and between educated people working in towns and their families back home at the mining site (see Bainton, this volume). These divisions, Macintyre noted, potentially made a mockery of negotiations between mining companies and the landowners they sought to consult:

> The issue then is *who* is to give consent? Is the question one of effect on a *community of people* who live, work and have rights to some areas of land? Or is the consent to be obtained from those who are indigenous and have or claim customary rights to *the land*, even when these are not recognised by the state? Is the group who is to give consent to be defined in terms of residential status, customary rights, legally recognised rights according to the national law or genealogical connection to the original customary owners? (2007, p. 55, emphases in original)

This list of potential axes of differentiation has implications that reach far beyond how a mining company can possibly identify 'landowners' from whom to gain consent. As fraught an issue as that is, it is not my primary concern in this chapter. Rather, I wish to point to this moment in the process by which an anthropologist who has moved from a classic village setting, presumed to be culturally homogeneous and with an intact system of social reproduction, to a setting in the midst of radical change, begins to query how social groups can even be identified at all and who can speak on their behalf or represent their interests.

Of course no rural community is the cultural isolate so beloved of anthropology in the mid-twentieth century, and no society exists outside of time and change. These propositions have been undisputed in our discipline since at least the end of the previous century. Here, I call attention to the figure of the anthropologist who is relocated from a classic setting on the periphery to one that is rapidly being transformed into a metropole, albeit a temporary one. Mines do not last forever, although they may be in operation for decades. What endures instead are people's experiences of the mine and its aftermath (Gilberthorpe, 2013; McKenna, 2015).

One might argue that the mining communities that became the focus of Macintyre's research are inherently unstable, boom-town economies prone to the host of social woes that crop up wherever a large extraction project appears. Debating the inevitability or otherwise of the 'resource curse' is not my project. My aim is instead to show how the axis of comparison so often presumed in anthropology—between a rich-country metropole and a poor-country periphery—becomes unsettled by Macintyre's trajectory. We have always known that even presumed peripheries include their own local metropoles. Less often is an anthropologist able to watch the formation of a metropole in action, with its uneasy relationship to the periphery it once was and may one day be again. In a position to precisely observe this process of transformation, first on Misima and then on Lihir, Macintyre has documented some of the ongoing effects of the emergence of the metropole itself.

I say 'ongoing', now that I have followed a roughly similar trajectory—not to a mining community, but rather to one of the more 'organic' metropoles in PNG. The relative newness of Lae, which itself began as a gold rush town in the 1920s, and of the city as a concept in the PNG cultural repertoire, is without question a factor in how debates around new social distinctions are played out as an element of life in the new metropoles, whether they emerge through urbanisation or economic transformation through resource extraction. Inequities are built into both modes of urban emergence; both the original colonial order and the neo-colonial order of resource extraction and the aid economy have advantaged foreign interests and priorities over those of Papua New Guineans. For example, many towns in PNG were never built with the intention of having any Papua New Guineans in them; the original colonial vision for these small urban zones was that they would be exclusively European in population, except for a necessary cohort of single, male Melanesian labourers (Gibson, 2019; Levine & Wolfzahn Levine, 1979). Papua New Guinean women, in particular, did not become a significant demographic in such towns until the late 1960s, shortly before independence in 1975 (Jackson, 1977). As the newest city dwellers in the country, women in PNG are still discovering what 'city life' might possibly mean for them (Demian, 2017). In its broadest sense, my own recent work has focused on exactly this. Although thematically focused on the topic of domestic violence, its actual remit has been to explore the ways in which social organisation has changed in the city, and how women are trying to navigate these changes in ways that might make urban life for them not only safe, but also satisfying.

The nature of city life in general is still very much a project under construction in PNG's cities and towns. There are issues that all urban Papua New Guineans confront every day: an infrastructure that is not adequate to the size of current urban and peri-urban populations, an insufficiency of jobs in the formal sector, and a quite spectacular insufficiency of housing accessible to families of the grassroots, to use the common PNG term for citizens with few educational qualifications or similar cosmopolitan achievements, usually but not always because they have started out life in the country's rural areas (Cox, this volume). Because there were no cities or towns of any kind in PNG prior to the colonial era, many urban Papua New Guineans are still learning how to negotiate, on a daily basis, interactions with people with whom they may have little or nothing in common. Whether these interactions occur briefly in one of the town markets or every day in the workplace, the relationships that comprise city life are largely unmoored from the structural expectations that might govern them in the more rural, ethnically homogeneous parts of the country.

This means that both men and women in PNG are experimenting with the imaginary of the city as a different kind of life, freed from the constraints of the village; there are any number of consequences to this experimentation (Foster, 2008; Goddard, 2010). For example, there is no popular consensus on who has ownership of which spaces in the city, how those spaces in the city are to be used, who is entitled to use them, and in what ways; the ongoing debate about the growth of settlements and unofficial markets is one expression of this lack of consensus. On a more intimate scale, many men may feel that their wives should be subject to the same constraints on movement that they might be expected to adhere to in a village setting or, perhaps, even greater constraints, because the perceived risk that they could leave their husbands for another man is higher.

A common complaint voiced by urban PNG women, both grassroots and middle class, is that those forms of action associated with 'modernity' that appear to be available to men in the city are not also available to them—or, if they are, the consequences are more severe (Demian, 2017; Spark, 2011). From romantic courtship and involvement in commerce, to consumption of alcohol and gambling, many women feel they are held to standards of behaviour that men are not, and given a threshold for their ambitions that men are not. So while city life appears to offer boundless opportunity to men and women alike, there are structural asymmetries that place multiple obstacles in the way of women who might like to imagine themselves stepping into those opportunities.

In her own consultation with women in Lae on the subject of policing, Macintyre noted the distinctions that women in the settlements did not draw—notably, between the violence of men engaged in criminal activity and the violence of police (2008, p. 182). Instead, women living literally on the periphery of the city regarded the immoderate consumption patterns valued by men, whether in established cities or in the mining boom towns, as precisely what presented a threat both to the safety of life in the city and to their own domestic lives. Whether because all the household income was being spent on beer, or due to the direct effects of its consumption on men aiming to become drunk and express their feelings in that manner, women in Macintyre's interview cohort pointed to the connection between styles of consumption coded as masculine as one of the primary obstacles to their being able to live lives they considered satisfactory in the city.

For Macintyre, this meant, among other things, that some of the more innovative theories generated by anthropology in PNG and other Melanesian contexts were re-opened for debate. The issue is not that they were faulty to begin with, but rather that the comparative scheme on which they were predicated—a 'Melanesian' conceptual framework on the one hand and a 'Euro-American' one on the other—has shifted significantly. As Macintyre put it:

> The emphasis on alterity and the invitation to use Melanesian concepts as tools for scrutinising Western ideas about persons, selves and embodiment has proved difficult in practice. It still appears most successful when applied to 'classical' anthropologically defined cultures or communities rather than people in towns, populations around mining developments or other industrial developments, or those marginalised young men who move from village to town in their desire to engage with modernity. (2008, p. 184)

Alterity remains in the picture; for anthropologists, at least, this must always be the case. The foundation of the discipline is that we are always others to each other. However, concerns about alterity now belong to a generation of Papua New Guineans whose sense of sociality has shifted profoundly as they grapple with life in a world of others who are no longer distinguished by the ramifications of exchange relationships and inalienable value. Rather, they are distinguished by emergent and, at times, violent divisions of gender, class and those exhausting imaginaries that anthropologists and other social scientists have sought to dismantle for decades—the country and the city, the collective and the individual, the traditional and the modern. All of these are rearing their heads again as young Papua New Guineans, and often their elders too, ask what it is that they now owe each other in social environments where anyone could be from anywhere, and the value of persons and things seems to be in free fall (Macintyre, 2011).

'When the "body politic" alters', Macintyre noted, 'so too do concepts of order, social obligation and sanction—and all the ideas which underpin harmonious sociality, indebtedness and the rights involving people and their products' (1995, p. 31). She was introducing, in this case, the way Tubetube classifications of persons as either potential kin or potential food were recorded in the oral history and language of the island, and retained even after the 'pacification' of the colonial era their connotations of objectification and violence. But Macintyre elicited these distinctions—the term used for the body of a person who is a relative and that used for the body of a captive—from her Tubetube interlocutors in the course of discussing other kinds of objects and other kinds of persons. The uncovering of an oral history of violent exchanges and their implications for present-day relationships suggested, for Macintyre, that no consideration of social organisation could ever only account for those elements of social life where persons were harmoniously integrated in an unchanging social and political landscape.

To Matriliny and Beyond!

It may seem odd to move from a discussion of the nascent conundrums facing Papua New Guineans to a topic as classic, not to say hoary, as unilineal descent. However, as with most themes touched upon in this chapter, my purpose is to highlight how old anthropological concerns and concepts are continually repurposed in a country with such a long engagement with anthropologists as PNG. These concepts are being used in ways that locate both Papua New Guineans in relation to other Papua New Guineans and anthropologists in relation to other Papua New Guineans, as in the vignette with which I opened the chapter. In the conversation with the NGO staff member in Lae, the matriliny with which I was presumed to be familiar from one part of PNG was set against the patriliny of much of the rest of the country, as a way of framing what I had yet to learn about why women could not act successfully without the support of their menfolk. The social and epistemological comparisons being made for my sake were between one part of PNG and another.

That is to say, any assumptions about what anthropologists are using as their environment or background for comparison—the way most, if not all, anthropological theory is generated—cannot be taken for granted. If Macintyre's work shows us anything, it is this: regardless of whatever anthropologists think they know about a place and their own perspective on that place, the rug will continually be pulled out from under them by people who have already located their visitor somewhere else, among some other people.

I began this chapter with a story from very recent fieldwork; here is a story so old that it predates my having travelled to PNG for the first time. I had decided, as a young and exuberant research student in the mid-1990s, that I was going to work in Milne Bay Province. The province had only recently lifted a five-year moratorium on the presence of foreign researchers, and as a condition of granting a research visa, required an invitation from someone within the province. My PhD supervisor had put me in contact with a local activist who was interested in having someone conduct research in her maternal village. But she had also offered a caveat to my being that researcher: 'I don't want a feminist, I want someone who can get the job done'.

It was an intriguing restriction. I half-joked to my supervisor that I would simply leave my feminist badge at home. There followed a discussion of what my sponsor meant by this statement. When I finally arrived in Milne Bay nearly a year later, the answer I discovered was not any of the reasons I had tried to anticipate. Again, we cannot know what kind of identity our interlocutors will choose to engage with, because identities are not stable objects. Upon my arrival in Alotau, the provincial capital, my sponsor informed me that I would be studying 'the matrilineal kinship'. This sounded very much like a feminist project to me, steeped as I was at that point in a regional literature that emphasised the political and cosmological authority of women (Lepowsky, 1993; Macintyre, 1987; Weiner, 1976). This was one of the most important incorrect assumptions I made about working in the province, one that would shape how I came to understand social life in Milne Bay over the next 20 years, later still in urban PNG, and how I continue to reflect on the practice of anthropology itself.

Following her first relocation within Milne Bay Province itself, Macintyre noted that Misimans had no trouble reconciling institutions that seemed on the face of it to be in conflict with one another, such as Methodism and a homegrown spirit cult originating in the 1930s. The position that the two spiritual practices ought to be mutually exclusive is an exogenous one, belonging to European missionaries and colonial administrators. The people of Misima and its neighbouring islands did not, in Macintyre's experience, perceive a cosmological inconsistency between Christianity and the local spirit cult, but instead regarded them as outgrowths or manifestations of each other. During her work on Misima, Macintyre became interested in 'the ways in which contradictions can be virtually ignored in one context because they are seen to be resolved in others' (1990, p. 99).

Macintyre effectively called the bluff both of the colonial fears of cargo cultism and its presumed incompatibility with Christianity, and of anthropology itself. Both depend, historically, on a model of alterity in which the axis of comparison is between the society under consideration and the anthropologist's own. However, in her consideration of how people on Misima find their own concepts of the person, of the spirit, and of relationships between the living and the dead in the ostensibly imposed institution of Christianity, Macintyre showed the adroitness with which Papua New Guineans relocate the comparative project. The church, as an institutional form, is a colonial import. Its nature then changes almost immediately in relationship to the local spirit cult, which in turn is inflected by its relationship to Christianity—because institutions, like entities on any other scale from pigs to gods, do not possess an *a priori* identity. The playfulness of the Misiman spirit cult, and its organisational references to both Christian and colonial administrative structures, is precisely the kind of move Macintyre went on to track with each of her own movements made throughout a career of the Papua New Guinean style of detaching and re-attaching persons, things and institutions to suit their own comparative schemes.

How does this relate to the theme of social organisation or, indeed, to inequality? In both the vignette with which I opened the chapter and the instruction I was given by my very first interlocutor in Milne Bay, the thorny question of matriliny was raised as the ground upon which I was told to build my understanding of social differentiations and the asymmetries that could arise from them. For the twentieth-century anthropologists working in this corner—as it is still imagined or presumed to be—of the country, matriliny became a way to talk about economic exchanges, political forms, and the magical capacities inhering in the domain of femininity. These exercises were fruitful and important ones, as they teased out the connections between social organisation and institutions on a 'larger' scale that have become part and parcel of how anthropology does its comparative work. The conversation has now shifted, for people both within the province itself and outside it, in a PNG experiencing internal mobility of a kind unprecedented in its history. I have heard a district court magistrate in Alotau, the provincial capital for Milne Bay, exhort his disputing parties to remember that they should think about their relationship to land in terms of matriliny, as a means of telling them not only who they are, but also who they are in the unfolding time of the dispute itself (Demian, 2011). I have heard a high court judge from another matrilineal part of the country, New Ireland Province, point immediately to matriliny as that which distinguishes him from most other Papua New Guineans, in that his status shifts as soon as he goes home. He may be an elite jurist in Port Moresby, but is also a clan member who knows his place vis-à-vis sisters, both literal and classificatory, who have the right to act as his 'boss'.

These are, on their face, rhetorical claims. They offer Papua New Guineans engaged in regional mobility the chance to reflect and act under the sign of place-based identities in one context, and institutional or class identities in another. Social group formation under these conditions of multiple contexts becomes 'more situational than ontological: they are the product of immediate interests rather than of fundamental essences' (Errington & Gewertz, 2004, p. 85). The gesture towards fundamental essences (such as 'the matrilineal kinship') is itself a way of describing a set of distinctions and interests that people may exercise under some conditions, but not others. One of the first things noted by Macintyre in her own work in Misima and New Ireland (2001, 2003) is that a matrilineal system of inheritance guarantees nothing in terms of the transformational effects of a mine offering any material benefits to women. The matrilineal buck, as it were, stops at the point where the emergence of a mining metropole creates new opportunities for training, employment, travel and control over the distribution of royalties. Matriliny still has work to do as an arbiter of distinction between people from Milne Bay or New Ireland and other parts of the country, but it is not imagined to be extensible into the new forms of social and economic action presented by a mining boom.

Matriliny and its limits present a case in point for the problem of alienability. To put the problem in alternative terms, some institutional forms appear to 'travel' more readily than others, just as some social researchers find themselves readily detached from one site and embedded in another, while also retaining an identification from the previous site.

What is retained, and what is left behind or replaced, is not a decision made by anthropologists themselves. It is one made by their host communities and interlocutors, and is liable to shift at any time. There is no stable axis of comparison that can be presumed, and there are implications here not only for anthropology, but also for development and other area studies in their considerations of the bases for inequality and any actions that might be undertaken to rectify it.

The societies of Milne Bay Province—and their colonial-era designation, 'the Massim'—exert a perennial gravitational pull on the anthropological imagination. This pull acted upon both Macintyre in the 1970s and myself in the 1990s, and continues to attract the interest of graduate students. The distinctiveness of this corner of PNG at times seems self-evident, certainly in the insistence of Milne Bay peoples that certain features of their societies, often with matriliny at the top of the list, continue to set them apart from the rest of the country. Milne Bay is not the only matrilineal corner of PNG, but this minority mode of social organisation has been picked up by other Papua New Guineans as a feature to identify both Milne Bay people and foreign visitors whose sojourns began in that province. The identification of matriliny with Milne Bay, as demonstrated in the conversation between myself and the NGO worker with which I opened this chapter, is telling. Matriliny itself had become detached from its original context and made to stand for something other than a system of reckoning inheritance and identity. It was now a synecdoche for a region of the country, and a way of demonstrating how relationships to land and to other persons changed as one moved from one place to another. In turn, these relationships became the starting point for understanding how inequality itself could not even be understood in the same way in different parts of the country. Actions imagined to stem from such inequality—such as violence—would conceivably have entirely different causes depending on where one was, where one had come from, and which relationships were at the forefront at any given time.

In the same way, a region that once contained a distinctive social feature has now become contained by it. So, too, are the persons—whether local or foreign—who are identified by others as belonging to that place and, therefore, to that social form. Never mind that the social form is itself subject to processes of re-containment and re-contextualisation in the face of the economic, political, religious, and other vicissitudes of history that Milne Bay peoples have engaged with over the past century and a half. If even the most fundamental way of thinking about kinship can be scaled up to contain an entire region, and can further be imagined to encompass the researcher who leaves that region and travels to other parts of the country, then what appears to be a loss of ethnographic detail can become, in the moment of identification by another, the revelation of an entire perspective on how distinctions in social relationships are configured that one never knew one possessed until the original context was left behind. This perspective is not that of the original host community or their region: that remains their own, always. Rather, it is perspective as a technique for detachment and re-attachment, as a means by which the ethnographer's new friends, colleagues, and interlocutors come to know who she is, and therefore what kind of knowledge she seeks.

References

Cox, J. (2018). *Fast money schemes: Hope and deception in Papua New Guinea.* Bloomington, IN: Indiana University Press.

Demian, M. (2011). 'Hybrid custom' and legal description in Papua New Guinea. In J. Edwards & M. Petrović-Šteger (Eds), *Recasting anthropological knowledge: Inspiration and social science* (pp. 49–69). Cambridge, England: Cambridge University Press.

Demian, M. (2017). Making women in the city: Notes from a Port Moresby boarding house. *Signs: Journal of Women in Culture and Society, 42*(2), 403–425.

Errington, F. & D. Gewertz. (2004). *Yali's question: Sugar, culture and history.* Chicago, IL: University of Chicago Press.

Foster, R. (2008). *Coca-globalisation: Following soft drinks from New York to New Guinea.* New York, NY: Palgrave Macmillan.

Gibson, L. (2019). Class, labour and consumption in urban Melanesia. In E. Hirsch & W. Rollason (Eds), *The Melanesian world* (pp. 164–179). London, England: Routledge.

Gilberthorpe, E. (2013). Community development in Ok Tedi, Papua New Guinea: The role of anthropology in the extractive industries. *Community Development Journal, 48*(3), 466–483.

Goddard, M. (Ed.). (2010). *Villagers and the city: Melanesian experiences of Port Moresby, Papua New Guinea.* Wantage, England: Sean Kingston Publishing.

Hukula, F. (2018, 26 September). Melanesian anthropology Em Nem Nating. *Fieldsights*. Retrieved from culanth.org/fieldsights/melanesian-anthropology-em-nem-nating

Jackson, R. T. (1977). The growth, nature and future prospects of informal settlements in Papua New Guinea. *Pacific Viewpoint, 18*(1), 22–42.

Lepowsky, M. (1993). *Fruit of the motherland: Gender in an egalitarian society.* New York, NY: Columbia University Press.

Levine, H. B. & Wolfzahn Levine, M. (1979). *Urbanisation in Papua New Guinea: A study of ambivalent townsmen.* Cambridge, England: Cambridge University Press.

Macintyre, M. (1984). The problem of the semi-alienable pig. *Canberra Anthropology, 7*(1–2), 109–122.

Macintyre, M. (1987). Flying witches and leaping warriors: Supernatural origins of power and matrilineal authority in Tubetube society. In M. Strathern (Ed.), *Dealing with inequality: Analysing gender relations in Melanesia and beyond* (pp. 207–228). Cambridge, England: Cambridge University Press.

Macintyre, M. (1990). Christianity, cargo cultism and the concept of the spirit in Misiman cosmology. In J. Barker (Ed.), *Christianity in Oceania: Ethnographic perspectives* (pp. 81–100). Lanham, MD: University Press of America.

Macintyre, M. (1995). Violent bodies and vicious exchanges: Personification and objectification in the Massim. *Social Analysis, 37,* 29–43.

Macintyre, M. (2001). Taking care of culture: Consultancy, anthropology and gender issues. *Social Analysis, 45*(2), 108–119.

Macintyre, M. (2003). Petztorme women: Responding to change in Lihir, Papua New Guinea. *Oceania, 74*(1–2), 120–134.

Macintyre, M. (2007). Informed consent and mining projects: A view from Papua New Guinea. *Pacific Affairs, 80*(1), 49–65.

Macintyre, M. (2008). Police and thieves, gunmen and drunks: Problems with men and problems with society in Papua New Guinea. *The Australian Journal of Anthropology, 19*(2), 179–193.

Macintyre, M. (2011). Money changes everything: Papua New Guinean women in the modern economy. In M. Patterson & M. Macintyre (Eds), *Managing modernity in the Western Pacific* (pp. 90–120). St Lucia, Qld: University of Queensland Press.

McKenna, K. (2015). *Corporate social responsibility and natural resource conflict.* London, England: Routledge.

Narayan, K. (1993). How native is a 'native' anthropologist? *American Anthropologist, 95*(3), 671–686.

Narokobi, B. (1983). *The Melanesian way.* Port Moresby, Papua New Guinea: Institute of Papua New Guinea Studies.

Rooney, M. N. (2014, 9 May). Reflections on how the Manus Island detention centre promotes gender-based violence. *Devpolicyblog.* Retrieved from devpolicy. org/reflections-on-how-the-manus-island-detention-centre-promotes-gender-based-violence-20140509/

Ryang, S. (2005). Dilemma of a native: On location, authenticity and reflexivity. *The Asia Pacific Journal of Anthropology, 6*(2), 143–157.

Spark, C. (2011). Gender trouble in town: Educated women eluding male domination, gender violence and marriage in PNG. *The Asia Pacific Journal of Anthropology, 12*(2), 164–179.

Strathern, M. (2004). *Partial connections.* Walnut Creek, CA: AltaMira Press.

Weiner, A. B. (1976). *Women of value, men of renown: New perspectives in Trobriand exchange.* Austin, TX: University of Texas Press.

5

Global Health, Tuberculosis and Local Health Campaigns: Reinforcing and Reshaping Health and Gender Inequalities in Lihir, Papua New Guinea

Susan R. Hemer

Introduction

The social inequalities that drive tuberculosis (TB) have long been known to and discussed by health professionals and researchers. Medical anthropologists such as Paul Farmer have commented that physicians and public health workers are well aware of the social forces that structure who becomes ill and who has access to care (2000). TB 'is quintessentially a social disease … a marker of the contextual impacts of disadvantage and social disruption' (Mason & Degeling, 2016, p. 32). Rates of TB incidence are 'closely correlated with social and economic determinants such as the human development index, access to water sanitation and child mortality' and cluster among the poor, hungry and ethnic minorities (Hargreaves et al., 2011, p. 654). Structural determinants such as global socioeconomic inequalities, population growth, population mobility and rapid urbanisation give rise to social determinants such as malnutrition, poor and overcrowded housing and a range of barriers to access to care

(Hargreaves et al., 2011, 655). Therefore, TB is a disease of poverty—those people most likely to be exposed to infection are precisely those least able to seek diagnosis and continue the lengthy treatment required for cure.

These insights have been difficult to translate into policies that shape clinical practice and knowledge of these broader structures and determinants is often suppressed (Farmer et al., 2006). In the translation to policy, targets and practice, the focus is generally narrowed to the clinical aspects of this disease. The social inequalities that drive TB become submerged, while individual cases and hosts become the centre of biomedical attention and blame. As Farmer and his colleagues have stated, 'structural violence is often embedded in longstanding … social structures … Because they seem so ordinary in our ways of understanding the world, they appear almost invisible' (Farmer et al., 2006, p. 1686). These elisions in the ways that TB is understood, spoken about and treated perpetuate structural violence against people with the disease, which reinforces or compounds existing inequalities.

Globally, TB is the leading cause of death from a single infectious agent. In 2017, approximately 10 million people developed it (World Health Organization [WHO], 2018). At the turn of the century, it was estimated that approximately 2 billion people, or one-third of the world's population, were infected with latent TB (Farmer, 2000, p. 184). The World Health Organization (WHO) classifies 30 countries as being 'High TB Burden' countries, and these account for 87 per cent of cases. Most high-income countries have low incidence rates—this is a clear indicator of the relationship between TB and poverty (WHO, 2018). Globally, it has been stated that three basic factors drive TB: malnutrition, indoor air pollution (e.g. that caused by the use of solid fuels for cooking) and smoking (Elbeck, 2015). Within countries, people of lower socioeconomic status are more at risk: TB's 'mode of transmission and disease aetiology (whereby transmission is exacerbated by extended and close contact with persons in settings with little sunlight and air circulation and by comorbidities that reduce immunity) ensures that deaths caused by TB are disproportionately found in persons of lower SES [socioeconomic status]' (Silva, Dawson & Upshur, 2016, p. 76). Farmer has commented that the presence of the disease is the 'biological expression of social inequalities' (2001, p. 262). Further evidence of inequality driving TB is observed in patterns of infection—there exist clear gender and age disparities in rates of TB. Rates of male to female infection range from 1:1 to 3:1, with an average of 1.7:1 (Mason et al., 2016), and those above the age of 50 shoulder the highest burden of TB. Researchers have debated whether these gender disparities are 'real' or an artefact of access to health care and diagnosis, or whether they perhaps reflect smoking and other comorbidities rather than a greater susceptibility of men to the disease (see e.g. Feng et al., 2012; Ting et al., 2014; Wingfield et al., 2016).

The first-ever United Nations (UN) General Assembly high-level meeting about TB was held in September 2018. A declaration followed to accelerate progress towards the 'End TB' target of disease eradication by 2030. The UN Deputy Secretary-General Amina Mohammed explicitly noted the social basis of TB, including 'poverty, inequality, urbanisation, migration and conflict', and the need for an 'all-systems approach that accounts for the social drivers that perpetuate its spread' (United Nations, 2018). However, Dixon and Macdonald have argued that 'for all the talk about systemic drivers and inhibitors at the meeting, the five "key asks" in the declaration remained highly biomedical in approach, focused on "reaching" "vulnerable" people with drugs, diagnostics and vaccines' (2018, p. 248). Such an approach, with a focus on biomedicine and targets for control, reinforces existing efforts in global health. There exists a distinct preference for work on health conditions where measurable targets can be set and progress then monitored, which helps to reassure donor bodies that funds are being spent appropriately. This emphasis on 'narrow, vertical, technologically driven disease programmes' (Dixon & Macdonald, 2018, p. 250) deflects efforts and funding away from comprehensive primary health care and from conditions that are not so easily measured.

In Papua New Guinea (PNG), high levels of TB infection have gained international focus, large aid donations, the attention of non-governmental organisations and the press, in addition to the label of 'emergency'— particularly in the case of the emergence of high levels of drug-resistant TB in Daru, Western Province, on the southern coast of PNG. Programs seek to identify 'hot spots' (areas of high infection) and people with active infections; they then work to control people's movement until they are non-infectious and survey medication compliance through the Directly Observed Treatment, Short Course (DOTS) program. Issues of treatment failure are generally explained in terms of individuals' noncompliance; the socioeconomic and gendered contexts of such 'failures' are rendered largely invisible and, therefore, irresolvable.

In this chapter, I focus on the TB situation in the Lihir Islands in New Ireland Province, to provide a case study of structural inequalities that shape TB and those ways in which TB compounds various inequalities facing Papua New Guineans. Due to the presence of a large-scale gold mine, and all the 'development' that extraction brings to an area, Lihir possesses some of the best health care available in the country. However, within the island group, there exist disparities in access to health care that shape people's access to TB diagnosis and treatment. Through an ethnographic analysis of specific cases of TB, in the context of the Lihir Islands, this chapter investigates how relations of inequality shape people's access to and experiences of diagnosis and treatment. In a country in which healthcare provision is often compromised or entirely lacking, there exist challenges of physical access to health services and healthcare information and education is not evenly distributed, how might TB be shaped by these inequities and, in turn, compound them? Finally, this chapter reflects on how inequalities are perpetuated and influence people's chances of life and death and, further, how large-scale mining exacerbates these issues.

Global Health and Tuberculosis

In recent years, anthropologists have analysed how global health policies and priorities are understood and applied locally (e.g. Janes & Corbett, 2009; Harper & Parker, 2014; Parker & Allen, 2014). Many of these contributions have critiqued the vertical nature of interventions that have a single-disease focus, rather than a comprehensive approach to health and healthcare systems, and that are driven top-down by the priorities of the Global North (Magnussen, Ehiri & Jolly, 2004). Until the 1980s, the WHO took a holistic view of health, following the agreements for broad primary healthcare initiatives at Alma Ata in the 1970s. The WHO has sought to develop broader programs for health and to create approaches that rely on more than a singular focus to manage diseases. Approaches such as preventive chemotherapy are often combined with disease management, broader research programs, a focus on health systems, health education and the provision of safe water, sanitation and hygiene (WHO, 2012, p. 5). This broader focus can also be observed in UN comments about the latest efforts in fighting TB.

However, these broader components of health programs set at international levels are frequently jettisoned when disease management targets are set at the local level because of contextual factors or insufficient funding. In the late 1980s and early 1990s, there occurred a shift to vertical or disease point programs rather than improving health services and comprehensive national health policies (Elbeck, 2015): a 'resurgence of selective forms of primary care and vertical public health programs' (Janes & Corbett, 2009, p. 174). This has been the case for diseases that were named in the Millennium Development Goals, such as TB (Harper, 2010) and the 'Neglected Tropical Diseases', which gained importance in the early 2000s. Since this time, the WHO has consistently developed policies that target specific diseases with specific interventions; funding models support this approach.

In 1993, the WHO declared a 'global health emergency' in relation to TB and developed DOTS as the key strategy for global control of the disease. DOTS includes diagnosis by sputum smear microscopy, a standardised supervised treatment regime, an uninterrupted drug supply and a recording and reporting system. The WHO 'began to claim that TB problem [sic] could be solved by new and expensive drugs, vaccines, and new technological developments that would enable the rapid diagnosis of resistant cases' (Elbeck, 2015, p. 75). DOTS remained central in the 2006 STOP TB strategy, which aimed to manage more complex forms of TB, including multidrug-resistant TB (MDR-TB) and HIV–TB coinfection (WHO, 2006).

Tuberculosis in Papua New Guinea

The most recent available statistics for TB in PNG indicate that there were over 28,000 case notifications to the WHO in 2018. This is an incidence of 432 in 100,000, which equates to the second-worst incidence in the Western Pacific (behind the Philippines) and the sixth-worst in the world. Mortality from TB alone (e.g. excluding HIV–TB) is 52 in 100,000 (WHO, 2019); this statistic has worsened in recent years from 40 in 100,000 in 2014 (WHO, 2015). Statistics for the number of case notifications have worsened in the last 10 years; however, it is unclear whether this is due to increased detection of cases or a worsening situation. The WHO estimated a total of 17,000 cases in the country in 2009— nearly double this number of cases were found in 2017 (Department of

Health, Government of Papua New Guinea, 2011). Despite considerable attention and funding in recent years, including the aim for an 85 per cent cure rate (for detected cases), only 68 per cent of treatment is successful in notified cases. However, this rate is slightly more successful (75 per cent) in cases of MDR-TB.

PNG's TB program attracts high levels of funding from external donors, such as the Global Fund and bilateral aid programs, resulting in pressure to comply with international standards and procedures. In recent years, Australia has also expressed significant concern about TB, due to the proximity of Daru to the Torres Strait and the tendency for people with TB to cross the border for treatment (Horner, Wood & Kelly, 2013; Thomas et al., 2010). With this in mind, donors have focused on identifying 'hot spots' of TB infection and increasing efforts in those areas—in particular, Western Province, Gulf Province, the National Capital and, more recently, West New Britain (Aia et al., 2018; Cross et al., 2014). Outside these areas, the TB program has generally garnered less attention and lower priority, although some epidemiological research has aimed to understand rates of infection in other places in the country, such as the recent overview of surveillance data (Aia et al., 2018) and work in the Eastern Highlands, Madang and Milne Bay (Ley, 2014; Ley, Riley & Beck, 2014; Ley et al., 2014).

PNG has adopted the WHO-recommended DOTS program to address TB. Ideally, pulmonary TB should be diagnosed through a sputum smear that is microscopically identified as positive for TB bacteria. The disease remains contagious for some weeks after treatment begins; often, if facilities are available, people are hospitalised and isolated during this time. Next, patients go home to continue daily treatment with a mixture of medications; their compliance should be monitored by a nominated person (often a health worker) who watches them swallow their medication. These medications are provided in standardised combinations and quantities through the global STOP TB campaign. PNG aims for 100 per cent DOTS compliance in all health facilities; yet, it seems that many facilities do not practice DOTS as fully recommended, sending patients home with months of drug supplies but little to no further monitoring (Aia et al., 2018).

Diagnosis, as recommended by WHO, depends on the availability of microscopy. As recently as 2016, there were only 114 laboratories in PNG with TB testing capabilities (for a population of approximately

8 million people). PNG delivers TB services to the population through its decentralised health service, comprising provincial and district hospitals, health centres, health sub-centres and aid posts. In 2012, there were 306 hospitals and health centres, 428 health sub-centres and nearly 3,500 aid posts (Department of Health, Government of Papua New Guinea, 2012). TB diagnosis and treatment is managed through 275 health facilities that are accredited as 'basic management units' (BMU): the initial point for collecting TB data (Aia et al., 2018). These numbers indicate that most health facilities do not have laboratory facilities, nor are they considered to be BMUs; further, many BMUs do not have laboratory capabilities. Chest x-rays are still used as a form of alternative diagnosis in many larger health facilities; however, in many parts of PNG, there are either no x-ray machines, no power or the chemicals required to perform an x-ray are out of stock. Therefore, this form of diagnosis is often unavailable (see e.g. Street, 2014). These variations in health service provision often depend on the remoteness of the area—many areas have no healthcare services at all, or services that are rarely staffed or are staffed but lacking in facilities or medications (Howes et al., 2014; Wiltshire & Mako, 2014). Further, almost half of TB cases that are diagnosed in PNG are extra-pulmonary, which is more challenging to diagnose (Norbis et al., 2014); therefore, considerable misdiagnosis and delayed diagnosis are likely.

Worldwide, MDR-TB is becoming an increasing problem; an average of 3.5 per cent of new cases are multidrug-resistant. In PNG, data is by no means comprehensive. Estimates range from 3.4 per cent of new cases (the official rate listed by the WHO [2018]) to as low as 2.8 per cent of cultured samples in a survey in three major towns across three provinces— Madang, Goroka and Alotau (Ley et al., 2014). At the upper end of the estimates, there was 9 per cent MDR-TB in samples from Gulf Province (Cross et al., 2014) to as high as 25 per cent in samples taken in the Western Province during 2000 to 2006 (Gilpin et al., 2008). Extensively drug-resistant TB (XDR-TB) has also been reported in PNG since 2012, suggesting that drug-resistant TB is becoming a very significant problem in PNG.

For the country as a whole, TB presents a major issue in terms of the rates of infection and mortality, management of drug-resistant TB and the provision of successful treatment. Within the country, variable rates of TB infection and treatment highlight socioeconomic inequalities in addition to the unequal provision of (and access to) health care.

Tuberculosis and Health Care Provision in Lihir

Lihir is a group of five islands located to the north-east of mainland New Ireland, comprising a large southern island, Niolam, which is approximately 14 km wide and 21 km long, and four smaller 'outer' islands to the north, the conjoined Malie and Sinambiet, Masahet and Mahur. I have worked in Lihir since the late 1990s, including doctoral fieldwork on the northernmost island, Mahur (1997–98), a research position located mostly on Niolam focusing on community health and gender with a mining company (2000–02) and independent return visits in 2003, 2004, 2011, 2012, 2014, 2016 and 2018, which primarily focused on health and gender.

Niolam has hosted a large-scale gold mining operation since 1997; mining is now predicted to continue until approximately 2050. Mining has brought 'development' to this formerly remote, subsistence-based island population in forms including a ring road and vehicles on the main island, wage employment and businesses, increased alcohol consumption, improved health and education services and migration from elsewhere in PNG. The population has swelled from about 7,000, in the late 1990s, to approximately 16,000 Lihirians and 9,000 migrants (some of whom are employed with local companies): a combined population of about 25,000. Early in the development of the mine, certain areas within Lihir were designated as 'affected areas'—those villages closer to mine lease areas that include the mine pit and plant site, township, accommodation areas and airport. These communities were given access to comparatively greater benefits in recognition of greater impacts in these areas (see Bainton, this volume). Benefits include electrification, road sealing, regular rubbish removal services, the provision of community infrastructure and specifically negotiated packages to compensate for village relocation or loss of land. Villages outside these areas were effectively designated as 'non-affected' and have comparatively less access to the benefits of mining; this has created an antagonistic situation (Bainton, 2010). There is a 'noticeable decline in the material standards of living with increasing distance from the SML [Special Mining Lease]' (Bainton, 2010, p. 118). In 2000, Malie and Sinambiet islands were recognised as 'affected' following community protests about impacts to the ocean (Bainton, this volume). Overall, these mining and 'development' changes have shaped life on the islands in the last 20 years, including patterns of ill health and the population's access to health care.

Initially, TB was not highlighted as an issue of concern in Lihir—the baseline health report for the mining project did not mention it once (Taufa et al., 1992). Prior to the commencement of mining, the death register at the Catholic Palie health centre—located on the south end of Niolam—recorded two deaths from TB, in 1991 and 1992, of a total of 18 and 23 deaths in those years, respectively. Records from the time suggest that most people sought care at the centre for births and acute conditions and there were relatively few deaths in the centre. However, data from medical workers of the late 1990s indicated that TB was a focus of medical efforts, with 30 and 39 inpatients treated for TB in 1999 and 2000, respectively. This was recorded at the Lihir Medical Centre (LMC)—the new centre established by the mining company in the northeast corner of Niolam. There were two TB deaths in Lihir in both 1999 and 2000, but five deaths in 2001. TB was noted as a concern in reviews of health in the early 2000s; since this time, the number of TB cases and concern about the disease only seem to have increased (Hemer, 2001). In the early 2000s, there existed sufficient concern such that the mining company commissioned a report on TB in the islands, which noted an increasing number of diagnosed cases from 1997 to 2003 (Johnson, 2004). More recently, there were 74 cases diagnosed in 2013, 88 in 2014 and 96 in 2015. By the end of June 2016, 51 cases had been diagnosed, indicating that another increase was likely. These numbers provide a rate of 384 in 100,000 notified cases in 2015—higher than the national rate of notified cases of 351 in 2014 (WHO, 2015). It was unclear whether this higher rate was due to higher infection rates or was an artefact of better detection—health workers with whom I spoke did not have a clear opinion on the issue. This relatively high rate has not been recognised on the national level as a 'hotspot' such as those in Western or Gulf Provinces, which may partly be due to the general lack of government attention to mining enclaves—in practice, these are often regarded as the responsibility of the resource companies operating there.

Prior to mining, from the 1930s onwards, the largest healthcare institution in Lihir was the Catholic-run health centre at the Palie mission station in the south of Niolam. This provided outpatient and inpatient services, with a very basic laboratory and some outreach services for maternal child health, often undertaken by boat. There were also several aid posts dotted around the islands that were staffed by aid post orderlies or, more recently, by community health workers and nurses—these provided basic first aid and medication and referral services. Healthcare services were relatively dispersed, and access to them often required lengthy travel by foot or boat. Prior to the construction of the mine and associated infrastructure, the Lihir islands were one of the more neglected areas in New Ireland Province. In her early visits to Lihir, as part of conducting social impact monitoring studies for the mining company, Martha Macintyre recalls that she was 'struck by the relative poverty of people there' (2010, p. x). However, it was hoped that the incoming mine would provide a range of benefits and improve lifestyles, including health.

In terms of current health services, the population of Lihir is served by the Palie Catholic health centre in the south of Niolam, the Masahet health sub-centre located on Masahet island, the LMC near the mining town in the north of Niolam and eight aid posts (six on Niolam, one on Sinambiet and one on Mahur). The LMC was built in 1997 by the mining company to provide services to employees in addition to having a public outpatient and inpatient department, x-ray and laboratory services and various public health outreach services. The LMC is staffed by PNG and expatriate doctors, with at least one doctor always on call, and is run by an international health service provider contracted to the mining company. The LMC provides some of the best health care available in PNG. However, one major issue for health service provision to the islands has been the coordination between different service providers—the government, the Catholic health service and the mining company. For a number of years, the landowners' association also attempted to establish a fourth provider. With a relatively small population, a contained geographical space and a range of providers, positive health outcomes should have resulted. However, in practice, there are many points of disconnection, overlap or confusion about service provision. This is a key contradiction of mining, in which an increase in resources has not necessarily led to improvements in health.

The LMC has been accredited as a BMU for TB; it is a key point of data collection and reporting. Interviewed staff were keen to emphasise that, since 2011, the LMC has been following national TB guidelines for diagnosis and treatment. In 2013, the LMC obtained one of the first GeneXpert machines in PNG for testing TB—in 2016, there were still only a dozen machines in the country. This acquisition improved diagnostic capabilities and permitted testing for some drug sensitivity. The GeneXpert machine has led to the early detection of more pulmonary cases. Concurrently, the LMC built a specialist ward to house TB patients, outside the air-conditioning system used for the rest of the hospital.

The procedure in Lihir is this: most patients, particularly pulmonary cases (due to higher infectivity), are to be admitted as inpatients for the first two to four weeks of treatment. During this time, the focus is on infection control, health care for serious complications of TB (e.g. collapsed lungs) and medication provided in fixed-dose combination. Drug supply in Lihir is excellent in comparison with many other places in the country—the presence of a major mining company means that transport and logistics are functional.

It was quite clear to me in my recent visits to the islands (2016 and 2018) that clinical management of TB follows global best practice health guidelines and is some of the best in the country. Moreover, Lihir has healthcare resources, such as staffing, facilities and medication supply that are difficult to procure elsewhere. Despite this, in the discussion that follows, I trace a number of cases of TB in Lihir that demonstrate the ways in which structural inequalities shape the diagnosis and treatment of this illness and its impact on people's lives.

Challenges in Accessing Health Care

Palie health centre is located almost at the end of a sealed road in the south of Lihir. The centre was due to be rebuilt in 2008; however, its current, somewhat dilapidated appearance and occasional holes in the walls signal a lack of updated facilities within. Debates over authority, responsibility and funding have meant that the planned rebuild has not yet occurred; maintenance needs have also largely been ignored. There is one nurse trained in TB management; however, there is no x-ray machine or laboratory facilities to enable diagnosis. Suspected cases of TB (based on clinical signs) are referred for diagnosis to the far superior facilities at the LMC. Treatment of post-diagnosis patients from the south of the island is mostly managed through Palie.

In the early 2000s, the sharp discord between the facilities and expertise available at the LMC and Palie health centre was mitigated by policies in place at the local level that allowed all patients access to the LMC, regardless of their village of origin. Further, LMC doctors provided regular physical visits, radio contact and support for staff at Palie. There was an agreement in place that gave the LMC responsibility for outreach and maternal child health clinics for the northern three islands and the north of Niolam, whereas Palie was responsible for the south of Niolam.

In more recent years, a growing population and decreasing per capita funding has resulted in the LMC now being responsible for outreach in the north of Niolam, but not on the outer islands—these are now overseen by the government-run Masahet health sub-centre. Although doctors are permitted to provide support to Palie, in practice, this is no longer routinised. Further, there is no longer a Health Extension Officer based at Palie; instead, the highest qualified staff member is a nurse. In terms of TB diagnosis and treatment, it is now considerably more difficult to access health care if a person comes from villages near Palie, because the facilities and expertise available at this health centre are minimal in comparison with those at LMC. Moreover, the ring road past Palie in south-western Niolam is unsealed and has deteriorated to the point that it is sometimes barely passable, creating a barrier to accessible health care for all villagers in that area. It is the responsibility of the local government to maintain (and ultimately seal) this part of the road, as one component of the agreed benefits package for the mining project. In the past, the mining company often took responsibility for maintaining the ring road around the entirety of Niolam; however, it no longer does so. The failure of the government to provide this agreed-upon service or to upgrade the road means that villagers in this area struggle to gain physical access to health care. It also exacerbates the divide between those in the south-west with those in the north and east of the island, who have relatively easy access to the LMC and its superior facilities. For people with TB located in villages on the south-western or western coasts of Niolam, access may sometimes require a boat trip to LMC or Palie. This is also the case for people located on the northern islands. This lack of physical accessibility was raised by one health worker, who stated that the LMC only undertook contact tracing on Niolam rather than the outer islands. Consequently, more cases might be missed or be detected later in the course of the disease. Further, according to this health worker, villages such as Samo and Mazuz (on the south-western coast of Niolam) are located the furthest from the LMC, on the section of unsealed road; therefore, issues of distance and transport cost make defaulting on medications much more likely.

Even when health care is apparently physically accessible, the design or policies of healthcare provision can create challenges for access. Guided by global and national health policies, at both the LMC and Palie, some workers specialise in TB; for example, at the LMC, two health workers under the auspices of the public health team work back-to-back shifts that focus on TB and HIV. This is an unremarkable arrangement; further, the link with HIV makes good clinical sense, due to the syndemic relationship between the two. However, for people seeking diagnosis or advice, a visit to the medical centre to see one of these workers may signal (incorrectly or otherwise) to others that the person has HIV. Stigma was raised as an issue for at least one patient who was defaulting on medication; he asked the health worker not to visit him in his place of employment due to fear of repercussions. However, it was unclear to me whether the stigma related to the perception of having TB or the potential link with HIV.

A newly diagnosed TB patient in Lihir, particularly a pulmonary case, will be expected to stay for two to four weeks in the TB ward at the LMC. Those who default on treatment are expected to return and stay for four to six weeks in the ward. To prevent the spread of infection, this ward is located outside the centre's main air-conditioning system, to prevent contagion. The ward is not segregated by gender. Neither is the small TB ward at Palie, which is simply part of the general male ward. A situation in which unrelated males and females sleep within the same room is beyond comprehension in Lihir and probably also other places in PNG. During her study of TB in Lihir in 2004, Penny Johnson recalled at least one female patient who raised this as a concern, because she had had to share space with two male TB patients at LMC, before the dedicated TB ward was built (Johnson, 2004). However, issues of gender collocation were not considered during the planning and building process. Further, in my research, no health worker ever raised this as a concern or even a possible deterrent to diagnosis and treatment.

Only two of the most highly qualified health workers offered information on patterns of infection in TB. One, a doctor, noted that there were three peaks of infection in Lihir: infants who are infected via close contact with their mothers, teenagers who are infected for the first time and older people whose latent TB infection is activated. Another health worker suggested that, some years earlier, it had appeared that migrants were diagnosed more often than locals; however, in recent years, Lihirians were being diagnosed more often. He thought that overcrowding in areas near the mine was an issue for TB infection; based on published accounts of factors contributing to TB infection, this is likely to have been true.[1]

---

1 At the time of writing, statistics on the distribution of diagnosed cases, defaulting cases or deaths by age, gender or village were unavailable for Lihir or New Ireland Province. Even the PNG data is relatively limited on this issue—the latest WHO report on TB is limited to gendered population distribution graphs (WHO, 2019). Therefore, it is impossible to test assertions about the spread of cases. This lack of data suggests the need for more research across the country.

These comments are suggestive of structural inequalities driving TB infection, diagnosis and treatment; however, these sorts of reflections were rare. During my fieldwork in Lihir, I was surprised that most health workers had not considered whether rates of TB differed in accordance with sex or age. Nor did they question whether diagnosis and treatment were evenly accessible to all within Lihir (both Lihirians and non-Lihirian migrants) or whether a TB diagnosis had different implications for different members of the population. The majority of health workers were firmly focused on the clinical aspects of work and the attempt to manage the burden of ill health. Even at the national level, structural determinants and inequalities are not prioritised. In searching the most recent statistics, it also became apparent that TB data that is segregated by gender only became available for the whole of PNG in 2019—such information had already been available for all other countries classified as having a high TB burden (WHO, 2019).

Despite mineral wealth and a relatively small land area and population, shifts in policy and accepted practice have exacerbated inequalities in access to health care, rather than fulfilling earlier hopes of improved living conditions. There exist clear disparities and barriers in access to TB-related health care, shaped by physical location, gender and the experience of stigma—challenges that have not been alleviated by the influx of large flows of capital. This is unsurprising because the literature on extractive industries in the PNG context has drawn connections between the income from such projects, social conflict and growing inequalities (Banks, 2008). There is little to no evidence that resource development reduces poverty; in fact, it may perform the opposite or, at minimum, increase disparities (Banks, 2005). Laura Zimmer-Tamakoshi has noted the ways in which both gender and generational inequalities have been exacerbated by mining activity (Zimmer-Tamakoshi, 2016, this volume). Betina Beer has argued that large-scale capitalist projects in the country 'create continuities as well as conflicts with earlier forms of inequality' (2018, p. 348). In the following section, I chart the ways in which social inequalities not only influence TB infection, diagnosis and treatment but also deepen inequalities and poverty.

Compounding Inequalities

In June 2016, when I returned to the northernmost island of the Lihir group, Mahur, I found that two girls in their upper teens within the same lineage had recently been diagnosed with TB. I sat with a woman I have known for over 20 years, who told me that her high school–aged daughter had lost a lot of weight and had been coughing. She had been suspected of having TB, and the nurse at the aid post had sent her to the LMC for diagnosis. The daughter was diagnosed with pulmonary TB and hospitalised for some weeks, as is usual practice in Lihir. Following discharge, her family had arranged for her to stay with her mother's sister in a village closer to the LMC (on Niolam) to facilitate easier access to treatment for the required six months. Despite this, when I briefly discussed her case with the LMC, it became apparent that she was behind in her medications and, therefore, considered to be in default on treatment.

Within days, I heard about the second girl in the same kin group, who had been diagnosed with TB of the spine and was being treated on Mahur at the time of my visit. Again, the nurse at the Mahur aid post had suspected TB and referred her to the LMC for diagnosis. Following diagnosis, the girl was sent home to Mahur with a recommendation for nine months of treatment, due to the involvement of the spine and the difficulties associated with using medication to kill bacteria in the bone. I asked the nurse on Mahur about her treatment and prognosis. The nurse was uncertain—about the diagnosis, about her prognosis and whether there would be permanent bone damage. The nurse had no involvement in the ongoing treatment process, which was entirely managed by the LMC on Niolam. Medications were to be picked up once a month by the girl's mother, involving a lengthy and costly round trip by boat to the largest island of Lihir, and given to her daily by her mother. This represents a case of family administration of medication, rather than DOTS by health workers, despite the family living near the Mahur aid post, which provides evidence of a disconnection between health facilities in Lihir and the practical implementation of DOTS.

Both of these girls had been in school prior to illness, but were now unable to attend due to treatment. The first was absent from school due to initial hospitalisation and her subsequent move to a different village to better access treatment. The second was absent from school because the TB in her spine caused difficulties with walking. Health workers confirmed that it is common to lose up to a year of schooling when a young person is diagnosed in Lihir. Further, it is likely that some people who develop TB never return to school, given the lengthy treatment process. Such disruption to education is likely to compound any pre-existing socioeconomic inequalities.

In reflecting on these two cases, I realised that both girls were the daughters of unmarried women. It is only via deep familiarity with the Mahur social context that I am able to know that these families were likely to have been less financially secure, with less access to disposable income and, therefore, were less likely to be able to purchase protein to add to meals, and perhaps had smaller houses and gardens than others. As the most distantly located island in the group, Mahur has also benefited the least from the mining project. These girls are likely to have been less well-nourished than some other young people in Lihir—there exist known relationships between poverty, malnutrition and TB (Elbeck, 2015; Ortblad et al., 2015). These families are also more likely to struggle to afford transport to collect medications. A lengthy illness such as TB is likely to compound the precarious position of such families, pushing them deeper into poverty—reflecting the global understanding that TB is a driver of poverty (Ortblad et al., 2015).

Individual and Collective Responsibility: Losing Sight of Structural Inequality

Most health workers with whom I spoke kept attention firmly on clinical aspects of cases and considered individual characteristics of those infected and cultural beliefs about TB as critical for understanding the spread of TB cases in the islands, rather than considering the relationship between TB and structural inequalities such as poverty and uneven development. The way in which patients who defaulted on treatment were discussed provides a salient example. An adult Lihirian man had been diagnosed by LMC staff with MDR-TB, following repeated defaulting on TB medications over a number of years. He lived in an 'affected-area' village near the mine on Niolam and LMC staff had been visiting him daily to ensure his compliance with medication and his continued presence at home, because it was likely that he was contagious. They had conducted contact tracing to ensure his family remained free of TB. Staff were concerned that he was developing XDR-TB, which has a high fatality rate. Despite their efforts and ongoing medication, the man's condition worsened, and he eventually died (after I left Lihir). During my time there, what most mattered to health workers was that he defaulted numerous times on ordinary TB treatment, which led to his TB becoming resistant to frontline medications. To them, the most relevant point was the man's noncompliance—he had, in their eyes, created his own difficulties.

It might have been predicted that, because the man lived in a relatively affluent 'affected-area' village, he would be less vulnerable to the influence of structural inequalities. However, such a prediction preferences the immediate relative wealth of these villages over other, more long-term inequalities. Prior to the commencement of mining, some of the villages close to the mine were some of the poorest in the islands. As a child— assuming that he had not moved there from elsewhere—this man would probably have been subject to the poverty faced by all Lihirian children. His family most likely cooked over solid fuels (as most families did and many still do), which is a practice clearly linked to susceptibility to TB infection that may stay latent in the body for decades. As an adult, it is also very likely that he smoked and may have been at risk for diabetes— this is becoming increasingly common in affected-area villages, as living standards and consumption patterns suddenly shift, causing significant impact to bodies that were never prepared for high amounts of fat and sugar. [2] Smoking is one of the key risk factors for TB, as is diabetes. None of the health workers with whom I spoke raised questions regarding where he had contracted TB, whether he had concomitant diabetes or if there was an immune-related reason that the latent TB, which affects the majority of the population, became active in his case. Nor were serious questions raised regarding why he had defaulted numerous times on his medication—he was simply perceived as a 'poor' or 'noncompliant' patient.

Discussions about adherence to TB treatment and noncompliant patients are common both in the literature and on the ground in PNG. As noted by Simpson from Cairns Base hospital, 'the main factors in the survival of tuberculosis [are] related to human nature—people stop taking medicine once they feel better' (2011, p. 759). Ungugo, Hall and Attia (2011, p. 427) have suggested that legislation may be required in PNG to

---

2 A 2010 demographic health study on the Lihir islands indicated a high prevalence of smoking, at over 55 per cent for all adults (Bentley, 2010, p. 44). The report also identified changing diets and increasing incidence of being overweight or obese as factors that were increasing the risk of diabetes among the population.

incarcerate noncompliant patients and enforce the compulsory screening of contacts. Sometimes such discussions cover difficulties associated with health system factors such as remoteness, poor transportation, closed health facilities and poor drug supplies, or factors more closely tied to patients such as the effect(s) of stigma or side effects of medication, these are generally concealed by discourses that position PNG patients as highly problematic and, further, as driving the spread of TB and drug resistance. Structural factors are submerged beneath discussions of individual (ir)responsibility.

Prioritising individual responsibility over structural social inequalities has several consequences. First, health sector attention is directed towards trying to alter the behaviour of individuals to make them more compliant. It also shifts focus away from the need for structural change: 'victim blaming … is a poor practice that misdirects attention away from assembling more qualified human resources, improving health infrastructure and building stronger health systems that coordinate effectively with the private sector' (Mason et al., 2016, p. 3). This is particularly critical in areas affected by mining, where structural inequities and coordination of services are crucial. Focus on individual behaviour serves as a sleight of hand that obfuscates issues and inequalities. Finally, individualising responsibility deepens the social inequalities between the health care workforce and people infected with TB, leading patients to become less likely to seek diagnosis and to continue treatment.

Health staff also cited cultural beliefs about TB as issues in both diagnosis and treatment adherence. A number of staff stated that symptoms and their cause(s) are frequently the subject of misunderstanding—patients and community members often believe that sorcery is a key issue. Some people believe that treatment with TB medications is pointless or fear that symptoms indicated ensorcellment; consequently, they sought health care too late to be effectively treated. In these discussions, cultural beliefs were posited as a problem and health staff attitudes varied from understanding to frustration and dismissal.

In my experience, it was certainly the case that Lihirians raised concerns about sorcery whenever someone was seriously ill. Some illnesses are perceived as relatively simple and resolvable through biomedical treatment. Yet, other illnesses, including those that do not resolve easily with treatment, are understood to be linked to the untoward actions of another human being. In these cases, it is believed to be important to consider the state of a person's relationship with others and take steps to discover the likely culprit and resolve the situation. The state of social relationships is of great importance for Lihirians, as it is for other Papua New Guineans, who understand positive relationships with others, often termed *wanbel*, to be a source of health (Street, 2014; Troolin, 2018). In the case of TB, Johnson identified a number of cultural models that explained TB spread or symptoms, including that it ran in families and could be inherited, that it was a disease of old people, that it could be passed through food or was caused by sorcery. Most people did not have a contagion model and did not understand germ theory (Johnson, 2004). This differs dramatically to my findings in relation to HIV/AIDS—health education had been readily absorbed and people were actively worried about catching HIV from others via the blood/fluids pathway, particularly from migrants to the islands or if they travelled away from the islands (Hemer, 2015).

In the case of one of the young women discussed above, her mother was unsure about the diagnosis—she was concerned that her daughter's illness was caused by sorcery instead of TB or, alternatively, that sorcery was causing the TB. Despite this, she ensured that her daughter was diagnosed and got treatment. While some literature on Melanesia notes a strict binary between *sik bilong marasin* (biomedically treatable illness) and *sik bilong ples* (local illnesses having causes like sorcery; see e.g. Cox & Phillips, 2015), in Lihir there is no fixed or strict boundary between the two; therefore, a plurality of healthcare approaches is often sought (Macintyre et al., 2005). In this way, suggestions of sorcery do not preclude biomedical treatment. In another reported case, a woman's lymph glands swelled enormously and eventually burst. She was brought into the health centre and diagnosed with extra-pulmonary TB. A nurse commented that people in the village did not believe it was TB, instead deeming it to be sorcery. This is perhaps unsurprising because health education in PNG firmly identifies TB with the principal symptom of coughing, rather than abscesses of the glands that might rupture. Johnson (2004) noted that Lihirians firmly linked TB to weight loss and coughing rather than other symptoms. However, despite these concerns, this woman was diagnosed and successfully completed treatment for TB.

These cases suggest that a belief in sorcery is not necessarily incompatible with biomedical diagnosis and successful treatment of TB. However, narratives at the national level place patient beliefs and compliance at the centre of understanding high rates of TB in PNG. The Chairman of Public Health at the University of Papua New Guinea, Louis Samiak, has stated (in relation to TB) that the 'biggest barrier for the moment is cultural beliefs about the causes of diseases … the first source of help is witchdoctors and local remedies' (cited by Wilson, 2015). This perspective is echoed by Ungugo et al. (2011, p. 423), in a publication that notes the 'clash of culture and science' in TB diagnosis and treatment. The paper lists a range of issues in relation to TB, including inadequate health facilities and drug supply, the lack of diagnostic facilities in the country, a lack of contact screening and physical accessibility of health care, among others. Yet, it lists 'sorcery' and 'witchdoctor' as two of the five article keywords, demonstrating the focus on cultural responsibility and the preclusion of structural inequalities.

Lepani (2012) has critically reviewed the ways in which 'culture' or cultural beliefs are employed in the health field. The key issue that she identified was how cultural attitudes to sexuality were seen as problematic in the Trobriands regarding HIV; however, her points apply equally to the case of TB in PNG. A narrow version of culture, often labelled as 'cultural beliefs', is frequently blamed rather than addressing more complex issues such as social structures and global economic or political forces that shape the spread of infections and methods of diagnosis and treatment. This placement of responsibility on individuals as noncompliant or cultural beliefs as barriers to health care transfers attention from the structural positioning of people who develop TB and the challenges they face in seeking and continuing treatment.

Conclusions

The field of global health, for all its rhetoric regarding the socioeconomic and political contexts of diseases such as TB, is the author of policies that pay lip service to the systemic contexts of health, but that are profoundly singular, vertical and removed from context, in practice. Such policies are singularly disease-focused—they pinpoint targets for control and eradication to provide something tangible and achievable on which to focus. These guidelines and targets are then translated to the national level in countries such as PNG, where experts and funding shape health policies and practices with a largely clinical focus.

It requires a concerted effort to trace the impact of the inequalities obfuscated by such policies and, further, to analyse the ways that the policies themselves then compound those inequalities. In the case of

TB in PNG, some inequalities in infection rates, access to diagnosis and treatment are readily apparent—there exists a clear concern regarding high levels of TB infection and MDR-TB in particular provinces or locations that are designated as hotspots. These locations attract attention, research and publications, funding, global expertise and new technologies for diagnosis. However, the intensity of this focus has overshadowed TB in the rest of the country.

Analysis of the TB situation in Lihir facilitates a clear illustration of the ways in which, even within relatively wealthy mining enclaves, TB is flourishing and the health system is struggling to maintain the pace. Despite the presence of some of the best health care available in the country, access to health care is not a simple matter for many people on the islands. Moreover, the kind of access required to properly treat TB, which involves inpatient treatment for weeks and then six or more months of daily medications, may be beyond the health system's capabilities. These challenges, rather than being met with understanding about the social inequalities that drive TB and limit access to health care, are often viewed as individual or cultural failures.

In the case of TB, social, political and economic inequalities coalesce in physical form to shape an individual's risk of infection and the development of active TB. Further, they mould that person's access to diagnosis and their course through treatment, in which inequalities may be compounded by the destructive processes of the illness.

References

Aia, P., Wangchuk, L., Morishita, F., Kisomb, J., Yasi, R., Kal, M. & Islam, T. (2018). Epidemiology of tuberculosis in Papua New Guinea: Analysis of case notification and treatment outcome data, 2008–2016. *Western Pacific Surveillance and Response*, 9(2), 1–11.

Bainton, N. (2010). *The Lihir destiny: Cultural responses to mining in Melanesia.* Canberra, ACT: ANU E Press. doi.org/10.22459/LD.10.2010

Banks, G. (2005). Globalisation, poverty, and hyperdevelopment in Papua New Guinea's mining sector. *Focaal – Journal of Global and Historical Anthropology*, 46, 128–146. doi.org/10.3167/092012906780786799

Banks, G. (2008). Understanding 'resource' conflicts in Papua New Guinea. *Asia Pacific Viewpoint*, 49(1), 23–34. doi.org/10.1111/j.1467-8373.2008.00358.x

Beer, B. (2018). Gender and inequality in a postcolonial context of large-scale capitalist projects in the Markham Valley, Papua New Guinea. *The Australian Journal of Anthropology, 29*, 348–364. doi.org/10.1111/taja.12298

Bentley, K. (2010). *Lihir social demographic health survey.* Canberra, ACT: Centre for Environmental Health Pty Ltd for Newcrest Mining Ltd.

Cox, J. & Phillips, G. (2015). Sorcery, Christianity and the decline of medical services. In M. Forsyth & R. Eves (Eds), *Talking it through: Reponses to sorcery and witchcraft beliefs and practices in Melanesia* (pp. 37–54). Canberra, ACT: ANU Press. doi.org/10.22459/TIT.05.2015.02

Cross, G. B., Coles, K., Nikpour, M., Moore, O. A., Denholm, J., McBride, E. S., … Pellegrini, M. (2014). TB incidence and characteristics in the remote gulf province of Papua New Guinea: A prospective study. *BMC Infectious Diseases, 14*(93), 1–10. doi.org/10.1186/1471-2334-14-93

Department of Health, Government of Papua New Guinea. (2011). *PNG National Tuberculosis Management Protocol. Waigani, Port Moresby.* Retrieved from www.adi.org.au/wp-content/uploads/2016/11/National-Tuberculosis-Management-Protocol-PNG-2011.pdf

Department of Health, Government of Papua New Guinea. (2012). *Health Service Delivery Profile, Papua New Guinea.* Retrieved from pdf4pro.com/cdn/health-service-delivery-profile-papua-new-guinea-254938.pdf

Dixon, J. & Macdonald, H. (2018). Globalised tuberculosis control in local worlds. *Anthropology Southern Africa, 41*(4), 247–256. doi.org/10.1080/23323256.2018.1547116

Elbeck, O. (2015). Ethical issues in tuberculosis control. *Turkish Thoracic Journal, 16*, 73–85. doi.org/10.5152/ttd.2014.4134

Farmer, P. E. (2000). The consumption of the poor: Tuberculosis in the 21st century. *Ethnography, 1*(2), 183–216. doi.org/10.1177/14661380022230732

Farmer, P. E. (2001). *Infections and inequalities: The modern plagues.* Berkeley, CA: University of California Press.

Farmer, P. E., Nizeye, B., Stulac, S. & Keshavjee, S. (2006). Structural violence and clinical medicine. *PLOS Medicine, 3*(10), 1686–1691. doi.org/10.1371/journal.pmed.0030449

Feng, J. Y., Huang, S. F., Ting, W. Y., Chen, Y. C., Lin, Y. Y., Huang, R. M., … Su, W. J. (2012). Gender difference in treatment outcomes of tuberculosis patients in Taiwan: A prospective observational study. *Clinical Microbiology and Infection, 18*, E331–E337. doi.org/10.1111/j.1469-0691.2012.03931.x

Gilpin, C. M., Simpson, G., Vincent, S., O'Brien, T. P., Knight, T. A., Globan, M., … Konstantinos, A. (2008). Evidence of primary transmission of multi-drug resistant tuberculosis in the Western Province of Papua New Guinea. *Medical Journal of Australia, 188*(3), 148–152.

Hargreaves, J. R., Boccia, D., Evans, C. A., Adato, M., Petticrew, M. & Porter, J. D. H. (2011). The social determinants of tuberculosis: From evidence to action. *American Journal of Public Health, 101*(4), 654–662. doi.org/10.2105/AJPH.2010.199505

Harper, I. (2010). Extreme condition, extreme measures? Compliance, drug resistance and the control of tuberculosis. *Anthropology & Medicine, 17*(2), 201–214. doi.org/10.1080/13648470.2010.493606

Harper, I. & Parker, M. (2014). The politics and anti-politics of infectious disease control. *Medical Anthropology, 33*(3), 198–205. doi.org/10.1080/01459740.2014.892484

Hemer, S. R. (2001). Illness and health care in the Lihir islands [Unpublished report]. LGL.

Hemer, S. R. (2015). Breaking silences and upholding confidences: Responding to HIV in the Lihir Islands, Papua New Guinea. *Medical Anthropology, 34*(2), 124–138. doi.org/10.1080/01459740.2014.944263

Horner, J., Wood, J. G. & Kelly, A. (2013). Public health in/as 'national security': Tuberculosis and the contemporary regime of border control in Australia. *Critical Public Health, 23*(4), 418–431. doi.org/10.1080/09581596.2013.824068

Howes, S., Mako, A. A., Swan, A., Walton, G., Webster, T. & Wiltshire, C. (2014). *A lost decade? Service delivery and reforms in Papua New Guinea 2002–2012.* Canberra, ACT: The National Research Institute and Development Policy Centre.

Janes, C. R. & Corbett, K. K. (2009). Anthropology and global health. *Annual Review of Anthropology, 38,* 167–183. doi.org/10.1146/annurev-anthro-091908-164314

Johnson, P. (2004). 'TB, well that is a long-term punishment. Some people give their life to the medicine to make themselves better': A short ethnographic perspective on tuberculosis and TB treatment from Lihir Island [Unpublished report].

Lepani, K. (2012). *Islands of love, islands of risk: Culture and HIV in the Trobriands.* Nashville, TN: Vanderbilt University Press.

Ley, S. D. (2014). Molecular epidemiology of tuberculosis in selected sites across Papua New Guinea (Unpublished doctoral thesis). University of Basel, Switzerland.

Ley, S. D., Riley, I. & Beck, H. (2014). Tuberculosis in Papua New Guinea: From yesterday until today. *Microbes and Infection*, *16*(8), 607–614. doi.org/10.1016/j.micinf.2014.06.012

Ley, S. D., Harino, P., Vanuga, K., Kamus, R., Carter, R., Coulter, C., … Beck, H. (2014). Diversity of mycobacterium tuberculosis and drug resistance in different provinces of Papua New Guinea. *BMC Microbiology*, *14*, 307. doi.org/10.1186/s12866-014-0307-2

Macintyre, M. (2010). Foreword. In N. Bainton (Ed.), *The Lihir destiny: Cultural responses to mining in Melanesia*. Canberra, ACT: ANU E Press. doi.org/10.22459/LD.10.2010

Macintyre, M., Foale, S., Bainton, N. & Moktel, B. (2005). Medical pluralism and the maintenance of a traditional healing technique on Lihir, Papua New Guinea. *Pimatisiwin: A Journal of Aboriginal and Indigenous Community Health*, *3*(1), 87–99.

Magnussen, L., Ehiri, J. & Jolly, P. (2004). Comprehensive versus selective primary health care: Lessons for global health policy. *Health Affairs*, *23*(3), 167–176. doi.org/10.1377/hlthaff.23.3.167

Mason, P. & Degeling, C. (2016). Beyond biomedicine: Relationships and care in tuberculosis prevention. *Bioethical Inquiry*, *13*(1), 31–34. doi.org/10.1007/s11673-015-9697-6

Mason, P. H., Snow, K., Asugeni, R., Massey, P. D. & Viney, K. (2016). Tuberculosis and gender in the Asia-Pacific Region. *Australia and New Zealand Journal of Public Health*, *41*(3), 227–229. doi.org/10.1111/1753-6405.12619

Norbis, L., Alagna, R., Tortoli, E., Codecasa, L. R., Migliori, G. B. & Cirillo, D. M. (2014). Challenges and perspectives in the diagnosis of extrapulmonary tuberculosis. *Expert Review of Anti-infective Therapy*, *12*(5), 633–647. doi.org/10.1586/14787210.2014.899900

Ortblad, K. F., Salomon, J. A., Barnighausen, T. & Atun, R. (2015). Stopping tuberculosis: A biosocial model for sustainable development. *The Lancet*, *386*(10010), 2354–2362. doi.org/10.1016/S0140-6736(15)00324-4

Parker, M. & Allen, T. (2014). De-politicising parasites: Reflections on attempts to control the control of neglected tropical diseases. *Medical Anthropology*, *33*(3), 223–239. doi.org/10.1080/01459740.2013.831414

Silva, D. S., Dawson, A. & Upshur, R. E. G. (2016). Reciprocity and ethical tuberculosis treatment and control. *Bioethical Inquiry, 13*(1), 75–86.

Simpson, G. (2011). Multidrug-resistant tuberculosis on Australia's northern border. *Internal Medicine Journal, 41*(11), 759–761. doi.org/10.1111/j.1445-5994.2011.02588.x

Street, A. (2014). *Biomedicine in an unstable place: Infrastructure and personhood in a Papua New Guinean hospital.* Durham, NC: Duke University Press. doi.org/10.1215/9780822376668

Taufa, T., Jones, M., Day, G. & Mea, V. (1992). *Baseline health survey of Lihir Islanders, April 1991* [Report]. Hawthorn, Vic.: NSR Environmental Consultants Pty Ltd.

Thomas, E. G., Barrington, H. E., Lokuge, K. M. & Mercer, G. N. (2010). Modelling the spread of tuberculosis including drug resistance and HIV: A case study in Papua New Guinea's Western Province. *Australia and New Zealand Applied and Industrial Mathematics Journal, 52,* 26–45.

Ting, W. Y., Huang, S. F., Lee, M. C., Lin, Y. Y., Lee, Y. C., Feng, J. Y. & Su, W. J. (2014). Gender disparities in latent tuberculosis infection in high-risk individuals: A cross-sectional study. *PLoS ONE, 9*(11), e110104.

Troolin, D. (2018). Wanbel: Conflict, reconciliation and personhood among the Sam people, Madang Province (Unpublished doctoral thesis). University of Adelaide, Australia.

Ungugo, K., Hall, J. & Attia, J. (2011). Implementing tuberculosis control in Papua New Guinea: A clash of culture and science? *Journal of Community Health, 36,* 423–430. doi.org/10.1007/s10900-010-9324-8

United Nations. (2018). *United to end tuberculosis: An urgent global response to a global epidemic* (Opening statement and Plenary 1). Retrieved from www.unmultimedia.org/avlibrary/asset/2245/2245992/

Wilson, C. (2015, 25 March). Multi-drug resistance adds to tuberculosis epidemic in Papua New Guinea. *Inter Press Service News Agency.* Retrieved from www.ipsnews.net/2015/03/multi-drug-resistance-adds-to-tuberculosis-epidemic-in-papua-new-guinea/

Wiltshire, C. & Mako, A. (2014). Financing PNG's free primary health care policy: User fees, funding and performance. *Development Policy Centre Australian National University & National Research Institute, PNG.* Retrieved from devpolicy.org/publications/reports/PEPE/Financing-PNGs-free-primary-health-care-policy-user-fees-funding-and-performance.pdf

Wingfield, T., Tovar, M. A., Huff, D., Boccia, D., Saunders, M. J., Datta, S., … Evans, C. (2016). Beyond pills and tests: Addressing the social determinants of tuberculosis. *Clinical Medicine, 16*(6), s79–s91. doi.org/10.7861/clinmedicine. 16-6-s79

World Health Organization. (2006). *The Stop TB Strategy: Building on and enhancing DOTS to meet the TB-related Millennium Development Goals.* Geneva, Switzerland: World Health Organization.

World Health Organization. (2012). *Accelerating work to overcome the global impact of neglected tropical diseases: A roadmap for implementation.* Retrieved from www. who.int/neglected_diseases/NTD_RoadMap_2012_Fullversion.pdf

World Health Organization. (2015). *Global tuberculosis report 2015.* Retrieved from apps.who.int/iris/handle/10665/191102

World Health Organization. (2018). *Global tuberculosis report 2018.* Retrieved from reliefweb.int/report/world/global-tuberculosis-report-2018

World Health Organization. (2019). *Global tuberculosis report 2019.* Retrieved from www.who.int/tb/publications/global_report/en/

Zimmer-Tamakoshi, L. (2016). Inequality and changing masculinities among the Gende in Papua New Guinea: The 'good,' the 'bad' and the 'very bad'. *The Asia Pacific Journal of Anthropology, 17*(3–4), 250–267. doi.org/10.1080/14442213. 2016.1186216

6

The Missionary's Dilemma: A Short History of Christian Marriage and its Impact upon Gender Equality in Maisin Society

John Barker

Martha Macintyre opened 'Better homes and gardens' with a description of contemporary Tubetube houses. 'These houses,' she observed, 'being made entirely from "bush materials", conform to Western notions of the primitive or traditional architecture appropriate to a small tropical island' (1989, p. 156). Tubetube people, however, attributed the houses to Islander teachers who served as the workforce of the Methodist mission that arrived on the island in 1892. Drawing upon oral histories and archival sources, Macintyre related how the teachers focused their evangelical campaign against the houses of chiefs, due to the presence of ancestral skulls and other items they reasonably presumed to be associated with 'heathen' spiritual beliefs, warfare and sorcery. The destruction of the houses corresponded to the undermining of chiefly authority that, along with severe population loss through disease, ramified over time, ending Tubetube's involvement in regional trade networks and changing local patterns of settlement. Having helped to destroy the old society, the teachers provided new models of houses, gardens and ritual activities, now centred around the church. Macintyre concluded: 'when we are confronted by a church-going community in Papua New Guinea [PNG] it is easy to assume that the adoption of Christianity is an accretion'. A careful comparison of past and present forms and practices, however, reveals 'underlying ramifications of enforced change' (Macintyre, 1989, p. 169).

Macintyre's description of Tubetube villages could equally be applied to the Maisin of southern Collingwood Bay on the eastern edge of Oro Province. Visitors, including Maisin who have settled in towns, frequently praise the beauty of the bush-material houses, outrigger canoes lining the shores and subsistence gardens as evidence of traditional continuity, ignoring the abundant evidence of a connection to the outside world. When my wife, Anne Marie Tiejten, and I began our fieldwork in November 1981, we were aware that the Maisin had abandoned their traditional house forms for a type of bush house promoted by the former colonial administration. Yet we had been told, by the Archbishop of the PNG Anglican Church no less, that the Maisin were the most determinately 'traditional' of the coastal people within the Anglican fold. Indeed, it seemed the case that the Maisin and Anglican missionaries had found a comfortable balance between Christianity and tradition, one based upon distinguishing between the two as existing in separate physical and action spheres. Villagers worshipped and sent their children to school on a demarcated mission station while also conducting mortuary rituals and other traditional ceremonies in the surrounding villages (Barker, 1990).

Marriage appeared as the chief exception to this happy arrangement. I knew from the archival documents I had consulted in Port Moresby that the missionaries had waged a long war to bring the marriage practices of converts into conformance with church standards. The Papua New Guinean priest in charge of the St Thomas parish, based at Uiaku village, identified marriage and divorce as the major challenges he faced. When conducting a village census, I learned that very few people bothered with church weddings. Members of the church council and Mothers' Union spoke to me of their frustrations in encouraging villagers to conform to church rules on marriage and their inability to break up polygamous unions, of which there were five in the village at the time. Such problems did not seem to trouble most villagers, including those under discipline for remarriage, with young children who had to wait until adulthood to seek baptism. Couples who were legally married in the eyes of the church told me freely of their youthful sexual adventures and tolerated the same behaviour on the part of their unmarried children. The stability of marriage depended upon seemingly traditional norms: the production of children and maintenance of balanced exchange relationships between the patriclans joined by marriage.

Yet, as with the 'traditional' houses on Tubetube, appearances can be deceiving. Marriage, in addition to attitudes on gender, has changed over the decades, as much due to economic circumstances as direct challenges by Christian or secular evangelists. Further, while they might resist overt pressure to change their ways, most Maisin would agree in principle that marriages should conform to church rules and that women and men should have complementary, if not necessarily equivalent, statuses.

In this chapter, I explore the history and local ramifications of the Anglican campaign to impose Christian standards of marriage upon the Maisin, as they appeared in the 1980s. I set the stage by relating my first impressions of Maisin marriage and then drawing out the distinctions between indigenous and missionary assumptions about marriage and divorce. The next two sections draw upon archival sources and oral testimonies to outline the missionary push to impose Christian standards and the shape of the Maisin response. In the final ethnographic section, I examine the influences the missionary campaign had upon local understandings of gender, focusing on the experience of the local church women's group, the Mothers' Union. In the conclusion, I briefly discuss more recent changes in Maisin marriage practices in terms of their relationship to gender equality.

A Maisin Wedding

The Anglican mission was run by high churchmen who prided themselves on their sympathetic appreciation of indigenous Papuan culture. They aimed to instil a form of village Christianity that merged seamlessly with the values of strong family ties and simple spiritual faith that they imagined characterised indigenous life at its best. While this view satisfied their theological principles, it also had a pragmatic basis. The mission was extremely poor, in terms of both financial support and staffing. White missionaries lived in not-so-splendid isolation in charge of large districts, relying upon staffs of poorly educated Melanesian teachers who were initially recruited from the Queensland sugar fields to provide the bulk of teaching and preaching at the village level. White and brown mission staff depended heavily upon local people for food and labour.

Consequently, campaigns against 'heathen' practices tended to be selective and vulnerable to local resistance. Missionaries spoke out against customs they considered harmful or offensive to Christian morality but did not require baptised villagers to separate themselves from their 'pagan' neighbours. In principle, Christians were held to a higher standard than unbaptised villagers, expected to regularly attend church services, to send their children to school and to observe church regulations in general (Wetherell, 1977). In practice, the missionaries' tolerance for indigenous culture amounted to a benign indifference to the contradictions between their own worldviews and those of their charges.[1] The assumption that Christianity could be grafted onto native society allowed the missionaries to focus their energies on rules rather than reform. Therefore, the school day was thoroughly regulated, with students punished for the smallest infractions of teachers' authority. Further, full membership of the church was reserved for those who met its sacramental requirements, including baptism, confirmation and respect of Christian marriage vows. Outside this sphere, Christians continued to participate in customary activities, including initiation ceremonies, traditional dancing and death ceremonies—albeit with some restrictions, depending on the nature of the ceremonies and attitudes of particular missionaries (Barker, 1987).

I chose Uiaku for my research base because I wished to obtain a sense of the long-term ramifications of the Anglican project. The mission had established a church and school there in 1902. Apart from 1917–20, during which time a white priest briefly resided in Uiaku, all the teachers and clergy had been Papuans or other Melanesians. When we arrived in 1982, the Anglican Church was about to celebrate its first decade of independence and most Maisin were at least second-generation Christians. Therefore, Uiaku seemed perfect for my purposes. No aspect of indigenous life occupied the missionaries more than marriage. The mission logbooks from Uiaku and the district base at Wanigela were replete with entries recording efforts by the district missionaries and visiting bishops to educate newly baptised Christians about the church's expectations and

---

1   There were exceptions, notably the Reverend James Fisher, who described himself as the 'warden of the coast' as he launched a vigorous campaign to stamp out a range of local customs such as female facial tattooing and all-night dancing. However, Fisher's campaign of moral reform soon faltered, particularly beyond the head station at Wanigela. Like his contemporary, the Reverend Jennings at Uiaku, he suffered a breakdown and left the mission in 1923 (Barker, 1987; Fisher, 1915).

interventions to break up marriages that were illegitimate in the eyes of the church. I was very interested in learning about marriage practices as a way of gauging the impact of the missionary practice of targeted intervention.

Prior to departing from Canada, I had received a letter from Sister Helen Roberts, a nurse-missionary who was based at Wanigela at the old mission regional headquarters and airstrip. She wrote that we would be most welcome at Uiaku, but that people would be very concerned about whether we had been 'properly' married in a church (we had). Upon arrival in Uiaku, however, nobody seemed interested in our legal marital status; instead, local people came up with a plan to seal our marriage with a customary wedding. Anne and I were promptly adopted by two clans, and, within days, I received a lesson on my obligations to in-laws (mainly plentiful gifts of tobacco and rice). A couple of months later, our romantic notion of Maisin traditions collided with reality. We were thrilled to be invited to a 'traditional' wedding at a small Maisin village to the east. Over the next four days, we sat on a shelter feeling increasingly bored, sweaty, dirty and itchy. Occasionally, an English speaker would pop by to check on us and to assure us that things were about to begin. Sometimes they did, for a short time, followed by long, tedious hours of waiting. It did not help that, after midnight, the local string band plugged a cheap guitar into a scratchy radio amplifier, serenading the assembled in loud falsetto harmony until dawn. I later learned that the action was taking place backstage in earnest negotiations to deal with various slights that threatened to upend the festivities. Thus, Anne and I were introduced to the rather improvised nature of Maisin customary rituals.

Therefore, it did not come as a total surprise to learn that customary wedding ceremonies were exceedingly rare, and church weddings were rarer still. We were relieved when talk of staging such an event for us quietly died down. People were very clear about what was supposed to happen. The delays and general confusion resulted from disagreements (and no doubt some posturing) regarding whether each of the participants had met their obligations and/or shown proper 'respect' to the other side. Given these challenges, most people acknowledged a marriage through a series of private exchanges of food between the extended families involved. Yet even in these cases, reaching a stable state of marriage proved to be anything but simple for many couples. I recorded many marriage narratives of byzantine complexity; tales of intrigue as clan leaders attempted to arrange advantageous marriages; forceful interventions when careful plans went array, sometimes leading to violence; elopements by starstruck lovers disowned by their disappointed parents; whispers of love magic, sorcery and abduction and more.

None of this seemed to have much to do with Christianity. Yet Maisin insisted that the mission had a distinct and necessary role to play. Marriages must be sanctioned by the church, people told me, if they were to be stable and the children baptised. Polygamous unions must be firmly opposed as exploitative, disruptive and, above all, un-Christian. However, each of these principles was compromised in practice. Most couples waited until one or more children had been born and their union felt stable before approaching the priest for a marriage blessing. At the time of my initial fieldwork, five households of the 90 or so in the village were polygamous.

Given first impressions, it would be easy to dismiss the Maisin's acceptance of Christian marriage as superficial, a case of 'Sunday Christians, Monday sorcerers', as an anthropologist working up the coast described local adjustments to mission introductions at this time (Kahn, 1983). The colonial missionaries had often described Maisin as 'recalcitrant' and would almost certainly regard the present-day situation as less of a compromise and more of a failure. Anthropologists might well be tempted to view the case of Maisin marriages as one of cultural continuity in change. Superficial changes in attitudes and practices may occur, but, for the most part, marriage practices conform to the exchange logic that permeates Maisin social action and thought (Barker, 2016). Yet, as I will demonstrate in the remainder of this chapter, the Maisin perception that Christianity is central to local marriage must be taken seriously. The Anglican campaign against customary marriage had a major impact on Maisin society, one that only becomes visible when we consider the wider ramifications of that project alongside the specific influences on marriage.

Marriage Principles

It was inevitable that missionaries and Maisin would clash over marriage because basic values were at stake. Marriage for Maisin exemplifies *marawa-wawe*—literally, the sharing of one's inner self with another—best translated as social amity based upon the balance between the exchange partners. Social amity as a perfect balance, however, is difficult to attain. In the past, Maisin favoured sister-exchanges (*daati*), often betrothing sons and daughters while they were very young. The frequency of such arrangements remains an open question—I recorded only one instance of a successful sister exchange among living Maisin. Older folk recalled two earlier instances, mostly because violence broke out after one of the engaged individuals broke the arrangement by eloping with someone else. Many older Maisin told me of being betrothed when entering their teens for a period of months or years, during which they were called 'husband' and 'wife' while working for their future in-laws, but often the children had other ideas and the engagement would be called off.

Marriage was and continues to be marked by exchanges of food and sometimes material items between the couple's families. One should marry outside one's patriclan and 'blood kin'—roughly figured as descendants of common grandparents. Normally, the women moved to the husband's residence. Maisin strongly preferred their daughters to marry into nearby families—not only for access to her labour but also to use rights to her husband's garden lands. In particular, the new husband marked his debt to his in-laws by providing regular small gifts of food and betelnut, assisting in gardening and other tasks and avoiding the use of their names. Such continuous informal exchanges prepared the ground for formal ceremonial prestations involving extended families. The husband's family reciprocated for the wife and her children either by fostering a child or providing a large bridewealth gift. In return, the wife's brothers organised the initiation of her first-born child. The cycle ended with the death of one or other of the married couple. The affines acquired the property of the survivor and, in return, took responsibility for overseeing their mourning, ending with a ceremony in which the widow or widower was decorated like a young person and released from their obligations to their in-laws (Barker, 2016; Hermkens, 2013).

These general principles permitted a wide variety of variations, depending on contingencies and the personalities involved. No doubt, *marawa-wawe* was less often achieved than referenced as a measure against which the actualities were measured. The point I wish to make here is that, as in other Melanesian societies, Maisin marriage ideals were firmly grounded in principles of reciprocal exchange.

The contrast with Anglican principles could hardly be greater. Adhering to Catholic teaching, the missionaries regarded Christian marriage as an institution ordained by God, one of seven Sacraments that were legally and spiritually binding upon Christians and regarding which no compromise could be allowed. As with baptism or participation in the Eucharist, marriage entailed a lifelong commitment not simply to one's partner but to the church itself. Christian marriage could only be formalised by an ordained priest, preferably in a church ceremony, but minimally with a blessing. Once properly married, the Christian was bound until death to his or her spouse. Divorce was not permitted and a Christian who left his or her spouse was subject to escalating discipline from the church (up to excommunication) unless the marriage was restored or the 'ring' spouse died.

Unlike their contemporaries in Protestant missions, the Anglicans, for the most part, did not justify their insistence on church-regulated marriage in terms of a larger project of regulating the behaviour of men and women within a sanctified Christian family (Jolly & Macintyre, 1989). One finds little rhetoric in Anglican writings that condemns the supposed degraded status of women in native society or the exaltation of Christian domesticity in converts' lives. Instead, they focused their efforts on the reformation of the person, particularly males. The Papuan's 'special weaknesses, from a Christian point of view', observed the first Bishop of the mission, 'are impurity, untruthfulness and a callousness in giving pain, especially to dumb animals' (Stone-Wigg, 1907). Stone-Wigg condemned the 'utter laxity' with which men carried on their affairs with women both before and after marriage. The Papuan's propensity for lying, however, suggested a modicum of guilt upon which the missionaries could work. The first step was to ensure that converts complied with the marriage rule.

In sum, the Anglican position on marriage was grounded in the Christian individual's obligation to obey the dictates of God as represented in the Sacraments. Customary practices complicated missionary efforts to impose Christian marriage. Parents, one missionary complained, arranged marriages 'with an eye more upon the payment made, than upon a girl's wishes. This leads to unhappiness, desertion, and later, perhaps, excommunication' (Somerville, 1945, p. 163). Yet, in principle, native customs, including betrothals, could be squared with the sacramental requirements of the church. The missionary's job was to enforce the rules on their unruly 'children'. If they could be made to respect their marriage vows, converts would themselves reform customary practices as needed.

Disciplining Marriage

In 1917, Bishop Gerald Sharp published a 36-page set of guidelines for priests in the New Guinea diocese that listed expectations, rules, procedures and resources. He devoted the longest sections to marriage, systematically laying out various permutations of acceptable and unacceptable unions, requirements for the marriage ceremony and forms of discipline to be applied to individuals and couples living 'in sin'. The Bishop found such detail necessary because 'lack of recognition of the marriage bond on the part of the natives has led to much difficulty, complication, and disappointment' (Sharp, 1917, p. 17). Ideally, an engaged Christian couple would have their banns read over the course of three weeks in the church before being married in a full Eucharist service by the district priest. The Bishop sorted through numerous complications arising from the fact that many of the first generation of baptised Papuans were already married or betrothed to pagans, setting out guidelines for distinguishing between 'legitimate' pagan marriage (which should continue) and 'concubinage' (which should not), the recognition of the 'true' wife or husband in cases of serial monogamy and the treatment of multiple wives in polygamous marriages.

'Fortunately,' the Bishop declared, 'we live in a country in which ecclesiastical discipline can be, and is, exercised' (Sharp, 1917, p. 14). He also stated that:

> Those living in a state of mortal sin, who have, that is to say, arranged their lives so that they are, for the time, being lived in a manner directly opposed to the plain meaning of the 7th Commandment,[2] must be excluded from all Christian services until they set right their lives. (1917, p. 14)

'Setting right' their lives should begin by asking permission and then faithfully attending Matins and Evensong services, sitting with catechumens in Sunday services and leaving following the recitation of the Nicene Creed. If they persist in sin, the Bishop had no option but to excommunicate:

---

2   The commandment that forbids adultery.

An excommunicated person should not be allowed to go on the mission station for any purpose whatever, except to enquire about his own restoration from the priest or the Bishop. He must not bring or send any food to the missionary for sale; and if he dies excommunicate, he cannot be buried with a service, nor in the Christian cemetery. His own people must bury him in their own way. (Sharp, 1917, p. 15)

Bishop Sharp concluded his list of prohibitions with instructions that missionaries should encourage all baptised Christians to shun the miscreant.

Some years passed between the establishment of the first mission station among the Maisin and the enforcement of marriage rules (Barker, 2005b). In 1902, an Australian lay missionary, Percy John Money, supervised the construction of a massive mission station at Uiaku, with a church capable of serving the entire population of approximately 500 souls. The mission, however, was unable to appoint a white missionary, and progress under a handful of resident Melanesian teachers was slow. In 1914, a newly arrived district missionary based at Wanigela (to the north of the Maisin territory) made Uiaku his special project, visiting the village weekly to prepare a catechumen class for baptism. Three years later, roughly 170 Maisin had become Christians, prompting the mission to turn the Maisin villages into a parish and assign the Reverend A. P. Jennings as its district priest.

Jennings did his best to enforce church authority, particularly with the adolescent boys and girls boarded under his charge on the mission station. Within a few months of his arrival, he was directing the flogging of schoolboys for 'fortification' and, in one incident recalled by Maisin elders more than 60 years later, suspended six girls from communion and ordered their heads shaved and ornaments removed. He records only one intervention in a marriage in the Uiaku logbook, writing of having recruited a government policeman to bring back a schoolgirl who had eloped with an older man who already had two wives. This may have reflected caution as much as need; following Jennings' disciplinary actions, he often had to send his boarders home after their parents refused to provide food for them. The isolation, bouts of malaria and intransigent parishioners steadily wore Jennings down, but it was drumming that eventually ended his short residence. A lover of classical music, the priest could barely abide the steady beat of drums accompanied by the rise and fall of chanting—it is also that Jennings suspected that young people found the greatest opportunities for sexual dalliances during such occasions. Initially, Maisin respected his requests to cease dancing before midnight, so that school children would not arrive exhausted the next day, but this did not last. The last straw occurred in 1920. In response to what the district missionary at Wanigela described as a 'strange snake cult' (to which I will return later), the people of Uiaku took up their drums and feathers, dancing dusk to dawn over the course of weeks. Close to a mental breakdown, Jennings fled.

St Thomas Parish in the Maisin villages continued to be staffed by Melanesian and, later, Papua teacher-evangelists who provided instruction in the schools and non-communal Sunday services. Unlike their Polynesian and Fijian counterparts in the Methodist and Congregationalist missions elsewhere in Papua, they did not aggressively seek to impose their notion of Christian morality upon villagers. Responsibility for instruction or discipline in 'proper' Christian behaviour in Uiaku now fell on the shoulders of the district missionary in Wanigela. Throughout the 1920s, one finds entries on the priest's and Bishop's attempts to enforce mission marriage laws on the Maisin. The following description is typical:

> Edric Mamatu or Emanu married Gameti by native custom but the marriage was not acknowledged. He then took Gertrude sister of Waiko? Rarara & Eric Tama who object to their sister being with Edric. If Edric wants Gameti & will send away Gertrude [sic] marriage with Gameti will be acknowledged. If not Edric & Gertrude will be excommunicated. (Wanigela Log Book, 28 November 1923)

The logbook does not provide a full or entirely reliable record of missionary interventions. The priest made only periodic visits to Uiaku for communion services; therefore, he relied mainly upon reports by teachers and members of the church council concerning sexual affairs and marriages. They were often uncertain of the names of unbaptised villagers and ignorant of the complex family negotiations surrounding marriages. To add to the unreliability, the degree of detail provided in the logbook waxed and waned over time, with some entries only listing numbers of excommunicates during one of the Bishop's visits or vague information regarding discipline. Still, there is enough information to indicate that the mission maintained its strict stance on marriage and divorce through succeeding decades. Eventually, there was some easing of enforcement, particularly once Papuan priests were appointed to the St Thomas Parish, beginning in 1962. The practice of excommunication effectively ended, and church marriages remained exceedingly rare. Most couples 'living in sin' in the eyes of the church sought restoration after the birth of one or two children. Divorced individuals who had remarried could remain under discipline, and their children were denied baptism until they reached adulthood at age 18.

Maisin Responses

Regardless of their own personal exasperation, the district missionaries listed the disciplined and excommunicated in the logbook with a bureaucratic hand. Anglican propagandists took a different tack, favouring purple prose and a heavy-handed paternalism. Taken together, these two styles reveal much of the missionaries' assumptions about their project to enforce Christian marriage. In a near-perfect example of the genre, the Reverend James Benson tells the story of Foa, 'the fairest, sweetest and best of the three of Mandarena, who was the "taumanuma" (i.e., the high chief) of the Uiaku tribe' (Benson, 1923, p. 104). Foa had been betrothed as an infant to Urakueta in Bonando village. After taking Christian instruction, the newly baptised Winifred lets it be known that she wants no part of Urakueta, known to be 'in truth, a worthless scamp'. Urakueta's people stage a raid and steal Winifred, causing her relatives to gather their clubs and spears and attack Bonando. In the fracas, an Uiaku man is clubbed to death. Shocked by their actions, the Maisin fall into a 'sober stillness' as they await the arrival of the district priest. The latter quickly sorts things out, sending the warriors to Tufi to stand trial and arranging for Bonando to compensate Uiaku with shell money— the customary payment for a homicide—on the neutral grounds of the Wanigela mission. When tensions flare up again, the missionary arranges a new home for Urakueta's kin at Wanigela. Winifred also settles at Wanigela, 'waiting for and looking for her true love, and he who wins her will win that which is more precious than all the jewels of a hundred Bonandos, for "a good wife is more precious than rubies"' (Benson, 1923, p. 104).

In this scenario, the missionaries regarded Maisin and other Papuans as childlike. They would only be brought to an understanding of the institution of Christian marriage through patient education and firm discipline. Maisin, however, did not regard marriage as an institution, but rather a locus formed by and around various exchanges. The information that may be gleaned through archival and oral sources strongly suggests that the fight over Winifred had little (if anything) to do with her Christian status. The entry in the Wanigela logbook reveals that Winifred's betrothed had also received baptism. The fight broke out when a senior man in Uiaku took Winifred as his second wife while her betrothed was away working on a distant planation. Therefore, the evidence indicates that the conflict was over a broken sister exchange.

I would suggest that, rather than seeing the mission as offering an alternative form of marriage, Maisin in the early years likely regarded the missionaries' actions as one complication among many that affected marriage negotiations at the time. Winifred's double removal—first to Bonando and then to the Wanigela station—occurred in the significant year of 1921. The previous year had seen the emergence in Uiaku of a 'snake cult' and the hurried departure of Jennings. This movement, an offspring of the so-called Baigona cult of a decade earlier, focused on a crisis of rampant sorcery and death. Ten days after removing Winifred, the district missionary visited Uiaku and took down the names of '84 men reputed to be using lime pots for nefarious purposes' (Wanigela Log Book, 25 April 1921). A month later, he returned to supervise the public destruction of lime pots and the sharing of food to assure that any man fasting would lose his power. The clans in conflict over Winifred symbolically destroyed war clubs at the same gathering.

The causes of the panic cannot be known, although it is noteworthy that it occurred during the years of the worldwide influenza pandemic. Sickness placed a premium on children. At the time, the Resident Magistrate noted that 'several people have taken a second wife on the plea that the first has not borne any children' (Muscutt, 1921). Other factors also likely affected marriage negotiations. Labour-recruiting began around 1910, and the absence of young unmarried men increased opportunities for polygynous marriages, at least initially. Young labourers returned with goods purchased in eastern plantations, challenging the authority of older men. During this same period, the resident magistrates and police had been putting increasing pressure on Maisin to rebuild their villages, plant coconut plantations to earn money from selling copra and serve as carriers on patrol. In 1918, the government further strengthened its hand by imposing a head tax on adult males, to be paid off either in cash or labour in the new village plantations. This provided an inducement to form larger families, as did the government's new policy of providing five shilling per annum bonuses for young children, a response to the crisis of rapidly declining populations in parts of the Territory. In this context, the case of Winifred's abduction appears as much more than a simple story of a contest between indigenous and Christian forms of marriage.

Such complexities must be kept in mind when reviewing the mission's campaign to establish Christian marriage during the colonial period. The logbook entries listing marriages, individuals under discipline and excommunications imply a one-sided battle that eventually sputtered and failed. There are clues, however, that Maisin drew the mission into local marriage negotiations. Early in 1925, for instance, the district missionary was approached by an unbaptised young couple who requested him to marry them 'thinking thereby to avoid the necessity of doing so in the villages where the subject was unpopular'. He sent them away, only to be visited by the girl's brother who asked if the mission would give permission for the girl to be returned to her mother: 'He too was told that he and the parties concerned must settle the matter themselves as it is not the practice of the missionaries to interfere in the affairs of heathen people' (Wanigela Log Book, 27 Jan. 1925). Evidently, some Maisin had come to accept the mission's participation in marriage negotiations, even if they did not necessarily understand the conception of marriage they worked to impose.

In the early 1980s, I interviewed several elders (who had come of age in the early 1920s) about their experience of the mission and their own Christian beliefs. They listed various things that missionaries opposed, including polygyny, but limited their positive contributions to two: the rudimentary education provided at the school and the bringing of peace. No one suggested that the mission had introduced a new conception of marriage, although a handful of people had been married in church (and some since divorced and placed under discipline for varying periods). Instead, when I introduced the subject of marriage and the mission, conversation inevitably turned to instances where the missionaries, church councillors or the Mothers' Union had intervened to separate a young couple or to prevent a polygynous union. People sometimes mentioned church law, but for the most part, they justified these interventions as preventing fights. One woman related a complex story of several young people who eloped with someone other than their betrothed. The Bishop came to the village and publicly destroyed a tapa cloth bearing the clan emblem of one of the parents to signify the end of the practice of child betrothals. 'There had been so much fighting,' she told me, 'that people were pleased when this law came in' (Interview with Ida Elsie Aibu, Uiaku village, 9 March 1983).

The elders' reference to 'peace' is significant. While missionaries did occasionally portray themselves as peacemakers, they placed far less emphasis on conversion as a dramatic movement 'from darkness to light' than Protestant missions elsewhere in Papua and New Guinea. The idiom of peace-making resonates more with indigenous conceptions of asymmetrical reciprocity (in general) and leadership (in particular). Maisin distinguish between two types of clans, with respective leaders (Barker, 2005a). The higher-ranked *kawo* have the prerogative of hosting feasts on the plaza before their houses, in addition to speaking first at gatherings. The *kawo* build alliances and, thus, make peace. They are assisted by lower ranked *sabu*, who provide food and dance during ceremonies. They are said to be passionate warriors. Maisin liken the relationship between *kawo* and *sabu* as between elder and younger brothers. The *kawo* provide guidance for supposedly hot-headed *sabu*, leading them in times of peace and unleashing them for war. In the 1980s, adult Maisin spoke of the clergy, teachers and missionaries of old in a similar fashion. Like *kawo* (or older siblings or wife-givers), the church gave villagers something of greater value than they received in turn—knowledge and blessings of the Christian God. In return, like *sabu* (or younger siblings or wife-receivers), the villagers owed them 'respect' (*muan*). 'Peace' (*sinan*), on which health, integrity and material success ultimately rely, depended in turn on bringing the mutual gifts offered by mission and village into balance, a state of social amity (*marawa-wawe*).

The attainment of social amity is also central to the Maisin conception of marriage, yet it is difficult to obtain. The most common frictions in Maisin society occur across the marriage line—these frequently cause accusations of sorcery. The involvement of the mission in local marriage arrangements added a complication that villagers no doubt found inconvenient, mystifying or annoying, depending on the circumstances. Yet this same involvement may be useful when marriage arrangements come unglued and tempers threaten to get out of hand. While the practice of infant betrothal does not appear to have been vanquished by the single act of a bishop, it did decline after Christian conversion and was abandoned by the early 1950s.

Over the decades, the mission's campaign to regulate Christian marriage among the Maisin also waned. Although divorce continued to be a problem for the church, the national priests who replaced the missionaries proved reluctant to intervene with young couples 'living in sin'. In a quiet compromise, priests and couples alike tended to wait until children had been born and a marriage appeared stable before conducting a brief blessing ceremony. Bishop Sharp's notion of Christian marriage would remain an ideal for most Maisin. Yet the intervention was not without profound effects. It added to the changes that were diminishing the power of male leaders, which had already been weakened by the forceful ending of warfare and young men's acquisition of new forms of wealth on the plantations. It also increased the ability of young adults to resist and foil their elders' marriage schemes. More subtly, it created a dilemma for more devout Maisin, who now had to come to seek balanced moral relationships not just with their affines, but with their church and God.

I gained a sense of this dilemma from several of the stories people told me of their marriages. Cuthbert, a man in his mid-70s in 1983, had been through short-lived marriages, one with the 'ring wife' of another man, before settling down with Linda. Linda's first marriage had been church-blessed, but her husband abandoned her to join the Papuan Constabulary. She had entered two succeeding unions, only to be rejected when no children were forthcoming. The district missionary and Bishop urged Cuthbert to send Linda away, but he refused. The couple was placed under discipline and denied entry to the church and the mission station. Many years passed and Cuthbert had a dream: 'I saw the church leaders sitting down. They asked, "Who are you?" And I asked, "Where is God?" They replied, "You can't see God and neither can we".' This occurred on Good Friday. The following December, Cuthbert and Linda brought fish and taro to the annual patronal celebration on the station. They continued to do this every year, although they did not attend church services.

Cuthbert explained to me that marrying Linda had been 'my first mistake and I don't want to have two or three mistakes'. 'Mistakes' (*daa*), in Maisin parlance, refer to breaches in reciprocal relationships that invite retaliation. Cuthbert did not blame the church for punishing him and Linda, but it still brought sadness and shame. His dream suggested that the breached relationship had harmed both parties—neither could see God. His and Linda's act of reconciliation marked a movement to restore the bond. The missionary's dilemma remained—Cuthbert and Linda still 'lived in sin'. Yet for Cuthbert, who wept as he told me his story, the weight of separation had been lifted, at least in part. The gathered had happily accepted his gifts at the St Thomas Day celebration, Linda had joined the women cooking the food for the communal feast and he had taken his place among the *kawo* elders garbed in traditional dress, to enjoy the traditional dancing and festivities.

While moving towards reconciliation, Cuthbert and Linda's actions could not overcome the church's strict prohibition on divorce. They remained on the list of former congregants banned from receiving communion. By the 1980s, concerns about reconciling Christian and indigenous marriage commitments were beginning to be overtaken by a fear that many young people were avoiding both. Many young people had taken advantage of the opportunities provided by both the mission and the government for advanced education in the post-War period and resettled in urban areas as they took up employment during the late colonial and early independence periods. Even as they lost some control over their migrant children, the ageing population in the Maisin villages scolded remaining 'school-leavers' for being self-willed in their sexual activities and choices of partners. As evidence, they pointed to the growing numbers of unmarried pregnant girls. In condemning this supposed trend, the clergy and villagers united in 'cleaning up' after sexual liaisons resulted in births, by forcing couples into marriage (although not always with the biological fathers). The 'traditional' wedding that Anne and I attended in the early months of our fieldwork originated as an effort to impose control over such an unsanctioned union.

Reconfiguring Gender Relations

The Anglican campaign to impose Christian marriage had wider implications for gender relations in Maisin society. In his seminal essay, 'Missionary occasions', Burridge wrote that 'the missionary's dilemma, which cannot be escaped, focuses on the crucial institution of marriage'. Christian marriage, he continued, 'connotes ideally the union in love of initially equivalent souls each of which finds salvation in the love of God, each other, and others'—that is, an ontological equivalence between women and men before God. Further, he explained 'that equivalent ontological status, whatever the imperfections of the transient social order, is all-important' (Burridge, 1978, p. 23). This principle lies at the heart of Christianity as a metacultural phenomenon; it creates endless problems for missionary and convert alike, because it is entirely unclear how or if any particular social order could live up to this ideal.

Protestant and Catholic missions operating in Papua approached gender in distinctive ways that reflect underlying theological and institutional differences. The London Missionary Society and Methodist missions in Papua built their local organisations around married couples. Whether a white couple in a head station or Islander teacher and his wife in a village, the missionary ideally modelled a 'civilised Christian home' (Langmore, 1989). Larger 'industrial' mission stations, such as Kwato near Samarai, provided men and women with training in their respective domestic skills, such as boat building for men and sewing for women, although their ability to enforce conformance to middle-class European norms (on which they modelled the family) tended to be limited to converts recruited to themselves become evangelists (Wetherell, 1996). The emphasis in the Roman Catholic and Anglo-Catholic missions, in contrast, was on 'the community, the total mission family' (Langmore, 1989, p. 82). They sought to impose a hierarchical Christian order, loosely based on a romantic notion of the medieval church, in which the local priest served as the 'father' over his parish, under the bishop and under God. Ideally, if not entirely in practice, the Anglican missionary was a celibate. Equally importantly, the focus of mission life was less on the family than on adherence to the daily round of worship and communal sharing. Whereas the better endowed Protestant missionaries hired servants to work in their households, Anglicans made a virtue of relying on the generosity of local villagers. Through vocation as much as necessity, they were prone to tolerate (or conveniently ignore) local behaviours that would have offended many of their Protestant colleagues—as long as the essentials of Christian membership were respected.

Such differences help to explain why Anglican missionaries focused narrowly on enforcing marriage vows, rather than undertaking a more ambitious project of reforming the family or gender relations. This is not to suggest, however, that the mission's intrusions were without effect. With the important exception of church offices, the Sacraments did not distinguish between males and females. From the beginning, girls and boys attended school and church together. They shared the experience of baptism, received Christian names, were confirmed as members of the church by visiting bishops, and were served the eucharistic host by district priests. Females and males sat in segregated areas in the classroom and church, but this shared experience still suggested a certain type of equivalency that was contrary to the indigenous social order that sharply differentiated the genders, both in their working roles and physical substance. Only males could advance to church leadership, but women assumed responsibility for preparing the church for worship, for gathering and cooking food for Christian festivals, and so forth. I have found no evidence that Maisin considered the church a feminine domain, as Ericksen suggested for Presbyterians on Ambrym in Vanuatu (Eriksen, 2008); nevertheless, it provided a space in which Christian women could gather, work together, gossip and joke away from the purview of brothers, fathers and mothers-in-law.

Ultimately, however, the mission had its most direct impact on Maisin gender relations through its long-running efforts to enforce its marriage rules by recruiting converts in good standing to the cause. In 1920, Jennings formed a church council whose main task was to assure compliance with church rules, especially marriage. The council, which comprised males who represented different hamlets in the village, does not appear to have been very active. A significant shift in the church's relationship with the Maisin began in the late 1940s, in the aftermath of World War II, in which Maisin had served as carriers for the Australian army in the Kokoda-Buna campaign. Inspired by the creation of a village cooperative at Gona under the supervision of an Anglican missionary, the Maisin, in addition to many others in the Northern District, began their own Christian cooperatives, starting plantations of coconuts and cacao in hopes of generating funds for local economic development. Initially encouraged by the mission, these efforts had a strong spiritual overtone that concerned local government officers, who were worried about 'cargoism' (Barker, 1996). These were entirely male endeavours, but during the same period, the mission began introducing chapters of the Mothers' Union at some of its district stations, under the supervision of female lay missionaries.

Maisin women took notice of this. By 1948, a small group of younger Christian women, who were in good standing with the church, had organised a chapter in Uiaku—others soon followed in the rest of the Maisin villages. Missionaries regarded the Mothers' Union as an auxiliary organisation. In addition to assisting women in their spiritual lives and during times of sickness, the Mothers were expected to assist the local clergy, particularly in cleaning the church for services, and help the all-male church council to enforce church discipline. The pioneers who formed the

Uiaku Mothers' Union saw it as something greater than this, associating the creation of the Union with the liberation of women from customs such as the shearing of a new wife's hair upon marriage and self-laceration at the time of deaths. They spoke of energetic intervention to prevent men from taking on multiple wives. They also took great pride in forming an organisation with officers and economic initiatives, specifically the sale of decorated tapa cloth through the mission, equivalent to those in the male-run cooperatives. As evidence of their success, they pointed to the sewing machines they had purchased from tapa sales in addition to their financial contribution to the building of the first iron-roofed church in 1962 and the mission's appointment of a Papuan priest to the St Thomas Parish.

In the early 1980s, the Mothers' Union appeared but a shell of its former self—small, with ageing members. But looks were deceiving. Its members included the most experienced artists in the traditional forms of tapa and facial tattoo design—women who enjoyed a steadier income than most—in addition to elders, who were knowledgeable in clan histories and traditional healing. On church festival days, particularly the annual Ladies Day, the Mothers proved adept at organising young women (including some under church discipline) to gather food, cook, serve and dance. Occasionally, during community meetings at which the senior men discussed economic development projects, the funding of the clergy or the unending failures of the village cooperatives, a Mother would stand up to remind the men that much of the funds came from their tapa sales—therefore, they needed to come up with their own ways of making money and not push the women so hard. The Mothers' Union came into its own during the late 1990s. The Maisin rejection of industrial logging attracted a wave of attention and support from international environmentalists and their allies (Barker, 2016). Tapa was immediately identified as a sustainable economic alternative to logging; consequently, sales increased enormously. Much of this sudden wealth was captured by men within houses and the political leadership. However, as happened elsewhere in the region, the non-governmental organisations took women's role in development as a key mandate and tended to regard women's voluntary organisations as more responsible with funds than men's. The Mothers' distinctive blue skirts became increasingly visible as the chapter expanded in membership; the Ladies Day celebration competed with the patronal feast day in size; the Union purchased its own dinghy, and its leaders regularly attended regional assemblies. Further, when the parish priest attempted to commandeer the dingy, the Mothers threatened to go on strike—he quickly backed down (Barker & Hermkens, 2016).

The Mothers' Union cannot be described as reformist, let alone radical, in terms of gender equality. Its views on marriage and the respective roles of men and women were extremely conservative. Rather than breaking with past gender relationships, the Mothers ratcheted up the already considerable authority of a mother-in-law over her sons' daughters and, to a lesser extent, the daughter-in-law's kin, who were obliged to offer her respect in the form of name avoidance and gifts of food, labour and wealth. In this way, the traditional ideal of *marawa-wawe*—a balanced exchange relationship—became fused with the ideal of Christian marriage, a domain now dominated not by clergy but senior church women.

Conclusion

On the afternoon of 24 October 1982, people gathered on the Uiaku mission station to discuss the problem of disobedient young people, who had not 'respected' the church by attending services or, in the case of those whose parents were under discipline, seeking baptism on their own. The parish priest opened by venting his frustrations with both the youth and their families. He urged them to mend their ways, as one never knew what the future would hold. He noted the case of R, who had been church secretary when he arrived in St Thomas Parish but then took a second wife. 'R', the priest continued, 'still is a faithful man. He bears the burden of being cut off from the church. He didn't expect to be in this position. One day, he might go back to his wife [i.e., send away his second wife]. He is a good Christian man.' R sat quietly through this speech—in fact, R had called the meeting. The missionaries had long since departed, but the dilemma over marriage persisted.

In the distant past, the 'big men' in Maisin society commonly practised polygyny. Yet it would be as misleading to argue that R's marital status represented a traditionalist's rejection of Christianity as to assume that, due to the continued use of thatch and sago, the design of village houses remained untouched by change. Indeed, in one important respect, the missionary project enjoyed considerable success. Limiting themselves to enforcing sacramental marriage, the missionaries generally left Maisin to work out the implications for family and gender relations. Various adjustments and compromises ensued. The Papua New Guinean clergy who had replaced the foreign missionaries learned to turn a blind eye to the previous sexual and marital histories of couples whose marriages they blessed and children they baptised; thus, they preserved the ideal of church-sanctioned marriage. Villagers quietly abandoned child betrothals and sibling exchanges while continuing to articulate marriages through a series of lifelong exchanges between affinal kin. Finally, when conflicts arose, as they regularly did, over matters such as an 'improper' marriage or overly delayed bridewealth payment, some senior voices would appeal to the values of Christian fellowship or urge a gift to restore social balance— often both—to maintain peace. This is not to suggest that peace could always be obtained. Breaches of ideals, real and imagined, fuelled near-constant gossip, recriminations and rumours of sorcery. Christian marriage and balanced exchange were ideals that existed in tension not only with each other but also with the subjective perceptions of fellow villagers. They oriented behaviour and its evaluation but did not determine it.

Marriage provides a privileged location in which to assess gender relations. As Macintyre noted in a recent essay, the 'study of gender and sexuality in Melanesia has long been structured in terms of the theoretical concerns of anthropology as a discipline' (2019, p. 285). Such concerns have largely centred around questions of male domination of females, gendered agency and conceptions of the person and gender in indigenous Melanesian culture. However, even as debates waxed and waned within and between these concerns, historical and anthropological research has revealed how wider social, economic and religious changes have profoundly transformed the contexts in which people 'interact and perceive themselves … The concomitant changes in gender relations have been profound and disruptive of earlier conceptualisations of male and female identity' (Macintyre, 2019, p. 288).

Through most of the twentieth century, the Anglican mission had the most direct impact upon Maisin gender relations, primarily through its campaign to impose sacramental marriage. At the time of my earlier fieldwork in the 1980s, the Maisin drew a sharp distinction between the 'village', 'government' and 'mission' spheres of social and political activities (Barker, 2007). This masked the degree to which the mission campaign ramified through society as a whole and affected not only the conception of marriage but also customary practices. Since this time, changes in gender ideologies and practices have become increasingly visible and profound. Several factors have contributed to this—the most immediate has been through engagement with international environmental activists, who (since the mid-1990s) have partnered with the Maisin to block industrial logging in their traditional territories, while also fostering alternate sustainable local development. Although vocally supportive of Maisin 'culture', many of these same activists are strongly committed to empowering women, whom they have insisted should serve in equal numbers on local committees (Barker, 2016). Over the long term, however, influences from beyond the villages have had a more lasting impact. Many Maisin have attended at least high school and, today, at least a quarter of those born in the villages now reside in urban areas, where many hold well-paying jobs. Many have married non-Maisin and/or left the Anglican Church for other denominations, exposing them to alternative traditions of gender and marriage. Although the villages are physically more isolated than in the late colonial and early postcolonial eras (due to the closing of local airstrips), considerable movement occurs between rural and urban areas. Maisin, particularly younger people, are increasingly exposed to representations of compassionate marriage in church sermons, television programs, commercial advertising and social media. Such representations are widely influencing young people's understandings of courtship, sexuality and marriage choice and mutuality (Cox & Macintyre, 2014).

In Uiaku, as elsewhere, such changes disrupt the old certainties, prompting confusion, resentment and resistance, particularly (but not only) from older generations. As Ryan Schram aptly described, in terms of the Auhelawa people of nearby Duau (Normanby Island), the Maisin appear to have entered a 'post-cultural' era, in which all the received guidelines for behaviour appear to be up for negotiation (Schram, 2018). All the same, memories of custom and the notion of sacramental marriage will likely continue to be touchstones as Maisin adjust their expectations and practices of marriage. On our last visit to Uiaku in 2007, Anne and I met a woman who had left an abusive relationship in town to marry (village-style) an old sweetheart. The couple clearly regarded their marriage as a relationship built on mutuality, yet they submitted to the customary demands of their respective in-laws, adhered to the traditional division of labour in the garden and at home and expected to arrange a bridewealth exchange in the near future. Couples continued to avoid church marriage in favour of blessings after the birth of several children, but a simplified version of the 'traditional' wedding ceremony, like the one we had experienced in 1982, continued and had become more common. We learned that we had become exemplars of the tradition because it was universally believed that our adoptive clans had married us in the 'traditional' fashion when we first arrived in the village.

References

Barker, J. (1987). Cheerful pragmatists: Anglican missionaries among the Maisin of Collingwood Bay, Northeastern Papua, 1898–1920. *Journal of Pacific History, 22*(2), 66–81. doi.org/10.1080/00223348708572553

Barker, J. (1990). Mission station and village: Cultural practice and representations in Maisin society. In J. Barker (Ed.), *Christianity in Oceania: Ethnographic perspectives* (pp. 173–196). Lanham, MD: University Press of America.

Barker, J. (1996). Village inventions: Historical variations upon a regional theme in Uiaku, Papua New Guinea. *Oceania, 66*(3), 211–219. doi.org/10.1002/j.1834-4461.1996.tb02552.x

Barker, J. (2005a). Kawo and Sabu: Perceptions of traditional leadership among the Maisin of Papua New Guinea. In C. Gross, H. D. Lyons & D. A. Counts (Eds), *A polymath anthropologist: Essays in honour of Ann Chowning* (pp. 131–137). Auckland, New Zealand: University of Auckland.

Barker, J. (2005b). An outpost in Papua: Anglican missionaries and Melanesian teachers among the Maisin, 1902–1934. In P. Brock (Ed.), *Indigenous peoples and religious change* (pp. 79–106). Leiden, Netherlands: Brill. doi.org/10.1163/9789047405559_006

Barker, J. (2007). Taking sides: The post-colonial triangle in Uiaku. In J. Barker (Ed.), *The anthropology of morality in Melanesia and beyond* (pp. 75–91). Aldershot, England: Ashgate.

Barker, J. (2016). *Ancestral lines: The Maisin of Papua New Guinea and the fate of the rainforest* (2nd ed.). Toronto, Canada: University of Toronto Press.

Barker, J. & Hermkens, A.-K. (2016). The Mothers' Union goes on strike: Women, tapa cloth and Christianity in a Papua New Guinea society. *The Journal of Anthropology, 27*(2), 185–205. doi.org/10.1111/taja.12193

Benson, J. (1923). The crown jewels of Bonando. *Australian Board of Missions Review, 15*(6), 103–105.

Burridge, K. (1978). Introduction: Missionary occasions. In J. A. Boutilier, D. T. Hughes & S. W. Tiffany (Eds), *Mission, church and sect in Oceania* (pp. 1–30). Lanham, MD: University Press of America.

Cox, J. & Macintyre, M. (2014). Christian marriage, money scams and Melanesian social imaginaries. *Oceania, 84*(2), 138–157. doi.org/10.1002/ocea.5048

Eriksen, A. (2008). *Gender, Christianity and change in Vanuatu*. Aldershot, England: Ashgate.

Fisher, J. E. J. (1915). The warden of the Coast. *Australian Board of Missions Review*, *6*, 167–169.

Hermkens, A.-K. (2013). *Engendering objects: Dynamics of barkcloth and gender among the Maisin of Papua New Guinea*. Leiden, Netherlands: Sidestone Press.

Jolly, M. & Macintyre, M. (Eds). (1989). *Family and gender in the Pacific: Domestic contradictions and the colonial impact*. Cambridge, England: Cambridge University Press.

Kahn, M. (1983). Sunday Christians, Monday sorcerers: Selective adaptation to missionisation in Wamira. *Journal of Pacific History*, *18*(2), 96–112.

Langmore, D. (1989). *Missionary lives: Papua, 1874–1914*. Honolulu, HI: University of Hawai'i Press.

Macintyre, M. (1989). Better homes and gardens. In M. Jolly & M. Macintyre (Eds), *Family and gender in the Pacific* (pp. 156–169). Cambridge, England: Cambridge University Press.

Macintyre, M. (2019). Gender relations and human rights in Melanesia. In E. Hirsch & W. Rollason (Eds), *The Melanesian world* (pp. 285–299). London, England: Routledge. doi.org/10.4324/9781315529691-16

Muscutt, C. A. (1921). Patrol report to Collingwood Bay, 25 April–26 May. Cape Nelson Station, Box 6518. Port Moresby: National Archives of Papua New Guinea.

Schram, R. (2018). *Harvests, feasts and graves: Postcultural consciousness in contemporary Papua New Guinea*. Ithaca, NY: Cornell University Press. doi.org/10.7591/9781501711015

Sharp, G. (1917). *Diocese of New Guinea: Its rules and methods*. Dogura.

Somerville, E. (1945). *Our friends the Papuans*. Sydney, NSW: Australian Board of Missions.

Stone-Wigg, J. M. (1907). The Papuans: A people of the South Pacific. In H. H. Montgomery (Ed.), *Mankind and the Church*. Retrieved from anglicanhistory.org/aus/hhmontgomery/mankind1907/stone-wigg01.html

Wanigela Log Book. (n.d.). Box 25, Anglican Archives, New Guinea Collection, Michael Somare Library, University of Papua New Guinea.

Wetherell, D. (1977). *Reluctant mission: The Anglican Church in Papua New Guinea, 1891–1942*. St Lucia, Qld: University of Queensland Press.

Wetherell, D. (1996). *Charles Abel and the Kwato Mission of Papua New Guinea 1891–1975*. Carlton South, Vic.: Melbourne University Press.

7

Gendered Ambition and Disappointment: Women and Men in a Vernacular Language Education Movement in Melanesia

Debra McDougall

Introduction

'They ruin us when they teach English first'

> –18-year-old man of Ranongga Island,
> Solomon Islands

Young people of Solomon Islands are expected to learn to read and write in English, a language that many do not speak or understand well. Most rural children grow up speaking one (sometimes several) of the country's more than 70 indigenous languages as well as the neo-Melanesian English-based creole Pijin; some urban children learn the indigenous language of their rural-born parents or grandparents, but most grow up speaking Pijin, which is the language of urban life (Jourdan, 2013). Multilingualism, rather than monolingualism, is the norm rather than the exception in Solomon Islands; people move fluidly between different indigenous languages, Pijin and English. Yet few feel entirely confident in English—the country's official language, the language of status and the language of schooling. Even tertiary-trained teachers often lack confidence in their mastery of English and use Pijin as the language of instruction (Tanangada, 2013). English-only education is particularly devastating for rural children, who are already disadvantaged in the Solomon Islands educational system.

For decades, scholars of multilingual education and language policy have argued that children learn best when taught in their first language (Ball, 2011; Lo Bianco, 2015; United Nations Educational, Scientific and Cultural Organization, 1953). Resistance to first-language education policies is often based on the false assumption that the sooner children learn a standardised national or global language, the more likely they are to master it. In fact, longer and more intensive study of a first language almost always leads to better levels of literacy in the national or global standard. Ten years ago, the Solomon Islands Ministry of Education and Human Resource Development (MEHRD) adopted a policy that embraces the right of children to be taught in vernacular languages for these sound pedagogical reasons and to affirm cultural diversity in the country (Jourdan, 2013; MEHRD, 2010). Unfortunately, the policy has not been implemented beyond two pilot projects.[1]

Outside the formal system, however, some individuals and communities have established schools that promote the use of vernacular language. Gegeo and Watson-Gegeo (2012), for example, describe an initiative among Kwara'ae people of North Malaita that began in the years following the 1998–2003 ethnic crisis. This crisis caused both a nation-wide disruption to schooling and a massive influx of Honiara residents whose parents or grandparents came from Kwara'ae, but who lacked linguistic and cultural knowledge that is essential to rural life. Such initiatives form part of the highly localised autonomy movements discussed in the Introduction (Bainton & McDougall, this volume)—instances in which remarkable leaders mobilise communities to do for themselves what colonial or postcolonial governments have failed to do.

---

1   Advocates of multilingual education in Solomon Islands are frustrated by the slow rollout of the policy; however, the fate of a similar policy in nearby Papua New Guinea (PNG) illustrates the negative consequences of hasty implementation. In PNG, transitional bilingual education was established in the late 1990s without sufficient teacher training or curriculum materials. Many parents and teachers blamed vernacular language education, in addition to other reforms including outcomes-based education, for poor educational outcomes. By the end of 2012, then prime minister Peter O'Neill led a return to a system that used English as both medium of instruction and subject of study from early primary school (Devette-Chee, 2015; Litteral, 2015; Merlan & Rumsey, 2015; Troolin, 2013).

My focus in this chapter is the Kulu Language Institute of Ranongga Island, a remarkable language movement that has allowed thousands of youth and adults to study their own language. I draw on material from more than 50 interviews conducted with people involved with the Kulu Institute in November 2017, follow-up work in September 2019 and two decades of study of Ranonggan social life and history (McDougall, 2016). *Kulu* comes from the names of two languages spoken on the Western Province island of Ranongga: Kubokota and Luqa. The work of the Kulu Language Institute began in 1998 as a modest attempt to teach villagers to read a Luqa language translation of the New Testament. Over two decades, it has grown to become a powerful force in the intellectual life of Ranongga. Hundreds of students each year pay modest fees for intensive courses (over one or two weeks) in language study. The curriculum is a sophisticated monolingual description of the structure of the language, authored by Dr Alpheaus Graham Zobule, a Luqa man with multiple tertiary degrees, including a PhD in theology. Like the middle-class Papua New Guineans described in this volume by John Cox, and an earlier generation of tertiary-educated men of the Western Pacific who led 'thought rebellions' in the era of global decolonisation (Banivanua-Mar, 2016, pp. 195–204), Zobule is committed to using his formidable intellect and training to help people of his home island. While other vernacular language programs in the country focus on basic literacy, students at the Kulu Institute move far beyond literacy to explore the underlying structures and expressive possibility of Luqa language (McDougall & Zobule, forthcoming).

The young man quoted in the epigraph grew up on his father's land, speaking Luqa as his first language. Like most speakers of Luqa, he understands Kubokota. He also speaks a language of Choiseul Province (his mother's first language), Solomon Islands Pijin and English, which he studied for 12 years in school. On the face of it, he seemed to be an education success story; he had passed the competitive examinations that push a majority of students out of upper secondary education. And yet he told me about how ashamed he always felt in school when he was called upon to stand in front of the class and read aloud. After taking the first intensive course in Luqa language in his home village, he decided to withdraw from his final year of secondary school to complete the sequence of courses on Luqa grammar. In the Kulu classrooms, he learned to enjoy reading and speaking in front of others. In this way, he lost his sense of shame.

Humiliation is an emotion that is too commonly experienced in schools all around the world, particularly for students from socioeconomically, ethnically or racially marginalised populations. As global and national programs promise 'education for all', and more and more young people invest their hopes in schooling, they often find their 'dreams made small'—the title of Jenny Munro's (2018) powerful study of the schooling experiences of Papuan Highlanders in Indonesia (see also Munro, 2013). Solomon Islanders rarely encounter the bald racism that Papuans suffer in secondary and tertiary schools dominated by non-Papuan Indonesians, but Munro's analysis of processes of 'belittlement' is nevertheless relevant to schooling within the independent nations of the Western Pacific. In Solomon Islands, like Papua (Munro, 2017), there is a gendered dimension to hope and humiliation in schooling. Many young men with whom I spoke expressed anger, frustration and dismay about schooling; they told me how disappointed and uncertain they were regarding their futures. Young women were also critical of English-only schooling, but they rarely seemed angry. They were far more optimistic about their futures than young men were.

Like others in the collection, this chapter draws inspiration from the work of Martha Macintyre. Across her writings, Macintyre has insisted that contemporary forms of gender inequality should be understood in the context of colonial and postcolonial histories, rather than some imagined traditional culture (see e.g. Macintyre, 2017). This approach is evident across her ethnographic work, from rural Tubetube (Macintyre, 1987, 1988), to mining compounds in Lihir (Macintyre, 2006, 2011a) and among urban working men and women (Macintyre, 1988, 2000, 2008, 2011b).

I also build on studies of contemporary masculinity in the Pacific (e.g. Biersack, 2016; Jolly, 2008), particularly work that has focused on the struggles of non-elite men who are increasingly excluded from positions of power in their own societies. These struggles have formed an ongoing concern for Laura Zimmer-Tamakoshi, who has documented intergenerational conflict and the increasingly chaotic modes of leadership that followed the decline of traditional 'big men' (Zimmer-Tamakoshi, 1997, 2016, this volume; see also Gibbs, 2016). Chapters in this volume by Deborah Gewertz and Frederick Errington and Dan Jorgensen highlight the violent behaviour in which some men engage, when faced with irrelevance or powerlessness. Fortunately, not all the emergent masculinities are so depressingly destructive of self and community. In the face of colonial humiliations, some Pacific men have re-embraced warrior identities (Tengan, 2008), often in the arena of sport (Calabrò, 2016). Moreover, like men all over the world, many men of the Pacific have been drawn to the gentle patriarchy of Pentecostalism, a form of Christian faith that scholars have argued is appealing to both men and women, due to the way that it curbs excesses of male power and draws men back into centre of domestic life as husband, father and head of the household (Brusco, 1995; Eves, 2016; Cox & Macintyre, 2014).

In this chapter, I analyse gendered experiences of education in Solomon Islands, expressed through the reflections of students and young teachers involved in the Kulu Language Institute. Inequality is obviously harmful to those of lower economic means, social status and educational opportunities. Scholarly research on inequality provides a more counterintuitive insight—socioeconomic inequality is also harmful to those who are on the top of the rankings (Wilkinson & Pickett, 2009). In the cases I discuss, young men enjoy privileged access to schooling. Until recently, parents were much more likely to pay school fees for boys rather than girls. Boys continue to undertake far less domestic work than girls and teenage boys are rarely expelled from school when they impregnate girls, nor are they burdened with the care of children born outside marriage. Yet these privileges do not necessarily benefit young men. Rather than feeling empowered, many feel worthless and unable to live up to expectations. The Kulu Language Institute has opened a path for some young men to reconceptualise their lives and envision a positive future for themselves and their communities.

Education and Gender Inequality in Solomon Islands

In Solomon Islands, and in many developing country contexts, women and girls face more significant barriers to education than their brothers, barriers poignantly illustrated by a recent report that built on the insights of adolescent girls themselves (Plan International, 2019). Most families struggle to pay for the costs of education. Where schooling opportunities are scarce, they choose to prioritise the education of boys over girls. With minimal access to contraception or sexual information, romantic relationships forged in school often lead to pregnancy, which is stigmatised and leads to young women—but not young men—being expelled from school. Women and girls are also subject to violence, including sexual violence, and often do not feel safe in school or while travelling to school. Girls and young women contribute far more labour—approximately 75 per cent more—to the functioning of urban and rural households than boys and young men. Despite ongoing inequity and the significant barriers to education faced by women, however, educational opportunities for women have expanded dramatically over the last generation.

Over 20 years of research on Ranongga, I have noticed shifts in attitudes among parents, who seem to be more committed to sending both daughters and sons to school. Many still worry that girls will fall pregnant if they are away from home at school. Yet there is also a sense that girls who obtain waged employment are more likely to use it to support their extended families than boys are. These shifting attitudes are evident in the life story of a woman whom I address as 'auntie'. She was the youngest of 14 children in a prominent post-War Ranonggan family and excelled in school, but her father and elder brother refused to pay her school fees. They had invested their hopes and funds in her brother and expected her to stay home and look after the family until she married and had a family. If she went to school, they reasoned, she would simply become pregnant, come home and their money would be wasted. Her mother quietly saved household money and paid her fees, allowing her to complete secondary school and then a nursing degree. 'Prove your brothers wrong,' her mother told her. This opposition to women's education did not end within this auntie's generation. When her niece wanted to continue her secondary education in the 1980s, she faced the same objections from her uncle and grandfather. Following a pattern established by her own mother, this auntie supported her niece, who is now a schoolteacher on her way to becoming a principal. Now retired from a successful professional career, this auntie mused on how wrong her father and brother had been. An elder brother who lives overseas sends money for large family endeavours, but she and her niece are the ones who have consistently used their modest salaries to support their rural kin.[2]

Such on-the-ground experiences combine with major shifts in policy, driven in part by aid-donor-driven agendas for increasing access to education and achieving gender equality. Recent MEHRD performance reports include close analysis of the changing levels of gender disparity,

2   Eriksen (2008, p. 80) has observed that remittances paid by educated North Ambrym women working in urban Port Vila are changing attitudes towards education for both women and girls.

reflecting a policy commitment to closing the gap between boys' and girls' levels of schooling. As of the 2009 census, 80 per cent of children aged 6–14 were enrolled in school, an increase from less than 60 per cent in 1999 and less than 40 per cent in 1986 (Solomon Islands Statistics Office, 2012, p. xxviii, 95). During the 1970s, girls were far less likely than boys to attend school. The census indicated that 40 per cent of all women in their 50s in 2009, but only 20 per cent of all men in their 50s, had never attended school. By 2014, boys and girls participated equally in early childhood, primary and junior secondary school. Gender disparity persisted in senior secondary school: in 2014, nine girls were enrolled for every 10 boys in Years 10–12 of schooling, resulting in a Gender Parity Index (GPI) of 0.9 (MEHRD, 2015, p. 6). By 2018, girls had achieved parity with boys in Year 10; further, the GPI of 0.94 in Year 11 and 0.9 in Year 12 also signalled a trend towards equal enrolments (MEHRD, 2019, p. 22). Although more than 90 per cent of all primary and secondary students in Solomon Islands are older than the official age of enrolment, girls are slightly less likely to be over-age than boys, which suggests that they are either more likely to start on time or less likely to be held back a grade (MEHRD, 2019, p. 21). By all measures, there has been a steady and significant expansion of educational opportunities for Solomon Islander girls and women over the last generation.

The commitment to expanding basic (Years 1–9) education has meant that more students are in school for longer periods all over Solomon Islands. Due to this expansion, the cost of education has become a significant burden for nearly all Solomon Islands families. Under the fee-free basic education policy of Solomon Islands, no fees are charged for students in Years 1–9. However, school boards have implemented various kinds of registration fees or parental contributions. On Ranongga, for example, community junior secondary schools (the least prestigious level of such schools, below provincial and national secondary schools) require 'parental contributions' of SBD 1,000–1,500 (AUD 200–270).[3] Senior secondary schools charge fees of several thousand Solomon Islands dollars, in addition to even greater contributions. If fees or 'contributions' are not paid, children are not permitted to attend school.

---

3   This is a considerable sum of money for large rural families. For context, in 2018 Solomon Islands GNI was approximately SBD 19,000 (USD 2,370), according to World Bank Data (data.worldbank.org/country/SB). Parental contributions alone approach 10 per cent of GNI, without including travel or school supplies, and net income is lower than the national GNI in rural areas.

It is not clear that the money spent to keep youth in classrooms for longer periods has positive results in terms of employability, which is the primary motivation that many parents and students see for education. Jobs that required Year 9 education 20 years ago now require a Year 12 education, and today's Year 12 graduates are rarely able to find work. Credential inflation is obviously one aspect of the problem (Dore, 1976). But there also appears to be a decline in the quality of schooling. High school graduates today are said to be less well-educated than their fathers or grandfathers, who only completed primary school. MEHRD reports reveal better results for numeracy than literacy, but generally low levels of achievement; at Year 6 in 2010, 40 per cent of students reached 'moderate' mastery, while 60 per cent demonstrated 'minor', 'minimal' or no 'mastery' (MEHRD, 2013, pp. 31–39). This data from standardised testing resonates with anecdotal evidence that many students are not achieving even basic literacy with six or more years of schooling. On my most recent visit to Ranongga, teachers at the Kulu Language Institute told me of students who came to the Kulu Institute entirely illiterate—unable even to write their names—despite completing nine years of school. They lamented this wasted time and wondered about the long-term effects of such prolonged experiences of failure.

Observers have linked the expansion of access to schooling to a decline in quality, often blaming inadequate teacher training or resourcing (Watson-Gegeo, 1987; Watson-Gegeo & Gegeo, 1992a, 1992b). Beyond problems of curriculum or teacher training, schooling is made more complex because authority and oversight are vested in provinces, which have limited capacity and minimal funding to implement goals (Maebuta, 2013, p. 124). Moreover, despite the rhetorical emphasis on the need for mass education, government expenditure is significantly skewed towards tertiary education (Whalan, 2011, p. 242)—the realm in which women and rural people of both genders are most disadvantaged. Perhaps the greatest overall problem with schooling, however, is its orientation towards narrowly economic outcomes. Even if the education system were more effective in teaching basic numeracy and literacy, it would not fulfil the promise of salaried employment, given that there are far more graduates than there are jobs available.

Goi Is.

Buri

Koriovuku

Vori

New Mala

Kolomali

Patu

Rava

Qeuru

New Bare

KUBOKOTA

Sabala

GANOQA

Pienuna

Kulu Language Institute

Modo

Vonga

Mt. Kela
864 m

Obobulu

Solomon Sea

Kudu

Suava

Baniata

Saevuke

LUQA

Paqe

Aena

Keara

Koqu

Ngaidavala

Ngaikeni

Lale

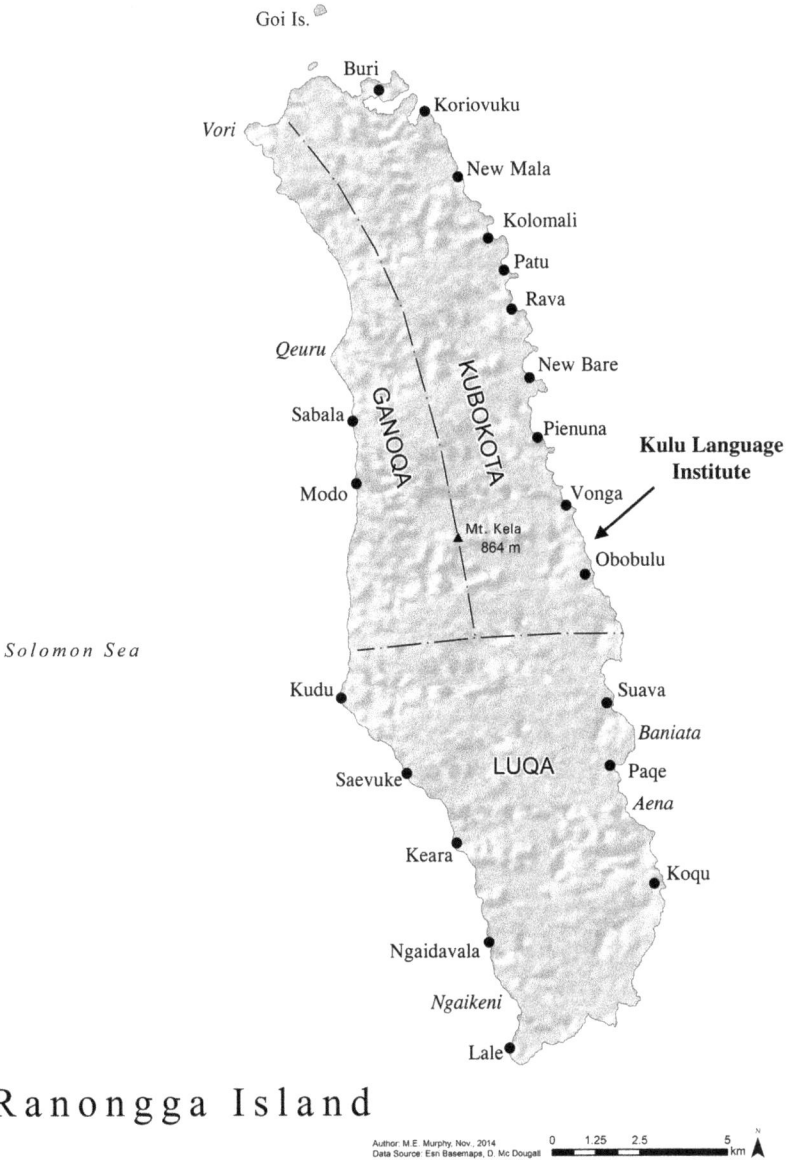

Ranongga Island

Author: M.E. Murphy, Nov., 2014
Data Source: Esri Basemaps, D. Mc Dougall

0   1.25   2.5   5
km

Figure 1: Ranongga Island.
Source: Map by M. E. Murphy. Data source: Esri Basemaps, D. McDougall.

With the massification of schooling, lineages and extended families no longer pool resources to support a single student in further studies. Today, it is mainly parents who struggle to find money for their children to attend school, raising money themselves or approaching the local member of parliament to pay the fees from his constituency development fund. Parents and politicians alike seem willing to support both girls and boys in education. Educational achievement in the 1960s and 1970s, when few men and even fewer women finished primary school, allowed the previous generation of men to move into positions of respect and authority. Despite ongoing inequality in access to upper secondary and tertiary education for women, it is true that young women today enjoy far more possibilities for advanced schooling than their mothers and grandmothers did. For young men today, education and career possibilities seem to be contracting at the same time that men seem to be playing a less important role in domestic life—I return to this point below.

The Kulu Language Institute of Ranongga

The Kulu Language Institute takes its name from the two languages spoken on Ranongga. Luqa is spoken by approximately 3,900 people in the southern half of the island and Kubokota is spoken by approximately 3,400 people in the northern half (see Figure 1).[4] When the first Luqa grammar teachers began in the late 1990s and early 2000s, classes were convened in community halls, under tents or simply in the shade of trees. Today, the Kulu Language Institute has a campus situated on a beautiful stretch of coastal land. Over the past five years, the Kulu school has grown exponentially. By 2018, some 1,500 adults or teenagers—approximately 20 per cent of the entire population of Ranongga—had undertaken at least one workshop or class on Luqa grammar (Zobule, 2018).

I have followed this movement since its beginnings (McDougall, 2012). On a visit back to Ranongga in 2016, I observed how it had grown and began conversations with the director of the Kulu Institute, Dr Alpheaus

---

4   The ISO 639-3 codes are 'lga' for Luqa and 'ghn' for Kubokota, which is also known in the literature as Ghanongga, Ganoqa or Ghanoga language. For further details about Kubokota, see Chambers (2009). Estimates for 2018 speaker populations are based on the 2009 Solomon Islands population census tabulated by ward with 541 people for North Ranongga, 2,514 for Central Ranongga and 3,305 for South Ranongga, with a two per cent annual growth rate for the province. Kubokota is spoken primarily in North and Central Ranongga and Luqa in South Ranongga (Solomon Islands Statistics Office, 2012).

Graham Zobule, about interviewing students, teachers and community members to understand its apparent success and potential challenges. In November 2017, I conducted more than 50 interviews in Honiara and on Ranongga and also observed a week of classes at the Kulu Institute. In 2019, I began work in digitising legacy materials from Ranongga, including my own field recordings, recordings from the now-disbanded provincial culture office and stories produced by Kulu Language Institute.[5] Zobule is a partner in this Endangered Languages Documentation Project, which involves Kulu staff who are transcribing the materials and beginning to produce new audio recordings of people talking about local values and histories. In August 2019, I worked with colleagues from Australian universities, in addition to Zobule and his colleagues in Ranongga and Honiara, to facilitate public lectures and a week-long workshop on vernacular languages (McDougall, 2019).

The Kulu Language Institute curriculum presents a challenging exploration of the structure of local language—it differs from other vernacular language initiatives around the country that teach very young children how to associate letters and sounds in their own language before quickly moving on to English (Burton, 2012; Cox, 2017; Glasgow, Ha'amori, Daiwo & Masala, 2011). Through dialogue with the first generation of Luqa grammar teachers, Zobule developed a corpus of materials, including eight textbooks and thousands of pages of text, that develops a new vernacular metalanguage for describing the grammar of Luqa. This metalanguage metaphorically expands existing vocabulary for family relationships, the structure of plants and words for cutting, grouping and searching.

Four texts comprise the core sequence of classes that are regularly offered at the Kulu Institute (Zobule, 2016). Book 1, titled 'Reading Luqa language', focuses on phonology, the idea of syllables and the meaning of words. Reading comprehension exercises focus on stories written by former students. Book 2 is titled 'The structure of words' and is focused on parts of speech—understanding how words function differently depending upon their relationship with other words in the sentence. Book 3, 'The structure of sentences', explores the structure of noun phrases, clauses and sentences. Book 4, 'Structure of complete writings', focuses on text composition and analysis. In addition to these four core

5   Recordings and texts from Ranongga, Solomon Islands. elar.soas.ac.uk/Collection/MPI1314450. Funded by an Endangered Language Documentation Program Legacy Materials Grant.

courses, Zobule has produced a guide to teaching, illustrated alphabet books in both Luqa and Kubokota and a preliminary course for adults or children with no literacy. Most of the instruction in the Kulu Institute is in and about Luqa; there is also a Kubokota version of Book 1. There are also two books on the grammar of English. Students are not admitted to study English grammar classes until they have completed the sequence in Luqa grammar.

Depending on the level of the class, Kulu classes last between five and 10 days, with six hours of instruction per day. The first-level classes are held in villages wherever and whenever there is sufficient demand. More advanced classes (Luqa Books 2–4 and English) are held on the Kulu campus. Kulu students pay modest fees of SBD 200–400 (AUD 35–70), depending on the length of the course. The fees cover the textbooks (bound photocopies of up to 200 pages), accommodation and food; they also generate a small quantity of revenue to support the Kulu school. In 2017, Kulu teachers began to receive a small payment of SBD 50 (less than AUD 10) for a week-long course. Zobule's wife, Sanny Zobule—who runs their family business, a low-cost rest house in Honiara—financially supports Kulu staff to pursue further training with her husband in Honiara.

The work of the Kulu Language Institute originated during the years when Zobule was leading the Luqa translation of the New Testament. When the first draft of the Gospel of Mark was produced in 1998, he realised that many Ranonggans could not read it; either they had never learned to read or they were unable to read their own spoken vernacular. Zobule's cousin John Tengana began teaching literacy to people of Saevuke village. Saevuke had never had a primary school and its people were ridiculed for their ignorance. Tengana found that Saevuke people were confused by English words such as 'consonant' and 'vowel'. He pressed Zobule to produce Luqa language terms that people would understand. In late 2000, a workshop on Luqa grammar was held in Saevuke, which drew people from all around the island into the study of grammar, including Izikeli Moata of Kudu village. When I interviewed him in 2017, Izikeli recalled that he was surprised by the way the language worked—it captured his imagination. He began to teach alongside Tengana, using materials that Zobule was developing, and the two were eventually joined by Danstone Beck of Paqe village. Zobule calls these men the 'pioneers' of the Kulu

Institute (see Figure 2). They taught Luqa throughout the 2000s, while Zobule was overseas, completing a second Master's degree and a PhD in theology.

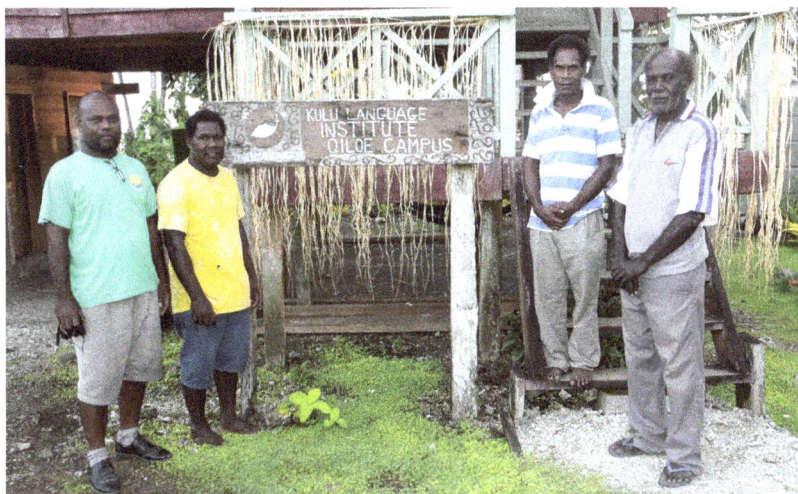

Figure 2: Kulu Director Dr Alpheaus Zobule, with head teacher Izikeli Moata, founding teacher John Tengana and principal Stephen Buka (November 2017).
Source: Photo by Debra McDougall.

In the 2000s, few Ranonngans perceived the value in formally studying a language that they already knew and that would not contribute to their socioeconomic mobility; the fact that the teaching of Luqa grammar persisted after the translation was completed is due to the tenacity of Tengana, Danstone and Izikeli. Tengana attended meetings of the Ranongga circuit of the United Church and inserted workshops on Luqa grammar into the annual schedule. In the absence of funding for transport, the three men walked for hours across and around the island, to deliver the courses. Often hungry and exhausted, they left their wives behind to look after children, garden and generate household income. Danstone was a builder by trade and he used his own funds to photocopy the Luqa materials, so that they would have enough copies for each student to read one during class. Danstone took up residence for nearly a decade in the hamlet of Qiloe to teach Luqa grammar, a relationship that eventually led to the gift of land to the Kulu Institute, which 'anchored' it and provided it with a place in which to grow. Izikeli was serving as head teacher when I stayed on the Kulu campus in 2017.

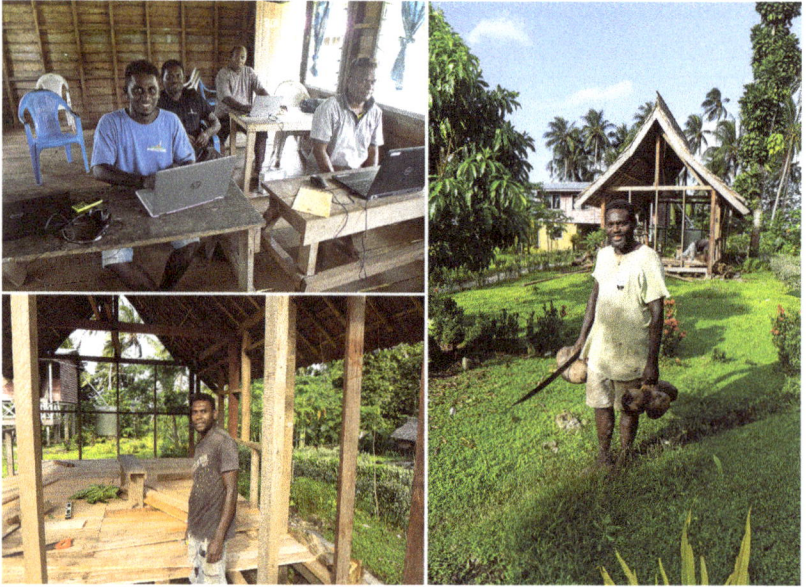

Figure 3: Kulu teachers (clockwise from top left): John Poa Lokapitu (Account Manager) and Aldrin Apusae, Samuel Bakson (Deputy Principal) and Nathan Manoa (Grounds Manager) (September 2019).
Source: Photos by Debra McDougall.

Figure 4: Radence Philipi, apprentice teacher (September 2019).
Source: Photo by Debra McDougall.

It is not a coincidence that the pioneers of the Kulu Institute were Men. These were not ordinary men—few would have made the sacrifices that Tengana, Izikeli and Danstone did. However, even if a Ranonggan woman were to have become as passionate about Luqa grammar as these three, I doubt that she would have been given permission to leave her husband and children behind in the way that these three men did. As of 2019, all leadership positions in the Kulu Institute—principal, deputy principal, finance manager and grounds manager—are held by men (see Figure 3). Most teachers and apprentice teachers are also men, but this is slowly changing. The first female teacher is an unmarried woman now in her 30s; in 2019, she was one of two women undertaking further study in Honiara with Dr Zobule. In September 2019, one of the two apprentices at the Kulu Institute was a young woman (see Figure 4).

Although they do not hold formal leadership positions, women are essential for the everyday running of the school. I have already mentioned Sanny Zobule's critical behind-the-scenes financial support of the school, the teachers and her husband's scholarly activities. Each time I have visited the Kulu campus, the principal and teacher's wives have organised meals for students and visitors. When large numbers of students enrol in Kulu classes during school holiday time, women from nearby hamlets are paid a small fee to assist with cooking. More often, they voluntarily contribute cooked food and garden produce, particularly when the Kulu school hosts visitors. Not all domestic work is done by women—both male and female students are rostered to assist with meal preparation, including late-night shifts baking bread for morning classes, and all students work in the school gardens in the afternoons. Male teachers and apprentices do construction work; they saw and carry timber and other housing materials and construct classrooms and staff houses.

In the very early days of the movement, men were the primary attendees. In the first Luqa grammar workshop held in 2000, for example, I was one of three women present and the only one who had travelled from beyond Saevuke. Most early students were men intending to study theology to become ministers in the United Church, who hoped that learning Luqa grammar would help them understand the new Luqa New Testament and understand English. As the movement grew and spread, women joined in the workshops offered in their villages. Today, young women enrol in the school in slightly higher numbers than young men.

Gendered Ambitions

The massive growth in attendee numbers in recent years is due almost entirely to an influx of youth who are currently enrolled in junior or senior secondary school, who have completed secondary school, or have quit or been forced out of school due to failing to achieve adequate exam results for entry into higher levels of schooling, failing to pay school fees or other circumstances. According to attendance lists and teachers' reflections, female and male students attend in approximately equal numbers. Their reasons for enrolling are simple—they expect it to help them in their formal studies, particularly the study of English. Increasing numbers of trained primary and secondary teachers are also attending the Kulu school, because they have witnessed these effects on their students.[6]

The young men and women who had completed all or some senior high school were critical of the fact that the instruction started with English. One young woman said that learning English grammar in school made learning Luqa grammar easier, but most of the others focused on the negative effects of doing things 'backwards'. Even those who were relatively successful in passing highly competitive exams to move onto higher grades said that everything was 'fuzzy' in normal school, whereas things were clear at the Kulu Institute. Several interviewees likened school learning to poorly prepared meals. As the first female Kulu Language Institute teacher told me, 'they give raw food to children, so they just eat it uncooked'. Some spoke of unripe fruit, and others described it as a jumbled pile, contrasting it with the Kulu curriculum, in which everything is laid out carefully, as one might lay out a feast. Many contrasted the rote learning of school to the more creative work in Kulu, remarking on the way that Kulu teachers 'played with the language' to understand and explain how it works.

Young women who were currently enrolled in secondary school mentioned that they hoped that studying Luqa would allow them to understand the Bible better and use language effectively in all realms of life. Nevertheless, it was clear that their primary goal was learning Luqa to

---

6   At a September 2019 gathering at Qiloe, Zobule addressed the increasing instrumentalisation of the Kulu Institute. Although he was pleased that the school was helping young people, he suggested that everyone, especially adults, should be trying to dig deeper into their own language. The gathering marked the beginning of a new branch of work at the institute—documenting and strengthening local values that are worth preserving in the face of changing ways of life.

succeed in school. One student told me how happy she was when she got to the English grammar section of the Year 11 exam—she found it easy because she had studied with the Kubokota, Luqa and English grammar books. When I asked them about their aspirations, each spoke of finishing secondary school and doing further training—one aspired to study law, another computer work, another teaching and a few were unsure. They also praised the Kulu curriculum for its coherence and seemed to find the intensive format of the Luqa grammar classes helpful. One secondary school student told me that, in school, they skip back and forth between subjects, with too much time between English lessons.

Although they were critical of conventional schooling, none of these young women was as scathing in their reflections as many of the young men. For example, none of them spoke of school ruining them in the way that the young man quoted at the start of this chapter did. This youth was speaking about something far deeper than mere academic failure—schooling seemed to have inflicted an injury to his very sense of self. The Luqa term I have glossed here as 'ruin' is *ngangulu*. Like the Pijin tem *spoil*, *ngangulu* refers to both physical damage and the metaphysical destruction of a curse or sorcery. Other young men told me that they felt that school had tricked or cheated them. Nearly every young man interviewed recalled the way that they felt ashamed of themselves and were unable to stand in front of a group to speak or read. They spoke not only of how much clearer and straightforward the Kulu curriculum was but also the way it has given them confidence. Several of the young men who became apprentice teachers or teachers in the Kulu school recounted how they completed secondary school with no sense of purpose. Even where they succeeded in school, they felt lost and useless; they were ashamed that they had let their families down because they had not found employment.

One young Kulu teacher said that he took a Kulu class only because his brother-in-law suggested it. He reluctantly asked his grandfather for school fees. At the time, he was mocked for studying his own language— people laughed at him for 'going back to kindergarten' after completing secondary school and asked why he was not doing something useful with his life. Yet he persisted, apprenticing himself to Tengana, Izikeli and Danstone and eventually becoming a teacher in his own right. Another teacher told me of his circuitous schooling journey and the feeling that he was disappointing his family, who had valued education highly for two generations. He eventually completed vocational schooling in marine training and worked on ships for several years before returning to his wife's village to be a 'farmer'. Still, he thirsted for some other kind of work and found his calling in the Kulu school, which he first attended simply because it was only a few hundred metres from his house. He was overjoyed when Zobule invited him to become an apprentice teacher. Another young man, a student at the Kulu Institute in 2017, told me of being unable to sit his Year 11 exam because his family could not pay the fee. He thought his future was over, but an uncle has sponsored him to study Luqa grammar, and he now sees work for himself in teaching kindergarten.

These young men spoke of profound personal transformation, a reorientation that was moral and spiritual as well as intellectual. One young man told me that he would probably be in prison if it were not for the Kulu school—before he studied Luqa grammar, he was a thief and smoked marijuana. Another had always been successful in school and had attended a prestigious provincial secondary school. Despite his success, he never felt any confidence in himself:

> It was as though I was chasing the shadow of something, but I couldn't actually grab the thing itself. I didn't know what I was doing, or what school was doing for me. It was though I was flailing around on the surface of the sea; I didn't know anything. Imagine you are on the surface of the sea and grab at a dry coconut floating past. If you don't get a good grip, it slips away. When I came to Kulu and finished the classes, it was as if I had dug down under the surface of the ground. Now I'm able to dig out something strong. It is as if I'm digging under the surface of the earth.

When he completed the vernacular language curriculum, he felt transformed: 'it was as though I was freed from prison'.

Who could have predicted that studying grammar would have such a profound effect on young men's sense of self and worth? Over and over, in my interviews and conversations with young men, they told me not only of their intellectual failures but also moral failings: drinking, stealing and spending all their money on betelnut or cigarettes. Somehow—and no one could really articulate precisely how this was the case—the study of a local language shifted their entire outlook on life. It made them stop feeling like failures and made them respect themselves.

Dispensable Men?

In a volume on how myths of matriarchy may paradoxically support male political dominance, Macintyre (1988) examined two forms of myth on matrilineal Tubetube. The first genre of myth depicts a woman born of sea creatures who leaves her mother to live with a husband. She is ultimately betrayed by her in-laws and abandons her husband to return to the sea. The second type of myth depicts quasi-human husbands who are lazy or stupid and are killed after they impregnate their wives. These 'mythic demonstrations of inadequacies of husbands', Macintyre argued, 'provide a moral basis for a matrilineally constructed social order that depends upon the unity of brothers and sisters' (1988, p. 188). In Tubetube reality, married couples move back and forth between husbands' and wives' families, with burdensome labour obligations to both sides of the family and complex sets of affinal and patrilateral exchanges constituting the flow of social life. In Tubetube myth, the matrilineal social order reproduces itself. Husbands are, ultimately, dispensable.

As in Tubetube and much of island Melanesia, Ranonggan clan identities are traced through mothers, as are deep and existential connections to ancestral land. Women, rather than men, are remembered as apical ancestors in genealogies. Oral historical accounts of events of the late nineteenth century and early twentieth century suggest that women played important roles in arranging marriages, allocating land and welcoming outsiders ashore (McDougall, 2016, pp. 64–91). Myths and humorous folk tales focus on sibling relationships, often depicting what happens when brothers and sisters do not properly take care of one another. Sisters and brothers were understood to be metaphysically linked—a woman who died in childbirth, like a man who died in warfare, became a 'bad ghost' and the moral infractions of a cross-sex sibling were seen as the cause of such a calamity. Despite underlying ideologies of matriliny, and this emphasis on cross-sex sibling complementarity, men possess more political power than women. As Macintyre (1987) argued was the case in Tubetube, this differential power seems to have once been strongly linked to men's engagement in warfare; men held a monopoly on physical violence.

Over the course of the twentieth century, a more straightforward kind of patriarchy emerged in the Western Solomons. Churches recognised fathers and husbands as heads of families and governments recognised brothers (but not their sisters) as leaders of matrilineal clans. Such developments arguably weakened the constitutive relations between sisters and brothers and undermined the cognatic ties among their descendants. The changing political economy has also shaped gendered identities and ownership. From the 1930s to the 1960s, when copra production formed the backbone of the colonial economy, patrilineal inheritance patterns seemed to dominate—coconut plantations belonged to individual men, rather than their matrilineages. When copra prices plummeted in the 1980s, however, things changed. Ranonggan families turned to market gardening to generate cash income. Families work together on both copra production and market gardening. Whereas copra plantations were identified as male property, gardens are mostly identified as belonging to women, and marketing is done entirely by women. Commercial logging commenced on Ranongga's steep hillsides only after more profitable forests elsewhere were exhausted. Battles over landownership in the context of resource capitalism are always fought in the name of matrilineal clans (so-called 'tribes'). Though matriliny lies at the centre of these battles, women are excluded; only men speak for their clans in court and in negotiations with companies. However, rather than bolstering men's authority, involvement in the sordid politics of logging has undermined their moral authority in all other realms. Women are taking on more central roles in the leadership of families and communities and even stepping into neo-traditional 'chief' roles that had always been seen as male (McDougall, 2014).

Macintyre did not directly relate the puzzles of matriliny to the challenges of contemporary PNG women, but her ethnographic studies of educated and employed women seemed to suggest that they are enacting the Tubetube mythic vision of the 'dispensable husband'. She argued that women in mining experience the classic 'double burden' with a vengeance, usually maintaining large gardens while also holding full-time work (Macintyre, 2006). Yet they use the freedom that their wages have given them to break the bonds they find most constraining—particularly relationships with abusive, neglectful or unfaithful husbands. For such women, 'money changes everything' (Macintyre, 2011b). A degree of economic independence has allowed them to reject bonds of marriage to husbands who have been taught for generations that they have the God- and custom-given right to dominate their wives (see also Zimmer-Tamakoshi, 1998; Spark, 2011, 2017). Such independent women are often savagely critiqued—accused of embracing global human rights discourses and the decadent individualist lifestyles that go with them

(Macintyre, 2000, 2012; see also Jolly, 1996; Taylor, 2008). Clearly, though, these women are reshaping, rather than rejecting, the networks of kin relationships that sustain them; they invest heavily in their own children as well as nieces and nephews, an investment that often takes the form of paying school fees.

As more women choose not to marry, marriage is increasingly portrayed as the quintessentially traditional social institution. In reality, marriage has been undergoing continuous change for decades in both rural and urban areas of the Western Pacific (see chapters in Marksbury, 1993). In Ranongga in the late 1990s, when I began my research, premarital sexual activity was common, but when women fell pregnant, marriage was usually arranged. Increasingly, young women have children and are not compelled to marry. Some children are looked after by their grandmothers, while mothers may be away working or studying or even living with a new husband. In the family that I have lived with most often on Ranongga, the generation of women now in their twenties all have children, but few have any relationship with the father of the children. The fathers seem to have no responsibility for the children, and young men seem increasingly inessential in domestic life.

Ranonggans speak of marriage as 'sitting down well'. Despite the fact that not all marriages allow partners to 'sit down well,' the metaphor aptly captures the sense of stability that is lost as marriage declines as a social institution. Prototypically, a husband clears the land for the garden and builds a house for his wife and children; the lack of anyone to help with such work is what unmarried Ranonggan women, and married women whose husbands are absent or neglectful, complain about. Nevertheless, gardening and care of children are primarily seen as the work of women. When women are unmarried, they perform this work within their natal families, continuing to be linked to kin and family. The state of not 'sitting down well' seems to have a more existentially powerful effect on young men, who have no paternal obligations and far fewer responsibilities to their natal families than young women. They are free but also detached—perhaps even dispensable. It seems to me that some of the malaise of young Ranonggan men I spoke to originates in this feeling of being dispensable.

Conclusion

During my most recent trip to Ranongga, I spent a weekend in the village that has become home to me—Pienuna, approximately a 45-minute walk from the Kulu Institute. Twice on Saturday night, my household was awakened by the howls of young men, drunk on home-brewed alcohol. They walked through the hamlet, swearing in Kubokota and English and gathering on the shore that is still referred to as the chief's landing place. Drunken behaviour of this sort is a breach of rules of interaction in Ranongga, where quiet indirect discourse—not shouting or haranguing—characterises public speech. In all my years living in Pienuna, I had only heard such outbursts a handful of times, and they were invariably followed by some sort of formal conflict resolution. Requests for compensation for swearing were often combined with some airing of the underlying problems that had caused the outbursts. Now, I learned, the young men drank and behaved in this way every weekend. No one even tried to stop them.

Young Ranonggan women often feel controlled—their labour is demanded and their sexuality is policed. But they rarely feel useless in the way that young men often seem to. The young men running amok in Pienuna enjoy much greater freedom of movement and behaviour than their sisters; however, this freedom counts for little when they cannot envision a worthwhile life. Their self-destructive behaviour seems like the 'negative agency' that Holly Wardlow (2006) discussed in relation to Huli women. Feeling manipulated, disrespected and disregarded by their natal families, Huli women engaged in casual sexual encounters for money or pleasure and, in the process, they ruined their reproductive capacity—the quality that their male relatives valued most. Might the performatively bad behaviour of young Ranonggan men also be a 'fuck you' (to quote one of the young men yelling in Pienuna village) to their kin and community, who make them feel worthless?

One way to understand the power of the Kulu Institute is to place it within the context of other movements that have promised to transform the lives of people of the Western Pacific. Perhaps the most powerful among these are charismatic Christian revival movements. I have long been interested in the gendered dynamics of these religious movements in Solomon Islands. They seem to provide not only a ground upon which women are able to organise and emerge as collective actors but also a vehicle for new kinds of masculine self-formation (McDougall, 2003, 2009, 2013, 2014; see also Maggio, 2016). Men, in particular, become passionate about religious teachings because they promise a way that they can transform their own lives from the inside out. I have been struck by the similarity between the kinds of testimonies I have heard as part of my research on new forms of Christianity and the testimony of young men involved in the Kulu Institute. Similar stories of profound transformation emerge in Nick Bainton's (2011) study of the Personal Viability movement in Lihir and beyond and John Cox's (2018) research on how fast money schemes continue to attract people, often through evangelical Christian networks.

The Kulu Language Institute resonates with other grassroots social movements that have re-valued local ways of life in periods of rapid social, economic and political change. One such movement has been thriving in Ranongga's nearest neighbour—the 'Simbo for Change' movement focuses on local livelihoods and has inspired a 'revitalised ethic of care for the island' (Suti, Hoatson, Tafunai & Cox, 2020). Many such movements have centred on what is known in neo-Melanesian languages as *kastom*. This term embodies a sense of opposition to European or Western forms of religion, politics or economic life; as David Akin (2013) has observed, *kastom* evokes a continuity with the past that is intended to assert dignity and the right of self-determination in the face of powerful outside forces. The materials of the Kulu Institute are devoid of any reference to *kastom*, nor is there much explicit discussion of the importance of preserving Luqa language or Ranonggan culture. Yet the very process of analysing vernacular language taps into a sense of continuity with the past, making young men like those I have quoted feel 'anchored' in solid ground (McDougall & Zobule, forthcoming).

It seems odd that studying grammar could have such a profound effect on the moral and emotional lives of young people. Unlike words of a language, grammar is not something that people often consciously reflect upon. For many, the power of the study of grammar comes from the way it enables them to move across languages, using insights and analytical skills that have been built up in a language they know to better master English. For some students, the process has also opened up a new understanding of broader sociopolitical and educational structure, allowing them to see that what they imagined as their own personal failures were, in fact, flaws in the system.

References

Akin, D. W. (2013). *Colonialism, Maasina rule and the origins of Malaitan kastom.* Honolulu, HI: University of Hawai'i Press.

Bainton, N. A. (2011). Are you viable? Personal avarice, collective antagonism and grassroots development in Melanesia. In M. Patterson & M. Macintyre (Eds), *Managing modernity in the Western Pacific* (pp. 231–259). St Lucia, Qld: University of Queensland Press.

Ball, J. (2011). *Enhancing learning of children from diverse language backgrounds: Mother tongue-based bilingual or multilingual education in the early years.* Paris, France: UNESCO. Retrieved from unesdoc.unesco.org/ark:/48223/ pf0000212270.locale=en

Banivanua-Mar, T. (2016). *Decolonisation and the Pacific: Indigenous globalisation and the ends of empire.* Cambridge, England: Cambridge University Press.

Biersack, A. (2016). Introduction: Emergent masculinities in the Pacific. *The Asia Pacific Journal of Anthropology, 17*(3–4), 197–212. doi.org/10.1080/144422 13.2016.1186215

Brusco, E. (1995). *The reformation of machismo: Evangelical conversion and gender in Colombia.* Austin, TX: University of Texas Press.

Burton, L. J. (2012). Building on living traditions: Early childhood education and culture in Solomon Islands. *Current Issues in Comparative Education, 15*(1), 157–175.

Calabrò, D. G. (2016). Once were warriors, now are rugby players? Control and agency in the historical trajectory of the Māori formulations of masculinity in rugby. *The Asia Pacific Journal of Anthropology, 17*(3–4), 231–249. doi.org/ 10.1080/14442213.2016.1191530

Chambers, M. R. (2009). Which Way Is up? Motion Verbs and Paths of Motion in Kubokota, an Austronesian Language of the Solomon Islands (Unpublished doctoral thesis). Endangered Languages Academic Programme, School of Oriental and African Studies, University of London.

Cox, J. (2017). Kindy and grassroots gender transformations in Solomon Islands. In M. Macintyre & C. Spark (Eds), *Transformations of gender in Melanesia* (pp. 69–93). Acton, ACT: ANU Press. doi.org/10.22459/TGM.02.2017

Cox, J. (2018). *Fast money schemes: Hope and deception in Papua New Guinea.* Bloomington, IN: Indiana University Press.

Cox, J. & Macintyre, M. (2014). Christian marriage, money scams and Melanesian social imaginaries. *Oceania, 84*(2), 138–157.

Devette-Chee, K. (2015). Attitudes toward the use of Tok Pisin and Tolai as languages of instruction in lower primary schools in Kokopo, East New Britain Province, Papua New Guinea. *Language and Linguistics in Melanesia*, *33*(2), 16–34.

Dore, R. (1976). *The diploma disease: Education, qualification and development*. Berkeley, CA: University of California Press.

Eriksen, A. (2008). *Gender, Christianity and change in Vanuatu: An analysis of social movements in North Ambrym*. Aldershot, England: Ashgate.

Eves, R. (2016). Reforming men: Pentecostalism and masculinity in Papua New Guinea. *The Australian Journal of Anthropology*, *27*(2), 244–259. doi.org/10.1111/taja.12196

Gegeo, D. W. & Watson-Gegeo, K. A. (2012). The critical villager revisited: Continuing transformations of language and education in Solomon Islands. In J. W. Tollefson (Ed.), *Language policies in education* (pp. 245–264). London, England: Routledge.

Gibbs, P. (2016). I could be the last man: Changing masculinities in Enga society. *The Asia Pacific Journal of Anthropology*, *17*(3–4), 324–341.

Glasgow, A., Ha'amori, B., Daiwo, J. & Masala, V. (2011). The Solomon Islands' initiatives to support and enhance the use of vernaculars in early childhood education. *Languages & Linguistics in Melanesia*, *29*, 86–94.

Jolly, M. (1996). 'Woman ikat raet long human raet o no?' Women's rights, human rights and domestic violence in Vanuatu. *Feminist Review*, *52*(1), 169–190. doi.org/10.2307/1395780

Jolly, M. (2008). Moving masculinities: Memories and bodies across Oceania. *The Contemporary Pacific*, *20*(1), 1–24. doi.org/10.1353/cp.2008.0010

Jourdan, C. (2013). Pijin at school in Solomon Islands: Language ideologies and the nation. *Current Issues in Language Planning*, *14*(2), 270–282.

Litteral, R. (2015). Changes in mother tongue education policy in Papua New Guinea. *Language and Linguistics in Melanesia*, *33*(2), 93–99.

Lo Bianco, J. (2015). Multilingual education across Oceania. In W. E, Wright, S. Boun & O. Garcia (Eds), *The handbook of bilingual and multilingual education* (pp. 604–617). Hoboken, NJ: Wiley.

Macintyre, M. (1987). Flying witches and leaping warriors: Supernatural origins of power and matrilineal authority in Tubetube society. In M. Strathern (Ed.), *Dealing with inequality: Analysing gender relations in Melanesia and beyond* (pp. 207–229). Cambridge, England: Cambridge University Press.

Macintyre, M. (1988). The unhappy wife and the dispensable husband: Myths of a matrilineal order. In D. Gewertz (Ed.), *The myth of matriarchy reconsidered* (pp. 185–195). Sydney, NSW: Oceania Monograph Series.

Macintyre, M. (2000). 'Hear us, women of Papua New Guinea!': Melanesian women and human rights. In A. Hilsdon, M. Macintyre, V. Mackie & M. Stivens (Eds), *Human rights and gender politics: Perspectives on the Asia-Pacific region* (pp. 147–171). London, England: Routledge.

Macintyre, M. (2006). Women working in the mining industry in Papua New Guinea: A case study from Lihir. In K. Lahiri-Dutt & M. Macintyre (Eds), *Women miners in developing countries: Pit women and others* (pp. 131–44). Aldershot, England: Ashgate.

Macintyre, M. (2008). Police and thieves, gunmen and drunks: Problems with men and problems with society in Papua New Guinea. *The Australian Journal of Anthropology, 19*(2), 179–193.

Macintyre, M. (2011a). Modernity, gender and mining: Experiences from Papua New Guinea. In K. Lahiri-Dutt (Ed.), *Gendering the field: Towards sustainable livelihoods for mining communities* (pp. 21–32). Acton, ACT: ANU E Press. doi.org/10.22459/GF.03.2011

Macintyre, M. (2011b). 'Money changes everything': Papua New Guinean women in the modern economy. In M. Patterson & M. Macintyre (Eds), *Managing modernity in the Western Pacific* (pp. 90–120). St Lucia, Qld: University of Queensland Press.

Macintyre, M. (2012). Gender violence in Melanesia and the problem of Millennium Development Goal No. 3. In M. Jolly & C. Stewart (Eds), *Engendering violence in Papua New Guinea* (pp. 239–266). Canberra, ACT: ANU E Press. doi.org/10.22459/EVPNG.07.2012

Macintyre, M. (2017). Introduction: Flux and change in Melanesian gender relations. In M. Macintyre & C. Spark (Eds), *Transformations of gender in Melanesia* (pp. 1–21). Canberra, ACT: ANU Press. doi.org/10.22459/TGM.02.2017

Maebuta, J. (2013). Solomon Islands: Adaptive leadership strategies in schools. In S. R. P. Clarke & T. A. O'Donoghue (Eds), *School level leadership in post-conflict societies the importance of context* (pp. 110–126). London, England: Routledge.

Maggio, R. (2016). 'My wife converted me': Gendered values and gendered conversion in Pentecostal households in Honiara, Solomon Islands. *The Australian Journal of Anthropology, 27*(2), 168–184. doi.org/10.1111/taja.12192

Marksbury, R. A. (1993). *The business of marriage: Transformations in Oceanic matrimony*. Pittsburgh, PA: University of Pittsburgh Press.

McDougall, D. (2009). Becoming sinless: Converting to Islam in the Christian Solomon Islands. *American Anthropologist, 111*(4), 480–491. doi.org/10.1111/j.1548-1433.2009.01157.x

McDougall, D. (2012). Stealing foreign words, recovering local treasures: Bible translation and vernacular literacy on Ranongga (Solomon Islands). *The Australian Journal of Anthropology, 23*(3), 318–339.

McDougall, D. (2013). Evangelical public culture: Making stranger-citizens in Solomon Islands. In M. Tomlinson & D. McDougall (Eds), *Christian politics in Oceania* (pp. 122–145). New York, NY: Berghahn Books.

McDougall, D. (2014). 'Tired for nothing'? Women, chiefs and the domestication of customary authority in Solomon Islands. In M. Jolly & H. Choi (Eds), *Divine domesticities: Christian paradoxes in Asia and the Pacific* (pp. 199–224). Canberra, ACT: ANU E Press. doi.org/10.22459/DD.10.2014

McDougall, D. (2016). *Engaging with strangers: Love and violence in the rural Solomon Islands*. New York, NY: Berghahn Books.

McDougall. D. (2019, 20 September). Reviving the spirit of vernacular languages. *ARC Centre of Excellence for the Dynamics of Language*. Retrieved from www.dynamicsoflanguage.edu.au/news-and-media/latest-headlines/article/?id=reviving-the-spirit-of-vernacular-languages-in-solomon-islands

McDougall, D. & Zobule, A. G. (forthcoming). 'All read well': Schooling on solid ground in a Solomon Islands language movement. *The Contemporary Pacific, 33*(2).

Merlan, F. & Rumsey, A. (2015). Language ecology, language policy and pedagogical practice in a Papua New Guinea highland community. *Language and Linguistics in Melanesia, 33*(1), 82–96.

Ministry of Education and Human Resource Development. (2010). *Policy statement and guidelines for the use of vernacular languages and English in education in Solomon Islands*. Honiara, Solomon Islands: Solomon Islands Government.

Ministry of Education and Human Resource Development. (2013). *Performance assessment report (2006–2013)*. Honiara, Solomon Islands: Solomon Islands Government. Retrieved from www.mehrd.gov.sb/

Ministry of Education and Human Resource Development. (2015). *Performance assessment report (2010–2014)*. Retrieved from www.mehrd.gov.sb/

Ministry of Education and Human Resource Development. (2019). *Performance assessment report 2018*. Retrieved from www.mehrd.gov.sb/

Munro, J. (2013). The violence of inflated possibilities: Education, transformation and diminishment in Wamena, Papua. *Indonesia*, *95*, 25–46. doi.org/10.5728/indonesia.95.0025

Munro, J. (2017). Gender struggles of educated men in the Papuan highlands. In M. Macintyre & C. Spark (Eds), *Transformations of gender in Melanesia* (pp. 45–68). Canberra, ACT: ANU Press. doi.org/10.22459/TGM.02.2017

Munro, J. (2018). *Dreams made small: The education of Papuan highlanders in Indonesia*. New York, NY: Berghahn Books.

Plan International. (2019). *Our education, our future: Pacific girls leading change to create better access to secondary education: Solomon Islands*. Retrieved from www.plan.org.au/-/media/plan/images/learn/who-we-are/blog-media-images/2019/200519-sols-report/our-education-our-future_policy-reportcompressed.pdf?la=en&hash=C58B84266055B5E31D8C0088475DA3942B258032

Solomon Islands Statistics Office. (2012). *2009 Population and housing census: National report* (Vol. 2). Honiara: Solomon Islands Government. Retrieved from sdd.spc.int/sb

Spark, C. (2011). Gender trouble in town: Educated women eluding male domination, gender violence and marriage in PNG. *The Asia Pacific Journal of Anthropology*, *12*(2), 164–179.

Spark, C. (2017). 'I won't go hungry if he's not around': 'Working class' urban Melanesian women's agency in intimate relationships. In M. Macintyre & C. Spark (Eds), *Transformations of gender in Melanesia* (pp. 115–140). Canberra, ACT: ANU Press. doi.org/10.22459/TGM.02.2017

Suti, E., Hoatson, L., Tafunai, A. & Cox, J. (2020). Livelihoods, leadership, linkages and locality: The Simbo for Change project. *Asia Pacific Viewpoint*. doi.org/10.1111/apv.12260

Tanangada, L. O. (2013). A study of language use in secondary school classrooms in the Solomon Islands: Conceptions, practices and proficiencies (Unpublished Master's thesis). Waikato University, Hamilton, New Zealand.

Taylor, J. P. (2008). The social life of rights: 'Gender antagonism', modernity and Raet in Vanuatu. *The Australian Journal of Anthropology*, *19*(2), 165–178. doi.org/10.1111/j.1835-9310.2008.tb00120.x

Tengan, T. P. K. (2008). *Native men remade: Gender and nation in contemporary Hawai'i*. Durham, NC: Duke University Press.

Troolin, D. (2013). Navigating contested terrain: Vernacular education in a Papua New Guinean Village. *Current Issues in Language Planning, 14*(2), 283–299.

United Nations Educational, Scientific and Cultural Organization. (1953). *The use of vernacular languages in education.* Paris, France: UNESCO.

Wardlow, H. (2006). *Wayward women: Sexuality and agency in a New Guinea society.* Berkeley, CA: University of California Press.

Watson-Gegeo, K. A. (1987). English in the Solomon Islands. *World Englishes, 6*(1), 21–32.

Watson-Gegeo, K. A. & Gegeo, D. W. (1992a). Keeping culture out of the classroom in rural Solomon Islands Schools: A critical analysis. *The Journal of Educational Foundations, 8*(2), 27–55.

Watson-Gegeo, K. A. & Gegeo, D. W. (1992b). Schooling, knowledge and power: Social transformation in the Solomon Islands. *Anthropology & Education Quarterly, 23*(1), 10–29.

Whalan, J. (2011). Aid for education in post-conflict Solomon Islands. *Prospects, 41*(2), 237–247.

Wilkinson, R. G. & Pickett, K. (2009). *The spirit level: Why more equal societies almost always do better.* London, England: Allen Lane.

Zimmer-Tamakoshi, L. (1997). The last big man: Development and men's discontents in the Papua New Guinea Highlands. *Oceania, 68*(2), 107–122.

Zimmer-Tamakoshi, L. (1998). Women in town: Housewives, homemakers and household managers. In L. Zimmer-Tamakoshi (Ed.), *Modern Papua New Guinea* (pp. 195–210). Kirksville, MO: Thomas Jefferson University Press.

Zimmer-Tamakoshi, L. (2016). Inequality and changing masculinities among the Gende in Papua New Guinea: The 'good', the 'bad' and the 'very bad'. *The Asia Pacific Journal of Anthropology, 17*(3–4), 250–267.

Zobule, A. G. (2016). *Kulu Language Institute curriculum* (Vols. 1–8). Solomon Islands: Kulu Language Institute.

Zobule, A. G. (2018, November). *Studying the vernacular in the vernacular by the vernacular speakers: The case of the Kulu Language Institute in the Solomon Islands* [Public lecture]. ARC Centre of Excellence in Language Dynamics, The Australian National University, Canberra, ACT.

8

Stingy Egalitarianism: Precarity and Jealousy at the Sisiak Settlement, Madang, Papua New Guinea

Deborah Gewertz and Frederick Errington

Martha Macintyre and Nick Bainton have described a Papua New Guinea (PNG) goldmine at Lihir that delivered such extraordinary affluence to landowners that they could become over-the-top makers and shakers—they could 'have it all' by staging remarkably elaborate customary rituals and by buying coveted four-wheel-drive vehicles. In this way, they were able to excel within traditional and modernist socioeconomies. In contrast to the past, in which 'exchange functioned as a levelling device, providing an important avenue for dispersing wealth and resources' (Bainton & Macintyre, 2016, p. 121), the flood of incoming money allowed a multiplicity of ceremonial distributions without significant depletion of resources. Indeed, the 'resulting efflorescence of custom has been a defining feature of their engagement with mining capitalism' (Bainton & Macintyre, 2016, p. 110). For those cash-fortunate Lihirians, theirs was a 'new world of surplus' (Bainton & Macintyre, 2016, p. 111). They had won big-time, and the mine handouts appeared endless.

For those less well-placed Lihirians (those who were not owners of mining land), the benefits of mining capitalism have been elusive. Certainly, some were given start-up money for small businesses, so as not to be entirely excluded from mine-based prosperity. Yet, their various enterprises frequently failed, and no further financing was offered. When their hopes 'for perpetual financing were foiled', these would-be entrepreneurs retaliated by 'allowing all the chickens to die, smashing the can crusher and letting several hectares of vegetables to rot in the ground' (Bainton & Macintyre, 2013, p. 156). As manifestations of what Macintyre and Bainton characterised as 'ferocious egalitarianism', these dramatic actions have 'less to do with the morality of distribution or social equality, and are more related to the feeling among certain individuals and groups that they have been slighted or have missed out on their just entitlement' (Bainton & Macintyre, 2016, p. 156; see also Bainton, this volume). The ferocity was a 'levelling' reminiscent of the 'negative agency' enacted by Huli women, living elsewhere in PNG. Feeling insufficiently appreciated for their productive and reproductive services, these women 'jump the fence', abandoning their homes and gardens and surviving largely through prostitution (Wardlow, 2006). Disappointed Lihirians, as with the Huli women, were asserting their efficacy. They were saying, in essence, 'fuck you'—'if you don't value me, I'll bring the house down'.

Our most recent work, among the Chambri at Sisiak settlement (outside Madang), provided an instructive contrast to the Lihirian case. If the Lihirians have won big and lost big, the Sisiak Chambri have simply lost out. If the Lihirians manifested Melanesian social life on steroids, the Chambri manifested Melanesian social life on life support. Rather than exhibiting ferocious egalitarianism, they exhibited 'stingy egalitarianism'. Clearly, this type of egalitarianism was intended to 'level'. The levelling was neither a product of an expansive 'giving it all away' nor a dramatic 'bringing the house down'. Instead, these Chambri engaged in a pre-emptive refusal to let anyone get ahead. However, as we shall see, for Lihirians and Chambri, the (largely) outside forces of global capitalism have, for better or worse, called the shots.

Thus, we offer our chapter as a complement to Macintyre and Bainton's fascinating study—as a (somewhat dark) contribution to an inventory of Melanesian social lives and concomitant egalitarianisms, as they emerge and transform in relationship to capitalism.

On Aspiration and Precarity

Our thoughts about social change in the Western Pacific have engaged Marshall Sahlins' distinction between 'develop*man*' and 'develop*ment*'. Although prompted by the encroaching Western capitalist economy, these modes of change differ in their historical trajectories. Developman can be a lengthy process in which people innovate with novel resources to become more of who they already are—where new wine gushes from old bottles, as contenders court allies and confound adversaries during increasingly intensified social and ritual events. Development is a modernist process in which people strive with novel resources to become other than who they already are. It is a process wherein 'each person takes the betterment of himself as his life project' (Sahlins, 1992, p. 13). If developman does shift into development, Sahlins argued, it is prompted by 'humiliation'—when the new wine, once embraced by the gallon, is understood as low-status swill.[1] That said, without necessarily discounting humiliation as an impetus for change, our PNG research indicates that people, particularly the young, may embrace a modernist process for a number of reasons. Principally among these may be the desire to escape the increasing demands of an elaborate system of developman. There is another possibility, as outlined above for those Lihirians made rich by the mine—a synthesis between developman and development, between the customary and the modernist. As Macintyre and Bainton showed regarding Lihir, people may want to become more of who they already are and to become different from what they are.[2] They may aspire to have the best of both worlds.[3]

For the Chambri living at Sisiak, aspirations were generally quite modest: for the most part, just to get by. For them, like those urban Papua New Guineans described by Sharp, Cox, Spark, Lusby and Rooney (and, again, unlike the revenue-rich Lihirians), their lives were constrained by 'precarity'—'by unpredictability and insecurity' (Sharp et al., 2015, p. 2). It must be noted that much of the literature concerning precarity comes from political science and positions precarious workers in a post-Fordist, neoliberal labour market. Considerations may include whether the

---

1 For more detail on 'humiliation' in Melanesia, see the essays in Robbins and Wardlow (2005).
2 See also Errington and Gewertz (2005, pp. 163–170) for a demonstration that development can be embraced without humiliation negating the aspirations of developman.
3 In this sense, to use Keir Martin's (2013) phrasing in his analysis of contemporary Tolai, they wished to be both 'big men' and 'big shots'.

precarious constitute a class—the precariat—and, if so, whether this class has the 'consciousness' necessary for revolutionary potential. Therefore, it is perhaps possible 'to identify or imagine precarious, contingent or flexible workers as a new kind of political subject, replete with their own forms of political organisation and modes of expression' (Neilson & Rossiter, 2008, p. 52). While the economically marginal at Sisiak have never known Fordist employment conditions and were not on the brink of class militancy, we nonetheless find the term 'precarity' useful in depicting their lives. After all, they have been affected by the same neoliberal policies that have caused massive insecurities worldwide. For instance, externally imposed 'structural adjustments'—beginning in PNG during 1994—have replaced an already minimal safety net with user-pay practices. This, in combination with PNG's commitment to a national economy based on capital-intensive resource extraction, including that of the Lihir goldmine, has left many local peoples hard-pressed and their economies stagnant.

The fact that those at Sisiak were hard-pressed—that their lives were precarious—has resulted in a widespread inability to achieve either developman or development. This inability, in turn, came to inflect a broadly Papua New Guinean expression of still-uncolonised consciousness—a persisting ethos of competitive egalitarianism.[4] Sisiak males, principally, would feel diminished by, and jealous of, any successes of another; at the same time, they generally lacked the material resources to push back directly. As John Taylor found in urban Vanuatu, most at Sisiak lacked both 'distributive' and 'possessive' agency (2015, p. 42). Consequently, because most did not have material efficacy, the few who did (the 'tall poppies') became targets of jealousy; correspondingly, the attack—the 'getting even'—took devious forms. Jealousy prompted revenge through sorcery, and the resulting complex became a compelling social fact within settlement life.[5]

---

4   Here, we reference Jean and John Comaroff's (1991) analysis of Christianity and its colonisation of the consciousness of indigenous South Africans.
5   Other scholars of Pacific societies have, of course, discussed sorcery. See, for example, Tonkinson (1981), Knauft (1985), Forsyth and Eves (2015), Kirsch (2006), Rio (2010) and Taylor (2015). Indeed, Chambri have long been concerned with sorcery. However, our focus here is not on sorcery per se, but rather on the jealousy under conditions of capitalist precarity that triggered sorcery fears (and perhaps practices) at Sisiak. That said, not all contemporary sorcery practices must be tied to capitalism, as Herriman (2015) has shown concerning Java. Moreover, unlike in parts of Africa, the precarity of Chambri life at Sisiak has not generated much speculation that capitalism was a mysterious process, one ramifying into an economy of the occult. On the latter, see Comaroff and Comaroff (2001) and Smith and Mwadime (2015).

Moreover, to the extent that this jealousy/sorcery complex was considered justified, at least by the perpetrator, it became part of the moral economy.[6] As James Carrier pointed out, the 'morality' of the 'moral economy' stems from material transactions reflecting—building on, looping back on— social obligations (Carrier, 2017; see also Bainton; Cox, this volume). This has been certainly true in Melanesia, where the value of transactions frequently lay in their sociality. Further, in the context of development, commodity transactions might have a 'gifty' aspect.[7] Accordingly, many settlers at Sisiak were jealous, not only of the (seemingly unwarranted) material success of others, but of the relationships that accompanied the success.[8] Among these resource-poor Papua New Guineans, the result was a multiple and moralistic levelling—one that coerced the prudent to keep their heads down (cf. Oppermann, 2016).

The tensions underlying everyday life at Sisiak were familiar to us from past work among rural and urban Chambri; yet, they were to flare up alarmingly when we joined a local household. Our money made just some lives notably less precarious; the affluence we bestowed aroused contention. Our presence provided 'unique opportunities for individuals to "rise above" others … [creating] a high degree of risk particularly as it … attract[ed] the jealousy of others' (Taylor, 2015, p. 42).

On the Chambri at Sisiak

Sisiak began as an official settlement of Madang in 1969, when the colonial administration purchased 220 acres of land near the native village of Sisiak to settle migrants. (For a brief history, see Gesch, 2017, p. 109.) These were employed in rebuilding, expanding or otherwise developing

---

6   Oppermann, writing about Buka, another Papua New Guinean group, suggested that sorcery is 'imagined as the anarchy of jealousies' (2016, p. 186). More specifically, he found that elites 'fear that it is "uneducated youth" and others jealous of their success that both spread rumours of sorcery and practice it … [T]he discourse of *poisen* can thus operate as a levelling critique of elites' (2016, p. 195). Comparably, Schwoerer reported, concerning the Eastern Highlands of PNG, that 'sorcery accusations are the result of uneven economic development and failure to deliver basic social services' (2017, p. 317). Additionally, see Maggio (2018) on sorcery accusations calibrating a moral economy within an urban settlement in the Solomon Islands.
7   James Carrier (2017) referenced his ongoing relationships with the proprietor and staff of his neighbourhood shop in Edinburgh.
8   As our colleague, Dr Bryant Allen, described in an email received on 15 July 2018: 'no chiefs in Melanesia. Most men feel they are as good as the next man. So, when one prospers and another does not, what can be the reason? It is either a personal failing or the other has some supernatural assistance, either to succeed, or to sabotage your success.'

the coastal town, whose strategic port was heavily damaged during World War II (see Sinclair, 2006, p. 258). Most of the labourers were drawn from villages proximate to the Sepik River or other lowland areas, from groups in which men competed for hard-won, if transitory, eminence.[9]

Chambri people, with whom we have long worked (Deborah since 1974 and Fred since 1983), comprised one of these egalitarian sociocultural groups.[10] By the 1970s, Chambri residing in their home villages on Chambri Island were engaged in developman—again, a process through which social and cultural innovation enabled people to become more of, and better at, what they already were. Senior men eagerly augmented their power through the appropriation of new opportunities in the form of cash and commodities. They pressured at least one of their sons to obtain an education and a well-paying job. Remittances, it was hoped, would enhance patriclan prestige and continuity by enabling bigger and better brideprices. By 1983, a sufficiently large cash brideprice was paid that the groom's father bragged that his clan could kill the bride, for her death compensation had already been given.

By 1987, that which allowed clan leaders to conceive of becoming more of what they already were was allowing their sons to conceive of becoming less of what their fathers wanted them to be. These sons insisted that they were 'young lives' and exercised their choices and decisions so as to participate in a system premised on personal choice: one that conjoined freedom of religious choice, freedom of commodity choice and freedom of marital choice.[11] Thus, they embraced development, whereby social and cultural innovation occurred such that people became 'modernist'—more and better at what they had not been. Often seeking new opportunities in town, they moved to urban settlements. Many moved to Chambri Camp in the town of Wewak. There, the road connection to the Sepik River made circular migration relatively easy and frequent. Women from

---

9   A comprehensive urban study of Madang indicated that 'the Sisiak programme has been specifically oriented towards the Sepiks' (Russell D. Taylor & Partners Pty Ltd, 1972, p. 23).
10   This is not to dispute the presence of hierarchical relationships between men and women.
11   The choices and decisions exercised by these young men were explicitly directed towards participating in another system, one that had been building since a variety of late nineteenth- and early twentieth-century 'first contacts' and becoming increasingly pervasive after Independence in 1975. They were self-styled 'young challengers', to use Pierre Bourdieu's term, who were struggling against orthodoxy to make their own choices and decisions—struggling to make 'their [own] mark ([or] 'epoch')' (Bourdieu, 1983, p. 60). This would not be possible 'without pushing into the past those who [had] an interest in stopping the clock, eternalising the present stage of things' (Bourdieu, 1983, p. 60).

the Chambri villages would occasionally bring smoked fish for sale at the market and as gifts for town-dwelling kin. Town dwellers would readily visit home villages for holidays and ritual events like funerals.

In contrast, in the absence of a road link from Madang to the Sepik River, those at Sisiak had only limited access to the people and resources of the home villages. Unfortunately, the period of post-war prosperity, which had encouraged many to migrate to Madang, proved to be of only limited duration. To some extent, Madang's current circumstances reflected the general shift in the PNG economy—an economy, as mentioned previously, that was increasingly focused on resource extraction at limited sites, leaving coastal towns with diminished economic opportunities. This was evident in our Sisiak data.

By 2018, Chambri at Sisiak were struggling to get by, significantly more so than Chambri elsewhere. According to the tenants' list constructed by Michael Kosai, our assistant and Sisiak resident, there were 54 houses at Sisiak inhabited by Chambri-identified people; these included 100 adults—73 Chambri and 27 non-Chambri affines.[12] (It should be noted that Kosai's list excluded children, some of whom were in their twenties, as well as elderly 'dependents'. Please note that we use Kosai's terms throughout.) For those operating within the informal economy, 41 were craftsmen, earning money by selling carvings, stencilled clothing, baskets, woven bracelets and shell jewellery to other Papua New Guineans and to the relatively few Western tourists still coming to Madang.[13] Some of these also sold betel nuts and cigarettes outside their houses. Although sales were variable and no records were kept, they claimed a fortnightly income of between PGK 20–200, with an average of PGK 51 for these two weeks. (As of 13 July 2018, shortly after receiving Kosai's data, PGK 1 = USD 0.33.)

Another 10 people were peddlers and resold small items, ranging from batteries to instant noodles. Their sales were comparably variable and unrecorded; however, they reported a fortnightly income of PGK 50–150, with an average of PGK 71. Others were similarly self-employed. One was a farmer, growing vegetables to sell at Madang's

---

12 All Chambri names are pseudonyms.
13 Tourism to PNG has dramatically declined in recent years. This has, in part, been due to the economic downturn of 2008 and to PNG's reputation as a dangerous place. Although some young backpackers did visit, most of the moneyed tourists arrived during sporadic visits by cruise ships, disembarking only for brief and highly regulated excursions.

main market, with a fortnightly income of PGK 200. One was a lay clergyman, whose congregation provided him with a fortnightly income of PGK 100. Three were businessmen who used their vehicles to transport passengers and goods. They earned an average fortnightly income of PGK 470. One was a consultant who sold business advice. His fortnightly income was PGK 500. Three were hired hands, with average fortnightly incomes of PGK 107. Two were seamstresses, with average fortnightly incomes of PGK 140. One was a housecleaner with a fortnightly income of PGK 170.

Within the more formal economy, three worked in factories, with an average fortnightly salary of PGK 325. Two worked for mining companies, with an average fortnightly salary of PGK 763. Four were carpenters, with an average fortnightly salary of PGK 318. One worked for the village court, with a fortnightly salary of PGK 150. One was a seaman, with a fortnightly salary of PGK 700. One worked as a counsellor for the local government, with a fortnightly salary of PGK 300. Three were teachers, with an average fortnightly salary of PGK 477. One worked as Madang's Commissioner of Boy Scouts, with a fortnightly salary of PGK 250. Two were security guards, with an average fortnightly salary of PGK 385. One was a mechanic, with a fortnightly salary of PGK 510. One was an electrician, with a fortnightly salary of PGK 276. One was a secretary, with a fortnightly salary of PGK 430. One was a store clerk, with a fortnightly salary of PGK 276. One drove a van, with a fortnightly salary of PGK 250.

It should be emphasised that income earned in the informal economy through market sales, as with craft items, was likely to be erratic. In the more formal economy, the range of pay varied from PGK 800 for a mineworker to PGK 350 for a factory worker. Some factory workers, who had to pay for their own transportation and, sometimes, uniforms, told us that it was hardly worth it. On the other hand, unmarried children in their twenties (who were not part of Kosai's survey) might well have contributed minor sums (perhaps through the sale of crafts) to family income. Many with a fortnightly salary attempted to supplement their incomes by selling crafts and, in a few cases, food (e.g. via buns purchased from a local bakery and resold). Finally, it was possible that money came in through illegal means, as with the sale of drugs, alcohol, sex and stolen items.

Overall, Sisiak's two-adult households, in which at least one Chambri was resident, earned approximately PGK 15,116 per fortnight, averaging PGK 151.12 per adult—the equivalent of USD 48.37 or approximately USD 97 per two-adult household. Of the combined adult income of some PGK 300 per fortnight, Chambri households spent the following on semi-obligatory purchases: PGK 20 on transportation to work and the market; PGK 20 on water; PGK 20 on electricity; PGK 60 on school fees and other children's needs; and PGK 40 on miscellaneous items (including betel nut). There was, as well, a limited amount of money available for food. This averaged PGK 140 (USD 46.20), which did not buy much during a two-week period. Food purchases tended to be basic and minimal: PGK 100 at the stores was primarily spent on rice, instant noodles, canned fish and meat, PNG-produced sausage, hard biscuits, bouillon cubes, small amounts of oil, tea, sugar, powdered milk and, occasionally, butter and eggs. PGK 40 at the town market was spent mostly on garden vegetables. Fresh meat would be a treat. Crucially, in our experience, many residents at Sisiak were frequently hungry.

We had known for some time that hunger was a chronic problem at Sisiak. In 2006, for example, we wrote about our old friend, Paul Kamboi, who was finding life in the settlement difficult. A former 'young life', he had fled to Sisiak to escape ensorcellment by senior Chambri men, who had chosen a different woman for him than the one he wished to marry.[14] Never returning to Chambri Island, he worked for a timber company. After it closed in the 1980s, he supported his family by selling carvings to tourists at the market. Sales were only occasional; sometimes, he could not afford the bus fare home and had to walk the long way back to Sisiak in the scorching tropical sun. Nor could he really afford the tuition for his younger son's education. Worst of all, he and his children sometimes had to go without food. While he did enjoy chatting with his mostly Chambri neighbours at Sisiak, he was often distracted by hunger. And, he could not let this be known, lest he be perceived as making a request of others, who were probably as short of food as he was. Correspondingly, Paul had to tell his youngest child, (then) 10-year-old John, that he was a big boy now—too old to cry if he was hungry.

---

14   For more detail about the prescribed Chambri system of mother's brother's daughter's marriage, see Fortune (1933) and Errington and Gewertz (1987, p. 50).

During 2011 and 2015, we visited Paul briefly; however, it was not until 2018, when Paul was 62, that we spent appreciable time with him. He had been diagnosed with prostate cancer, and we had been sending him money to pay for medical costs and John's school fees. In response to his invitation, we moved in with him at Sisiak. His area consisted of his house, several outbuildings, a shower enclosure and an outhouse, all demarcated from the narrow, unpaved road and from neighbouring areas by carefully tended ornamental bushes. We were given two rooms in his house, displacing his two unmarried daughters, Faith and Alberta, and their young children. They moved into an outbuilding, where John ordinarily slept by himself. On occasion, David (Paul's divorced, older son) resided in one of the outbuildings. Other active participants in the household lived nearby and visited daily—these were Paul's eldest daughter (Pauline), her Chambri husband (Peter) and their three children.

In urging us to join him, Paul was obviously pleased that we could pay for the electricity to be turned on and for his overdue water bill to be covered. He was also anxious; he was unsure how his Sisiak neighbours would react to our daily presence. Indeed, as we were to discover, of all those Chambri we knew at Sisiak—many for over 40 years—Paul was virtually the only one willing to take responsibility for us. The others were concerned that we, as affluent white people—the lone white people, they told us, ever to live at Sisiak—would bring trouble. Certainly, trouble might come from other Chambri. Moreover, Sisiak was a 'mixed' community of migrants from a variety of linguistic and cultural groups; most were Sepiks, but many were unentailed to Chambri. Criminally inclined youth, either in small groups or in larger gangs, were regularly (extremely) intoxicated with locally distilled spirits and marijuana. They were known to burgle houses and assault occupants. At the very least, these youths 'heeded the authority of no one' and 'disturbed everyone' as they roamed up and down the narrow roads, their loud music and boisterous shouts lasting throughout most nights. Their conspicuous good times as (later-day) 'young lives' kept the rest of us awake in intimidated silence. To protect us from actual incursion, Paul arranged for 'security'. He enlisted the help of his now 22-year-old (and somewhat alienated) son, John, to keep his fellow gang members—again, Sepiks from a number of groups—at arm's length. Despite this logic, the plan backfired.

Our arrival at Sisiak was noticed. Neighbours stood by as we unloaded a heavy suitcase and bulky, if basic, items such as foam mattresses, pillows, bedding, mosquito nets and cooking utensils, plus luxury items as a fan and a sturdy kerosene stove. Finally, we unloaded freshly purchased household provisions, including a 10 kg bag of rice. Previously in PNG, we had cooked for ourselves and shared with others. This time we provided money for food and Paul's daughters shopped and cooked for us. Consequently, everyone had plenty to eat, even if it was mostly rice augmented with instant noodles, canned fish and market vegetables. Everyone had more energy and visibly put on weight. And, Paul was less discomfited by his illness.

Much as during our previous stints living in Chambri Camp in Wewak (as recently as 2015), things seemed to be working out well enough at Sisiak. Even though we were frequently kept awake by the raucous youth, their activities remained outside our immediate household area. Faith and Alberta, and sometimes Pauline and Peter, went daily to the town market to sell their handicrafts. On returning, they reported how the market had been for them. A 'good market' was earning PGK 10–15 through the sale of a stencilled t-shirt. This said, there were many market visits for which transportation costs (a round trip cost of PGK 2 per person) were not met, as nothing was sold. Before we arrived, the family would have simply gone to bed hungry. Subsistence had been largely hand-to-mouth, as remained the case for many Sisiak residents.[15]

Given the prevalence of these straitened circumstances, the lift in their fortunes was a source not only of gratification but of concern to Paul and his family. Others might easily become 'jealous' (*jelus*).[16] It was best that we white people not sit or, especially, eat on the porch, lest those passing by be reminded of our presence in this household. It was better that we all ate in darkness or, at the very least, inconspicuously (in fact,

---

15   Some limited food sharing did occur, particularly among proximate neighbours, if a family happened to have a minor windfall.

16   Francis Mihalic, author of the classic *Jacaranda dictionary and grammar of Melanesian Pidgin* (1971), does not list '*jelus*' as a Pidgin entry. As a synonym for the English word 'jealous', he lists '*ai tudak*', which literally means 'He is blind. He is jealous' (1971, p. 58). The implication is of someone who is blind with jealousy. The other provided synonym for 'jealousy' is '*mangal*' (1971, p. 129), attributed to speakers in New Hanover. This means 'to covet, to long for, envy, yearn for, desire strongly' (1971, p. 129). It may be that the concept of jealousy has become more directly invoked and is no longer metaphorically related to blindness. Additionally, it has become more universalistic—no longer tied to an obscure regional language. Further, its meaning has, perhaps, expanded from merely coveting to actively resenting.

most Chambri did eat indoors, circled around a little lamp). Despite these precautions, Paul's family soon became aware of jealous gossip from Chambri and others.[17] It was rumoured that, with these white people there, Paul's family could now 'eat meat every day', could eat fresh (not canned) beef, chicken, mutton or pork.[18] In fact, most of our meals featured canned fish or beef; sometimes, we did splurge. Undoubtedly, the live chicken that Faith and Alberta carried home from the market one afternoon was noted by the community.[19]

Further, John, influenced by his fellow gang members, made it clear that he did not want our help in continuing his education. Recently, we had sent money to pay for 'top-up' courses so that he might improve his grades and progress in school. His friends demanded to know why he should receive special help from us while they, whose scores had been as bad as his, did not have white people sponsoring them. Paul became alarmed that these friends, and possibly others (Chambri and non-Chambri), were jealous of his relationship with us. He began a disquisition on jealousy and the sorcery that it prompted. At Sisiak, anyone and everyone might feel jealous and be thought capable of enacting sorcery.[20] Both of these fostered the moral economy of levelling.

On Jealousy, Sorcery and the Moral Economy

As part of Paul's disquisition, he brought out a notebook containing information that he wished to possess in consultable form. It contained the names of totemically significant rocks on Chambri Island—these were names that his sons should have learned if they had been initiated.

---

17 Taylor quoted an informant saying that, 'in town, all we eat is money. Town isn't safe because it is too mixed. There is too much mixing of people from different places and too much mixing of *kastom*. There is also too much jealousy' (2015, p. 43).

18 Lamb flaps (sheep bellies), once eaten by many Papua New Guineans, have become a treat, largely displaced by locally produced sausage. On lamb flaps, see Gewertz and Errington (2010).

19 For a differently inflected set of relationships linking jealousy, sorcery, white men, money, and food under urban circumstances in PNG, see Bashkow (2006, pp. 134–144).

20 The social role of sorcerer had once been part of the persona of knowledgeable men on Chambri Island, including during the florescence of the developman economy. At Sisiak, the role had become much more generalised, and it was unclear who the practitioner might be and, much less, who might have enlisted the practitioner's help. Moreover, although the Chambri did have techniques of sorcery detection, these never resulted in a clearly identifiable culprit against whom definitive action could be taken. In this latter regard, they were unlike the Gebusi described by Knauft (1985).

It contained the birth dates of all his children and grandchildren. Finally, it contained the names of those living throughout the mixed community at Sisiak from whom he sensed some grudge—these were people that he and his children should avoid to forestall possible sorcery. Despite his precautions, his daughter, Faith, had already encountered jealousy. She was singled out by her teachers due to her academic success and encouraged to progress to high school; however, Paul had insisted that she drop out lest sorcery ensue. Undoubtedly, some had been jealous of him and his family for the help Deborah had given over the years.

Paul continued with the suggestion that his stepbrother, Jacob, had undoubtedly been killed by sorcery that had emanated from jealousy. Like Paul, Jacob had worked closely with Deborah since her first fieldwork stint on Chambri Island, which began in 1974. By 1987, he had begun to call himself a 'traditional anthropologist'. His various (self-designed) projects included seeking analogues between 'traditional' Chambri stories and the Bible.[21] Additionally, after he had settled relatively permanently at Chambri Camp in Wewak, he became preoccupied with soccer. Eventually rising to the rank of a 'Level Three Soccer Referee', he presided over matches with verve augmented by his official Fox 40 soccer referee whistle—a gift from 'the coach of America', the soccer coach at Deborah's university.

Jacob died in 2007. It was not until 2014 that we were able to visit his widow who, following his last instructions, unlocked for us the box containing his papers and memorabilia. Inside, we found hundreds of hand-written pages. There were accounts of debts owed to, and incurred by, him. There were lists of secret names and ritual prerogatives possessed by his clan. There was a carefully drawn family tree that depicted his descendants from his sequence of three wives. There were traditional Chambri stories, perhaps ultimately intended for us. There were originals of letters that had been faxed to various business interests and politicians (including several prime ministers), requesting sponsorship of his activities as a traditional anthropologist. There were descriptions of soccer matches. There were accounts of wrongs against him and, sometimes, others in his family (including a 17-page account of an assault on a daughter), all written to claim compensation if not legal redress. There were documents of infractions he witnessed as an auxiliary policeman, as when

---

21   See Gewertz and Errington (1991, pp. 154–168).

several youths taunted a woman by cutting down her flowers. We were unsurprised that, in pursuing his urban opportunities, he had become an auxiliary policeman.

Finally, as he lay dying of what was formally diagnosed as mouth cancer, he listed those whose grudges against him might have prompted the sorcery that, he was certain, was killing him. Principal contenders were a mixed group of those with traditional and more modernist grievances: those he had charged in the assault on his daughter; one or more of his jealous former wives, each striking out at the others through him, and, most likely, fellow soccer referees envious of his successes. Of the latter group, he surmised that a specific Chambri referee was the assailant.

Paul, in recounting the circumstances of Jacob's death, was certain that he had been killed by the other Chambri referee. For our part, we observed sadly that, of his various endeavours, Jacob was most proud of his accomplishments as a referee. Paul agreed and, with some bitterness, talked of the 'negative thoughts of jealousy' that led to sorcery, with the end result that everyone was brought 'down to the same level'.[22] He then announced that our continuing presence was making him and his family uncomfortably conspicuous and putting them at risk; it was best that we leave within a week—we agreed.

The following night was again sleepless. Emerging at dawn, we found that the household was already up and vigilant. Faith and Alberta stood outside, looking warily at the road where the revellers remained active. As Fred walked onto the porch, Paul immediately pushed him back inside, stating most emphatically, 'they must not see you; do not show yourself. It is no longer safe for you to stay. You must leave immediately'. We were soon to discover that John, during the night, had taken a brief leave from fellow gang members. So drunk that he could barely stand, he had demanded money from Paul to buy more alcohol and had threatened his older brother, David, with a gun.[23]

Agreeing with Paul that our continued presence endangered ourselves and our hosts (John being the exception), we threw our things together. With transport quickly arranged, we departed later that morning for a hotel in town. Subsequent to our departure, perturbations continued. Two of our research assistants were menaced with knives by gang members seeking

22　For a moving account of frustrated ambition caused by sorcery, see Smith and Mwadime (2015).
23　For a discussion of the salience in PNG of the image of the drunken and/or stoned young man with a gun, see Macintyre (2008).

money. Then, the night after our departure, members of John's gang left the road and entered Paul's immediate area to obtain the money they assumed that we had left with him. After David, in response to this act of trespass and household intimidation, ordered them out, John again threatened him—this time with a knife.[24]

In conclusion, our presence had become a major disruption in an ongoing moral economy, one in which Sisiak residents were alert to the accomplishments of others. This was especially the case if those accomplishments could be construed as resting on advantageous relationships. The jealous did not feel that they lacked ability or virtue; instead, they felt that they had been unfairly excluded from the relationships benefiting others—that they had been unfairly diminished by the enabled eminence of others. In this sense, by striking back at the (undeserved) advantages we had provided, sorcery and violence perpetrated by youths (at least as a possibility) served as a mode of moral re-equilibration.[25]

On Levelling among the Economically Precarious

By 2018, few at Sisiak had either the means or the inclination to stand out. The extravagance and flamboyance of a wide range of ceremonies we had witnessed on Chambri Island had (as far as we know) never been a part of Sisiak life. These were ceremonies in which 'big men' mobilised their followers, arranged for the playing of sacred flutes to summon ancestral presences, and 'strutted their stuff'. Instead, at Sisiak, 'traditional' ceremonies were primarily limited to occasions of mourning; these had become culturally generic and modest—in this regard, the contrast with Lihir could not be sharper. One mourning ceremony that we witnessed in 2011, although well attended by the deceased woman's Chambri and non-Chambri family, friends and neighbours, was minimally financed through PGK 20 contributions from her children and grandchildren. The 'thanks' to those attending—instant noodles, garden vegetables and portions of lamb flaps—were limited and laid out with the utmost care to ensure that everyone received exactly the same amount.

---

24   We and Sisiak residents were fortunate that no one was actually injured due to our stay. In this regard, our circumstances were quite unlike the tragic ones related by Don Kulick (1991).

25   Although sorcery and physical violence operate in different ways, they can be used in concert. See Cox and Phillips (2015) for an elaboration.

Moreover, and relatedly, in response to our inquiries—in conversation and a questionnaire—we were to discover that what it meant to be a Chambri at Sisiak had become truncated. Neo-Melanesian (Tok Pisin), rather than Chambri, was the language of everyday life within families and between others, whether Chambri or non-Chambri. Many Chambri at Sisiak did not speak any Chambri at all. Aside from those of Paul's generation, few had ever visited the home villages for more than a week or so. Nevertheless, just having a Chambri father was usually enough to make one a Chambri.

This said, there was a sense that a Chambri should know, or at least value, Chambri things. Certainly, some (including those who did not speak the Chambri language) mentioned that being a Chambri was to be heir to a distinctive language, one strikingly different from those spoken in neighbouring Sepik River villages.[26] And, there were still senior men, including Paul, who were not only fluent Chambri speakers, but also (because they had been initiated) possessed impressive cosmological knowledge. For instance, in reminiscing with us, Paul recounted with pride the stories about the creation of Chambri as a place of ancestral power. These stories included restricted knowledge conveyed to initiated men and everyday knowledge literally conveyed at a mother's knee. Among Paul's pleasant childhood memories was that, after supper on Chambri Island, his mother would tell him and his sister traditional stories. In response to our direct question about social reproduction, he regretted that his kids knew nothing about Chambri Island and would not want to live there; hence, there was no point in trying to pass any of this information on to them.

In asking about what it was to be Chambri at Sisiak, we probed people's likes and dislikes of life there. Our questionnaire revealed virtual unanimity (among our 30 respondents). They welcomed the proximity to the town, with its hospital, schools, stores and market. Unsurprisingly, they wished there were more opportunities to earn money to access these urban resources. They thought they could get on well enough with most of their neighbours. However, they strongly disliked the behaviour of some of the young men, such as their periodical criminal activities and nightly carousing, including shouting obscenities and harassment.

We asked them if they ever planned to leave Sisiak. Some talked vaguely about buying a block of land somewhere and building a house where it would be 'more peaceful' than in town. Nevertheless, this was well

26   Iatmul, belonging to the Ndu language family, is spoken in these neighbouring Sepik River villages. The Chambri language belongs to the unrelated Nor Pondo language family.

beyond the means of most. Very few wished to return to Chambri Island. Land there had become somewhat scarce; most at Sisiak had not fulfilled ritual obligations in the home villages for many years. Village people simply did not know them and would ask, resentfully, 'who are you and where have you been?' Perhaps the most adequate answer to this question would be to demonstrate success during their time of absence. Thus, one said he would like to return to Chambri and take his father's place, provided that he had accumulated enough money (e.g. by winning the lottery) to build a large, permanent-materials house.[27] Another anticipated a welcome home once he was dead; by then, he hoped to have saved enough money (through the sale of carvings) for his children to buy a coffin and arrange its transport to Chambri for burial.

Life on Chambri Island did have some appeal; it was less cash-driven than life in town. Nonetheless, few at Sisiak had, and fewer wished to acquire, the skills necessary for village life. Women did not look forward to paddling a canoe, setting fishing nets, cutting firewood and smoking fish. Even if they were willing to learn, they anticipated derogatory comments about their competence from an elderly mother-in-law. Paul's daughter, Pauline, had received a sufficiently biting critique on her one visit to Chambri that she never wanted to go back. Finally, expecting a tepid welcome, many feared returning to Chambri Island. Chambri Island remained a place of ancestral power; therefore, resentments encountered there could be acted on. To the extent that those living on Chambri Island were in place, those visiting felt out of place, socially and cosmologically.[28]

---

27 Michael Kosai, our research assistant, estimated that approximately one-third of those Sepik people living at Sisiak believe in 'fast money schemes' (Cox, 2018) and have invested in the likes of Papalain, SP Can, Uvisitract, RD Tuna Condom Case and Blood Diamond. He also said that there are currently (as of 2019) no lottery games in Madang.

28 In earlier descriptions of the Chambri as they lived in their home villages, we wrote about their active totemic division of labour, with its mix of competition and cooperation. Living there, we were often awakened by booming slit-gong drums, calling men to converge in elaborate men's houses to debate, in archaic Chambri, about their ritual prerogatives. Displaying immense 'communicative competence … the knowledge and ability to speak in socially appropriate ways' (Bauman, 1975, p. 293)—debaters would mingle dance and oration. They would allude to their secret totemic names and attendant special powers that ensured the vitality of their patriclans and their capacity to attract wives, made their rivals fearful, regulated their portion of the universe in its succession of seasonal changes and anchored them in a landscape of signification. Indeed, walking through Chambri Island with ritually knowledgeable senior men was a lesson in the identity between people and place. Pausing every 20 or 30 yards at a succession of rock monoliths, we would hear the (often esoteric) polysyllabic names of, for example, the ancestor who, taking the form of a python, had moored his canoe there as part of the process of bringing the island into being. For these guides, Chambri Island was not just their home—it was central to their being as Chambri.

Given that most had little alternative other than to remain at Sisiak, with its ups and downs, what were their prospects?[29] Chambri there did take pride in their creativity and resilience. Based on their cultural history as carvers of traditional ritual objects and elaborately decorated touristic items, they enjoyed visualising complex designs. Now that international tourism to PNG had significantly diminished, these designs appeared on stencilled t-shirts for sale to other Papua New Guineans. Most mornings, Chambri did go to town to take their chances at the market, sometimes joking about their role in the 'informal economy'. (Once, when a little naked boy at Sisiak stood behind a table occasionally used in vending betel nut, someone quipped that he, too, was engaging in the informal economy.)

They did think about ways to earn more money—to improve the quality of their houses and more easily pay for electricity, water, school fees and food. In addition to selling handicrafts, their plans included raising chickens for sale; buying a drum of kerosene and offering small amounts for sale; finding a better job than at the local fish processing plant, where their pay barely covered the expenses of getting to work; acquiring power tools to make employment as a carpenter more viable; creating an online presence for the sale of stencilled t-shirts and carvings; learning computer skills; or qualifying as teachers. In following these aspirations, they knew they would have to step carefully. For example, the woman who wished to sell chickens once had her chicks killed and was threatened at knifepoint by one of the local criminal youths. (She was afraid to report him; as it turned out, he was later killed by the police.) Further, one of those who wished to continue her education had earlier left school because her success as a student was attracting jealousy.[30]

---

29   It has become increasingly common throughout PNG for settlement dwellers to become alienated from village kin and village-based resources, such as access to land. Whether they thereby become 'lumpenproletariat' is interesting to contemplate.

30   Forsyth and Eves note that fear of sorcery, linked with jealousy and envy, leads 'to an unwillingness of some … to work towards advancing their own living standards. Setting up businesses and becoming successful (especially if wealth is shown outwardly, such as in building new houses) is widely seen as being risky and as inviting a premature death through a sorcery attack' (2015, p. 11).

Schizmogenesis Among the Economically Precarious

Clearly, many living at Sisiak were economically insecure. Many of those Chambri who did work in the formal economy (e.g. in the fish factory or as a security guard) were ill-paid if regularly employed. Some, as with labourers, were engaged in 'non-standard employment which is poorly paid, insecure, unprotected, and cannot support a household' (Munck, 2013, p. 758). Others, the majority, relied on the informal economy with small and uncertain market or roadside transactions. The Chambri experience at Sisiak appeared widespread in PNG:

> Today, precarity characterises the experience of many urban Papua New Guineans, whether in formal employment or business, or earning a living through informal economic activities. For many Papua New Guineans, there is a disappointing gap between their aspirations for prosperity and their daily experiences of making a living. (Sharp et al., 2015)

As we have seen, that many Chambri living at Sisiak were short of cash forms only part of the story. Their economic precarity—and that of many other urban-dwelling Papuan New Guineans—was inflected by an ongoing ethos of competitive egalitarianism. Since developman at Sisiak never flourished and development had floundered, economic precarity ramified in a distinctive fashion. This precarity resulted in a moral economy of 'stingy'—if not downright mean—egalitarianism, one in which success was downplayed and appreciation, withheld.

Central to Sisiak's moral economy was jealousy—this, given and received by virtually everyone, had become a fact of social life. Jealousy was pervasive and made consequential due to ensuing sorcery and, to some extent, youth violence. The result was schizmogenesis, a negative feedback loop in which aspiration led to levelling, which then perpetuated precarity.[31] John Taylor came to a similar conclusion concerning the 'deeply affective nature of sorcery'. Working with urban Vanutuans, he argued that the fear of sorcery 'exacerbates social and economic inequalities particularly as it contributes to the discouragement or advancement, especially among those already disempowered' (Taylor, 2015, p. 48).

31　See Taylor (2015) on the socially and psychologically pernicious effects of witchcraft.

Conceivably, some collective action might eventually emerge at Sisiak from a common threat—perhaps of a mass eviction from government-owned land.[32] Nevertheless, in the context of poverty inflected by jealousy and sorcery, it is difficult to imagine sustained community-building among Chambri, much less between them and their non-Chambri neighbours.[33] While the Chambri and many of their Sisiak neighbours did suffer from precarity, they were neither solidary nor shared a consciousness of their condition. They did not, thus, constitute part of a social class of the precariat. Since jealousy at Sisiak seemed to feed (literally) on hunger, their best hope for the future might lie in a general easing of economic strictures. Still, this would seem outside their capacity to effect or compel.

Of course, those at Lihir also have little capacity to control their future economic circumstances, at least as these concern mining incomes. Certainly, the mining bonanza will pass and, with it, the capacity to achieve spectacular success of both developman and development. Correspondingly, ferocious egalitarianism, as a grand gesture of negative agency, may eventually lose its symbolic and practical feasibility. Yet, since not all their land has been subsumed by the mine, precarity may be forestalled. That said, for many Papua New Guineans living in cash-based, urban circumstances, the moral economy of places like Sisiak may increasingly prevail.

References

Bainton, N. & Macintyre, M. (2013). 'My land, my work': Business development and large-scale mining in Papua New Guinea. In F. McCormack & K. Barclay (Eds), *Engaging with capitalism: Cases from Oceania* (pp. 139–165). United Kingdom: Emerald Group Bingley.

Bainton N. & Macintyre, M. (2016). Mortuary ritual and island riches in island Melanesia. In D. Lipset & E. Silverman (Eds), *Mortuary dialogues: Death ritual and the reproduction of moral community in Pacific communities* (pp. 110–132). New York, NY: Berghahn.

Bashkow, I. (2006). *The meaning of whitemen: Race and modernity in the Orokaiva cultural world*. Chicago, IL: University of Chicago Press.

---

32   Michelle Rooney (2013) has documented a comparable eviction in Port Moresby.
33   But, for a more optimistic account of community members working together to address common problems, including those of crime, see Craig and Porter (2018).

Bauman, R. (1975). Verbal art as performance. *American Anthropologist, 77*(2), 290–311.

Bourdieu, P. (1983). *The field of cultural production.* Cambridge, England: Cambridge University Press.

Carrier, J. (2017). Moral economy: What's in a name? *Anthropological Theory, 18*(1), 13–35.

Comaroff, J. & Comaroff, J. (1991). *Of revelation and revolution: Christianity, colonialism and consciousness in South Africa.* Chicago, IL: University of Chicago Press.

Comaroff, J. & Comaroff, J. (Eds). (2001). *Millennial capitalism and the culture of neoliberalism.* Durham, NC: Duke University Press.

Cox, J. (2018). *Fast money schemes: Hope and deception in Papua New Guinea.* Bloomington, IN: Indiana University Press.

Cox, J. & Phillips, G. (2015). Sorcery, Christianity and the decline of medical services. In M. Forsyth & R. Eves (Eds), *Talking it through: Responses to sorcery and witchcraft beliefs and practices in Melanesia* (pp. 37–54). Canberra, ACT: ANU Press. doi.org/10.22459/TIT.05.2015

Craig, D. & Porter, D. (2018). *Safety and security at the edges of the state: Local regulation in Papua New Guinea's urban settlements. Justice for the poor.* Washington, DC: World Bank. Retrieved from documents.worldbank.org/curated/en/184231530596208653/Safety-and-security-at-the-edges-of-the-state-local-regulation-in-Papua-New-Guinea-s-urban-settlements

Errington, F. K. & Gewertz, D. (1987). *Cultural alternatives and a feminist anthropology.* Cambridge, England: Cambridge University Press.

Errington, F. K. & Gewertz, D. (2005). On humiliation and class in contemporary Papua New Guinea. In J. Robbins & H. Wardlow (Eds), *The making of global and local modernities in Melanesia* (pp. 163–170). Burlington, England: Ashgate.

Forsyth, M. & Eves, R. (2015). The problems and victims of sorcery and witchcraft practices and beliefs in Melanesia: An introduction. In M. Forsyth & R. Eves (Eds), *Talking it through: Responses to sorcery and witchcraft beliefs and practices in Melanesia* (pp. 1–19). Canberra, ACT: ANU Press. doi.org/10.22459/TIT.05.2015

Fortune, R. F. (1933). A note on some forms of kinship structures. *Oceania, 4*(1), 1–9.

Gesch, P. F. (2017). Varieties of local leadership in three peri-urban communities in Madang. *Contemporary PNG Studies*, *26*, 109–120.

Gewertz, D. & Errington, F. (1991). *Twisted histories, altered contexts: Representing the Chambri in a world system*. Cambridge, England: Cambridge University Press.

Gewertz, D. & Errington, F. (2010). *Cheap meat: Flap food nations in the Pacific Islands*. Berkeley, CA: University of California Press.

Herriman, N. (2015). The morbid nexus: Reciprocity and sorcery in rural East Java. *The Australian Journal of Anthropology*, *26*(2), 255–275.

Kirsch, S. (2006). *Reverse anthropology*. Stanford, CA: Stanford University Press.

Knauft, B. (1985). *Good company and violence*. Berkeley, CA: University of California Press.

Kulick, D. (1991). Law and order in Papua New Guinea. *Anthropology Today*, *7*(5), 21–22.

Macintyre, M. (2008). Police and thieves, gunmen and drunks: Problems with men and problems with society in Papua New Guinea. *The Australian Journal of Anthropology*, *19*(2), 179–193.

Maggio, R. (2018). 'According to kastom and according to law': 'Good life' and 'good death' in Gilbert Camp, Solomon Islands. In C. Gregory & J. Altman (Eds), *The quest for the good life in precarious times: Ethnographic perspectives on the domestic moral economy* (pp. 57–86). Canberra, ACT: ANU Press. doi.org/10.22459/QGLPT.03.2018

Martin, K. (2013). *The death of the big men and the rise of the big shots*. New York, NY: Berghahan.

Mihalic, F. (1971). *The Jacaranda dictionary and grammar of Melanesian Pidgin*. Milton, Qld: The Jacaranda Press.

Munck, R. (2013). The precariat: A view from the South. *Third World Quarterly*, *34*(5), 747–762.

Neilson, B. & Rossiter, N. (2008). Precarity as a political concept, or, Fordism as exception. *Theory, Culture and Society*, *25*(7–8), 51–72.

Oppermann, T. (2016). Coral roads and their sorcery: Lost authority and spectral commodification in Buka. *Oceania*, *86*(2), 186–207.

Rio, K. (2010). Handling sorcery in a state system of law: Magic, violence and kastom in Vanuatu. *Oceania, 80*(2), 182–197. doi.org/10.1002/j.1834-4461. 2010.tb00079.x

Robbins, J. & Wardlow, H. (Eds). (2005). *The making of global and local modernities in Melanesia: Humiliation, transformation and the nature of cultural change.* Burlington, England: Ashgate.

Rooney, M. (2013, 5 April). *Another Port Moresby community bulldozed.* Retrieved from www.devpolicy.org/another-port-moresby-community-bull dozed-2013040/

Russell D. Taylor and Partners Pty Ltd. (1972). *Madang urban study.* Konedobu: Department of Lands, Surveys and Mines.

Sahlins, M. (1992). The economics of develop-man in the Pacific. *Res: Anthropology and Aesthetics, 21,* 12–25.

Schwoerer, T. (2017). Sorcery and warfare in the Eastern Highlands of Papua New Guinea. *Oceania, 87*(3), 317–336.

Sharp, T., Cox, J., Spark. C., Lusby, S. & Rooney, M. (2015). *The formal, the informal and the precarious: Making a living in Papua New Guinea.* Retrieved from dpa.bellschool.anu.edu.au/experts-publications/publications/1292/formal-informal-and-precarious-making-living-urban-papua-new

Sinclair, J. (2006). *Madang.* Madang, Papua New Guinea: Divine Word University Press.

Smith, J. & Mwadime, N. (2015). *Email from Ngeti: An ethnography of sorcery, redemption and friendship in global Africa.* Berkeley, CA: University of California Press.

Taylor, J. (2015). Sorcery and the moral economy of agency: An ethnographic account. *Oceania, 85*(1), 38–50.

Tonkinson, R. (1981). Sorcery and social change in southeast Ambrym, Vanuatu. *Social Analysis: The International Journal of Social and Cultural Practice, 8,* 77–88.

Wardlow, H. (2006). *Wayward women: Sexuality and agency in a New Guinea society.* Berkeley: University of California Press.

9

Inequalities of Aspiration: Class, Cargo and the Moral Economy of Development in Papua New Guinea

John Cox

Introduction

This chapter explores the contours of contemporary Papua New Guinean (PNG) ideologies of nation-making and development and examines how narratives of development are constructed by the nation's urban middle class, based on aspirations for their own personal advancement and the development of the nation as a whole. These aspirations are changing relationships between urban professionals and their rural kin; remittance payments, for example, are being reframed in a developmental idiom as 'projects' or 'business' (see also Filer, this volume). However, the changes are not simply transactional; at a more affective register, I argue that middle-class Papua New Guineans are demonstrating something like the 'sentimental cosmopolitanism' identified by Black (2009) in the connections between donors and recipients of the KIVA Microfinance program.

These developmental aspirations and reworking of relationships are founded on a moral valuation of particular classes of people, usually glossed as 'elites' and 'grassroots' (Cox, 2013). As Gregory and Altman argued in their preface to a recent volume that explored theories of domestic moral economy, 'a study of values, then, must examine the social relations of the valuers and note the differences between points of view and moral environments' (Gregory & Altman, 2018, p. xviii). This chapter analyses a distinctive middle-class PNG moral economy, one that is profoundly shaped by discourses of development and citizenship (see also the differently situated but complementary moral economy analyses by Bainton; Filer; Gewertz & Errington; Zimmer-Tamakoshi, this volume). It seeks to understand how PNG professionals come to view their rural kin as having a 'cargo cult mentality' (bearing in mind that the grassroots also demonstrate a moral critique of this hierarchy) (Gewertz & Errington, this volume; Golub, 2014, p. 172; Smith, 2018, p. 46ff.).

In popular PNG articulations of ideal relations between classes, middle-class 'elites' are imagined as mobile, both spatially and temporally, because their lives move through various experiences and usually along a professional career path that accumulates financial, social and cultural capital. The grassroots, by comparison, are denied these same mobilities and are imagined, if in their rightful place, as static—rooted in traditional subsistence village life, where they provide for all of their own needs as an 'innocent population' (Golub, 2014, p. 160ff.). When the grassroots display aspirations that imply mobility beyond their prescribed place, their desires are likely to be delegitimised by accusations of exhibiting a 'cargo cult mentality'. As Golub put it, 'grassroots who … seek development, wealth and modernity are excoriated by urbanites for betraying the nation's deepest values' (Golub, 2014, p. 162).

The term 'cargo cult' was originally coined to describe Melanesian social movements that wrestled with the meaning of colonial rule, and the attendant inequalities of wealth and racial subordination, in a search for 'moral equivalence' (Burridge, 1960). Many cargo cults flourished after World War II, when the Australian colonial order had been disrupted. Some were millennial movements that sought to change the situation through spiritual power, emphasising a fusion of traditional Melanesian mythology and Christianity (Bainton, 2008; Lattas, 2007; Lawrence, 1964; Lindstrom, 1993; Macintyre, 2013). Others, such as Maasina Rule in Solomon Islands, were more secular organisations that challenged colonial power through activism and negotiation with British authorities (Akin, 2013).

Today, a number of these movements persist. Some have even taken ownership of the term cargo cult, but in common parlance, the 'cargo cult mentality' is a pejorative term. As I demonstrate below, with the case of the PNG community development worker Andrew, it is frequently used to disparage the expectation of rural people regarding access to wealth and development by implying that they expect material rewards to appear as if by magic. Gamblers are sometimes referred to in this way as people who expect to gain money without work (Macintyre, 2011). A further implication is that the grassroots are lazy and, rather than working for their own living, prefer dependency on their relatives, the state or aid programs. Cargo cult mentality is now a synonym for 'handout mentality'; the use of this phrase marks class privilege.

These disparities of power notwithstanding, middle-class aspirations are not purely selfish. Many urban professionals do maintain close relationships with the grassroots and aspire to better the lot of their rural kinsfolk. Indeed, the 'moral career' of most professionals in PNG includes ideals of scaling a career ladder and accumulating sufficient resources to be able to 'give back' to village relatives. As Debra McDougall shows in her chapter in this volume, this sometimes results in sustained and creative projects that have considerable legitimacy and impact on the ground. More often, however, townsfolk simply imagine themselves returning to 'the village' in their retirement and those who have not made ongoing contributions to the life of the village community may find themselves less welcome than they anticipated (Dalsgaard, 2013; Macintyre, 2011; Rasmussen, 2015; Zimmer-Tamakoshi, 1997).

Relationships between town and village are increasingly being articulated in the idiom of development. The grassroots are becoming recipients of the generosity of their middle-class relatives, who sponsor small-scale 'projects' or business activities that are within the financial means of the donor (Rasmussen, 2015). Sometimes, they are even able to attract development projects funded by external aid agencies (e.g. Suti, Hoatson, Tafunai & Cox, 2020). These practices echo Melanesian systems of political patronage in which any residual visions of equitable and reliable state-run services are displaced by personalised disbursement of goods (Cox, 2009). The dependency implied is disparaged as 'cargo cult mentality', but the grassroots are also disciplined into accepting their clientelist position, while their aspirations for basic health and education services are ignored.

Class Distinction and Development in Papua New Guinea

Alongside Martha Macintyre, several of the other contributors to this volume have made significant contributions to scholarly understandings of how class distinction in PNG is being shaped through moral evaluations of people that are based in ideas of modern development. Deborah Gewertz and Fred Errington, in a 1998 article titled 'Sleights of hand and the construction of desire in a Papua New Guinea modernity' (see also Gewertz & Errington, 1999), documented a now-familiar process of the production of narratives of blame to account for economic inequality in PNG. These insights into class, development and inequality have also been advanced by Nick Bainton's work on the social effects of mining in Lihir and Paige West's studies of conservation projects in the PNG highlands (see below).

Let me begin with the work of Gewertz and Errington—they tell the story of a microenterprise organisation operating in Wewak, the provincial capital of East Sepik Province. The organisation was founded to provide assistance and relief to women who produce handicrafts but struggle to sell them at a profit. This organisation did so through training programs that instilled entrepreneurial disciplines and aspirations, such as participating in a trade fair in Jayapura, across the border in Indonesia. Gewertz and Errington viewed these ideologies of business as justifications of personal accumulation in a society where this invites jealousy and where such accumulation is regarded as immoral. However, as their analysis proceeded, it became apparent that these new entrepreneurial disciplines of the self and other features of the training did not deliver success in business. If anything, the programs set women up to fail and to accumulate debts that had not burdened them previously. But, another outcome was a new moralising of money and business; women who had not succeeded in their business ventures could now be judged—by others and also by themselves—not to have been working hard enough and, therefore, as undeserving, poor and failed citizens. Gewertz and Errington located this within the nascent PNG class system:

> These processes, reflecting middle-class expectations, were based on a modernist claim that almost anyone could gain access to a certain quality of life. Almost everyone had the potential opportunity and capacity, indeed the right and virtual obligation, to work and save in order to consume self-evidently desirable goods and services.

Correspondingly, according to this formulation, those unable or unwilling to accumulate and therefore acquire these goods and services would have primarily themselves to blame. Any ensuing and persistent inequality would thus be understood as less the product of unfair exclusion or repudiation of kin obligations than of personal failure to fulfil reasonable expectations. (Gewertz & Errington, 1998, p. 346)

This observation of the dynamics of self-blame and its alienating effects mirrors anthropological analysis of similar phenomena in different contexts and times, such as Cahn's (2006, 2008) work on multi-level marketing in Mexico; the critical feminist literature on microfinance, such as Karim's 2011 study of Bangladesh; Schuster's 2015 work in Paraguay or Schiffhauer's (2018) study of pyramid schemes in Siberia. Neoliberal ideologies of individual opportunity have been highly successful in obscuring the structural factors that entrench inequality everywhere. Moreover, in an era of the retreat of social protections provided by the welfare state—or, in the case of PNG and similar developing countries, the failure of the postcolonial state to build an effective welfare system— the financialisation of people's 'social collateral' (Schuster, 2015) undermines existing social safety nets that sustain the poor. Indeed, in the Western Pacific, the so-called '*wantok* system' is a keystone of a national ideology of the resilience of kin-based social protection. The grassroots are imagined as existing in a realm of subsistence affluence and traditional social harmony, in which all their needs are met without cash nor the state; therefore, this ideology justifies both middle-class accumulation and inadequate state services (Cox, 2016, 2018; Cox & Phillips, 2015; Schram, 2015; cf. Rooney, 2019).

In PNG and other countries in the Global South, these ideologies are deeply embedded in private sector developments, such as large-scale mines or the massive Papua New Guinea Liquefied Natural Gas Project (see Bainton; Main, this volume). Bainton has written of the long-running 'Personal Viability' (more commonly known as 'PV') program: a private company, led by a well-known PNG businessman of Chinese descent, who has developed his advice on how to prosper in business and life into a very popular personal development course (Bainton, 2010, 2011; Bainton & Cox, 2009). PV is highly moralistic in tone. It begins by asking its participants the pointed question, 'are you viable?' (Bainton, 2011), by way of introducing a personal stocktake of income and expenditure that leads people on a path of accumulation and of exactly the kind of moral justification of the refusal of kinship obligations envisaged by Gewertz and Errington.

In Lihir, PV was adopted by elite local leaders as the foundation for their long-term development manifesto that mapped out a future 'road' to a prosperous and 'viable' society that would maximise the benefits of mining and reduce the so-called 'resource dependency syndrome'. Their commitment to the PV program was a contemporary 'rational' response to an actually-existing cargo cult that had flourished in Lihir in the pre-mining era, which cultivated visions of 'instant wealth' (Macintyre, 2013) and the transformation of Lihirian villages into a metropolitan city (Bainton, 2008). An older generation of Lihirians has interpreted the mine as the (partial) fulfilment of these earlier prophecies, which partly explains the heightened expectation for the company to 'deliver the goods'. But, if the ideology of PV encourages grassroots business activities and promises to unleash an entrepreneurial spirit that will free people from their reliance upon the company, it also mystifies the inequalities in how the financial benefits of the mine are distributed and provides a moral justification for the accumulative practices of Lihirian elites (Bainton, 2010).

Similar practices and ideologies are also found within government (sometimes exactly: in 2007, I observed notices advertising PV training for high-level public servants in Honiara, the capital of Solomon Islands) and in bilateral development programs sponsored by donor partners, such as Australia (where the official aid program is intensifying its commitment to business and entrepreneurship). They also characterise many of the community programs run by international non-governmental organisations (NGOs), including conservation initiatives (West & Aini, this volume). At local and national scales, in the private and not-for-profit sectors, development is increasingly articulated as a modernising and moralising project of capital accumulation by individuals.

In her 2001 article, 'Environmental NGOs and the nature of ethnographic inquiry', Paige West provided a compelling analysis of how these class-based discourses of development disparage and infantilise the rural poor (see also West, 2006). West described the essentialist expectations of Western conservationists who were disappointed with the failure of Gimi people to conform to their fantasies of what indigenous rainforest people should be. By assuming Gimi to be culturally inauthentic, conservationists legitimised their own ways of seeing land and the environment and rendered the landowners and their (misunderstood) foraging and gardening practices as 'threats to biodiversity'. West has continued to document these processes of dispossession in a now substantial body of work (e.g. West, 2016), but here I wish to focus on her critique of the paternalistic dispositions of middle-class Papua New Guineans working for the international NGO Conservation International, particularly their use of the term 'cargo cult mentality'.

West described an incident where villagers, unsatisfied with the minimal benefits of their participation in the conservation scheme, had dared to confront NGO workers with a list of their unmet needs. These included medicine, a water supply, unspecified consumer goods and food for children (West, 2001, p. 64). None of these seems unreasonable or overly ambitious—they represent aspirations for basic needs that many middle-class Papua New Guineans simply assume as an entitlement. However, the response from the NGO worker was highly aggressive and condescending, accusing the villagers of having a 'cargo cult mentality'—of not wanting to work for their own benefit, but expecting material goods and wealth to 'magically' appear. As West argued, 'dismissing the development needs of Maimafu village by referring to local desires as a "cargo" mentality is an exercise in power' (West, 2001, p. 65).

Accusations of 'cargo cult mentality' are exercises in class-based power—discursive exercises that imagine the urban middle class as hard-working modern citizens and 'grassroots' villagers as primitive, superstitious and backward (Golub, 2014, pp. 171–177). These discourses occupy a prominent place in public discussions of development and fears of aid dependency, in addition to politics. I have previously argued (Cox, 2009) that cargo cult accusations in Solomon Islands are used to discipline villagers who ask for the wrong kinds of benefits from NGOs, as is also clearly demonstrated by West's example. However, this experience also points to a practice where villagers learn to second-guess these self-appointed catalysts of development; therefore, it reflects the same kinds of relationships that characterise political patronage in Melanesia (Cox, 2009). These dynamics closely parallel the racialised and gendered hierarchies that Papua New Guineans, especially women, experience in working with Australian and other international aid programs (Spark, 2020).

Politicians establish and retain their influence through distributions of favours, goods and money, a practice that has been deeply entrenched by increases to constituency development funds (public money that can be disbursed at an individual member of parliament's discretion) in both Solomon Islands and PNG (Cox, 2009; Wood, 2019). Although these relationships are often analysed in terms of reciprocity, in practice, it is the patrons, not the clients, who benefit from these highly extractive patronage systems. Politicians routinely complain that they are 'not ATMs' (in reference to frequent requests for financial assistance) and label their constituents as having a cargo cult mentality or a 'handout mentality' (Okole, 2003). In common parlance, the two terms have largely merged, but the former emphasises credulous waiting for wealth to appear by supernatural means and the latter laziness and dependency. Thus, in one simple and familiar step, cargo cult discourse legitimises the accumulative practices of 'big shots' (Martin, 2013) and renders the aspirations and demands of their followers immoral, greedy and superstitious or backward. For anthropologists, this step was first taken by colonial administrators who were threatened by indigenous movements that questioned the inequalities of the colonial system (Akin, 2013; Burridge, 1960; Lindstrom, 1993). Therefore, it is disappointing (but not entirely surprising) to observe the long life of this colonial trope now being weaponised by the postcolonial elite and even becoming entrenched as a mainstream theme in nation-making discourses (Cox, 2018, pp. 71ff.; Lattas, 2007, p. 157; Lindstrom, 1993, pp. 15ff.).

Class, Cargo and Money Schemes

These dynamics played out in a similar way in my research on 'fast money schemes', the epidemic of pyramid schemes that captured the imagination of PNG's middle class in the late 1990s and that has never really subsided (Cox, 2019). As Verdery (1995) argued, pyramid schemes provide an invaluable window into social transformations and class-based aspirations. Fast money schemes remain a part of 'popular economies' (Krige, 2012) in PNG. Some, such as the Bougainvillean fraud U-Vistract and the Papalain scam from Morobe Province, have had a remarkable 'long tail' and, more than 20 years later, continue to operate, albeit largely within their core regional constituencies, rather than among the national middle-class (Cox, 2018, 2019). In the heyday of the fast money schemes, the scale of participation and money contributed was driven by middle-class investors who were drawn not only by the promise of 100 per cent monthly returns on their money, but also by a heady cocktail of (unfulfilled) promises: being able to realise national development, embodying entrepreneurial dispositions, finding favour with God and bridging what Burridge called the 'moral equivalence' with the cosmopolitan world of the global middle-class, imagined largely through the lens of white Australia (Cox, 2015).

In the years following the crash of the fast money schemes in 1999, a cargo cult narrative emerged that was explicitly structured around class. Those who had lost their money in the schemes were imagined to be acting according to a cargo cult mentality—unthinking, credulous and having a magical view of the production of money, consumer goods and wealth that was divorced from the realities of labour or the discipline of saving. The following editorial in *The National* provides a typical example:

> Why do people 'invest' in these schemes? At first, when U-Vistract hit the headlines, it appeared that many initial investors had indeed reaped huge returns on small investments. That is precisely the way in which these schemes operate. The first investors will always receive large dividends—but, as the scheme continues, and more investors take part, the returns diminish until no returns are paid. That is why these schemes are referred to internationally and in PNG as 'pyramid schemes'; the pyramid shape reflects the diminishing returns to those who have entrusted their money to these frauds. Some of the more sophisticated investors back in those days began to realise the truth of the situation. They and other educated potential investors put their money elsewhere.
>
> Today, and for some years past, these cruel and unlawful schemes target the simplest of our people, very often squatters and simple village people. These people believe what they are so enthusiastically and persuasively told. And, of course, the golden promises have been added to by dark suggestions that the established banks and the government have some vested interest in blocking the people from the rightful gains such organisations could provide. We still have not succeeded in persuading these thousands of our countrymen and women that such fast money is nothing but a pipe dream, more allied to the cargo cults of old, than to modern schemes designed to improve people's incomes. The old adage 'nothing for nothing, and precious little for sixpence' is accurate when describing the whole field of making money. Broadly speaking, there is only one sure way of making money, and that is through hard work. That is not, of course, a palatable answer for thousands of our people living at or beneath the poverty line.

Anything that can promise some relief from their present situation is bound to be seized upon with enthusiasm. It is not until they learn the hard way, by not only not making profits, but by losing what they have been able to invest, that they come to realise the nature of these schemes. ('Modern Shylocks', 2005)

This account draws on classic 'cargoist' (Lindstrom, 1993) themes—it articulates a popular ideology of class-based inequalities of aspiration. The lower classes of the rural poor and urban squatters are represented as poor, simple, gullible and not understanding the link between labour and the accumulation of capital and unable to handle money (Rooney, 2019, p. 164). However, it could be argued that the extremely low wages that these classes of people have access to are insufficient to meet basic survival needs (Gibson, 2019; Hukula, 2019; Sharp et al., 2015); therefore, they understand the relationship between work and accumulation only too well.

This kind of popular narrative is also used to explain why young men turn to petty and violent crime—they crave goods and lifestyles that are beyond their financial reach and so attempt to gain them by force. While there exist realities of crime and violence in urban settlements (Gewertz & Errington, this volume), blaming urbanisation ignores the prevalence of rural violence and rests on a national mythology that romanticises village life (Macintyre, 2008, p. 181).

Returning to the editorial in *The National* (see above), the middle classes are acknowledged as also having been fooled by the fast money schemes' promises of great wealth. However, they are not represented as being gullible or greedy. Rather, they are represented as sophisticated and even discerning, taking the returns of the pyramid schemes and then reinvesting their money elsewhere. This may have been the experience of a tiny fraction of the elite, but this was certainly not a typical outcome. In interviewing dozens of middle-class fast money scheme investors since the quoted editorial was published, I have only met two who made money from the scheme (and one who had his principal returned to him without interest after having thought twice about his investment). Nevertheless, the underlying understanding is that middle-class financial aspirations are legitimate and informed, whereas grassroots aspirations follow a cargo cult mentality that threatens the social order.

Very often, cargo cult discourse is located within a modernist narrative of cultural development, in which rural villagers are imagined as living traditional lives without access to—or need for—cash. This supposed naivety in relation to money leaves them vulnerable to cargo cult thinking. As my friend Roga, a lecturer at Divine Word University in Madang, explained to me:

> It's something that comes out from deep inside our culture. When they see a white man coming, they think, 'Oh yes, here comes some money. How can we get some of that money?' It started after the war with the cargo cults—they wait for the big ship to come, full of money! Now Noah, he's the latest one in Bougainville. And here in Madang we had the Black Jesus—he was promising all his followers, 'If you join with me, you can have so much money!'

This account provides a typical culturalising explanation that conflates cargo cults with money schemes, such as Noah Musingku's U-Vistract scheme. The account is also national in scope. Noah is in Bougainville, but Madang also has its own contemporary cargo cult, the Black Jesus cult—led by Steven Tari, an infamous cult leader from villages in the Transgogol area outside Madang. Tari claimed to be the son of the 1960s cargo cult leader Yali (Lawrence, 1964) and also the incarnation of the Black Jesus. In 2007, Tari was arrested, charged with murder and rape and subsequently imprisoned. It is not clear whether the so-called Black Jesus actually promised his followers money, but in Roga's account, he has been assimilated into the prevailing cargo cult narrative—a feature of an unchanging Melanesian culture that is ill at ease with modernity and at risk of lapsing into an irrational quest for wealth driven by an untameable desire.

In practice, however, fast money schemes cultivated visions of grassroots national development (Cox, 2011, 2018, pp. 127ff.). Thomas, a Sepik labourer resident in the 'Public Tank' settlement outside Madang (on the way to Sisiak, discussed by Gewertz & Errington, this volume), described his rational, well-thought-through aspirations in anything but the mad, magical rush expected of the cargo cult mentality:

> If this is paid and our rewards are given, with our group we have all these development proposals—we have bridges, schools. On the personal level, we have a good house, water, schools, I think the best schools. The guys with me have these little plans and someone who is in the Public Works Department helped them to type everything up. There must be some contribution to the LLGs [local-level governments], having the same treatment.

There will be something for everyone. There's no selfishness or greediness. We'll share it with others. Also, the people who say bad things about us, we'll show them they're wrong and share with them too. We have AusAID but we can share our own aid program back to our own communities. There will be some controls—you have to have your own plan for large monies.

Thomas presents himself not only as the grassroots planner and organiser that he is (he has also led delegations to successive Madang Governors requesting better services for the settlements) but also as a responsible developmental citizen. Although he has no qualifications himself, he identifies with an ideal of planning by experts, such as his friend from the Public Works Department. Not only does Thomas demonstrate good moral credentials in his commitment to sharing, but his aspirations are for public goods and services, presented and accounted for properly—rather than irresponsible consumption (Cox & Macintyre, 2014; Cox, 2014; Barnett-Nagshineh, 2019, p. 232). The reference to AusAID, the (now-defunct) Australian government aid agency, is a rejection of dependency (another signal of moral worthiness) and foreshadows the argument made below about Papua New Guineans taking development into their own hands.

Global Aspirations and the Place of the Poor

What, then, are acceptable aspirations for the lower classes? Robert Foster (2008) and Alex Golub (2014) have both proposed accounts of contemporary PNG popular national ideologies that imagine the urban middle class as prospering from modernity, while the grassroots remain in a traditional state. The rural grassroots are conceived of as living in a temporal stasis, in which they maintain old cultural traditions. As Macintyre put it:

> The lives, experiences and worldviews of town dwellers, of industrial or office workers, have tended to be viewed through the lens of interactions between urban and rural, in which the authentic or base cultural template of values, aspirations and social relationships is located in the rural village. (2011, p. 92)

What Gewertz and Errington have called 'incommensurable differences' in class become starkly differentiated in relation to what are considered to be legitimate aspirations. Villagers are expected to be able to provide for themselves through subsistence agriculture, perhaps augmented by some small-scale cash cropping or micro-enterprises so that they might afford a few basic commodities: kerosene and soap, tea or tinned fish (Dundon, 2004; Foster, 2002). They are not expected to fully partake in the benefits of modernity, including the benefits requested by West's Maimafu informant from the NGO: medicine, good water supply and access to consumer goods. Such goods are implicitly restricted—temporally, spatially and morally—to the modern, urban professional class, that understands the proper relationship between labour and consumption and, therefore, possesses a worthy moral disposition that equips them to enjoy these benefits without lapsing into the excesses of a cargo cult mentality.

Middle-class aspirations often embrace a cosmopolitan lifestyle modelled on Australia, the former colonial power, or broader ideas of a prosperous global middle class. These aspirations have multiple sources and are stimulated by images seen on television, such as Australian soap operas; new shopping malls, such as Vision City in Waigani, which has an iconic status within Port Moresby as a modern urban space; new housing schemes that allow professionals to live in gated communities in new residential areas and through international travel for study, workshops, church activities and, increasingly, for tourism. Perhaps most accessibly, aspirations are stimulated through social media; for example, Facebook is now the dominant platform and allows transnational connections to flourish (Barbara, Cox & Leach, 2015; Foster & Horst, 2018). Social media use is no longer limited to the middle class; the pull of these global imaginaries extends well beyond PNG's urban elite to many other communities. Those who are faced with the possibility of a mine or other large-scale resource development may imagine their villages turning into cities (Bainton, 2010; Macintyre, 2003: 121; Main, this volume).

The cosmopolitan urban lifestyle is not merely a fantasy. Many middle-class Papua New Guineans enjoy relatively prosperous circumstances that allow them to travel internationally for holidays (typically to Australia, Fiji, Indonesia or Israel, where the pull of Christian pilgrimages to the Holy Land is strong), to eat out regularly or to live in new condominiums. This fortunate group typically occupy higher levels of the business, professional or aid management elite and have grown up in urban centres with educated parents and siblings. Macintyre (2011) has documented how these changed circumstances allow contemporary middle-class Melanesian women greater individual freedoms than in any previous generation. Ceridwen Spark (2014) showed that new, more assertive and creative dispositions are flourishing and being valourised in the language of empowerment and personal success among this class of young women in PNG and across the Pacific region (see also Brimacombe, 2016). Although Melanesian cities have been male-dominated spaces since their establishment by colonial powers, women are now negotiating these spaces, often quite independently of male companions or protectors, and following paths of their own career advancement and other projects of personal development (Demian, 2017; Spark, 2011). Urban Pentecostal churches often provide a sympathetic community for modern professionals and mediate some of the moral perils associated with the individualism inherent in global middle-class lifestyle aspirations (Cox & Macintyre, 2014; Marshall-Fratani, 2001).

However, this description of prosperity and liberation paints far too rosy a picture. Melanesian professional women find working with condescending Australian aid program managers to be both humiliating and infuriating (Spark, 2020). Anxiety, disillusionment and 'downward mobility' are also prevalent. In addition to other scholars, I have previously written of the economic precarity of the PNG middle class (Cox, 2013; Gibson, 2019; Macintyre, 2011; Rooney, 2019; Sharp et al., 2015). The costs of living in Melanesian cities exceed what most wage-earners can sustain; therefore, household budgets are often strained. The obligations of urbanites to their rural kin are perpetually troubling because demands for school fees, medical expenses and funeral or brideprice contributions cannot be ignored indefinitely (Monsell-Davis, 1993). Managing these demands is difficult, but many in the middle class are aware of their own privileges. As Spark (2018) observes:

> While the middle class in PNG are maligned for turning their backs on their grass roots counterparts, internationally educated and cosmopolitan women … are acutely aware that they are products of a context in which some are afforded more opportunities than others. (p. 279)

For the most part, middle-class people do recognise the legitimacy of these needs, even as they try to protect themselves from an impossible deluge of demands. Some are more disparaging and fear that their generosity creates an unhealthy dependency that makes the grassroots unproductive and fosters a 'handout mentality' (Foster, 2008, p. 111; Gewertz & Errington, 1999, p. 49; Martin, 2007). 'Handout mentality' is a variant of 'cargo cult mentality'. Some fear that if they fail to meet expectations, their relatives may punish them with sorcery (Dalsgaard, 2013, p. 292). Therefore, maintaining good relations is important for avoiding this, particularly for those who imagine themselves retiring to a peaceful village life.

Many have reached an understanding with their kinsfolk that realistically acknowledges the limitations of their capacity to meet demand. Peter, a New Irelander in his 50s, who works in Madang as a secondary schoolteacher, provided an example of how these agreements are negotiated:

> We tell our folks—we're saving this much and we'll give it to you but when we don't have anything we'll tell you. They're not jealous of our savings because we help them a lot. So, they don't have any bad feelings about what we do. We have our budget and we live by that and we have some savings for requests from our relatives but, if we don't have it, we don't go asking others for it. If we borrow something it must be returned very quickly. I don't like living with debts. In fact, we don't have any debts! We don't make commitments or if we do, we save for it.

Peter exemplifies the rational, financially disciplined, middle-class subject who saves money and spends within his means. In the eyes of the self-help scheme described by Bainton (2011), he would be considered well and truly 'viable'. However, the moral economy of accumulation for Peter is not focused on personal advancement. Rather, it extends to an active role in maintaining good relations with (and redistributing money to) his family back 'home':

> What's the point of saving money if you have relatives in need? It's important to us because we understand their situation. Life is home but we only go every two years because we spend a lot of money there—much more than we would in four weeks back here. We admire our people for living the kind of life they live—garden food, fishing, pigs, chickens and when they have the money canned stuff. The cost of goods in Kavieng is more expensive than here but it's even more expensive in the village. We feel we have to contribute to the village economy but the local trade stores are much more expensive. We decide to support them because we see that they really struggle and we want to support the village economy.

In Peter's case, these enduring family connections mediate the structural divisions of class. Peter maintains contact with his relatives through mobile phone contact, which helps him to manage their demands and expectations, particularly for visits to town. He describes the impact of the mobile phone on these relationships as follows:

> It's the answer to the lack of transport and the cost of transport. You can say, 'Don't waste your money on transport, wait'. It's more economical for me to pay for credit on their phones than to house them and feed them when they visit.

Like many urban wage-earners (Dalsgaard, 2013, pp. 292ff.), Peter anticipated retiring to the village. However, he passed away in 2014 and missed the opportunity to enjoy that return.

Peter's case may represent one mode of close and amicable connection between extended families that are stretched between town and village. Certainly, much love exists in these relationships, rather than only burdensome obligations. When, for instance, educated women save their own money to reinvest in the education of their nieces or other children within the extended family (Macintyre, 2011), they are identifying closely with individuals and trying to set them up for social mobility and economic independence or, at least, to do what they can to provide them with this opportunity (see also McDougall, this volume).

At a more elite level, the Business and Professional Women's Club of Port Moresby provides an institutionalised mode of addressing such needs and aspirations. The Club brings successful career women together to fund scholarships for girls whose families do not have the means to support their education. The Club also provides mentoring and networking opportunities that assist its members to negotiate their careers in male-dominated workplaces (Spark & Lee, 2018). Rasmussen has also documented a Port Moresby–based club of Manusians (the Mbuke Islands People's Association) who gathered together to raise funds for projects back in Manus and even established a 'business arm' for this purpose (Rasmussen, 2015, pp. 143ff.).

Where the Business and Professional Women's Club or the Mbuke Islands People's Association may exemplify the formalised charitable activities of the Port Moresby business community or a distinct provincial or cultural group, there is also a relatively recent parallel trend in which the internal remittance economy is taking a developmentalist turn within PNG families. Remittances to close kin are being construed as development projects; professionals send money 'back to the village' for specific 'projects', such as building a water tank or installing solar panels. Others try to set up their rural relatives in small businesses that they hope will allow them to be more financially independent, fulfilling a role as productive labourer-citizens in the national economy. This trend echoes the global turn in development policy towards microenterprise and income generation projects across both not-for-profit and private sector actors alike. In PNG, this includes mining companies that set up small projects for women and other groups not likely to receive royalties directly (Macintyre, 2003).

Sometimes, this business activity is not actually located in the village (the paradigmatic locus of development); rather, it extends to creating markets for products that villagers have grown or made. Others have set up relatives in small kiosks or driving taxis in Port Moresby or other towns. An enterprising Manusian friend of mine has used her free time to set up a stall at a fashionable Port Moresby market (augmented by a Facebook page), where she sells handicrafts made by her relatives on Manus. She enjoys the benefits of a well-paid position, comes from a well-educated family and does not complain of burdensome requests from her relatives. However, she does feel for their disadvantaged circumstances and has begun this business expressly to create income-generating opportunities for the people 'back home'. These new commodity chains are not lacking in interpersonal warmth, nor do I think they turn kin relationships into market transactions. Indeed, much of the evidence from research into commodity chains in Melanesia suggests that commodities gain their mobility through good relationships and friendships (Sharp, 2016, 2019). However, some subtle shifts occur in the distribution of power through these networks of kin.

My previous work has described how middle-class desires to be catalysts for development among their rural kin were exploited by the fast money scheme U-Vistract (Cox, 2018, pp. 141ff.; Cox & Macintyre, 2014). In my analysis of these dynamics, I have argued that, as middle-class Papua New Guineans begin to see their relatives through the lens of the development project, they adopt a 'sentimental cosmopolitanism' akin to that fostered by international NGOs in their fundraising (Black, 2009). Black studied KIVA, a large microfinance NGO that connects donors in the Global North with recipients in the Global South, through the exchange of stories over the internet. The success of KIVA depends on donors feeling not only that they have done some good by helping someone in need, but also that they have made an emotional connection with the recipients. Middle-class Papua New Guineans are adopting similar dispositions as they begin to see their rural kin as subjects who must be mobilised for development. As Thomas, the mercurial Sepik from Public Tank settlement put it, imagining himself in the position of a wealthy patron enriched by a money scheme, 'we can share our own aid program back to our own communities'. These dispositions contain disparities of power that become a form of 'Christian patronage', in which well-intentioned Christian professionals position themselves as personalised disbursers of development in ways that mirror Melanesian systems of political patronage (Cox, 2018, p. 152; cf. Main, this volume). Patrons are the more powerful parties in patron–client relationships; they are able to determine the kinds of development projects that they are willing to fund. Moreover, the role of the state as a provider of routine expert services is replaced by the patron's petty disbursements and projects (Cox, 2009).

Situating Social Mobility: The Village Cargo Cult Mentality versus Middle-Class Vocation

If the rural poor are subaltern subjects that require developing, this constitutes a constraint on other aspirations they may have. Moralistic narratives of blame, such as cargo cult discourse, play a powerful role in legitimating the place of patrons and shaping the kinds of desires to which the grassroots may properly aspire. In my own fieldwork, I have encountered almost identical scenarios to the one documented by West, in which middle-class development program staff lambaste villagers for having a 'cargo cult mentality'. Here, I focus on the account of a middle-class development NGO worker, rather than on the villagers whom he was trying to influence. My informant, Andrew, was a well-educated Sepik man in his late twenties who had been working for an environmental NGO in Madang province on efforts to reduce illegal logging through small-scale 'eco-forestry', using portable sawmills and trying to improve market access for locally harvested timber.

At the time I interviewed him in 2009, he held a new position at Divine Word University. Despite the judgemental attitude that I document below, I liked him and was fortunate enough to catch up with him a few months after the completion of my fieldwork, when he attended a conference in Melbourne. In Madang, he had been describing the activities of Pentecostal pastors as 'cargo cult', another common application of the term (Cox, 2018, p. 117). When I pressed him on exactly what he meant by this; he responded as follows:

> I'd like to talk about two examples from my work with an NGO from the Sogoram area in Madang. It's in the TransGogol LLG and the other is in the Usina-Bundi LLG. People are scattered around with limited access to resources. The Japan and New Guinea Timber Company was active in that area, so they have high expectations because they had an easy start with royalties. They don't want to work but expect that NGOs will bring money. I have to explain to them that we are not bringing bulldozers and that kind of equipment.

> It's a cargo cult mentality—they want access to resources to change their lifestyles but they don't want to work for it. It was hard working with them. When we were doing an activity in the village people give excuses—they say they're working on their gardens or have other commitments. This is something the timber company has done. It promotes laziness among people—a cargo cult mentality. They have land and they can till the soil but they don't want to, they just sit around.

In Andrew's (middle-class) mind, the people expect something for nothing. However, in this case, their (to him unrealistic) expectations are not inherent, nor are they provoked by the promises made by his NGO (as in West's example) or their politicians. Rather, their lack of interest in bettering themselves is the result of being spoiled by logging company largesse. Like many town dwellers, mining companies and development agencies, Andrew imagines rural life as paradisaical, where life is timeless and work in subsistence horticulture is easy. For him and many others, the work that people do in their gardens could not be as important or rewarding as participation in a development program.

For Andrew, the 'noncompliance' of the villagers with his project was unacceptable and needed to be dealt with strictly—by 'scolding' the people. Scolding is not uncommon in PNG, although the term has fallen from use in contemporary English elsewhere, and seems to reflect a mode of exercising authority that derives from the colonial period. Alice Street, in her ethnography of Modillon Hospital in Madang, has observed nurses who hector patients and demand that they demonstrate their moral worthiness (2014). Stephanie Lusby has documented the violent practices of the PNG security industry, in which security guards are beaten into submission by their overseers (2017, pp. 30ff.). This violence is understood as reforming them into good citizens. In Andrew's case, despite his age, a similar disciplining role for him as a development worker overturned the traditional intergenerational hierarchy. This suggests that class is a more important form of privilege than age:

> As a young man it's difficult but I have to scold at old people when they are stubborn and don't want to do the activities for their own benefit.

Andrew admitted that this was not very effective; therefore, I asked him if he changed his approach when he realised it was not working. He answered as follows:

> Sometimes I try. People are people. It's too much to deal with human beings like they're inferior objects like pigs or dogs. So to scold someone is treating them like a dog. I always use that approach. I talk hard at them and then later I explain why I had to speak like that. At times I tell them I'm just wasting my time with such people who have such an attitude to development. 'You're lazy', I used to tell them, 'you're lazy'. They're remote, hungry for development. The government is not likely to do that for them, so they need NGOs but they are unwilling to work hard for those changes.

I asked him more about scolding: 'but this approach of scolding them didn't work?' He said:

> I'd change my approach. When we go to the villages, normally we buy some food items. But people come for rice and biscuits, not to work, so I'd do away with manufactured items. Because we are there for them, it's their obligation to provide stuff. If they don't give it, we can buy from them.

Andrew's attempts to soften his approach seemed to run into conflict with his own impatience and his ideological investment in the victim-blaming cargo discourse. I pressed him further on whether his scolding was effective, and he revealed how ingrained the discourse of self-blame is in developmental interactions in PNG:

> It's effective because some of them said I have to talk harder in order to have the mandate and have authority over them. This contradicts my own values and opinion. I only scold the dogs.

This extraordinary disparagement of noncompliant villagers is remarkable; not only does Andrew judge them as lazy, but this judgement also removes some of their humanity, meaning that they must be treated like dogs. This is an almost exact re-enactment of colonial racist authority that, historically, has driven the cargo cult trope (Buck, 1988; Lindstrom, 1993) and is remembered by many as the origin of inequality (Rousseau, 2015). Andrew justified his scolding as a departure from normal manners and ethics that was required by the context. Some villagers who supported the project urged him on, supporting his sense that cargo cult villagers require much less respectful treatment than he would usually extend to normal, middle-class people like himself. The acceptance of scolding by some villagers implies an acceptance or internalisation of the middle-class moral valuations of rural life and subsistence work. This is an example of the developmental paternalism documented by West, in which villagers are to be scolded like naughty children. The village context was a revelation to Andrew:

> I didn't know about cargo cult until I was here and then I saw the pattern of their behaviour. I may have heard it as a child and have heard of examples of some activities when people want free stuff. But I wasn't able to know what cargo cult is until I've seen cargo cult in the village. Understanding cargo cult came from being confronted with such attitudes working with the people, in the village but not just village groups but other organisations.

The horror of the inertia of villagers, whom he saw as subject to a cargo cult mentality, was confronting for Andrew. However, for him, the lack of temporal momentum shown by these noncompliant and backward villagers stood in contrast to his own social and temporal mobility:

> I used to tell them, 'I'm a young man. I want to go for further studies. I can't waste my time with you, who don't want to see development. I'd rather spend time with those who are willing to work.' This experience, on the other hand, was a good one. It improves myself as a community development worker. It helps to change strategies to work with communities. One strategy is not acceptable. It has to be flexibility. I have to change my approach. People have to work.

Placed in a difficult context and confronted by inequality, Andrew retreated into a middle-class narrative of his own 'moral career' (Chu, 2010). Here, we may observe a different side of these 'developmental' interactions than was visible to West in her village fieldwork or to Gewertz and Errington in Wewak. For Andrew, the unfruitful interaction with a noncompliant village was reinterpreted as an experience that he could learn from, and that would form part of his portfolio of moral and professional progression.

Academic discussions of careers in PNG have largely focused on the dilemmas of professional women (Macintyre, 1998, 2011; Spark, 2011, 2020); or accounts of young men without a clear 'moral career' (e.g. Gewertz & Errington; McDougall, this volume). But the place of career progression and vocation as a constitutive element of class identity has largely been overlooked. Through his (albeit challenging) work for the environmental NGO, Andrew accumulated not only financial capital from his wages, but also professional cultural capital that would advance his career. He even demonstrated his credentials along this career trajectory via using modern managerialist buzzwords, such as 'strategy' and 'flexibility'.

However, this flexibility was not entirely open-ended. Although Andrew may have needed to adapt his strategies, the goal remained the same—'[grassroots] people have to work'. The work ethic of the poor is foregrounded as the primary obstacle to development, just as in the microfinance program studied by Gewertz and Errington and in the self-help course documented by Bainton. Like the would-be entrepreneurs envisaged by these two programs, Andrew demonstrated the drive to 'get ahead' and advance himself, though this was through study and professional work rather than the pursuit of business.

This narrative of middle-class career progression is nested within a broader nation-making narrative of productive (professional, urban) citizens contributing to the collective project of national development. The nation itself is seen as suffering from a pathological dependency on aid and foreign multinational companies; therefore, it must become economically independent. PNG Prime Minister James Marape has made ambitious public statements that draw on this sentiment, stating that he intends to make PNG 'the richest black nation in the world' (Graue, 2019) and pledging that PNG will not be dependent on Australia in 10 years' time (Lyons & Davidson, 2019). U-Vistract articulated a similar vision, boasting that PNG would become an aid donor to smaller countries in the region (Cox, 2018, p. 197). Perhaps, Marape's muscular economic nationalism exhibits echoes of the global populist zeitgeist, but it also represents a response to perceptions of the failure of the O'Neill government (in which Marape served as Treasurer) to put the benefits of the resources boom towards public services that might improve the wellbeing of the majority of the population.

Conclusion: Inequality of Aspiration

PNG's middle-class may struggle with the cost of living, but they experience this as a failure of the system to provide the benefits that they feel they should enjoy, given their education, work ethic and overall position in society. As individuals, many imagine themselves called to a particular career path that God has planned for them and hope to work their way into promotions and social mobility (Macintyre, 2011). The religious element of this vocation or moral career has fallen from most Western accounts of career progression, but it remains fundamental to imaginings of the life course in PNG. Perhaps the most distinctively PNG feature of this 'vocation' is the way that it is nested within a narrative of national development. As the nation's skilled professionals advance through their careers, they fulfil part of the developmental destiny of PNG (Cox, 2018).

Looking down the ladder of class, the grassroots cannot access the same career mobility. Rather, they are regarded as stationary custodians of the nation's traditional cultural heritage, grounded in subsistence agriculture. Urban grassroots are usually regarded as dangerously out of place, particularly in the case of women and young men (Lepani, 2008; Macintyre, 2008). Their aspirations are severely constrained and, when articulated to middle-class actors, typically met with condescension or explicit moral condemnation.

Nevertheless, even as they condemn the handout mentality, middle-class Melanesians still extend a hand to their less fortunate kin. I have argued that this increasingly takes the form of 'projects' and that new forms of inequality are taking shape as a result of this developmentalist language. Middle-class 'donors' (this is not a term I have heard used in PNG) to rural kinsfolk are occupying positions of patronage that are analogous to Melanesian political clientelism, based on the disbursement of favours. Disturbingly, aspirations for more equitable development in the form of basic health and education services give way to patronage that systematically neglects public goods and cultivates a dysfunctional governmentality of low expectations, where grassroots no longer have confidence that they are entitled to the rights of citizens.

References

Akin, D. (2013). *Colonialism, Maasina rule and the origins of Malaitan kastom*. Honolulu, HI: University of Hawaii Press.

Bainton, N. (2008). The genesis and the escalation of desire and antipathy in the Lihir Islands, Papua New Guinea. *The Journal of Pacific History, 43*(3), 289–312.

Bainton, N. (2010). *The Lihir destiny: Cultural responses to mining in Melanesia*. Canberra, ACT: ANU E Press. doi.org/10.22459/LD.10.2010

Bainton, N. (2011). 'Are you viable?' Personal avarice, collective antagonism and grassroots development in Papua New Guinea. In M. Patterson & M. Macintyre (Eds), *Managing modernity in the Western Pacific* (pp. 231–259). St Lucia, Qld: University of Queensland Press.

Bainton, N. & Cox, J. (2009). *Parallel states, parallel economies: Legitimacy and prosperity in Papua New Guinea* (SSGM Discussion Paper 2009/5). Canberra, ACT: The Australian National University.

Barbara, J., Cox, J. & Leach, M. (2015). *The emergent middle classes in Timor-Leste and Melanesia: Conceptual issues and developmental significance* (SSGM Discussion Paper 2015/4). Canberra, ACT: The Australian National University.

Barnett-Nagshineh, O. (2019). Shame and care: Masculinities in the Goroka marketplace. *Oceania, 89*(2), 220–236.

Black, S. (2009). Microloans and micronarratives: Sentiment for a small world. *Public Culture, 21*(2), 269–292.

Brimacombe, T. (2016). Trending trousers: Debating kastom, clothing and gender in the Vanuatu mediascape. *The Asia Pacific Journal of Anthropology, 17*(1), 17–33.

Buck, P. (1988). Cargo-cult discourse: Myth and the rationalisation of labor relations in Papua New Guinea. *Dialectical Anthropology, 13*, 157–171.

Burridge, K. (1960). *Mambu: A Melanesian millennium*. Princeton, NJ: Princeton University Press.

Cahn, P. (2006). Building down and dreaming up: Finding faith in a Mexican multilevel marketer. *American Ethnologist*, *33*(1), 126–142.

Cahn, P. (2008). Consuming class: Multilevel marketers in neoliberal Mexico. *Cultural Anthropology*, *23*(3), 429–452.

Chu, J. (2010). *Cosmologies of credit: Transnational mobility and the politics of destination in China*. Durham, NC: Duke University Press.

Cox, J. (2009). Active citizenship or passive clientelism: Accountability and development in Solomon Islands. *Development in Practice*, *19*(8), 964–80.

Cox, J. (2011). Prosperity, nation and consumption: Fast money schemes in Papua New Guinea. In M. Patterson & M. Macintyre (Eds), *Managing modernity in the Western Pacific* (pp. 172–200). St Lucia, Qld: University of Queensland Press.

Cox, J. (2013). The magic of money and the magic of the state: Fast money schemes in Papua New Guinea. *Oceania*, *83*(3), 175–191.

Cox, J. (2014). Fast money schemes are risky business: Gamblers and investors in a Papua New Guinean ponzi scheme. *Oceania*, *84*(3), 289–305.

Cox, J. (2015). Israeli technicians and the post-colonial racial triangle in Papua New Guinea. *Oceania*, *85*(3), 342–358.

Cox, J. (2016). Value and the art of deception: Public morality in a Papua New Guinean ponzi scheme. In L. Angosto-Ferrandez & G. Presterudstuen (Eds), *Anthropologies of value: Cultures of accumulation across the global North and South* (pp. 51–74). London, England: Pluto Press.

Cox, J. (2018). *Fast money schemes: Hope and deception in Papua New Guinea*. Bloomington, IN: Indiana University Press.

Cox, J. (2019). Money schemes in contemporary Melanesia. In E. Hirsch & W. Rollason (Eds), *The Melanesian world* (pp. 180–193). Routledge Worlds Series. London, England: Routledge.

Cox, J. & Macintyre, M. (2014). Christian marriage, money scams and Melanesian social imaginaries. *Oceania*, *84*(2), 138–157.

Cox, J. & Phillips, G. (2015). Sorcery, Christianity and the decline of medical services in Melanesia. In M. Forsyth & R. Eves (Eds), *Talking it through: Responses to sorcery and witchcraft beliefs and practices in Melanesia* (pp. 37–54). Canberra, ACT: ANU Press. doi.org/10.22459/TIT.05.2015

Dalsgaard, S. (2013). The politics of remittance and the role of returning migrants: Localising capitalism in Manus Province, Papua New Guinea. *Research in Economic Anthropology, 33,* 277–302.

Demian, M. (2017). Making women in the city: Notes from a Port Moresby boarding house. *Signs: Journal of Women in Culture and Society, 42*(2), 403–425.

Dundon, A. (2004). Tea and tinned fish: Christianity, consumption and the nation in Papua New Guinea. *Oceania, 75*(2), 73–88.

Foster, R. (2002). *Materialising the nation: Commodities, consumption and media in Papua New Guinea.* Bloomington, IN: Indiana University Press.

Foster, R. (2008). *Coca-globalisation: Following soft drinks from New York to New Guinea.* New York, NY: Palgrave Macmillan.

Foster, R. & Horst, H. (Eds). (2018). *The moral economy of mobile phones: Pacific Islands perspectives.* Canberra, ACT: ANU Press. doi.org/10.22459/MEMP.05.2018

Gewertz, D. & Errington, F. (1998). Sleights of hand and the construction of desire in a Papua New Guinea modernity. *The Contemporary Pacific, 10*(2), 345–368.

Gewertz, D. & Errington, F. (1999). *Emerging class in Papua New Guinea: The telling of difference.* Cambridge, England: Cambridge University Press.

Gibson, L. (2019). Class, labour and consumption in urban Melanesia. In E. Hirsch & W. Rollason (Eds), *The Melanesian world* (pp. 164–179). London, England: Routledge.

Golub, A. (2014). *Leviathans at the gold mine: Creating indigenous and corporate actors in Papua New Guinea.* Durham, NC: Duke University Press.

Graue, C. (2019, 30 May). James Marape elected as PNG's new Prime Minister. *Australian Broadcasting Corporation.* Retrieved from www.abc.net.au/radio-australia/programs/pacificbeat/james-marape-elected-as-pngs-new-prime-minister/11165242

Gregory, C. & Altman, J. (2018). Preface. In C. Gregory & J. Altman (Eds), *The quest for the good life in precarious times: Ethnographic perspectives on the domestic moral economy* (pp. xvii–xix). Canberra, ACT: ANU Press. doi.org/10.22459/QGLPT.03.2018

Hukula, F. (2019). Morality and a Mosbi market. *Oceania, 89*(2), 168–181.

Karim, L. (2011). *Microfinance and its discontents: Women and debt in Bangladesh.* Minneapolis, MN: University of Minnesota Press.

Krige, D. (2012). Fields of dreams, fields of schemes: Ponzi finance and multi-level marketing in South Africa. *Africa: The Journal of the International African Institute, 82*(1), 69–92.

Lattas, A. (2007). Cargo cults and the politics of alterity: A review article. *Anthropological Forum, 17*(2), 149–161.

Lawrence, P. (1964). *Road belong cargo: A study of the cargo movement in the southern Madang District, New Guinea.* Melbourne, Vic.: Melbourne University Press.

Lepani, K. (2008). Mobility, violence and the gendering of HIV in Papua New Guinea. *The Australian Journal of Anthropology, 19*(2), 150–164.

Lindstrom, L. (1993). *Cargo cult: Strange stories of desire from Melanesia and beyond.* Honolulu, HI: University of Hawai'i Press.

Lusby, S. (2017). Securitisation, development and the invisibility of gender. In M. Macintyre & C. Spark (Eds), *Transformations of gender in Melanesia* (pp. 23–43). Canberra, ACT: ANU Press. doi.org/10.22459/TGM.02.2017

Lyons, K. & Davidson, H. (2019, 26 July). Papua New Guinea will not be dependent on Australia in 10 years, new PM says. *The Guardian.* Retrieved from www.theguardian.com/world/2019/jul/26/papua-new-guinea-will-not-be-dependent-on-australia-in-10-years-new-pm-says

Macintyre, M. (1998). The persistence of inequality: Women in Papua New Guinea since independence. In L. Zimmer-Tamakoshi (Ed.), *Modern Papua New Guinea* (pp. 211–31). Kirksville, MO: Thomas Jefferson Press.

Macintyre, M. (2003). Petztorme women: Responding to change in Lihir, Papua New Guinea. *Oceania, 74*(1/2), 120–133.

Macintyre, M. (2008). Police and thieves, gunmen and drunks: Problems with men and problems with society in Papua New Guinea. *The Australian Journal of Anthropology, 19*(2), 179–193.

Macintyre, M. (2011). Money changes everything: Papua New Guinean women in the modern economy. In M. Patterson & M. Macintyre (Eds), *Managing modernity in the Western Pacific* (pp. 90–120). St Lucia, Qld: University of Queensland Press.

Macintyre, M. (2013). Instant wealth: Visions of the future on Lihir, New Ireland, Papua New Guinea. In M. Tabani & M. Abong (Eds), *Kago, kastom and kalja: The study of indigenous movements in Melanesia today* (pp. 123–146). Marseilles, France: Pacific-CREDO Publications.

Marshall-Fratani, R. (2001). Mediating the global and local in Nigerian Pentecostalism. In A. Corten & R. Marshall-Fratani (Eds), *Between Babel and Pentecost: Transnational Pentecostalism in Africa and Latin America* (pp. 80–105). Bloomington, IN: Indiana University Press.

Martin, K. (2007). Your own buai you must buy: The ideology of possessive individualism in Papua New Guinea. *Anthropological Forum, 17*(3), 285–298.

Martin, K. (2013). *The death of the big men and the rise of the big shots: Custom and conflict in East New Britain.* New York, NY: Berghahn Books.

Modern Shylocks [Editorial]. (2005, 10 November). *The National.*

Monsell-Davis, M. (1993). Urban exchange: Safety-net or disincentive? *Canberra Anthropology, 16*(2), 45–66.

Okole, H. (2003). Enhancing nation building through the provincial government system in Papua New Guinea. In D. Kavanamur, C. Yala & Q. Clements (Eds), *Building a nation in PNG: Views of the post-independence generation* (pp. 51–67). Canberra, ACT: Pandanus Books.

Rasmussen, A. (2015). *In the absence of the gift: New forms of value and personhood in a Papua New Guinea community.* London, England: Berghahn.

Rooney, M. N. (2019). Sharing what can be sold: Women haus maket vendors in Port Moresby's settlements. *Oceania, 89*(2), 154–167.

Rousseau, B. (2015). Finding the diamond: Prosperity, secrecy and labour in Vanuatu. *Oceania, 85*(1), 24–37.

Schiffhauer, L. (2018). Dangerous speculation: The appeal of pyramid schemes in rural Siberia. *Focaal: Journal of Global and Historical Anthropology, 81*, 58–71.

Schram, R. (2015). Notes on the sociology of Wantoks in Papua New Guinea. *Anthropological Forum, 25*(1), 3–20.

Schuster, C. (2015). *Social collateral: Women and microfinance in Paraguay's smuggling economy.* Oakland, CA: University of California Press.

Sharp, T. (2016). Trade's value: Relational transactions in the Papua New Guinea betel nut trade. *Oceania, 86*(1), 75–91.

Sharp, T. (2019). Haggling highlanders: Marketplaces, middlemen and moral economy in the Papua New Guinean betel nut trade. *Oceania, 89*(2), 182–204.

Sharp, T., Cox, J. Spark, C., Lusby, S. & Rooney, M. (2015). *The formal, the informal and the precarious: Making a living in urban Papua New Guinea* (SSGM Discussion Paper 2015/2). Canberra, ACT: The Australian National University.

Smith, R. (2018). Changing standards of living: The paradoxes of building a good life in rural Vanuatu. In C. Gregory & J. Altman (Eds), *The Quest for the good life in precarious times: Ethnographic perspectives on the domestic moral economy* (pp. 33–55). Canberra, ACT: ANU Press. doi.org/10.22459/QGLPT.03.2018

Spark, C. (2011). Gender trouble in town: Educated women eluding male domination, gender violence and marriage in PNG. *The Asia Pacific Journal of Anthropology, 12*(2), 164–179.

Spark, C. (2014). An oceanic revolution? Stella and the construction of new femininities in Papua New Guinea and the Pacific. *The Australian Journal of Anthropology, 25*(1), 54–72.

Spark, C. (2018). Hybridity in Port Moresby: Gender, class and a 'tiny bit of feminism' in postcolonial Papua New Guinea. In J. Wallis, L. Kent, M. Forsyth, S. Dinnen & S. Bose (Eds), *Hybridity on the ground in peacebuilding and development: Critical conversations* (pp. 271–285). Canberra, ACT: ANU Press. doi.org/10.22459/HGPD.03.2018

Spark, C. (2020). 'Two different worlds': Papua New Guinean women working in development in Port Moresby. *Asia Pacific Viewpoint.* Advance online publication. doi.org/10.1111/apv.12271

Spark, C. & Lee, J. (2018). *Successful women's coalitions in Papua New Guinea and Malaysia: Feminism, friendships and social change* (Developmental Leadership Program Research Paper 50). Birmingham, England: University of Birmingham.

Street, A. (2014). *Biomedicine in an unstable place: Infrastructure and personhood in a Papua New Guinean hospital.* Durham, NC: Duke University Press.

Suti, E., Hoatson, L. Tafunai, A. & Cox, J. (2020). Leadership, linkages and locality: The Simbo for Change project. *Asia Pacific Viewpoint.* Advance online publication. doi.org/10.1111/apv.12260

Verdery, K. (1995). Faith, hope and caritas in the Land of the Pyramids: Romania, 1990 to 1994. *Comparative Studies in Society and History, 37*(4), 625–699.

West, P. (2001). Environmental NGOs and the nature of ethnographic inquiry. *Social Analysis, 45*(2), 55–77.

West, P. (2006). *Conservation is our government now. The politics of ecology in Papua New Guinea*. Durham, NC: Duke University Press.

West, P. (2016). *Dispossession and the environment: Rhetoric and inequality*. New York, NY: Columbia University Press.

Wood, T. (2019). The clientelism trap in Solomon Islands and Papua New Guinea and its impact on aid policy. *Asia Pacific Policy Studies*, *5*, 481–494.

Zimmer-Tamakoshi, L. (1997). The last big man: Development and men's discontents in the Papua New Guinea Highlands. *Oceania*, *68*(2), 107–122.

10

Exiles and Empty Houses: Contingent Events and Their Aftermath in the Ok Tedi Hinterland

Dan Jorgensen

Introduction

Not long ago I had a conversation with Martha Macintyre in which she explained how she got into anthropology. A historian by training, she was recruited as bibliographer to the Cambridge Kula Conference (Leach & Leach, 1983; Macintyre, 1983a, 1983b; see also Gregory, this volume). One of the things that struck her then was that it seemed time for a historical approach to some of the classic themes of Melanesian ethnography (see e.g. Macintyre, 1994).[1] Macintyre's historian's sensibility is also evident in her work with Rolf Gerritsen on mining on Misima, which is located in the chain of island communities engaged in *kula* exchanges (Gerritsen & Macintyre, 1991). For me, what stands out in that account is how the temporal unfolding of the project resulted in a reversal of Misiman positions on whether the workforce should reside on Misima

---

[1] In fact, Macintyre's initial fieldwork on Tubetube formed part of the broader *kula* project, in which she filled gaps and brought aspects of the historical southern Massim record up to date (1983b, p. 379).

or operate on a fly-in fly-out (FIFO) basis. Published five years after their initial social impact study, their chapter stands as a detailed postscript that reflects events and their aftermath in real time.

Historians cannot remain indifferent to events and the passage of time; as Macintyre took pains to argue, neither can ethnographers. This is clear in the course of initial fieldwork (Jorgensen, 1980, 1981a), where expectations are continually revised in light of events in the field. But things keep on happening after the ethnographer leaves, as anyone who has made follow-up visits realises. In my own case, much of my subsequent fieldwork in Telefomin in the highlands of Papua New Guinea (PNG) has been inadvertently historical and twice occurred in response to explicit Telefol requests. In each case, the request was triggered by what local people understood to be significant and potentially game-changing events—the first being the emergence of revival evangelism less than four years after my fieldwork on Telefol religion (Jorgensen, 1981b). This was later followed by work on the prospects of large-scale mining (Jorgensen, 1983, 1990a, 1990b, 1997).

In what follows, I take up problems posed by focusing on events as contingent interruptions of the usual flow of things. Here Sally Falk Moore's ideas are particularly relevant. In two striking pieces she made a strong case for what she terms 'processual anthropology' and the ethnography of the present (Moore, 1987, 1994). These are firmly situated in her conception of the importance of temporality in ways that dovetail well with Macintyre's sense of a properly historical anthropology. This is not reducible to the oft-adopted expedient of juxtaposing the past and the present:

> Chopping up the social facts of fieldwork and putting them into two conceptual bins marked 'old' and 'new' is not the way to address the temporal problem. Such a sorting sounds as if it were saying something about sequence. But the effect of this classification is to remove the connections from view and treat time simply as an exercise in a dualistic categorization. (Moore, 1994, p. 371)

The point instead is that a processual attitude moves beyond retrospectives on the past and not only imagines the present as an emerging moment but also conceives of the present as a time from which the next moment will emerge. The focus is on the unfolding of events and on close inspection of the baggage that is brought to them and what is carried away afterwards (Moore, 1994, p. 371).

This historical perspective sees the ethnography of the present as necessarily pointing towards the future. Events that claim our attention often sit at the intersection of different interests and aims and in that sense may be 'up for grabs' and connected to outcomes not clearly given in advance. Both conjunctural and contested, they may mark turnings along different pathways, foreclosing some possibilities and opening others.

Many of Moore's ideas were taken up by Liisa Malkki in an important piece on the ethnography of events as transitory phenomena (1997). Two parts of Malkki's account seem particularly relevant here. One is the question of the relation between news and culture. When PNG newspapers—and, after that, blogs and social media—became accessible on the internet in the 1990s, I was struck by the gap between what we as ethnographers wrote and the events we read about in the news. What struck Malkki as problematic was the relationship between ethnography and journalism, which often started and ended with an invidious comparison couched in ideas of comprehensiveness, depth and seriousness versus superficial, ephemeral and somewhat flighty coverage. But she suggested this gap was maintained by a self-conscious distancing between ethnographic traditions of regularity and durability against the irregular and evanescent. Here she agreed with Moore, arguing that an anthropology of the present is particularly important when it takes note of the unusual and even ephemeral, and on two counts—as analysis, and as witnessing. The former is important in understanding the historical process and the latter in appreciating what we increasingly have come to recognise as crisis.[2]

Without suggesting that ethnographers become journalists, Malkki argued for rethinking habitual distinctions between our respective tasks. Ethnographers of the present are concerned with accounts that make space for or are founded on the flow of events. However, this flow does not cease when the ethnographer leaves the field. In her case, she attempted to follow what was happening in and around the refugee camps she was working with, but this had to be done remotely and in a necessarily patchwork fashion, based on what she was able to gather from correspondence, phone calls, agency reports and news stories.

---

2   Here Kirsch is an honourable and early example (2006).

In the remainder of this chapter, I turn to two cases in which unexpected events dramatically affected Telefolmin and others in the hinterland of PNG's Ok Tedi mine. In both instances, the terms of everyday life were disrupted and called into question; the term 'crisis' is not too strong to describe the situations in which people found themselves. The key events were wrenching but played out at different scales and with different dynamics. The first was an unprecedented outbreak of violent attacks against alleged witches in a rural village; the second was a prolonged period of drought across the region that led to the shutdown of the Ok Tedi mine and wholesale evacuation of the neighbouring town of Tabubil. These are the events referred to by the title of this chapter, and I have already published on them in some detail elsewhere (Jorgensen, 2014, 2016). But the burden of this chapter is to consider these events in light of their further trajectories and consequences—their aftermath. To anticipate my conclusions, I will argue that tracking events and their consequences after we leave the field provides us—even with imperfect information—a useful perspective on local futures and how they take shape.

At the time of my first fieldwork in 1974–75, the Ok Tedi mining project had gone from a source of occasional work clearing trails and drill pads to an exciting if vague presence on local horizons. A few years later, hundreds of men from Telefomin and surrounding areas were building the town of Tabubil; by the time I read Macintyre's Misima work, many had taken up permanent work at Ok Tedi and were soon followed by families who joined them in town. The two examples I discuss played out in a wider context in which the mining economy and the town of Tabubil had become familiar features of the landscape of local lives. For Telefolmin and many of their neighbours, the mining economy has been a source of prosperity and a range of benefits, including better access to educational and health services. But as we shall see, these benefits are not evenly distributed, even in relatively prosperous communities, nor is their continued availability assured.

Sorcery-related Killings in Telefomin

While most Telefolmin regard a village as their home, for the past generation the rural economy has been supported by remittances from absent kin,[3] many of whom fly home to visit their villages at Christmas. The events I discuss here occurred in the village of Talavip in late 2011, as people began arriving for the holidays. Some returned from various coastal towns, but most arrived from Tabubil (near the Ok Tedi mine) or from the Frieda River project to the north (see Figure 1).[4] Among these was Samuel, who had planned to stand for parliament in the 2012 elections but died suddenly while awaiting his flight home.[5] Not long afterwards, a group of village youths—described to me as 'The Boys'—began what they called an 'Operation' to identify and punish those they suspected of killing Samuel by *wiskrap* ('witchcraft') (for further detail, see Jorgensen, 2014; see also Zimmer-Tamakoshi, this volume).

Operating from their 'men's house' on the margins of the village, The Boys enacted a program of intimidation and public torture as part of an effort to 'weed the garden' of those suspected of *wiskrap*. This culminated in the disappearance and murder of two men who had also returned home for Christmas. The Boys also accused a third man residing in Tabubil of *wiskrap*, but the latter's friends phoned to warn him not to come.[6] He escaped, but his village house was ransacked, his family beaten and his sister raped.

These killings were unprecedented, in both the form that they took and in their degree of violence. The alleged *wiskrap* bears no discernible relationship to traditional (and long-discarded) varieties of sorcery and

3   This dependence intensified with the increasing size of bridewealth payments since the mid-1980s (Jorgensen, 1993). A rough estimate of Telefolmin living in Tabubil and surrounding environs at the time runs to several hundred, including families of Ok Tedi Mining Ltd (OTML) employees who enjoyed company housing in town. Workers from Telefomin district have for some years formed the core of the OTML labour force (see Jorgensen, 2006; Jenkins, 2016a).
4   Tabubil is the town associated with the Ok Tedi mine, and serves as the administrative, logistical and commercial centre for the project, including an international airport.
5   His death was described by a villager as caused by a heart attack, with which Telefomin are familiar (for further details, see the discussion of Haslam's visit to Telefomin below).
6   A killing of an accused youth in a neighbouring village (who had just won a scholarship to a coastal vocational school at this time) was also reported, but I have few details. There was also an attack against a villager employed by the government on the station who managed to escape (see below for further details).

was said to be a recent import of Western origin.[7] In fact, there was broad scepticism about the *wiskrap* allegations, which many regarded as spurious. Finally, Telefomin had possessed a 'quiet' reputation for decades; these killings were the most violent incident that had occurred since the 1953 'Telefomin Murders', in which two Australian patrol officers and two native police constables were killed (Craig, 1990).[8]

The Boys possessed little standing in the community; villagers referred to them as 'useless' (cf. McDougall, this volume). By most measures, they were disaffected and marginalised—unlike many elder brothers or uncles with mining jobs, The Boys were unemployed, largely unschooled and reportedly grew marijuana, which they both smoked and fed into the long-distance trade in drugs for guns (Alpers, 2005; Bell, 2006; Macintyre, 2008).[9] The contrast between them and others was thrown into sharp relief at Christmas—the time when those with education or jobs returned to the village. I suspect that this fuelled The Boys' evident rage and displays of public sadism, including a penchant for forcing villagers to watch them torture their victims. Their effect on others was summed up by one villager in this way:

> The Boys were 'terrorising' the community. They kept themselves apart in their *haus man* and everybody avoided them. At this time, people were afraid to go outside, especially at night. People didn't let their children go out and people didn't want to go to their gardens because they were afraid. Before they started one of their 'operations', they would strike the stones on the road with their weapons until sparks flew. They had axes, bushknives, sharpened iron rods and some guns. They didn't listen to or respect the elders, and they made war with (*birua long*) the community. The public servants on the station were so frightened that they quit work at 2:00 and stayed home. People relieved themselves in their houses rather than go outside. When people from other villages walked to the station, they would keep away from the village and take the other road by the school instead.

7   Traditional sorcery was not avenged through physical violence; people relied instead on unknown sorcerers in their midst to even scores on their behalf. It is important to note that such attacks were said to occur *between* villages, *not within them*—as in the present case. For further details, see Jorgensen (2014).
8   Only two homicides occurred in the valley over the nearly 60 years separating the two events.
9   Note that high school subsidies ended when the Telefomin District Development Agreement was terminated by the national government in 2004. From that point forward, rural families had to be selective about paying school fees. This was likely a factor in at least some young men's situations.

Contingency, Rupture, Change

Retrospective analysis may detect a combination of sudden death, elections and a holiday gathering that highlighted pre-existing fault lines; however, the evidence suggests that, to most villagers, the torture and killings arrived out of the blue. This is about as unambiguous a case of rupture as one could hope to find—the violence surrounding the *wiskrap* accusations caught everyone (except the perpetrators) by surprise.[10] However, while it is obvious that the attacks were radically new in Telefomin, it is difficult to see how this would count as change *unless the attacks were repeated.* To make that case, we must look beyond the events themselves and ask: will this happen again or have we seen the last of it? This, I would argue, was also the most pressing question facing the villagers among whom these events played out.[11]

We can get some sense of this by tracking how people responded to these events. During the time the attacks were taking place, the local police detachment was aware of what was happening but failed to intervene. Explanations offered after the fact included claims that more personnel would have been required, but that fuel budgets were insufficient to fly in additional staff from the provincial capital; the local lockup did not have the capacity to house the numbers involved in the attacks; and personnel and budgets were already stretched to the limit to provide security for the coming elections. Although the plausibility of each explanation is open to challenge, they serve as an indication that The Boys operated with effective impunity, as was common in many other parts of the country at the time.

In the period immediately after the killings, individuals who had been attacked or whose family members had been targeted effectively became exiles and sought safety by relocating elsewhere. A sense of unravelling is unmistakable in an email from one villager who travelled home for Christmas:

---

10   But the perpetrators were *not* surprised. A lengthier treatment would note that the attacks were entirely consistent with well-publicised patterns of sorcery-related killings in PNG, which reached a 20-year peak in 2011 (Forsyth et al., 2017). The torturers' playbook and talk of imported Western sorcery are quite familiar (see Englund & Leach, 2000; Gibbs, 2012; Haley, 2008, 2010).
11   Here I must mention the serious and concerted efforts of colleagues to address the future of sorcery-related killings as a practical matter; these are informed by a backlog of experience and considered advice on policy and interventions (Forsyth & Eves, 2015). Although I cannot pursue the matter here, Gibbs' (2015) outline of pragmatic responses matches quite closely the local efforts arrived at in Telefomin over the course of subsequent events.

> For the *avip kasel* (village people), they are not really okay … the
> village especially is now at the state of breaking up the community,
> with each family [leaving] and moving to another location. Now
> the village is facing leadership crisis coz all the men are afraid.
> That's why my Christmas at home was not good. Anyway it's not
> a good story.

The widow of one victim moved to Mt Hagen, while his mother took his
children into her care and established a separate household away from the
village in the bush, where she felt safer. The government employee who
was attacked at the station fled with his family to a neighbouring valley
under the cover of darkness and subsequently moved to the provincial
capital. The man in Tabubil who had been forewarned was able to fly
his family to safety and flee with them to a distant town where he and
his wife could find new employment. Yet another shifted with his family
to a different valley in the region among a neighbouring ethnic group,
where they have now settled. In each of these cases, empty and often
derelict houses stand as reminders of those forced to seek safety elsewhere.
The possibility of further attacks was not far from their minds.[12]

In the first half of 2012, the sister of Samuel (the man whose death
The Boys claimed to avenge) also died suddenly of an apparent heart
attack. Her family insisted on a post-mortem examination and paid for her
body to be flown to the hospital in Tabubil for autopsy, which confirmed
a heart attack as the cause of death. The family asked the physician in
charge, Dr Nick Haslam, to present his findings to the *haus krai* (funeral)
gathering in the village, which he did (Haslam, 2015; cf. Cox & Phillips,
2015). His view was that this effort was effective, and it is noteworthy
that Samuel's family went to extraordinary lengths to forestall further
accusations or violence. Later that year, I received word of an intoxicated
youth armed with a pistol who tried to disrupt a local funeral; I was told
that the crowd shouted him down and drove him off, despite the fact that
he was armed. Mourners reported him to local police, who confiscated his
pistol, although he was later released without charge.

---

12   At least one other man who had been set upon by The Boys remained in the village but kept
to himself and had few dealings with his neighbours, preferring to shift his church attendance to the
congregation at the government station.

After the 2012 elections, the new member of parliament (MP) for the area ordered the construction of a larger lockup facility at the station and recommended a strengthening of the local police detachment. That Christmas, he joined with a prominent villager in attempting to broker a reconciliation between the victims of the attacks and the families of The Boys, aiming to prevent any possible payback attempts. This was not successful—some of the victims' kin refused any attempt at reconciliation, while the family of another set the compensation demand so high that it would have been impossible to pay. When it was suggested that the possibility of charges against The Boys be dropped, one victim's family replied that their wish was that 'the law should take its course'.

After many delays, homicide charges were brought against three of The Boys; they were arrested and transported to the provincial capital to appear in court in 2014. The charges and witness testimony were heard in national court, but the presiding judge found that there was no case to answer, because the victims' bodies had not been found: the defendants were discharged.

Now, nearly eight years later, the 2017 election has taken place with no violence reported in Telefomin, nor have I received any word of further attacks associated with *wiskrap* accusations of any sort (and nor have I heard anything further about The Boys). While the future remains open, it appears that such accusations and attacks—a variant of PNG's sorcery-related killing epidemic—have not become established as a 'local practice'. To the extent that this is true, it seems likely to be the result of the efforts of Samuel's family and the local MP to put the 2011 killings behind them.

If There is a Moral to this Story ...

... it is that contingent events may leave permanent traces without becoming precedents or being normalised. People died, empty houses remain and villagers have departed in the wake of The Boys' violence— nobody is likely to discount the after-effects of their rampage. But facing the possibility of a darker future, Samuel's family and the new MP (among others) undertook their own efforts at repair whose most apparent effect may be the welcome *absence* of discernible change.

The El Niño Drought and the Ok Tedi Shutdown

In 2015 I returned briefly to PNG to pursue mobile phone research when the El Niño drought intervened. By mid-2015 conditions were deteriorating in many parts of the country and my main concern quickly became reporting on the drought's impact on the Min people straddling the boundary of West Sepik (Sandaun) and Western Provinces. This was part of a broader effort by Bryant Allen, Mike Bourke and others to gather information on the drought and responses to it across PNG. The data was compiled, mapped and forwarded to government and non-governmental agencies in an effort to help coordinate relief efforts (Bourke et al., 2016). At the end of September, Paul Barker presented my preliminary report at the Institute of National Affairs in Port Moresby as I made my way back to Canada. This report became the nucleus of my subsequent paper on the drought and its impact (Jorgensen, 2016).

Although the effects were not as severe as in some parts of the country, the drought's consequences for Min people were complicated by the fact that they live in the Ok Tedi hinterland centred on the mine and the town of Tabubil (Jorgensen, 1996, 2006; see Figure 1). As the residential and logistical hub for Ok Tedi, Tabubil had become the largest town in western PNG, with a population of over 18,000 in 2009 (National Statistical Office, 2009).[13] Both the town and the mine depend on shipping via the Fly River port of Kiunga for fuel, food and supplies, and low water had made the river unnavigable.

---

13 Population figures for Tabubil are notoriously inconsistent. Compare, for example, figures in Filer and Jenkins (2017, p. 242) with figures in two reports by the National Statistical Office (2014, 2009, conducted in collaboration with the PNG Sustainable Development Program). Carr and Filer put the 2009 population of the town and environs at around 23,000, whereas Howes and Kwa's assessment puts the population of Tabubil at 25,000, 'including adjacent settlements and villages' (Howes & Kwa, 2011, p. 15). I use the 2009 National Statistical Office figures here, which include four adjacent villages and one migrant settlement; these lie outside the formal boundaries of OTML's lease, but comprise part of Tabubil's everyday network of activity. The National Statistical Office lists the total number of households in Tabubil as 2,673.

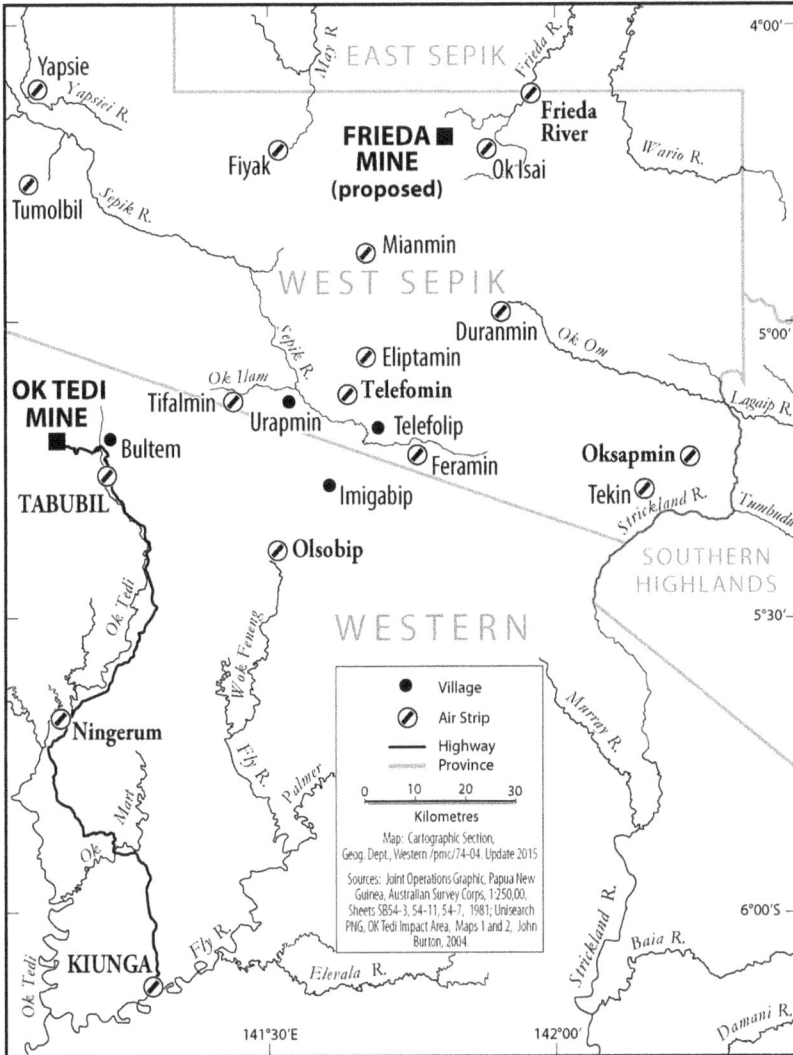

Figure 1: The Ok Tedi hinterland.

Cut off and unable to deliver ore to market, OTML declared *force majeure* and suspended operations in early August 2015. To ease pressure on supplies, workers and their families were sent to their home areas across PNG pending an end to the crisis. The departure of an estimated 2,000 families (James, 2017) amounted to a diaspora that affected the Ok Tedi hinterland and beyond, amplifying pressures and dislocations in the

277

drought-affected communities to which they returned. In the hinterland, the evacuation was a solution to problems at Ok Tedi; however, it became a source of problems for rural people who were already struggling.

After my return to Canada I tracked local conditions via phone, text messaging and social media. In October 2015 I submitted a manuscript—with a postscript on updates—to *Oceania*. The reviewers were receptive and argued for speedy publication in view of the ongoing crisis. However, there was to be an important revision: noting my previous update, one of the reviewers asked for a further update on events since October. The resulting addition amounted to a postscript to a postscript (Jorgensen, 2016, pp. 35–36), the gist of which may be summarised in two sentences from a statement made by OTML in December. Under the title 'Coming back to OTML—what's different?' CEO Peter Graham said:

> As the majority of employees will be FIFO, the residential makeup of Tabubil town will change. Generally families will not be on-site and employees will be in dongas and share accommodation. (Ok Tedi Mining Limited [OTML], 2015c)

Ok Tedi, FIFO and Tabubil

When the evacuation began in August, the *Papua New Guinea Post-Courier*'s Jeffrey Elapa reported that:

> Many police men from MacGregor Barrack MS [Mobile Squad] 1 have joined their friends from MS 19 to take part in the eviction of the employees and their families from company houses in Tabubil and Kiunga, putting them on the plane back to their point of hire or home provinces. (Elapa, 2015a)[14]

The evacuation and shutdown immediately drew critical reactions, including a declaration in Parliament by the Telefomin MP that the layoff of employees and contractors was unjust and that OTML management failed to give advance warning of the repatriation exercise (Gunga, 2015; cf. Mann, 2015; Peter, 2015).

Despite these reactions, there was a certain familiarity with the process of shutting down the mine and evacuating Tabubil—OTML did the same in the El Niño drought of 1997–98, a suspension that lasted roughly seven

---

14 In another report, Elapa stated that over 200 police personnel assisted the eviction and that an estimated 300 families left the OTML Kiunga compound at the same time (2015b).

months as well. But there was a key difference: arriving near the end of the drought, OTML's December announcement was an unprecedented game-changer. The plainest meaning was that those families who had been sent to home areas because of the drought were now to stay where they were after the drought had passed. Even if the mine shutdown was temporary, their repatriation was intended to be permanent—they had been evicted from Tabubil, not merely evacuated.

When interviewed, OTML's CEO claimed that FIFO was the dominant practice in the mining industry and was clearly preferred by operators; from this point of view, OTML had been out of step with the industry and was simply catching up (Business Advantage Papua New Guinea, 2015; Garrett, 2015). However, arguments and negotiations about FIFO are not new in PNG (see e.g. Bainton, 2010; Gerritsen & Macintyre 1991; Jackson, 1988; McGavin, Jones & Imbun, 2001).[15] FIFO was the subject of early negotiations surrounding the establishment of Ok Tedi, and the government position stressed national participation in a project with the state as an equity partner. As early as 1978 government negotiators emphasised the importance of establishing a township that was open to local people. Beyond that, there was a stated interest in limiting the ratio of single to married mine employees and in the provision of training facilities to enable the participation of local people in the project (Jackson, Emerson & Welsch, 1980; Pintz, 1984).

The Ok Tedi impact study argued that typical models of enclave development were self-destructive, with tensions between local people and the outside workforce at the Bougainville mine serving as a negative example (Jackson et al., 1980; cf. Nash & Ogan, 1990). The aim was to integrate local people with the project rather than insulate them from it; an open township was integral to this position. There was also a preference for family settlement: plans for Tabubil assumed two dependents per employee, with married employees predominating over singles. The reasoning behind this was evident in fears regarding what a massive influx of single outsiders might bring: 'rascals, involvement with local women and brawling as a result of drinking' (Jackson et al., 1980, p. 274; cf. Bainton & Banks, 2018).

---

15   Public debates about FIFO have recently played out in PNG newspapers and social media. See, for example, Kenneth (2019), Vari (2019), Kepmewato (2019) and a series of articles in *The National* (e.g. 2013, 2014, 2018a, 2018b).

The state's plan for Tabubil as a residential community prevailed; Tabubil was to offer employment in addition to medical and educational services for the surrounding region. Access to family housing was an important issue for workers and became an element of early labour strife. In 1988 striking workers supported their demands for housing by digging up roads, blocking airstrips and cutting telephone lines (Jackson, 1993, p. 187). OTML management had contemplated declaring *force majeure* but resolved the issue and agreed to build an additional 200 family houses over the following 18 months. Family housing thus has a history in labour relations at Ok Tedi: all the more striking, then, that OTML decided to eliminate such accommodation after a generation of employees' families had made their homes there.

From Tabubil Futures to FIFO

Ok Tedi was PNG's first large post-independence mine and, in its haste to bring it on stream, the state permitted it to commence operations without a tailings dam. Massive quantities of mining waste were dumped in the Ok Tedi River, which led to a lawsuit by local people and a transnational coalition against the operator and chief shareholder (BHP). The case was brought to court in Melbourne amid great publicity and did not go well for BHP. The result was an out-of-court settlement for damages (Banks & Ballard, 1997) that ultimately led to BHP's 2002 exit from the project to avoid future liability. Subsequent legislation governing Ok Tedi permitted the mine to operate until 2009 and then to 2015; in 2011–12, OTML was preparing a submission to extend mine operation to 2025 (see Carr & Filer, 2011; Jenkins, 2016a). Such plans required approval by landowners and villages along the Fly River that had been affected by the mine's pollution, and had also to be approved by the PNG government.

When BHP left the project, its shares were vested in the PNG Sustainable Development Program (PNGSDP), a not-for-profit company whose mandate is to 'support and promote sustainable development through initiatives that will benefit the people before and after closure of the Ok Tedi Mine' (PNGSDP, 2019). Since then, PNGSDP had funded numerous local development projects in Western Province and the rest of PNG. As the mine's majority shareholder, PNGSDP also had a strong voice in the direction of OTML. When Inmet, OTML's last private shareholder, exited Ok Tedi in 2011, the mine's remaining shareholders were PNGSDP (64 per cent) and the state of PNG (36 per cent). Nigel

Parker, OTML's CEO, argued that this altered the calculus of corporate priorities. He observed that when Inmet was a shareholder, there was a mix of the commercial mandate with the social mandate:

> Inmet were very good in the social mandate side of it but now Inmet has exited it is *full social mandate* so everything we do has a focus on the Papua New Guinean people, what we can deliver to the economy, to the peoples of the Western Province and, of course, to a wider group of people that are not just impacted by the mine. (Garrett, 2013, emphasis added)

In line with these statements, OTML and PNGSDP developed plans for Western Province after mine closure.[16] These included the Tabubil Futures project, which aimed to transform Tabubil into a mixed-economy town with 'a college in the clouds' as its centrepiece: the Star Mountains Institute of Technology (Business Advantage Papua New Guinea, 2012a; Jenkins, 2016a; Nalu, 2012; PNGSDP, 2011).

Things did not go smoothly in 2013, however, and Parker described the year as 'like riding a tiger' (Wilkins, 2013). Profits fell sharply due to a drop in copper prices, declining ore grades and ageing equipment. More importantly, 2013 saw another change of ownership as the recently elected O'Neill government expropriated PNGSDP and took control of OTML and its assets (Howes, 2013a, 2013b). This unsettled period marked a shift in OTML's fundamental orientation.

In 2011 and 2012, OTML's public statements stressed corporate social responsibility (Business Advantage Papua New Guinea, 2012b, 2012c).[17] However, after the expropriation, OTML emphasised what Parker called the commercial mandate:

> The new OTML vision is: We are a sustainable, efficient and well-regarded operating company that delivers value to all our stakeholders. The new mission is: We mine gold, silver, and copper from PNG reserves. (OTML, 2013, p. 6)

---

16   PNGSDP's most successful project of this period was the 2011 construction of a telecom tower network that provided mobile phone coverage to most of the population of Western Province. For information on the relationship between OTML and PNGSDP, in addition to mine extension plans, see Carr and Filer (2011), Filer and Jenkins (2017), Jenkins (2016a), Howes (2013b) and Morauta (2014). I discuss the crucial role played by PNGSDP's Long Term Fund (LTF) below.

17   For example, OTML's 2012 annual review contained the following vision statement: 'our hope and our vision is to empower local communities such that they are healthy, educated and economically diversified' (OTML, 2012, p. 7).

OTML's 2013 annual review mentions plans for Tabubil Futures for the following year; however, the 2014 review merely reported that no progress had been made 'due to legislative delays' (OTML, 2014, p. 23). Tabubil Futures disappeared altogether from subsequent OTML reports without further comment.[18]

During this time OTML embarked on a program of restructuring and by the end of 2014 had cut a third of its workforce and introduced new rosters for those who remained (James, 2017; OTML, 2013, 2014; see also Jenkins, 2016b, p. 11).[19] The groundwork for these changes was laid in 2013, when a Brisbane consulting firm was hired to produce streamlined work rosters to extend mine life to 2025 (Middleton, 2014; Shiftwork Solutions, 2014). Here, however, it is important to note that their brief was not only to work towards more efficient rosters but also to 'reduce impacts on the local economy associated with the termination of a residential mine in a remote location' (Middleton, 2014). One of their findings was that existing rosters resulted in 'the character of the site to be more residential than FIFO' (Middleton, 2014). What is implied, but left unstated, is that a residential workforce presented a problem. One remedy was to revise accommodation arrangements; these appear in OTML's 2014 annual review as new single accommodation blocks for FIFO staff (OTML, 2014, pp. 23, 46).[20]

Phrased as a matter of efficient timetabling and employees' working conditions, the rostering project nonetheless reveals a preoccupation with FIFO and Tabubil's post-closure residential configuration. Parker addressed the relationship between FIFO and the township in an article that appeared at the same time (Oxford Business Group, 2014). Although OTML built Tabubil with over 1,000 single-family houses for residential employees, Parker suggested that the FIFO alternative would be attractive to employees from other parts of PNG. Arguing that his main concern was the viability of a post-mining township, he also claimed that special purpose mining leases—as at Tabubil—were unsuitable for long-term development. He went on to say that sustaining a township

---

18   There was no OTML annual review for 2015, though the 2016 review includes some data from 2015. Note that the eclipse of the social mandate at Ok Tedi parallels what Kemp and Owen (2018) have termed 'corporate refusal'.

19   Most mines operate on a 24/7 basis, which makes shift timetabling (rostering) crucial for smooth operations. Shiftwork Solutions reported that Ok Tedi rosters were relatively uncoordinated and chaotic, which made flight schedules for FIFO employees particularly complicated and costly.

20   These became known as the 'Parker Dongas'. Note the move away from family housing.

requires massive investment and concluded by asking, 'whether a resource company should be required to develop a supportive township'. Although he stopped short of endorsing FIFO as a transition to a post-mining Tabubil, the door to that option had clearly been opened.

Implementing FIFO

When Peter Graham succeeded Parker as CEO in May 2015, an expanded FIFO model was on the table. Recalling that time, Graham noted the declaration of *force majeure* and the relocation of employees' families as his first order of business. This was followed by further retrenchments, new rosters and the move from a residential to a FIFO operation (James, 2017). Shortly after the FIFO announcement, he explained that 'being residential just costs a lot to run a town, and providing all of the services and maintaining the houses and providing schooling for residents' families … [are] just a cost the business can't afford' (Garrett, 2015). He later argued that Ok Tedi was 'on death row', but that cost-cutting had extended the mine's future, bringing it to a sweet spot (James, 2018).

The drought provided OTML with the opportunity to finesse the FIFO transition without the complications of dealing with a resident population in Tabubil. On return to work in 2016 all employees had to agree to new roster assignments and conditions of employment before being re-hired.[21] The FIFO transition was in this sense a 'done deal' by the time that operations resumed (Australian Broadcasting Corporation, 2016). Despite this, there existed signs of dissatisfaction among returning workers. One assessed the new situation this way:

> Very hectic working environment, understaffed and overloaded. The company was once one of the very best employer until recently taken over by the government and was forced to undergo a lot of changes including cut in work force, restructure, ceased of all incentives, change of rosters and do away with residential status to FIFO. These are changes that are really affecting my interest and my approach to the company. (Indeed, 2019)

---

21   OTML reports that 99 per cent of their employees accepted offers under these terms (2016, p. 3).

Another said:

> Ok Tedi Mining Limited was once a company that most people would wish to work with. The operation was a residential type where employees are accommodated with their families onsite and most staff gets weekend offs accept (sic) the shift workers who are compensated very well. Things have changed and the operation is now a FIFO operation where the employees were told to move their families out of the mining township to their point of hire/origin. I am currently on 4 week and 2 weeks off. (Indeed, 2019)

Area residents welcomed the return of OTML employees but noted that many came merely to pack belongings and leave for good.

Over the following year, there were general complaints about abandoned buildings or disused facilities (e.g. the golf club or tennis courts); some described Tabubil as a ghost town, even two years after the drought. However, these observations were juxtaposed with other comments that insisted that families had returned and moved back into their former houses. One social media post helped to put these discrepant parts of the picture together:

> Mate it's like a ghost town all employees are on FIFO and the houses are given to local employees only … almost half the town has empty houses … now it's no more the Tabubil that we used to know.

These remarks suggest a slippage between stated policies and the actually existing FIFO arrangements. Official announcements stressed that the FIFO policy covered *all* employees (OTML, 2015c, 2016, p. 42). But in April 2016 it emerged that workers whose point of hire was Tabubil or nearby areas of the North Fly and Telefomin Districts[22] were allowed to return to family housing for a rental fee (Papua New Guinea Resources, 2016). The reason given was the desire to minimise travel time for workers on short-cycle rosters, and in 2017 this number accounted for more than 400 employees and their families (OTML, 2017, p. 44).

Housing reappeared as a labour issue in early 2018, when around 100 workers staged a sit-down protest over roster changes that they had been disputing since operations resumed. OTML management sacked them within hours and flew them out of Tabubil the following day (Mauludu,

---

22 This was known as the 'Preferred Area' (see Jenkins, 2016a).

2018a, 2018b).[23] This was not the end of it however: six months later OTML and the employees' union signed a new contract that encompassed 'benefits for the workers such as housing' (Gware, 2018). This agreement allowed 'employees who work the three-week roster[24] eligibility to reside in Tabubil … As a result, it is expected that an additional 110 families will relocate to Tabubil during 2019' (OTML, 2018, p. 46; cf. EMTV, 2018).

By January 2019 the number of preferred-area families at Tabubil had risen to 420. Together with the 110 additional families, a total of 530 employees' families resided in company housing early in the year (OTML, 2018, p. 46). This accounts for about one-third of the current workforce, suggesting that done deal or not, OTML's move to full-on FIFO lost ground within two years of its launch.

Tabubil Futures Redux?

The most consequential outcome of 2015 for many in Ok Tedi's hinterland was the shift to FIFO, and the event that set this in motion was not the El Niño drought, but the government takeover of OTML. Local views see FIFO as a threat to Tabubil and, with it, the future of the North Fly region. Social media commentary highlighted the damage that closing down Tabubil would inflict on the regional economy and took aim at the premise that the mine's viability hinged upon scaling back support for the town. Others argued that the mine owed its existence to a commitment to the North Fly region in agreements that permitted OTML to operate at all (as discussed above; cf. Banks & Ballard, 1997; Filer & Jenkins, 2017): 'closing down the township would be against the spirit of the mine continuation' (Pinen, 2015).

Phillipa Jenkins, much of whose work focused on mine continuation negotiations, registered similar misgivings based on her research *before* the drought. Considering Tabubil's viability after the state stripped PNGSDP of its equity, she went on to say that:

---

23 North Fly MP James Donald unsuccessfully called for the Mines Minister to intervene (Mou, 2018; Poriambep, 2018). OTML's public response pointed out that the employees' contracts included 'a 10 per cent wage increase on restart after dry weather associated with a new FIFO roster' (Business and Human Rights Resource Centre, 2018).
24 That is, the short-cycle roster.

With this national government takeover of OTML, the future sustainability of Tabubil and the other villages above Ningerum becomes less likely. The people of Western Province are *unlikely to benefit at all* from the national government's appropriation of PNGSDP's share in OTML. (2016a, p. 133; emphasis added)

What she perceived clearly was that the expropriation was more than a simple assertion of nationalistic control; it signalled a fundamental change in the relationship between the mine and the surrounding population.

Ok Tedi's takeover occurred against the backdrop of a burgeoning debt load that threatened state finances. Capturing the entirety of Ok Tedi's revenue stream was an important motivation, and although the mine had no private shareholders, the state behaved as any privately owned mining company might: it sought to extract as much value as possible by cutting costs to enhance the bottom line. In the process, the FIFO strategy effectively declared the state's interests and those of the mine's hinterland to be at odds.

In the overall scheme of things, however, OTML's dividends may have been a sideshow for the O'Neill government. From the beginning it was evident that the government's attention was focused on a much bigger target: the USD 1.4 billion Long Term Fund (LTF) established by PNGSDP. Since its founding in 2002, two-thirds of PNGSDP's dividends were allocated to the LTF; these were to become available to the people of Western Province after mine closure. This fund was invested in low-risk securities administered from Singapore, where PNGSDP was incorporated—a fact intended to place the assets beyond the reach of PNG politicians (Howes, 2013b; Morauta, 2014). One of the government's first actions following the takeover was an attempt to seize these funds, leading to prolonged litigation in Singapore (Howes, 2013a, 2013b; McLeod, 2019; PNGSDP, 2019).

As of 2019 the future of Tabubil looked as uncertain as ever, but the year also held surprises for the O'Neill government. In early April the Singapore courts found in PNGSDP's favour and rejected the state's claim to the LTF. Before the month was out, Prime Minister O'Neill resigned; James Marape became PNG's new prime minister at the start of May. In mid-June, Marape travelled to Singapore and, a week later, visited Tabubil. There he met with local leaders and OTML executives and gave a public speech in which he put both OTML and the Western

Provincial Government on notice. He took them and previous national governments to task, arguing that through the Ok Tedi mine the people of Western Province had helped the country to generate hundreds of millions in revenue but had received little benefit in return. He charged Provincial Governor Awi Yoto with the responsibility for improving the situation through a number of measures, including finding common ground with PNGSDP and putting an end to FIFO for OTML workers (Gerega, 2019).

While it would be unwise to place too much credence in the contents of a single speech, Marape's position seemed to have been directly aimed at repairing the relationship between OTML and the people of Western Province—and especially Tabubil and the North Fly—by pushing for specific measures. One indicator may be the following month's announcement that OTML, through the state's tax credit scheme, was undertaking to seal the 136 km highway connecting Tabubil to Kiunga for the first time since it was built in 1981 (Loop Business, 2019). At a cost of an estimated PGK 100 million and a construction schedule of three years, the project suggests that Tabubil does indeed have a future beyond the current mine termination date of 2025.

On the Mining Economy and Inequalities in Ok Tedi's Hinterland

In closing, I venture a few remarks on this volume's theme of inequality. We have known for some time that large resource projects produce new forms of inclusion, exclusion and marginalisation at different scales (see e.g. Ballard & Banks, 2003; Jacka, 2001, 2015; Main, this volume), and much of this chapter is set within the context of inequalities arising from the Ok Tedi mine at both local and regional levels.[25] The exiles of this chapter's title are families forced to leave their home village in the face of The Boys' violence, while the empty houses are those left behind by workers and families who were evicted from Tabubil in OTML's FIFO scheme. The events surrounding these circumstances can be traced to the distribution of advantage and disadvantage in the regional mining economy.

---

25 One obvious dimension of inequality at Ok Tedi is the contrast between the people in the foothills and mountains of the hinterland and those who have been subject to the environmental effects of the mine on downstream portions of the Ok Tedi and Fly River systems. I have discussed these matters in more detail elsewhere (Jorgensen, 2006; see also Kirsch, 2006).

In the case of The Boys, inequalities at the local level are evident and clearly fuelled the animus they showed in their attacks. In this they have much in common with disenfranchised Ipili youth, who may become self-styled 'Rambos' (guns for hire) on the fringes of the Porgera mine (Jacka, 2019). Unlike the latter, however, The Boys' violence was directed within their own community rather than in intertribal conflicts. In Telefomin the axis of inequality manifested itself most powerfully at close range, rather than following traditional lines of political cleavage (see note 7 above). This difference notwithstanding, however, both the Ipili and Telefol cases also hint at emerging issues of intergenerational equity (Jorgensen, 2019, pp. 109–110)—a factor that was long ago identified by Filer as a feature underlying aspects of the Bougainville conflict (1990). This would suggest that, as at Bougainville, inequality may develop relatively slowly over time, as fissures grow between early beneficiaries and disadvantaged successors (see also Bainton & Macintyre, 2016).

Less obvious, perhaps, is the way that inequality figures in understanding the dynamics of OTML's FIFO policies. Here the most telling form of inequality is that between the national government and the people of Ok Tedi's hinterland, who—despite a range of legal provisions, agreements and consultations—have had little say in large decisions affecting their lives. This structural inequality is similar to what we are used to seeing in the relationship between transnational corporate developers and local people, with the added irony that—because the state itself is now the developer—the state's role as protector of local interests is compromised by interests of its own. In the case of FIFO, the material consequences of closing Tabubil raised the prospect of permanent regional marginalisation: an entrenchment of inequality through what Ferguson has termed the 'global disconnect' (1999).

Having said this, however, this chapter's larger point is that the aftermath of these events has not yet run its course. As we have seen, apparent changes are themselves subject to change: FIFO policies became attenuated, a terminal date for Ok Tedi now appears more notional than real, and the question of the LTF and its disposition at the end of mine life remains open. An ethnography of the present in the Ok Tedi hinterland will have to be one from which the region's future can be seen to emerge.

Postscript: On Doing Remote Ethnography of the Present (November 2019)

The events I have focused on were disruptive in both the technical sense of unsettling things as they were and in the human sense of disturbing people's lives. My intent in writing this chapter was in the spirit of Malkki's remarks, which is to provide both analysis and a form of witnessing. To close, I'd like to venture some brief comments on doing ethnography at a distance while events continued to unfold.

These two sets of events posed the question: what happens next? Email and SMS contacts with villagers were crucial in tracking the aftermath of The Boys' violence after leaving the field, and I also became a close follower of news reports (though these yielded little).[26] But the single most helpful contact occurred by chance, when Nick Haslam emailed me to discuss the post-mortem and the funeral of Samuel's sister. What I came to know was largely adventitious and depended upon Haslam's intervention.

Things were different in the case of Ok Tedi's shift to FIFO, not least because the nature of the event itself was not immediately evident. The move to FIFO came as a surprise to workers and families but was in fact a decision by OTML management that had been contemplated well in advance of the drought that provided cover for it. What had been a story of drought and recovery became a story of displacement instead. But the details only became clear after following OTML documents, published interviews with OTML executives, news reports and social media commentary. My dependence on journalistic and internet sources underscores both the possibility and difficulty of following events and subsequent developments in absentia.

I would also argue that providing an account of the sources of the FIFO transition brings something into view that was always significant but rarely discussed—the importance of national policy on Ok Tedi in shaping the future of Tabubil and its hinterland. Tabubil's urban infrastructure, sealed airstrip, communications network and road connection to Kiunga provide not only a gateway to the Ok Tedi mine: it is also the only reliable portal to the outside world for the people of the northern reaches of Western

---

26 Contacts with colleagues were also useful, particularly Richard Eves, Philip Gibbs, Tom Strong and (especially) Miranda Forsyth.

Province.[27] Anything that jeopardises Tabubil's viability threatens a 'return of remoteness' for the entire region and guarantees perpetual 'Last Place' (*las ples*) status for its inhabitants (cf. Saxer & Andersson, 2019). For this to happen in the aftermath of Ok Tedi's closure would represent an unacceptable externalisation of risks and costs by an enterprise that is owned by the state in the name of the people of PNG (cf. Bainton & Holcombe, 2018). Being able to trace the links back to the state's takeover counts as a vindication of the approach taken here.

Having said this, what about events on the ground and the present state of play in Tabubil? One of my frustrations is that most of my Telefol contacts who lived in Tabubil did not return there after the shift to FIFO; therefore, I have little access to first-hand accounts of local conditions, aside from the social media commentary alluded to above. What we do know is that Ok Tedi is widely expected to operate through at least 2030, although this will require a further continuation agreement.[28] In addition to the sealing of the Tabubil–Kiunga highway, there are roads currently being extended out from Tabubil east to Olsobip and north to Telefomin (Elapa, 2019). All of this would seem to suggest that Tabubil will remain a regional hub for the foreseeable future. As to life in Tabubil, two unexpected sources of information provided hopeful news in the latter part of 2019. A friend working in parliamentary circles in Port Moresby reported that 'by next year 2020 all OTML employees will be going back with families—it has started already'. Not long after this, I learned that Emma Gilberthorpe was working on a project in one of Tabubil's peri-urban villages. In response to my queries, she replied:

> It's quite amazing … They rent the houses out to local people. Schools are bustling. There are projects going on, rice farm, fish farm, chicken farm. It's really looking good … The Min highway is being built. It has passed Bolangun already.

Second Postscript (May 2020)

In the five months since the previous postscript was written, the situation in the Ok Tedi hinterland has dramatically changed. The World Health Organization declared the coronavirus pandemic in February and, in

---

27 This is especially so given the closure of smaller airstrips in the northern part of Western Province, as at Olsobip and Nomad (see Knauft, 2019).
28 This scenario is corroborated in part by the fact that OTML recently invested in upgrading and relocating one of the mine's crushers.

March, the PNG government announced a State of Emergency (SoE) that was subsequently extended to the end of June. The strategy was to impede the virus' spread by imposing travel restrictions, closing schools and universities, prohibiting large gatherings and enforcing a general lockdown in urban areas (Lyons, 2020).

National borders were an immediate focus of concern; ports and international airports were closed and security assumed particular importance regarding Indonesia's border with PNG's West Sepik and Western Provinces (Blades, 2020). Politicians called for new or expanded border posts at Tumolbil and Yapsiei (Nanau, 2020) and at least one provincial governor called for enforcement on a 'shoot to kill' basis along the border (Radio New Zealand, 2020a).

Border anxieties were not confined to politicians: news of coronavirus deaths in Indonesia led scores of villagers from Tumolbil and Yapsiei to flee to Ok Isai, roughly 60 km to the east (see Figure 1).[29] At Tabubil, two employees returning from overseas leave were suspected to be infected with coronavirus and were quarantined pending (negative) testing (Post-Courier, 2020a).[30] Not long after, three traditional border-crossers who tested positive for the virus were intercepted at Bige, along the Ok Tedi River, between Tabubil and Kiunga.

The meaning of these developments for the people of Tabubil and the hinterland was not immediately clear. One result was an increase in army deployment at both Kiunga and Tabubil, and OTML security established checkpoints along the Kiunga-Tabubil Highway to prevent outsiders entering the area (Loop Business, 2020a, 2020b). Strengthened travel restrictions requiring government authorisation for flights out of both towns underscored the point that the North Fly region was seen not only as vulnerable but also as a potential threat to the rest of the country (Radio New Zealand, 2020b, 2020c).

There are also safety issues about large industrial sites such as the mine, and these couldn't help but conjure the possibility of a replay of the El Niño shutdown. In the face of such concerns, OTML CEO Graham announced that mine production would continue during the SoE, arguing that sufficient safety measures were already in place.

---

29   Coronavirus fears fuelled new or borrowed conspiracy theories, with quack cures and apocalyptic pronouncements flooding social media.
30   Elsewhere, calls for an end to FIFO were repeated (Papua New Guinea Post-Courier, 2020b).

In late April Tabubil went into enforced lockdown: all entry points were barricaded, and inspections were conducted to locate unofficial residents or visitors, who were required to leave.[31] All employees' families were given the option of remaining in OTML housing or returning to their villages, and workers who left to join families when the SoE was imposed were stood down for the duration (Esila, 2020). In the meantime, widespread testing and contact tracing were announced for remaining workers and their resident families, with reports that employees who tested positive would stand down but continue to draw full pay.[32]

Despite these efforts, it is not clear that the mine will be able to continue to operate, and my optimism about Tabubil's future at the end of last November may have been premature. Among other things, the closure of the port of Kiunga suggests that there may be a limited capacity to absorb and stockpile further production. Beyond this, there is no guarantee that Tabubil will be able to remain free of the coronavirus, nor even that it will not become a hotspot for the dissemination of further outbreaks across the hinterland. The history of clandestine entry to Tabubil associated with the traffic in marijuana, guns or even betel nut makes it clear that there are unofficial routes of access to the town. There is no reason to believe that keeping infection out will be any more reliable than it has proven to be anywhere else. If that is the case, the future of the mine, the town and the region may be up for grabs.

The irony of Tabubil's situation—and that of its hinterland—is one that it shares with many other parts of the globe today. Where its future was once predicated on its connections to the world at large, its continued viability seems—at least in the short run—to depend on its insulation from that same world. Its success in escaping Last Place remoteness may come at a high price. Spillover is the pandemic's signature process, and nobody can yet say where it will all lead. This is as true for me, writing from the security of my home in the sixth week of Canadian lockdown, as it is for the people of Tabubil and its environs. The best one can do at present is wish them (and one another) well.

---

31 Local contacts suggest that those wishing to enter Tabubil from outside are housed in tents at town entrances pending results of COVID-19 testing; however, I have been unable to confirm this.
32 I was told that those who tested positive would not be permitted to return to their rural villages until they had undergone a 14-day quarantine and later tested negative.

Acknowledgements

This chapter developed from a paper I wrote for Aletta Biersack's 2018 American Anthropological Association panel on modelling change under the title 'Expectations of permanence? Events, exiles and empty houses in the Ok Tedi hinterland'. The panel provided a testbed for some of the ideas presented here, and I am grateful to Aletta for her comments and suggestions concerning them. I also owe much to each of the following for suggestions and information (but none of them is to blame for my use of their help): Nick Bainton, Snoky Bowin, John Cox, Julian Craig, Terry Dagayok, Yon Dagayok, Robert Dripal, Colin Filer, Miranda Forsyth, Don Gardner, Emma Gilberthorpe, Nick Haslam, Phillipa Jenkins, Michael Main, Debra McDougall, Jackson Pinen, Gons Samson, Simon Soltumnok, Steve Sumengim, Musje Werror and Mike Wesch. Finally, Imke Jorgensen provided candid feedback in addition to an indispensable leavening of good humour and good sense.

References

Alpers, P. (2005). *Gun-running in Papua New Guinea: From arrows to assault weapons in the Southern Highlands*. Geneva, Switzerland: Small Arms Survey. Retrieved from smallarmssurvey.org/fileadmin/docs/C-Special-reports/SAS-SR05-Papua-New-Guinea.pdf

Australian Broadcasting Corporation. (2016, 8 February). Ok Tedi to resume next month after El Niño suspension [broadcast]. *ABC News Pacific Beat*. Retrieved from abc.net.au/radio-australia/programs/pacificbeat/ok-tedi-to-resume-operations-next-month-after-el/7148028

Bainton, N. (2010). *The Lihir destiny: Cultural responses to mining in Melanesia*. Canberra, ACT: ANU E Press. doi.org/10.22459/LD.10.2010

Bainton, N. & Banks, G. (2018). Land and access: A framework for analysing mining, migration and development in Melanesia. *Sustainable Development*, *26*(5), 450–460.

Bainton, N. & Holcombe, S. (2018). A critical review of the social aspects of mine closure. *Resources Policy*, *59*, 468–478.

Bainton, N. & Macintyre, M. (2016). Mortuary ritual and mining riches in Island Melanesia. In D. Lipset & E. Silverman (Eds), *Mortuary dialogues: Death ritual and the reproduction of moral community in Pacific modernities* (pp. 110–132). New York, NY: Berghahn Books.

Ballard, C. & Banks, G. (2003). Resource wars: The anthropology of mining. *Annual Review of Anthropology, 32*, 297–313.

Banks, G. & Ballard, C. (Eds). (1997). *The Ok Tedi settlement: Issues, outcomes and implications.* Canberra, ACT: National Centre for Development Studies.

Bell, J. (2006). Marijuana, guns, crocodiles and submarines: Economies of desire in the Purari Delta. *Oceania, 76*(3), 220–234.

Blades, J. (2020, 24 April). Pandemic exposes weakness of PNG's border security. *Radio New Zealand.* Retrieved from rnz.co.nz/international/pacific-news/415003/pandemic-exposes-weakness-of-png-s-border-security

Bourke, R. M., Allen, B. & Lowe, M. (2016). *Estimated impact of drought and frost on food supply in rural PNG in 2015* [Policy brief 11]. Retrieved from devpolicy.org/publications/policy_briefs/PB11PNGdrought.pdf

Business Advantage Papua New Guinea. (2012a). *Tabubil: A college town in the clouds.* Retrieved from businessadvantagepng.com/tabubil-a-college-town-in-the-clouds/

Business Advantage Papua New Guinea. (2012b). *Beyond mining: Interview with Ok Tedi's Nigel Parker.* Retrieved from businessadvantagepng.com/beyond-mining/

Business Advantage Papua New Guinea. (2012c). *Ok Tedi's Nigel Parker on social responsibility in mining.* Retrieved from businessadvantagepng.com/ok-tedis-nigel-parker-on-social-responsibility-in-mining/

Business Advantage Papua New Guinea. (2015). *Restructure will see 25% reduction of Ok Tedi staff and switch to 'fly in-fly out' operation at Papua New Guinea mine.* Retrieved from businessadvantagepng.com/restructure-will-see-25-reduction-of-ok-tedi-staff-and-switch-to-fly-in-fly-out-operation-at-papua-new-guinea-mine/

Business and Human Rights Resource Centre. (2018). *Ok Tedi Mining's company response.* Retrieved from business-humanrights.org/en/papua-new-guinea-ok-tedi-mining-terminates-191-employees-following-protest-to-request-better-work-conditions-benefits

Carr, P. & Filer, C. (2011). Plans to close the Ok Tedi Mine in Papua New Guinea. *Exploitation et Gouvernance Minière dans le Pacifique*, 1–5. Noumea, New Caledonia: Institut de Recherche pour le Développement. Retrieved from nouvelle-caledonie.ird.fr/content/download/41887/318828/version/1/file/carr+filer.pdf

Cox, J. & Phillips, G. (2015). Sorcery, Christianity and the decline of medical services. In M. Forsyth & R. Eves (Eds), *Talking it through: Responses to witchcraft and sorcery beliefs and practices in Melanesia* (pp. 37–54). Canberra, ACT: ANU Press. doi.org/10.22459/TIT.05.2015.02

Craig, B. (1990). The Telefomin murders: Whose myth? In B. Craig & D. Hyndman (Eds), *The children of Afek: Tradition and change among the Mountain Ok of Central New Guinea* (pp. 115–150). Sydney, NSW: Oceania Publications.

Elapa, J. (2015a, 4 August). Financial crisis hit Kiunga, Tabubil as Ok Tedi mine scales down. *Papua New Guinea Post-Courier*.

Elapa, J. (2015b, 10 August). OTML to open in early 2016. *Papua New Guinea Post-Courier*.

Elapa, J. (2019, 2 September). Road brings hope for Bolangun. *The National*. Retrieved from thenational.com.pg/road-brings-hope-for-bolangun/

EMTV. (2018, 12 August). OTML signs agreement with OTM Allied Workers Union. *EMTV Online*. Retrieved from youtube.com/watch?v=61qJlIb8w SU&t=4s

Englund, H. & Leach, J. (2000). Ethnography and the meta-narratives of modernity. *Current Anthropology*, *41*(2), 225–248.

Esila, P. (2020, 15 April). Mine unaffected so far. *The National*. Retrieved from thenational.com.pg/mine-unaffected-so-far/

Ferguson, J. (1999). *Expectations of modernity: Myth and meanings of urban life on the Zambian Copperbelt*. Berkeley, CA: University of California Press.

Filer, C. (1990). The Bougainville Rebellion, the mining industry and the process of social disintegration in Papua New Guinea. *Canberra Anthropology*, *13*(1), 1–39. doi.org/10.1080/03149099009508487

Filer, C. & Jenkins, P. (2017). Negotiating community support for closure or continuation of the Ok Tedi Mine in Papua New Guinea. In C. Filer & P. Y. Le Meur (Eds), *Large-scale mines and local-level politics: Between New Caledonia and Papua New Guinea* (pp. 229–259). Canberra, ACT: ANU Press. doi.org/10.22459/LMLP.10.2017.08

Forsyth, M. & Eve, R. (Eds). (2015). *Talking it through: Responses to sorcery and witchcraft beliefs and practices in Melanesia.* Canberra, ACT: ANU Press. doi.org/10.22459/TIT.05.2015

Forsyth, M., Putt, J., Bouhours, T. & Bouhours, B. (2017). *Sorcery accusation-related violence in Papua New Guinea: Part 4: Trends over time and geographic spread* (Department of Pacific Affairs, In Brief, 31). Canberra, ACT: The Australian National University.

Garrett, J. (2013, 6 January). PNG's Ok Tedi: From disaster to dividends. *Australian Broadcasting Corporation.* Retrieved from abc.net.au/news/2013-01-07/an-radio-doco3a-ok-tedi/4455092

Garrett, J. (2015, 8 December). Ok Tedi to shed more than 100 workers in PNG. *ABC News Pacific Beat.* Retrieved from abcmedia.akamaized.net/news/pacificbeat/audio/201512/PABm_OkTediCuts_0812_nola.mp3

Gerega, L. (2019, 24 June). Marape tells Awi Yoto to improve Western. *Papua New Guinea Post-Courier.* Retrieved from postcourier.com.pg/marape-tells-awi-yoto-improve-western/

Gerritsen, R. & Macintyre, M. (1991). Dilemmas of distribution: The Misima gold mine, Papua New Guinea. In J. Connell & R. Howitt (Eds), *Mining and indigenous peoples in Australasia* (pp. 35–53). Sydney, NSW: Sydney University Press.

Gibbs, P. (2012). Engendered violence and witch-killing in Simbu. In M. Jolly, C. Stewart & C. Brewer (Eds), *Engendering violence in Papua New Guinea* (pp. 107–136). Canberra, ACT: ANU E Press. doi.org/10.22459/EVPNG.07.2012.03

Gibbs, P. (2015). Practical church interventions on sorcery and witchcraft violence in the Papua New Guinea Highlands. In M. Forsyth & R. Eves (Eds), *Talking it through: Responses to sorcery and witchcraft beliefs and practices in Melanesia* (pp. 309–327). Canberra, ACT: ANU Press. doi.org/10.22459/TIT.05.2015.17

Gunga, T. (2015, 29 July). Mirisim: OTML employees and contractors layoff is an injustice. *EMTV News.* Retrieved from emtv.com.pg/mirisim-otml-employees-layoff-is-an-injustice/

Gware, C. (2018, 12 August). OTML industrial agreement signed. *Loop PNG.* Retrieved from www.looppng.com/business/otml-industrial-agreement-signed-78857

Haley, N. (2008). Sung adornment: Changing masculinities at Lake Kopiago, Papua New Guinea. *The Australian Journal of Anthropology, 19*(2), 213–29. doi.org/10.1111/j.1835-9310.2008.tb00123.x

Haley, N. (2010). Witchcraft, torture and HIV. In V. Luker & S. Dinnen (Eds), *Civic insecurity: Law, order and HIV/AIDS in PNG* (pp 219–35). Canberra, ACT: ANU E Press. doi.org/10.22459/CI.12.2010.11

Haslam, N. R. (2015). Post-mortem as preventative medicine in Papua New Guinea: A case in point. *Rural and Remote Health, 15*(4), 2861.

Howes, S. (2013a). PNG Sustainable Development Program to exit Ok Tedi. *DEVPOLICYBLOG.* Retrieved from devpolicy.org/sdp-to-exit-ok-tedi-2013 0604-2/

Howes, S. (2013b). The remarkable story of the nationalization of PNG's largest mine and its second largest development partner, all in one day. *DEVPOLICYBLOG.* Retrieved from devpolicy.org/ok-tedi-sdp-20130924/

Howes, S. & Kwa, E. (2011). *Papua New Guinea Sustainable Development Program review.* Retrieved from www.pngsdp.org/independant-reviews/

Indeed.com (2019). *Ok Tedi Mining Limited employee reviews.* Retrieved from ca.indeed.com/cmp/Ok-Tedi-Mining-Limited/reviews?fcountry=ALL

Jacka, J. K. (2001). On the outside looking in: Attitudes and responses of non-landowners towards mining at Porgera. In B. Imbun & P. McGavin (Eds), *Mining in Papua New Guinea: Analysis and policy implications* (pp. 45–62). Waigani, Papua New Guinea: University of Papua New Guinea Press.

Jacka, J. K. (2015). *Alchemy in the rainforest: Politics, ecology and resilience in a New Guinea mining area.* Durham, NC: Duke University Press.

Jacka, J. K. (2019). Resource conflicts and the anthropology of the dark and the good in highlands Papua New Guinea. *Australian Journal of Anthropology, 30*(1), 35–52. doi.org/10.1111/taja.12302

Jackson, R. (1988). LDC: Has long-distance commuting a future in Papua New Guinea? *Impact Assessment, 6*(2), 109–125. doi.org/10.1080/07349165.1988.9725639

Jackson, R. (1993). *Cracked pot, or copper bottomed investment? The development of the Ok Tedi project 1982–1991, a personal view.* Townsville, Qld: Melanesian Studies Centre, James Cook University.

Jackson, R., Emerson, C. A. & Welsch, R. (1980). *The impact of the Ok Tedi project.* Boroko, Papua New Guinea: Department of Minerals and Energy.

James, D. (2017, 14 February). Ok Tedi likely to have extended mine life, says CEO. *Business Advantage PNG*. Retrieved from businessadvantagepng.com/ ok-tedi-likely-to-have-extended-mine-life-says-ceo-peter-graham/

James, D. (2018, 12 June). Ok Tedi has moved from 'death row' to a 'sweet spot', says CEO. *Business Advantage PNG*. Retrieved from businessadvantagepng. com/ok-tedi-has-moved-from-death-row-to-a-sweet-spot-says-ceo/

Jenkins, P. (2016a). *The politics of mine closure and sustainable development at the Ok Tedi Mine, Papua New Guinea* (Doctoral thesis). The Australian National University, Canberra, ACT. doi.org/10.25911/5d7637756a8c5

Jenkins, P. (2016b). *Sustaining community through the FIFO transition at Ok Tedi mine—Development, maintenance and staged closure in the North Fly*. Paper presented at the Development Policy Centre conference 'PNG Update: Sustaining Development Beyond the Resource Boom'. Retrieved from devpolicy.org/Events/2016/PNG-Update/4a_Jenkins.pdf

Jorgensen, D. (1980). What's in a name: The meaning of meaninglessness in Telefolmin. *Ethos, 8*(4), 349–366. doi.org/10.1525/eth.1980.8.4.02a00060

Jorgensen, D. (1981a). *Taro and arrows: Order, entropy and religion among the Telefolmin* (Doctoral thesis). University of British Columbia, Vancouver, Canada. Retrieved from open.library.ubc.ca/cIRcle/collections/ubctheses/ 831/items/1.0095526

Jorgensen, D. (1981b). Life on the fringe: History and society in Telefolmin. In R. Gordon (Ed.), *The plight of peripheral people in Papua New Guinea* (pp. 59–79). Cambridge, MA: Cultural Survival.

Jorgensen, D. (1983). Some notes on the geography of the Afek myth cycle from a Telefolmin point of view (Appendix 7.6). In P. Swadling (Ed.), *How long have people been in the Ok Tedi impact region?* Boroko, Papua New Guinea: PNG National Museum.

Jorgensen, D. (1990a). Telefolip, Telefolmin: The architecture of ethnic identity in the Sepik headwaters. In D. Hyndman & B. Craig (Eds), *The children of Afek: Tradition and change among the Mountain Ok of Central New Guinea* (pp. 151–160). Sydney, NSW: Oceania Monographs.

Jorgensen, D. (1990b). Placing the past and moving the present: Myth and contemporary history in Telefolmin. *Culture, 10*(2), 47–56.

Jorgensen, D. (1993). Money and marriage in Telefolmin. In R. Marksbury (Ed.), *The business of marriage: Transformations in Oceanic matrimony* (pp. 57–82). Pittsburgh, PA: Pittsburgh University Press.

Jorgensen, D. (1996). Regional history and ethnic identity in the Hub of New Guinea: The emergence of the Min. *Oceania, 66*(3), 189–210. doi.org/10.1002/j.1834-4461.1996.tb02551.x

Jorgensen, D. (1997). Who and what is a landowner? Mythology and marking the ground in a Papua New Guinea mining project. *Anthropological Forum, 7*(4), 599–627. doi.org/10.1080/00664677.1997.9967476

Jorgensen, D. (2006). Hinterland history: The Ok Tedi mine and its cultural consequences in Telefolmin. *The Contemporary Pacific, 18*(2), 233–263. doi.org/10.1353/cp.2006.0021

Jorgensen, D. (2014). Preying on those close to home: Witchcraft violence in a Papua New Guinea village. *The Australian Journal of Anthropology, 25*(3), 267–286. doi.org/10.1111/taja.12105

Jorgensen, D. (2016). The garden and beyond: The dry season, the Ok Tedi shutdown and the footprint of the 2015 El Niño drought. *Oceania, 86*(1), 25–39.

Jorgensen, D. (2019). Afterword: Dark anthropology in Papua New Guinea? *The Australian Journal of Anthropology, 30*(10), 104–116.

Kemp, D. & Owen, J. R. (2018). The industrial ethic, corporate refusal and the demise of the social function in mining. *Sustainable Development, 26*(5), 491–500.

Kenneth, G. (2019, 24 June). Govt to review FIFO—minister. *Papua New Guinea Post-Courier*. Retrieved from postcourier.com.pg/govt-review-fifo-minister/

Kepmewato, R. (2019, 3 July). Fly-in, fly-out tactic only leaves us shortchanged [Letter to the editor]. *The National*. Retrieved from thenational.com.pg/fly-in-fly-out-tactic-only-leaves-us-shortchanged/

Kirsch, S. (2006). *Reverse anthropology*. Stanford, CA: Stanford University Press.

Knauft, B. (2019). Finding the good: Reactive modernity among the Gebusi, in the Pacific and elsewhere. *The Australian Journal of Anthropology, 30*(1), 84–103. doi.org/10.1111/taja.12303

Leach, J. & Leach, E. (Eds). (1983). *The kula: New perspectives on Massim exchange*. Cambridge, England: Cambridge University Press.

Loop Business. (2019). Tabubil-Kiunga highway to be sealed. Retrieved from www.looppng.com/business/tabubil-kiunga-highway-be-sealed-85877

Loop Business. (2020a). OTML sets-up COVID-19 screening station. Retrieved from www.looppng.com/coronavirus/otml-sets-covid-19-screening-station-91416

Loop Business. (2020b). Ok Tedi Mine continues to operate. Retrieved from www.looppng.com/business/ok-tedi-mine-continues-operate-91558

Lyons, K. (2020, 23 March). Papua New Guinea declares state of emergency after first coronavirus case. *The Guardian*. Retrieved from theguardian.com/world/2020/mar/23/papua-new-guinea-declares-state-of-emergency-after-first-coronavirus-case

Macintyre, M. (1983a). *The kula: A bibliography*. Cambridge, England: Cambridge University Press.

Macintyre, M. (1983b). Warfare and the changing context of 'Kune' on Tubetube. *Journal of Pacific History*, *18*(1), 11–34. doi.org/10.1080/00223348308572456

Macintyre, M. (1994). Anthropology's histories: Dealing with time and transformation in the Pacific. *Reviews in Anthropology*, *22*(4), 275–283. doi.org/10.1080/00988157.1994.9978071

Macintyre, M. (2008). Police and thieves, gunmen and drunks: Problems with men and problems with society in Papua New Guinea. *The Australian Journal of Anthropology*, *19*(2), 179–193. doi.org/10.1111/j.1835-9310.2008.tb00121.x

Malkki, L. (1997). News and culture: Transitory phenomena and the fieldwork tradition. In A. Gupta & J. Ferguson (Eds), *Anthropological locations: Boundaries and grounds of a field science* (pp. 86–101). Berkeley, CA: University of California Press.

Mann, A. (2015, 30 July). Writing was on the wall for Ok Tedi mine [Letter to the editor]. *The National*. Retrieved from thenational.com.pg/writing-was-on-wall-for-ok-tedi-mine/

Mauludu, S. (2018a, 22 February). Mine group sacked. *The National*. Retrieved from thenational.com.pg/mine-group-sacked/

Mauludu, S. (2018b, 23 February). OTML confirms sacking. *The National*. Retrieved from thenational.com.pg/otml-confirms-sacking/

McGavin, P. A., Jones, L. T. & Imbun, B. Y. (2001). In country fly-in/fly-out and national HR development: Evidence from PNG. In B. Y. Imbun & P. A. McGavin (Eds), *Mining in Papua New Guinea: Analysis and policy implications* (pp. 113–132). Waigani, Papua New Guinea: University of Papua New Guinea Press.

McLeod, S. (2019). A billion reasons: The future of PNG's Sustainable Development Program. *The Lowy Institute Interpreter*. Retrieved from www.lowyinstitute.org/the-interpreter/billion-reasons-future-png-sustainable-development-fund

Middleton, A. (2014). *Rostering overhaul extends Ok Tedi mine life.* Retrieved from miningnews.net/leadership/news/1194966/rostering-overhaul-extends-ok-tedi-life

Moore, S. F. (1987). Explaining the present: Theoretical dilemmas in processual ethnography. *American Ethnologist, 14*(4), 727–736. doi.org/10.1525/ae.1987.14.4.02a00080

Moore, S. F. (1994). The ethnography of the present and the analysis of process. In R. Borofsky (Ed.), *Assessing cultural anthropology* (pp. 362–376). New York, NY: McGraw-Hill.

Morauta, M. (2014, 15 September). PNGSDP not drawing down on Long Term Fund [Press statement]. *PNGBlogs.* Retrieved from www.pngblogs.com/2014/09/pngsdp-not-drawing-down-on-long-term.html

Mou, F. (2018, 26 February). MP calls for probe in OTML staff sacking. *Papua New Guinea Mine Watch.* Retrieved from ramumine.wordpress.com/2018/02/26/mp-calls-for-probe-in-otml-staff-sacking/

Nalu, M. (2012, 5 September). Tabubil: after mine closure. *The National.* Retrieved from www.thenational.com.pg/tabubil---after-mine-closure/

Nanau, E. (2020, 30 April). More funding needed to safeguard borders. *Papua New Guinea Post-Courier.* Retrieved from postcourier.com.pg/more-funding-needed-to-safeguard-borders/

Nash, J. & Ogan, E. (1990). The red and the black: Bougainvillean perceptions of other Papua New Guineans. *Pacific Studies, 13*(2), 1–17.

National Statistical Office. (2009). *Western Province socio-economic urban survey report 2009.* Port Moresby, Papua New Guinea: National Statistical Office.

National Statistical Office. (2014). *2011 national population and housing census ward population profile: Southern Region.* Waigani, Papua New Guinea: National Statistical Office.

Ok Tedi Mining Limited. (2012). *Annual review: Our journey continues.* Port Moresby, Papua New Guinea: Ok Tedi Mining Ltd. Retrieved from oktedi.com/who-we-are/annual-performance/annual-performance-2012/

Ok Tedi Mining Limited. (2013). *Annual Review: A new dawn securing our future.* Port Moresby, Papua New Guinea: Ok Tedi Mining Limited. Retrieved from oktedi.com/who-we-are/annual-performance/annual-performance-2013/

Ok Tedi Mining Limited. (2014). *Annual Review.* Port Moresby, Papua New Guinea: Ok Tedi Mining Limited. Retrieved from oktedi.com/who-we-are/annual-performance/annual-performance-2014/

Ok Tedi Mining Limited. (2015a). Toksave: Resetting the business and dry weather action. Tabubil, Papua New Guinea: Ok Tedi Mining Limited.

OkTediMiningLimited.(2015b).Importantupdateandinformationforemployees. Electronic document available at: www.oktedi.com/attachments/article/227/TOKSAVEImportantUpdateandInformationForEmployeesOnStandDown. pdf (accessed 12 December 2015).

Ok Tedi Mining Limited. (2015c, 3 December). Toksave: Coming back to OTML: What's different? Online bulletin. Electronic document available at: www.oktedi.com/media-items/news-releases/228-toksave-coming-back-to-otml-what-s-different (accessed 12 December 2015).

Ok Tedi Mining Limited. (2016). *Annual Review 2016.* Port Moresby, Papua New Guinea: Ok Tedi Mining Limited. Retrieved from oktedi.com/who-we-are/annual-performance/annual-performance-2016/

Ok Tedi Mining Limited. (2017). *Annual Review 2017.* Port Moresby, Papua New Guinea: Ok Tedi Mining Limited. Retrieved from oktedi.com/who-we-are/annual-performance/annual-performance-2017/

Ok Tedi Mining Limited. (2018). *Annual Review 2018.* Port Moresby, Papua New Guinea: Ok Tedi Mining Limited. Retrieved from oktedi.com/who-we-are/annual-performance/

Oxford Business Group. (2014). *Nigel Parker, managing director & CEO, Ok Tedi Mining, on the roles of townships and fly-in-fly-out employees in Papua New Guinea.* Retrieved from oxfordbusinessgroup.com/viewpoint/building-lasting-legacy-nigel-parker-managing-director-ceo-ok-tedi-mining-roles-townships-and-fly

Papua New Guinea Post-Courier. (2020a, 16 March). Two staff at Ok Tedi mine quarantined. *Papua New Guinea Post-Courier.* Retrieved from postcourier.com.pg/two-staff-at-ok-tedi-mine-quarantined/

Papua New Guinea Post-Courier. (2020b, 2 April). Take back PNG by banning fly-in fly-out. *Papua New Guinea Post-Courier.* Retrieved from webcache.googleusercontent.com/search?q=cache:4xLtmRJKHCEJ:postcourier.com.pg/yu-tok-2-2/

Papua New Guinea Resources. (2016, 2 April). Ok Tedi implements fly in – fly out rosters. *Papua New Guinea Resources.* Retrieved from pngresourcesonline.com/ok-tedi-implements-fly-in-fly-out-rosters/

Papua New Guinea Sustainable Development Program (PNGSDP). (2011). *Annual Report, 2011.* Electronic document available at: www.pngsdp.org/annual-reports/

Papua New Guinea Sustainable Development Program (PNGSDP). (2019). *PNG Sustainable Development Program Ltd.* Retrieved from pngsdp.org

Patjole, C. (2020, 24 April). Porgera mine extension application refused. *Loop PNG.* Retrieved from www.looppng.com/business/porgera-mine-extension-application-refused-91723

Peter, J. (2015, 3 August). OTML hiding truth about mine closure. *The National.* Retrieved from thenational.com.pg/otml-hiding-truth-about-mine-closure/

Pinen, J. (2015). Is it a social responsibility of the company to provide services such as schools? Comment on discussion of Fly-in, Fly-out policy at Ok Tedi in *Abip Family* Facebook group. Retrieved from www.evernote.com/shard/s2/sh/14952083-f96d-4b65-b927-763ab644f544/69cd821136e54c9ad6ce6d9ac82b41f3

Pintz, W. (1984). *Ok Tedi: Evolution of a third world mining project.* London, England: Mining Journal Books.

Poriambep, C. (2018, 27 February). Minister will not intervene in Ok Tedi mine sacking. *Papua New Guinea Mine Watch.* Retrieved from ramumine.wordpress.com/2018/02/27/minister-will-not-intervene-in-ok-tedi-mine-sacking/

Radio New Zealand. (2020a, 3 April). PNG governor wants 'shoot to kill' order at border. Retrieved from rnz.co.nz/international/pacific-news/413325/png-governor-wants-shoot-to-kill-order-at-border

Radio New Zealand. (2020b, 9 April). Emergency controls tighten on PNG borders. Retrieved from rnz.co.nz/international/pacific-news/413883/emergency-controls-tighten-on-png-borders

Radio New Zealand. (2020c, 30 April). Tight control of movement in PNG's Kiunga, Tabubil. Retrieved from rnz.co.nz/international/pacific-news/415506/tight-control-of-movement-in-png-s-kiunga-tabubil

Saxer, M. & Andersson, R. (2019). The return of remoteness: Insecurity, isolation and connectivity in the new world disorder. *Social Anthropology, 27*(2), 140–155. doi.org/10.1111/1469-8676.12652

Shiftwork Solutions. (2014). *Rostering for a sustainable future: A case study by Shiftwork Solutions.* Retrieved from shiftworksolutions.com/assets/Uploads/CaseStudy-OkTedi-Final.pdf

The National. (2013, 25 June). Fly-in, fly-out concerns backed. *The National*. Retrieved from thenational.com.pg/fly-in-fly-out-concerns-backed/

The National. (2014, 19 February). Fly-in, fly-out slammed. *The National*. Retrieved from thenational.com.pg/fly-in-fly-out-slammed/

The National. (2018a, 31 July). Morobe opposes fly-in fly-out for Wafi-Golpu mine workers. *The National*. Retrieved from thenational.com.pg/morobe-opposes-fly-in-fly-out-for-wafi-golpu-mine-workers/

The National. (2018b, 27 November). Fly-in fly-out system praised. *The National*. Retrieved from thenational.com.pg/fly-in-fly-out-system-praised/

Vari, M. (2019, 23 January). MP Mirisim supports no fly-in fly-out. *Papua New Guinea Mine Watch*. Retrieved from ramumine.wordpress.com/2019/01/24/mp-mirisim-supports-no-fly-in-fly-out-for-frieda-mine/

Wilkins, A. (2013, 9 December). 'Just like riding a tiger': Ok Tedi's CEO reflects on a momentous year. *Business Advantage Papua New Guinea*. Retrieved from businessadvantagepng.com/just-like-riding-tiger-ok-tedi-minings-ceo-reflects-momentous-year/

11

Transforming Inequalities and Uncertainty: Gender, Generational and Class Dimensions in the Gende's *Longue Durée*

Laura Zimmer-Tamakoshi

Introduction

Generalisations about patriarchal custom in Papua New Guinea (PNG) have long been challenged by works that investigate the power of women in societies where women participate in local exchange systems and the fulfilment of obligations to exercise control over the distribution of important items of exchange. While many traditions of male–female relations allow women little voice in political decision-making (see Macintyre, 1998, pp. 212–217), the traditions of the Gende people of Madang Province empower women of all ages and instil stability in systems built on intergenerational and brother–sister cooperation and marital ties between kin-based groups (Zimmer, 1985; Zimmer-Tamakoshi, 1997a; elsewhere in PNG, see Faithorn, 1976; Goodale, 1983; Warry, 1986). Throughout the *longue durée* of the Gende's pre- and post-European contact history, and in the face of uneven access to education and money, women have tenaciously held onto gender equality. However, new forms of economic inequality have transformed local moral economies, given rise to new subjectivities and class relations and driven intergenerational conflict between men.

My anthropological research has always been driven by questions of inequality. I was inspired by anthropologists Louise Morauta and Dawn Ryan, who demonstrated that villages were not the homogenous and mythical 'homeland' or '*ples*' that some (including the government) wished for, where migrants were welcomed back regardless of their success or failure in the urban workforce and their remittances and exchange performances (Morauta, 1979, 1981a, 1981b; Ryan, 1968; Morauta & Ryan, 1982). As part of Jane Goodale's Bryn Mawr 'mafia' and a Philadelphia-area Women and Development Study group, I was schooled in the importance of women and men of all ages in both traditional and changing exchange systems (Zimmer-Tamakoshi & Dickerson-Putman, 2008; Zimmer-Tamakoshi, 2008; see also Goodale, 1971, 1983; Sexton, 1982, 1986; Weiner, 1976). Hoping to further the study of the impacts of urban migration and inequality on rural and urban communities by bringing gender and generational issues to the foreground, and with Morauta as my in-country sponsor and mentor, I undertook fieldwork in 1982–83 among Gende people living at Yandera village. They were off the beaten track of development projects and had high outmigration rates of both men and women, most of whom were living permanently in town. I was also interested in whether mining projects—as foreign mining companies had been prospecting in the area since the 1960s—might compound rural inequalities that had already emerged as the result of unequal urban remittances.

My engagements with the Gende have continued over my career. After finishing my dissertation (Zimmer, 1985), I taught at the University of Papua New Guinea for three and a half years and have returned often to work with the Gende (most recently in 2016). When mining took off in the 1990s and 2000s, I undertook consulting projects at the Ramu Nickel site at Kurumbukare (beginning in 1995) and witnessed the aggressive copper exploration undertaken by Marengo Mining near Yandera village and its far-flung impact zone (beginning in 2007). Since 1982, I have studied the impacts of development (or its absence) on both powerful and less powerful Gende men and women in village, town and mining camp settings. Much of my early work focused on how migration and urbanisation have transformed gender relationships. At a time when gender was often equated with women's studies, Jeanette Dickerson-Putman and I explored how development transformed men's lives and how the changed situations of men affected women and vice versa (Dickerson-Putman & Zimmer-Tamakoshi, 1994). As my work has shown, men's success or failure is intersected or imbricated with women's varied situations and choices (e.g. Rosi & Zimmer-Tamakoshi, 1993; Zimmer-Tamakoshi, 1993a, 1993b, 1996a, 1996b, 1997a, 1997b, 1998).

The Gende have dealt with periods of extreme inequality and uncertainty for countless generations. Centuries ago, when they lived in PNG's interior, they were forced from their lands by tribal warfare. While many Gende sought refuge with nearby allies and in-laws, some younger Gende travelled to the less-populated northern Bismarck mountains and favourably positioned themselves along ancient trade routes. With flexible and egalitarian traditions, young men and women created ties with new neighbours through marriage and trade and, over time, established generational bonds and exchanges with their own offspring. Without the direct support (and control) of elders during the transition, bands of Gende youths, siblings and young couples nonetheless succeeded in making a new place for themselves, a place they eventually populated from the Ramu foothills back up into the tallest mountains in Chimbu territory.

Beginning in 1932, an influx of traders and missionaries and their goods unsettled the Gende's position as middlemen, setting off waves of migration for wage labour in towns and on plantations built by German and Australian colonists. Recent mining developments are generating return mobilities as migrants hope to cash in on jobs and royalties flowing to village people (Zimmer-Tamakoshi, 2012, 2014a, 2016; see also Bainton & Banks, 2018). 'Big men' who strove to hold society together by promising development and levelling rural–urban inequalities have been replaced by wealthy younger men who are more interested in personal glorification than social cohesion and in dominating their wives than partnering with them. This chapter tracks the emergence of relations of inequality over the long term of Gende history, including the more than three decades of my own research, which has spanned an era in which wage-migration has been supplanted by mining as the dominant form of economic engagement. It focuses particularly on relationships between genders and across generations in an era when Gende society has appeared to fracture and ends with a discussion of whither the Gende moral economy in an era of big mining and its extreme inequalities.[1]

---

1   See Bainton (this volume) for comparable processes around the Lihir gold mine and Cox (this volume) and Gewertz and Errington (this volume) for complementary discussions of moral economies in Melanesia.

A Resilient Past and Moral Economy

According to linguistic evidence and oral history (Aufenanger, 1979; Hughes, 1977; Kituai, n.d.; Z'graggen, 1975; Zimmer, 1985), the Gende once lived in the eastern highlands near what is now the town of Goroka. Fleeing their homeland due to tribal warfare, bands of Gende migrated north over the tall Bismarcks to the sparsely-populated hills and lowlands near the Ramu river (see Figure 1). While many Gende stayed behind and were taken into neighbouring highlands groups, those who ventured into new territory eventually made it their own, making ties with new neighbours through marriage and trade. Soon, clusters of men and women descended from these pioneers made their way back up the Bismarck mountains, following the tracks of Gende traders through rugged terrain and extending their social and political networks to include both the smaller and dispersed Ramu river peoples and the powerful Chimbus on the other side of the Bismarck divide and the Jimi river peoples to the west.

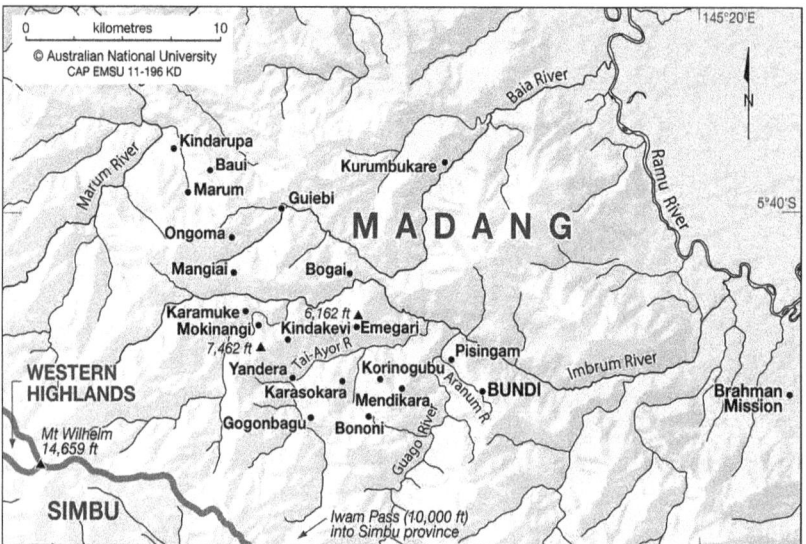

Figure 1: Gende villages are located in a mountainous region of Madang Province that borders Simbu Province.

Source: Education and Multimedia Services, College of Asia and the Pacific, Australian National University.

The Gende settlers were soon joined by other men and women, who preferred the cooler, less malarial and less snake-infested mountains, where traditional staples like sweet potatoes could be cultivated and pandanus fruit and nuts consumed and traded in the rainy season. By the time I arrived in Yandera village in 1982, six generations of men and women had descended from Bamdi, the eponymous founder of one of the seven sub-clans in Yandera. Bamdi himself was allegedly the descendant of Kabizhi, a Gende and Warakai clansman who had travelled from the Ramu foothills unknown generations before to establish Tundega clan in what became Yandera.

With strategic marriages and exchange relations, Gende men and women fashioned strong links within and between north–south and east–west trade routes. Valuable resources, such as shells from the north coast and stone suitable for axes and arrow points from the highlands, flowed through the hands of the most connected and skilled traders (Hughes, 1977). Women from all the different peoples involved in these regional trade routes travelled back and forth between their places of birth and their husbands' hamlets. Those who were still alive during my visits proudly told me about the stone axes and shells that were included in their brideprices, exchanges that reflected their value and desirability as women who were able and willing to work hard raising pigs and children. During hikes in the higher mountains, several were quick to point out vantage points from which one could see from mountain to sea. The first time, in 1982, we stood on a mountainside not far from the border with Chimbu Province on a clear day and saw the north coast—some 50 miles away. Karkar and Manam islands were visible, as was an ash-laden plume from Manam's active crater. I knew then that women had the same opportunities as men to see the Ramu river plains, coast and paths followed by shell valuables, traders and, later, by white men.

Moving along their migration routes, the Gende practised a system of exchange that encompassed their lives. Reciprocity was at the core of the Gende social contract, and young people were obligated to respect and support the elders who had nurtured them as children and invested in their ritual transition to adulthood and marriage. Flexible enough to accept outsiders as 'children' or 'parents', the system of reciprocity provided a means of judging humanity and a motivation to be 'good'. Gende who were very 'good' were considered 'big' (*nambaio*); big men and women (*wana nambaio* and *ana nambaio*) promoted the wellbeing of their kin groups and settlements by looking after more than their immediate family, investing widely in child wealth payments, initiations and marriages. Above all, the generosity of 'big men' and 'big women' was demonstrated through large, coordinated exchange events, called *poi nomu* (literally 'pig house'). These included competitive gifting and other exchanges timed to coincide that cemented ties with allies, assuaged enemies, showed off young male and female initiates and women's industry and ensured peaceful ancestor-hood for the elderly and the fair distribution of the deceased's rights to land (Zimmer-Tamakoshi, 1996a, 1997a, 1997c, 1998).

Two kinds of rituals, called *kwiagi* and *tupoi*, continue to be critical elements in smooth intergenerational and other relations among the Gende. In *kwiagi*, or death payment parties, the deceased's grown children and their spouses give large quantities of cooked pork and other gifts to pay off the debts of the deceased and to ease the grief of the deceased's relatives. If children fail to give generously in *kwiagi*, they may lose land rights associated with the deceased and incur ancestral ill will. Those husbands and wives, brothers and sisters, and any others who work to ensure a *kwiagi*'s success may earn the status of 'owners' or caretakers of land in their own, or even their spouse's, clan territories. Rather than understanding land ownership as inherited by birth, the Gende consider whoever works the land and pays off their own or the previous owner's debts to be *papamama bilong graun* (the 'landowner'). This not only allows smaller clans to grow or to be absorbed into other clans, but also may be used as a negotiating tool—as when the first Gende who settled in the Ramu river area used it to convince Ramu and allies to grant them land and hunting rights in the foothills near Kurumbukare and allow them to marry Ramu women.

In addition to taking leading roles in these *kwiagi*, women could attain considerable power through a women's ritual known as *tupoi*. Before a woman's marriage, her parents and married elder siblings spent days and nights advising her about her rights and obligations to her own and her future husband's clans, about sex and childbirth and about her intrinsic value as an individual. Such training helped to equip young women to set off for the unknown with their brothers or young husbands. As in many parts of PNG, the husband's family gave pigs and other wealth to the bride's family, binding the families together and transferring some rights over the woman's labour and children from her natal to her affinal kin. However, among Gende, married women were expected to redeem their brideprices through *tupoi*, a ritual of 'returning the pigs' that granted them greater authority in their dealings with family and in-laws. In the past, a recently married husband would help clear gardens for his wife under the watchful eye of his mother; however, the young couple was forbidden to have sex until the bride fulfilled this rite. One can see that this was a useful taboo for all sides in the transaction—the in-laws were assured that their daughter-in-law was not lazy, her parents knew she was respected, and the young couple was ready to take on social adulthood and parenthood. As brideprices have risen and other customs have changed, couples no longer wait to have sex; however, *tupoi* is still a measure of a woman's status and a doorway to many freedoms. One such freedom is divorce. Another is her right to use any pigs or wealth she gains in the future to her own ends, including investing in others' marriages, children and so on. In doing so, a woman becomes vested in land rights in her own and other clans' territories. Although she may not be a big man walking up and down a line of slaughtered pigs, loudly declaring his generosity and greatness, she has as much (if not more) political influence over who is going to receive that pork. Even today, with great sums of cash in the hands of few men and even fewer women, women raising herds of 10 or more pigs are a force to be reckoned with.

These rituals linked Gende people from the foothills of the Bismarck ranges to the highlands and their Chimbu, Ramu and other allies and affines; however, they did not always prevent violent conflicts. A critical divide among the Gende—which continues to this day over mining and landowner issues—was the alliance of clans spread out in a swath of settlements near present-day Bundi and Emegari and Karasokara villages. Their closest combatants and competitors in the north–south trade route were a large, more or less parallel strip of allied clans composed of people living near Kurumbukare and in the taller mountains.

The Gende's last major conflict began shortly before foreign missionaries arrived in 1932 and within the memories of persons still alive in the early 1980s. The conflict started between Karasokara and Yandera villages. The two had a history of tension, but the fight began prosaically enough. Three Yandera women were insulted by Karasokara suitors who told others that the girls had sex with them so that they might marry rich men. At the time, the boys' elders were seething over the small amount of pork they had received from Yandera exchange partners at a recent pig kill. Conflict erupted when the young women returned their suitors' insults by lifting their skirts and shouting that they would never marry them and that their naked backsides were all the boys would ever see of them. Outraged,

Karasokara warriors and their Emegari allies drove the outnumbered Yandera villagers from their land. Tundega and Yandima clan members began returning to their lands after the missionaries arrived, but sporadic fighting continued up until World War II over areas of land that had been lost. Resolving the deaths of warriors on both sides was a focus of exchanges between Karasokara and Yandera leaders at Yandera's last *poi nomu* in 1982. More recent conflicts revolved around mining and land ownership as Yandera sought to cut off affinal ties with Karasokara and their allies.

The Transformation of Regional Economies, Migration and Inequality

The arrival of the missionaries and government patrols in the 1930s sparked massive economic, social and political shifts throughout Gende society. Bringing in large quantities of cowry shells from the coast, the outsiders caused the inflation and rapid collapse of the shell economy and undermined the Gende's role as middlemen. Wage labour changed the balance between elder and younger kinspeople, as younger workers soon had alternative means of accumulating wealth and choosing their own routes to success. Christianity had its own impacts on marriage and other customs. Importantly, engagement with the colonial economy created lasting inequalities across Gende society and between the Gende and their former trading partners, particularly their relationships with the Chimbu, who would soon be wealthier than they.

In 1932, Catholic missionaries travelled to the highlands from the north coast, having heard there were as many people behind the tall Bismarck mountains as there were leaves on a tree. The first actual highlanders they ran into were Gende, who had long before resettled on the Bismarcks' northern flanks in Guiebi village. A man from Utu, a small Sepu village near the Ramu river, showed Father Alfons Schaefer and Brother Anthony Bass the steep path up to Guiebi. While Utu undoubtedly had ties with the Gende through trade and possibly marriage, he feigned fear of the Gende long enough to convince Schaefer to give him a pair of his pants. When they finally came across a garden in which women were working, the Sepu man discreetly disappeared, leaving the German missionaries and their carriers on their own. The women were startled, cried out and were soon joined by their menfolk.

While some Gende were frightened and called the white-skinned men 'ghosts', most were excited by the cowry shells the newcomers used to pay for things. Traditionally, a pig traded to the Gende by their Chimbu trading partners would fetch a string of cowry shells the length of the pig. Through helping the missionaries build missions at Guiebi and then Bundi, where they also built an airstrip, it was not long before many ordinary Gende—women and men—had more cowry shells than most big men. Big men found themselves in the embarrassing position of having to work alongside lesser men and children to maintain their status as leaders and middlemen in the north–south trade route.

Chimbu trading partners soon wondered about the explosion of Gende wealth. In early 1933, a prominent Chimbu leader, Kavagl, visited the mission at Bundi (his Gende wife's home village) with his wife and hundreds of his followers on a trading trip to buy brides and attend a large *kaima* (or *singsing*) festival hosted by his Gende in-laws. Seeing their apparent prosperity, Kavagl invited Father Schaefer to visit his people in the highlands. Initially, Schaefer hesitated; however, in November, after receiving news of the Leahy brothers' expedition into the highland valleys, he took up Kavagl's offer and started a mission in Mingende. Other Catholic missionaries followed, making their way into the Wahgi Valley and leaving a string of airstrips and missions in their wake.

The missionaries and colonial government were keen to develop the densely populated central valleys and airlifted tons of shells and other goods into the highlands. The effects on the Gende were significant— their middleman role was eliminated and massive inflation occurred in the local economy. Marriages and other ties based on worthless shells collapsed, and reputations were ruined.

Finding themselves suddenly massively disadvantaged in relation to their highland allies, the Gende began to forge new translocal connections through the mission, Allied forces, European commercial interests and the colonial government. Father Heinrich Aufenanger, who had replaced Father Schaefer in 1934, sent catechists to Gende villages to promote the learning of Tok Pisin and Christian principles. Soon, Gende catechists were travelling far and wide. During World War II, Gende men were carriers and orderlies for Allied forces fighting the Japanese in the Ramu valley. After the war, men headed south to the new towns of Goroka, Kundiawa and Mt Hagen, where they worked as cooks and servants or joined construction gangs, building the airstrip in Goroka and other developments. Others worked on coastal plantations as far away as Kavieng and Port Moresby, at the Wau-Bulolo goldfields or as carriers and native police on government patrols into uncontrolled areas of the highlands. When migrants came home and distributed imported goods, more Gende left home, including women. While women had few job opportunities other than as 'house girls' (*haus meri*), they cooked and washed clothes for their husbands and younger clan brothers, tended small gardens and raised a pig or two, providing stability and a certain independence among the younger generation. Some couples became permanent urban dwellers, raising families and sending them to urban schools.

By the mid-1950s, migration became a regular part of young men's lives as parents expected cash as part of their daughters' brideprices. Older villagers and wives who stayed behind often suffered from a lack of male labour and unfulfilled exchange obligations, because not everyone was successful in finding a job, wanted to return home or was welcome if they did. Coffee plantations were opening in the central highland valleys, and patrol posts were becoming towns in need of carpenters and other labour. Roads were built in other parts of the country, linking some villagers to the coffee market—but not the Gende.

In 1958, Father Mike Morrison opened the first English-speaking school in the highlands at Bundi. Those Gende who helped build it envisioned a positive shift in Gende fortunes, with future migrants making more money and sharing it with their extended families; conversely, the church saw it as a way of creating a class of educated Catholics living in nuclear households and practising Western ways. The first class had 36 boys. Later, at Morrison's insistence, 20 girls were admitted. English was taught to prepare children for higher education in business, clerical, managerial and other skills needed in an expanding urban job market. As the school grew, teachers were brought in from Australia. In 1965, a first graduating class of 30 students (mostly male) was flown to Madang to continue their education. While fewer girls went on to higher education, those who did used their education to promote their independence and status, some helping extended families and others less so. Ultimately, school and education were major sources of inequality among Gende society.

The years leading up to national independence in 1975 were a time of both promise and concern for Gende villagers. There were roads to build, coffee to plant, local councils to elect and national politics to understand. More cash flowed into the exchange system as individual growers carried coffee to markets over the mountains, mining companies explored for copper near Yandera village and nickel and cobalt at Kurumbukare, beginning in the 1960s, and some of the first graduates from the school at Bundi became doctors, teachers, secretaries, bank clerks and government workers. Unfortunately, individual remittances and earnings were vastly unequal; mining companies were not finding viable deposits and their high turnover added uncertainty to the economy. Further, roads were difficult to build in the steep environment and had little support from the government; wealthier Chimbu neighbours, with better roads connecting them to coffee markets, drew many Gende brides while escalating prices for Chimbu brides made them unaffordable for most Gende bachelors and their families (Zimmer-Tamakoshi, 1993a).

Intergenerational Conflict and Troubled Masculinities

When I arrived in Yandera, 50 years after the missionaries, my census showed that only one of 57 men between the ages of 18 and 24 and only 37 of 67 between the ages of 25 and 34 were married. Most older men had married in their mid-20s. The fallen middlemen of the 1930s had been unable to help their sons contract marriages, and some also lost their own wives. Unmarried men felt great shame over their inability to attract marriage partners to achieve social adulthood (Zimmer, 1984). Bachelors responded to the challenges facing them by trying their luck in town. Parents and other family members complicated their situations by investing in migrants or returnees who had more money, granting them land rights and brideprice support in return for the fulfilment of exchange obligations that their sons were not meeting. Traditions intended to provide stability were being used by the older generation to balance their own obligations while also placing their sons in liminal positions (Zimmer, 1990a). Parents justified their choices as temporary, hoping children would strike it rich and regain land rights during *kwiagi*; however, they rarely did.

One migrant who benefited from intergenerational conflicts with a judicious return to Yandera was Ruge Angiva. I have detailed the lives of Ruge and his family in many publications (Zimmer-Tamakoshi, 1996a, 1997b, 2016); these are instructive of the different paths Gende have taken to navigate the possibilities and trials of social and political change.

They shatter any illusion that Gende society is one integral, undivided community. As the stories of Ruge's family illustrate, local power dynamics shift as individuals and coalitions manage their relationships through exchange and other means. Anything that disturbs parts of the webs of exchange also disturbs or provides opportunities for others.

When the missionaries came, Ruge's father (Angiva) became one of their helpers, establishing a Tok Pisin school and church in Yandera. He also served as village *Tultul* (counsellor), assisting Australian officers in getting Gende to live in compact villages, where they were enumerated and taxed and where Western medicine and other services were administered. Spurning polygyny and other traditions, Angiva worked hard to help his community benefit from the presence of outsiders, believing Christianity and modernity were the way to go. Although he was poorly paid, he shared what little he earned, and his wife Amokai worked hard in her gardens and raised many pigs. For these reasons, many considered him a good man and named their sons after him. Even so, when he died in his early fifties, around 1960, he left many traditional exchange obligations unfulfilled and his only son landless (Zimmer-Tamakoshi, 2016, pp. 255–256).

Ruge and his sisters were among the first Gende to attend the Tok Pisin school established by their father. Learning Tok Pisin made it easier to interact with the missionaries and colonial officials, in addition to finding work in towns and elsewhere. Believing a catechist that initiation was heathen, Ruge ran away to Kundiawa, a town in the eastern highlands, where he worked for years as a male servant (*haus boi*) for Australians. In the home of one *masta*, Ruge cautiously drank alcohol with the young Australian while shrewdly observing his behaviour for insights into the *waitman*'s ways. When Ruge returned to Yandera for a visit, his uncles— annoyed with their brother and wanting to groom their oldest nephew to be a leader of his own generation and a generous supporter of theirs— complained that he had not completed his initiation, arguing that this would bring ill fortune to him. Not believing them but wanting to marry, Ruge agreed on an abbreviated initiation. His uncles and his mother then negotiated a brideprice for a woman from Yandera's other clan. Rosa, following tradition, stayed with Ruge's mother to raise pigs for her *tupoi* obligation to her in-laws. Leaving it to others to clear gardens for Rosa, Ruge went off to Goroka in the late 1950s with another girl, Elizabeth, who snuck away from her home village (Karasokara) to be with him. Ruge worked as a cook and Elizabeth as a house girl for an Australian family.

Saving AUD 70, Ruge helped pay brideprice for Elizabeth, making him one of the first Gende to contribute cash to his wife's brideprice. In the seven years they lived in Goroka, Ruge and Elizabeth hosted many of Ruge's younger cousins that were seeking jobs. For a time, they were joined by Rosa, who posed as Elizabeth's sister because polygyny was frowned upon by their employers. Soon after, in 1958, Elizabeth bore a daughter—Betty. When Rosa, too, became pregnant, she returned to Yandera and began raising pigs for an expected child wealth payment to her clan (Zimmer-Tamakoshi, 2016, pp. 256–247).

Realising that there was little future for him in town and encouraged by his uncles to work towards becoming a big man with knowledge of white men's ways, Ruge returned to Yandera. His father had forfeited land rights in helping the church; however, Ruge's uncles invested plentiful land—and their wives and his mother invested plentiful pigs—to support Ruge's ambitions. His family grew to include three wives and 15 children. Elizabeth, having seen the benefits of education, registered her oldest daughters at the boarding school in Bundi in the early 1960s. By 1982, all their hard work and planning had paid off. Cash from Elizabeth's oldest daughter Betty (then an Air Niugini stewardess) and Elizabeth's trade store, along with the many pigs and other contributions from his wives, mothers and aunts, supported a large *poi nomu* that validated Ruge's big man status.

Though much of Ruge's wealth was in pigs and his extended social network, access to cash was changing traditional pathways to success and who was winning. Another man to achieve big man status in the 1982 *poi nomu* was Peter Tuma, the young local camp manager for the mining company developing the Yandera prospect. He had only one wife, but was supported by the many villagers who had received school fees for their children and other cash payments from him over the years. They supplied him with the pigs and pork that he distributed at the *poi nomu*. Noteworthy among the seven big men in Yandera was Lapun ('old man') Gene, the reigning and oldest big man in Yandera and one of the most influential in Gende society. Gene owned much of the land in which copper deposits lay and his adult sons, many with lucrative jobs in town, had also held well-paid jobs with the mining companies that came and went. Together, Gene and his sons timed Gene's 'retirement party' to coincide with the *poi nomu*. A big man for decades, Gene staged his own final death payment exchange, a *kwiagi* at which all his debts and obligations were paid off by him, his wives and his sons and their wives, resulting in his land rights in Yandera turning over to the younger generation. After the event, Gene and his wives intentionally moved to one wife's home village near Kurumbukare where they continued investing in land rights there, betting that one day prospectors (and they and their children) would strike it rich.

Sometimes, such attempts to amass or even just acquire land rights result in violence. In 1982, a cousin of Ruge who had returned to Yandera from town argued furiously with his uncles and Ruge about rights to his father's land. When this cousin's father died years before, Ruge paid most of his *kwiagi* debts and became the rightful owner of the land. Although Ruge allowed his cousin's wife to use some of the land, his cousin's anger continued unabated. In 1990, he assaulted Ruge so badly that he died. Most of the time, such violence was held in check through the maintenance of a large network of ties that would ensure some access to land and other resources (Zimmer, 1990b). An inventive card-playing system and other means of spreading wealth around to an extent also helped (see Zimmer, 1986, 1987) as did the realisation that, while the mining company was creating temporary inequalities, there was nothing certain about its long-term success.

Rising inequality affected women differently to men. The escalation in brideprice meant that they had to raise more pigs to repay their own brideprices and to help sons marry. Some older village women even took up part-time work at a spice company near Bundi; however, they quit and brought down the whole operation when they realised that younger women who had the time to sort cardamom into different grades all day were being paid higher wages and, thus, contributing to brideprice inflation for everyone (Zimmer-Tamakoshi, 1996b; see also Filer, 1985). However, women always had access to land and were not ashamed of renting and working on others' land in the way that men tended to be. While men resented women for having it 'easier', physical violence against Gende women was uncommon in both village and town. Married women at Okiufa and other urban settlements, who could only raise a pig or two on the land they rented from local landowners, nonetheless led respectable lives managing their husbands' modest incomes, scrimping and saving, keeping husbands away from temptations and alcohol on paydays, investing in children's education and maintaining exchange ties with villagers in expectation of future mining and other developments. Paradoxically, perhaps, women married to more prosperous townsmen or working in two-income professional families struggled to manage extended households of in-laws and others with little support from husbands and other male relatives (Zimmer, 1990a; Zimmer-Tamakoshi, 1993a, 1993b, 1998). Yet, even women who were abused by their urban husbands could escape by returning to the village and raising pigs to pay back brideprices. In 1983, I witnessed a young woman quietly face down her angry brother who had expected to use her brideprice from a prosperous townsmen to acquire his own bride. The woman had the moral support of many at Yandera's crowded village market in addition to her parents, who had already returned the brideprice to their daughter's in-laws to reduce conflict. The young woman planned to marry a returned migrant, who had not prospered in town but was willing to work with his wife-to-be to raise many pigs for her parents and brother. The angry brother was virtually booed off the school playing field where the market was held.

Even if, in this context, women tend not to experience shame as intensely as men, emerging inequalities among women are also evident even in the same family. Ruge's oldest daughter, Betty, intentionally avoided being controlled by in-laws by marrying Australian men and building a business empire (Zimmer-Tamakoshi, 1993b, 1996a). Not long after her father's *poi namu*, she set up a coffee-buying business in Yandera village with the intention of 'helping' her kin (see Cox, this volume); however, this venture was marred by resentment and competition. She continued with other enterprises: a farm to provision urban markets along the Highlands Highway (and, later, two mining operations), PNG's first trout farm and a successful tourist business and lodge for people wanting to hike to the top of the nation's highest mountain. Each of these endeavours required a large labour force, which she drew from her extended family in Yandera. While Betty prides herself in being the 'mother of all' and the hardest working member of the crew (which is true), she enjoys privileges such as international travel and a large modern house that her siblings and relatives do not. Unsurprisingly, her enterprises were targeted by dissidents in the area who destroyed government vehicles in addition to her trout farm.

Although less privileged women undoubtedly resent the privilege of their middle-class or elite sisters, even poor women retain a public role in a way that men who are unsuccessful in the formal economy do not. While older women can still earn respect raising gardens and pigs and helping their children and grandchildren, older men have receded from the public eye—hiding in their homes after helping their wives in the gardens, selling buai in the marketplaces or playing cards along the side of the road.

Broken Promises and the Ushering in of New Power Dynamics during the Extraction Boom

The intergenerational inequality that emerged in force with the bachelorisation of Gende society in the 1970s and 1980s made younger men angry with their elders (particularly fathers) and resentful towards younger women who they perceived as having certain advantages. Gende power dynamics were again transformed by the resurgence of mining prospecting and mining projects in the mid-1990s and afterwards. The social and economic trends since that time threaten to fracture Gende society and identity permanently: leaving 'the boys' and the equivalent of some 'good old boys' in charge, sending a traditional older generation to their graves (or hiding in their garden houses), undermining women's equality with men and intensifying inequality, class relations and different subjectivities such that the once-egalitarian Gende society would be a thing of the past.[2] Earning high salaries, younger men are able to challenge senior men's control of land through ancestral gerrymandering and to pay their own brideprices. While many younger women have sought status through paid employment or raising more pigs to fulfil *tupoi*, others forgo marriage or escape through divorce and remarriage or return home to work with their families and less prosperous brothers. Gende families are fragmenting as some members try to keep significantly higher salaries for themselves; Gende society itself is fragmenting as those who have a mine in their backyard are closing off social relations with those who do not.

In 1982, Ruge touted himself as 'the last big man'—a prescient assertion. The *poi nomu* that drew hundreds of exchange partners from towns throughout PNG, every Gende village and bordering Ramu and Simbu villages was one of the last. The crisis that bachelors faced, in addition to the opportunities education and capitalism were offering some young men, was encouraging a generational shift, one that was obvious at the 1982 *poi nomu* (see Zimmer, 1985). Alienated migrants who had turned to petty crime (*raskolism*) in town came home to prey on those who had rejected them, and prosperous townsmen spent more time conferring with one another on what should be done to kickstart development than with

---

2   I have written about these transformations in scholarly articles (e.g. Zimmer-Tamakoshi, 1997c, 2001, 2006, 2007, 2012, 2014a, 2014b, 2016, 2018) and in reports for Highlands Gold/Pacific (1995, 2000) and Marengo Mining (2007, 2008a, 2008b, 2009, 2010a, 2010b, 2011a–c, 2012, 2014).

Ruge and other big men. Further, the shame, frustration and anger of former migrants who felt cheated by older relatives simmered and boiled over as others monopolised the interest of potential brides and investors.

Several migrants who had returned to Yandera to participate in the *poi nomu* organised what they called the 'Bundi Strike'. Challenging local big men's authority, the strike's leaders demanded that government leaders meet them at the district station at Bundi to explain what had happened to funds set aside for a road in the provincial budget. One organiser, a former government worker, wanted to help the Gende develop a stronger stance in relation to the government and mining companies. He saw big men and the older generation as uneducated and locked in the past, worried more about status and competition than the futures of younger generations. Early on the morning of 28 March 1983, a plane carrying invited national and provincial government officials landed on the Bundi airstrip. Within minutes, several thousand Gende, many armed with axes, bows and arrows, surrounded the delegation and prevented the plane from taking off. The organisers delivered a list of grievances and demands. Foremost was the request for funds to complete the road to connect with both Madang and the Highlands Highway. Demonstrators challenged the officials to treat them like 'men' or face the consequences, which included the Gende joining Simbu Province. Having disbanded the local government council and posted sentries at the district headquarters to prevent police interference, the strikers' threats were taken seriously, and the 'disbanded' Gende Council—many of whom were on the airstrip—received promises for future support in addition to cheques in the amount of PGK 25,000 (worth approximately USD 37,500 in 1983), to be used for the Bundi school and to finish part of the road between Bundi and Yandera.

The strike's organisers claimed that they cared about village society; however, very few established leaders were impressed. Ruge refused to be part of the strike, brushing it off as 'a young man's thing' and a way of promoting their own interests. Several of the organisers were already absentee landowners who were benefiting from their less fortunate brothers- and sisters-in-laws, who paid rent for the use of the land in pigs. The local catechist and the manager of the Yandera mining camp also declined to participate, arguing that the church and the mining company would solve the Gende's problems.

However, they did not. Not the government. Not the church. Not the mining companies. Not even big men like Ruge who worked hard to build extended networks of exchange partners who one day would find marriage partners for his many young sons and their cousins, should he be unable to do so. The promising prospecting initiated by the mining company, which coincided with my departure from Yandera in May 1983, fizzled and it was the middle of the 1990s before the Ramu prospect took off, sparking a whirlwind of divestment in what were thought of as inconvenient exchange relations and investing in relations that the investors hoped would place them in more favourable positions to receive benefits from the extraction industry.

In a 1995 landowners survey at the Ramu Nickel project (Kurumbukare), I found Gende families moving into the sparsely-populated area, contesting the same land blocks with conflicting origin stories. Some Gende, who I had interviewed long before for my 1982 census of Yandera village, claimed new clan identities, one boldly telling me that his wife was a member of a Yandera clan, not him, and that I had got it all wrong. It was obvious that genealogies were futile proof of land ownership. People were using *kwiagi* ceremony to establish new or reverse ancestral ties. Nightly card games and *kwiagi* fuelled what I came to term 'ancestral gerrymandering' (Zimmer-Tamakoshi, 1997c, 2001, 2006, 2007). During the day, people I had already interviewed would come to me and say 'I forgot to tell you', before changing their stories. Deals were made, and outsiders were buying their way into others' genealogies. I experienced hostility whenever I questioned these revised versions.

When I returned to the Ramu Nickel project in 2000, women and their unmarried sons confronted me. They were angry because the company and leaders of landowner groups had falsely claimed that I had listed only male heads of household as rightful 'landowners' in my 1995 census, omitting sisters, widows, wives and unmarried sons. The man who was representing Gende to Ramu Nickel, David Tigabu, was the son of a man who had preposterously claimed the whole of Kurumbukare as his own when I interviewed him in Port Moresby in 1995—a time when both father and son were *personae non gratae* at the proposed mine site. In both 1995 and 2000, and during later meetings with the Chinese company (MCC) that would eventually develop the Ramu Nickel project, I stressed that no single Gende could afford to control the entirety or even major portions of the mine site through *kwiagi* investments.

Shortly after my 2000 visit, MCC had negotiated to operationalise production; by 2005, local positions at the mine were being filled by Gende migrants returning to reap the benefits of having sent home remittances for many years (see Zimmer-Tamakoshi, 2014a). In 2007, I began a multi-year census/survey of over 20 Gende and non-Gende villages to be affected by the development of the copper project at Yandera, a pipeline and coastal depot.[3] The Australian company Marengo Mining acquired the prospect in 2005 and quickly began digging new holes and expanding their area of exploration. From 2007 through 2012 and 2014, my team and I collected extensive data on all households in the region, including those of migrants who returned from elsewhere to be counted in Gende country, who were interviewed in town or whose information was provided by their village kin.[4] Many of the migrants were living (some working) at the Ramu Nickel project. Therefore, while the focus was on the impact of the proposed Yandera project, I learned a lot about events in the Kurumbukare area.

Perhaps the most important finding was that the Gende were committed to mining, despite its negative impacts on the environment and society, because it was ending bachelorisation in Yandera and nearby villages. Men were able to obtain jobs with salaries ranging between PGK 5,000 and tens of thousands of kina; thus, they were able to marry. Returned migrants with special skills drew the highest salaries, allowing some to have more than one wife and play at being 'big shots' (Martin, 2013). Real big men were a thing of the past, much like large pig feasts and networking with the entire tribe. Unsurprisingly, gambling with company employees was rampant and aggressive, unlike the more sociable and 'good' gambling that still occurs in villages farther away from Yandera and among close kin in garden settlements (Zimmer-Tamakoshi, 2014b, 2016; see also Pickles, 2019). To protect their workers from all-night card games, supervisors at the Yandera project built worker accommodation and camps that are off-limits to anyone not working for the company.

---

3   The aims of the surveys went far beyond those of the work contracted at Ramu Nickel. The interview schedule I constructed covered many areas, including kinship relations and clan affiliations, work histories, income sources, participation in traditional exchanges such as *tupoi*, education and more. The interview took approximately three hours to complete. Land tenure and measurements were carried out by a separate team.

4   My team was composed of university-educated Papua New Guineans who had worked with anthropologist Nancy Sullivan on other projects. We received logistical help from Gende working for Marengo and others I had worked with over the years. Many of my findings are discussed in recent publications and presentations (see Zimmer-Tamakoshi, 2012, 2014a, 2014b, 2016, 2018).

One surprisingly happy segment of Gende society—to me, at least—was the merry widows of Yandera (see Zimmer-Tamakoshi, 2012), some of whom had been married to former big men. They are happy that their sons can now help pay higher brideprices and help pay off their fathers' *kwiagi*, thereby cementing land rights for both mothers and sons. However, in general, young men's windfall and new independence come at a heavy price. Young men are paying their own brideprice; therefore, they are no longer indebted to either the parents of their wives or their own families, and they may be more likely to treat their wives as their own personal property (Zimmer-Tamakoshi, 2016, p. 262).

Younger wives were less happy about having to raise large pig herds to achieve *tupoi* and, in some cases, deal with domestic conflict involving co-wives. Nevertheless, census data showed just how hard even women who had grown up in town were willing to work, raising five, six, even 10 pigs at a time to redeem their brideprices and invest in other exchanges, or to sell to wealthier villagers for prices as high as PGK 1,000. Very few women have enviable positions working for the mining companies and, from time to time, there were spats over who had the 'right' to do so. One young woman who returned from town as a fully qualified secretary was driven out of Yandera in less than a week by older women with lesser qualifications who felt that, having lived in Yandera all or most of their lives, they deserved the job more than the young woman did. Those women who fit quite easily back into the village had helped their husbands keep up with exchange relations while they lived in town before coming back to work at the Yandera project (or at Ramu Nickel).

An alarming side effect of mining prosperity was the dissolution of many Gende marriages—Gende people living near mining projects had begun divorcing distant spouses and remarrying closer to home. The primary motive was to narrow ties, so that future royalties and other benefits did not disperse among distant in-laws. However, this was a risky strategy. When several of the new prospects drilled near Yandera turned out to be duds, in areas where villagers from Snopass and Karasokara villages had long intermarried with Chimbu partners, suddenly brothers had to rely on old ties with their sisters' Chimbu husbands to raise cash crops (coffee) on their in-laws' land or return to town in search of work. Some Gende men, who had attracted Chimbu and Gende wives due to the possibility of striking it rich, lost their wives because they and their parents could not or could no longer front or promise the brideprices.

'The Boys' and the Generational Split

This section focuses on the individuals benefiting most by the presence of mining—the former bachelors and younger men working at Ramu Nickel and at Yandera (who head most of the Landowner Associations) and a few older men rich enough to wield considerable influence in the local politics of mining—and presents examples of just how much the Gende's moral economy has shifted due to mining's daunting intrusion into Gende society. 'The Boys' or Gende *mavi* ('wild dogs'), as they often call themselves, make it clear in person, email and a variety of Facebook groups that they base their hopes for the future on mining and that no one (including the anthropologist) is to obstruct their goals with inconvenient facts. These facts include mining's destructive and unsustainable nature, the ongoing lack of reliable roads, decent health care and schools in most villages and settlements and the exclusion of many Gende, who are unable to achieve political influence through exchange and who can no longer rely on bygone egalitarian expectations.

Figure 2: 'The Boys', Yandera Mining Camp (2007).
Source: Photo by Laura Zimmer-Tamakoshi.

The obvious generational split is unnerving, as is evidence of growing gender inequality and difference between haves and have-nots. Boys with jobs that make PGK 5,000, PGK 6,000 and up to PGK 30,000 or more per annum are using *kwiagi* and other exchanges to become big landowners, leaving others earning PGK 250 or less a year landless. The Boys, an expression harking back to traditional male initiations where youths grouped together for years in activities in the forest to become men, are now supporting one another more than anyone else.

In the past, initiates hunted wild animals, ate the meat and shared valuable skins and feathers with parents and others who would help them with brideprices. Today, Boys of 20, 30 and, sometimes, 40 years of age are now turning their backs on older men, resenting their handling of development in the past (see also Gewertz & Errington, this volume). Before and after the Ramu Nickel census, for example, many men vying to be included as 'landowners' left their wives and unmarried sons to tend gardens hacked from the rainforest while they met up in town and spent any money they received (or expected) as landowners to participate in *kwiagis*, drink beer and even establish second marriages (as opposed to helping their sons acquire wives). The young men and their mothers were used as placeholders. Less of this happened in association with census work conducted at Yandera, because family ancestries and land rights were better known; however, deals were being made, and younger men with money were more in control of those deals.

The phenomenon of young males increasingly bonding with one another has been noted in other mining contexts (see Bainton, 2008). Among the Gende, young men who benefit most from mining favour dealings, compatible with ongoing market participation (see Zimmer-Tamakoshi, 2016), spurn the society-wide networking of their elders as an ineffective use of resources. One such deal occurred during an infamous sex party in Kundiawa. Six or so Boys from Yandera, who were in their 40s, paid thousands of kina for hotel rooms, alcohol and prostitutes, outspending each other over a month, before deciding among themselves who would take on the leadership of the landowner association. This act of conspicuous consumption, reminiscent of national politicians, had regrettable consequences. One contestant for leadership was Ruge's son, a local schoolteacher, who spent his entire superannuation (retirement) savings but did not win the position. The winner of the landowner association leadership role held a well-paid management job at the Yandera mine site.

He contracted AIDs and died a few years later. The wives of both men were unhappy about their husbands' use of money but had little or no influence over their decisions.

Not long after the sex party incident, the Gende millionaire, security firm owner and then member of parliament, Peter Yama, bought his way into Ruge's clan through his son, the ex-teacher who was desperately in need of cash. Yama already had many financial deals and land claims with Ramu Nickel. When Marengo extended its area of interest beyond Yandera and began prospecting in the area of Yama's father's people, Yama sent two young men to give me his census data in the village of Snopass. When the new prospect did not pan out, Yama claimed that he had 'ancestral' ties to the land in Yandera. Ruge's son was the ideal dupe. Inconveniently for Yama, I knew (and he knew)—from the fieldwork and censuses carried out over the years in Yandera, Snopass and other Gende villages—that he had gerrymandered his way into Yandera at the expense of others less wealthy than he. Several years later, in 2014, Yama's sons menaced me and my female Gende assistant at the Madang Resort Hotel. It was only through subterfuge that I managed to get both of us safely out of Madang.

The 2014 incident was not the first time that my research had become politically inconvenient. In 2007, in a meeting with Ramu Nickel senior management, I was asked 'how do you verify Gende landowners' claims?' When I explained that traditional *kwiagi* exchanges were being used by wealthier Gende to become members of landowning groups, I was abruptly dismissed. This was inconvenient and threatening knowledge. They were not interested in understanding Gende culture or mining's impact on Everyman (or Woman), and they definitely did not like the idea of flexible kin relations. However, The Boys had a fervent interest in simplifying that process for them. As far back as 1995, it was obvious that The Boys and other powerful players did not want the process of ancestral gerrymandering advertised or explained in too much detail. That week, in 2007, as I was preparing to go to Yandera, and just after my discussion with Ramu Nickel management, young Gende associated with Yama confronted me over a chapter I had written on ancestral gerrymandering at Ramu Nickel (Zimmer-Tamakoshi, 2001), claiming that it was false and that I should retract it. They had accessed the article online. I was being tracked—the perils of long-term research and knowing too much! What is inconvenient for me, however, is more troublesome for Gende who might disagree with Yama—now Governor of Madang—and others like him who wish to dominate the directions development is taking, for their own enrichment.

Whither the Gende's Moral Economy?

Can the Gende's aptitude for resilience and egalitarian practices continue to temper capitalism's onslaught? Alternatively, will toxic inequality and deepening capitalist-oriented subjectivities among some Gende create an unequal class system? Or, has this already occurred? As I have shown, the inequalities among Gende individuals and families are significant. At the same time, the future of mining revenues and mining projects is uncertain. Gende have dealt with uncertainty over the generations by utilising egalitarian practices. However, contemporary uncertainty may lead to a deepening of class interests, another period of ancestral gerrymandering or a return to older forms of egalitarianism. Just as nation-builders and policy-makers of the past mistakenly assumed that a village necessarily takes care of its own, regardless of their successes or failures in town, it would be a mistake to summarise the Gende's story here and not continue to watch the various trajectories of big and small players.

While villagers may continue raising pigs and sweet potatoes and practising partial customs, there exist deep differences among them in terms of access to mining and other revenue and radical demands on their land and other resources that make egalitarianism difficult if not impossible. While the current existence (and future) of many Gende is grim when contrasted with those benefiting the most from mining operations and other sources of local economic inequality, there exists uncertainty about where the Yandera prospect is headed and a growing discontent with Ramu Nickel's disdain for the general population of 'landowners', in addition to a shared sense among Papua New Guineans that they are being ripped off by foreigners and corrupt politicians. Ramu Nickel has paid relatively little in benefits and compensation to the community in relation to both its corporate profits and benefits and payments accorded to key middlemen.

Seeing the landowners' discontent as a political opportunity, Governor Peter Yama made a rare public appearance, declaring that he wanted Ramu Nickel investigated. Nothing came of this during the political turmoil over Peter O'Neill's alleged corruption and his recent stepping down as prime minister. However, when the even more recent toxic spill into the ocean at the Basamuk refinery caused major outrage, Governor Yama called for a shutdown—possibly a permanent shutdown—of Ramu Nickel. While many expected this would rattle the Chinese administrators at MCC, MCC simply claimed it had cleaned up the mess and paid for any damage in a strongly worded article in the *Papua New Guinea Post-Courier*. Unsurprisingly, The Boys said little about the poor royalty payments at Ramu Nickel and even the toxic spill, being leery of upsetting the powers that be at Ramu Nickel or Yandera and losing their jobs and incomes.[5]

While there is no open class war, there are plentiful signs that most Gende are angry about extreme differences in individual living conditions and wellbeing. Looking at gender in/equalities and generational differences, even rural–urban inequalities, is no longer sufficient. Relations of production and class differences—be they defined as such or as a national proletariat and labour aristocracy (see Filer, this volume)—must be added to the intersectional equation, particularly when land and other forms of wealth are ending up in the hands of only some people.

References

Aufenanger, H. (1979). The Gende of Central New Guinea: Of the life and thought of a tribe in the Bismarck Ranges, Papua New Guinea (P. W. Holzknecht, Trans.). *Oral History, 7*(8 & 9). Boroko, Papua New Guinea: Institute of Papua New Guinea Studies.

Bainton, N. (2008). Men of kastom and the customs of men: Status, legitimacy and persistent values in Lihir, Papua New Guinea. *The Australian Journal of Anthropology, 19*(2), 194–212.

Bainton, N. & Banks, G. (2018). Land and access: A framework for analysing mining, migration and development in Melanesia. *Sustainable Development, 26*(5), 450–460.

Dickerson-Putman, J. & Zimmer-Tamakoshi, L. (Eds). (1994). Introduction: Women, development and stratification in the Pacific. *Urban Anthropology, 23*(1), 1–11.

Faithorn, E. (1976). Women as persons: Aspects of female life and male-female relations among the Kafe. In P. Brown & G. Buchbinder (Eds), *Man and woman in the New Guinea Highlands* (pp. 86–95). Washington, DC: American Anthropological Association.

Filer, C. (1985). What is this thing called 'brideprice'? *Mankind, 15*(2), 163–183.

---

5   On Facebook, The Boys have been openly critical of Yama's claim that he funded 100 scholarships for Madang Province youth to attend school in the Philippines. They and other suspicious Gende demand to know the names, districts and sex of those '100' students.

Goodale, J. C. (1971). *Tiwi wives: A study of the women of Melville Island*. Seattle, WA: University of Washington Press.

Goodale, J. C. (1983). Siblings as spouses: The reproduction and replacement of Kaulong Society. In M. Marshall (Ed.), *Siblingship in Oceania: Studies of the meaning of kin relations* (pp. 275–305). Lanham, MD: University Press of America.

Hughes, I. (1977). *New Guinea stone age trade: The geography and ecology of traffic in the interior* (Terra Australis Vol. 3). Canberra, ACT: Research School of Pacific Studies, The Australian National University.

Kituai, A. (n.d.). 'From over the Blue Mountain range came the white men': Impact of the Divine Word missionaries in Gende (Bundi) 1932–1965. (Unpublished manuscript in author's possession.)

Macintyre, M. (1998). The persistence of inequality: Women in Papua New Guinea since independence. In L. Zimmer-Tamakoshi (Ed.), *Modern Papua New Guinea* (pp. 211–230). Kirksville, MO: Thomas Jefferson University Press.

Martin, K. (2013). *The death of the big men and the rise of the big shots: Custom and conflict in East New Britain*. New York, NY: Berghahn.

Morauta, L. (1979, September). *Rural-urban exchanges and the analysis of Papua New Guinea's towns*. Paper presented at the Sociological Association of Aotearoa (New Zealand) Conference, Canberra, ACT.

Morauta, L. (1981a). Mobility patterns in Papua New Guinea: Social factors as explanatory variables. In G.W. Jones & H. V. Richter (Eds), *Population mobility and development: Southeast Asia and the Pacific* (pp. 205–228). Canberra, ACT: The Australian National University.

Morauta, L. (1981b, September). *Redistribution within the village: Can we rely on it?* Paper presented at the Fourteenth Waigani Seminar, University of Papua New Guinea, Port Moresby.

Morauta, L. & Ryan, D. (1982). From temporary to permanent townsmen: Migrants from the Malalaua district, Papua New Guinea. *Oceania, 53*(1), 39–55.

Pickles, A. J. (2019). *Money games: Gambling in a Papua New Guinea town*. New York, NY: Berghahn.

Rosi, P. & Zimmer-Tamakoshi, L. (1993). Love and marriage among the educated elite in Port Moresby. In R. Marksbury (Ed.), *The business of marriage: Transformations in Oceanic matrimony* (pp. 175–204). Pittsburgh, PA: University of Pittsburgh Press.

Ryan, D. (1968). The Migrants. *New Guinea, 2*(4), 60–66.

Sexton, L. (1982). Wok meri: A woman's saving and exchange system in highland New Guinea, *Oceania, 52*(3), 167–198.

Sexton, L. (1986). *Mothers of money, daughters of coffee: The wok meri movement.* Ann Arbor, MI: University of Michigan Press.

Warry, W. (1986). Kafaina: Female wealth and power in Chimbu, Papua New Guinea. *Oceania, 57*(1), 4–21.

Weiner, A. B. (1976). *Women of value, men of renown: New perspectives in Trobriand exchange.* Austin, TX: University of Texas Press.

Z'graggen, J. A. (1975). *Languages of the Madang District, Papua New Guinea.* Canberra, ACT: Australian National University Press.

Zimmer, L. J. (1984, November). *Pigs, money, migrants or men? Identity crisis in the Highlands of PNG.* Paper presented at the 83rd Annual American Anthropological Association, Denver.

Zimmer, L. J. (1985). The losing game: Exchange, migration and inequality among the Gende people of Papua New Guinea (Unpublished doctoral thesis). Bryn Mawr College, Pennsylvania.

Zimmer, L. J. (1986). Card-playing among the Gende: A system for keeping money and social relationships 'alive'. *Oceania, 56*(4), 245–63.

Zimmer, L. J. (1987). Playing at being men. *Oceania, 58*(1), 22–37.

Zimmer, L. J. (1990a). Conflict and violence in Gende society: Older persons as victims, trouble-makers and perpetrators. *Pacific Studies, 13*(3), 205–224.

Zimmer, L. J. (1990b). When tomorrow comes: Future opportunities and current investment patterns in an area of high outmigration. In J. Connell (Ed.), *Migration and development in the South Pacific* (pp. 82–96). Canberra, ACT: Australian National University Press.

Zimmer-Tamakoshi, L. (1993a). Bachelors, spinsters and 'pamuk meris'. In R. Marksbury (Ed.), *The business of marriage: Transformations in Oceanic matrimony* (pp. 83–104). Pittsburgh, PA: University of Pittsburgh Press.

Zimmer-Tamakoshi, L. (1993b). Nationalism and sexuality in Papua New Guinea. *Pacific Studies, 16*(4), 20–48.

Zimmer-Tamakoshi, L. (1996a). Role models for contemporary Gende women. In H. Levine & A. Ploeg (Eds), *Work in progress: Essays in New Guinea Highlands ethnography in honour of Paula Brown Glick* (pp. 317–341). Germany: Peter Lang.

Zimmer-Tamakoshi, L. (1996b). The women at Kobum Spice Company: Tensions in a local age stratification system and the undermining of local development. *Pacific Studies, 19*(4), 71–98.

Zimmer-Tamakoshi, L. (1997a). Empowered women. In W. Donner & J. Flanagan (Eds), *Social organization and cultural Aesthetics: Essays in honor of William H. Davenport* (pp. 45–60). Philadelphia, PA: University of Pennsylvania Press.

Zimmer-Tamakoshi, L. (1997b). The last big man: Development and men's discontents in the Papua New Guinea Highlands. *Oceania, 68*(2), 107–122.

Zimmer-Tamakoshi, L. (1997c). When land has a price: Ancestral gerrymandering and the resolution of land conflicts at Kurumbukare. *Anthropological Forum, 7*(4), 649–666.

Zimmer-Tamakoshi, L. (1998). Women in town: Housewives, homemakers and household managers. In L. Zimmer-Tamakoshi (Ed.), *Modern Papua New Guinea* (pp. 195–210). Kirksville, MO: Thomas Jefferson University Press.

Zimmer-Tamakoshi, L. (2001). Development and ancestral gerrymandering: David Schneider in Papua New Guinea. In R. Feinberg & M. Ottenheimer (Eds), *The cultural analysis of kinship: The legacy of David Schneider and its implications for anthropological relativism* (pp. 187–203). Urbana, IL: University of Illinois Press.

Zimmer-Tamakoshi, L. (2006, February). *Uncertain futures, uncertain pasts.* Paper presented in working session on Mine Closure in the Pacific: Past Experiences and Anticipated Futures at the annual meeting of the Association of Social Anthropology in Oceania, San Diego.

Zimmer-Tamakoshi, L. (2007). Gende land management practices and conflicts over land: A patrilineal case. In R. J. May (Ed.), *Land management and conflict minimisation projects: Review of the historical context of current land management and conflict management situations in the Pacific* (pp. 59–68). Fiji: Pacific Islands Forum Secretariat.

Zimmer-Tamakoshi, L. (2008). It's not about women only. In L. Zimmer-Tamakoshi & J. Dickerson-Putman (Eds), *Pulling the right threads: The ethnographic life and legacy of Jane C. Goodale* (pp. 56–76). Urbana, IL: University of Illinois Press.

Zimmer-Tamakoshi, L. (2012). Troubled masculinities and gender violence in Melanesia. In M. Jolly, C. Stewart & C. Brewer (Eds), *Engendering violence in Papua New Guinea* (pp. 57–81). Canberra, ACT: ANU E Press, doi.org/ 10.22459/EVPNG.07.2012.02

Zimmer-Tamakoshi, L. (2014a). Natural or unnatural partners? Inequality and the Gende's relations with mining companies. In P. D'Arcy, P. Matbob & L. Crowl (Eds), *Pacific-Asia partnerships in resource development* (pp. 86–101). Madang, Papua New Guinea: Divine Word University Press.

Zimmer-Tamakoshi, L. (2014b). 'Our good work', or 'the Devil's work'? Inequality, exchange and card playing among the Gende. *Oceania, 84*(3), 222–238.

Zimmer-Tamakoshi, L. (2016). Inequality and changing masculinities among the Gende in Papua New Guinea: The 'good', the 'bad', and the 'very bad'. *The Asia Pacific Journal of Anthropology, 17*(3–4), 250–267.

Zimmer-Tamakoshi, L. (2018). Fieldwork interrupted: The politics of fieldwork in Papua New Guinea. In L. Zimmer-Tamakoshi (Ed.), *First fieldwork: Pacific Anthropology, 1960–1985*. Honolulu, HI: University of Hawai'i Press.

Zimmer-Tamakoshi, L. & Dickerson-Putman, J. (Eds). (2008). *Pulling the right threads: The ethnographic life and legacy of Jane C. Goodale*. Urbana, IL: University of Illinois Press.

12

From Donation to Handout: Resource Wealth and Transformations of Leadership in Huli Politics

Michael Main

In the decade since ExxonMobil's vast Papua New Guinea Liquefied Natural Gas (PNG LNG) project began construction work in what is now Hela Province in the Papua New Guinea (PNG) highlands, the Huli owners of the gas resource (referred to in this chapter as 'landowners') stand as a prime example of a population cursed by the unequal distribution of extracted resource wealth. In the case of PNG LNG, these inequalities are global in scale and include the enrichment of offshore investors in addition to a corrupt political elite that retains power in PNG, no matter how starkly their fraudulent means to power are exposed (see Haley & Zubrinich, 2018). Frustration over the lack of promised development benefits from the project, including the non-payment of landowner royalties, has fuelled a history of conflict and unresolved grievance within the population—who are the customary landowners of the resource area—that has resulted in the most resource-rich province in PNG also experiencing the most extreme levels of violence.

In the wake of the development failure that is the PNG LNG project, traditional forms of leadership that ushered the project into existence are also seen to have failed, as Huli society experiences increasing levels of frustration and social disorder. Traditional methods of obtaining political power have given way to a more pragmatic leadership style that no longer relies on mythological and cosmological understandings of development and wealth. The failure of Huli elites to deliver on the development promises of the PNG LNG project has resulted in a transformation of leadership forms and the emergence of the honorific title 'paramount chief' in a system that has no tradition of chiefly leadership roles.

The PNG LNG project's reneging on its development promises at the local level is, at least in part, a reflection of its deficiencies in delivering on its much-lauded macro-economic benefits to the PNG state. Constructed at the cost of USD 19 billion, the PNG LNG project is the largest resource extraction project in the history of the Pacific region. At the time of writing, the project is producing 8.8 million tonnes per annum (MTPA), which is well above its nameplate production rate of 6.9 MTPA.[1] In its first four years of operation, the project is estimated to have generated USD 18.8 billion for ExxonMobil alone, which owns a 33.2 per cent stake in the project (Barrett & Gloystein, 2018). In November 2018, the PNG treasury halved its forecast for expected revenue from the project to USD 11 billion over 26 years to 2040. However, according to a recent World Bank report, the PNG LNG project:

> is authorised to hold its foreign currency earnings in offshore accounts without first having to pass it through PNG's domestic spot market. Together with generous tax concessions, this means that without a large rebound in LNG [liquefied natural gas] prices, the project is unlikely to be a major source of foreign currency inflows for at least the first 10 years of production. (World Bank, 2019, p. 19)

The macro-scale inequalities of the PNG LNG project have fed into inequalities experienced at the local level. Huli landowners of the gas resource are enraged that the project has delivered very little of the infrastructure that they were promised. Before project construction began in 2010, landowners and the state signed Landowner Benefit Sharing Agreements that promised roads, power supply, schools and hospitals. These agreements were not signed by ExxonMobil. Therefore, it is to the state that Huli landowners look in their expectation of benefits and infrastructure projects. Huli attitudes towards ExxonMobil are best described as ambivalent. The ideal model of the state collecting

---

1   'Nameplate' is the industry term used to denote a nominal rate of expected production.

resource revenues and using those to provide services is broadly embraced by landowners. However, in the face of state failure to deliver on its expectations, many landowners expect the company to take up the slack. Oil Search, via the Oil Search Foundation,[2] has been operating in PNG long enough to have learned this lesson and has made large investments in the Hela provincial health system. ExxonMobil makes largely symbolic gestures; however, as a matter of corporate policy, it does not engage in state-like development programs. ExxonMobil is criticised for this, sometimes publicly, as detailed later in this chapter. However, it remains the case that the advent of the PNG LNG project has resulted in heightened expectations of the state, which have given rise to a profound reinterpretation of traditional Huli hierarchies and understandings of leadership because Huli recognise that access to resource benefits can only be gained via the hierarchical structures that connect Huli landowners to state power. Hierarchies are necessarily unequal, requiring certain individuals to be endowed with more social efficacy than is held by other individuals in the general population.

In this chapter, I argue that Huli desire an effective hierarchy that supports individuals who have access to state power and are capable of accumulating wealth via access to power. The ideal Huli leader has become a wealthy and powerful individual who can facilitate the development of Hela Province for the benefit of the people. This chapter examines ways in which traditional forms of Huli leadership have been eclipsed by expectations of resource wealth and development, culminating in the construction of the PNG LNG project. In recent years, these Huli leaders have proven to be adept at accumulating wealth for themselves, but have not applied their wealth and power towards improving the lives of the people of Hela.

The Huli Paramount Chief

In her analysis of leadership in the Southern Massim region, Martha Macintyre critiqued a myth, frequently expressed in anthropological writings on Melanesia, that traditional leadership was both ahistorical and based on some egalitarian ideal (1994). Writing of Massim communities,

---

2   The Oil Search Foundation is the development arm of Oil Search Limited (OSL). Founded in 1929 and incorporated in PNG, OSL is the largest oil and gas company in PNG; it operates all PNG's oil fields, in addition to having substantial interest in all its gas fields.

Macintyre argued that there was great flexibility in the nature of power and that leadership could be both hereditary and newly forged. Exposing the myth of 'first among equals' as an 'oxymoron' (p. 259), Macintyre uncovered a logic of underlying inequality in Massim societies. This analysis finds parallels in patterns of leadership among Huli, especially in the current era of LNG extraction. In particular, the relatively recent adoption of the terms 'chief' and, more recently, 'paramount chief' among Huli to express admiration for various leaders must be understood in the context of shifting power relations and the exploitation of natural gas reserves since the 1990s. Huli have been surprisingly late to adopt these titles, which have been in widespread use across PNG for many decades and have done so in the absence of any equivalent Huli term or understanding. Macintyre wrote that use of the term 'paramount chief' in PNG can be traced to Malinowski, via his supervisor Charles Seligman, who accepted the term that was invented in 1896 by the Lieutenant-Governor of British New Guinea, Sir William Macgregor. Whereas 'the Trobriands as the site of an endogenous hereditary hierarchy' was an invention of Malinowski (Macintyre, 1994, p. 248), the recent Huli adoption of chieftainship is a response to the exploitation of oil and gas reserves within Huli territory. In both cases, new forms of leadership have been adopted as 'an opportunistic response' (p. 251) to new opportunities afforded by access to external sources of wealth and power.

Similar 'inventions of tradition' have been documented for other sites of resource extraction in different parts of PNG. Like Huli, Lihirians 'had no customary institution of hereditary chieftainship'; however, unlike Huli, they decided to invent a 'Council of Chiefs' 'through which to regulate the process of development' that was expected from the Lihir gold mine (Filer, 1997, p. 177). Huli apply the title to individuals who might be able to facilitate the process of development from the PNG LNG project. Macintyre's radical proposal is that the invention of tradition is not a feature of modernity, but rather a fundamental component of tradition itself. In her analysis of the adoption of the title 'paramount chief' sometime in the 1920s by a prominent man on the island of Murua, Macintyre (1994) argued that this transformation of Muruan social relationships should be read in terms of the capacity for a particular Maruan individual to 'adapt, transform and transcend' these relationships and cultural norms. Macintyre was revisiting the work of Fred Damon (1983), who argued that the title had been adopted 'even though there is no such position in the culture' (p. 45). For Macintyre, such a statement 'is to reify, conceptually and temporally, an array of set characteristics that are not susceptible to change' (1994, p. 250). In other words, it was not a case of culture being abandoned, but rather culture as a historicised and transformative process that responds, often via the specifics of individual agency, to new opportunities and new realities. In the case of the Muruan leader, it was an opportunistic response to colonial understandings of land ownership so that he could obtain ownership of a resource that had previously been held communally. The new Huli 'chiefdom', and particularly the more recent 'paramount chiefdom', is explicitly related to the desire to access resource wealth.

The first Huli ethnography, undertaken by Robert Glasse during the 1950s, states that 'Huli have no chiefs or hereditary offices vested with political authority' (1968, p. 21). Subsequent ethnographies of Huli (barring my own contribution) make no mention of chiefs; however, newspaper articles and social media posts since the PNG LNG project began construction make frequent reference to the Huli 'paramount chief' in describing certain individuals who hold great leadership status. Prior to the addition of the adjective 'paramount', the use of the term 'chief' in Huli has been traced directly to the actions of British Petroleum (BP) in 1989 when drilling an exploratory well at Angore in what is now Hela Province. In his Corporate History of Hides, the former Community Affairs Adviser for Oil Search wrote:

> It is worthwhile explaining how the title 'chief' has come to be used among the Huli, since the practice is linked to the drilling of the Angore-1A well. Traditionally, Huli does not have a hierarchical society—there are no chiefs.

> In 1989, when the Angore well was being drilled, BP employed a number of the local leaders, basically on sinecures, to advise BP which people should be taken on as labour – according to their clan ties. The senior person amongst these was Minule Arawi, as the senior landowner. A BP drilling supervisor at the time was Ernie Hardman. He gave Minule a hard hat with the word 'chief' stencilled on it. From that time the practice has grown among the Huli and now every clan leader in the general Hides/Karius area is styled a 'chief'. (Clapp, 2002, p. 44)

Although Clapp is correct in stating that, traditionally, there were no Huli chiefs, Huli society was, and remains, hierarchical. It is this hierarchy that was transformed in the adoption of chiefly titles.

The earliest reference I have found to 'paramount chief' for Huli is in a February 2007 article in the *Papua New Guinea Post-Courier*: 'paramount chiefs from the Hiwa Komo clan in the Hides gas project area are in Port Moresby to see the Ombudsman Commission to push for a possible referral of the deal to the watchdog' (Papua New Guinea Post-Courier, 2007). The article refers to a proposed deal between PNG Power Limited and Hides Joint Venture Limited to supply gas-generated electricity to the Ramu Nickel mine site. Hiwa is a major clan group that has been involved in disputes over land related to the extraction of gas at Hides since 1990 (Clapp, 2002, p. 217). The phrase 'paramount chief' does not appear in any of the numerous 'social mapping reports'[3] that were produced by anthropologists as part of the suite of baseline studies undertaken prior to the beginning of the PNG LNG project. A 2005 letter from the Hiwa Tuguba Hides Association to the Minister for Petroleum and Energy, highlighting landowner issues at Hides that they wanted the minister to resolve, refers to Wandiago Gihamua as 'Chief of Hiwa tribe'. It is possible that the term 'paramount chief' was introduced to Huli via an act of journalistic flair. Whatever the case, there are important differences in the deployment of this term between its Huli use and its much earlier use on the island of Murua.

Although I encountered the term many times during my fieldwork in Hela, it was always in the context of a leader being described by someone else. I never heard anyone describe themselves in that way, although I did meet some people who had the title bestowed upon them. In Huli, 'paramount chief' is more often an expression of admiration for a particular individual and of the desire for such a hierarchical structure to exist. It is also performative—a particularly salient example of this was the moment in 2015 when the (former) PNG prime minister Peter O'Neill visited Tari, the capital of Hela Province, and was accorded the status of 'a paramount chief when he was presented the unique Huli wig and headdress that is only worn by Hela chiefs' (Elapa, 2015). O'Neill had arrived in Tari to announce the commitment of PGK 600 million 'for infrastructure developments' for the province—money that was supposedly coming from the PNG LNG project, but that would never materialise. There is certainly no such wig that is used to identify Hela chiefs, except that on this particular day there was—the point of the exercise was to reinforce

---

3 'Social mapping and landowner identification studies' are a requirement of the PNG Oil and Gas Act. These studies are to identify and describe landowning groups, including their social organisation and cultural methods of land ownership.

a link to wealth and political power that could be harnessed for the benefit of the province. Huli paramount chiefs are usually the heads of major clan groups and, when things become really serious, several can gather together—the veritable full bench of paramount chiefs—to make their case to the national government in Port Moresby. The term is deployed loosely, in a way that reflects the nebulous nature of Huli leadership, which I describe below. To understand these transformations of Huli culture and social relationships, it is necessary to revisit early Huli ethnography that has itself become a historical artefact.

Transformations of Huli Leadership

In 1959, the American anthropologist Robert Glasse published the first two ethnographic works on Huli, in the form of two journal articles: 'The Huli descent system: A preliminary account' and 'Revenge and redress among the Huli: A preliminary account' (Glasse, 1959a, 1959b). In these papers, Glasse described two parallel hierarchies that exist in Huli society. In 'The Huli descent system', Glasse pointed out that it is only certain 'experts' who possess extensive genealogical knowledge; these people are called upon to facilitate in dispute resolution and to officiate in ritual ceremonies. These experts are holders of an inherited form of knowledge that is passed agnatically though particular family lines.

In 'Revenge and redress', Glasse described the existence of great disparities in wealth and social status between people, which are based on differences of individual ability and volition. Different people will own different numbers of pigs, have more or fewer wives and maintain residence rights over greater or lesser portions of land. Glasse even divided male Huli into three categories of person: those with low, average and high social status. Glasse avoided stating that these three categories find certain analogy with class distinctions observed in Western societies. However, the comparisons are obvious: one major difference being that Huli status distinctions were based on individual ability and desire, rather than the structural conditions of society. This was certainly the case during my fieldwork in 2016, when I found that status differences are, to an extent, understood in moral terms and resonate with the neoliberal economic ideal of individual responsibility. Therefore, there is an element in the persistence of Huli inequality that is seen to mirror immoral behaviour.

There is an ethos of individualism in Huli that cannot be overstated. Unlike other highlands groups, Huli cultural praxis is oriented towards the service of the individual rather than the collective. Huli prioritise and respect individual ambition and choice. Conflict always occurs between individuals rather than clans and group alliances form around individuals, based on a combination of kinship, clan affiliation, residence and friendship. Different people display different levels of individual ambition and ability and the stratification of Huli society into different levels of social efficacy, and material wealth has encountered the era of resource extraction and the opportunities for great wealth and prosperity with no small degree of familiarity.

Thus, there are two parallel leadership systems that exist for Huli: one that is based on inheritance and the other on effort. Both systems exclude women—the first on the basis that genealogical knowledge is agnatic and the second on the basis that land ownership is agnatic. Holly Wardlow (2006, p. 69) described the exclusion of Huli women from taking positions of power in terms of a 'collective agency' that is less available to women. Genealogical knowledge and land ownership are intimately related. The type of leadership bestowed upon certain people whom Glasse described as 'experts' is inherited and based on the knowledge that is passed from father to son within particular genealogical units. This form of leadership is also stratified and includes clan leaders in addition to regional leaders. Every clan has a family line that holds detailed genealogical and historical information about the clan.

The men who hold this information are known in Huli as *agali haguene*, or 'head man'.[4] *Agali haguene* are relied upon for their trusted knowledge in the complex system of land ownership and to assist in the resolution of disputes over claims to land. The average man, as accurately described by Glasse, has extensive knowledge of his own genealogical history, but not the vast trove of historical knowledge possessed by the *agali haguene*. This system should not be thought of as rigid, as claims to land are strongly influenced by competition between individuals and land disputes occur between those who claim to have superior knowledge. To possess knowledge and to use that knowledge in disputes over land are two different things. Further, prior to the influence of resource extraction projects, Huli historical knowledge, called *dindi malu*, or 'land history',

---

4   *Agali* = 'man' and *haguene* = 'head'. Note that this noun is not pluralised. *Agali* means 'men' in the plural context, with the plural form indicated by the context and verb suffix.

was considered to be a shared resource, albeit one that only came to the surface during disputes over land. Land disputes, where *dindi malu* is spoken and contested, are public performances held in open space, referred to in Huli as *hama*. Ultimately, Huli believe that a singular truth binds everyone together; land disputes are contested in the pursuit of that truth.

The Huli word *gimbu* means 'bind' or 'join together'; the establishment of the Hela Gimbu Association in the 1960s constituted an attempt to bring together the definitive set of knowledge required to complete the Hela historical narrative. Huli despaired at the loss of knowledge that was successively occurring for each new generation—they still do this. Loss of Huli *mana*, which 'encapsulates a socio-historical accounting of knowledge' (Goldman, 1983, p. 67), was part of the perceived 'entropic' decline that included the fertility of the land and people. However, it is simultaneously true that those with superior knowledge and rhetorical skill are likely to win the argument in a land dispute and that knowledge is constantly being created in the prosecution of land disputes. Rhetorical skill in the construction of an argument in itself provides evidence for objective truth. Therefore, individuals possess the power to create truth, and Huli social structure is in a constant state of 'becoming' (Goldman, 1993, p. 23). Thus, individual desire for accumulation of wealth and social status goes hand in hand with the desire to accumulate knowledge and create new truth.

At the regional scale, holders of inherited knowledge are known as *dindi pongoneyi*, or 'land root man'.[5] These days, *dindi pongoneyi* are sometimes referred to in English by Huli as 'high priests'. 'High priest' is not an unreasonable analogy, as the *dindi pongoneyi* possessed very restricted knowledge about ritual practices and had access to the most sacred sites in Huli territory. There are only a handful of family lines that hold *dindi pongoneyi* status; these are widely known among Huli today. In Glasse's time, the role of the *dindi pongoneyi* was, quite literally, to prevent the world from ending and ensure the maintenance of the health and fertility of both land and people. Currently, they are called upon to facilitate in claims over clan rights to benefits from the PNG LNG project.

---

5   *Pongone* = 'root' and the suffix '-*yi*' = 'man'. Note that this noun is not pluralised. The plural form is indicated by the context and verb suffix.

I came to know one *dindi pongoneyi* named Allan Ango; the extent of his influence was extraordinary. Ango was born in Koroba and gave much of his land to the Koroba Catholic mission after it established itself during the 1950s. Allan Ango was among the last generation of Huli to have lived his school-age years prior to the establishment of an Australian administration presence and the arrival of mission schools. Ango was fluent in the languages of neighbouring groups but spoke no English. However, Ango, like many other Huli, instantly recognised the importance and value of the white man's education and the access it granted to the wider world of material wealth and wellbeing that was rapidly being introduced into the PNG highlands. Huli ritual leaders such as Ango wasted no time in their reinterpretation of Huli mythology and cosmology, to the effect that the coming of Western modernity had been clearly prophesised by the ancestors. In this way, Western modernity, including its education and health systems, were pre-encompassed by Huli and already formed part of a prophesised Huli destiny. In embracing Western education, Huli were embracing something that (from their perspective) already belonged to them, and that was already part of what it meant to be Huli.

Ango seemed to be constantly on the move, travelling slowly with his walking stick but never stopping and forever in the process of checking in with his extended network. This network stretches all the way from Koroba to the Papuan Plateau. After spending time with Ango in Koroba, I travelled with him by car all the way to Komo, a journey of several hours. Ango had to sit in the back of the car hidden from view; if people knew that he was there, we would have been constantly stopped by anyone wanting a piece of his knowledge—this was an issue for us along the entire journey. At Komo, I went to church with Ango, who was surrounded by people asking for all kinds of advice and knowledge. A local schoolteacher even said to me, 'I want to know about the names for birds. In school, we are only taught one word, *ega*, but *ega* just means "bird". Huli have words for all the different types of birds.' During Ango's stay with us in Komo, we were visited by the president of Bosavi district, Efela Babe. Bosavi district straddles the southern part of Hela Province, from the southern side of Mt Sisa to the Papuan Plateau. Ango met and conversed with Babe in fluent Etolo. Babe had earlier consulted with Ango over Etolo genealogical connections with Hela, the apical ancestor who, in the Huli narrative, united all the clans of Hela Province and many beyond. Babe had sought this information during his campaign for election as Bosavi president. Babe had witnessed the success of the revered Southern

Highlands Governor and later Hela Governor, Andisen Agiru, after he had turned to Ango for knowledge that he used for his political campaign. In turning to Ango for information, both Agiru and Babe were emulating the 'expert' leadership style described by Glasse.

Agiru came to power in 1997, more than 10 years before the PNG LNG agreements were signed. He had been instrumental in negotiations over the PNG LNG project and was a very popular leader. Agiru, I was told, was descended from a *dindi pongoneyi* with the ancestral name of Pawa. I am unable to verify Agiru's genealogical origins; however, the critical point is that Agiru constructed his own identity in these terms and was revered as such by his supporters. One person explained to me his view of Agiru and his role in the PNG LNG project as follows:

> He brought negotiations, agreement with that he came. It's like Moses in the Bible who led Israel from Egypt to the Canaan land on the mountain he died. So, after negotiations and then the gas flow the people to get payment he died.

The *dindi pongoneyi* families had been quick to adopt Christianity, through which they readily reinterpreted their own traditions. The adoption of Christianity by Huli reflected a self-positioning of Huli as always being at the centre of the universe, both economically and cosmologically. Therefore, Christianity was not interpreted as something foreign, but rather as something that had been prefigured in Huli tradition and to which Huli were ancestrally entitled. Agiru embraced an evangelical form of Christianity; he was convinced that Huli were descended from the Israelites and even made trips to Israel, where he was said to have purchased land (Cox, 2015). The analogy of Moses leading the Israelites is a typical example of Huli use of Christianity to place Huli at the centre of matters of importance. This also reflects a Huli desire to support the elevation of their leaders to positions of great authority. In the transcript of Agiru's speech at Kokopo provided below, Agiru describes the PNG LNG gas as 'spiritual gas to fulfil the great commission *blong* [of] world evangelism'.

Agiru was from a distinguished Huli family line and had received a good education that resulted in him attending university in Port Moresby. When Agiru decided that he wanted to run for political office, he realised that, to win Huli votes, he needed to be able to speak to the people in terms of their own shared Huli identity. To relate to the majority of Huli living in bush-material houses, raising pigs and tending sweet potato gardens, Agiru referred to their shared Huli *dindi malu*. That is, by invoking the names of clans and ancestors and associated landscape features, their praise terms and patronyms, he was able to tap in to deeply held sentimental feelings that Huli possess concerning their homeland. By displaying such a wealth of knowledge spread across the vast expanse of Huli territory, he could demonstrate a superior intellect that was governed by benevolent intentions.

Agiru returned to his Huli homeland and set about learning all he could about Huli *dindi malu*. As a descendant of a *dindi pongoneyi*, Agiru was able to call upon the services of Allan Ango and other Huli elders. Agiru's political genius was explained to me by Michael Ango, the son of Allan Ango. Michael had witnessed Agiru's transition into a politician when Agiru came to live with Allan Ango to learn from him. Michael explained that:

> He praised the mountains, he praised the rivers, he praised the clans and then 'you are the son of this man, you are the son of this man, you are my relative, you are my people, you are my daughter, your village is here, your house is here, your river is this one.' And 'how did this man know my mountain? How did this man know my clan? How did this man know my family?' Okay then we go to put this man first. So the people realised that 'Oh Agiru called my name, I have never known Agiru before. He called my father, he called my name, he called my river, he called my village, he called my garden, he called my mountain'. Everybody started thinking of Agiru. 'We want Agiru, we want Agiru'. From kids to old men. Because other candidates they never call our village, our place, our home, our family tribes, family names, our clan. So this man called our clan names, our mountain, our village, our place, our fathers.

It is difficult to convey via translation just how deeply sentimental the Huli language is. Sentimental expression is conveyed via 'the mechanics of synonym substitutions and metamorphoses of sound shape' (Goldman, 1998, p. 66). The calling of genealogical names and associated landforms includes the deployment of a vast trove of praise names; metaphoric replacement terms charge the language with extraordinary pathos. To 'be a competent communication' in Huli 'demands an understanding of the structural and discoursal salience of renamings' (Goldman, 1998, p. 66).

Anderson Agiru had an extraordinary gift for Huli political rhetoric and, in the social and political context of his day, political power in Huli was accessible via the deployment of such rhetorical gifts. Agiru was also a confirmed bachelor—this aspect of his life had deep connections to traditional Huli beliefs about moral purity. Huli traditionally maintained a belief in the polluting power of women and, particularly, the extraordinary danger posed by menstrual blood. Huli men and women lived separate lives and men maintained their own gardens and avoided eating food that was grown and harvested by women. The Huli bachelor cult, known as *haroli*, involved young men living for two to three years together in the bush, learning complex rituals and spells, particularly relating to how to avoid becoming contaminated by female contact. When organising hunting trips into the high forest, Huli men would prepare by avoiding sex for several months to purify themselves. The multitude of moral codes of behaviour are known in Huli as *ilili* (forbidden acts); many of these relate to purity and the avoidance of female contact. Agiru maintained a reputation for moral purity and stood as an example of a *Huli ore*, or 'pure Huli', partly via his status as a bachelor.

Death of a Great Language

During the Umbrella Benefits Sharing Agreement meeting for the PNG LNG project held at Kokopo in April 2009, Andisen Agiru gave a speech to the attendees in Huli. Agiru's speech was reportedly much lauded and laden with Huli mythology and traditional knowledge that he skilfully linked to the project and the expected future for the Huli people. Agiru's speech in Huli was not recorded; however, a recording does exist of the speech that he gave in English on day three of the forum, which begins: 'the greatest river unbreached is the river of time'. This does not correspond to any known Huli speech form or saying, and it is likely that nobody exactly knew what he was talking about. However, it is both evocative and typical of Agiru's style of harnessing devotion through the deployment of pathos and rhetorical skill. Agiru then went on to credit himself for the return to power of the then prime minister Michael Somare. According to Agiru, in 2001, he made a prophecy that Somare would return to power and that the speaking of his prophetic words put into action events that resulted in the return of Somare to the prime ministership:

Let us pause for a while [no pause]. The date 2nd August 2001, at a village called [indecipherable] the speaker for the National Parliament then, Dr Narakobi, Mr Alfred Kiabe, member for Komo-Margarima, Bart Philemon, then was in government now the member for Lae, the then-member for Wapenamanda, Masket Langalio, myself and my brother Somare. We stood there and on that day doing ground breaking ceremony to connect the peoples of [indecipherable]. We did that ground breaking ceremony on that day and I spoke and prophesised that Grand Chief will form government again in 2002. That was on the 2nd August 2002 [Agiru means to say 2001]. Two weeks later, he was sacked as foreign affairs minister, Minister for Foreign Affairs. If I had not made that statement, he would not have been sacked. I made that statement and, as a result, the ball started rolling for the emergence of the government we have today, our government. It is thanks to the government of Sir Michael that there is going to be a PNG LNG project.

Agiru simultaneously credits himself for the existence of both the Somare government and the PNG LNG project.

This belief in the material agency of the spoken word is very much part of a Huli ontology of speech. For Huli, 'saying words is a production of material effects' (Goldman, 1983, p. 36). With the power of speech at his disposal, Agiru then went on to make various promises, many of which had little or nothing to do with any of the signed agreements:

A child at school in the Hela world today will have the know-how. I will lend him my torch to search. He may then come and make an offer to buy out ExxonMobil! [applause]. My today's limitations will be something of the past then … I need to build and seal a highway from the Gulf at Kikori, through Kutubu to Tari [cheers]. I need to build and seal a highway from Kiam to Kisina Pori at Ialibu. I need to upgrade and seal Mendi to Lake Kopiago highway … I need to upgrade and seal the road from Margarima to Kandep into Wabag. Seal the road from Hides to Fugua. [Several roads later] Telefomin to East and West Sepik. Build a new road from Juha down to the Fly. And of course, why not? I'll build a freeway from Tari International Airport to the Hides gas plant into Komo … The airport at Kikori has been talked about, it's part of decision 24 of 98. I need to build a wharf, international wharf through private public partnership at Kikori [applause]. Why build a road if there is no wharf? Cities around the world are built around airport. Why have an international airport up in Tari? I need to build Hela City [applause]. And that is one of the most critical projects because royalty, na equity, na em blo' papa graun tasol, and the provincial government, local level. Minister blo' trade and industry, or commerce and industry, I want Tari declared a tax-free zone [applause]. I want to expand Mendi township and the township of Ialibu. [Several townships and several hospitals later] Education is dear to my heart. For my people there must be a university in the Southern Highlands, especially the Hela area. That university must be built in the Komo-Margarima electorate. Hela Technical College, those who fail to go to university must go there to upgrade their learning. That technical college must be built in the Tari-Pori electorate. The Hela International School of Culture, Language and the Arts. The culture and arts of Melanesia is fast diminishing. We need to go back and start teaching art and craft and culture back at school so that we do not lose our identity. And that institution must be built in the Koroba-Lake Kopiago electorate … Future generations fund. Applying the Alaskan and Norwegian models we propose to invest part of our benefits accruing from the oil and gas business, the Southern Highlands Provincial Government and Hela Provincial Government will invest fund blo' future. Whatever money is given to our province we will give priority to investment in women and youth development. We will because it is our spiritual gas to fulfil the great commission blong world evangelism. Provincial government blong tupla province by setting money aside lo displa fund. We will insist that landowners do the same.

In his chapter for this volume, John Cox writes of the differentiation between what are seen as the 'legitimate aspirations' of the 'rural grassroots' versus those of the 'urban middle class'. When Agiru declared that he wanted to build a Hela City, he was legitimising the aspirations of those living a more traditional lifestyle—the subsistence farmers living in bush-material houses who were looking for a leader to deliver them into modernity. The populist largesse of Agiru's rhetoric makes sense in the context of a Huli understanding that material reality is brought into being via the act of speech. Agiru's words had brought Somare back to power, and his words would likewise bring to fruition his vision for the future of Hela. Agiru was reaching deep into traditional Huli understandings of the power of the act of speech. He had been emboldened by his success, thus far, in returning Somare to power and bringing the PNG LNG project into material reality. At Kokopo in April 2009, Agiru gave it everything he had.

The day that Agiru died, I was in Tari; all around me, the people of Hela had gone into a deep mourning. The most immediate and obvious impact of his death was a cessation of the fighting that had ravaged Tari for months. The conflict had arisen from a complex dispute related to compensation payments for Tari airport land after it was expanded to accept heavier aircraft that were needed during the construction of the PNG LNG project. Out of respect for Agiru, all fighting was suspended and even the two rival candidates for his replacement, Francis Potobe and Philip Undialu, restrained themselves from politicising the situation. However, by that time, some had begun to complain openly about Agiru's failure to deliver on his promises. Many people even spoke to me about Agiru's ill health and death being the direct result of him giving away their gas for nothing. This particular observation relates to a Huli prophecy associated with the mountain that hosts the gas resource. According to the prophecy, underneath Hides ridge (known in Huli as Gigira) is an eternal fire—a giant, smouldering piece of wood. One day a man with red legs will come and ask for the fire. The landowners of Gigira may share some of the fire with him, but they are not to give all the fire away, lest the world come to an end. The failure of the PNG LNG project to deliver on its promises is widely viewed in terms of the fulfilment of this prophecy.

In many ways, Agiru was the last of a kind; however, PNG LNG had transformed him into something unique. The absence of benefits from PNG LNG had exposed Agiru's beautiful rhetoric as something hollow and powerless; it seems unlikely that a leader such as Agiru will ever emerge again.

It's About the Money, Stupid

Agiru left behind a political environment that was vastly different from the one that had existed when he first came to power. The rivalry between his would-be successors Potobe and Undialu centred around the issue of development and who was best placed to address frustrations over the failure of the PNG LNG project to live up to its promises, not to mention the failure of Agiru's vision. When these two politicians spoke to the people, they did so in the language of development rather than culture or tradition. On 5 October 2016, a public ceremony marked the handover of Tari hospital administration to the Oil Search Foundation and the appointment of the Oil Search Managing Director, Peter Botten, as chair of the Tari Hospital Board. At the time, the governorship had been assumed by Francis Potobe; however, he was later successfully challenged by Undialu.

During the ceremony, Francis Potobe gave a speech in English that perfectly captured these feelings of frustration and spoke directly to the needs and desires of the Huli population. Potobe's speech was delivered to a large Huli crowd in Tari; however, it contained almost no reference to Huli culture or tradition, apart from a negative allusion to the Huli practice of fence building:

> Now as the new Governor of Hela Province [cheers] … It is not easy to be a public servant in this part of the country. Plenty of public servants want to enjoy a better life. But for Hela public servants whether policemen, nurses, doctors, teachers, life em hard … here. Me together with minister Marape and Peter O'Neil together with man blong here and meri blong here we grew up in the area where Hela leaders are fence builders. Hela leaders are fence builders … Hela go bush, haus sik [hospital] go bush, community school go bush, airport bagarap [broken]. No got telephone, no power line, no nothing because our leaders are fence builders. [cheers] … road project … rate of return is nothing! The Highlands Highway go down, the Tari hospital go down, Tari airport go down, everything go down in the land where we produce oil and gas our leaders are the fence builders. Minister Marape, Member Undialu … must never be fence builders. We are not here to build fence. We are here to make sure haus sik em alright. When we are producing power in Hides. The power producers are leaving it for the government when power bypass us for many years because our leaders are fence builders … Last 20 years, 40 years we are fence builders … You must not be a fence builder, you must be a service provider. Haus sik must change, development must come … I say thank you to Mr Peter Botten and the Oil Search team … it's about time Oil Search put the foot down. I am yet to see ExxonMobil following in the footsteps of Oil Search … Mr Botten when the doctors were pulling out you came on board and prime minister Peter O'Neil and … we were forgotten by the health department for a long time. We were forgotten by education department for a long time. The mothers were delivering babies using the candle light or bamboo light. We were producing LNG and we don't produce leaders … when I quit politics I will look back and say when I was a member of parliament I did these things. When you have leaders who are

fence builders, when you have government who doesn't want to know what is happening in Koroba, Komo, Tari, Margarima, Benaria. School bagarap, haus sik bagarap, airport bagarap … you are going to produce a society that is growing up without education, know nothing and what you expect lawlessness. Lawlessness … Police … police now 100 men for Hela. Koroba will have 40 policemen, Komo will have 40 policemen, Nogoli will have 20 policemen, Margarima will have 20 policemen. Tari will have two to three hundred policemen. Then we know we are almost there … their children need to go to school, their family need to do shopping, they need a reliable airport, they need the reliable power and a company must work. We are launching big things. You look at the Komo airport, a big white elephant sitting in the countryside doing nothing … Hela must be peaceful … we happen to be the last people in this country all the time. Why? because the Highlands Highway stop here, everything stop here. So if that is the name of the game we play the game … lock him up in the police station but there is nowhere else to keep them so they let them out and the next day they committing the crime again. That is the story blong Hela Province …

Potobe's repeated references to fence building constituted a direct appeal for Huli to abandon their traditional approach to politics. A defining feature of Huli culture is the construction of mud walls around clan boundaries. Known as *gana* in Huli, these have the dual purpose of marking territory and providing defensive protection in times of war. On land that is unsuitable for the digging of trenches and the construction of mud walls, Huli construct wooden fences. Therefore, Potobe was calling for structural change in the ways that Huli have traditionally related to each other, to assist in producing the desired level of development. Melissa Demian (this volume) calls our attention to the figure of the anthropologist, who is relocated from a classic setting on the periphery to one that is rapidly being transformed into a metropole. In the context described above, I was witnessing the express desire of Huli to do exactly this—the struggle to transform Hela into a city was the struggle to relocate Hela from the periphery to an important, industrialised urban centre (for comparable aspirations in Lihir, see also Bainton, 2008, p. 293, this volume).

In the months that followed Agiru's death, Michael Ango announced that he intended to run for the Hela governorship during the upcoming elections. Michael had witnessed the way Agiru had prepared himself for politics and reckoned that, as the son of the *dindi pongoneyi* to whom Agiru had turned for knowledge, he was ideally placed to follow in his footsteps. Like Agiru, the younger Ango had received a Western education and obtained a tertiary degree in Port Moresby. Michael's degree was in civil drafting; the qualification took him to employment in Rabaul, where he also married. While Michael's education could not have been more different from that of his father, the elder Ango had encouraged his son's education as a desired form of Huli development and change. During a long hike with Michael, from Komo down to Bopole (the Etolo village of Efale Babe), Michael collected a type of moss from one of the river crossings that Huli use for bathing. Michael showed me this moss and told me that his father had said to him, 'now you use this moss in the river to clean yourself every day so that you are ready for school'. An embodied Huli tradition was being deployed in the preparation of a new and desired Huli future.

In 2009, Michael Ango returned to his Huli homeland from Rabaul, at the beginning of the construction phase of the PNG LNG project. Like many other diaspora Huli, Michael wanted to stake his claim to promised royalty payments from the project and to take advantage of the promised employment and business opportunities that were expected to flourish. Although Michael's knowledge of Huli genealogical clan history was a disrupted and truncated version of his father's expertise, it was nonetheless extensive. The younger Ango believed that he was well placed to assist in the highly complex 'clan vetting' and 'landowner identification' process that had begun prior to 2009 to identify the beneficiaries of the PNG LNG project, and still continues to this day (see Filer, 2019). Michael was recruited by a well-respected Duguba[6] leader named Stanis Talu to assist with clan identification issues in the Nogoli area that were associated with Petroleum Development License Area 1. Michael was engaged in this (unpaid) work at the time of Agiru's death.

However, Michael was poor; he knew that he could not compete with the well-funded politicians of his day. With some funding, Michael had a vision for his political success and a vision for himself as the second coming of Andisen Agiru:

---

6   Duguba is the Huli name for the southern clans that exist on either side of the Karius Range and Mt Sisa. Some Duguba are Huli in language and practice, whereas others exist beyond the limits of Huli cultural identity, such as the Etolo clans. Duguba is both a cardinal term and a genealogical identifier.

But just because I am poor in the vehicle and poor in campaign … if someone support me for the campaign and maybe 500,000 for the truck and the campaign rally. This is in my brain so I will just campaign from Kopiago come to here, go from Tuandaga, go to Margarima, go to here, come … No Agiru is not dead, Agiru is alive, there is someone like Agiru here already. Mike I'm telling the truth that if someone wants to back me even for the member or even for governor. Mike, Berabuli clan is everywhere in the three electorates of Hela Province. Koroba, Kopiago side, Tari side, Tari-Pori side, Komo-Margarima side.

Ango's Berabuli clan is extensive and has a complex history that links its members to many locations in Hela. However, Michael's Beraboli relatives and friends openly mocked him for his political ambition. They accused him of having a mindset that belonged in the 1980s. In those days, they said, people used to gather up what money they could and donate to the political campaigns of their clan leaders. Now, in the era of PNG LNG, the people instead hold out their hands expecting to be paid for their votes.

Michael's friends were right and, in the months that followed, the only candidates who made any kind of impact were part of an elite group of Huli with access to power and money. The only candidate who ran on a platform that highlighted his expertise and skill was the CEO of the Tari hospital, Dr Hewali Hamiya. However, even Dr Hamiya was unable to compete with the political connections of the two main rival candidates, Philip Undialu and Francis Potobe. Huli voters wanted to be represented by a person with impressive leadership qualities, who had access to money and power. As such, the ideal Huli leader has become a benevolent strongman who is able to accumulate great wealth and influence that he will then use to develop Hela Province and improve the lives of the Huli people. Huli had no vested interest in a person like Michael Ango—who was poor, just like everyone else. Huli respect the ability of individuals to accumulate wealth, and they recognise that wealth accumulation is necessary to finance the development of the province. Huli desire the existence of wealthy and powerful leaders; therefore, they also desire the inequality that is necessarily part of the hierarchy that supports such leaders.

Transformations of Morality

The leadership styles of contemporary Huli politicians draw on the interplay between two traditional styles of leadership, originally described by Glasse. Today, as in Glasse's time, Huli have great scope to determine for themselves what type of lives they want to lead, the ways in which they choose to express a Huli identity, the extent they wish to engage with the rich and complex palette of Huli culture and tradition and the degree of wealth and prestige that they are motivated to accumulate for themselves. The type of leadership embodied by the current Hela Governor is that of the man of great wealth and prestige described by Glasse in 'Revenge and redress'. When Anderson Agiru first came to power, he was more a reflection of the 'expert' Glasse described in 'The Huli descent system'. Prior to the PNG LNG project, Huli put their faith in the power of traditional knowledge to improve their lives, even if this knowledge had been reconfigured in response to Christianity and new material opportunities. In the era of PNG LNG, Huli have instead put their faith in the material wealth and political power that their leaders are able to accumulate and deploy on behalf of their own people. In both cases, Huli desire a form of leadership that depends on the unequal distribution of resources. In the first case, the most valuable resource is knowledge; in the second case, the most valuable resource is material wealth and power.

With the advent of PNG LNG, Agiru became an amalgamation of both types, who made much of Huli prophecy and mythology, which were perceived to underpin the project, while also accumulating great wealth for himself. However, by the time of Agiru's death, these had failed to deliver any of the expected benefits from the project; consequently, the power and salience of Agiru's knowledge had also failed. I have been unable to find any evidence of Agiru carrying the title 'paramount chief'— he both preceded and eclipsed the introduction of that term. However, contemporary leaders are often described in this way. Contemporary leadership continues to carry a strong moral component; however, the moral component has also changed and is now largely based on contemporary rather than traditional beliefs.

In contemporary Huli politics, the married status of politicians is largely irrelevant. The moral component is reflected in the way people dress, by maintaining a healthy lifestyle and, particularly, honesty and integrity in the stewardship of resource wealth. Politicians display campaign photos of themselves in clean-cut suits and with smiling white teeth. My host while I was living in Komo, Charles Haluya, was a local-level politician who avoided chewing betel nut and did not smoke or drink. Charles has political ambition, and his concern for his appearance is part and parcel of the moral purity that he must maintain for political success. His approach has borne fruit and, since 2016, Charles became president of the Komo-Margarima electorate, before being elected Deputy Governor of Hela Province. Charles' constituents do not expect the same of themselves; however, they do expect this of their leaders, whom they desire to be an ideal version of Huli potential. Charles had also built a guesthouse with funds made available during the construction phase of the PNG LNG project. The only guests that Charles ever hosted were myself and (before me) a police mobile squad contingent that were sent to protect the assets of the PNG LNG project. The accommodation of these police was paid for by ExxonMobil; however, Exxon paid the money to the police department in Port Moresby and Charles, inevitably, went unpaid. Charles was forced to eject the police from his guesthouse; they then found accommodation elsewhere. However, Charles maintained the large guesthouse, replete with mess hall and laundry, as a way of displaying himself as a hard-working individual who was able to solicit the support of friends and clansmen in the realisation of his goals. As an ordinary person living in a bush-material house, Charles would have no chance of political success. However, as a person who could demonstrate both the ability to accumulate wealth and influence and to manage that wealth in a sensible way, which includes the management of his personal life, Charles was giving himself the best chance of gaining the support of his community.

Conclusion: Inequality and Urban Utopia

Huli do not desire to be represented by an equal—rather, by a first among the people, who is able to achieve the development aspirations of the province. Further, Huli have never been egalitarian—the Huli example reinforces the point that 'claims for indigenous egalitarianism' in PNG (Macintyre, 1994) are contradicted by a logic of inequality upon which various forms of leadership depend. For the Huli case, I would go so far as to suggest that a tradition of individualism and respect for self-advancement has parallels with the much-derided neoliberal economic ideal of the capitalist West. After all, Agiru did envision a day when a Huli would come to buy out ExxonMobil. With the exploitation of oil and gas resources in Huli territory, development aspirations have become supercharged; consequently, the desire for great leaders to exist—leaders who are unequal and better able than others to achieve results—has transformed traditional forms of Huli leadership into something that had hitherto been unheard of in Huli parlance: the Huli paramount chief.

This process has occurred partly due to the failure of traditional forms of knowledge to engage with the world of development adequately, resource extraction and global economics. However, this process also continues a tradition of Huli creativity in engaging with and adapting to a changing world. To paraphrase Macintyre (1994), writing about the transformation of Muruan culture, this transformation of Huli culture must be read not as 'estrangement from' Huli culture 'as a set of norms, institutions and social relationships', but of Huli 'capacity to adapt, transform and transcend it'. What remains is the desire for a better life and the inexhaustible search for ways in which to achieve what Huli not unreasonably believe to be their entitlement from the exploitation of their gas resource: a Hela city for all.

References

Bainton, N. (2008). The genesis and the escalation of desire and antipathy in the Lihir Islands, Papua New Guinea. *The Journal of Pacific History*, *43*(3), 289–312.

Barrett, J. & Gloystein, H. (2018, 7 March). Shakes and superstition: Exxon faces backlash in Papua New Guinea. *Reuters*. Retrieved from www.reuters.com/article/us-papua-quake-exxon-insight/shakes-and-superstition-exxon-faces-backlash-in-papua-new-guinea-idUSKCN1GJ12S

Clapp, G. (2002). *Corporate history of hides*. Sydney, NSW: Oil Search Limited.

Cox, J. (2015). Israeli technicians and the post-colonial racial triangle in Papua New Guinea. *Oceania*, *85*(3), 342–358.

Damon, F. H. (1983). On the transformation of Muyuw into Woodlark Island: Two minutes in December, 1974. *The Journal of Pacific History*, *18*(1), 35–56.

Elapa, J. (2015, 20 October). Spokesman hails O'Neill's K600m pledge. *Papua New Guinea Post-Courier*.

Filer, C. (1997). Compensation, rent and power in Papua New Guinea. In S. Toft (Ed.), *Compensation for resource development in Papua New Guinea* (pp. 156–189). Canberra, ACT: The Australian National University.

Filer, C. (2019). *Methods in the madness: The 'landowner problem' in the PNG LNG project* (Development Policy Centre Discussion Paper 76). Canberra, ACT: Crawford School of Public Policy, The Australian National University.

Glasse, R. (1959a). The Huli descent system: A preliminary account. *Oceania, 29*, 171–184.

Glasse, R. (1959b). Revenge and redress among the Huli: A preliminary account. *Mankind, 5*, 273–289.

Glasse, R. (1968). *Huli of Papua: A cognatic descent system*. Paris, France: Mouton & Co.

Goldman, L. (1983). *Talk never dies: The language of Huli disputes*. London, England: Tavistock.

Goldman, L. (1993). *The culture of coincidence: Accident and absolute liability in Huli*. Oxford, England: Clarendon Press.

Goldman, L. (1998). *Child's play: Myth, mimesis and make-believe*. Oxford, England: Berg.

Haley, N. & Zubrinich, K. (2018). *2017 Papua New Guinea general elections: Election observation report*. Canberra, ACT: Department of Pacific Affairs, The Australian National University.

Macintyre, M. (1994). Too many chiefs?: Leadership in the Massim in the colonial era. *History and Anthropology, 7*(1–4), 241–262.

Papua New Guinea Post-Courier. (2007, 27 February). PNG Power deal smells fishy. *Papua New Guinea Post-Courier*.

Wardlow, H. (2006). *Wayward women: Sexuality and agency in a New Guinea society*. Berkeley, CA: University of California Press.

World Bank. (2019). *Papua New Guinea economic update, January 2019: Slower growth, better prospects*. Washington, DC: World Bank.

13

Measuring Mobilities and Inequalities in Papua New Guinea's Mining Workforce

Colin Filer

Introduction

Just before Christmas 2011, I got a call from a contact in the Australian aid agency to ask if I would be able to organise a 'country study' of Papua New Guinea (PNG) for the World Bank's forthcoming World Development Report on 'Jobs'. The study would have to be initiated by the end of January 2012, and a summary report of our preliminary findings would have to be delivered by June of that year. Furthermore, the study would have to involve some kind of collaboration with counterparts in PNG and should ideally involve the collection of new information about jobs in that country.

I cannot say that our study had much impact on the contents of the World Development Report itself (World Bank, 2012) because our summary report was only five pages long and the World Bank team had already decided what they were going to say about each of the countries that featured in it. But the team leaders had already promised to produce a 'companion volume' in which the authors of seven country studies, including ours, would have the opportunity to tell their stories at greater length. And so it came to pass (Betcherman & Rama, 2016).

Our own contribution to that volume (Filer et al., 2016) was constrained by the questions that the World Bank was attempting to answer. But the dataset that our team assembled can be used to answer some other questions as well. The World Bank team was trying to figure out what sort of jobs were 'good for development' and what national governments could or should do to create more of them. In this chapter, I focus on the question of how the jobs occupied by those who work in PNG's resource sector or mining industry are implicated in local, national and global forms of social inequality and social mobility.

Much has been written about the interactions between mining or petroleum companies and the landowners or local communities affected by their operations in PNG. A lot less has been written about the Papua New Guineans employed in the extractive industry sector, some of whom have been recruited because they belong to project-affected communities, while others have been recruited from further afield. There are good reasons to believe that the extractive sector workforce is more mobile, in both a geographical and social sense, than any other sectoral workforce in PNG, and elements of this workforce may even be considered as a sort of 'labour aristocracy' within the wage-earning population. This chapter considers the relationship between the social and geographical mobility of these workers, the inequalities within and beyond their ranks, and the extent to which they have become detached from the moral economy that binds other Papua New Guineans to networks of kinship and affinity within the so-called 'wantok system'.

Alternatives to Conventional Wisdom

Our decision to conduct a survey of extractive industry workers could be read as a challenge to the conventional wisdom, endorsed by the World Bank (2012, p. 203), which says that jobs in this sector are *not* 'good for development' because of the so-called 'Dutch Disease' (Filer et al., 2016, p. 103). According to this line of argument, a dominant or booming resource sector tends to depress the level of economic activity in other sectors of a national economy, so each new job created in this sector is likely to come at the expense of several jobs elsewhere. Instead of attempting to test this hypothesis against non-existent labour market statistics, we tried a rather different approach.

First, we wanted to examine the common assumption that workers in this sector must be socially isolated from the rest of the population because major resource projects constitute 'enclaves' that are isolated from the rest of the national economy. Second, we wanted to find out if jobs in this sector had some positive social qualities that might be shared, to a greater or lesser degree, with jobs in other sectors. One example of this could be the level of discipline imposed on the workforce through the routines of 'health and safety' that are familiar to anyone who has visited the site of a major resource project.

A third consideration was flagged by industry representatives at our inception workshop, and this turned out to be the most important one when we came to the analysis of our findings. They complained that their companies had gone to considerable expense to train Papua New Guinean workers to occupy some of the more specialised jobs in the sector, only to find that some of their money had been wasted on workers who promptly sold their new skills to employers in other countries where the global resource boom had created as many new job opportunities as it had in PNG. Naturally, they were inclined to think that this kind of 'brain drain' constituted a loss to PNG, as well as to their own companies, even though some economists have argued that the emigration of highly skilled workers from developing countries can sometimes have a positive impact on 'human capital formation' in their country of origin (Beine, Docquier & Rapoport, 2011; Bollard et al., 2011; Gibson & McKenzie, 2011; Packard & Nguyen, 2014).

In this case, we already knew how hard it was for a Papua New Guinean to get any kind of job in Australia, let alone a well-paid job in the resource sector, so there would be an extra bonus if we could demonstrate the existence of what the World Bank calls a 'positive spillover'. What might that consist of? The best example we could find during the course of our own study was one that even appealed to our friends in the Bank. This was the case of a man who ended up in a box in the published version of our country study, where he was described as 'a high-flying migrant worker, generating positive spillovers for his country':

> Peter (not his real name) is a highly qualified petroleum engineer. He was among the last cohort of Papua New Guinean students to undertake the final two years of secondary education at a boarding school in Australia under a scheme supported by the Australian government's aid program. While still at school he watched news coverage of the 1991 Gulf War, and when told that it was basically

a war about oil, he decided that he would try to make a career out of understanding this vital substance. At that time, it was not possible to get an undergraduate degree in petroleum engineering at any Australian university, let alone a PNG university, so he enrolled for a degree in medicine at the University of PNG. After completing his science foundation year, he was lucky enough to win a scholarship to an American university to study his preferred subject. Having obtained a postgraduate certificate from a Japanese institution, he worked in PNG's Department of Petroleum and Energy for a while and then completed his higher education with a Master's degree from a Scottish university. He got a job in the Australian gas industry, and on that basis secured permanent residence in Australia. He now lives in Sydney with his Papua New Guinean wife and six children, but has recently taken a job back in PNG on a fly-in-fly-out basis, with twenty-eight days working on site alternating with twenty-eight days of field break. During his field breaks, Peter normally spends a week doing development work in his home village in one of PNG's highland provinces. His main project for the past year has been to plant hundreds of trees to make up for a serious shortage of timber suitable for building houses. His next project is to build a guesthouse and other facilities that will attract tourists to the area. (Filer et al., 2016, p. 124)

I would not have been able to write this little story if I had not had a chance encounter with Peter himself and realised that he had been one of the workers included in our survey. We never found out what his wife thought about his activities, since she was not one of our respondents, but we did think of a way that the emigration of highly skilled men from PNG's resource sector, even if only temporary, might be good for the women employed in the same sector, and hence for the cause of gender equality. For we began to suspect, during the course of our survey, that the companies were beginning to react to the loss of these male employees by seeking to employ more women as their substitutes on the grounds that women would be less likely to follow the same path out of the country (Filer et al., 2016, p. 125).

Our own dataset does not supply me with a case in point to match our 'bloke in the box'. But here is one whose real name is Hillary in what appears to be a press release issued to one of PNG's national newspapers:

Hillary Turnamur from Toma in East New Britain is the first female in the country to be awarded a certificate of competency as mine manager works. This is according to records of the

Mineral Resources Authority (MRA). Turnamur is a manager at Ok Tedi Mining Ltd (OTML), Kiunga operations. She received notice of the award from the MRA after meeting the experience requirements and successfully completing an oral and written examination. OTML managing-director and chief executive officer Peter Graham said: "We are particularly proud of Hillary's achievement. She is a role model for young women in Papua New Guinea, demonstrating that women can successfully develop rewarding careers in mining, including into senior operating roles." Two years ago, the miner established the Ok Tedi Women's Network (OWN) for female employees to address safety and security concerns, identify development and career pathways and barriers to entry and progression, and to encourage mentoring and training for women. Graham added: "In 2019, 14 of the 27 trainees selected for our two-year graduate development programme and our apprentice programme are women. We are also reaching out to schools to encourage young girls to consider science, technology, engineering and maths subjects, reviewing relevant employment policies and sharpening our recruitment messaging. Women are currently underrepresented in Ok Tedi's workforce and while it will take time, we plan to change that." (The National, 2019)

The question, then, is how to stitch such anecdotes or narratives into a statistical profile of the extractive industry workforce.

Four Fields of Inequality

From the existing literature on PNG's extractive industry sector we can discern four different 'fields of inequality' between the people employed in it. The combination of these four fields creates a distinctive social and economic landscape within which the workers in question occupy particular positions at any one time, and also move between these various positions during the course of their careers.

Zones of Entitlement

The PNG government has long pursued what is commonly called the 'preferred area policy', which effectively creates a set of concentric rings or zones of entitlement to a number of 'benefit streams' derived from each major resource project. The first zone is occupied by the customary owners of the land covered by development licences, the second by 'project area people' or communities directly impacted by the project, the third by the people or government of the host province, and the fourth by the population or government of the nation as a whole (Filer, 2005). Direct or indirect employment on the project constitutes one of the income streams that flow through these zones of entitlement, along with compensation payments, royalties, business contracts and so forth. Jobs are generally the most valuable source of such incomes (Finlayson, 2002).

The spatial extent of these zones of entitlement, and the size of the population contained within each zone, varies a good deal from one project to another. A survey conducted by the PNG Chamber of Mines and Petroleum in 2010 found that 62 per cent of the Papua New Guineans employed directly by the operators of the Porgera mine had been recruited from within the first two zones of entitlement, while only 37 per cent of those employed directly by the operators of the Lihir mine had been recruited from the first three zones of entitlement. In the case of the Ok Tedi mine, 33 per cent had apparently been recruited from the first two zones of entitlement, but these zones have included two whole districts in two separate provinces ever since the original development agreements were formulated. In 2011, these two districts had a combined population of roughly 112,000, while the number of Papua New Guineans employed by OTML was just over 2,000. For most mining projects, including Lihir and Porgera, the inner two zones do not extend beyond the boundaries of a single local-level government (LLG) area, but these areas can also vary in the size of their population. The Porgera LLG area had more than 45,000 residents in 2011, whereas the Lihir LLG area had less than 26,000. The smaller the size of the national workforce employed on any major project, the easier it is for the operators to fill its ranks with local recruits. At the peak of its operation in the late 1990s, 90 per cent of the 714 national workers employed by the operators of the Misima mine were recruited from the first two zones of entitlement (Finlayson, 2002).

Relations of Production

Benedict Imbun and various colleagues have argued that this distinction between zones of entitlement under the preferred area policy has given rise to a specific form of industrial relations in which (generally expatriate) managers are able to manipulate divisions within the national workforce to their own advantage. On the basis of interviews conducted with members of the national workforce at a number of mine sites since the 1990s, Imbun (2006a) concluded that workers recruited from the first two zones of entitlement can reasonably be described as a 'tribal workforce'. This is because they still primarily think of themselves as customary landowners and retain some kind of role in the local subsistence economy, whereas those recruited from further afield constitute a sort of 'labour aristocracy' or 'national proletariat' who are 'further on the path to complete socialization into the industrial way of life than their local counterparts' (Imbun, 2006b, p. 122). Imbun thinks that this division is reflected in the reluctance of the locally recruited 'tribal miners' to join a trade union, and their inclination to take the side of management in the event of an industrial dispute, because they think their managers are 'like their typically traditional but benevolent village bigman or chief' (Imbun, 2006a, p. 329). This line of argument conjures up the image of a doubly asymmetrical relationship in which expatriate managers regard the 'tribal miners' or their leaders as their clients, whereas local community members or their leaders regard the mining company as a sort of corporate tenant (see Bainton, this volume).

If these divergent perceptions serve to enhance the self-esteem of local 'big shots' (Martin, 2013), they provide no comfort at all to members of the 'national proletariat', who are excluded from any role in the politics of the mine-affected area, and who suffer the double indignity of being paid less than half the wages or salaries paid to expatriate workers or managers with the same formal qualifications (Imbun & Morris, 2001). That is why Imbun (2006b, p. 122) reserves the term 'middle class' for the expatriate section of the workforce, including those in the non-managerial stratum, whose members reap the benefits of the so-called 'dual salary system'. This also helps to explain why some members of Imbun's national 'labour aristocracy' have jumped at the chance of securing jobs in other countries where there is no such discrimination.

Projects in Motion

The exodus of disgruntled labour aristocrats is only one of many forms of physical and social movement that take place around major resource projects during the different phases of the project cycle. The construction workforce is generally much larger than the operational workforce, only a small portion of it can normally be recruited from the first two zones of entitlement, but the rest of its members disappear when the building work is done. At that juncture, the occupants of the first zone of entitlement, the 'true landowners', become entitled to a stream of royalties that replaces or supplements the stream of compensation payments that they would have received during the construction phase. This makes it less likely that the recipients of such benefits would want to dilute their status as 'landlords' by exercising their entitlement to low-skilled and low-paid jobs within the project workforce. However, if it is old men who get to hoard these benefits, a younger generation of 'landowners' may not be so reluctant (Filer, 1990).

In a paper based on their own assessment of the likely social impact of the Misima mining project, Rolf Gerritsen and Martha Macintyre (1991) discussed sequential changes in the distribution of jobs and other benefits between members of a mine-affected community through the different phases of the project cycle—from exploration through to closure. They argued that these changes are the predictable results of a form of 'capital logic' that governs the investment decisions of the mining company, including decisions about when and how they choose to invest in the formation of a local pool of 'human capital'. However, their analysis did not consider the way in which variations in the scale or duration of a resource project might affect the outcomes of these decisions.

Once operational, mining projects that are bigger than the Misima project tend to act as magnets for people often described as 'opportunists'. These are people who have not been formally recruited by the operating company from the outer zones of entitlement, but who still seek to take up residence in one of the two inner zones. In doing so, they make claims of kinship or affinity with the local landowners, or may even be recruited by the landowners themselves, or at least by the 'big shots' among them, as their own clients or employees (Bainton, 2017; Bainton & Banks, 2018). In this way, the spatial hierarchy entailed in the relative distance of a landowner's land from the point of production is replaced or supplemented by a social hierarchy in which patron–client relationships emanate outwards from the mine manager's office. However, this whole edifice is liable to collapse at the moment of mine closure. When the mine manager's office is also closed, the royalty and compensation payments cease to flow to the local landlords, and locally recruited workers can only hope that their preferential training has qualified them to become members of the labour aristocracy and find a job on another resource project if they want to remain in the formal sector workforce. At that point, the relative scale and duration of the project, and the relative complexity of the social relations that have come to surround it, no longer matter so much.

Gendered Exclusions

Martha Macintyre (2011a, 2011b) has provided us with a number of reasons why we should not expect companies in PNG's resource sector to make a positive contribution to the cause of gender equality. The first is that Papua New Guinean men get seriously jealous at the thought of their wives working alongside other men to whom they are not related. This is not an issue restricted to the resource sector, and may well explain a good deal of the domestic violence reported from urban households in PNG (Rosi & Zimmer-Tamakoshi, 1993; Toft, 1986). However, the willingness of mining company managers to tackle this issue may be diluted by the peculiar features of their relationship with local community 'big shots' who are almost invariably men.

Formal employment in the resource sector has special characteristics that are also likely to exclude women from the workforce. One is the arduous pattern of shift work for some sections of the workforce, which makes the 'double shift' more problematic for women from the inner zones of entitlement, who are expected to maintain their customary roles in the subsistence economy, as well as in child care, once they are married. If the companies provided decent childcare facilities, this might at least signal a desire to address this problem, but Macintyre has reported a purely token effort at the Lihir project, and there is no evidence that other projects have done any better.

Women from the outer zones of entitlement are subject to a separate, but related, form of disadvantage because of the specific form of circular migration entailed in a practice now common in the resource sector. Workers travel from their normal place of residence to their place of work at intervals of more than a week but less than a month, work for several days at a stretch while sleeping in dormitories, and then travel home again for 'field breaks' that also last for several days. There is no way that companies would provide travel and accommodation for the children of women engaged on this basis, so it is hard to imagine how mothers in this situation could possibly manage their domestic responsibilities.

Survey Design and Implementation

Our initial plan was to conduct a survey of employers in PNG's resource sector as well as a survey of individuals currently or formerly employed in that sector. However, we soon abandoned the first of these surveys since it was hard enough to get the employers to collaborate in the survey of their own employees, let alone respond to a separate set of questions about their employment practices. In order to get access to their employees, we first made a list of the companies that were members of the PNG Chamber of Mines and Petroleum, and of the government agencies involved in the regulation of the resource sector, and made a rough estimate of their relative size. Our aim was to interview a random sample of 20 per cent of the people employed by small organisations (with fewer than 50 employees), 10 per cent of those employed by medium-sized organisations (with 50–500 employees) and 5 per cent of those employed by large organisations (with more than 500 employees).

For those people who had formerly been employed in the PNG resource sector, but were now employed elsewhere, we adopted a three-pronged strategy. First, we asked the PNG University of Technology and the University of PNG if they could supply us with contact details for their graduates in the fields of mining engineering and geology. Only the former was able to do so. Second, we tried to locate former employees of Bougainville Copper Ltd and Misima Mines Ltd, whose operations had closed in 1989 and 2004, respectively. The companies were unable to provide us with the relevant contact details, so we had to resort to networks of personal contacts. This kind of 'snowballing' technique also had to be applied to the discovery of Papua New Guineans now working in the resource sector outside of PNG, since the companies still operating in PNG had no record of where these people had gone.

As a result of these efforts, our team managed to conduct interviews with a total of 285 individuals between February and April 2012. These were divided into eight categories by reference to the nature of their current employers (see Table1). Four of these (categories 4, 6, 7 and 8) were outside the resource sector, and the 45 workers in these categories do not appear to constitute a sub-sample that has any particular coherence, so I have left them out of the dataset under consideration in this chapter. That leaves us with a sample comprising 240 workers who were currently employed in the resource sector, including 15 from the MRA, which is the national government agency that regulates the mining industry (but not the oil and gas industry), and one individual who performed the same function for the Autonomous Bougainville Government.

Table 1: Individual survey respondents by type of current employer

Type of Employer		Respondents
(1)	Mainstream resource (mining or petroleum) company	186
(2)	Landowner company contracted to mainstream company	16
(3)	Other private company contracted to mainstream company	22
(4)	Other private company not in resource sector	14
(5)	Mining industry regulators (public servants)	16
(6)	Other government department/agency/company	27
(7)	Educational or training institution	1
(8)	Other type of organisation	3

Source: Interview data.

The MRA was one of only three organisations with more than 50 employees that were willing and able to provide us with access to 5 or 10 per cent of them for the purpose of this study, though none of these could reasonably be described as a random sample of their total workforce. The others were OTML and Morobe Mining Joint Venture (which was responsible for the Hidden Valley mining operation). As a result, we ended up with 55 workers from the Ok Tedi mine site and 67 from the Hidden Valley mine site in our sample. Leaving aside the 16 public servants, the rest of our sample consists of a very mixed bunch of people employed on different resource projects, including 24 who were formerly employed on the Misima mining project and had since found work with other resource projects in PNG.

It is difficult to distinguish a group of 'preferred area' workers from the rest of our sample because I could not think of a survey question that would serve this purpose while making sense to all our respondents. The best approximation is the group of 45 workers who were born in the province or provinces that constituted the third zone of entitlement for the project on which they were employed and who had at least one parent born in the same province. This group mainly comprises people born in Western Province or West Sepik Province who were employed on the Ok Tedi project and people born in Morobe Province who were employed on the Hidden Valley project.

SAMPLE OF 240 WORKERS IN PNG'S EXTRACTIVE INDUSTRY SECTOR

45 'PROVINCIAL'

(32 men + 13 women)

150 'NATIONAL'

(117 men + 33 women)

45 'INTERNATIONAL'

(40 men + 5 women)

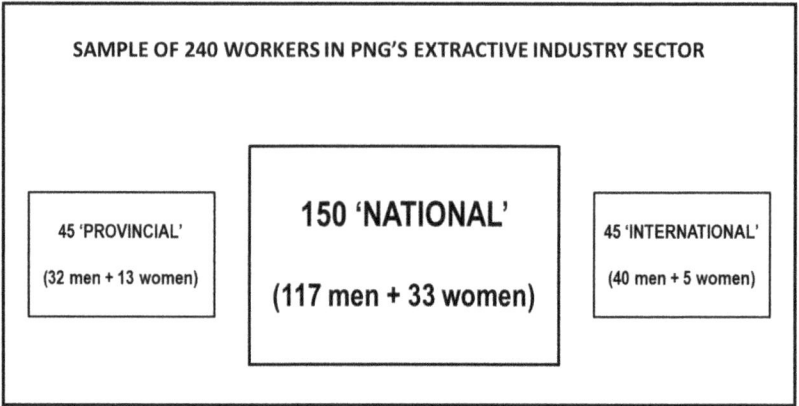

Figure 1: Distribution of respondents between three sections of the workforce.
Source: Interview data.

This group happens to be the same size as the group of 'exiles' included in our survey. Thirty-nine of these 45 workers were resident in Australia at the time, while six were located in other countries. If we regard this group as the 'international' section of our sample, and the previous group as the 'provincial' section, then the remaining 150 workers can be counted as the 'national' section located in between the two (see Figure 1).

Our sample of 240 workers represents around 1 per cent of all the Papua New Guineans who were formally employed in the resource sector at the time of our survey, including those who were (temporarily) employed in construction of the PNG LNG project, as well as those who were employed outside of PNG. But there is no sense in which this could be regarded as a sample that is representative of the larger population of workers in this sector. As we have seen, it is heavily biased towards two major mining projects in PNG, even if these were at opposite ends of the project cycle, one being an old mine and the other relatively new. It is also heavily biased towards the mining sector as opposed to the petroleum sector, and towards the larger, as opposed to the smaller, employers in the resource sector as a whole.

Survey Findings

The central question addressed in our survey might now be framed as a question about whether the 'mobility gap' (the difference between the three sections of the workforce) or the 'gender gap' (the difference between male and female workers) is more significant in explaining the other features of the group that we surveyed. However, the number of variables in the dataset raises other questions that might preclude any simple answer to this central question.

Gender and Generation

The proportion of women in both the national and provincial sections of our sample—22 and 29 per cent, respectively—was higher than we would predict from other sources of information about the resource sector. Women accounted for only 10 per cent of the workforce in the previously mentioned survey of three major mining projects conducted by the PNG Chamber of Mines and Petroleum in 2010 (Filer et al., 2016, p. 114), and only account for 11 per cent of the workers in the international section of our own sample. However, the number of women in the sample makes it easier to investigate the opportunities and constraints that women face in this sector.

Eighty-five per cent of the women in the national section of our sample were under 40 years of age, compared to 46 per cent of the men. In the provincial section, the proportion of younger women was slightly lower (77 per cent), and the proportion of younger men was slightly higher (53 per cent). However, the proportion of women under 30 years of age was higher in the provincial section (54 per cent) than in the national section (27 per cent). In the sample as a whole, there were 26 men in their 50s or 60s, but only one woman, and she was in the international section—a 'senior environmental adviser' working for a Brisbane-based contractor. If the resource sector is no country for old people generally, it certainly seems to be no country for older women.

These disparities are consistent with Macintyre's suggestion that a sizeable proportion of young female workers, especially those from a 'preferred area', are liable to drop out of formal employment when they get married, and even those who remain are liable to do so once they have a certain number of children to look after. Thirty per cent of the women in the national section of the sample, and 31 per cent in the provincial section, said they were not yet married. Across the sample as a whole, the women reported an average of 1.9 children in their care, whereas the men reported a considerably larger number—an average of four children in the national section of the sample, 3.4 in the provincial section and 2.5 in the international section. Our sample contained 166 married men (88 per cent of all the men in the sample), and 107 (or 64 per cent) of these married men said their wives were not formally employed. By contrast, only one of the 31 married women (61 per cent of all the women in the sample) said her husband was not in the formal workforce.

Income and Education

All our respondents were asked to locate their net fortnightly income (after deductions) in one of four different income brackets. Sixty-seven per cent of workers in the national section of the sample, and 89 per cent of those in the provincial section, said that they earned less than PGK 2,000 each fortnight, whereas 10 per cent of those in the national section, but only 2 per cent of those in the provincial section, said that they earned more than PGK 4,000. This would seem to support Imbun's suggestion that most of the highly paid jobs occupied by Papua New Guineans in PNG's resource sector are claimed by members of a 'labour aristocracy' who are recruited from outside the areas of preference.

The figures provided by respondents in these two sections of our sample appear to be consistent with those derived from a subsequent survey of employers. Jones and McGavin (2015, p. 176) reckon that the average gross fortnightly wage in the 'mining and quarrying' sector in 2013–14 was PGK 3,377, while the median was PGK 2,142. However, these numbers include the wages and salaries paid to expatriate members of the workforce, which are generally much higher than those paid to their national counterparts. The workers in the international section of our sample were paid at rates much closer to those paid to the expatriate members of the PNG workforce, which only serves to underline the similarity between these two groups of workers. Twenty-two of the workers in this group of exiles were receiving at least 4,000 Australian or United States (US) dollars a fortnight,[1] which meant that this was the median net income for the whole group.

---

1   Note that at the time of our survey in 2012, the Australian dollar and US dollar were roughly at parity.

We would expect net fortnightly incomes to be closely associated with the educational qualifications of the workers, and this is broadly the case. All 16 of the workers in the national and provincial sections of the sample who earned at least PGK 4,000 a fortnight had undergraduate degrees, sometimes with additional postgraduate qualifications, and all but one of these workers would seem to count as members of Imbun's 'labour aristocracy'. Likewise, all but one of the workers in the international section of our sample who earned at least 4,000 Australian or US dollars a fortnight were similarly qualified. Degree holders accounted for 85 per cent of workers in the international section, 49 per cent in the national section and 22 per cent in the provincial section. At the other end of the scale, all but five of the 81 workers in the national and provincial sections who had not completed the 12th grade of secondary schooling had incomes of less than PGK 2,000 a fortnight.

However, there were some rather peculiar anomalies. We were somewhat surprised to find that five of the workers in the international section of the sample had not completed the 12th grade of secondary schooling, yet were still earning more than most of the workers in the other two sections of our sample, including those with university degrees. There were four degree holders in the national section, and another three in the provincial section, who were earning less than PGK 800 a fortnight, which was the lowest of the four income brackets in our survey, but which only accounted for 17 per cent of all the workers in our sample. These anomalies are largely explained by differences in the work experience of the workers.

The concentration of women at the lower end of the pay scale is not quite so easily explained. In the national section of the sample, 76 per cent of the women, as opposed to 64 per cent of the men, were taking home less than PGK 2,000 a fortnight, but in the provincial section, 100 per cent of the women, as opposed to 84 per cent of the men, had this level of income. Overall, the women in the sample had a narrower range of educational qualifications than the men. All the women had a minimum of 10 years of formal schooling, but only five had postgraduate qualifications, and three of these were in the international section of the sample, while one of the remaining two was a public servant. Nevertheless, 54 per cent of the women, compared to 41 per cent of the men, in the national and provincial sections of the sample had university degrees. If female graduates were not earning as much as their male counterparts, the difference might be partially explained by their relative youth or inexperience, but could also be due to some form of gender discrimination. It might also be explained in part by the concentration of men in more specialised technical jobs and the greater likelihood that women tend to occupy clerical jobs of the sort found in many parts of the national economy. However, while 41 per cent of the women in the sample did indeed have clerical jobs, 28 per cent had more specialised technical jobs—the same proportion as the men.

Four Forms of Mobility

There are four distinct forms of mobility for which evidence was collected in our survey. The first is the peculiar form of long-distance commuting to which I already made reference in my discussion of gendered exclusions. It was difficult to think of a survey question that would distinguish long-distance (or long-rotation) commuters from those workers who commute to work on a daily basis. Some of them fly from their home to their workplace, while others drive or take a bus. A question about the time it takes to get to work will not serve the purpose either, and when you ask Papua New Guineans where their home is, they sometimes take this to be a question about their place of origin rather than their current place of residence.

From what we know of the employment practices at different resource projects, it was nevertheless possible to make an approximate distinction between these two groups of workers in our sample. Roughly half of the workers in the international section were long-distance commuters, 44 per cent of those in the national section, but only 9 per cent of those in the provincial section. That is not surprising, given that nearly all of the workers employed on the Ok Tedi project were normally resident in the townships of Tabubil and Kiunga at the time of the survey, and a substantial proportion of those employed on the Hidden Valley project were recruited from areas within daily commuting distance of the mine site. Only seven of the long-distance commuters in the national section of the sample, and none of the four in the provincial section, were women. While this might be taken as evidence in support of Macintyre's argument that this form of employment tends to discriminate against women, it is interesting to note that all seven of these women had children, who presumably had to be left at home for days at a time, even though only four of them were currently married.

The most distinctive group of long-distance commuters in the national section of our sample was a group of 24 workers from the island of Misima who had worked at the Misima mine site before the mine was closed in 2004. This group illustrates a second form of mobility that is evident in the results of our survey. Just as the 45 workers in the international section of our sample would formerly have counted as members of the national or provincial section of PNG's resource sector workforce, so these Misiman workers had 'migrated' from the provincial to the national section by finding work in the resource sector outside of Milne Bay Province. There was even one man from Misima discovered in the international section of our sample, so he had gone one step further.

There had never been more than 40 women among the locally recruited workforce on the Misima mining project when it was still in operation, and they accounted for only 6 per cent of local recruits (from the inner two zones of entitlement) when the size of the total workforce peaked in the late 1990s (Finlayson, 2002). It was predicted that very few of these women would remain in formal employment once the mine closed, either because of family commitments on the island or else because of their limited qualifications (Jackson, 2000, p. 40). Our own evidence bears this out. Although we cannot be sure how many Misimans were still formally employed in the resource sector in 2012, only one of the 24 who turned up in the national section of our own survey sample was a woman—a 'land rehabilitation officer' who was employed to clean up the mess when the mine closed and who then got a similar job at the Porgera mine. This lady was the only member of this group of 24 Misiman workers who had a university degree. None of the men in the group had more than 10 years of formal schooling and, although some had received additional technical training while working on Misima, none had obtained any additional qualifications since the mine closed. All 24 members of this group—even the female degree holder—were earning less than PGK 2,000 a fortnight, and therefore fell within the two lowest income brackets in our sample. If these workers were now members of a national labour aristocracy, they still appeared to be largely stuck in its lower ranks.

The second form of mobility can be considered as a particular instance of the third form, which not only consists of the movement of workers between provinces or countries, but also between jobs within the same geographical area, or even with the same employer. But if we think of this as occupational mobility, we still need to consider that people are not only moving between jobs within the formal sector of the economy but also moving in and out of the formal sector altogether. In order to get a handle on this third form of mobility, we asked our respondents to tell us about the jobs they had held before they took on their current job. In each case, we asked for the title of the job, whether it had been with the same employer or a different employer, and the number of years for which it had been held. We were able to combine the results with answers to a separate set of questions about the educational history of our respondents to determine whether they had been undergoing some kind of education or training during periods when they were not in formal employment.

If we just count the number of years that our respondents had spent in each of the jobs they had occupied, then it appears that the women had a considerably higher rate of occupational mobility than the men. In the national section of our sample, the women had spent an average of 2.7 years in each of their jobs, whereas the men had spent an average of four years in each of theirs. In the provincial section of the sample, the corresponding figures were 3.5 years for the women and 4.4 years for the men. The most plausible explanation for this discrepancy is that workers tend to stay longer in the same job as they grow older, so the higher rate of turnover among the women may be due to their lower average age. The discrepancy is much smaller if we only consider the number of jobs that individuals had held over the previous decade rather than the whole of their careers in the formal workforce. In the national section of our sample, the men and women had both spent an average of 7.5 years in formal employment during that period, the women had held an average of three jobs and the men had held an average of 2.8 jobs. In the provincial section of the sample, the men had spent an average of six years in formal employment and held an average of 1.8 jobs over the course of the previous 10 years, while the women had spent an average of 5.9 years in formal employment and held an average of 1.9 jobs.

The trouble with averages like this is that they mask a wide range of variation between individuals in the sample. Eleven of the men in our sample, but only one of the women, had been in their current job for more than a decade, the record being set by one man in the provincial section of the sample who had been in his current job as a 'community relations officer' for 31 years. We find a similar story if we look at the number of years that workers spent 'out of work' between finishing their previous jobs and starting their current ones. Four of the men in our sample, but none of the women, had spent more than a decade apparently 'unemployed' before landing their current jobs. In this case, the record was set by a 70-year-old man in the provincial section of the sample who said he had spent 41 years outside the formal workforce before being hired as an 'equipment operator', having previously been employed to do similar work in the 1960s. If we look at the number of years in which our workers had neither been formally employed nor undergoing some form of education over the course of the previous decade, we see that the average was 1.4 years in the national section of our sample, 1.5 years in the international section and 2.2 years in the provincial section. But there were 20 men and three women in the sample, including one man in the international section, who had been 'out of work' in this sense for at least five of the previous 10 years. Interestingly enough, six of these 20 men were Misimans, which reflects the fact that workers previously employed at the Misima mine generally took several years to find alternative employment in the resource sector after that mine had closed.

The final form of mobility is the one reflected in answers to questions about the province in which our respondents, their parents and their spouses were born. This is both a geographical and a social form of mobility in the sense that it reflects the extent to which individuals are enmeshed in networks of kinship and affinity that cut across provincial boundaries and ethnic identities. It has long been noted that Papua New Guineans, like other Melanesians, have a propensity to marry people from other 'tribes' and provinces, once provided with an opportunity to do so (Beer & Schroedter, 2014; Chowning, 1986; Lind, 1969; Rosi & Zimmer-Tamakoshi, 1993), and we should therefore expect members of a national 'labour aristocracy' or 'middle class' to be at the forefront of this particular tendency.

In the analysis of our survey results, I sorted our respondents into four categories according to the number of 'provincial affiliations' specified in their answers to our questions. The workers in the provincial section of our sample could not have more than three affiliations, given the way that this group had been defined. Nevertheless, 42 per cent of workers in this section had either one parent or a spouse born in a province other than their own birth province, and three of these 45 workers had both a parent and a spouse born elsewhere. In the national section of the sample, 32 per cent had two provincial affiliations, while 20 per cent had three or four. In the international section, 44 per cent had two provincial affiliations, but only 11 per cent had three or four. Across the sample as a whole, there was some evidence of a correlation between the number of provincial affiliations and the size of people's pay packets, but not as much as we might have expected.

A second way of dealing with the fourth form of mobility was to assign a provincial and regional identity if the workers and at least one of their parents were born in the same province, or if both of their parents were born in the same province. We could then determine whether those from one region were more 'parochial' than those from other regions, either because they only had the one provincial affiliation or else because they were married to someone with the same provincial identity. This was a way of revisiting the argument that the level of parochialism, in this sense, is inversely related to the length of time for which members of different ethnic groups have been exposed to contact with the Western or modern world (Levine, 1979, pp. 97–98). Given the construction of our own sample, the question could only be posed as one about the difference between respondents from the highlands region and those from the other three 'lowland' regions, where most of the population was subject to colonial administration before the highlanders had any contact with it.

Across the sample as a whole, there were 223 workers who could be assigned a provincial and regional identity, of whom 63 were highlanders and 160 were lowlanders. The difference here was that 65 per cent of the highlanders, but only 46 per cent of the lowlanders, had only one provincial affiliation. Of all these workers, 176 had a spouse to whom they assigned a provincial identity. The difference here was that 69 per cent of the 54 highlanders, but only 53 per cent of the 122 lowlanders, had married someone from the same province. Both of these disparities would be greater if the collection of lowlanders in our sample had not included a group of people from Morobe Province who were employed on the Hidden Valley mining project, and another group from Milne Bay Province who were formerly employed on the Misima mining project, since both of these groups were even more parochial than the highlanders.

Three Forms of Remittance

Our survey respondents were asked to specify their contributions to development 'at home' in the previous year (2011) under three main headings: goods supplied as gifts to relatives outside of the worker's own nuclear family; payments of cash to meet a variety of expenses on behalf of such relatives; and accommodation of rural relatives for various periods of time by workers resident in urban areas. Academic discussion of 'remittances' in PNG has generally focused on the first two types of transaction (Boyd, 1990; Carrier, 1984; Clunies Ross, 1984; Cox, this volume; Dalsgaard, 2013; Hayes, 1993; Morauta, 1984; Rasmussen, 2015; Sykes, 2017), but the third type may be no less significant as a distinctive aspect of rural claims on a share of urban wage incomes (Ryan, 1985, 1993; Zimmer-Tamakoshi, 1998).

The first point to be made here is that only six workers in the whole sample of 240 said that they did not make any of these three types of remittance. Two were in the national section of the sample and four in the provincial section; five were men and one was a woman; four earned less than PGK 800 a fortnight; and four were either divorced or not yet married. The one thing that all six had in common was that they were currently resident in Morobe Province and working on the Hidden Valley mining project. Another 87 workers, all in the national and provincial sections of the sample, gave equivocal answers to some of our questions, either by failing to state whether or not they had hosted rural relatives, or else by stating that they had made contributions in cash or in kind to relatives at home, but then failing to specify the value, substance or purpose of these contributions.

There were 219 workers who specified the value, substance and purpose of one or other of the first two kinds of contribution, of whom two-thirds (147) specified both while the rest only specified one of them. To limit the burden placed on their memories, we only asked them to name the 'four main things [they] bought' by way of an in-kind contribution, or the 'four main types of contribution [they] made', by way of a cash remittance, and in each case to say how much they spent on each commodity or payment. This could mean that we have failed to capture the entire value of the contributions made by some of the workers in the sample, even when they gave specific answers to both of these questions.

There were 96 workers in the national section of the sample, and another 28 in the provincial section, who specified the value and substance of their in-kind remittances. The combined value of these contributions was approximately PGK 836,000 in the national section and PGK 300,000 in the provincial section. The higher average value of the in-kind remittances made by workers in the provincial section—PGK 11,094, as opposed to PGK 8,616 in the national section—might be taken to reflect the greater ease with which workers in this group were able to supply commodities, rather than money, to villages within their own province. Yet in the international section of the sample, the combined value of the in-kind remittances made by 41 workers was more than 155,000 Australian or US dollars, which meant that the average was 3,790 dollars (then equivalent to PGK 9,475), so the distance between the worker and his or her 'home' does not seem to be the only factor at work here.

There were 129 workers in the national section of the sample, and another 34 in the provincial section, who specified the value and purpose of their remittances in cash. The combined value of these contributions was approximately PGK 1 million in the national section and PGK 209,000 in the provincial section. In this instance, the direction of the difference between the average value of the contributions made by workers in these two sections of the sample was reversed, being PGK 8,260 in the national section and PGK 6,144 in the provincial section. In the international section, 38 workers made cash contributions worth a total of approximately 145,000 dollars, which meant an average of 3,824 dollars (equivalent to PGK 9,560), so this group of workers turned out once again to be slightly more generous than those in either of the other two groups.

The combined value of the different types of commodity specified as components of the in-kind remittances made by 166 workers in our sample varied a good deal between the different sections of the sample. In the national section, 46 per cent of the money was allocated to means of transport (including vehicles, motors, parts and fuel), while 25 per cent was allocated to construction and building materials and 6 per cent to household furniture and appliances. In the provincial section, 68 per cent was allocated to construction and building materials, 10 per cent to household furniture and appliances, and only 6 per cent to means of transport. The international section was somewhere in the middle of this range of variation: the workers in this section spent 34 per cent of their money on construction and building materials, 27 per cent on means of transport, and 9 per cent on household furniture and appliances. Other types of commodity, such as food, working tools and equipment, clothing and accessories, or mobile phones and digital devices, each accounted for less than 10 per cent of the spending in all sections of the sample. The only exception was in the international section, where 11 per cent of the money was spent on food. We did not ask our respondents to tell us how these various commodities reached the hands of their recipients.

The purchase of means of transport or construction and building materials was also mentioned by some of our respondents as purposes for which they sent money to their relatives at home, but in no section of the sample did these account for more than 10 per cent of the value of total spending. In the national section, school fees accounted for the largest share of expenditure (24 per cent), followed by funeral expenses (13 per cent), then means of transport (9 per cent). In the provincial section, school fees again came top of the list (22 per cent), followed by compensation payments (11 per cent) and funeral expenses (10 per cent). In the international section, compensation payments came first (31 per cent), followed by school fees (21 per cent) and then brideprice payments (10 per cent).

Here again, the averages mask a range of variation between individual responses that might lead us to wonder whether some of these responses actually make sense. In the national section of the sample, there was one man who said he had spent PGK 114,000 on buying means of transport for his relatives in the space of a single year, and another who said he had spent PGK 108,000 on the same sort of thing. Together, these two accounted for more than half of all the money that people in this section of the sample had spent on such things, and that in turn helps to explain why means of transport accounted for almost half of all the money allocated to in-kind remittances by workers in this section of the sample. Admittedly, both of these men were employed in managerial positions (by the same mining company), and were making more than PGK 4,000 a fortnight, so perhaps they could afford remittances of such a size. However, if they were buying mini-buses or four-wheel-drives for their relatives, as seems likely, one might still wonder whether these could really be counted as 'gifts' to others rather than 'investments' in their own family businesses.

To get around this difficulty, we can calculate the median, rather than the mean, amounts that workers in our sample claim to have spent on one or both of the first two types of remittance before seeking to establish a relationship between the level of spending and the size of their fortnightly pay packets. Once we do that, the relationship seems fairly close. In the national section of the sample, the median annual expenditure by workers earning less than PGK 800 a fortnight was PGK 2,250; in the three higher income brackets, this rose to PGK 5,650, 9,650 and 22,000, respectively. In the provincial section of the sample, the equivalent amounts in each income bracket were PGK 2,500, 6,600, 34,400 and 17,000. And in the international section, the median level of spending by workers earning less than 4,000 dollars fortnight was 3,500 dollars (or PGK 8,750), whereas those earning more than 4,000 dollars a fortnight had a median spending level of 4,195 dollars (or PGK 10,488). The only obvious anomaly here is the reported level of spending by the four workers in the provincial section who were in the second highest income bracket, and that was because three of them reported unusually high levels of expenditure. Otherwise, it appears that workers in the international section of the sample were somewhat more generous in absolute terms, but still spent a smaller proportion of their net incomes on remittances than workers in the national and provincial sections.

Once we take income levels into account, the median levels of spending on these first two forms of remittance appear to be a function of marital status as much as a function of gender, but the association is not constant across the different sections of our sample. In the national section, it was married men who ranked first (with PGK 4,300), and unmarried women who ranked second (with PGK 3,575), while married women and unmarried men shared third place (with PGK 2,700). This pattern was repeated in the international section, with married men again spending the largest amount (7,779 dollars or PGK 19,447), again followed by unmarried women (3,575 dollars or PGK 8,938), then by married women (2,933 dollars or PGK 7,333), and finally by unmarried men (2,500 dollars or PGK 6,250). But in the provincial section, it was unmarried women who spent the most (PGK 13,000), followed by married men (PGK 4,000), then unmarried men (PGK 3,200), and finally married women (PGK 1,650). Given the small number of respondents in some of these categories, it is hard to attribute much significance to these numbers, let alone to their further breakdown into different forms of spending.

When we turn to the third form of remittance—if that is what it really is—we find that 165 town-based workers in the national and provincial sections of the sample had similar dispositions to entertain their rural relatives, so there is no point in counting them separately. Eighty-eight (or 53 per cent) of these workers said they accommodated some relatives over the course of the previous year. There were 415 guests altogether, of whom 259 (62 per cent) were said to have stayed for more than a month, and 146 (35 per cent) for more than six months. Our respondents also said that 108 (or 26 per cent) of their guests were mainly helping with child care, while 92 (or 22 per cent) were receiving some form of education at their hosts' expense.

One might suppose that workers in the international section of the sample would be much less hospitable, partly because of their distance from the relatives they might entertain, and partly because of political barriers to international migration. We were somewhat surprised to find that 19 (or 42 per cent) of the 45 workers in this group managed to surmount these obstacles by entertaining a total of 38 relatives, of whom 29 (or 76 per cent) were said to have stayed for more than a month. Eight of these guests were said to have been helping with child care, but only one stayed for more than six months, and none were apparently being educated at their hosts' expense. In the national and provincial sections of the sample, we have no reason to assume that guests could not be helping with child care while receiving some form of education at the same time, but it is safer to assume that most of the guests who engaged in one or both of these activities would have been among those who stayed for several months.

In the sample as a whole, there were 72 married men who said that they hosted 321 rural relatives between them, and 19 married women who said that they hosted 102. There is no indication that any of our respondents were married to each other, so these can be taken as the responses of 91 different households. If the wives appear to have been slightly more hospitable than the husbands (with an average of 5.37 as opposed to 4.46 guests), we cannot infer that our respondents were only counting their own relatives rather than those of their spouses. One might suppose that assistance with childcare would be especially important for those of our respondents who were single parents, but our entire sample only contained two single fathers and two single mothers who said that they obtained such support from visiting relatives. There was one unmarried mother (with two children) who said that she hosted three rural relatives for a period of more than six months, but she did not say that they provided such support. If child care does not figure very prominently in the relationship between this collection of urban hosts and their rural guests, then it does make this relationship seem more like a form of remittance from the former to the latter.

Orientations and Aspirations

In order to assess the orientations and aspirations of the workers in our sample, we posed three distinct sets of questions. First, those who had occupied one or more jobs before their current job were asked to specify the reasons why they had left each of those previous jobs. Second, we asked each of our respondents what they most liked, and what they least liked, about their current job. Finally, we asked them what job they would like to have in five years' time, and what was the best job they thought they could get during the rest of their careers. These were open-ended questions, so we had to devise some way of separating a remarkable variety of responses into a limited number of mutually exclusive categories. This process of classification may have obscured some important features of the variation we encountered.

Since 27 per cent of the workers in the provincial section of our sample, and another 5 per cent in the national section, were new entrants to the formal labour market, whose current job was the first one they had occupied, they could give us no answers to our first set of questions. This explains why the total number of responses from the provincial section was only 61, while the number of responses from the international section, with the same number of workers, all of whom had held at least one job before their current one, was 114. Some respondents gave more than one reason for leaving a previous job, in which case we inferred what the main reason had been so that each response could be assigned to a single category.

Very few of our respondents cited factors such as poor management, the work environment, commuting time, job location, family or personal reasons as significant factors in their departure from a job. Out of a total of 507 responses from the whole sample, only 11 per cent made reference to any of these factors, nor were such responses any more likely to come from women than from men. Even in the international section of the sample, the opportunity to emigrate was only specified in four of the 114 responses. Our respondents were mainly concerned with the extent to which a change of job had come about as a result of their own action, as opposed to that of their employers, and with comparing the terms and conditions of each job they had held.

There was a predictable difference between the reasons given by workers in the international section of the sample and those given by workers in the national and provincial sections. Only 18 per cent of the reasons given by members of the international section referred to a promotion or transfer by their existing employers, whereas 44 per cent pointed to a better job offer from a new employer, which was sometimes framed in terms of greater remuneration and benefits, and a further 21 per cent made explicit reference to the respondent's search for a better career path. Of 393 reasons given by workers in the national and provincial sections, more than 21 per cent cited a movement between jobs in the same organisation, but only 29 per cent cited a better job offer from a new employer, and only 14 per cent made explicit reference to the search for a better career path. A further 18 per cent of the reasons given by workers in these two groups made separate reference to redundancy (including mine closure), whereas this misfortune figured in less than 4 per cent of the reasons given by workers in the international section. These appear to reflect the greater mobility and autonomy of the international section of the mining workforce.

Within the national section of the sample, workers in the top two income brackets were more likely to say that they had been promoted rather than simply transferred when changing jobs within the same organisation, but this discrepancy was even more notable when comparing the responses of the women and the men. More than 31 per cent of the reasons given by the women, but less than 12 per cent of those given by the men, made reference to promotion, whereas 6 per cent of the reasons given by the men, but less than 2 per cent of those given by the women, only made reference to a transfer. A similar pattern is evident in the references made to the search for a better career path. While workers in the top two income brackets were more likely to mention this as the main reason for departing their previous jobs, this disparity was only evident in the national section of the sample. But in the national and provincial sections taken together, this accounted for 24 per cent of the reasons given by the women, but only 11 per cent of those given by the men. Like workers in the top two income brackets, women were also less likely to cite redundancy as a reason for departure.

In the national and provincial sections of the sample, 53 per cent of the workers said that the things they most liked about their current jobs were the qualities of the job itself, while another 8 per cent made separate reference to remuneration and benefits. The equivalent proportions in the international section were 40 per cent and 16 per cent. Three of the workers in this section, but only one in the national section, especially liked the commuter mining work schedule. Across the sample as a whole, there was a separate collection of workers who were more enthusiastic about the quality of their relationships with other people, especially colleagues, subordinates, trainees, local community members or other outsiders. This group accounted for 31 per cent of workers in the national section and 24 per cent in both the provincial and international sections. However, there were only two workers in the international section, and none in the other two sections, who extended this sentiment to their own managers or supervisors. Across the sample as a whole, there was only one male worker in the national section who said he liked nothing at all about his current job, but he was matched by another male worker who said he liked everything.

There was a wider spectrum of opinion when it came to sources of dissatisfaction. Aside from the 32 workers who could not think of anything they did not like about their current jobs, there were 52 (22 per cent) who grumbled about their relationships with other people (including managers or supervisors), 47 (20 per cent) who did not like the qualities of the job itself or the physical work environment, 42 (18 per cent) who complained about their working hours or commuting schedules, and 18 (8 per cent) who were frustrated by bureaucracy. The number who complained about the lack of opportunities for further training or advancement was surprisingly small—only four in the national section of the sample and one in the provincial section. This was the same as the number in the international section who complained instead about missing their friends and relatives at home. Otherwise, there were no significant differences between the responses from workers in the three different sections of our sample.

It was hard to discern any significant relationship between income levels and sources of satisfaction or dissatisfaction in the national and provincial sections of the sample. In the international section, six of the seven workers who specifically complained about their commuting schedules were earning less than 4,000 dollars a fortnight, but it is rather more puzzling that nine of the 10 workers who complained about their relationships with colleagues or subordinates were earning more than that. Across the sample as a whole, there appears to be no significant difference between the responses of men and women, and certainly no evidence that women were more likely to cite the quality of their relationships with other people, inside or outside of the workforce, as a specific source of satisfaction or dissatisfaction with their jobs.

While our third and final set of open-ended questions was meant to elicit a distinction between the short-term and long-term goals of our respondents, many of the responses suggested a measure of confusion on this score, because an answer to one of the questions sounded as if it would have been more appropriate as an answer to the other one. In any case, answers to both questions have been grouped into the same six categories, so answers to both questions can readily be combined to give a sense of the general aspirations of our respondents. This means that the number of aspirations or goals is twice the number of respondents, and some of our respondents have expressed two aspirations that do not appear to be consistent with each other.

Seventeen per cent of the answers given to our questions could not be assigned to any of our six categories because they were insufficiently specific. In all three sections of our sample, the most common aspiration was promotion within the respondent's existing line of work, which was sometimes expressed as a desire to be a supervisor or a trainer. This accounted for 50 per cent of the aspirations expressed in the national section, 51 per cent in the provincial section and 67 per cent in the international section. Some respondents expressed a higher level of ambition by saying that they aimed to occupy a senior managerial role, though it was sometimes difficult to tell whether or to what extent this would entail a departure from their existing line of work. This higher level of ambition accounted for 7 per cent of the aspirations expressed in the national section of the sample, 11 per cent in the provincial section and 17 per cent in the international section. It is understandable that workers in the international section should have greater hopes of further promotion than those in the other two sections, but somewhat strange that those in the provincial section should have greater hopes than those in the national section.

There were more workers who aspired to own their own business than to occupy a senior managerial role within a mining company, but these workers were more unevenly distributed between the three sections of our sample. This accounted for 17 per cent of the aspirations expressed in the national section, and 13 per cent in the provincial section, but none at all in the international section. This disparity is reduced when we add a second group of workers who specifically said that they aspired to be consultants to the mining industry, presumably making use of the skills already acquired in their existing line of work. This accounted for 12 per cent of the aspirations expressed in the international section of the sample, 6 per cent in the national section, but only 1 per cent in the provincial section. The remainder of the aspirations expressed by our respondents consisted of a desire to find an alternative form of employment or an alternative to any form of employment. These accounted for 21 per cent of the aspirations expressed in the national section of the sample, 11 per cent in the provincial section, but only 1 per cent in the international section.

The desire for promotion within one's existing line of work was inversely related to the size of a worker's fortnightly pay packet, while workers with higher incomes were more likely to aspire to a senior managerial role. In the national section of the sample, the desire to own one's own business was largely confined to workers in the middle income brackets, who were earning between PGK 800 and PGK 4,000 a fortnight, but in the provincial section, it was largely confined to those in the lowest income bracket, who were earning less than PGK 800 a fortnight. In the national section, it was workers in the top income bracket, earning more than PGK 4,000 a fortnight, who were most likely to say that they wanted to find an alternative form of employment or drop out of the labour market altogether.

In the national section of our sample, the desire for promotion within one's existing line of work accounted for 94 per cent of the aspirations expressed by women, but only 50 per cent of those expressed by men. This disparity could not be detected in the other two sections of the sample, where the number of female respondents was relatively small. Only one woman in the entire sample envisaged promotion to a senior managerial role in one of her responses to our two questions. There was no such gender disparity in the articulation of a desire to own one's own business, or even to be a consultant to the mining industry, at least in the national and international sections of the sample. In the national and provincial sections, there was a higher proportion of women who said they wanted to find an alternative form of employment, but no equivalent difference in the proportion who said they wanted to drop out of the labour market altogether.

Discussion and Conclusion

If our survey enabled us to answer some questions about the composition of PNG's mining workforce and the nature of its contribution to 'development', it is equally important to acknowledge the limitations of this study and the number of questions to which it can only provide some very partial answers, if any answers at all. For example, the evidence presented in this paper does not speak to the distinction that Imbun (2006a, 2006b) has drawn between the parochial or 'tribal' section of the mining workforce and those whom he describes as members of a 'national proletariat' or 'labour aristocracy'. We cannot tell how many of the 45 individuals in the provincial section of our sample belong to the first two zones of entitlement, as opposed to the third one, and might therefore think of themselves, or else be treated, as the customary owners of land in the vicinity of the project on which they are employed. Even if we did know the number, it might be so small as to preclude any attempt to treat these individuals as a representative sample of some larger 'tribal' population. We do know that the 24 workers formerly employed on the Misima project belonged to the first two zones of entitlement when they were working there, but they are now working on other mining projects where they no longer have this status.

What we do know is that another section of the mining workforce is clearly under-represented in the national and provincial sections of our sample. This consists of individuals employed by the contractors who supply various goods and services to mining or petroleum companies, including those contractors who are engaged under the terms of the preferred area policy, and may thus qualify as 'landowner companies'. There is no reason to assume that this group of workers enjoys the same terms and conditions as those employed directly by mining and petroleum companies, nor is there any reason to assume that those employed by landowner companies are themselves recruited from the first two zones of entitlement and therefore count as 'landowners' in their own right (Bainton, 2017). The absence of landowner companies and their workers from our sample is one of the main reasons that our evidence does not speak to debates about the relationship between the distribution of formal employment and the social dynamics or internal stratification of mine-affected communities (Bainton & Banks, 2018).

Imbun's distinction between the two sections of the mining workforce is not meant to cast additional light on that particular problem, but it is meant to explain why some members of the workforce are inclined to join trade unions while others are not. By some accounts, the level of unionisation has been remarkably high in PNG's mining industry (Hess, 2001, pp. 71–72), and that is why union membership can be regarded as a qualification for membership of Imbun's 'national proletariat' or 'labour aristocracy'. However, we did not ask our respondents to tell us whether they were members of a trade union, so our own evidence is also silent on the question of how this variable might relate to the others that we investigated.

At least one of these other variables does relate to Imbun's distinction, since it is partly based on the distinction drawn by Bedford and Mamak (1976) between the three different 'strategies' adopted by members of the Bougainvillean mining workforce in the early 1970s. One of these they called the 'proletarian' strategy, which would obviously be the strategy adopted by members of Imbun's 'national proletariat', since it entails a certain level of commitment to formal employment as the source of one's identity as well as one's livelihood. The others, which they called 'peasant' and 'entrepreneurial' strategies, could be those adopted by members of Imbun's 'tribal' workforce, and the choice between them might then depend on the perceived capacity of these workers to elevate themselves from the status of mere 'landowners' to the status of successful entrepreneurs, possibly as directors of landowner companies (Bainton & Macintyre, 2013).

Only one of the workers in our sample expressed a desire to exchange his current job for what might conceivably be described as the life of a 'peasant', cultivating his own customary land. There was indeed a larger group that appeared to possess an 'entrepreneurial' strategy, but the evidence does not enable us to say how many of them were thinking about a business based on their status as customary landowners. Those who aspired to be 'consultants' were clearly not thinking along these lines at all, but were mostly aiming to shift their positions within the mining workforce from direct to indirect employment by the major companies. Some of those who said they wanted to own their own business may have had similar aims. The majority of workers in our sample were mainly concerned with the prospects of occupational mobility within the extractive industry sector. In that sense, we could say that they had a 'proletarian' strategy, although this term does not readily accommodate the small number who already occupied managerial positions or the larger number who aspired to follow in their footsteps.

This kind of debate about the orientations and aspirations of wage-earners in PNG is just one tiny part of a very old—if not positively old-fashioned—debate about the factors that inhibit the formation of a proletarian 'class consciousness' and thus prevent such people from behaving in accordance with their own 'economic interests'. Imbun and his colleagues may have found some traces of such thinking among the trade unionists in PNG's mining workforce. But even in this context, it is mainly construed as a reaction to the perceived injustice of a neo-colonial dual salary system. The question that goes begging here is whether the jobs that people occupy in the formal sector workforce, or the incomes they derive from these occupations, determine their social values and practices outside the workplace.

In their own analysis of the absence of class consciousness in this wider social sphere, two of Imbun's colleagues observe that there is a 'very small sub-set of the population, primarily politicians, ex-politicians or members of landowning groups benefiting from mineral resource rents [who] live an opulent lifestyle mimicking every excess of the non-indigenous lifestyle that they seek to emulate' (Jones & McGavin, 2015, pp. 9–10). The rest of the population, including members of the formal sector workforce, cannot accomplish this act of emulation because the number of their dependents, inside and outside of their own households, grows in proportion to the size of their incomes, and thus inhibits the accumulation of private wealth. While this observation is not based on their own data, it does accord with the general tenor of political discourse in PNG and with many of the observations made by other social scientists. What therefore seems to matter to most Papua New Guineans is not the relations of production that give rise to their incomes, but the property relations through which these incomes are (or are not) redistributed.

That is how the concept of the 'remittance economy' came to be incorporated into our own contribution to the World Bank's companion volume. On the basis of our own evidence, we estimated that the combined value of the three forms of remittance we identified could amount to as much as one-quarter of the net incomes of the workers in our sample. Even if the proportion appeared to be somewhat smaller in the international section, it was still substantial. We also argued that this should not simply be construed as a set of gifts, or the acquittal of a set of social obligations, but as a form of investment that was creating 'positive spillovers for development'. However, I have to concede that this is not the only way to interpret the evidence.

In her own study of what she calls 'transnational [Papua New Guinean] households' in Australia, some of which relied on wage incomes from the mining sector, Karen Sykes has come up with a new version of Bedford and Mamak's 'peasant strategy', but one that does not lead anywhere. She says that the wage-earners she interviewed thought of their own jobs as 'their only remaining gardens', and she takes this to mean that they saw themselves as 'environmental and economic refugees seeking a substitute for making a living from horticulture' (Sykes, 2017, p. 126).

She is thus inclined to regard these people as an extreme case of the 'dislocation' induced by geographical mobility, apparently because their greater distance from their home villages eliminates the capacity of their remittances to provide a guarantee of future access to clan land, either for themselves or their children (Sykes, 2017, p. 131).

We did not ask our own respondents *why* they made remittances. I doubt whether the inclusion of such a question in our survey would have produced a sensible set of responses, even if we partially begged the question by providing a limited set of possible answers. If the remittance economy is such a pervasive phenomenon, it would seem like asking people why they did what they thought was right and proper. But if Sykes is correct in her own interpretation of the motives of Papua New Guineans in Australia, there is no reason to think that those still living in PNG would have any other motives, even if they had a greater chance of securing the desired outcome. So should we regard the 'positive spillovers'—if there are any—as the unintended consequences of action that is primarily self-interested? And if so, how do the actors react to the prospect of their own failure to achieve their own objectives?

Even though there was a wide range of variation in the volume and value of the remittances reported by our respondents, we could not identify any other variables in our dataset, aside from the relative size of people's pay packets, that might explain this variation. Men and women were equally likely to participate in the remittance economy, so it seems reasonable to assume that married men and women were looking after their own relatives rather than those of their partners. If our workers were travelling towards some form of possessive individualism, most of them do not seem to have made too much progress.

If the workers in the international section of our sample spent a somewhat smaller proportion of their net incomes on remittances, we cannot necessarily take this as a reflection of their greater sense of alienation from relatives in PNG, or even the dawn of a recognition that they might not go back home. In the informal conversations that accompanied their interviews, they appeared to be quite happy with the improvement in their material circumstances, and certainly did not regret their decision to emigrate, even if five of them did say that they missed their friends and relatives at home (Filer et al., 2016, p. 123). Perhaps it was Peter—our 'bloke in the box'—who epitomised the peak of their desire, since he was only a member of this section by virtue of having his family home in

Sydney, even while he spent more than half his time back in PNG. Peter did not tell me that his tree-planting program was intended to secure his customary land rights, as well as to produce a new form of 'development' in his natal village. Perhaps he had a mix of motives that defies any simple distinction between self-interest and the common good. But his was surely not a 'peasant' strategy.

We did not ask the workers in the international section of our sample whether or how they proposed to follow Peter's example, but anecdotal evidence indicates that their capacity to do so was being thwarted by the refusal of some mining companies in PNG to treat them as 'expatriates' and reward them accordingly (N. Bainton, personal communication, 7 March 2019). This form of circular migration would simply add to the resentment caused by the dual salary system that had partly motivated their initial decision to move overseas. At the same time, the window of opportunity that had been opened by the 'resource boom' was already beginning to close. If that made it harder for well-qualified Papua New Guineans to opt out of the system, it did not make it any easier for the companies to justify the employment of 'genuine expatriates' who cost so much more than their national counterparts. When resource booms come to an end, cost-cutting imperatives become the order of the day. The financial incentive to speed up the localisation of the mining workforce has only added to the political pressure that can no longer be alleviated by the safety valve of emigration.

If Peter was the odd man out in the international section of our sample, then what are we to make of Hillary's status as a woman who was absent from our own sample, but who did figure in a mining company's own story about its contribution to the cause of gender equality? Women like Hillary were certainly present in the national section of our sample, and our evidence does seem to indicate a recent growth in the number of women employed in technical and managerial roles. Furthermore, the women in our sample distinguished themselves from the men by reference to their experience of promotion, or their hopes for further promotion, within their current line of work. None of the unmarried women expressed a desire to exchange their jobs for a life of domesticity as mothers and housewives, even if this was the fate that awaited them. But in this respect our sample is clearly one-sided. Although we asked the married workers in our sample if their spouses also had wage-earning jobs, we did not ask the women whether they were married to men who were also working in the mining industry or whether this had helped them to retain their own places in the formal workforce. Nor did we ask the married men what their unemployed wives got up to in their spare time, so we cannot tell whether these women were victims of the 'jealous husband syndrome' that is said to restrict the social and economic activities of many women in PNG's urban households (Gustafsson, 1999; Strathern, 1984).

In the period since our study was completed, there has been a noticeable increase in the number of corporate press releases advertising the recruitment and advancement of women in PNG's extractive industry workforce. These could be read as a somewhat belated response to the national 'women in mining' program initiated by the World Bank in 2002, even if that program was primarily aimed at strengthening the position of women as representatives of mine-affected communities in the first two zones of entitlement (Eftimie, 2011). Yet manifestations of corporate social responsibility, like the dispensation of remittances, can also be read as expressions of economic self-interest. Maybe women resemble the 'tribal' section of the workforce to the extent of being less recalcitrant, less likely to join a trade union, and less likely to leave their employer, or even leave the country, in search of a better job. That was the gist of the argument we made in our contribution to the World Bank's companion volume (Filer et al., 2016, p. 125), but it must be said that our evidence is largely circumstantial. If that argument was based on the opportunities created by a resource boom that was coming to an end at the time of our survey, there is no reason to assume a simple and constant relationship between the different forms of mobility and inequality that we were able to detect.

Acknowledgements

It would not have been possible to assemble the data discussed in this paper without the hard work of a dedicated team of interviewers, namely Marjorie Andrew, Rosemary Benjamin, Philippa Carr, Casper Damien, Benedict Imbun, Jennifer Krimbu, Bill Sagir and Deane Woruba. Ingrid Ahlgren did a great job of sorting the orientations and aspirations of the workers into a set of discrete categories. The author would also like to acknowledge the funding provided by the former Australian aid agency, AusAID, for the conduct of the original study, and the collaboration of the workers who were interviewed and some of the organisations in which they were employed. Nick Bainton and Debra Mcdougall provided detailed comments on an initial draft of this chapter, but should not be held accountable for anything in the final product.

References

Bainton, N. A. (2017). Migrants, labourers and landowners at the Lihir gold mine, Papua New Guinea. In C. Filer & P.-Y. Le Meur (Eds), *Large-scale mines and local-level politics: Between New Caledonia and Papua New Guinea* (pp. 313– 352). Canberra, ACT: ANU Press. doi.org/10.22459/LMLP.10.2017.11

Bainton, N. A. & Banks, G. (2018). Land and access: A framework for analysing mining, migration and development in Melanesia. *Sustainable Development, 26*, 450–460. doi.org/10.1002/sd.1890

Bainton, N. A. & Macintyre, M. (2013). 'My land, my work': Business development and large-scale mining in Papua New Guinea. *Research in Economic Anthropology, 33*, 139–165. doi.org/10.1108/S0190-1281(2013) 0000033008

Bedford, R. D. & Mamak, A. F. (1976). Bougainvilleans in urban wage employment: Some aspects of migrant flows and adaptive strategies. *Oceania, 46*(3), 169–187. doi.org/10.1002/j.1834-4461.1976.tb01241.x

Beer, B. & Schroedter, J. H. (2014). Social reproduction and ethnic boundaries: Marriage patterns through time and space among the Wampar, Papua New Guinea. *Sociologus, 64*(1), 1–28. doi.org/10.3790/soc.64.1.1

Beine, M., Docquier, F. & Rapoport, H. (2011). Brain drain and human capital formation in developing countries: Winners and losers. *Economic Journal, 118*(4), 631–652. doi.org/10.1111/j.1468-0297.2008.02135.x

Betcherman, G. & Rama, M. (Eds). (2016). *Jobs for development: Challenges and solutions in different country settings.* Oxford, England: Oxford University Press. doi.org/10.1093/acprof:oso/9780198754848.001.0001

Bollard, A., McKenzie, D., Morten, M. & Rapoport, H. (2011). Remittances and the brain drain revisited: The microdata show that more educated migrants remit more. *World Bank Economic Review, 25*(1), 132–156.

Boyd, D. J. (1990). *New wealth and old power: Circulation, remittances and the control of inequality in an Eastern Highlands community, Papua New Guinea.* Canberra, ACT: National Centre for Development Studies.

Carrier, J. G. (1984). *Education and society in a Manus village* (Educational Research Unit Report 47). Waigani, Papua New Guinea: University of Papua New Guinea.

Chowning, A. (1986). The development of ethnic identity and ethnic stereotypes on Papua New Guinea plantations. *Journal de la Société des Océanistes, 42*(82), 153–162. doi.org/10.3406/jso.1986.2829

Clunies Ross, A. (1984). *Migrants from fifty villages*. Boroko, Papua New Guinea: Institute of Applied Social and Economic Research.

Dalsgaard, S. (2013). The politics of remittance and the role of returning migrants: Localising capitalism in Manus Province, Papua New Guinea. *Research in Economic Anthropology, 33,* 277–302. doi.org/10.1108/S0190-1281(2013)0000033013

Eftimie, A. (2011). *Striking gold: Women in mining initiative in Papua New Guinea*. Washington, DC: International Finance Corporation.

Filer, C. (1990). The Bougainville rebellion, the mining industry and the process of social disintegration in Papua New Guinea. *Canberra Anthropology, 13*(1), 1–39.

Filer, C. (2005). The role of land-owning communities in Papua New Guinea's mineral policy framework. In E. Bastida, T. Wälde & J. Warden-Fernández (Eds), *International and comparative mineral law and policy: Trends and prospects* (pp. 903–932). The Hague, Netherlands: Kluwer Law International.

Filer, C., Andrew, M., Imbun, B. Y., Jenkins, P. & Sagir, B. (2016). Papua New Guinea: Jobs, poverty and resources. In G. Betcherman & M. Rama (Eds), *Jobs for development: Challenges and solutions in different country settings* (pp. 102–138). Oxford, England: Oxford University Press. doi.org/10.1093/acprof:oso/9780198754848.003.0004

Finlayson, M. (2002). *Sustainable development policy and sustainability planning framework for the mining sector in Papua New Guinea: Benefit stream analysis* (Working Paper 2). Port Moresby, Papua New Guinea: Papua New Guinea Mining Sector Institutional Strengthening Project.

Gerritsen, R. & Macintyre, M. (1991). Dilemmas of distribution: The Misima gold mine, Papua New Guinea. In J. Connell & R. Howitt (Eds), *Mining and indigenous peoples in Australasia* (pp. 35–54). Sydney, NSW: Sydney University Press.

Gibson, J. & McKenzie, D. (2011). Eight questions about brain drain. *Journal of Economic Perspectives, 25*(3), 107–128. doi.org/10.1257/jep.25.3.107

Gustafsson, B. (1999). *Traditions and modernities in gender roles: Transformations in kinship and marriage among the M'Buke from Manus Province.* Boroko, Papua New Guinea: Papua New Guinea National Research Institute.

Hayes, G. (1993). 'MIRAB' processes and development on small Pacific islands: A case study from the Southern Massim, Papua New Guinea. *Pacific Viewpoint, 34*(2), 153–178. doi.org/10.1111/apv.342002

Hess, M. (2001). What about the workers? Mining and labour in PNG. In B. Y. Imbun & P. A. McGavin (Eds), *Mining in Papua New Guinea: Analysis and policy implications* (pp. 63–80). Waigani, Papua New Guinea: University of Papua New Guinea Press.

Imbun, B. Y. (2006a). Local laborers in Papua New Guinea mining: Attracted or compelled to work? *The Contemporary Pacific, 18*(2), 315–333. doi.org/10.1353/cp.2006.0020

Imbun, B. Y. (2006b). Multinational mining companies and indigenous workers in Papua New Guinea: Tensions and challenges in employment relations. *Labour, Capital and Society, 39*(1), 112–148.

Imbun, B. Y. & Morris, R. (2001). Labour and mining in remote areas: Toward an assessment of benefits. In B. Y. Imbun & P. A. McGavin (Eds), *Mining in Papua New Guinea: Analysis and policy implications* (pp. 81–93). Waigani, Papua New Guinea: University of Papua New Guinea Press.

Jackson, R. T. (2000). Kekeisi kekeisi: A long term economic development plan for the Misima gold mine's impact area (Unpublished report). Papua New Guinea: Government of Papua New Guinea.

Jones, L. T. & McGavin, P. A. (2015). *Grappling afresh with labour resource challenges in Papua New Guinea* (Discussion Paper 96). Port Moresby, Papua New Guinea: Institute of National Affairs.

Levine, H. B. (1979). *Urbanisation in Papua New Guinea: A study of ambivalent townsmen.* Cambridge, England: Cambridge University Press.

Lind, A. W. (1969). *Inter-ethnic marriage in Papua New Guinea* (Bulletin 31). Canberra, ACT: New Guinea Research Unit, The Australian National University.

Macintyre, M. (2011a). Modernity, gender and mining: Experiences from Papua New Guinea. In K. Lahiri-Dutt (Ed.), *Gendering the field: Towards sustainable development for mining communities* (pp. 21–32). Canberra, ACT: ANU E Press. doi.org/10.22459/GF.03.2011.02

Macintyre, M. (2011b). Money changes everything: Papua New Guinean women in the modern economy. In M. Patterson & M. Macintyre (Eds), *Managing modernity in the Western Pacific* (pp. 90–120). St Lucia, Qld: University of Queensland Press.

Martin, K. (2013). *The death of the big men and the rise of the big shots: Custom and conflict in East New Britain.* New York, NY: Berghahn Books.

Morauta, L. (1984). *Left behind in the village: Economic and social conditions in an area of high outmigration.* Boroko, Papua New Guinea: Institute of Applied Social and Economic Research.

Packard, T. & Nguyen, T. V. (2014). *East Asia Pacific at work: Employment, enterprise and well-being.* Washington, DC: World Bank.

Rasmussen, A. E. (2015). *In the absence of the gift: New forms of value and personhood in a Papua New Guinea community.* New York, NY: Berghahn Books. doi.org/10.2307/j.ctt9qdb0f

Rosi, P. & Zimmer-Tamakoshi, L. (1993). Love and marriage among the educated elite in Port Moresby. In R. A. Marksbury (Ed.), *The business of marriage: Transformations in Oceanic matrimony* (pp. 175–204). Pittsburgh, PA: University of Pittsburgh Press.

Ryan, D. (1985). Bilocality and movement between village and town: Toaripi, Papua New Guinea. In M. Chapman & R. M. Prothero (Eds), *Circulation in population movement: Substance and concepts from the Melanesian case* (pp. 251–268). London, England: Routledge & Kegan Paul.

Ryan, D. (1993). Migration, urbanisation and rural-urban links: Toaripi in Port Moresby. In V. S. Lockwood, T. G. Harding & B. J. Wallace (Eds), *Contemporary Pacific societies: Studies in development and change* (pp. 219–232). Englewood Cliffs, NJ: Prentice-Hall.

Strathern, M. (1984). Domesticity and the denigration of women. In D. O'Brien & S. Tiffany (Eds), *Rethinking women's roles: Perspectives from the Pacific.* Berkeley, CA: University of California Press.

Sykes, K. (2017). A moral economy of the transnational Papua New Guinean household: Solidarity and estrangement while 'working other gardens'. In C. Gregory & J. Altman (Eds), *The quest for the good life in precarious times: Informal, ethnographic perspectives on the domestic moral economy* (pp. 105–138). Canberra, ACT: ANU Press. doi.org/10.22459/QGLPT.03.2018.06

The National. (2019, 14 January). Turnamur gets competency certificate as mine manager. *The National.* Retrieved from https://www.thenational.com.pg/turnamur-gets-competency-certificate-as-mine-manager/

Toft, S. (Ed.). (1986). *Domestic violence in urban Papua New Guinea* (Occasional Paper 19). Boroko, Papua New Guinea: Papua New Guinea Law Reform Commission.

World Bank. (2012). *World Development Report 2013: Jobs.* Washington, DC: World Bank. doi.org/10.1596/978-0-8213-9575-2

Zimmer-Tamakoshi, L. (1998). Women in town: Housewives, homemakers and household managers. In L. Zimmer-Tamakoshi (Ed.), *Modern Papua New Guinea* (pp. 195–210). Kirksville, MO: Thomas Jefferson University Press.

14

Menacing the Mine: Double Asymmetry and Mutual Incomprehension in Lihir

Nicholas Bainton

In September 2012, Newcrest Mining Limited, the operator of the massive Lihir gold mine in Papua New Guinea (PNG), reached a settlement with the local landowning communities over a set of issues concerning their compensation and benefits sharing agreement and the process for reviewing these commitments. Towards the end of the previous month, the customary landowners of the mine lease areas had placed taboo markers made from the leaves of a ginger root plant—known locally as *gorgor*—on numerous locations across the mine and the processing plant, bringing operations to a sudden halt. Their specific grievances were set against a backlog of impacts related to the mine and mounting frustrations over the failure of the benefits package to counter these unruly forms of change. This peculiar form of protest forced the mine to close for several days and created the conditions for landowners to negotiate their demands on their terms successfully. The unusual expression of the dispute grabbed the attention of local and international media outlets, as journalists tried to understand how a traditional taboo marker could be used to shut a large-scale mine, while market analysts speculated on the potential impact that this event would have on the share price of Newcrest, which had only acquired the mine as their flagship operation in 2010.¹ This was not the first time that Lihirians had invoked the *gorgor* to disrupt the mine, but it did result in one of the largest forced payments in the history of the operation.

Several days after this settlement was signed, a large crowd of people gathered in Putput village, one of two communities relocated in 1995 to make way for the mine. The group included members of the landowning community, representatives of the local-level government, company personnel and political leaders from New Ireland Province, who were involved in the formal review of the compensation and benefits sharing agreement that was then underway. The crowd had assembled around a men's house enclosure, which belonged to one of the matrilineal clan groups who claim customary ownership of land within the mining lease, to commence the ceremonial feasting activities that followed the removal of the *gorgor* and signalled an end to the latest dispute with the company. The feast was an opportunity to reaffirm a sense of unity among the landowners and to remind the company and the government of their obligations to the Lihirian community.

As proceedings began, the former Chairman of the Lihir Mining Area Landowners Association, Mark Soipang, stood in front of the crowd and, speaking into a microphone that carried his voice across the hamlet setting, reminded the community that the power of the *gorgor* rested upon their collective unity. He then appealed to the landowners to maintain their customs of cooperation, which would help them to secure future social and economic development from the mine. This Lihirian capacity for unity was rhetorically contrasted with an imagined fragmentation of highland New Guinea societies that would, for example, prevent them from working in a similar unified way to force the closure of a mine on their own land. The *gorgor* was cast as a morally superior way of registering issues, compared to the barbaric practices to which some other Papua New Guineans supposedly resort. Building on this sense of Lihirian cultural and moral exceptionalism, Soipang triumphantly declared:

---

1   The exploration program and feasibility studies for the Lihir project were conducted by a joint venture between Rio Tinto and Nuigini Mining Limited. Under the terms of the original project approvals, the Lihir project was transferred to a new Papua New Guinean company—Lihir Gold Limited (LGL). As the parent company, Rio Tinto established the Lihir Management Company to develop and operate the mine on behalf of LGL. In 2005, Rio Tinto divested its interests in Lihir, allowing the Lihir operation to become owned and operated by LGL, until a merger occurred in 2010 with Newcrest Mining Limited.

Now Newcrest knows the power of the *gorgor*. The power of the landowners can stop this project without any fighting. When we use the *gorgor* the whole plant site and all other work activities will stop. This is true power, and now they realise. This is great power, and now they have received the message. Since Newcrest took over the project it has taken them until now to realise that the landowners can exercise their power without resorting to violence and they can stop this project at any time. Now they realise you have power, so they will no longer be able to play with you. This kind of mindset will help us in the agreements review.

Soipang's strident statements were met with nods of approval from the assembled landowners. His speech then shifted to the details of the settlement they had recently obtained. This included, among other things, various concessions from the company to provide more funding to support landowner participation in the agreements review process and the administration of the association, commitments to complete the agreements review process in a timely manner and an unprecedented payment of PGK 40 million that the landowners association claimed was outstanding under the terms of the existing compensation and benefits agreement.[2]

This dispute pivoted on a combination of specific and widespread grievances that the landowners association used to mobilise a moment of mass collective action. It was also illustrative of a longer pattern of engagement between the company and the community—the company has consistently acknowledged this form of protest to avoid the kinds of violent confrontations witnessed at other mining projects. As one Australian journalist reported at the time, landowner stoppages are just one of the 'hazards' of doing business in PNG and, in the case of Lihir, 'it's happened before, and I am sure it will happen again' (Zappone, 2012). Indeed, it did. Over the years that followed, the customary landowners of the mine lease areas resorted to the use of the *gorgor* to force the hand of the company and the state on a range of interrelated issues. While these

---

2   This PGK 40 million payment has been an ongoing source of community dispute and the subject of much public debate, largely due to the inability of the landowners association to demonstrate how it has used this money to benefit the community. The Lihir Agreements Review process began in 2012 and, at the time of writing this chapter, it was still underway, due to the inability of the parties to reach an agreement over the size, content and structure of the new package and persistent divisions within the Lihirian community that have led to a crisis of representation. For a description of the Lihir agreements, known as the Integrated Benefits Package agreement, and the first agreement re-negotiation process from 2000 to 2007, see Bainton (2010).

sorts of 'community risks' may form part and parcel of resource extraction in a country such as PNG, this tells us very little about why these kinds of conflicts occur so frequently or their underlying causes.

The purpose of this chapter is to demonstrate how this particular form of protest has taken root in Lihir—how it has become the means through which the people of Lihir seek to assert their own sense of justice and affirm their ongoing power over the land. Although this practice bears some resemblance to other well-documented 'landowner tactics', such as roadblocks and simple brute force, the consistent use of this method deserves further scrutiny. This practice is not a 'weapon of the weak', in the sense conveyed by James Scott (1985). It is not a hidden form of resistance or insubordination, but rather an act of open defiance that contests any attempt by the company or the state to exercise exclusive authority over Lihirian lives and land. To be sure, most Lihirians recognise the 'limited authority' of the company to operate the mine (within the constraints of national laws and local agreements and the obligations these entail). However, when the company is seen to behave as though it holds a 'singular authority' that privileges corporate interests over local welfare—when community rights and entitlements are not upheld—this violates a local vision of justice and a confrontation will occur. To avoid reducing the history of landowner protests to an abbreviated economistic picture—a series of spasmodic responses to the political economy of resource extraction—we require a more explicit way of contextualising these events. I propose that the persistence of the *gorgor* can be understood as a version of Karl Polanyi's 'double movement', in which the authority of the company to extract and develop the natural resources contained in Lihir is continually challenged by the reassertion of customary land rights. The company and state seek to put a clear price on land (and the resources it contains) and attempt in good faith to negotiate what that price might be in terms of compensation, royalties and other benefits. Landowners often eagerly accept these payments, but not the terms on which they are made, and continue to assert rights over land that cannot be bought and sold on a market. Although this struggle partly arises from the uneven development and entrenched inequality generated by the mine, and the failure of the company and the state to enact certain obligations, the underlying reasons can be identified in the different ways that the company and the community understand their relationship and their common inability to reconcile these differences. The net result is a doubly asymmetrical relationship that is reinforced by a form of mutual incomprehension and a pervasive sense of moral indignation.

Indignant Landowners and the Double Movement

When Polanyi set out to develop his idea of the double movement, he aimed to show how market societies are constituted by two opposing movements. As different groups have attempted to expand the scope and influence of self-regulating markets, protective counter-movements have emerged to insulate society from these destructive market forces. What we now understand as capitalism is the product of both forms of movement. Polanyi's primary objective was to expose the idea of the self-regulating market as a purely utopian vision—to show how the market economy has been built upon a fictitious foundation that necessitates the constant intervention of the state. This argument rests upon his well-known account of 'real' and 'fictitious' commodities. If commodities are defined as 'things' that are 'produced' for sale on the market, then labour, land and money—the core components of industrial mining—must count as 'false' commodities, since labour and land are nothing more than human activity and subdivided nature and money is merely a token of one's purchasing power (Polanyi, 2001, p. 75). Quite simply, these 'things' were not originally produced for sale on a market. Therefore, the markets of these three things are inherently unstable—Polanyi suggested that, since the power of the state is required to maintain the stable supply and demand of these 'commodities', such power could also be used to counter their harmful impacts on society and the environment.

He insisted that it was morally wrong to treat nature and human beings as objects whose price will be determined entirely by the market and that such a concept violates their inherent sacredness. In the case of land, a double movement emerges as different social actors resist the enclosure, commodification and destruction of the natural environment (as they fight for the very foundations of life itself). These sorts of movements have a long history in countries such as PNG, where people commonly claim a special attachment to the environment and regularly reject the idea that land is merely a commodity—as the common refrain proclaims, 'land is life'. This belief is one aspect of the double movement in Lihir, whereby landowners assert a bundle of perceived and legal rights arising from their relationship to the land. Polanyi's approach has the added merit of decoupling these contests from narrowly defined class-based interests, which allows us to identify a broader ensemble of social actors involved in these struggles. Throughout PNG, these processes of encroachment and commodification have also contributed to the emergence of a particular kind of modern political identity that sustains a broader double movement of immovable property rights across the nation (Ballard, 1997; Filer, 2014).

Many years ago, Colin Filer described how an 'ideology of landownership' had begun to emerge in postcolonial PNG (1997). He claimed that there was a sense in which Papua New Guineans had only recently become 'landowners', although most of the population has maintained customary ownership of their land since the pre-colonial era. The contemporary concept of the 'customary landowner' can be traced to various activities in the colonial era that sought to demarcate traditional land tenure patterns and boundaries. These initiatives helped birth notions of 'traditional culture' and 'customary law'—expressed through the neo-Melanesian term *kastom*—which was, for the most part, conceptually opposed to ideas of 'the law', 'the government' or 'business' as separate domains of activity, even if they remained entangled in practice (Filer, 2006; Foster, 1995). Postcolonial legislation recognised the legal status of customary landowners and confirmed the requirement to pay compensation for damages or loss of land held under customary forms of ownership; in the context of large-scale mining, this can be understood as a form of 'ground rent' accruing to these owners. These processes also had the effect of creating a kind of collective status and a sense of opposition between this novel entity and external forces—for example, between 'landowners' and outsiders wanting to gain access to their lands, or between ideas of 'custom' and the prospect of 'development' (Filer, 1997, p. 163).

As the resources boom began in PNG in the 1980s, the term *landona* (or landowner) soon entered the lexicon of the national lingua franca (Tok Pisin), which completed the conceptual separation of 'the landowners' from 'their land', even where it might be commonly assumed that this kind of separation cannot be achieved in practice (Filer, 1997, p. 164). Filer argued that adherents to this ideology generally hold that 'development', which the state has singularly failed to deliver, will be obtained through the compensation and benefits provided by extractive companies in return for access to the land and natural resources that are held under various forms of customary tenure. Following a long history of political and economic marginalisation, and more than three decades of engagement with exploration companies and large-scale mining activities, this ideology has gained a firm grip on the entire Lihirian population and thoroughly determines their ideas of development and their interpretation of events (Bainton, 2010). When Lihirians make claims on the company, and when they use the *gorgor* to assert their rights, this can be understood as the performance of this ideology or the dramatisation of the double movement and the social relations of resource compensation.

Around the same time, Filer also argued that there is no real moral message or purpose to the multitude of ways in which Melanesian landowners 'menace' the mining industry (Filer, 1998, p. 166). This might well appear to be the case at the aggregate level because the convolution of social and political interests and geographical complexities often makes life very difficult for the industry; however, this does not mean that we should assume there is no moral basis to individual actions or forms of collective protest. Even when the stated objectives underpinning community protests appear incoherent, more often than not, landowners are motivated by a distinct belief that some form of fairness, justice or a sense of what 'ought' to occur, has been violated. These sentiments may be influenced by the feeling of entitlement that this ideology of landownership tends to foster, but in most cases, the injustices and impacts are experienced in material ways. In Lihir, these are rarely baseless claims, even when they appear to be overt forms of rent-seeking behaviour.

To understand how this sense of moral outrage motivates the double movement in Lihir, we can turn to E. P. Thompson's (1971) work on the moral economy of the rioting crowd in eighteenth-century England.[3] Thompson helps us to understand how ordinary people make their suffering visible and force those in power to respond. However, his original concern was also to demonstrate that the riot was, really, epiphenomenal.

---

3   The idea of the moral economy has a long genealogy that can be traced to the work of medieval scholars (Owen, 2009). The concept was most famously elaborated in the second half of the twentieth century by the social historian E. P. Thompson and later popularised by James C. Scott, when he adopted the term in his study on early–twentieth century peasant rebellions in South-East Asia (Scott, 1976). As Thompson would later write in his reflections on the theory of the moral economy, this idea has taken off in multiple amorphous directions; and since then, scholars have been discovering moral economies everywhere (Thompson, 1971). This is partly due to the popular tendency to focus on values rather than obligations—where the term is used to describe certain economic activities and the social relations and values that inform them, rather than the obligations that emerge through certain transactions. Further, the term has come to serve as a convenient slogan for any kind of economic activity ostensibly opposed to the self-serving materialism that supposedly underpins modern market-based societies or neoliberalism in general. Moral economy has become a symbol to be invoked, rather than a substantial concept. Nevertheless, just as Thompson sought to rescue the poor stockinger and other obsolete artisans from the condescension of posterity, several scholars have also attempted to rescue Thompson's original meaning in the idea of the moral economy and to correct the muddled state of the concept (e.g. Carrier, 2018; Edelman, 2005; Götz, 2015; see also Cox; Gewertz & Errington; Zimmer-Tamakoshi, this volume).

He wanted to show that historians had been placing the analytical punctuation mark in the wrong spot—after the riotous eruption—which, in turn, obscured their understanding of the reasons why crowds gathered and acted as they did. Thompson built his idea of the moral economy upon three foundational elements: a focus on the economic interactions between incipient class groups and the obligations that arise through transactions over time, the customs and rituals that shape these interactions and the idea of a 'legitimising notion' that motivates and justifies collective action. It is not my intention to make a case for a 'moral economy of extraction' in Lihir. But by drawing attention to the moral content of 'extractive ethics', we may better understand what makes Lihirians so angry and what is likely to generate an explosive situation. That is, if we are going to understand why the *gorgor* has become so thoroughly grounded as a form of protest, we would do well to place this punctuation mark at the trigger point, at the point of offence, rather than after the resulting explosion. Therefore, we might say that one particular feature of this double movement is the mutual reinforcement of the ideology of landownership and a pervasive feeling of enragement. Notwithstanding the fact that some demands are simply cunning claims, my objective is to rescue the sense of indignation that frequently justifies or 'legitimates' the claims that landowners make on the company, the state and fellow community members and how this leads to specific forms of political action.

In the following section, I sketch the development context that provides the material basis for the double movement in Lihir. I then describe the traditional beliefs and protocols surrounding the use of the *gorgor* and customary ways of dealing with conflict and the innovative ways that Lihirians adapted this customary practice to suit a new industrial context. This is followed by an overview of the form and content of the specific issues that typically trigger the use of the *gorgor* and successive attempts to reform the so-called 'abuse' of this customary practice. By way of conclusion, I provide an extended discussion on the source of mutual of incomprehension between the company and the community, the limits of the double movement and the prospects for a less antagonistic future.

Compensation as Development

In 1995, after a prolonged period of negotiations, Lihirian leaders reached an agreement with the state and the developer of the mine and signed a compensation and benefits sharing agreement known as the 'Integrated Benefits Package' (or the 'IBP agreement'). This bundled package included the compensation and relocation agreements between the company and the community, the Memorandum of Agreement (MOA) between the community and the three tiers of government and the company's environmental monitoring and management plan. The state was inclined to regard this agreement as the successful outcome of the recently established Development Forum process, which entailed a set of tripartite discussions between the national government, the New Ireland Provincial government and the project area landowners to secure their joint endorsement for the terms of the project and to spell out the distribution of the costs and benefits, and roles and responsibilities arising from the development of the mine (Filer, 1995). The IBP agreement contained a substantial set of commitments for royalty and compensation payments, equity in the mine, preferential employment and business contracts and community development projects and services for the 'affected-area communities'. Therefore, the state was probably also inclined to regard this as the manifestation of its own 'preferred area policy', which generally holds that the people living closest to new mines should receive the greatest access to the social and economic benefits generated by these projects.

From the vantage point of some corners of the community, the IBP agreement represented the outcome of their own supernatural powers, previously conceived and exercised in the form of various sociopolitical (or millenarian) movements that arose in the late colonial era and that forecast the transformation of Lihir into a type of Arcadian 'city' (Bainton, 2008; cf. Main, this volume). From this perspective, the landowners have always been in little doubt regarding the ownership of the mine and the wealth that it would generate. This perhaps also explains the belief among some community leaders that compensation is a 'process of providing a permanent substitute for the losses and impacts associated with the development of the mine', and their very genuine concern about the prospect of being 'passive observers on their own land' (Lihir Mining Area Landowners Association, 1994). These ideas and fears were first presented in the form of a memorandum to the PNG Law Reform Commission.

The landowners drafted this memorandum during the final stages of the Development Forum process, to explain the details of their position paper on the matter of compensation for social and environmental impacts. The final structure of the IBP agreement reflected their own version of the 'compensation principle', which the landowners had expressed as a kind of compensation formula, whereby 'Compensation = Destruction + Development + Security + Rehabilitation'. From their perspective, this encompassed the full range of payments and provisions that would offset the losses they would suffer and reflected their desire to control the development of their resources.[4] In other words, this formed an expression of their expectation that mining would provide the springboard to propel Lihirians into a desired development future.

Following the 1995 signing of the IBP agreement, a 'special mining lease' was issued for the development of the mine and processing facilities on the main island of Aniolam, which required the relocation of Putput and Kapit villages. By 1997, construction was complete, and gold production was underway. An additional 'lease for mining purposes' was also set in place on land close to Londolovit, Kunaie and Zuen villages, to house the development of a mining camp, a residential town site and business centre and an airstrip and other infrastructure to service the operation. These five villages were classified as 'affected-area' communities, which seemed to imply that the rest of Lihir was somehow 'non-affected'. This distinction was the basis of a new socioeconomic hierarchy that has since persisted. However, not all affected-area communities are 'equal'. Just as some communities are more affected than others, some have also benefited more. In short, mining has generated profound intra-Lihirian inequalities.

For example, the relocations of Putput and Kapit villages have resulted in two entirely different outcomes. The relocation of Putput was relatively successful—the community relocated to their own land outside the mine lease area, the new village looks like a model Melanesian suburb, and the villagers have access to economic opportunities and services (even if they remain highly dependent upon the company and have become deeply fractured as a group). They also wield a greater degree of power and influence because they own critical parcels of land within the mining lease. On the other hand, the Kapit community have experienced numerous forms of ongoing

4   For a more detailed description of this compensation formula, see Filer (1997, p. 160) and Bainton and Macintyre (forthcoming).

depredation since 1995, as successive attempts to physically relocate this community off the mining lease and re-establish the security of land tenure and livelihoods have failed, due to insufficient planning and resourcing for the process (Hemer, 2016). Unlike Putput, the Kapit community did not own sufficient land outside the lease to which they could relocate as a group. The community was to be scattered around Lihir over 12 different relocation sites; these were selected on the basis that individual households had some claim to land or close links to relatives living in those areas. This strategy has been unsuccessful; consequently, the Kapit community has been torn apart, and many households have experienced chronic immiseration, despite the vast amounts of wealth generated by the mining economy. Further, as I demonstrate below, the effects of these development failures have generated a deep sense of moral outrage.

Within years of signing the 1995 IBP agreement, it was also evident that many Lihirians rejected the view that this agreement satisfactorily balanced the adverse social, economic and environmental impacts of the project; further, people from the 'non-affected' villages argued that they were also affected. The company may have ideally regarded the fulfilment of the agreement as a settlement of debts in ways that are endorsed by the state. But for many Lihirians, the continued presence of the company and the persistent absence of the state, along with mounting frustrations over the flawed implementation of the agreement, create the conditions for the ongoing re-negotiation of mining benefits and wealth redistribution. And as the opening scene attests, as more issues and impacts become entangled over time, it is likely that no amount of compensation will ever suffice. In this environment, the *gorgor* is a primary means to assert a local vision of justice.

Changes and Innovations in the Use of a Traditional Taboo Marker

Traditional taboo markers, such as the *gorgor*, are commonly found throughout the Pacific. They are used for a variety of closely related purposes, such as signalling property ownership or restricting access to particular areas or resources. These taboo markers are often considered to be highly potent, and they may be used with forms of magic or sorcery, with the intention that individuals who breach these taboos will be afflicted by illness or even death. Different materials are used in different cultural settings, including coconut fronds, ferns or ginger and cordyline plant (*tanget*) leaves. Lihirians use the twisted leaves of the white flower variety of the ginger plant (Zingerberaceae) as a taboo marker (Figure 1). Although Lihirians and company employees more commonly use the Tok Pisin term *gorgor*, in the Lir language this taboo marker is termed *galgal* or *golgol* (depending upon the dialect), and these are also the names for the ginger plant itself. Lihirians use the *gorgor* in a range of quotidian ways to prevent people from accessing resources or demarcate spatial restrictions. It is also used to warn people of potential peril, including the pollution or dangerous power associated with death and ritual practices. In daily contexts, it is common to see the *gorgor* tied to fruit trees (e.g. coconut or betel nut stands), marking them as off limits. Essentially, the primary meaning implied by the *gorgor* is 'keep off' or 'no trespassing'. As explained by some Lihirians, a landowner cannot guard all their resources all the time; so there exists a need to signpost their ownership. As it was once explained in a Lihirian briefing paper to the company, the *gorgor* means the same as 'The Seventh Commandment: Thou shalt not steal' (Kabariu, 1998).

Lihirians place a strong emphasis upon demonstrating respect to maintain unity and harmony; consequently, they will often resort to indirect methods to address their grievances and conflicts. Although the qualities of leadership have changed over time, as new pathways to status and influence have emerged, and as contemporary circumstances demand a broader set of leadership skills (Bainton, 2008), there remains a general expectation for leaders to personify qualities of restraint and dignity. In this context, the *gorgor* plays an important role as a less confrontational and non-violent way of signalling the need to resolve an issue.

Traditionally, the *gorgor* was highly respected because people believed it to be imbued with certain supernatural powers. For example, after a person has died, Lihirians will place a *gorgor* on the garden of the deceased during the mourning period. Relatives are restricted from harvesting garden produce, as a sign of respect. Some Lihirians claim that, in the past, people who 'broke the rules' would develop visible signs of illness and infection (symptoms that would now be regarded as a case of yaws). By the late 1990s, it was evident that some of these restrictions had already broken down. Some people admitted that, rather than let good produce go to waste, they might harvest the yams of their deceased relatives. With the increased availability of penicillin to treat yaws, it is likely that some people concluded that the *gorgor* was no longer as potent as before. These changes may also relate to the general erosion of traditional forms of social control.

Figure 1: *Gorgor* **at Kapit village (2011).**
Source: Photo by Nick Bainton.

Most importantly, the *gorgor* is used to signal a dispute over the use or ownership of land and other resources. When it is used in this way, the *gorgor* conveys an important message about leadership status and the right to assert ownership over resources. In the past, senior male leaders exerted greater control over the ownership and use of land within their clans and lineage groups. When leaders use the *gorgor* to assert their rights, it is not simply a present claim made manifest, but also a statement about past transactions and anticipation of future claims. It marks their knowledge of the history of ownership surrounding the resources under question and their claim on future use. As an indirect way of signalling an issue, the *gorgor* also plays an important function in the maintenance of relationships. Here, the purpose of the *gorgor* is best characterised by the Lihirian term *tupakie*, which can mean 'order' or 'to stop a dispute'. In Lihirian terms, the *gorgor* is an extension or 'part' of the person who places it—the embodiment of property rights. This means that when someone ignores or cuts a *gorgor*, when they deliberately rip it off, this is akin to 'cutting' the owner of the *gorgor*—a direct assault upon their status and authority and an overt act of disrespect. In the past, the assumed potency of the *gorgor* generally prevented these kinds of acts. These sorts of breaches required the payment of shell money and pigs and the hosting of a small feast. In this context, the relational logic of personhood and property is brought to the fore, as property rights are experienced as a type of social relation.

As the opening scene in Putput village shows, certain customary protocols surround the removal of a *gorgor*, particularly when it marks a dispute over resources. The 'owner' of the *gorgor* is required to host a small feast once the *gorgor* is removed and the dispute is settled. This serves two purposes. It establishes or reconfirms the legitimacy of the owner of the resource, as they have killed a pig 'on top' of this resource—their authority and leadership is manifest in their capacity to mobilise the resources to host this feast. Ideally, the feast also reconciles the two parties and restores a certain degree of social harmony. The pig is not regarded as compensation, but rather as an ameliorative gift and a demonstration of power.

One of the earliest incidences of Lihirians using the *gorgor* to signal an issue with the company occurred in 1989, when the exploration company damaged the sacred Ailaya rock during the construction of the road around the Luise Harbour where the mine is located (Bainton, Ballard & Gillespie, 2012). This moment of innovation paved the way for future practices. In her annual social impact assessment reports to the company,

Martha Macintyre documented a growing pattern of discontentment and escalating claims against the company, as people from the affected-area villages sought new ways of gaining access to mine-related wealth during the early years of the operation. Following the first rush of compensation money, after the lease areas were cleared and construction had commenced, but before the mine was fully operational, she noted several occasions in which people had 'blocked access or threatened to do so as a strategy for gaining further benefits, or in order to make a complaint' (Macintyre, 1997, p. 19). Macintyre recalled a definite sense of ambiguity surrounding these early protests. Landowners were not entirely sure how the company would respond to the *gorgor* or whether white people were susceptible to its power. At this point in time, Lihirians clearly understood the *gorgor* as more than just a sign; much debate ensued as to whether it was appropriate to use the *gorgor* in this way and what consequences might arise. But when the company stopped work and responded to their complaints, any doubts surrounding its efficacy in this new industrial context were soon removed. If some landowners were surprised that it had 'actually worked', others quickly understood their newfound power and, with this novel realisation, the *gorgor* was soon transformed into a potent political sign.

In the second year of gold production, a large group from Putput village entered the mine and the processing plant and placed *gorgors* on the plant site and the mine entrance. The group threatened violence and demanded that the mine be shut down due to outstanding compensation payments and noncompliance with the terms of the compensation and benefits agreement. Mine equipment was shut down, and plant equipment was maintained on limited capacity while a solution was negotiated over the next few days. In her advice to the company, Macintyre wrote that this particular dispute highlighted the difference in the relationship between the company and affected-area communities, as compared with other villagers around Lihir: 'it shows that these villagers are volatile in their responses and willing to take direct action in pursuit of their interests' (Macintyre, 1998, p. 8). Their demands related to disturbances to village life from mining operations (from noise, dust and light pollution from the mine at night) and the failure to construct a vegetation buffer zone between the mine and Putput village. The negotiations demonstrated that the demand was essentially one for more monetary compensation rather than a response to intolerable disturbance, since the leaders did not want immediate practical resolution, but rather more 'rent'. These demands were somewhat undermined (although not retracted) when the same community leaders demanded street lighting for security reasons.

When Macintyre spoke with people from the non-affected villages about these demands, some people dismissed them, cynically, as 'proof' of landowner greed. These discussions also revealed underlying hostilities towards the affected-area villages, who were seen as having benefited disproportionately. People from Putput were viewed as being particularly 'opportunistic and wasteful' (Macintyre, 1998, p. 8). Some people interpreted these demands for more compensation as a sign that the Putput community had already misspent previous payments on beer and other consumables and were now dependent upon compensation as a source of income. Others were more ambivalent, suggesting that no quantity of money could really compensate for the permanent loss of land, which justified their demands. Women from Putput community expressed their concerns about the need for practical solutions to mining impacts and also stressed their need for cash, complaining that other people did not realise how difficult it was to now be dependent upon store-bought food.

In the first year of the new millennium, a large group of villagers from Malie Island (the closest outer island to the main island where the mine was built) stormed the company's community relations office in the public town site and placed *gorgors* on the office door. Community relations staff were essentially held hostage to force negotiations. Angered by the sediment plume from the mine that had washed onto their reefs and affected their marine environment, the villagers demanded recognition as an affected-area community and access to the compensation and benefits that this status entailed. This was one of many environmental claims that arose during the early years of the project; as people witnessed changes to their natural environment these became a source of general anxiety. Although some of these changes could be linked directly to the operation of the mine, others were not; however, this signalled a growing awareness and politicisation of environmental issues (Macintyre & Foale, 2004).

These early disputes captured the newly established tensions in Lihir. Some people were now more engaged in the cash economy or had more access to 'development', but were also reliant upon the mine for continuing access to cash and modern lifestyles, whereas others looked on with resentment. These conflicts demonstrated that compensation demands would only increase with time and that people would seek novel ways of expanding the basis for compensation from the company. More importantly, these disputes signalled that some Lihirians were beginning to regard environmental impacts as a 'resource', particularly people from outside the affected areas who could not appeal to landowner status as a form of leverage.

In most cases, the company responded to community issues and demands, investigating claims and paying some form of compensation. If these responses reflected the capacity of Rio Tinto (as the owner of the mine) to absorb some lessons from its experiences in Bougainville, where a local rebellion forced the permanent closure of the Panguna copper mine (Regan, 2017), they also served to reaffirm villagers' views that they were right and that this constituted a successful ploy for gaining money. Meanwhile, the scientific reports investigating environmental claims had little effect on local ecological knowledge and were often dismissed as a kind of corporate smokescreen designed to obfuscate the issue (Macintyre & Foale, 2000, p. 49). Within the first five years of the mining operation, it had become obvious to everyone that this was the most effective means for raising issues and leveraging outcomes. By 2001, Macintyre had observed that there was now a 'greater propensity to threaten *gorgors* or mine closure as an "opening gambit" in any argument or expression of discontent. This was not necessarily reflected in an increase in the number of *gorgors* actually put up, but was noticeable in discussions with villagers whenever they spoke about impact issues' (Macintyre & Foale, 2001, pp. 4–5). The strength of these threats derived from the customary expectation that, once a *gorgor* has been placed, the area is then off limits and work should cease immediately and the fear among company managers of a violent uprising if the *gorgor* was ignored.

Consistent Contentions

Since the early years of the operation, landowner grievances have remained reasonably stable in form. The specific issues have changed over time, in response to the initial development of the mine, subsequent expansions and land acquisitions, further environmental impacts, competition over new economic opportunities, shifting political divisions and alliances or changes to the content and governance arrangements of the IBP agreement. However, for the most part, the typology of grievances has remained consistent—these mostly relate to the unequal distribution of the benefits and burdens of extraction. These inequalities have a temporal and spatial dimension because some impacts are more contained to specific communities or locations (while others are more widespread) and because others may be experienced at specific moments in time (while others endure over much longer periods). This point is amply illustrated in the difference between the relocations of Putput and Kapit villages.

Other common grievances relate to frustrations around the non-fulfilment or delayed implementation of obligations in the IBP agreement, including infrastructure projects, service delivery and community development programs or specific compensation payments. These issues are compounded by the failure of the government to fulfil its duties under the terms of the MOA and the historical failure of the company to fully resolve outstanding grievances, some of which have developed into complex multi-layered 'legacy issues' that can now be understood as cumulative impacts. Many landowners maintain the belief that the company has not adequately compensated them for the permanent alteration of their land and the wider environmental effects of the operation. The broader community has often argued that all Lihirians have experienced these impacts in one way or another, not just the affected-area communities; and, therefore, they should all receive some form of compensation. In this environment, it is often very difficult to untangle one set of issues from another. The overall experience has reinforced the feeling that 'the mine' has failed to deliver the expected forms of development.

As the mining operation has expanded, there has been an increase in economic opportunities or 'commercial participation' through employment or contracts to provide services to the mine. Most landowners maintain high expectations to access these business contracts, which many regard as a form of compensation for the loss of land, or a form of rent for the activities occurring on their land. These expectations derive from Lihirian ideas about what it means to be a landowner, which are expressed idiomatically through the regular demand 'my land, my work' (Bainton & Macintyre, 2013). Whereas the wider community, with less access to mining-related benefits, often press for more contracting opportunities, landowners typically demand first priority on the basis that they have experienced the brunt of the impacts and made the greatest sacrifice—a position somewhat reinforced by the state's preferred area policy. Consequently, local competition over access to business contracts has become a source of acrimonious conflict and a daily point of contention with the company, because only some people are able to establish businesses and only some businesses are successful.

Dispossessed and Sidelined

These constant conflicts and controversies have generated a deeply felt sense of indignation and injustice across the broader Lihirian community and, particularly, among the landowners. The feelings of humiliation and resentment that are created by these issues find expression in multiple ways, including occasional violent outbursts at company staff and destructive forms of sabotage or 'negative agency' (Wardlow, 2006; also Main, this volume) directed at fellow community members. Specific issues that arise at particular moments in time may trigger confrontations with the company, prompting individuals to invoke the *gorgor* and threaten operations. But these are not simply irregular responses to regular impacts. These moments of protest are grounded in a growing sense of collective outrage over the wider state of affairs and individual feelings of desperation.

In their many letters to the company and in countless public forums, Lihirians have accused the company and the state of reducing them to mere 'beggars' or 'spectators' on their own land, confirming their earlier fears about simply 'observing' rather than 'participating' in the development of their resources. As the company has expanded its operations and increased gold production, many Lihirians feel that someone else is reaping the fruits of their land, while they continue to be consumed by their own internal differences. Company managers and state representatives would probably agree that Lihirians have been (wilfully) divided, to their own detriment. However, they would probably also make the case that Lihirians are involved in a range of major commercial ventures that support the mine, and they would just as likely cite annual expenditure under the terms of the IBP agreement and the company's commitment to local education, training and employment opportunities as a form of 'proof' that Lihirians are fully participating in the development game. These kinds of claims make little impact upon community sentiment, not least of all because they fail to acknowledge who controls the flow of benefits; and many Lihirians would respond that the company has played a game of 'divide and rule' that has prevented them from realising their development aspirations on their own land. Even if some Lihirians have benefited significantly from the mine (at the expense of others), for the vast majority, this has been an extended experience of frustrated development, because the anticipated levels of social and economic change have simply not materialised.

When Lihirians describe themselves as 'spectators on our own land', this is one specific aspect of the ideology of landownership. This common turn of phrase represents a particular kind of subjectivity that accompanies large-scale mining; it also reflects a definite sense of loss and the feeling that someone else is benefiting from 'their birthright'. Lihirian leaders may have willingly signed up to this mining project in the hope of a better future; however, few Lihirians accept the persistent conditions of structural inequality that it has produced. In everyday terms, this sense of dispossession pivots on the basic feeling that someone has taken something away from them—whether it be their land, their home or their justified entitlement to meaningful development—regardless of any legal agreements that may have been signed. For the Kapit community, this is a kind of double dispossession. Not only have they given up their land for the mine (which they believe has erased their cultural identity), but they have also failed to benefit from this unequal exchange in the same way as the Putput community and those elites or 'big shots' who have somehow captured the various benefit streams that should have flowed their way. They feel that they have been robbed of the opportunity to convert their relocation into a lasting form of development. The fact that the company and other Lihirians have gained from their specific loss has produced a special kind of bitterness. As a young Kapit leader once explained to me, 'Nick, you have to understand, it's like another man has taken your wife and children and he is the one sleeping with your wife and raising your children'. This kind of scenario is more or less what Karl Marx had in mind when he developed his theory of 'original' or 'primitive' accumulation or what David Harvey (2005) now calls 'accumulation by dispossession'.

These structures of dispossession also entail a deeply affective component, as lamentations for past connections to place inform local responses to the mine and related inequalities. These sentiments are manifest in a kind of existential distress—or what Glenn Albrecht and his collaborators (2007) have termed 'solastalgia'—which may be understood as a psychological response to the death of place. In 2016, this type of sorrow was on full display during the ceremonial events that marked the restoration of the old Kapit village in the special mining lease area as part of an agreed obligation to preserve some of their original hamlets, graves and ceremonial grounds. A senior female leader from Kapit named Theresia Giar composed the following song with an accompanying female dance. The women wept as they performed in front of the assembled crowd.

Oo a tadanis sina hanio imen kinge	Oo very sorry for our home has been destroyed
Oo a tadanis sina hanio imen kinge	Oo very sorry for our home has been destroyed
A company sa rangsenie a hanio imen kinge	The company destroyed this home of ours
Kai men gele gen a kakien a miniel erton iiyen kinge	Today we want to mark a sign of coming together for all of us here
Kai mil, ge kasiri herton na hiyen si na sa ben	Later there will be no more coming together for us here
Oo a tadanis, sina bertume men gesa hinego imen e Kapit	Oo very sorry for our ancestors with you all and we will be leaving you all at Kapit
Oo a tadanis si na e tume gesa hin endie imen ni Kapit	Oo very sorry for our ancestors leaving them now at Kapit
	[repeat]

If these feelings of sadness, resentment and indignation are the price that some people have paid for development in Lihir, these emotions are also a source of motivation that drives the double movement. In the case of Kapit, this sense of loss and outrage has underpinned their rational demands for development (including the fulfilment of basic relocation obligations) and fuelled the many times that they have invoked the *gorgor* to resist the presence of the company on their ancestral land and to press for better outcomes. Although some moments of protest may be aimed at capturing more concessions, these moments and movements almost always register dissatisfaction with the existing terms of engagement and reassert an attachment to land.

Mineras Interruptus

Over the years, Lihirians have used the *gorgor* no less than 60 times to interrupt some aspect of the mining operation. On at least 12 of these occasions, this has resulted in the total shutdown of the mine, lasting from less than one day to more than one week. The frequency with which Lihirians threaten to use the *gorgor* is, of course, much higher. Almost every year since mining has begun, there has been some form of partial or total disruption to operations due to landowner grievances. Not all these events have received media coverage, or been reported in annual company reports or market notifications; however, every time the *gorgor* is used in this way, it generates considerable public attention in Lihir and consumes a great deal of energy and resources within the company as staff rush to respond and re-coordinate their operations. Although we may find comparable levels of disruption at other extractive projects, there is often more variety in the chosen methods (see Figure 2 and Video 1 for an example of the use of the *gorgor*).

These patterns of (partial) disruption are closely related to customary land tenure arrangements in the mining lease areas. The leases are divided into some 140 numbered 'blocks' that roughly correspond to the customary boundaries of the different parcels of land owned by different lineages and clans. Some of these blocks are larger than others, and some are more 'valuable' than others—for example, the blocks that contain the processing plant and administration offices or the mining pit are more important for daily operations. The ability to leverage the company is contingent upon the patterns of land ownership; a 'non-landowner' has no customary right to use the *gorgor* on the mine, whereas landowners can only assert their rights on their own lease area blocks. In this way, contemporary economic and political inequalities roughly map against the customary geography underpinning the mining lease areas.

Figure 2: *Gorgor* on mine lease area gates (2012).
Source: Photo by Nick Bainton.

Most of the time, issues are raised by individuals and their immediate lineage, which can restrict the effect or impact of the *gorgor*, depending upon which lease area blocks they own. When issues are raised at a broader community level, the different clans (or 'block owners') must agree on a collective plan of action. Lihirian society has undergone a steady process of atomisation; therefore, it now requires much more effort to mobilise different lineages and factions, even within the same clan or village, many of whom now have competing interests and agendas.

For the most part, the company has 'respected' the *gorgor* as a cultural practice and has not intentionally removed a *gorgor* before negotiations have begun. Company managers have generally recognised that the *gorgor* has prevented the kind of physical violence found at other resource extraction projects around the region. But as Macintyre has previously observed, in practice, this tends to further validate the use of the *gorgor* as a legitimate way of gaining political traction and a means for expressing landowner status. Even when issues are not resolved to the satisfaction of the community, this typically has the same effect.

In 2015, the national regulator of the industry, the Mineral Resources Authority, instructed the police force to remove the *gorgors* that had been placed on the mine during one particular moment of protest that involved the landowning community and their association. The actions of the state only served to strengthen local antipathy towards the company—widely thought to have requested the state to intervene in the dispute—and further politicised the *gorgor* as a cultural institution that symbolised the rights and autonomy of the community vis-à-vis the state. This was also the first time in the history of the mine that a *gorgor* had been 'ignored' and removed before the issue was resolved, which only strengthened the determination of the landowners and deepened their sense of indignation.

From a community perspective, using the *gorgor* in this way can function as a pressure release valve. As tensions rise over specific issues and the pressure for direct action increases within the community, this public act of resistance can have a cathartic effect. Having reasserted their status as landowners, drawn attention to the issue and reminded the company and the state of their obligations (perceived, contractual or otherwise)—defining the terms of engagement—the leaders are then able to begin resolving matters. However, these constitute highly stressful moments in the life of the community. Leaders come under immense pressure to maintain control of events and to achieve favourable outcomes to justify their actions. Factions may threaten to negotiate side deals with the company or the government or seek to sabotage events for their own personal gain. While some observers might rejoice in these cases of counter-movement, these moments weigh heavily upon the community, which serves to highlight the importance of the customary feast once issues have been 'resolved'.

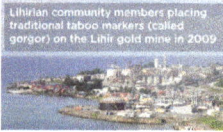

Video 1: Lihir community members placing traditional taboo markers (*gorgor*) on the Lihir gold mine as a sign of protest (2009).
Source: Compiled by Nick Bainton.
Video content is available online: press.anu.edu.au/ publications/series/pacific/unequal-lives

In acting out this ideology, Lihirians have also created a form of hegemony. Lihirians have managed to liberate a key symbol of male authority, which has been scaled up and loaded with new meaning to enable it to perform much heavier work in an industrial context. In doing so, Lihirians have literally and metaphorically transferred power from the 'ground' or the 'base' to the 'top' of the hierarchical structure that is occupied by the company and the state. This power is then transferred back 'down', in the form of a dominant Lihirian ideology, as company managers and state representatives reinforce a certain pattern of behaviour through their mutual acceptance (at least momentarily in practice) of these terms of engagement. A form of cultural ascendancy is then evidenced in the language that is sometimes used by company staff to describe these events—such as 'code red', a 'big *gorgor*' or a 'major *gorgor*'. This, in turn, animates the *gorgor* and suggests a certain fetishisation—it is the *gorgor* that has closed the mine rather than the landowners who placed it. Although some Lihirians might interpret this as proof that some company managers have come to understand the *gorgor* as more than just a sign, most Lihirians would regard this as evidence of their ability to influence the company or to penetrate corporate consciousness. As Lihirians have come to use the *gorgor* in more militaristic ways—as a direct assault upon the company—they have instilled a constant fear of 'mineras interruptus' or operational disruption (Owen, 2016). A transferal of power occurs as the *gorgor*—a symbol of leadership and property ownership—has come to dominate the thoughts of senior leaders in the company and the state, forcing them to accept Lihirian ideas about the relationship between resource ownership and development. In these moments, Lihirians have managed to thoroughly menace the mine.

Reforming Custom

Many Lihirians are concerned about the apparent abuse of this customary practice. These concerns stem from the belief that there are times when the *gorgor* has been used in inappropriate ways, without a genuine reason, appropriate authority or regard for the customary protocols for removal. Some Lihirians have even argued that the *gorgor* should not be used in a modern industrial setting, that it belongs 'in the village' (along with other customary practices) and that quarantining custom is the most effective way to maintain 'traditional authenticity'.

Lihirians are also highly critical of people who use the *gorgor* when they are drunk; however, many concede that it has become common for people to get drunk to precipitate arguments that they would otherwise be too ashamed to raise (due to the prevailing emphasis upon showing respect) and that men, in particular, will get drunk to gather the courage to confront the company directly. These changes are directly mirrored in everyday village contexts. Placing a *gorgor* when drunk is considered to be antithetical to the calm assuredness expected of leaders and also unnecessary, if there is a genuine cause. Similar arguments are made against the practice of placing the *gorgor* on the mine by stealth during the night.

Many Lihirians find it problematic when institutions such as the local-level government or the landowners association use the *gorgor* in their battles against each other, but less so when they use the *gorgor* against the company. When these institutions use the *gorgor*, they will rely upon their members with customary ownership rights over the location in question to place the taboo. However, for some observers, the *gorgor* is thought to be the preserve of the owners of a resource, rather than a representative or corporate body. From the perspective of the company, when the landowners association mobilises landowners to place a *gorgor* on the mine, the association appears to be using the community to fight its own institutional battles. From the perspective of the association, this is a false distinction, because its leadership and legitimacy are derived from the same community. These moments also draw attention to the emerging crisis of representation in Lihir, because not all Lihirians support the association—and this is a point that the company has often sought to convey.

The *gorgor* has sometimes been used by drunken youths to signal intergenerational struggles with maternal uncles over the inheritance of land and mine-related wealth. The *gorgor* has frequently been used to escalate relatively minor issues that might otherwise be resolved in less contentious ways, which often highlights greater, underlying sociopolitical fault lines. Non-Lihirian labourers have also appropriated the *gorgor* on some occasions to signal industrial disputes with the company. In 2011, drunken landowners from Kapit village attempted to place a *gorgor* around the neck of an expatriate manager from the company as a sign of their frustration over specific relocation impacts. Taken as a whole, these kinds of practices are considered by many Lihirians as a perversion of tradition, but in some ways, they might also be interpreted as the inevitable outcome of the liberation of symbols.

Notwithstanding these local critiques, most Lihirians vehemently maintain their right to use the *gorgor* to signal an issue with the company, as long as people follow the proper customary laws, expressed locally as '*ol i mas bihainim ol kastom lo*'. What this actually means, in practice, has been the subject of intense debate and numerous initiatives designed to formalise the use of the *gorgor*. These concerns about the *gorgor* form part of a much broader set of concerns that originated during the colonial period about the preservation of traditional values and practices, or *kastom*, in the face of rapid social change (Bainton, 2008). At various times, the landowners association and the local-level government have tried to codify the use of the *gorgor*. This has precedents in their previous attempts to codify local land rules to help reduce disputes generated by the mine (Kabariu, 1998) and in their ongoing efforts to document customary feasting protocols to 'strengthen' and 'preserve' Lihirian culture (Bainton, 2010; Bainton & Macintyre, 2016).

In 2008, the landowners association developed the first of several policies for regulating the use of the *gorgor*. This was not the first time Lihirians had produced a set of *gorgor* 'rules'; however, it was the most significant attempt to integrate the *gorgor* into more formalised dispute-handling processes with the company. The policy contained a set of procedures and 'customary penalties' for deviation. This included the requirement to 'register intent' to place a *gorgor* and the establishment of a 'dispute resolution committee' who would then decide whether cases are 'genuine' or not. This was intended to provide some steps to slow the *gorgor* reflex. The idea was to create a kind of *gorgor* circuit breaker that would facilitate more 'peaceful' and orderly dispute resolution processes. Many

Lihirians highlighted the irony of this proposition, arguing that the *gorgor* is their peaceful solution. These efforts to control landowner practices ultimately foundered, much like other Lihirian attempts to codify customary activities.

At the time, and in the absence of an alternative dispute-handling mechanism, this policy was somewhat supported by the company and it influenced how some managers responded to *gorgor* events. For example, when threats were made against the company, managers might ask whether the aggrieved party had complied with 'their own policy' and whether the resulting *gorgor* should be considered 'legitimate' and observed; at the very least, this had the effect of buying some more time in the negotiation process. The company has never formally supported the use of the *gorgor* on its operations, and it certainly could not legally endorse a policy that effectively sanctions landowners to disrupt the mine.

From the perspective of the community, the place of the *gorgor* in company–community dispute resolution processes has never really been satisfactorily resolved. Suggestions have been made in different forums to allow the *gorgor* to be used in a purely symbolic way to raise an issue—but without actually disrupting operations—or to create a dedicated '*gorgor* zone' in which it might be used. Lihirians have rejected both suggestions for the obvious reason that it removes the power of the *gorgor* and because a dedicated zone would logically be restricted to the customary owners of that area. These incongruities highlight the incompatibility between the *gorgor* as a cultural institution and conventional company-driven dispute-handling mechanisms, because the *gorgor* is not merely a means for signalling an issue, but also specifically entails the performance of power and identity.

The company has found itself caught between its stated support for Lihirian customs and traditions—as part of its corporate social responsibility policies—and an industrial ethic that demands uninterrupted operational output and adherence to the law. These tensions are mirrored at the level of the state, between the constitutional commitment to acknowledge 'worthy customs' and the terms of the Mining Act that deem any community disruption to mining operations to be illegal. If there was any ambiguity in the state's position, this was resolved in 2014, when the managing director of the Mineral Resources Authority (MRA) issued a public notice in Lihir clarifying the legal status of the *gorgor* (which was then put to good effect in 2015). The notice acknowledged the *gorgor* as a traditional practice that 'has a time and a place' and stated that, should the invoking of the *gorgor* obstruct the execution of the company's rights under the Mining Act, this would amount to a punishable offence. The issuing of this public notice may have strengthened the resolve of the company to hold the line against the 'illegal' use of the *gorgor*, but for most Lihirians, it has done little to change their belief in their inalienable customary right to protest in this way.

Development Failure and Corporate Social Confusion

Lihirians have made use of a variety of means to publicly air their grievances regarding the impacts and inequities generated by the mine, including rallies and avoidance strategies, media campaigns and public notices and social media debates and position papers directed at the company. However, on their own, these tactics generally gain limited traction. On the other hand, the *gorgor* has become a deeply grounded and proven form of protest, which reflects the centrality of land as both the source of many struggles and the source of sovereignty underpinning these collective actions.

The continual complaint about being spectators on their own land serves to emphasise the failures or inconsistencies of the corporate ideology of development, as much as it also reflects a certain idealisation inherent in the Lihirian ideology of landownership. This repeated reference to the role of spectators also suggests that we could conceptualise the double movement in Lihir as a kind of football match between the company and the community. If we follow this line of thought, the question becomes whether the *gorgor* is a kind of (political) football, a goal scored by the community, a linesman's flag, a referee's whistle or even a pitch invasion by the spectators. As we have seen, it may represent different things on different occasions. If the *gorgor* represents a referee's whistle, it could signal a stoppage in 'play' (and possibly a penalty, as witnessed in Putput village) or a half-time or full-time mark in a particular match (or dispute). If the *gorgor* serves as a referee's whistle, the community also plays the role of referee as they attempt to interpret, and even make up, the rules of the game that is being played. Further, as they have directed the field of play (and set the 'rules of the *gorgor*'), this has been one particular way to demonstrate their superiority over the company.

Therefore, if the spectators are fed up with being spectators, the question is whether they want to be players or referees or rule-makers instead (or whether they just want to mount a pitch invasion). This also raises a troublesome question concerning the role of Lihirian labourers working for the company and whether they are permitted to take part in this game, or whether they too must spectate from the sidelines. If this is the case, there is no reason to assume that they will consistently support either side and, in practice, many have hedged their bets. The state has periodically abdicated its role as referee, even if the MRA has stationed an officer in Lihir to adjudicate disputes. At different junctures, both sides have surely suspected certain actors of covertly transferring to the other team, even while the state has maintained some responsibility for the entire league to ensure the sport endures. However, as the games continue, and the rules are adapted to suit increasingly complex circumstances, it becomes ever more difficult to determine the difference between a point scored and a home goal because minor victories often produce lasting legacies and inadvertent consequences for both sides. The ground upon which this unholy match is being played might be one of many locations for some greater battle between the forces of industrial greed and 'collectivist' counter-movements, but it also represents the prize that will be awarded to the victor in a very specific contest. Consequently, access to land within the lease areas has become a zero-sum game—the company argues that it has already paid for exclusive occupancy, while the community continually forces the company to renegotiate its access to this bounded arena.

This analogy, like all analogies, is liable to break down at some point; however, it does help to highlight the different motivations and entanglements between the different social actors within this space, the complex ways that Lihirians have responded to the inequalities and dispossessions of extraction and the assorted ways that the *gorgor* has been used and understood. To simplify this situation, we might say that Lihirian acts of protest are deliberate attempts to remove any form of wealth and power that makes them feel inferior or dependent in their relationship with the company (Filer, 1997, p. 182). If this is the case, it is very unlikely that the company will ever be able to settle upon a 'fair trade' that balances out the benefits and burdens of extraction to the satisfaction of the entire community—the agreements review process may well continue in one form or another for the life of the mine, as a perpetual manifestation of this double movement. More precisely, if Lihirian demands are really about wrestling control of the processes of developing their natural resources, it seems that some Lihirians are less interested in trying to balance out this necessarily asymmetrical relationship—even while they actively try to redirect the flow of wealth—than in demonstrating that a foreign company is powerless on their land. This is certainly one inference we can make from the hostile ways in which some landowners invoke the *gorgor*.

At the outset, I suggested that the fundamental reasons for this stalemate can be found in the different ways that Lihirians and the company regard their relationship. As Filer notes in his chapter of this volume, we commonly find that most senior (male) landowners throughout PNG tend to view themselves as being in a landlord–tenant relationship with mining companies, whereas most (expatriate) mining company managers prefer to see themselves in a patron–client relationship with these same community leaders. This is the source of a persistent double asymmetry. In Lihir, some of these managers also tend to see themselves as the heralds of modernity and the benevolent benefactors of economic development through the employment opportunities, training, business contracts or community development programs that the company can provide under their direction. Although these magnanimous acts are sometimes subject to the whims of individual managers, or the conditions within the benefits package, they are also presented as evidence of the company's commitment to the values of corporate social responsibility.

The leaders of the landowners association would rather see themselves as the vanguards of a cultural and socioeconomic movement that will harness the wealth from the mine to achieve their idea of development on their own terms—what an earlier generation of leaders called the 'Lihir society reform' program and the current generation now call the 'Lihir Destiny' vision (Bainton, 2010). These positions are premised upon rather different ideas of development, and this is one source of the state of mutual incomprehension between the company and the community. If the company is convinced that successful operations are good for the Lihirian population (because more corporate profits will supposedly create more opportunities to invest in Lihir), it seems that most Lihirians have concluded that this looks too much like a trickle-down theory of development or a form of 'drip-feeding' that is likely to benefit the company before it benefits the community. This corporate ideology of development constitutes an affront to Lihirian ideas of land ownership and their role as 'landlords' and exacerbates their sense of subordination and indignation.

A second reinforcing reason for this condition of confusion can be found in the particular brand of corporate social responsibility (CSR) to which the company subscribes. For some managers, the very notion of CSR is perplexing for reasons other than the belief that it represents a set of global policy constraints on their primary commitment to shareholder-capitalism. The first reason is the double asymmetry itself, where company managers struggle to reconcile their dual roles as both patrons and clients. The second reason is the fact that, in the Lihir context, CSR commitments are partially mandated by the state's preferred area policy that had become a feature of the nation's mineral policy landscape by the time the Lihir IBP agreement had been signed in 1995. In practice, this policy effectively creates a set of concentric rings or 'zones of entitlement' around each major mining project, starting with the innermost ring, which is occupied by the customary landowners of the mining lease areas, followed by the project area people, the residents of the region, and the outermost ring, which is occupied by the population or government of the nation as a whole (see Filer, this volume). If this policy was originally a response to the threat of succession from the province that hosted the ill-fated Panguna mine, where the landowners argued that they most certainly did not receive any preferential treatment, this commitment was not framed in the international language of CSR, because this policy was developed before the notion of CSR had begun to permeate the discourse of the mining industry in the 1990s (Dashwood, 2012; Filer, Burton & Banks, 2008).

In 1998, when Rio Tinto was still the owner of the Lihir gold mine, and when the lessons from Panguna were still fresh, the World Bank was leading an initiative to assess the extent to which the world's largest mining and petroleum companies were committed to the emerging principles of CSR. The World Bank had asked Rio Tinto, in addition to several of their peers, to indicate which of their own operations might be taken as an example of good practice in terms of managing social and environmental issues. Rio Tinto duly nominated the Lihir operation as its own best example of CSR in practice (Filer et al., 2008). Although the decision to nominate Lihir appeared to contradict the findings of the early social impact monitoring reports, part of the reason for this decision may have been due to a belief within the company that the significant size and scope of the recently settled IBP agreement should be matched by a corresponding degree of community support for the project.[5]

---

5   As Filer, Banks and Burton observed, it was probably also due to the pre-existing relationship between Lihir Gold Limited and the World Bank, since the project's risk insurance was covered by the Multilateral Investment Guarantee Agency (Filer et al., 2008, p. 167).

This declaration happened to coincide with a set of proclamations from the chairman of the board about the need to shift from a 'cost culture' to a 'value culture', supposedly expressed in a commitment to the idea of the 'triple bottom line'.[6] Shortly afterwards, Rio Tinto came to the conclusion that no degree of patronage dispensed to the Lihir community would actually secure its 'social licence to operate'—this is presumably one reason why Rio Tinto then decided in 2005 to divest itself of all interests in Lihir. It is entirely possible that Newcrest will reach the same conclusion, even if its rhetorical commitments to CSR are now framed by its subscription to various international norms and standards as a newly admitted member of the International Council of Mining and Metals. It remains to be seen whether these events will translate into substantially different outcomes on the ground or whether they will simply reinforce the state of incomprehension.

The point of this brief excursion is to highlight the fact that each successive operator of the Lihir gold mine has reverted to a 'cost culture' every time they have encountered 'hard times', whichever way this may be defined during different historical periods. Even if the overall quantum of compensation and social and economic benefits has increased, much of which exists as legal obligations under the terms of the IBP agreement, there is always room to devise strategies to essentially shrink the size of the preferred area and, therefore, the number of clients who need patronage of one form or another. This may arrive in the form of fewer resources to implement existing obligations and services, or less discretionary spending on so-called CSR programs or simply tighter contract management procedures for landowner companies, which may result in smaller profit margins. The company may publicly claim that these initiatives are justified to create new efficiencies or to address program failures and, thus, to enhance the positive effect of future activities. Even if these shrinking schemes seem to be consistent with the same 'network-cutting' strategies of those 'big shots' who aim to keep their wealth contained to the inner zone of entitlement (Bainton, 2009; Martin, 2013), these same landowners will invariably argue that these strategies still constitute a symbolic violation of the original IBP agreement. This is the source of immense frustration within the community and the cause of ongoing bewilderment for all.

---

6   The 'triple bottom line' represents an attempt to broaden the 'bottom line' from a primary concern with profits to include environmental and social considerations in the operation of a business.

Colin Filer once suggested to me that this state of affairs could be represented as a kind of formula whereby: the ideology of landownership + CSR= double asymmetry + mutual incomprehension. I am inclined to call this 'Filer's formula for development failure', because it seems to explain the terminal outcomes experienced in Lihir and the unlikeliness of ever finding an acceptable solution to the development puzzle. This also helps to explain why the original compensation formula proposed by the landowners association has not produced the sorts of outcomes they had once envisioned.

We might then ask where this leaves Thompson's concept of the moral economy. There is, at least, one important difference between Thompson's eighteenth-century England and contemporary Melanesia. The social and economic transitions that Thompson described played out over approximately a hundred years or more. This meant, among other things, that a moral economy had formed through the history of transactions between different groups based upon a system of mutuality. In some circumstances, the crowd was supported by the authorities as they threatened or actually rioted against perceived violations of customary norms and entitlements. The authorities were sometimes prisoners of the people and were complicit in these riots and the validation of local legitimising notions. There is very little evidence of this kind of shared understanding between the different groups who are present in Melanesian 'mining arenas' (Bainton & Owen, 2019), much less so in Lihir. In other words, the community is not responding to the violation of a pre-existing social contract by creating an ideologically serviceable past to defend the norms and practices of an earlier order—although there are definite parallels to be found in the degree of restraint that accompanies the use of the *gorgor* and the distributive actions of Thompson's rioting crowd. Rather, from a community perspective, it is the company who is mystified about the real social order of extraction; the community must, therefore, set the company straight, to defend their interests. The very act of transferring power from the ground and creating a form of cultural hegemony forces some degree of mutual understanding or 'custom in common', as Thompson might have it. The net result of this is to make the company and the state prisoners of the people—if only for a limited moment in time—and to create the conditions in which their moral failings can be comprehended, to produce the desired outcome based upon a Lihirian understanding of development.

By way of conclusion, it is worth considering the limits of this kind of protest by indignant crowds. From the preceding discussion, it is evident that Lihirians are not able to act in the way that Polanyi imagined that a state could, to limit the injustices that accompany the commodification of labour, land and money. In asserting their non-commodifiable rights to land, some Lihirians have successfully extracted money and benefits; however, some have been extraordinarily excluded. Even if local leaders genuinely want to ensure just outcomes for all Lihirians, they do not have the scale to achieve this outcome, and one result of their *gorgor* activism has been greater inequality in Lihir. In the absence of the state and effective governance, these re-assertions of highly localised sovereignty have not slowed or halted the broader processes of dispossession that form part of capitalism more broadly. Lihirian landowners cannot tame the market—they can merely menace it.

The question then becomes whether Lihir can transcend this double movement or whether Lihir is doomed to remain firmly in its grip. In their work on 'extractive relations', my colleagues John Owen and Deanna Kemp have argued that the only practical solution to address this constant state of 'trading in powers' is for the global mining industry to internalise the social, environmental and human rights costs or 'externalities' that it creates (Owen & Kemp, 2017). Among other things, this would require companies to adopt a strategy of 'shared authority' with the custodians of the natural resources they seek to access and exploit. Companies will minimally need to internalise a set of 'countervailing powers', in the form of a new communities architecture or enhanced CSR management capabilities that can moderate the industrial ethic that motivates the industry. Until such time, large-scale mining will remain a harm industry that produces both slow and structural violence and inescapable conflict. This kind of corporate reformation might just decrease some of the destructive impacts of mining capitalism and reduce some of the reasons for moral outrage. Such reformation might even go some of the way towards creating the sorts of global institutional forms that Polanyi had in mind, to support a new social and economic paradigm. But in the end, some critics would probably respond that such initiatives only tinker at the edges of capitalist expansion, just as some Lihirians would argue that there is no acceptable form of shared authority. So long as a foreign company is operating on their land, it will be impossible to escape this doubly asymmetrical relationship and the corresponding state of mutual incomprehension, which will only compel some people towards further acts of resistance until the mine is eventually closed. The lesson to be gained from the closure of the Misima gold mine in the nation's southeastern corner suggests that, at this point, these levelling acts will be redirected with even greater vigour towards fellow Lihirians until all traces of this mine-derived wealth and inequality are removed. Perhaps only then will the double movement come to an end, or it may just assume another form, as Lihirians are further subsumed within the global system. It then remains to be seen if they will lose their ideologies and desires but retain their customary practices.

Acknowledgements

This chapter has benefited from extensive conversations with Colin Filer and John Owen and comments from John Cox and Debra McDougall. I am most indebted to Luke Kabariu from Lihir for his careful explanation of the *gorgor*. I also thank members of the Kapit community for graciously sharing their experiences with me. Naturally, any mistakes and misinterpretations are entirely my own.

References

Albrecht, G., Sartore, G. M., Connor, L., Higgenbotham, N., Freeman, S., Kelly, B., … Pollard, G. (2007). Solastalgia: The distress caused by environmental change. *Australasian Psychiatry, 15*(1), S95–S98.

Bainton, N. A. (2008). The genesis and the escalation of desire and antipathy in the Lihir Islands, Papua New Guinea. *The Journal of Pacific History, 43*(3), 289–312.

Bainton, N. A. (2009). Keeping the network out of view: Mining, distinctions and exclusion in Melanesia. *Oceania, 79*(1), 18–33.

Bainton, N. A. (2010). *The Lihir destiny: Cultural responses to mining in Melanesia.* Canberra, ACT: ANU E Press, doi.org/10.22459/LD.10.2010

Bainton, N. A. & Macintyre, M. (2013). 'My land, my work': Business development and large-scale mining in Melanesia. In F. McCormack & K. Barclay (Eds), *Engaging with capitalism: Cases from Oceania* (pp. 139–165). United Kingdom: Emerald Books.

Bainton, N. A. & Macintyre, M. (2016). Mortuary ritual and mining riches in island Melanesia. In D. Lipset & E. Silverman (Eds), *Mortuary dialogues: Death ritual and the reproduction of moral community in Pacific modernities* (pp. 110–132). New York, NY: Berghahn.

Bainton N. & Macintyre, M. (forthcoming). Being like a state: How mining companies assume government roles in Papua New Guinea. In N. Bainton & E. Skrzypek (Eds), *Absent presence: Resource extraction and the state in Papua New Guinea and Australia*. Canberra, ACT: ANU Press.

Bainton, N. & Owen, J. R. (2019). Zones of entanglement: Researching mining arenas in Melanesia and beyond. *The Extractive Industries and Society*, *6*(3), 767–774.

Bainton, N., Ballard, C. & Gillespie, K. (2012). The end of the beginning? Mining, sacred geographies, memory and performance in Lihir. *The Australian Journal of Anthropology*, *23*, 22–49.

Ballard, C. (1997). It's the land, stupid! The moral economy of resource ownership in Papua New Guinea. In P. Lamour (Ed.), *The governance of common property in the Pacific Region* (pp. 47–65). Canberra, ACT: National Centre for Development Studies and Resource Management in Asia-Pacific Project.

Carrier, J. G. (2018). Moral economy: What's in a name. *Anthropological Theory*, *18*(1), 18–35.

Dashwood, H. (2012). *The rise of global corporate social responsibility: Mining and the spread of global norms*. Cambridge, England: Cambridge University Press.

Edelman, M. (2005). Bringing the moral economy back in … to the study of 21st century transnational peasant movements. *American Anthropologist*, *107*(3), 331–345. doi.org/10.1525/aa.2005.107.3.331

Filer, C. (1995). Participation, governance and social impact: The planning of the Lihir gold mine. In D. Denoon (Ed.), *Mining and mineral resource policy issues in Asia-Pacific: Prospects for the 21st century* (pp. 67–75). Canberra, ACT: The Australian National University, Research School of Pacific and Asian Studies, Division of Asian and Pacific History.

Filer, C. (1997). Compensation, rent and power in Papua New Guinea. In S. Toft (Ed.), *Compensation for resource development in Papua New Guinea* (pp. 156–189). Canberra, ACT: The Australian National University.

Filer, C. (1998). The Melanesian way of menacing the mining industry. In L. Zimmer-Tamakoshi (Ed.), *Modern Papua New Guinea* (pp. 147–177). Kirksville, MO: Thomas Jefferson University Press.

Filer, C. (2006). Custom, law and ideology in Papua New Guinea. *The Asia Pacific Journal of Anthropology*, *7*(1), 65–84.

Filer, C. (2014). The double movement of immovable property rights in Papua New Guinea. *The Journal of Pacific History*, *49*(1), 76–94.

Filer, C., Burton, J. & Banks, G. (2008). The fragmentation of responsibilities in the Melanesian mining sector. In C. O'Faircheallaigh & S. Ali (Eds), *Earth matters: Indigenous peoples, the extractive industries and corporate social responsibility* (pp. 163–179). Sheffield, England: Greanleaf Publishing.

Foster, R. J. (1995). *Social reproduction and history in Melanesia: Mortuary ritual, gift exchange and custom in the Tanga Islands*. Cambridge, England: Cambridge University Press.

Götz, N. (2015). 'Moral economy': Its conceptual history and analytical prospects. *Journal of Global Ethics*, *11*(2), 147–162. doi.org/10.1080/17449626.2015.1054556

Harvey, D. (2005). *The new imperialism*. Oxford, England: Oxford University Press.

Hemer, S. R. (2016). Emplacement and resistance: Social and political complexities in development-induced displacement in Papua New Guinea. *The Australian Journal of Anthropology*, *27*(3), 279–297. doi.org/10.1111/taja.12142

Kabariu, L. (1998). Lihir land rules. (Unpublished typescript.)

Lihir Mining Area Landowners Association. (1994). Memo to PNG Law Reform Commission. (Unpublished typescript.)

Macintyre, M. (1997). Lihir gold mine project: Social, political and economic impact 1996. (Unpublished report to Lihir Management Company.)

Macintyre, M. (1998). Social and economic impact study, Lihir, 1998. (Unpublished report to Lihir Management Company.)

Macintyre, M. & Foale, S. (2000). *Social and economic impact study Lihir 2000*. Abbottsford, England: Charlotte & Allen Associates.

Macintyre, M. & Foale, S. (2001). *Social and economic impact study Lihir 2001*. Charlotte Abbottsford, England: Allen & Associates.

Macintyre, M. & Foale, S. (2004). Politicised ecology: Local responses to mining in Papua New Guinea. *Oceania*, *74*(3), 231–252.

Martin, K. (2013). *The death of the big men and the rise of the big shots: Custom and conflict in East New Britain*. New York, NY: Berghahn.

Owen, J. (2009). *A history of the moral economy: Markets, custom and the philosophy of popular entitlement*. Melbourne, Vic.: Australian Scholarly Publishing.

Owen, J. (2016). Social licence and the fear of Mineras Interruptus. *Geoforum*, *77*, 102–105.

Owen, J. & Kemp, D. (2017). *Extractive relations: Countervailing power and the global mining industry*. London, England: Routledge.

Polanyi, K. (2001). *The great transformation: The political and economic origins of our time*. Boston, MA: Beacon Press.

Regan, A. (2017). Bougainville: Origins of the conflict and debating the future of large-scale mining. In C. Filer & P.-Y. Le Meur (Eds), *Large-scale mines and local-level politics: Between New Caledonia and Papua New Guinea* (pp. 353–414). Canberra, ACT: ANU Press. doi.org/10.22459/LMLP.10.2017

Scott, J. C. (1976). *The moral economy of the peasant: Rebellion and subsistence in Southeast Asia*. New Haven, CT: Yale University Press.

Scott, J. C. (1985). *Weapons of the weak: Everyday forms of peasant resistance*. New Haven, CT: Yale University Press.

Thompson, E. P. (1971). The moral economy of the English crowd in the eighteenth century. *Past and Present, 50*, 76–136.

Wardlow, H. (2006). *Wayward women: Sexuality and agency in a New Guinea society*. Berkeley, CA: University of California Press.

Zappone, C. (2012, 29 August). Landowners halt mining at Lihir. *The Age*. Retrieved from www.theage.com.au/business/landowners-halt-mining-at-lihir-20120828-24ypo.html

15

Intersecting Inequalities, Moving Positionalities: An Interlude

Margaret Jolly

Introduction

The breadth and depth of Martha Macintyre's scholarship and humanity are celebrated across this volume. As a long-term colleague and friend, I am honoured to add some words that, although they were invited as an 'Afterword', are perhaps better described as an 'Interlude', that sits between the feast of scholarly reflections presented in the preceding chapters and some more personal engagements yet to come. These include a biographical interview between Martha and Alex Golub, some moving and hilarious tributes to her and a long, enticing list of Martha's publications to date—an assortment of after-dinner treats, if you like. Anyone who has had the pleasure of feasting at Martha's table, in addition to reading her writing, will appreciate the aptness of the gastronomic analogy.

Following the diversity of a dozen chapters and the elegant integration offered by Neil Maclean in the Prologue and Nick Bainton and Debra Mcdougall in the introductory chapter, I offer my own exegeses and distillations of connecting themes. I highlight three critical characteristics of Martha's scholarship to which the authors in this volume attest and have engaged with in various ways. First, I witness her staunch and sustained critique of inequalities—in particular, gender and class and their intersection in Papua New Guinea (PNG). This has manifested in her intimate ethnographic work, in which she has shown how those aspects of matriliny in Milne Bay that enhanced women's power in the past have been eroded by the male domination inherent in colonialism and capitalist development, particularly in extractive industries. It is also apparent in her writing on the persistence of gender inequalities across PNG, as indigenous and exogenous patriarchies have creolised to create novel and, sometimes, more malign forms of male domination—for example, in her argument that the beauty and danger of indigenous masculinities were remixed in the figure of the Melanesian Rambo (see Macintyre, 2008; Maclean, this volume). Second, I observe how, from her very first writing, in collaboration with Edmund Leach on a classic volume on the *kula* (Leach & Leach 1983), in her bibliography of the *kula* (Macintyre, 1983a) and in her own ethnography of Tubetube (e.g. Macintyre, 1983b) she has exposed the chimera of closed, persisting cultures, conceived in antithetical opposition rather than relation to foreign influences. This, as Maclean elaborates in the Prologue, was fundamental to her critique of the dichotomy of the gift and the commodity and of Marilyn Strathern's influential *The gender of the gift* (Macintyre, 1995; see also Jolly, 1992). This view was also fundamental to our collaboration (Jolly & Macintyre, 1989), which argued that any idea of an unchanging domestic domain in the Pacific was at odds with the dramatic reconfigurations of indigenous domesticities catalysed by colonial economies and Christian conversions. Third, I observe how Martha has always positioned herself as a critical anthropologist, sustaining a strong ethic of ethnographic fidelity to her interlocutors in many sites and challenging lingering romanticisation of culture in provocative scholarly analyses and revealing reports, often in the fraught contexts of researching extractive industries and gender violence in PNG (e.g. Macintyre, 1995, 2011, 2012, 2017; Macintyre & Spark, 2017).

In/Equality?

Any consideration of inequality must rely on a vision of what equality is or might be. However, I do not dwell on the protracted debates about this in the canon of Western philosophy and political science or in grand theories about the alleged difference between hierarchical holism and egalitarian individualism, proposed by Louis Dumont (see Jolly & Mosko, 1994; Strathern, 1987, 1988). Rather, I merely note the extraordinary difficulty of pursuing equality in a global context in which inequality is deeply sedimented and exponentially expanding. As the editors observe in their introductory chapter, 'we are witnessing its extensification globally and its intensification locally' (Bainton & McDougall, this volume).

Liberal theorists in Western contexts have often differentiated between equality of opportunity (given diverse, unequal origins) and equality of outcome (of equal endpoints). More recently, some corporate primers and even some neoliberal feminists have distinguished equality (which entails that everyone is at the same level) and equity (which denotes impartiality or lack of discrimination). Simple poster charts, now available online, suggest that equality is about sameness and quantity, whereas equity is about quality and fairness (see Figure 1). Such linguistic niceties in English and conceptual oppositions focusing on the rights of individuals within states, corporations or communities may occlude the deeply structural inequalities of our world, the sedimentation and the intersection of gender, race and class.

Figure 1: Commonly used image depicting the difference between 'equality' and 'equity'.
Source: Interaction Institute for Social Change (Artist: Angus Maguire).

In the early anthropology of PNG and the broader Pacific, there existed a tendency to contrast the allegedly more egalitarian polities of the Western Pacific 'Melanesia' and the more hierarchical polities of the Eastern Pacific 'Polynesia'. In the introductory chapter, the editors allude to Sahlins' influential antinomy of big man versus chief (1963)—the first based on personal generosity and redistribution and the second derived from inherited genealogy and divine power. This seemed consistent with a claim that Eastern Pacific polities were more advanced and proximate to European civilisation than the Western Pacific, a story that had roots in the gendered racial logics of early European exploratory voyages (see Jolly, 2012), but that also persisted in popular stories of cultural evolution prevalent in some anthropological writings into the twentieth century, at least (for a critique of this, see Hauʻofa, 1975; for a RePresentation of Melanesia, see Kabataulaka, 2015). Sahlins, at least, saw the irony in reversing the imperial 'time's arrow', observing that Polynesian chiefdoms were more akin to feudal lords and Melanesian big men closer to capitalist entrepreneurs.

A library of subsequent ethnographies and comparative analyses refuted this simplistic dualism, documenting the presence and sometimes collapse of many hierarchical chiefly systems in the Western Pacific, both hereditary and achieved, and the crucial importance of performance and not just inheritance in all forms of power, albeit a chief, a big man, a great man, a big shot (e.g. Godelier & Strathern, 1991; Martin, 2013). Increasingly, claims of 'egalitarianism' in the Western Pacific and the masculinist bias in such formulations have been challenged—by evidence of both profound gender inequalities in many allegedly 'egalitarian' societies in PNG (e.g. Jolly, 1987) and of those rarer women who were acknowledged as 'big women' or chiefs (Zimmer-Tamakoshi, this volume).

Intersectionality

Equally foundational to this volume, if implicit rather than explicit in most of the chapters, is the notion of intersectionality. American lawyer and civil rights activist Kimberlé Crenshaw is usually credited with coining the concept (1991). Crenshaw developed a robust sense of how, in the particular context of the United States (US) legal system, identifications of being black and being a woman intersected and interacted. Her insights proved profoundly important in both critical race studies and intersectional feminism. She popularised the concept in public addresses and TED

Talks, stressing its salience and urgency in confronting contemporary inequalities in the US. However, there were also precursors, such as the British socialist feminist scholars who opposed the essentialism of white radical feminists—they were effectively arguing for the intersectionality of gender, race and class. Writers such as Nira Yuval-Davis and Floya Anthias (1989) have spoken of the need to think beyond the additive terms of layered, multiple oppressions, to analyse how inequalities have interacted and mutually shaped one another. Also in 1991, Australian feminist scholars published a volume, titled *Intersexions*, that was inspired by similar visions and values (Bottomley, de Lepervanche & Martin, 1991), in which I published a chapter reflecting on the politics of feminism in Vanuatu, in the context of colonialism and decolonisation (Jolly, 1991).

The editors of this volume aspire to develop an intersectional approach to inequality in the Western Pacific, akin to that recently espoused by Holly Wardlow (2018) in her research with Huli women in the PNG highlands. In opposition to those who lament an undue fixation with 'suffering subjects' in anthropology (Robbins, 2013), they instead argue that this is an urgent need, given the 'increasingly harsh conditions that characterise many rural and urban settings' (Bainton & McDougall, this volume) due to the exponential expansion of inequalities. Their poignant opening vignettes—juxtaposing the PNG government's purchase of a posse of Maseratis for foreign dignitaries visiting the Asia-Pacific Economic Cooperation meeting, while young children were dying in a resurgent polio epidemic—consummately evoke the surreal horror of the situation. They allude to Crenshaw's model of a traffic intersection, a junction of fast-moving inequalities, but suggest a more Oceanic image of a person caught in the vortex of converging currents. Like them, I see intersectionality, not as a grand theory, but rather as a practical prism that distils, reflects and refracts a complex reality.

Indigenous and Exogenous Inequalities: Gender and Generation, Race and Class

In its subtitle, this volume privileges what some have seen as the 'holy trinity' in formulations of intersecting inequalities—gender, race and class. On first glance, we might conceive of gender as an indigenous inequality (in addition to the inequalities of generation or elder/younger, also discussed in this volume). We might consider race and class to be exogenous since they originate in white colonialism and capitalist modes of development. However, as Martha Macintyre's corpus has demonstrated and several chapters in this volume reveal, indigenous inequalities of gender and generation have also been changing dramatically, partly through interaction with these introduced inequalities of race and class.

This is clearly revealed in Debra McDougall's chapter on the Solomon Islands, which examines a vernacular language education movement on the island of Ranongga. In this context, race is relevant in that the English language introduced by diverse white colonial agents still occupies a privileged position in the formal education system. This primacy disadvantages rural children in particular; they often feel humiliated by the difficulties of learning in a foreign language and may leave school functionally illiterate and, thus, unable to compete for the few jobs available to young Solomon Islanders. The vernacular language movement, named the Kulu Institute and headed by Dr Alpheaus Zobule, now has a beautiful campus and over a thousand students per year. Its pedagogy involves a challenging exploration of the structure of the local language and a well-sequenced series of lessons taught in an intensive format. This has enabled students to perform far better in their formal studies that are taught in English. Students have described their lessons in English as trying to eat raw food as compared to their cooked, digestible and delicious lessons in the vernacular.

McDougall reveals the dynamics of gender and generation involved in the movement, its students and the local context. The first leaders were three local men who had the autonomy to leave their families to catalyse the movement; they were later joined by women teachers, and there has been a recent influx of female students, as numbers have grown. Boys and girls have responded differently to their educational experiences at school and in the movement. Young men were often angry about being taught in English, feeling that they were being 'ruined' by this and suggesting that such humiliations led them to lives of dissolution and crime. Their education at Kulu instead gave them a sense of self-respect: as one young man said, 'it was as though I was freed from prison' (McDougall, this volume). Girls evinced far less anger about school and a greater sense of heightened opportunity, although they are still more disadvantaged than boys, in terms of familial support for their schooling; they are engaged in far more domestic work than boys and bear the risks of possible pregnancy and of gender and sexual violence while at, or travelling to, school.

However, these gendered differences are also deeply generational. The grandfathers and fathers of these boys moved into positions of respect and authority in accordance with the expanded opportunities for men in the colonial and postcolonial periods. As male power expanded with the incursions of copra plantations and logging, women were more focused on their gardens, domestic life and local authority. The grandmothers and mothers of girls now attending school experienced far more barriers— barriers that have now been redressed by both government and aid policies directed towards gender equality. Young women now sense far more opportunities and husbands and partners are increasingly seen as more dispensable in forming families; McDougall (this volume) cites Macintyre (1988) on the 'dispensable husband' of Tubetube oral tradition. Some young men experience a sense of worthlessness due to being so excluded from domestic responsibilities and satisfying work and may express anger in response (the negative agency of 'fuck you'). An interesting alternative is emergent in charismatic Christian revivals, in what McDougall terms the 'gentle patriarchy of Pentecostalism' (McDougall, this volume; see also Cox & Macintyre, 2014), which puts men at the centre of domestic life. As Macintyre consistently insisted and McDougall affirms, 'contemporary patriarchy is not a holdover from traditional patriarchy' (McDougall, this volume; see also Cox & Macintyre, 2014).

John Barker's analysis of marriage and gender relations among the Maisin of Collingwood Bay, Oro Province, similarly reveals that what may appear as 'tradition' may not be indigenous, much like Macintyre's 'better homes and gardens', which have been dramatically reconfigured by colonial influences and Samoan missionaries in Milne Bay (Macintyre, 1989). Based on a conjoint exploration of Anglican mission archives and Maisin oral histories, he charts the dramatic changes in marriage and gender relations precipitated both by Christianity and economic circumstances. In his view, these changes derived from friction between the basic values believed by white Anglican missionaries and Maisin people to be inherent in marriage. Marriage was a preoccupation of high church Anglican missionaries, who saw it as a sacrament with crucial ramifications for church membership. It was a lifelong commitment, ordained by God, to both the partner and the church; therefore, divorce caused excommunication. Conversely, Maisin people saw marriage as akin to all reciprocal exchanges, wherein exchange partners shared their inner selves with each other through the materiality of food and valuables.

The contemporary shape of Maisin marriage is the result of both historical friction and accommodation. Early Anglicans distinguished legitimate marriage from Maisin 'concubinage' (particularly polygyny) and lamented the 'laxity' of Maisin married life, given the prevalence of affairs. They punished sexual exchanges between adolescents at mission boarding schools and excommunicated couples who were living sinful lives. Later Papuan missionaries were more forgiving and ended excommunication. However, the shape of Maisin marriage was also moulded by other external influences. The global flu pandemic of 1918–1920 (locally perceived as sorcery) elevated the desire for fertility, as did the child bonuses paid during the colonial period. The head tax on adult males and their recruitment as labourers to work on plantations and then as carriers in World War II all influenced marriage and gender relations.

The Indigenous diarchy (*kavo/sabu*) between the feasting, peace-making clans and the warrior clans, between elder brothers and younger brothers, was transposed onto the relationship between the church and the congregation, which was enjoined to offer respect. The church was seen to be effecting peace, by stopping conflicts over contested betrothals and marriages. Infant betrothal had waned by the 1950s; however, some polygynists persisted. Today, full *kastom* weddings are rare; Christian weddings are rarer still. Couples often wait until they have several children before they seek the church sanction to bless their union as Christian. The Anglican campaign to impose Christian marriage had wider implications for gender relations, given the ontological equivalence of woman and man before God. Still, this entailed both sharing and segregation. Whereas the London Missionary Society and the Methodists focused on the married couple and domestic life, high Anglicans (like the Catholics) focused on collective hierarchies. The male-dominated church and the Mothers' Union functioned as an auxiliary that both supported the clergy and challenged its hegemony, instituting a female hierarchy in which older women exerted power over younger women.

Changing relations of gender and generation are also central to Laura Zimmer-Tamakoshi's chapter on the Gende of the PNG highlands. She shows how the *longue durée* of Gende life has been influenced by complex historical processes: their enforced movement northwards as exiles in tribal warfare, their changing positions as mediators in networks of trade moving from north to south between Chimbu and Gende, the impact of male urban migration, coffee growing and roads and, most recently, the regional position of Gende in relation to extractive industries (e.g. Ramu Nickel and Marengo Mining). This example clearly shows how inequalities generated between and within ethnic groups by the dynamics of mining, the declaration of the zones of those affected (as defined by the PNG state) and the formation of landowner groups interacts powerfully with gender and generational dynamics.

Zimmer-Tamakoshi observes dramatic shifts in both gender and generational dynamics, due to the emergence of class differences. In her earlier work, she witnessed more egalitarian and agreeable relations between men and women. Young women were taught about sexuality and birthing and about their rights as individuals and in relation to their husbands' claims. Moreover, through the practice of *tupoi*, Gende women were able to redeem their brideprice through the hard work of raising pigs and accumulating valuables and cash. This led to increased authority and control over land belonging to their own and other clans and control over pig herds. Zimmer-Tamakoshi has witnessed the power of both big men and big women, who alike promoted the wellbeing of the collective.

However, during her fieldwork in the 1980s, she also observed how young men were suffering from long periods of bachelorhood and, thus, not attaining the status of full adults. Older men were inclined to invest in migrants and returning labourers rather than their sons, which generated intergenerational conflict. However, the arrival of mining ended this bachelorisation, as young men secured jobs in and around mining sites, used their newfound wealth to pay their own brideprice (and even take several wives) and to cement their land rights through payments to their fathers. These changing generational dynamics have also generated new gender dynamics, whereby young women are increasingly seen as the property of their husbands and, as brideprices increase, women find it harder to redeem their brideprice. Marriages are increasingly concentrated around the Ramu Nickel site—this is to narrow ties and concentrate claims for royalties and other benefits. There are fewer jobs for women in mining and any jobs are also less well paid. Women also often experience conflicts with co-wives.

Zimmer-Tamakoshi sees these intersecting processes as generating a new moral economy. There has been a fracturing of Gende society, which she describes as 'unnerving generational splits' (Zimmer-Tamakoshi, this volume). Young men invest their hopes for the future in mining, even though they also acknowledge it as destructive and unsustainable. Increasingly, men evince a selfish desire for the pleasures of sex and alcohol;

'Boys' as old as 40 rent hotel rooms and pay sex workers, emulating the style of those corrupt politicians that they often criticise. Women who have secured new wealth (e.g. Betty) have started local enterprises such as trout farms—these are often still dependent on family labour. However, the differences between her glamorous large house and the 'smoky huts of her sisters' (Zimmer-Tamakoshi, this volume) are palpable. Local critics killed all her fingerling trout. This is not 'open class war', suggests Zimmer-Tamakoshi; however, there clearly exists extreme sensitivity about differences that emerge from the cash economy (see Gewertz & Errington; Bainton, this volume).

Class, *Landonas* and the Moral Economy of Extraction

Several chapters raise questions about these new socioeconomic inequalities, the language of class and the pivotal place of extractive industries in both the PNG economy and what has been termed the 'moral economy'. As the editors astutely observe, although class has exogenous origins, it has assumed a very distinctive form in the Western Pacific. John Cox observes that the distinction between the 'elites' and the grassroots is still predominant in discussions of emergent class distinctions in PNG. However, he does not resile from discussing the 'middle class' and their problematic relationship to the 'grassroots'. As the botanical metaphor suggests, poorer people are often thought to be immobile and their material desires seen as naive and greedy. This contrasts with the spatio-temporal mobility and legitimate modern desires of urban elites, exercised in shopping malls, watching TV, imbibing the internet and prosperity gospels in Pentecostalist churches.[1] This is apparent in newspaper articles and media reports about fast money schemes in which middle-class investment is legitimated (even though few have gained even meagre financial rewards), whereas the poor are accused of having a 'cargo cult mentality'.

In deploying the old colonial trope of 'cargo cult', the postcolonial middle class have (according to Cox) 'weaponised' it, justifying their own accumulation of wealth as a sign of their economic and moral discipline

---

1   In a reversal of the same class-based dualism, the life of the rural poor can also be romanticised as harmonious and non-violent (a fantasy that is belied by many of the chapters in this book).

while critiquing the laziness or poor discipline of the poor. Schemes such as the Personal Viability scheme operating at Lihir (see Bainton, 2010) legitimate the refusal of kin obligations on the part of the wealthy and mystify the structural inequalities created by the mine with neoliberal notions of individual opportunities. Moreover, as social collateral becomes financialised, it undermines pre-existing social safety nets and converts kin relations into ones of paternalist patron-clientage (see Cox, 2018).

Even when middle-class Papua New Guineans manifest good intentions to help rural kin pay school fees, contribute to medical or funeral needs, pay brideprice or to establish locally beneficial development programs, the ensuing dependency often co-exists with a sense of moral superiority in doing good. This sits in parallel to the 'sentimental cosmopolitanism' promoted by big international non-governmental organisations (BINGOs) in fundraising for aid, argues Cox (this volume). Mobile phones and social media make it far more difficult to refuse poor distant kin and fears may be stoked that, if they fail to be generous, they will incur revenge of material or divine kinds. However, if money is used in what is perceived as 'bad' ways or if development projects fail, it is the poor rural kin who are 'scolded' like children and blamed. This occludes the failure of the PNG state to meet the basic health and education needs of its citizens.

Colin Filer also debates the discourse of class in his fascinating study of the mining workforce in PNG, pondering whether they can be described as either a 'national proletariat' or a 'labour aristocracy'. Based on an exhaustive survey of 285 wage-earners working or previously employed in the mining industry, he addresses several questions. The first was posed by the original World Bank funders who commissioned the study with the question 'what were good jobs for development?'—this was framed in terms of their broader social value rather than the income generated for the individual. It is difficult, observes Filer, to view mining jobs as good for development, given that a very high dependency on mining and petroleum co-exists with PNG ranking very low on the human development index in the region. The other questions addressed by Filer are whether the 'enclave' development of mining sites is reflected in mining workers being socially detached from others and whether mining jobs do have positive social qualities akin to jobs in health and education.

This survey generated a series of fascinating findings. I will focus on those about gender, the moral economy of giving to kin and class consciousness. First, it is apparent that, despite the often-attested absence of women in mining, there is a growing percentage of women employed at provincial, national and international levels and, increasingly, in technical and managerial roles. Second, it emerges that most of those surveyed, both women and men, were heavily engaged in a remittance economy, redistributing their wealth to kin and others. They could not emulate an opulent lifestyle nor evince what has been called 'possessive individualism' because they (both men and women) were redistributing rather than accumulating wealth. The variation between individuals in how much was redistributed depended on the size of the pay packet—this likely meant that men remitted more. Finally, Filer adjudges an absence of class consciousness among these mining industry workers and, perhaps especially, among women. Although the results of the survey were not definitive, they seem to suggest that women working in the mining industry were less likely to join trade unions, more compliant and less recalcitrant in relation to bosses and less likely to leave their employer for a better job.

It proves interesting to compare the national scale, quantitative survey and interview methods of Filer's study with Michael Main's more ethnographically focused study of the Huli people of the PNG highlands. This is a region that has been dramatically reshaped by the promise and the disappointment of the large PNG Liquefied Natural Gas (PNG LNG) project. This was, as Main relates, supposed to generate bounty both for the national economy and, particularly, for those living proximate to the project and most affected by it, such as the Huli people. Although there have been some benefits in compensation and royalties to those men adjudged to be landowners and the arrival of PNG LNG has assisted the formation of the separate Hela Province, both national and local benefits have proved to be profoundly disappointing. At the national level, profits have been siphoned off by corrupt politicians and held in offshore accounts, while local dynamics have reconfigured political economies in a way that Main describes as a passage 'from donation to handout' (this volume).

He suggests that Huli people evince a strong ethos of both materialism and individualism in the pursuit of inequality; however, in this chapter, we see this manifest only in men. He deploys a distinction drawn by a much earlier ethnographer, Robert Glasse, between two types of Huli leaders: those relying on expert genealogical knowledge used in land disputes and rituals and those who, by individual ability and volition, accumulated wealth and, thereby, social status. He acknowledges that both forms of leadership excluded women. These two forms of male authority are manifest in the respective careers and the speeches of Allan Ango and Andersen Agiru—the first more reliant on expert genealogical knowledge, whose truth claims were widely respected, and the second inspired by visions of wealth through materialist modernist development, and who credited his own speech with prophetic efficacy. However, in the next generation, male authority has been reshaped by the experience of the PNG LNG project and the two forms converge; expert knowledge about land and genealogy may form the basis for capturing significant wealth from the PNG LNG project and translating this into political authority. Further, Main suggests that, as elsewhere in the Western Pacific, the position of paramount chief has been newly created to justify elite pre-eminence in a period of turbulent conflict and intense economic competition.

Nick Bainton's chapter moves our focus to the Lihir goldmine in New Ireland Province and highlights the crucial connections between those inequalities generated between the mining company Newcrest and all Lihirians and those inequalities among Lihirians, on the basis of their location in regions more or less affected by the mine. He consummately analyses the situation on Lihir in terms of Polanyi's notion of the 'double movement' of increasing marketisation (which is dependent on the myth of a self-regulating market free of state intervention) and a counter-movement against marketisation (which insists on the sanctity of land and labour). This clearly resonates with the widespread claim in PNG, and the Western Pacific more broadly, that 'land is life' and with resistances to the enclosure and commodification of land and the destruction of the environment, not only on the basis of class interest.

In Lihir, this counter-movement is expressed in the periodic, almost annual, practice of closing down the mine through the use of the *gorgor*—an indigenous taboo whereby a male authority places a ginger plant imbued with sacred potency to ban the use of a resource (e.g. a garden or a fruit tree) or to enforce a boundary. The *gorgor* has been repurposed to 'menace' the mine, scaling up this symbol of male authority, imbuing it with potent new meanings and avoiding the violent conflicts of blockades and destruction that occur at other PNG mining sites. The *gorgor* evokes the irreparable loss felt by the *landona*—a novel individual and collective identity emergent in the context of PNG's extractive economy (Filer, 1997). The separation of people from their land and the consequent destruction and pollution can never be truly compensated. Mine closures are often effected to secure promises—the cash compensation, royalties, company equity, business contracts or community development of the Integrated Benefits Package agreement—or to protest the dust, noise and light of the mine and its pollution of soil, rivers, reefs and ocean. As Bainton argues, a seemingly extractive ethos is imbued with a clear moral message, with parallels to the 'moral economy' E. P. Thompson discerned among the English working class. The *gorgor* represents a way for Lihirians to demonstrate that they are not humiliated beggars; they are landlords, not tenants, and patrons, not clients. Protests are not only about accumulating wealth, but also about demonstrating local power. There exists a mutual incomprehension between the company and Lihirians— cash is offered, health and education benefits are given (where the state has failed miserably); however, this will never suffice to compensate the irrevocable loss experienced.

However, not all Lihirians experience this equally. Those more proximate to the mine receive more benefits, according to the protocols of the nationally regulated zones of entitlement. Consistent grievances are expressed about the unequal distribution of benefits and the unequal burdens imposed. Some relocations, such as that of Kapit village, failed miserably and people are now experiencing difficulties with housing and gardens and with food and water insecurities. Such differences may be manipulated by the company, exacerbating the atomisation of Lihir.

Susan Hemer's chapter examines the health dimensions of inequality in the Lihir group of islands, with a particular focus on tuberculosis (TB). Globally, TB is a marker of poverty and, as Paul Farmer has suggested, a symptom of the structural violence that is inherent in global health inequalities. In PNG, TB is resurgent, and drug-resistant forms of TB have also emerged, particularly in Daru (which has provoked selfish concern in Australia about the biosecurity risks due to its proximity to the Torres Strait). Hemer argues both that inequalities shape TB and that TB compounds inequalities in Lihir. The development of the gold mine (from 1997 to the present) has been accompanied by improved infrastructure, a ring road around the island, increased opportunities for waged work, improved health and education and an influx of migrants. The health care in Lihir (i.e. on the main island, Niolam, in the local language) and particularly that available at the Lihir Medical Centre (LMC) is among the best in the country. However, the rates of diagnosed TB are increasing, although it is unclear whether the increase is due to higher infection or better detection. There exist some differences by age and sex; infants, teenagers and elderly show peaks of infection, but men are more likely to be diagnosed than women. Hemer discerns a link to poverty; for instance, two teenage girls who were diagnosed with TB were both daughters of poor unmarried mothers. However, the main inequality is that experienced between those who have access to the LMC facility, which has superior facilities for detection and treatment, and those who do not—between those in the north-east and those in the southern and western parts of the main island of Lihir.

Hemer detects another important inequality in the politics of knowledge about and treatment of TB. This is part of a broader problem in global health care, whereby the broader primary health focus on improved nutrition, water and sanitation and better education is displaced by a narrower biomedical focus on the disease itself and preventive chemotherapy. Programs directed to narrower biomedical ends are more easily funded and monitored by quantitative methods (see also Foale, this volume; Lepani, 2012). This leads to a focus on the individual and their clinical diagnosis rather than broader structural determinants. On Lihir, health workers tend to focus on the individual responsibility of patients to comply with complex and protracted chemotherapy regimes. This leads to victim blaming and may deepen the inequalities existing between health workers and their patients in a way that compromises recovery and wellbeing.

Moving Positionality and Increasing Precarity: The Ethics of Ethnography

Finally, I distil and connect several chapters in this volume that address the positionality of the anthropologist, questions of ethnographic fidelity and authority and persisting inequalities of race in the creation and dissemination of knowledge.

The chapter co-authored by John Aini and Paige West confronts these problems directly. John Aini is a New Ireland man who has long been involved in the work of the local, environmentally attuned non-governmental organisation (NGO) Ailan Awareness and also a long-time collaborator with Paige West in her ethnographic work on dispossession and environment in New Ireland (see e.g. Aini & West, 2018). West's wider work on coffee production and the politics of ecology and conservation in PNG has been suffused with a decolonising sensibility and method (West, 2006, 2012, 2016). Through a forensic examination of the documentation of visits by young white researchers working with environmental NGOs or arriving as university graduate students, they demonstrate how locals such as Aini can bear large material and social costs in providing advice and hospitality. Either from her office at Colombia University in New York or while travelling herself, West is often involved in mediating these requests and brokering some of the more naive and excessive presumptions of these novice researchers. Aini and West demonstrate that the production of their knowledge entails dual exploitation—one grounded in the racialised inequalities between whites and PNG people and the other between BINGOs and local NGOs, which is similarly racialised.

Through the analysis of anonymised email correspondence, they show how the good intentions of these young, white people (who wish to work on urgent environmental issues) are regularly vitiated by an ignorance of the local situation and a presumption that local NGO staff have the time and resources to smooth the passage of their visit. Aini and West reveal the sheer quantity of time, hard work and mobilisation of both material resources and social networks expended in arranging the transport, accommodation and feeding of such folk—some visitors fail to acknowledge or even notice their indebtedness. Much of this work is not paid or calculated in commodity terms; therefore, it becomes invisible, and visitors are able to simply construe it as 'island hospitality'. This, they argue, occludes the profound inequalities of race and class that underlie the creation and dissemination of knowledge. This echoes the way in which Amelia Moore (2019) has exposed the confluence between environmental science and climate change tourism in the Bahamas.

This raises questions not only about short-term or novice research visitors, but also the long-term relationships created between anthropologists and their hosts. In their introductory chapter, the editors adjudge that much anthropological knowledge and anthropological careers are also grounded in 'debts that cannot be repaid' (Bainton & McDougall, this volume). The long-term connections that anthropologists have sustained with the peoples of their primary field sites—embodied by Martha Macintyre and several senior authors in this volume—are cherished and celebrated by the discipline. However, some authors in this volume honestly acknowledge that this does not ensure continuing congenial relations, particularly in situations of conflict and economic precarity. Laura Zimmer-Tamakoshi describes how one of her studies of 'ancestral gerrymandering' among the Gende in the context of the Ramu Nickel mine was angrily disputed by young men who had downloaded her work (which is now available online). The pervasiveness of the internet and social media means that anthropologists are now held even more accountable for their representations of the people who host them—their hosts may not necessarily agree with such representations.

The chapter by Deborah Gewertz and Frederick Errington, respected senior ethnographers of the Chambri people of the Sepik and the Duke of York Islanders in East New Britain and analysts of class in PNG (Gewertz & Errington, 1999), reveals the perils of doing ethnography in situations of economic precarity. They relate the disturbing story of their time living in a Sepik settlement on the edge of Madang. In contrast to the efflorescence of customary exchanges afforded by mining wealth in Lihir (see Bainton & Macintyre, 2016), they witnessed a 'stingy egalitarianism' borne of economic precarity; as they express it, 'Melanesian life on life support not steroids' (Gewertz & Errington, this volume). This precarity derives from the marginality of these settlement residents in an increasingly commoditised economy—they are not beneficiaries of mining wealth and have no trade flows or easy connections back to Chambri kin living in villages. Indeed, many who had settled near the town to access money, schools and hospitals did not wish to return to villages where they feared their rights to land would not be recognised. They have neither a social safety net nor support from a government in which neoliberal principles of 'user-pays' prevail. Food is scarce and not shared, incomes are uncertain, and settlement life is unpredictable. Jealousy exists, both of the material success and the sociality of others. A ferocious insistence on levelling, an 'egalitarianism' that constrains and vilifies individuals who do better than others, has emerged as a survival strategy. Expressions of jealous rage erupt in collective outbursts of violence on the part of drunken young men (see also Zimmer-Tamakoshi; McDougall; Jorgensen, this volume).

When Gewertz and Errington arrived to stay with their host (Paul), their very presence and their obvious white wealth presented problems. Although they avoided the display of alluring material goods, the very fact that their hosts were now eating meat and gaining weight caused jealous words and, ultimately, violent conflicts. They swiftly decamped to a hotel to quieten the resentment; however, menaces and threats against their hosts persisted. Quite rightly, the authors view their presence as causing a major disruption in an ongoing moral economy. Their long-term relations and congenial reciprocity with other Chambri people in the past could not protect their hosts or themselves against the jealous rage provoked by inequality in such a situation of extreme precarity. As the authors suggest, the lives of these Chambri people living on the edge of Madang are not only economically precarious but also culturally diminished, without the language and the distinctive knowledge and power associated with being 'Chambri'.

In her chapter, Melissa Demian poses the question of the shifting positionality of the anthropologist in both her own life trajectory in PNG and that of Martha Macintyre. Her reflections were prompted by a conversation with a woman in an NGO office in Lae; this woman noted the differences between the power of women in the matrilineal region of Milne Bay, where Demain first worked, as compared to those parts of PNG where men assume sole entitlement to land and 'block women's spiritual power' (Demian, this volume). Demian plays with Macintyre's reflections on possession in her classic paper on the 'semi-alienable pig' (Macintyre, 1984) as she poses the problem of the 'semi-alienable anthropologist'. She suggests that PNG people see Martha and herself both as white foreigners and as embedded in place, linked by language and familiarity to specific locales. However, what happens when the anthropologist shifts locales? Further, what happens when the anthropologist is Papua New Guinean?

For Demian herself, the shift from Milne Bay to Lae involved not only a shift in place and language but also a shift in her source of funding and in her modes of listening and reporting. A shift in location can also entail a shift in scale—for example, from a more local ethnographic to a national scale (from the perspective of Port Moresby), which is a move visible in Macintyre's own trajectory and published corpus. However, inspired by Marilyn Strathern (1991/2005), Demian queries a simple nesting model of scale, showing how similar relations or antinomies can recur at successive scales (e.g. men/women or young/old) and suggests that scaling up can represent both loss and gain.

Demian brings these ideas into her study of women in Lae town who are seeking to make their urban lives safer and more satisfying. She alludes to the way in which Europeans imagined towns as both white and male. Anne Dickson-Waiko's writings (e.g. 2007) on how PNG women were often excluded from towns and the commodity economy in both colonial and postcolonial periods is relevant to this. This legacy persists, in that PNG women sense that modernity is less available to them—they do not possess the same freedom to romance, drink and gamble that men do. They are imperilled by the violence both of male gangs and the police. Men fear the untrammelled freedom of women in town and try to constrain them through forms of physical and symbolic violence.

Whereas Demian engages Macintyre in relation to location and spatiality, Dan Jorgensen engages with questions of time and historical change posed for him by Macintyre's history of changes in *kula* (1983a) or the changes consequent in mining in Misima and Lihir (Macintyre, 2011). He records dramatic changes in the lives of Telefomin people living near the giant Ok Tedi gold and copper mine and its hinterland in Sandaun and Western Province. In 2011, in the wake of the unexpected death of a prominent man at an airport on his way home, a number of village youths (The Boys) engaged in widespread intimidation, public torture, murder and rape of those they accused of killing him using witchcraft. These Boys were disaffected, uneducated and unemployed young men who were getting high not just on the marijuana they were cultivating and selling but the dangerous datura vines ('devils trumpets'), which are endemic in the region. They menaced their victims with axes, bushknives, sharpened iron rods and guns. They particularly targeted those people who had returned to home villages for Christmas and who were wealthier, educated urban dwellers. Initially, police did not intervene, citing lack of sufficient men and resources. The youths were eventually arrested and charged; however, in the absence of the victims' bodies, the charges were eventually discharged by a judge. This violent episode had permanent effects, fragmenting communities and causing many to flee in fear. However, as Jorgensen notes, partly due to the restraint of the victim's family—who wanted to 'put the past behind them' (Jorgensen, this volume)—similar episodes of youth violence did not recur or become normalised.

The second crisis involved the El Niño drought, which had devastating effects on agriculture in this region (as in many parts of PNG) and coincided with the closure of both the Ok Tedi mine and the Tabubil township, which had been the residential and service hub for the mine. This resulted in the widespread movement of families back to home villages, where kin were already struggling with the severe effects of the drought. Ostensibly, the drought was the cause of this closure, because the Fly River (which had been the passage for ore going out and supplies coming in through the port of Kiunga) was no longer navigable. However, as Jorgensen shows by outlining the complex history of the ownership of the mine and the tensions between its commercial and social mandate, this suited the company and, ultimately, the government. The government gained control of Ok Tedi Mining Limited in this period to focus on maximising profits by making the evacuation of the town a permanent eviction and instituting a fly-in fly-out system of engaging workers, despite this being a long-contested system in PNG. However, in the years since this crisis, it seems that the social mandate of the mining company and the vision of town as a centre of development in Western Province has been reanimated and the future of Tabubil as a residence for local families has now been re-envisaged.

In exploring the conjunction of these two crises, Jorgensen reflects on how we might consider change, beyond the dualisms of old and new, and a teleological view that involves retrospecting on times past and prospecting on times to come. The work of historian Koselleck on temporal horizons (2002) and Chris Ballard's critical work on Oceanic historicities (2014) are both relevant here. However, Jorgensen instead seeks inspiration in processual anthropology and an ethnography of the present, as espoused by Sally Falk Moore. How can ethnographers deal not only with regular and durable cycles of events but also with irregular and evanescent phenomena, such as those that more often engage journalists? Further, how in this age of connectedness across time and place can ethnographers such as Jorgensen complement their embodied insights with the ephemera of 'news' gleaned from phone calls and social media?

In his chapter, Simon Foale offers a reflection on how anthropology's ethnographic method and qualitative research is often devalued by those who espouse the superiority of sciences that are based on quantitative methods and large datasets. Simon began his professional life as a marine scientist but later pursued a PhD in anthropology and collaborated with Martha Macintyre on a range of projects, which brought the perspective of political ecology to the study of environmental movements and conservation dynamics in the Western Pacific (e.g. Foale & Macintyre, 2005).

In his contribution to this volume, Foale singles out conservation biology, suggesting that it rules supreme in the marketing of iconic images to promote environmental awareness and action—for example, turtles, dugongs and coral reefs. He critiques the neofunctionalism of conservation biology and how coral reefs are inaccurately portrayed as crucial for fisheries. In fact, reefs are deficient in nutrients; therefore, they constitute poor fishing grounds, as compared to other parts of the ocean. They are biodiverse but unproductive compared to other fishing areas.

He is particularly critical of those 'opinion leaders in coral reef science', who sought to dilute the importance of coral bleaching caused by carbon emissions and warming oceans by 'framing it differently', casting it as only one of the 'multiple drivers of coral reef destruction, along with fishing of herbivorous fish and sediment and nutrient runoff' (Foale, this volume). Such analyses led to austerity programs, the declaration of no-take marine protected areas and huge uncompensated costs for many very poor, and often landless, fishing people in low-income countries. Such paradigms led to the development of resilience theory (e.g. at the Stockholm Resilience Centre)—this, as with the use of resilience in other contexts of climate change, puts the emphasis of responsibility on the local poor rather than the global rich whose emissions are the primary cause (see Jolly, 2019a; McDonnell, 2019). According to Foale, this 'studiously ignored the role of colonialism and global capitalism in driving poverty and environmental destruction in the global economic periphery' (this volume).

Moreover, by claiming to speak on behalf of other species or entire ecosystems, environmental scientists may also intervene in ways that have negative effects on other human beings. He expresses alarm and dismay at the 'undeserved hegemony of natural scientists' (Foale, this volume) in cross-disciplinary projects. He contends that natural scientists are often 'wantonly oblivious to power/knowledge relations' and perpetuate a reductionist and managerialist colonial science (Foale, this volume). They appropriate, dumb down and marginalise the insights of social scientists and, particularly, anthropologists.

Foale's specific case studies form part of a wider critique of how the 'hard' natural sciences are wielding ever-greater hegemony over the 'soft' social sciences and humanities with claims that only quantitative methods and large datasets constitute legitimate 'evidence'. This complements the work of Sally Engle Merry (2017) on the seductions of quantification. Foale sees this epistemic inequality as being buttressed by the neoliberal character of contemporary universities and the administration of research funds by governments and international agencies. The pervasive metric fixation in higher education management and research funding abets the hubris and hegemony of the natural sciences. He proposes only partial solutions; anthropologists must collaborate more and adopt a more strategic approach to publishing, grant-writing and communicating our knowledge to broader public audiences to enhance impact. However, would this entail further capitulating to the hegemony of natural science models?

The Fossil-fuelled Inequalities of Climate Change

Foale's insights into the deeply unequal relations between natural scientists and anthropologists engaged in research on the environment are deeply disturbing for those of us who are struggling to redress the inequalities inherent in the current global crisis of climate change. As I see it, the global inequalities created by the fossil-fuelled capitalist overdevelopment (see Figure 2) of the world are both cause and consequence of our current climate emergency (see Jolly, 2018, 2019a, 2019b). However, it is difficult to raise resistant hope when sceptics and deniers of climate change are wilfully spreading disinformation (with the support of fossil-fuelled interests). The urgency and gravity of the situation surely require a coalition between scholars and activists and between natural and social scientists, involving epistemic equality and mutual respect (see Jolly, 2020).

The papers in this volume are intensively, although not exclusively, focused on PNG (Mcdougall's chapter focuses on the Solomon Islands). This intense focus is justified, not least because PNG is the primary place in which Martha Macintyre conducted her research. This primary focus perforce raises comparative questions about how, given the dominance of extractive industries in PNG's past, present and envisaged future development, the country will fare as the global climate crisis intensifies and dramatic shifts continue in the proportion of global energy supplied by fossil fuels compared to renewables such as solar, wind or hydropower. Other independent states in the Western Pacific have also witnessed the burgeoning inequalities and environmental devastation that are consequent on capitalist models of overdevelopment. However, for example, in Vanuatu, the gender and generational inequalities of land commoditisation and dispossession are linked to an economy that is dependent on tourism, real estate speculation and tax haven schemes and the corruption of a shadow state (see McDonnell, 2017), rather than the extractive industries of logging and mining. These divergent modes of capitalist development have likely generated differences in how gender, race and class inequalities intersect that we do not have space to further explore here (however, see McDonnell, Allen & Filer, 2017; Patterson & Macintyre, 2011; Chapter 1, this volume).

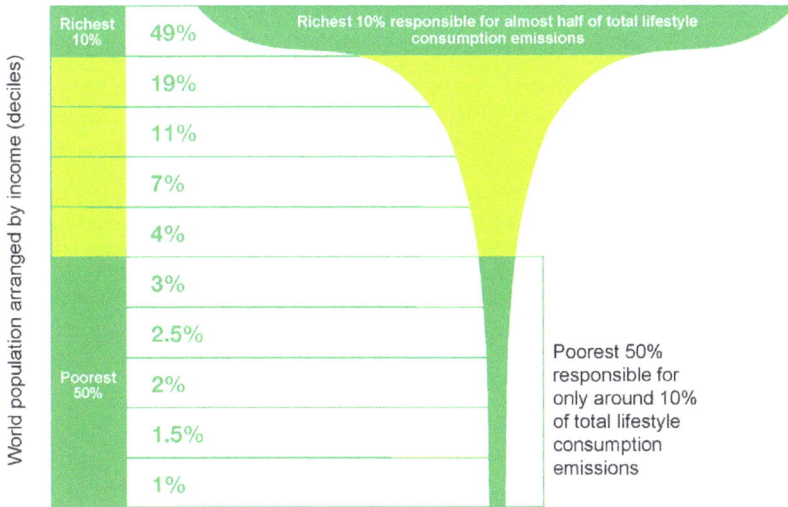

Figure 2: Percentage of CO$_2$ emissions by world population.
Source: Gore (2015).

However, it remains clear that all these independent states of the Western Pacific—PNG, Solomon Islands and Vanuatu—are embedded in broader patterns of global inequality in their experience of climate change, whereby those poor who produce the least carbon emissions are also those who suffer the most. We are all painfully familiar with the iconic, globally circulating images of sea-level rise and king tides engulfing the low-lying atolls of Kiribati, Tuvalu and the Marshall Islands. However, as dire as this situation is, the consequences of climate change across the Pacific reach even further. Sea-level rise and coastal inundation and erosion are also being experienced on the coasts of high, volcanic islands, including those in PNG, Solomon Islands and Vanuatu. This threatens freshwater sources and imperils major food crops (e.g. taro and yams) with greater salinity. Changing patterns of rainfall and seasonality and droughts of greater severity and frequency disturb the patterns of growing and harvesting those garden and tree crops on which many peoples of the Western Pacific still rely for daily food. The warming and acidification of the ocean bleach and kill protective coral reefs. Increased storm surges, floods and more intense and frequent cyclones and hurricanes devastate crops and houses, cause landslides and threaten both lives and livelihoods.

At the Pacific Island Forum in Tuvalu in August 2019, the assembled Pacific leaders issued a radical and solidary declaration that climate change was an existential threat to all people of the region. They insisted that this was their pre-eminent concern for future security, more important even than the geopolitical rivalry, which captures primetime attention in Australia (see Jolly, 2019b; Teaiwa, 2019). Given this, the indifference and condescension shown by the Australian government at Tuvalu—the attempts to dilute the words of the final communiqué and the cheap racist and sexist quips by Australian politicians and shock jocks afterwards—has been extraordinary (see Regenvanu, 2019). Climate sceptics and critics of the Paris Agreement, who argue that Australia contributes only 1.3 per cent of the world's global greenhouse emissions, must confront the harsh reality that (per capita) we are one of the worst polluters in the world. Moreover, our greenhouse emissions are rising and will exponentially increase with the opening of large mines at Adani and in the Galilee Basin in Queensland. Australia's national government must make fundamental changes to its climate change policies and work urgently to reduce its emissions—this is clear to all in the Pacific. It is for this reason that the preferred diplomatic language of Australia as a close neighbour to the Pacific (or even, in Scott Morrison's evangelical Christian vision, 'family') has such a hollow, false resonance in the region (Kabutaulaka & Teaiwa, 2019; McDougall, 2019). Such language obscures the deep inequalities between Australia and the Pacific, inequalities that derive from colonial legacies but still lie at the heart of the contemporary climate emergency. Therefore, the perpetuation of 'unequal lives' might continue in ways that are even more tragic than those we are presently witnessing.

References

Aini, J. & West, P. (2018, June). *Communities matter: Decolonising conservation management*. Plenary Lecture, International Marine Conservation Congress, Kuching, Malaysia.

Bainton, N. A. (2010). *The Lihir destiny: Cultural responses to mining in Melanesia*. Canberra, ACT: ANU E Press. doi.org/10.22459/LD.10.2010

Bainton, N. A. & Macintyre, M. (2016). Mortuary ritual and mining riches in island Melanesia. In D. Lipset & E. Silverman (Eds), *Mortuary dialogues: Death ritual and the reproduction of moral community in Pacific modernities* (pp. 110–132). New York, NY: Berghahn.

Ballard, C. (2014). Oceanic historicities. *The Contemporary Pacific, 26*(1), 95–114.

Bottomley, G., de Lepervanche, M. & Martin, J. (1991). *Intersexions: Gender/class/culture/ethnicity*. Melbourne, Vic.; Sydney, NSW: Allen & Unwin.

Cox, J. (2018). *Fast money schemes: Hope and deception in Papua New Guinea.* Bloomington, IN: Indiana University Press.

Cox, J. & Macintyre, M. (2014). Christian marriage, money scams and Melanesian social imaginaries. *Oceania, 84*(2), 138–157.

Crenshaw, K. (1991). Mapping the margins: Intersectionality, identity politics and violence against women of color. *Stanford Law Review, 43*, 1241–1299.

Dickson-Waiko, A. (2007). Colonial enclaves and domestic spaces in British New Guinea. In K. Darian-Smith, P. Grimshaw & Stuart Macintyre (Eds), *Britishness abroad: Transnational movements and imperial cultures* (pp. 205–230). Carlton, Vic.: Melbourne University Press.

Engle Merry, S. (2017). *The seductions of quantification: Measuring human rights, gender violence and sex trafficking.* Chicago, IL: University of Chicago Press.

Filer, C. (1997). Compensation, rent and power in Papua New Guinea. In S. Toft (Ed.), *Compensation for resource development in Papua New Guinea* (pp. 156–189). Canberra, ACT: The Australian National University.

Foale, S. & Macintyre, M. (2005). Green fantasies: Photographic representations of biodiversity and ecotourism in the Western Pacific. *Journal of Political Ecology, 13*(1), 1–22.

Gewertz, D. & Errington, F. (1999). *Emerging class in Papua New Guinea: The telling of difference.* Cambridge, England: Cambridge University Press.

Godelier, M. & Strathern, M. (Eds). (1991). *Big men and great men: Personifications of power in Melanesia.* New York, NY: Cambridge University Press.

Gore, T. (2015). *Extreme carbon inequality: Why the Paris climate deal must put the poorest, lowest emitting and most vulnerable people first* [Policy Paper]. Retrieved from www.oxfam.org/en/research/extreme-carbon-inequality

Hau'ofa, E. (1975). Anthropology and Pacific Islanders. *Oceania, 45*(4), 283–289. doi.org/10.1002/j.1834-4461.1975.tb01871.x

Jolly, M. (1987). The chimera of equality in Melanesia. *Equality and inequality: Papers in memory of Chandra Jayawardena. Mankind, 17*(2), 168–183.

Jolly, M. (1991). The politics of difference: Feminism, colonialism and decolonisation in Vanuatu. In G. Bottomley, M. de Lepervanche & J. Martin (Eds), *Intersexions: Gender/class/culture/ethnicity* (pp. 52–74). Sydney, NSW: Allen and Unwin.

Jolly, M. (1992). Partible persons and multiple authors (contribution to Book Review Forum on Marilyn Strathern's *The Gender of the Gift*). *Pacific Studies*, *15*(1): 137–149.

Jolly, M. (2012). Women of the East, Women of the West: Region and race, gender and sexuality on Cook's voyages. In K. Fullagar (Ed.), *The Atlantic world in the Antipodes* (pp. 2–32). Newcastle, NSW: Cambridge Scholars Press.

Jolly, M. (2018). Horizons and rifts in conversations about climate change in Oceania. In W. Anderson, M. Johnson & B. Brookes (Eds), *Pacific futures* (pp. 17–48). Honolulu, HI: University of Hawaii Press.

Jolly, M. (2019a). Engendering the anthropocene in Oceania: Fatalism, resilience, resistance. In T. Neale & W. Smith (Eds), *Elemental Anthropocene: Cultural Studies Review*, *25*(2), 172–195.

Jolly, M. (2019b, October). *Blue Pacific, polluted ocean*. Paper presented at the Rethinking Pollution Symposium, School of Culture, History and Language, The Australian National University, Canberra, ACT.

Jolly, M. (2020). Moving beyond disciplinary boundaries to respond to climate change. In M. Sawer, F. Jenkins & K. Downing (Eds), *How gender can transform the social sciences: Innovation and impact* (pp. 187–197). Cham, Switzerland: Palgrave MacMillan (Pivot Series).

Jolly, M. & Macintyre, M. (Eds). (1989). *Family and gender in the Pacific: Domestic contradictions and the colonial impact*. Cambridge, England: Cambridge University Press.

Jolly, M. & Mosko, M. (1994). Transformations of hierarchy: Structure, history and horizon in the Austronesian world. *History and Anthropology*, *7*(1–4), 87–108.

Kabutaulaka, T. (2015). Re-presenting Melanesia: Ignoble savages and Melanesian alter-natives. *The Contemporary Pacific*, *27*(1), 74–145.

Kabutaulaka, T. & Teaiwa, K. (2019, 21 August). Climate, coal, kinship and security in Australia-Pacific Relations. *Australian Outlook*. Retrieved from Australian Institute of International Affairs website: internationalaffairs.org.au/australian outlook/climate-coal-kinship-and-security-in-australia-pacific-relations/

Koselleck, R. (2002). *The practice of conceptual history: Timing history, spacing concepts*. Stanford, CA: Stanford University Press.

Lepani. K. (2012). *Islands of love, island of risk: Culture and HIV in the Trobriands*. Nashville, TN: Vanderbilt University Press.

Macintyre, M. (1983a). *The kula: A bibliography*. Cambridge, England: Cambridge University Press.

Macintyre, M. (1983b). Warfare and the changing context of Kune on Tubetube. *The Journal of Pacific History, 18*(1–2), 11–34.

Macintyre, M. (1984). The problem of the semi-alienable pig. *Canberra Anthropology, 7*(1–2), 109–123.

Macintyre, M. (1988). The unhappy wife and the dispensable husband: Myths of a matrilineal order. In D. Gewertz (Ed.), *The myth of matriarchy reconsidered* (pp. 185–195). Sydney, NSW: Oceania Monograph Series.

Macintyre, M. (1995). Violent bodies and vicious exchanges: Personification and objectification in the Massim. *Social Analysis, 37*(April), 29–43.

Macintyre, M. (2008). Police and thieves, gunmen and drunks: Problems with men and problems with society in Papua New Guinea. *The Australian Journal of Anthropology, 19*(2), 179–193.

Macintyre, M. (2011). Modernity, gender and mining: Experiences from Papua New Guinea. In K. Lahiri-Dutt (Ed.), *Gendering the field: Towards sustainable livelihoods for mining communities* (pp. 21–32). Canberra, ACT: ANU E Press. doi.org/10.22459/GF.03.2011

Macintyre, M. (2012). Gender violence in Melanesia and the problem of Millennium Development Goal No. 3. In M. Jolly, C. Stewart & C. Brewer (Eds), *Engendering violence in Papua New Guinea* (pp. 239–266). Canberra, ACT: ANU E Press. doi.org/10.22459/EVPNG.07.2012

Macintyre, M. (2017). Flux and change in Melanesian gender relations. In M. Macintyre & C. Spark (Eds), *Transformations of gender in Melanesia* (pp. 1–22). Canberra, ACT: ANU Press. doi.org/10.22459/TGM.02.2017

Macintyre, M. & Spark, C. (Eds). (2017). *Transformations of gender in Melanesia*. Acton, ACT: Australian National University Press.

Martin, K. (2013). *The death of the big men and the rise of the big shots: Custom and conflict in East New Britain*. New York, NY: Berghahn Books.

McDonnell, S. (2017). Urban land grabbing by political elites: Exploring the political economy of land and the challenges of regulations. In S. McDonnell, M. G. Allen & C. Filer (Eds), *Kastom, property and ideology: Land transformations in Melanesia* (pp. 283–304). Canberra, ACT: ANU Press. doi.org/10.22459/KPI.03.2017

McDonnell, S. (2019). Other dark sides of resilience: Politics and power in community-based efforts to strengthen resilience. *Anthropological Forum*, 29, 1–19. doi.org/10.1080/00664677.2019.1647828

McDonnell, S., Allen, M, G. & Filer, C. (Eds). (2017). *Kastom, property and ideology: Land transformations in Melanesia*. Canberra, ACT: ANU Press. doi.org/10.22459/KPI.03.2017

McDougall, D. (2019, 13 June). Singing the same tune? Scott Morrison and Australia's Pacific Family. *Australian Outlook*. Retrieved from Australian Institute of International Affairs website: internationalaffairs.org.au/australian outlook/singing-same-tune-scott-morrison-australias-pacific-family/

Moore, A. (2019). *Destination anthropocene: Science and tourism in the Bahamas*. Berkeley, CA: University of California Press.

Patterson, M. & Macintyre, M. (Eds). (2011). *Managing modernity in the Western Pacific*. St Lucia, Qld: University of Queensland Press.

Regenvanu, R. (2019, 19 August). Vanuatu will host the next Pacific Islands Forum. We want to know if Australia really wants a seat at the table. *The Guardian*. Retrieved from www.theguardian.com/world/2019/aug/20/vanuatu-will-host-the-next-pacific-islands-forum-we-want-to-know-if-australia-really-wants-a-seat-at-the-table

Robbins, J. (2013). Beyond the suffering subject: Toward an anthropology of the good. *Journal of the Royal Anthropological Institute*, *19*(3), 447–462. doi.org/10.1111/1467-9655.12044

Sahlins, M. (1963). Poor man, rich man, big-man, chief: Political types in Melanesia and Polynesia. *Comparative Studies in Society and History*, *5*(3), 285–303.

Strathern, M. (1987). *Dealing with inequality: Analysing gender relations in Melanesia and beyond*. Cambridge, England: Cambridge University Press.

Strathern, M. (1988). *The gender of the gift*. Berkeley, CA: University of California Press.

Strathern, M. (2005). *Partial connections*. Walnut Creek, CA: AltaMira Press/ Rowman and Littlefield Publishers. (Original work published 1991.)

Teaiwa, K. (2019). No distant future: Climate change as an existential threat. *Australian Foreign Affairs*, 6, 51–70.

Wardlow, H. (2018, December). *Thinking through intersectionality and gender inequality in Papua New Guinea*. Paper presented at the European Society for Oceanists Conference, London and Cambridge.

West, P. (2006). *Conservation is our government now: The politics of ecology in Papua New Guinea*. Durham, NC: Duke University Press.

West, P. (2012). *From modern production to imagined primitive: The social life of coffee from Papua New Guinea*. Durham, NC: Duke University Press.

West, P. (2016). *Dispossession and the environment: Rhetoric and inequality in Papua New Guinea*. La Vergne, TN: Columbia University Press.

Yuval-Davis, N. & Athias, F (Eds). (1989). *Woman-nation-state*. Houndsmills, Basingstoke, England: The Macmillan Press.

Coda: A Legacy of Engaged Anthropology

Encountering Anthropology: An Interview with Martha Macintyre

Martha Macintyre and Alex Golub

The following is an edited excerpt from a 2018 interview with Martha Macintyre, conducted by Alex Golub in Melbourne. Martha traces her entry into anthropology, important personal influences that have shaped the trajectory of her career (from her early historical anthropology of *kula* exchange systems to her applied work with mining companies and the police force in Papua New Guinea [PNG]) and her various forms of activism. The discussion concludes with some timeless advice for students. The full interview transcript has been deposited in the Melanesian Archives at the University of California, San Diego.

Beginnings

Alex: So how did you get interested in anthropology originally?

Martha: I came from a very left-wing family. My mother was secretary of the industrial nurses' union in Victoria, and she worked as an industrial nurse from the time when I was about nine years old. My father worked in a factory as a laboratory assistant and later went to night school and qualified as an industrial chemist. My parents were both very active in the Labor Party and as well as in the trade unions.

I started university in 1964; during this time, I had been involved in two big political campaigns—anti-apartheid and opposition to the war in Vietnam. The Australian Trade Unions organised international solidarity campaigns, so my parents inspired me to activism. My generation was the first group of people in Australia to be conscripted into fighting in Vietnam, so I was very involved in the anti–Vietnam War movement.

Then, of course, there was Women's Liberation. All of those things involved me at university. We campaigned to have a women's studies subject at the University of Melbourne, when I was a tutor in history. I was also involved in student theatre. I acted in several productions and at one stage thought I might be an actress.

At Cambridge, when I first arrived in 1972, it was the height of the women's movement, and we had a big campaign for child care, which they there call nurseries. I got involved in that, thinking this is going to be useful to me (I was pregnant). And through that, I met a lot of people who were involved in feminist studies. We campaigned and won the battle for a subject in Sociology—The Women's Paper. Two things came out from that. One was a book called *Women and society*, which was the name of the subject, and I have a jointly authored chapter in that. The other one was *Nature, culture and gender*. Elena Lievin, a psychologist, Ludi Jordanova, a historian, Carol McCormack, an anthropologist, and I organised a seminar called 'Nature, culture and gender' and we invited people over the course of the year to give papers in it.

I had not encountered anthropology before I went to England. It wasn't offered in Melbourne. I went to Cambridge with the intention of doing a PhD in history. But that proved problematic because I didn't have much money. I thought I would get a scholarship, and I didn't. I was going to do my PhD in the area of history of ideas, history and philosophy of science.

My husband and I went together to Cambridge and then I discovered I was pregnant. I thought, 'With no money, I cannot do a PhD and have a baby'. I decided I'd better quickly get a job before I looked pregnant. I had made friends because I was teaching on the women's studies course. They wanted people who had some experience in women's studies, and I had had experience in Melbourne. I was teaching the history of feminism, and I'd met Christine Hugh-Jones, who was completing her PhD, supervised by Edmund Leach. I said to her, 'I've got to get a job quickly. Do you know anybody who can give me a research assistant job or anything?' And she said, 'I think Edmund Leach needs someone to fix up his library'.

She put in a word for me with Edmund, and I got the job working four or five mornings a week. His library was a beautiful conservatory in the Master's Lodge because he was then the Master of King's College. When I went into it, it was a midden! Offprints of his own and other authors, letters, notes, lectures, drafts of articles and copies of various journals. After several months I realised that under the pile was a table! There were papers that went six feet up the wall one end and he said to me, 'Just start anywhere and catalogue and put them into files'.

It took me about two years to catalogue the whole library. I would take things home and read them, and sometimes he'd just say, 'Have a look at this. What do you think?' Or he'd give me things he was writing himself. Anyway, I got more and more absorbed in anthropology, so I thought, 'I now know more about anthropology than I know about history'. Well, after three years of doing that, I thought, 'I think I better do the certificate course'.

It's now called an MPhil. It was one-year intensive. It was an incredible course. You sat four exam papers: one on judicial and legal anthropology, one on kinship, one on the economy and one on religion and ritual. But there were no lecture courses attached to any of them. You just went to any lecture that appeared to be relevant, and you had a supervisor who set you specific topics.

My husband Stuart was at St John's College where he became very close friends with Jack Goody. Jack offered to supervise my studies. But Jack Goody and Edmund Leach were at loggerheads, so I felt conflicted about accepting his offer. In his office, Leach used to have a Sarawak machete—a long-bladed sword with human hair on the end. And when I was pregnant and couldn't sleep, in the last stages of pregnancy, I used to lie there and invent detective stories whereby one of them would be found with the Sarawak blade lodged in his head.

I thought, 'I can't have Goody as a supervisor'—although he did supervise me for a little while on the kinship paper, so I said to Leach, 'Well, who should I get?' And he said, 'You're not going to be supervised by me?' I said, 'No'. By that stage, I'd worked for him for three years, and I think our relationship was quite different. He was my boss, but there was a very easy friendship too. We'd sometimes sit in the garden behind the library and have lunch together. I just didn't want it complicated as I knew that I would disagree with him on some things. He said, 'Well there's this woman who's just returned from PNG. She can't get a job because her husband's already employed. Her name's Marilyn Strathern. Go and see if she'll supervise you.'

I went over to the Haddon Library and got out her thesis. As I read it, I thought, 'Oh this is terrific. I'd love being supervised by her.' But, then I flicked to the front, and it's got a disclaimer that her work is all her own and not her husband's. You know, that's pretty weird! And, of course, his thesis was right next to hers, so I opened it up. He has no disclaimer!

Kula

Alex: Can you tell me about how you got interested in PNG?

Martha: Well, I did the certificate course, and I did very well in it. Stuart, by that stage, had a postdoctoral fellowship. I didn't have a job, so I said to Edmund, 'Can I still come back?' He said, 'I've got this plan to have a conference on the *kula,* and I want you to get everything that has ever been written on the *kula* and prepare a bibliography for all the conference people'. I had never heard of the *kula.*

Alex: You hadn't read any Malinowski?

Martha: No, I'd never read Malinowski at that stage because much of my reading had been on Africa and South-East Asia. For my major essay, I had done a history of the ideas on the debate about African models in New Guinea Highlands. I was interested in Melanesia and, of course, Marilyn introduced me to quite a lot of Melanesian material. But I'd never read Malinowski. So, I went to the University Library and looked up '*kula*'— because he'd written it down for me—and there was one book! It was on a tribe in Sri Lanka called *The kula.* I took it out and I read it, and I thought, 'How are we going to have a conference on this?' It was written in 1906! So I went back to him said, 'Look, I could honestly only find one book and nobody has written anything about this group ever since'. He said, 'Really?' And I said, 'No'. He said, 'Except that I've got that whole shelf there!', pointing to all the works of Malinowski and a whole lot of stuff on Melanesia. He pulled out *Argonauts* and said, 'Take this home and read it over the weekend and come back and start the bibliography'. I took it home, read it, and then I walked in the next day, and he asked me, 'What did you make of it?' I said, 'People don't believe this, do they?'

He took a dark double take, and I said, 'Look, that place has been swarming with plantation owners, with pearlers, with missionaries and traders'. You know, I'm always a historian in some ways. I said to him, 'These people have been involved in employment. There has been pacification in the region for many years. There are missionaries everywhere. They barely get a mention in this bloody book!' And he was really taken aback. But, he was interested in my criticisms. He said, 'Well go and read all about it and see if people respond anthropologically in the way that you do'. But, of course, they didn't then.

I became more and more interested. When I produced the bibliography, it was really for him. Then he said to me, 'Oh, I'm just going to send this off to Cambridge University Press, as it is'. I didn't even have time to do anything to it, which is why it's sort of in this funny note form.

None of the people I mixed with in anthropology were working in Melanesia. Chris Gregory was in economics, but we hit it off personally and we have maintained that friendship from the time of the *kula* conference. But, in the seminars and lectures, I found the few Melanesian ones that I attended much more interesting. The one that really inspired me was Gilbert Lewis. Gilbert was a fantastic lecturer. I'll never forget the lecture about 'What is a ritual?' Which is part of the book *Day of shining red*. He just started ambling around, demonstrating the way that people walk about as a platform or ritual space is being prepared. He posed the question, 'How do you know when the ritual starts, when everyone's just of walking around, absorbed in practical tasks?' He gave us a sense of what it was like to be in a village and trying to work out what was happening, knowing that this was a ritual, but when does it start? And then, who are the protagonists and, then, how do you analyse and interpret what's essentially a chaotic social idea?

Fieldwork in Tubetube

Alex: How did you end up on Tubetube?

Martha: Having done all the research, I thought 'Where is the area that's least known?' If you look at the map in the *kula* book, there's a circle around the southern part because everyone knew that it was the centre of the *kula* in the south, but nobody had worked there, except for Cyril Belshaw, who got it completely wrong. Well, no, he didn't get it completely wrong. But, he just didn't understand that what he called *kune* and *leau* was the *kula*. *Kune* is what it's called in the Tubetube language, and he thinks they're different systems. It's just the same word in two different languages, you know. He has *kune* one and *kune* two … I can see why, because you get there and it doesn't work like Malinowski said it did, so he thinks it's a different system.

I got to Moresby, I got my research permit from the National Research Institute. You had to apply to the province and get permission from the local-level government and the provincial government. I was told I had permission from the local-level government. In fact, they didn't even inquire but, because I had the provincial one, I just set off, because they were the ones who were responsible for getting local-level government approval for your presence there. They didn't want to go out to Tubetube. Who would want to? Trek out all that way. And in those days there were no fast boats, it was a day's trip. Nobody on Tubetube was expecting me.

I went to The Australian National University to have Michael Young as a supervisor, who had worked in the region, who really knew it well and he prepared me very well for what I would need. I was used to living fairly frugally, so I wasn't set back by any of the privations of living in a village. The thing that bothered me most was that I left behind two small children. I had no means of contacting them. Once you were out on the island, there was no radio. Sometimes, there were no boats. So, that was my main source of anxiety.

They were in Perth. I was on a grant. I had so little money. To get to Perth from Canberra was about $600, but I just couldn't bear to go off, for me not to be there for my daughter's birthday. I blew my money and went there and I said 'No, you know, I can't do this, I can't'. Stuart convinced me, 'You've done so much work on this, you've got to go'. I went, actually quite reluctantly. And a lot of people have since asked me, 'Should I take my children along?' I don't think I could've taken my children there. It's such a malarial area. I think it's a terrible thing to do, to leave small children for months. Really, I've thought many times that if I could go back in time, I would not go to Tubetube. It's very strange, as my life from that time has been dominated by work in PNG, but I now know how hard it was for the people I love most.

Alex: What was fieldwork like? What did your day consist of?

Martha: Well, when I couldn't speak the language, the first thing I did was walk around and I'd have either Mary or Catherine or Fred—my three assistants, you know, they all have English names because it's been missionised for so long. I'd been taught how to map. I mapped villages, gardens, paths. And I just constantly tried to learn the language, all the time we were walking. It takes about two and a half hours to walk around the island and I would just point to things and ask for words and, gradually, built it up. For the first four months, I concentrated on learning the language.

Because I had my tape recorder, I just used to tape everybody. Because I said, 'This is how I'm going to learn the language. I'll just listen to what you talk about. Can I turn it on? And anything you say will be on that thing.' They used to laugh listening to it, hearing their conversations back again. If we sat down and other people were talking about something else I didn't understand a word of, I'd have the tape running. When we'd get back, I'd say, 'Fred, what's that word? What's that word?' I did all the usual things, you know, getting family names and genealogies. I mapped the whole place, and I collected a lot of data on gardening. For the first six months, I concentrated on things that I could just watch and describe and later ask questions about. But, after I could speak the language, I started working on the historical material and the *kula*.

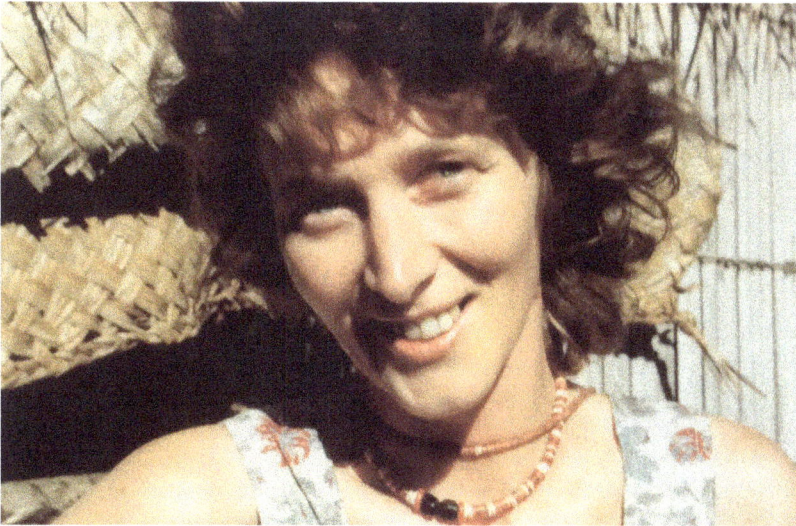

Figure 1: Martha Macintyre, Tubetube (1980).
Source: Photo by James Weiner.

477

If you look at my thesis, it's an historical ethnography. That's what I set out to do and that's what I did. I really wanted to understand how it had changed in the context of the colonial period; what the effect of pacification had been; what the effect was of things moving in and out. I knew from Malinowski that stone axe blades go out up in the north—they don't go out in the south, as you see from Debbora Battaglia's work. They're still circulating down there. And, in the past, those things were circulating with *mwali* and *bagi*—items such as *sapisapi* belts, boars' teeth, turtleshell ornaments and stone axes. All of those things were *kula* objects in the Malinowskian sense of the word. And what intrigued me was: 'When did some things drop out?' and 'How come up north they've only got these two things while down south all of those things are called *kune*?' Canoes are called *kune*. And you pay for them with your valuables. I was just trying to reconstitute not only what it was now, but what it was in the past.

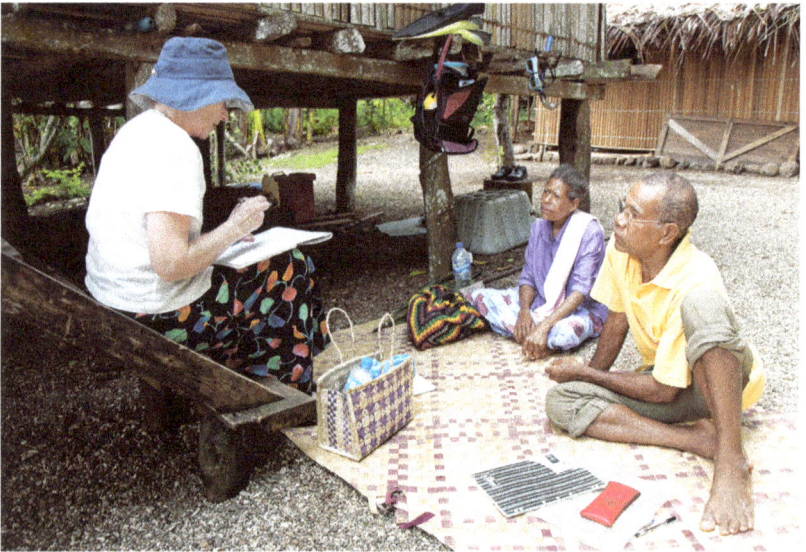

Figure 2: Martha at Lagisuna, Tubetube, checking material collected a decade earlier (2010) with Fred Boita and Catherine Arthur.
Source: Photo by Simon Foale.

The Australian National University (ANU)

Martha: Michael Young and Roger Keesing were my supervisors. Michael kept in touch with me while I was in the field, as much as was possible in those days. Tubetube was very remote. There was no radio contact, I was very dependent on boats coming by with mail and dropping it off.

And I had the classic thing—all my field notes went missing. I had them in a box, and when I went to get on the plane, they made me put it in the hold. They wouldn't let me take it as carry-on luggage. When I got to Canberra, it wasn't there. I was so horrified that I didn't tell anyone, I just went home and cried. And I started writing.

Six months later, one of the academics, Gehan Wijewardena, arrived back from fieldwork in Sri Lanka, no, Thailand, opened his door—there's a box. And it was so funny because we were all sitting there having a cup of coffee with several other people and Gehan emerges with this box and says, 'Martha, this has got your name on it. What's it doing in my room?'

Stuart moved to the University of Melbourne from Perth, which made things a lot easier. So, during that stage, when I was in the field, he moved over to Melbourne. When I was writing up … he applied for a visiting fellowship in Canberra and came up, and we all lived there. And that made life a lot easier for the last year of my research and for the first bit of my postdoc.

Canberra was a really interesting place to be then. Roger Keesing—I have a lot of criticism of him on various fronts, but he was someone who brought people in, had interesting seminars going. He set up this project with sociolinguistics, which brought in a lot of young scholars, to discuss and develop research based on Dell Hymes' work. I'd never really encountered sociolinguistics until then, but I attended some of the seminars, and I found them very absorbing. There were a lot of Pacific scholars there. Marie Reay, Michael and Roger in the Research School and in my cohort, Jimmy Weiner and Wayne Warry. Darryl Feil finished his PhD shortly after I arrived. Anthony Forge was head of department in the faculties. Don Gardner was there, Robert Attenborough, Patrick Guinness, Jadran Mimica, Shirley Campbell and Deane Fergie were in the other department—all doing research in Melanesia.

And visitors came, such as Deborah Gewertz and Fred Errington. So, you really felt a buzz of ideas around gender and issues of Pacific ethnography. Similarly, because at that stage, there were other people doing PhDs, I had people to talk to who I found interesting. Later, when I graduated, there was another crop who I was in touch with all the time as they were doing their PhDs. Chris Ballard, John Burton, Klaus Neumann, Nicholas Thomas. Exchange was a really important topic, the networks of exchange and, increasingly, people in both history and anthropology were studying the effects of colonisation on Melanesian economies. Because I had taken a historical approach to the *kula* exchange system, I found that the archaeologists there were interested in my research. It was a fantastic Archaeology Department, with Jack Golson, Jim Allen; Chris Gosden was there for a while and other people who were interested in the exchange of material objects and migration in Melanesia. You always had people feeding new ideas into your own work.

PhD Thesis

Alex: Could you tell me a little bit about what your thesis was about? You said it was a historical approach to *kula*.

Martha: I was interested in the *kula* because of the ways it embodied values placed on specific material objects. I kept thinking, 'How did these objects, which are shells, have so much other meaning once they are transformed?'

My hypothesis before I went was that whatever Malinowski saw in his fieldwork, in the early twentieth century, was not an enduring tradition. It had to have been utterly transformed by pacification, by missions, by the imposition of colonial government and by the changed economy. Because he has very little about the changed economy. You know, it's just on the side. Oh, there are these pearlers there, and people give Hancock [G. F. B. Hancock] pearls for money, and goods, and *kula* shells and all this sort of stuff. And it doesn't get drawn into his analysis at all. Then I realised I had a predecessor, J. P. Singh Uberoi, who made a very similar argument about the effects of pacification. I still think he is absolutely right in his reinterpretation of the *kula* in terms of the political changes that occurred in the context of pacification and the imposition of colonial rule. So, that was what I wanted to do, was to look at the effects of social and economic change on the *kula* system and, in so doing, perhaps try to do some reconstruction. Well, as you can imagine, this was somewhat iconoclastic. Malinowski was just appalled at any kind of conjectural history, as he called it.

But, I thought, I will at least be able to talk, at that stage, to old people who might recall stages in the economic changes and discuss what they saw. I concentrated on what was within living memory, although I also had some conjectures about the changes that had occurred prior to this. When I was doing the bibliography of the *kula* and at the first *kula* conference, we realised that although Seligman and Malinowski both designate Tubetube as the southern major axis, this tiny little island was very odd. Why would such a minute place be so important as the route, the southern route? That interested me, because I knew from the reading I'd done that Tubetube was one of the first places, after Dobu, that was missionised.

That intrigued me too. There was a long history of the missionaries being there. As I read all the government reports, I also realised that it had experienced interventionist government control, because Tubetube people were seen as warlike, which they were. I had that kind of historical dimension, that people should look at ethnography through a historical lens, take into account the effects of colonisation. This is not considered very strange now but, in 1979, it was viewed with some suspicion. I remember there was a debate of who could possibly examine my thesis because it wasn't really anthropology. Donald Denoon was one of my examiners because of that.

Alex: Was Michael Young's approach influential on you or maybe your approach was influential on him? How did he fit into this?

Martha: Michael Young was very encouraging of it, but he hadn't published very much of that stuff at that stage. I think we influenced each other. He agreed with me that, yes, historical change is very important. And a lot of people would now agree, but, then, how you studied it and how you inserted, or enmeshed, sources of different types: literature, and memoirs, and government reports—what Tubetube people were up to. Just what kind of value did you place on it? And there was much more scepticism and antagonism. At the second *kula* conference in Charlottesville, Nancy Munn was scathing in her criticism of any anthropological 'reconstruction' and insisted that there would be no available data on Gawa anyhow.

John Barker's work was thought about similarly. I remember when he contacted me about contributing to a piece he was doing on religion in Oceania. He said there were so few people who talked about the fact that there were churches in every village. They would just ignore them. Or schools in every village. And the view that people weren't really Christian, whatever that might mean, was very strong. It came out in Mimi Kahn's work—because they didn't seem to be conventionally Christian, it must be a veneer. She called them Sunday Christians, Monday sorcerers.

Whereas, when I was there, well, I suppose I had expected them to be Christians, having been the second place in Milne Bay to have a resident missionary. In fact, when I got there, I found out that the missionaries had left very soon after the station was built because they all started dying of malaria. They had a very peculiar form of Christianity, which now, because I've written about it, I gather upsets the local—some of the more educated—Tubetube people. Some of them went across to Bunama, to Normanby Island, where the mission school was based, and learned to speak English and to become good Christians and pastors. For a while, there were Samoans on the island, Samoans and Rarotongans, missionaries. But, it was not quite the kind of total immersion that the Dobuans had had in Wesleyan Christianity. It was quite intriguing. I haven't written a lot about that, partly because I realised now that it's much more sensitive now even than when I was there. The only books they had in their own language, which they used to teach people to write in their own language, were the hymn book, a sort of abbreviated version of Bunyan's *The pilgrim's progress* and the *Gospel of Saint Luke*.

I suppose the religious thing turned out to be quite different from the way I had expected. I thought it would be much more institutionalised, much more recognisably Wesleyan. I'd read a lot about the Wesleyan Church in New Ireland and other places in PNG, and I expected it to be like that, and it wasn't. It was local, very idiosyncratic. My argument about the transformation of the *kula* was messier than I had hoped. I still feel there are some problems there that I haven't solved but, in effect, I would say, I would almost say now that the *kula* didn't exist before colonisation. I wouldn't have dared say that then. I remember sitting with Roger once and saying, 'I think perhaps I should write my thesis referring to this system as it's referred to, as *kune* and *leau*, in Tubetube, and never mention *kula*. And see if people twig to the fact that this was the *kula*.'

Because I found that *kula* valuables were used in so many other more contexts than I had known, and remain constantly in use, going in and out of the *kula* ring, my image of the *kula* is entirely different from Malinowski's.

ANU Postdoctorate

Martha: Roger said I could get into the Gender Relations in Melanesia project if I finished my thesis six months early. Its aim was to be a kind of discussion that would produce new material on gender. It was based in the Research School of Pacific Studies, as it was then. It was a brainchild of Roger Keesing.

I wrote like a demon and finished it in time to be in on the beginning. Marilyn Strathern was the person chosen to be the leading light in that project. Margaret Jolly was also a postdoc, and me, and various other people, who came and went as visitors. Anyway, that was a real buzz, because I guess it was a time when the whole debate about women, anthropology, the influence of Western feminism on ways of viewing all academic disciplines, were in question. It was a really exciting project. Lots of seminars and discussions.

The book that came out from it was called *Dealing with inequality*, that Marilyn edited. That was the result of a very interesting series of discussions and seminars, where each of us gave something related to the theme: 'What is inequality and what is gender inequality?' All the time I was involved in that I was really inspired: 'This is it!' I think that was the time when I really got excited about anthropology being a very dynamic, changing discipline, in a way that I never felt about history. You know, history is different, history builds. You don't get these dramatic turns. It also provided me with the opportunity to learn how to supervise, as my first three supervisions were when I was a young postdoc. And when you've got a lot of time like that and you're intellectually engaged yourself, it is quite a good thing to be engaged with other people's work. I was the co-supervisor for Jim Fingleton, who wrote on Tolai, Maureen McKenzie and Klaus Neumann.

I moved back to Melbourne and in 1985 was appointed to a lectureship at La Trobe University. From that time on, I started doing occasional consultancies. By that time, things were getting tight financially at

La Trobe, so funding for research was nil. I wanted to get back to PNG, and I thought, 'Oh, this will get me back into the field'. So, I did the Misima work. I moved to Melbourne University in 1998.

Activism

Martha: My activism has been kind of sporadic. On women's issues, I've always had some commitment and involvement. For example, I was very involved with the women's movement here, before England. For many years, it was the movement for gun control. I was involved with it because I met a young bank teller who had been completely traumatised by being held up at gunpoint and having someone holding a gun to his head. And I asked myself: 'What kind of country is it, that I can just get a gun and walk into a bank, for heaven's sake?'

The longest political campaign that I was involved with was to do with the post-de-institutionalisation of mentally ill people, which, in Australia as in other countries, had many disastrous side effects. They are put out on the street. The park that we went walking in used to house the big mental hospital. And I think quite literally, they just said, 'Well, you're not in here anymore' to people who had been there for many, many years. All around this area here, you would encounter people who really couldn't function in the world. The mentally ill and people in prison are the two least glamorous sorts of activism to be involved in.

But, I just felt so badly about it, I contacted a minister in the church over in North Melbourne and said, 'Something's got to be done about getting these people some housing, some proper services to help them readjust to living in the community.' For 10 years, I was involved in what was called the Macauley Association. We were a non-government organisation (NGO). We had to apply for funding and support everywhere, to employ people and set up housing and assistance for mentally ill people to adjust to living in the community.

For the last few years, I have been a member of the Grandmothers against Detention of Refugee Children. We held demonstrations and lobbied politicians. It took a long time but, in the end, almost all the children were moved from offshore detention. Alas, many are now detained in Australia.

I should say the other thing about where my academic interests and my feminist politics overlap. For a long time, I was involved with the International Women's Development Agency, which began as a kind of ginger group to attempt to get the Australian aid agency to look at things to do with women in the Pacific region where it gave aid. Women were never given any kind of place in aid; it was all agricultural projects for men in cash cropping and things like that. What started as a little political movement is now an independent NGO. I was on the board of that for a while too. That was a real crossover because, by that time, issues of violence against women in PNG and the Solomons and other places had become an issue for NGOs.

Misima Consulting

Alex: Let's shift to talking about your consulting work and how and why you got into consulting.

Martha: In 1985, I was approached by EFIC, the Export Finance and Insurance Corporation, which is a commercial arm of the government in Australia. Although I didn't realise at the time, they were the insurers for Placer Pacific for the Misima project. They asked me if I could help prepare what was part of a much larger feasibility study to weigh up and decide whether or not they would finance it and what kinds of constraints they'd put on the company. In retrospect, they didn't explain their role very well to me. I thought this would be a good way of getting back to PNG. I did negotiate that any report I wrote—and this was the same for Lihir—had to be of value to the government of PNG and to the local people, so that decisions made in respect of my report would be clear and open.

But, I think, perhaps I was somewhat naive, because it was a fairly narrow consultancy, that one. I thought, 'Oh, this will be very helpful, because they always stuff up land tenure arrangements and have peculiar ideas about communal ownership and things like that'. It was clear when they were talking to me that they really had no idea, neither the company nor these EFIC people, of how people held their land and what kinds of relationships they had. There was also the idea that there was land there that belonged to no one. I thought, 'Well at least I can be helpful in that and identify the ways in which people own or transmit or in other ways have claims over their land'. Although it was called a social impact study, the terms of reference were not very clear.

I read a lot about social impact analysis, which was very geared to Western countries, where you had lots and lots of data. You could do a social impact study at a desk in Australia. I thought, 'Oh God, I'll have to put in some of these other things'.

I was working with Rolf Gerritsen, who'd done social impact studies because he was going to do the economic/business side of it. Rolf was in Development Studies at ANU then. He had worked in PNG. But, he'd done a lot of research on economic development—in Ghana, PNG and in Australia. He was trained in economics and interested in the ways in which small-holder agriculture worked in developing countries, the transformation from subsistence to cash cropping, that kind of thing. He was much more experienced working with those guys than I was.

I couldn't work out how EFIC had heard of me but, apparently, they'd asked who had worked in that region, not realising that every island has a different language. Because at least they did realise that someone would have to be able to communicate, which in fact was not really true, although a lot of Misimans can speak Tubetube, it's not easy to work in a different language in the field. But, a lot of Misimans also speak English because of the mission school they had for decades. It was one of the early places that had missions, and they taught in English. Very highly educated group, the Misimans.

They'd also had previous mining. This was the 16th mining operation. They were not little innocent people who had no experience in mining. They have had very large mining projects there for over a century. And I felt—and this really changed over the period of my time working in PNG—the Department of Minerals and Energy, as it was then, was protective of the interests of local landowners. They really tried to protect the interests of local people. I recall my meetings with the various public servants before I went to Misima and I did believe that they supported landowner interests and conservation.

But, it was clear that, higher up the food chain, the PNG government wanted Misima to go ahead and were not really interested in the social or the environmental impact. They thought it was small enough in scale, people were very enthusiastic about it, and they were used to mining.

Obviously, fussing away about drawing up new sorts of arrangements, as happened in Porgera, at the development forums and things like that, would mean they were not going to get it up and running quickly. Those people who I initially dealt with had very little influence over what eventually happened. That kind of disturbed me, to be honest. I felt bad about that because ideas about ways of implementing processes for improved housing, standards of roads and a whole lot of things were just swept aside. Things that the mining company could do and that everybody wanted. The people wanted a big flashy high school. Rolf argued against it on the grounds that it would not be sustained by the government when the mine closed.

Alex: How long did it take you to do the study?

Martha: I was there for about three months. Some things were just checking how similar they were to Tubetube. All across that region, ideas of kinship and land, relations to land and transfer of land and property are very similar. I was confident that I was on firm ground. But, as happens in lots of places, the company wants to constantly restrict the number of people whom they acknowledge as having a stake in this process. They designate landowners, and they're the people who they restrict their benefits to as much as possible. Which was crazy on Misima. It's a small island; everybody is affected. And I think, in retrospect, I didn't speak strongly enough about that. I was bullied by them into, you know, 'But these people are losing their land and those people aren't'.

There was some opposition from women, which I found interesting. This was because of the disruption that they remembered previously and the marginalisation of women in the mining industry, so that women didn't have access to money. I called a meeting of women at the mission station and I was amazed how many came. The old ladies got up and spoke about the effects of previous mine projects, of prostitution in the community, of illegitimate children to miners, that kind of talk. But, everybody thought that that could be controlled, including the women. They wanted the mine, you know. They just wanted people to acknowledge that this might happen, so you control it. They were enthusiastic about bringing in laws restricting how women can dress or, you know.

The mine took on board some quite good things, such as schooling and the employment of women. Only a few in 'non-traditional' jobs, but at least they tried. One later became the head of IT at the Lihir gold mine. But, Placer did things on the cheap there. The roads were not well-made and fell apart in the rainy season.

I was interested in what was happening in PNG. And I also think that the best teaching is informed by research. I think that people who just do their research when they are doing their doctorate and teach on that for the rest of their life become very boring teachers. You teach what you're studying. I have very rarely taught exclusively on PNG. But, it engages you with theoretical developments that you think, 'How do I deal with this material?' When you're writing reports, I think people quite incorrectly see them as atheoretical. The theory is implicit, and it's heavily descriptive, but you do have to keep abreast of how people are thinking about economic change, how people are conceptualising the demise of a whole lot of institutions that occur in the context of mining. I like doing research, even though, as we've discussed, it's often very uncomfortable.

Lihir

Alex: You ended up doing the Misima consulting and then Lihir was right afterwards?

Martha: Not really, it was almost 10 years later. I did work in Australia because having children restricted travel. I tried to get back to Tubetube a few times, but it was always very short periods of time because the kids were at school and I was teaching. I did a study of El Salvadoran refugees, and I did a couple of pieces of research combining with people at Melbourne University in the medical faculty, on refugees' experience of the health system in Australia. In that period of time, up until 1995, I wasn't working on mining, but that was when Bougainville was happening I was reading about it and thinking, 'My God!' Ok Tedi was becoming more and more crazy in terms of environmental damage, so when I was approached to do the Lihir social impact study, at first I did it with Rolf again, but because he worked exclusively on what would be the associated business development and how to work in Lihir. He dropped out, and they asked me to stay on and do annual monitoring, so I did that.

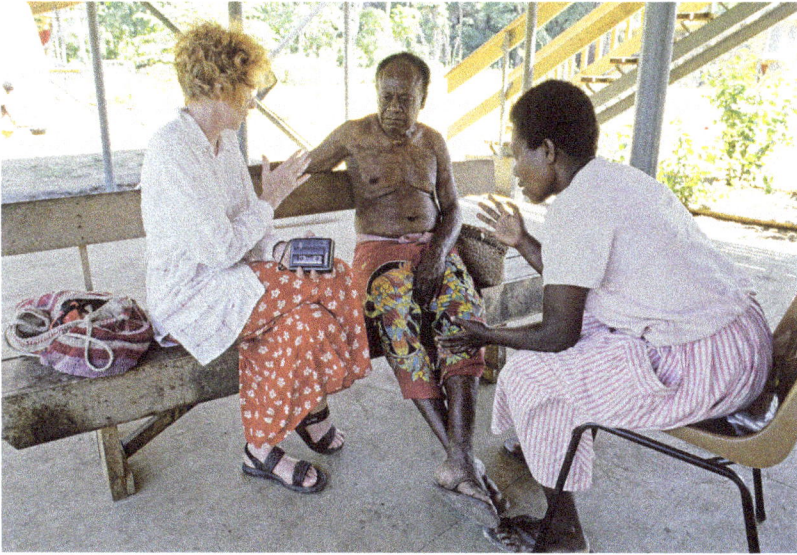

Figure 3: Martha Macintyre and Emma Zanahien interviewing John Pae underneath a new relocation house in Putput village, Lihir (1996).
Source: Martha Macintyre research archives.

Social monitoring requires you to collect a lot of information on health and I became very interested in health in PNG. The Human Development Indicators that are accepted by the United Nations and the World Health Organization include maternal health and mortality, infant health and mortality, injuries and deaths from injury, infectious diseases and endemic diseases as well as health service provision. I'd immersed myself in the international literature when I was working out what would be monitored.

My work with refugees introduced me to another area of research. Refugees arrive with massive health problems, often psychological or psychiatric problems, but they have children, and they have to negotiate a new health system. They often have babies shortly after their arrival. I did a comparative study of refugees from Russia, Ukraine, China, Latin America, Iraq and Turkey.

With all things, you can always find someone who's prepared to sit down and say you should read this and you should read that. I talked a lot with others who had worked on mining—Richard Jackson, with Colin Filer who was an old friend from Cambridge anyhow. John Burton taught me so much about demography, just from his own extraordinary knowledge of the subject and ways of dealing with it. Robin Hide is the most amazing bibliographer and generous with his time and knowledge. People can give you reading to do and advice; you kind of muddle along.

By the time I started working on Lihir, I felt doing that kind of work was more tricky, both ethically and in terms of the way in which you were understood by the community you were working with.

The other thing is that I really felt very strongly that, although people say, 'Well you shouldn't work with big business or whatever'. For someone like me, who in one stage of my life was a member of the Communist Party, politically I really felt very uncomfortable about working with Rio Tinto. But, on the other hand, by that time, I was much more confident than when I was working on Misima. I felt that I had knowledge and expertise that could be useful in representing the community in ways that were important. However, you have to make compromises; you can never keep yourself nice.

Alex: Well, I think you can. You just end up being an activist pushing the process from the outside.

Martha: But then you're outside, and you don't have access to what is going on. Your knowledge is partial and skewed. That was the thing that I found very interesting working there—I really followed what decisions were being made within the company and what information or pressure influenced change because mining companies, every day, do these extraordinary searches about what activists are doing and saying and how it is being disseminated, so they really know who writes about them, what they're saying. This is as well as reports of injuries, accidents, oil spills from all over the world. At that stage, there was quite a lot of activism around Porgera. I would see the things coming off the fax machine on Porgera and occasionally discuss them with managers, to see what they thought of the tensions elsewhere. I would get into work early at the Community Relations office and read through the faxes.

The people who affect the mining company policy, the one great opposition strategy I felt, was PARTiZANS (People Against Rio Tinto Zinc and Subsidiaries). Have you read about them? PARTiZANS were people who bought shares in order to get up at meetings and protest about something or try to change policies by the company. They really scared the hell out of them, whereas MiningWatch and organisations like that, who get their facts wrong so often, they just get shrugged off. The big changes and adjustments are made in London or Toronto by members of the board who make judgements almost entirely in terms of money—shareholder interest. Civil unrest, threatened lawsuits, that might change company policies for the better, but much as I deplore what mining does to the environment and to communities, I am sceptical about fly-in/fly out activists who campaign 'on behalf of Papua New Guineans'. I saw my role as an 'honest broker'. I am deeply suspicious of people who see themselves as 'anthropological heroes' for 'their people'. Writing an anthropological monograph is not being an activist. It's an entirely different business.

Alex: You really brought students through. You must've brought a half dozen students through Lihir.

Martha: I got one who did a thing on women's health. She was an Honours student, Emma Kowal. She shifted from being a medic. She did graduate as a doctor, but she got the bug when she did that work in Lihir and is now a professor of anthropology at Deakin University. She did a really good study with Lihirian women and their attitude to birth control and Western medicalisation of women's health. Kate Morton did a terrific study, an Honours thesis, on modern land use. The company gave us access to aerial photography, which was very detailed and so she was able to do that. Simon, of course, Nick Bainton, Susan Hemer. Susan worked on the outer islands, looking at the indirect impacts. Alana Burley, who undertook the tree study, the study of forestry, was able to demonstrate that, in fact, there was no pristine rainforest, that it had been planted. Lots and lots of things had been planted over a long period of time. A lot of people came through.

All of the PhD students got university grants. Some of the others came on money from my research fund—so, yes, indirectly, on mine money. I could pay some of them during holiday breaks as research assistants to go and do little studies. Michael Fabinyi did research on fishing with Simon. It just expanded what we could really study.

Alex: Did you put people up in the mine? Did they use mine accommodation?

Martha: I had built a little house down in Samo [on the opposite side of the island to the mine]. When I first went there, I initially thought that I couldn't stay in the mining town site all the time, because I didn't want to be identified with the mine. But, in fact, it wasn't easy, because you have to have a computer and you have to be buzzing around to the court, to the police station, to the schools, to offices. You're not just strolling around the island chewing the fat with people—you have to be getting numbers. I used to spend some time down in Samo in my matchbox; they thought it was the funniest little house because I'd said, 'I just want a little, tiny house'. The mining company would put them up sometimes, if there was space in the dongas [prefabricated accommodation huts], which there often was.

Alex: And that didn't compromise you irredeemably with the Lihirians?

Martha: No, with my own students who were doing PhDs there, I'd encourage them to have cross-links with the mining company. Nick Bainton had a little bush-material house in Kinami village, where he was based. Towards the end of the time I was working there, they would usually put me up in a place that was shared with other consultants, and I would base myself there. There's no way that you can't be linked to the mining company if you're doing that kind of work because you're asking questions. And I'd have to drive around in one of their cars [because there were no other vehicles on the island].

Alex: Do you honestly think that the work you did in Lihir changed what happened on the island?

Martha: On some things, yes. The policies for health treatment and particularly health treatment for women. There were objections by the mine manager, but I got the other managers onside. There was such a high rate of gynaecological problems associated with having too many children. Cervical cancer is a big problem in PNG, and very young women in their forties would die. They lost a few secretaries, women who worked closely with them, whom they respected. Those managers got upset about it. I said, 'Okay, we need to have someone come in on the medical team, who is a trained obstetrician and gynaecologist, to deal with these health problems that woman have'.

First of all, it was confined to the women workers, who would then have an automatic check-up. I don't know if it was compulsory, but they were all very keen to have it. But then, of course, the doctors say, 'We can't just pick and choose which women we deal with', as the women were coming into the maternal and child health clinic. Something like that is the direct policy that you influence.

Some of the other things were indirect because you can get something started, or you can become part of another process of change that is coming from the local people, which it occasionally was, for things like water supplies and housing. You're endorsing a process of local people and that gives weight to it. Mining companies mistake community relations for public relations, for PR, right? So, for a lot of the suggestions, I'd say, 'This will be good PR'. That works.

Here's one thing I'm really proud of that we did, which was stopped, but I got a ball rolling. I brought in Simon Foale after I'd been there for a year or two when I realised that deep-sea tailings disposal in Lihir was going to be a big environmental issue. I thought, 'I need a marine biologist because I can't tell whether the reefs are being wrecked or the fish are gone'. He worked with their other consultants, doing surveys with them too. That was another check, his own observations, and with CSIRO [Commonwealth Scientific and Industrial Research Organisation], the Commonwealth scientific body that the company hires to do the environmental impact studies. He would go out on the boat with them and dive and go and see what they're doing, look at their results and look at what they're analysing.

We realised that a lot of what local people thought were the environmental impacts were not environmental impacts. What they really needed to be worrying about were other things like acid rock drainage, which is long term and has dire effects on the environment. Often, they would be demanding roads through here and roads through there, which the mine would be prepared to do because that was a relatively cheap thing. It was just cutting swathes through forests or wrecking rivers. I thought long and hard, and I talked to lots of people. They'd say, 'Smoke, right? Pollution.' They'd read the papers about acid rain, and they'd say, 'We've got acid rain falling all over our island'. I thought 'If they're going to ever have to mount some kind of lawsuit and say they've got acid rain, I'm afraid they'll just be laughed out of court'. I looked into all these stories they had about what kinds of pollution there were and their effects. It was fascinating, that research. I realised it came from bits and pieces that they'd hear on the radio about acid rain or water pollution or chemicals. I realised what they thought was air pollution was in fact the steam coming from the geothermal vents. The one ecologically good thing that the mine introduced is the generation of electricity by geothermal plant, and everyone is worried about this steam that rises up.

The tailings are bad enough, but the silting up of rivers kills anything before the tailings do. It just wrecks the whole ecology. At Porgera, the rivers are really stuffed because of soft waste, which is not toxic but has completely altered the courses of rivers and the flow and everything. I got very absorbed in that gap between what people worried about and what all the scientists working on it were telling me. I found out as much as I possibly could. It was good working with someone like Simon, who was trained as a marine biologist and has a science degree, and understood it when they were talking about these various chemicals and their effects and when they're neutralised.

I thought we're not really going to change the older people, but we could try to get them at schools to institute education that directly gives them the knowledge to understand the processes. I worked very hard with Simon to set up an education program with the Department of Education in PNG. We fitted it into the normal curriculum so that when they are learning about acids, for example, they would learn about things like the effect of exposure of rocks to the air and why that made acid and that kind of thing. And with pollution on Lihir, in particular, we saw the density of population and shortening of fallow, which people really knew was the problem. But they would say, 'It's pollution from the air. We're not getting big yams. They're poisoning the ground.' I applied for independent funding to do research that would build on the effects of the shortening of fallow right through the island and the trees and tree cover. We did independent research that could feed back both into this education program and to a more considered and well-informed discussion of a combination of environmental and social impacts.

Lihir Environmental Education

Martha: We did a pilot project working with the Education Department, people in the school and Maureen Mackenzie. She'd been the first person I'd ever supervised. She was a graphic designer, though she's not anymore, who had taught in PNG's School of Art. She really had great ideas about how to produce things that would be used, so we got the school curriculum, and we designed it. We used pictures of Lihir, schematic pictures of Lihir. We used Papua New Guineans as much as possible, and we just went through these things with the science teachers in Lihir and in Moresby at the Curriculum Development Branch. This bit is for the teacher, and this is what the students have.

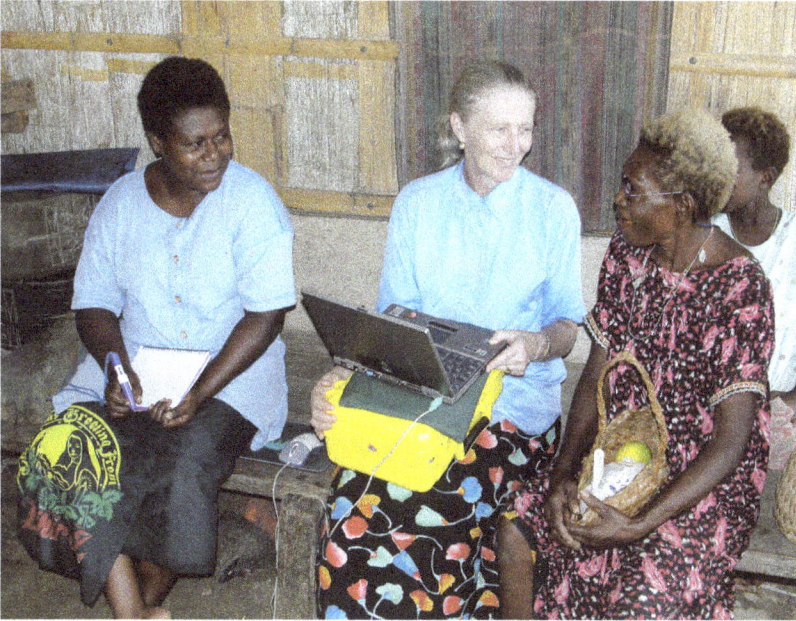

Figure 4: Emma Zanahien and Martha Macintyre discussing traditional healing techniques with Bridgit Moktel on Malie Island, Lihir (2002).
Source: Martha Macintyre research archives.

Then we tested it. Raising questions that students raised, testing their knowledge. You can see we used on the cover a schematic picture of a Tolai chemist who was on the island. So people could recognise him as 'the scientist'. And this woman was a renowned gardener, we used the pattern on her dress that people would also recognise—and a very familiar, if schematised, face.

We tested it on New Ireland as well as in Lihir, at 13 different schools. And we discovered that people loved learning new words. The kids all said, 'We want to learn the meanings of all these words properly'. We added a glossary. We were saying to them, 'Really you didn't have to worry about acid rain on Lihir, the stories you've heard refer to China'. We did that for acid rain, smoke, what is dangerous smoke, what happens to smoke and steam—the difference between smoke and steam. And they could do little exercises on smoke and steam.

We got some funding from the mining company to begin the research, but that vanished when the person who supported it in the company left. In the end, I used my own money to print the booklets, because we thought that the mining company and the Education Department were going to finance printing the booklets and they both refused. [laughs] But, getting the cooperation of the Education Department to design and test the pamphlets was wonderful. The one we prepared on acids, that was great, that was probably the one that students liked best. Because we made it all up ourselves—they had very poor teaching on this at the local level.

Then, being an eclectic anthropologist, I had taken an interest in the traditional ways of building houses. When they were preparing the brown matting that Lihirians use on blinds, on their houses, they used noni fruit roots. And if they're mixed with an acid, it goes brown, and if they're mixed with a base, it goes yellow. We could suddenly get all the kids doing litmus tests and finding out what was acid and what was base. We did that in the hope that eventually people understand acid rock drainage. I see this as my sort of activism. I would rather contribute to the education of PNG kids than wave a flag saying, 'I'm more radical than you' or write books that are read by very few people.

We did one booklet on gardening and fertility, once again using these very famous gardeners as the caricatures or avatars. That was the one that students and teachers on New Ireland really responded to. Partly, they recognised all the things from the pictures as being their own plants. We also did one project with primary school kids that was on useful plants. They would have a day when they would bring in useful plants, and they planted them, and they made gardens with useful plants. I really felt that that was what was needed to build up, both a kind of pride in their environment, and in the knowledge that they had, because they had to go and ask their elders about all these plants. We did one on *bilas*, decorations worn at feasts, which of course was the most popular, and everyone had to come dressed in traditional items. They discussed it ahead of time in class, and each child came with one piece of *bilas*. They had to find its local name, its habitat, and how it was made, that kind of thing.

That was a great project too. I really enjoyed doing that with them. We also did some that were more scientific. We did a big study on yams, when I persuaded a colleague John Petheram, an agronomist, to look at the effects of shortening fallow. By chance, he was supervising a PNG student, Bazakie Baput. They came to Lihir and Bazakie wrote his Master's thesis on the problems of short fallows in Lihir. I think that I used some of my funds and the company gave them accommodation. That project involved women because they were the only ones who knew the names of the plants, how they grow and the important fallow plants. We made big posters to go in the schools on yams. We also did the same with fish and traditional fishing techniques.

Police Project

Martha: While I was working in Lihir, I was approached by AusAID to help with the design of a project aimed at improving relations between police and local communities. This was because I succeeded in getting a policewoman stationed at Lihir. Someone in the police force had said, 'There's this woman who is very concerned about having more policewomen'. AusAID had this large project with the Royal PNG Constabulary where they were trying to improve community relations and the involvement, conditions and status of women in the police force. They hired me to do that in conjunction with their HR consultant. I was initially asked to do the design of just that component of the project. I had to work with the person who was doing the design for assistance with criminal matters and with another person dealing with the finances because they're shambolic in the police force. There was a person who was also like the quartermaster, dealing with equipment and uniforms and all that kind of thing. There were several of us who did that design.

That was such an eye-opener; I was really excited by that project. I went around to every province. I had hardly been out of the islands. Milne Bay and New Ireland were the only parts of PNG I'd worked in. I'd got to work in Moresby for quite a while, and then you did it a month at a time, here and there.

Aid project people shouldn't be paid the rates they are, in my opinion. It's kind of worse than making money out of mining. That sort of boomerang aid is something I really got concerned about when I worked with AusAID. I had no idea how it worked until then.

Anyway, I went around and I had to interview people in villages. Some of it was ethnographic, more sociological, but with an ethnographic component in the interviewing with all the women police, and there's not a lot of them. But, I chose places where there was a critical mass of policewomen, such as Wabag, Madang, Goroka, Moresby and Lae, and interviewed all the policewomen there about their careers, about problems they'd faced in getting promotion, discrimination against them in various forms.

In towns, they would get the Chamber of Commerce people and the government people and local representatives of churches and other organisations. It was fascinating. You'd have day-long meetings where they would discuss law and order issues from the perspective of 'how do we improve policing?' It was just the most wonderful research to do. I just learned so much about what Papua New Guineans think in that context. And, because people wanted to participate, you weren't trying to draw people out. People really wanted to tell you things.

What they wanted varied across different places. I found real regional variation that made me puzzle over, 'Why is this such an issue here and it's not seen as an issue there? And why are these sorts of behaviours common in this area?' It just presented so many questions. I like that sort of research. I like pondering.

I'd go home every night exhausted because, boy! Aid work is really hard work. You have to do the research and that night you have to prepare the report. If you get behind, you're stuffed. We would work until midnight, every night, typing up what we'd learned during the day and what the implications were for the design. I discovered all kinds of things. A lot of people wanted to talk about things that were not directly related to anything we could do. It was like learning about contemporary PNG in this concentrated way, and comparative, and overall and just fascinating. That was why it was wonderful.

It plunged me into a lot of other research about 'what do they do with community policing?' It had been very big in some areas of the United States, and in some areas of Canada and in some places in Germany. I embarked on reading all this literature on community policing. The gender aspect I could quickly deal with. I was very familiar with arguments about improving women's status in the workplace. So, I'd have meetings with policewomen. But, that was also fascinating, seeing people in their jobs, seeing the difficulties they faced and having a lot more sympathy for policewomen than I did when I started.

When you study hard problems, it's often very sad and even very depressing at one level. But, I also think—and I faced this the most in studying El Salvadoran refugees from a horrendous civil war—you also are forced to confront the kinds of issues of representation that have been left out of academic debates. What do you write about, as an anthropologist, when you are having to deal with human cruelty, with horrifying discrimination, with real criminality and evil sometimes?

The challenges of confronting things like, 'What causes these problems? What can possibly be done? How can anthropology write about these subjects in ways that have any purchase, that can assist with people understanding them?' I find those the kind of real challenges and sometimes, I'll admit, in some of my writings, I express the frustration that people don't want to know these things. I have written so much about violence against women in PNG and all these people who come to it as if it's something new and some new problem that is arising because of modernity. I just thought, 'I'm sick of this'.

And I'm also sick of people saying there's not enough research on it. Who needs to do more research to find out that there is too much violence against women in PNG and something should be done about it? I wrote that. I wrote critical things about some of the ways that aid programs intervene in these things. Mainly because I think they don't do the sort of research that I've done over the years to really understand what's going on, to see why these violent people are tolerated and why they do it. That's why they come in with assumptions about middle-class Australia or Canada or whatever as solutions. Finding a safehouse is a very difficult thing anywhere, and it's impossible in a PNG village. Why do you fund a project that costs millions, that's allegedly for safehouses and then say it doesn't work? You could have known from the outset that was not going to work.

Alex: We were talking earlier about the perception that some people have that you're not a critical voice in mining. But it seems to me that you have expressed the fact that you are a critical voice.

Martha: Yeah. One of the reasons I have never chosen to be or become one of the, what Colin [Filer] calls, the radical opponents of mining, is partly because I thought, well at this stage in my career it was going to appear terribly hypocritical, and I'm going to have to do all sorts of self-justifying nonsense now, I don't want to engage in. Partly because, coming from Australia, you're ultrasensitive of speaking for others. I felt I could join forces. If anyone on Lihir objected to that mine, I would have been behind them, to be honest. But, I didn't find any people objecting to the mine. If I objected to the mine, it would be only as an outsider.

That's why I worked so hard on this education thing. I'd rather engage with the Papua New Guineans and have a generation of kids who grow up being able to understand what is happening to their environment, rather than clutching at this bit of half-baked information that they gave about acid rain or water pollution.

Alex: The result of this police study, was it published, was there a report?

Martha: Yes, but that was an utterly internal thing and, of course, because you're dealing with criminal material, I think that's quite right for that to be private. I did a report dealing with human rights abuses by the police, and since they often weren't charged, these are just allegations.

I wish I'd been asked by Human Rights Watch to do the police project report because they had a public report which drew on my report. They had access to it, which really pissed me off because I asked AusAID if I could publish some things from that report and not disclose names or people or places even and they said no.

Alex: There'd be some people who would say if you have a certain kind of material then you have no choice but to breach your contract.

Martha: Yeah, and never get back into PNG again and be sacked by the university for breaching contracts. I made myself unpopular enough with the police commissioner as it was, and that was seen as overstepping the mark. I was never asked to do any more work for the Australian government because of that.

The Australian Journal of Anthropology (TAJA)

Martha: When I retired, in 2008 technically, I had seven postgraduates whom I had to see through, most of them nearly at the end of their candidature. I knew the end was in sight, or thought it was. I realised when I resigned from my job that I had a lot more recognition than I had thought I had within my own profession. I thought, 'What are the skills that I have? I can write, and I'm a good judge of what's interestingly written.'

TAJA had been in-house, based in New South Wales at the University of Sydney, and all the editorial board were from Sydney. I thought, 'I'll make it a national and international editorial board, so we can send things to people, like Fred Myers for items on Australian Aborigines'. That it's not quite so parochial. I got people from other places to be on the board, who worked in regions where a lot of Australians worked, in South-East Asia, in the Pacific, in Australia. I did come in with a change agenda, if you like that terminology.

Advice to Students

Alex: My last question for you is, what are some of the things that you've learned in the course of your career that younger scholars need to know?

Martha: I suppose the thing that I do push is: keep reading. Don't get stuck in your own little groove. Read widely, not just anthropology. The other thing is a piece of advice I got when I was going into the field. Bill Heaney was teaching at University of Papua New Guinea. He gave me a pen as a present as I went into the field and his advice was, 'No matter how ill you are with malaria, no matter what's happened, write every day'. That was the best advice I think I got. It just forced me to think: 'I've got to write every day; I've got to write what happened'. Because even when I didn't have time or a lamp was out of kerosene, when I got to writing up, those notes were just so useful. Even those sketchy little things like what happened would remind me of other things that day. Regarding fieldwork, that's the best advice that I got, and I always give it to my students.

The thing that bothers me most with a lot of academic life is the lack of scholarly humility in many people's writings. They don't acknowledge that these questions have been asked, in a variety of ways, many times before. It annoys me when we see these constant claims of novelty and originality. Maybe it's from studying history, where you have to be aware of who preceded you and where you fit into that. I think too often anthropologists get an inflated sense of their own importance.

Personal Reflections and Tributes to Martha Macintyre

First Contact with Martha

Chris Gregory

Over the course of one's life, one acquires many good friends and colleagues, but it is often hard to remember the exact day you first met. Not so with Martha. I have very vivid memories of our first meeting because it was a most memorable encounter. It was in July 1978, at a conference at King's College (Cambridge), to discuss recent ethnographic and theoretical developments on the *kula*—an enduring form of exchange in the south-eastern archipelago of Papua New Guinea (PNG). The Who's Who of British Social Anthropology were there: Professor Sir Edmund Leach, Professor Sir Raymond Firth and the next generation of Big Men of British Social Anthropology, such as Andrew Strathern and Michael Young. Also invited were Big Women of American Cultural Anthropology, such as Nancy Munn and Annette Weiner. The conference gathered all the ethnographers who had worked on the *kula* since Malinowski's time. It was a very select audience and I must say that I felt very ill at ease among the august company. As a PhD student, I was one of the least qualified people to be there. The only reason I was invited was that Jerry Leach, one of the organisers, thought that someone trained in economics (like me) might have something to contribute to the discussion. The only person less qualified than me to be there—I mistakenly thought—was this Aussie sheila named Martha. Unlike me, she had never even been to PNG and had not even begun her PhD. Moreover, she was not even a participant at the conference. She was employed as the conference rouseabout. Her job was to record the proceedings, prepare the coffee and so on.[1]

---

1   Her recordings, I note, are available online from the Smithsonian Institute: sova.si.edu/search?q= Kula. However, her role as recorder is not acknowledged.

The conference got off to a very inauspicious start with an introductory paper by Jerry Leach, a junior lecturer at Cambridge at the time. Professor Sir Edmund Leach, the co-organiser (but no relation of Jerry Leach), was at his cranky, irritable best. He had little respect for Jerry as an ethnographer and theorist and unleashed an attack on Jerry after his introductory speech, an attack that persisted throughout the next five days of the conference. Professor Sir Edmund's irritation with Jerry's theoretical position even frames the book that came from the conference, which they co-edited together (Leach & Leach, 1983). It contains a foreword by Jerry Leach that sets out an agenda and a cranky afterword by Professor Sir Edmund Leach that dismantles the argument in Jerry's Foreword, point by point.

When the conference proper got under way, I was amazed to hear the Aussie sheila ask the first question from her perch in the audio recording section. I confess that I had an attack of the Aussie cultural cringe. 'Jesus, love,' I thought to myself, 'you must learn to shut up. You are not even a participant at this conference.' So stunned was I by her intervention that I did not take in what she said—but I do remember the reaction. Far from being savagely attacked by Professor Sir Edmund and others, they listened sagely to what she was saying, nodding their heads and stroking their chins as if to say, 'hmm, interesting question'. This continued for the next five days of the conference. When I allowed myself to listen to what she had to say, I found myself thinking, 'hmm, yes, that *is* a well-informed question'.

This was because this young Aussie sheila was the best-informed person at the conference. As part of her job as Professor Sir Edmund's rouseabout, she prepared a bibliography of everything that had ever been published on the *kula*. At the time, Martha was transitioning from history to anthropology and—as are the ways of the historian—she had read not only every ethnographic account on the *kula* but also every relevant historical document she had been able to find in the archives. At that time, anthropologists were not into history, and they had little idea of the historical context of Malinowski's fieldwork, let alone a knowledge of, or interest in the writings on the *kula* that predated Malinowski.

During the conference, it became clear that the missing link in our understanding of the *kula* was the island of Tubetube. It was universally agreed that Martha would be the ideal person to fill in this gap in the literature by conducting fieldwork there, which, of course, she did when she took up a PhD scholarship at The Australian National University the following year (1978). I can say without fear of contradiction that Martha was the best-prepared PhD student in the history of the discipline. Her review of the literature, which became her first book (Macintyre, 1983a), was exhaustive. Further, the conference gave her face-to-face access to the combined wisdom of all the ethnographers who worked on the *kula* ring. Her grasp of the history of the *kula*, and the extant comparative ethnography, was second to none.

Another world-first for Martha was the fact that she is the only PhD student in the history of the discipline who wrote her first article in the field after just one week's fieldwork. Such was the desire on the part of the *kula* volume editors to acquire up-to-date evidence on the *kula* in Tubetube that they delayed publication of the volume until her contribution arrived (Macintyre, 1983b).

That conference shaped the course of Martha's academic career over the next 40 years. She has maintained an active interest in PNG, revisiting the place many times. Martha's research interests have, of course, widened and moved on; however, what has remained unchanged is her capacity to keep asking the hard, thought-provoking questions based on well-grounded archival research and her lived experience as an anthropologist. Evidence for this comes in a recent essay of hers (January 2018) with a classic Martha-esque title: 'Was Derek Freeman "mad"?'

Classic Martha. What other Aussie sheila would be game enough to ask such an important question? Good luck in your future career, Martha. I look forward to reading some more of your pearlers.

References

Leach, J. W. & Leach E. (Eds). (1983). *The kula: New perspectives on Massim exchange*. Cambridge, England: Cambridge University Press.

Macintyre, M. (1983a). *The kula: A bibliography*. Cambridge, England: Cambridge University Press.

Macintyre, M. (1983b). Kune on Tubetube and in the Bwanabwana region of the southern Massim. In J. W. Leach & E. Leach (Eds), *The kula: New perspectives on Massim exchange* (pp. 369–382). Cambridge, England: Cambridge University Press.

Macintyre, M. (2018). *Was Derek Freeman 'mad'?* Retrieved from insidestory.org. au/was-derek-freeman-mad/

Martha and Me in the 1990s

Bronwen Douglas

I want you to recall 1990—or imagine it, if you are too young to remember. I had been teaching Pacific history at La Trobe University for nearly 20 years, but the subject's once-exotic glamour had seriously faded and too few history students wanted to take it. What, I asked myself, could I teach that would be relevant, trendy and fitted my commitment to reading texts for Indigenous presence. I know! Women! So, I circulated this memo (see Figure 1) to three people, including Martha Macintyre, an anthropologist in the Sociology Department. I do not recall if the others replied, but Martha did, saying something like, 'this is terrific. I want to teach it with you!'

These days, our exchange would have been via email, and I would still have her reply. But, it was three years before the History Department gained any email access at all—in the form of a single computer in an administrator's office, on which we typed our messages in DOS and could not edit them after hitting return at the end of a line. My memo to Martha was typed on my own desktop computer (one of those small square Macs), which is why I can find a copy—I'm a compulsive electronic hoarder. I then printed it and sent it through the internal mail system in a yellow reusable envelope, in which Martha no doubt returned her reply. This is doubly bizarre in today's terms—not only communication by snail mail but also a university mail system that actually functioned.

La Trobe University
MEMORANDUM

TO   Martha Macintyre
SUBJECT   New subject proposal
DATE   22 March 1990.

Attached is a tentative outline of a subject I am thinking of offering in 1992.   The proposed program may be too ambitious - indeed, Theme IV could probably be a half unit in its own right.   I shall be able to be more precise when I have examined the texts available in more detail.

I am interested in combining exploration of traces of actual women acting in the past with a consideration of conceptual, categorical and 'political' dimensions of a variety of modes of discourse, both contemporary and later, male and female, and including formal representations by historians and anthropologists.

I should be grateful to know your reactions to the proposed subject, including its likely relevance to the majors in Family and Gender and Anthropology.   Any suggestions you might make will be gratefully received.   Perhaps we could have a chat about it over coffee at some stage.

Bronwen Douglas.

Figure 1: Memorandum to Martha Macintyre (22 March 1990).
Source: Memorandum composed and sent by author.

Over the next year, we formulated a new subject proposal (see Figure 2). The La Trobe approval process was still fairly casual, though sociology took longer to accept it than history. The subject began in 1992 as 'Images of women in the Pacific'; however, in the second year, we renamed it 'Gender, colonialism and postcolonialism' because Martha (rightly) suggested that 'images' was a bad, Eurocentric term. We taught together for four years, though Helen Lee helped one year when Martha was on leave. The subject was more popular with anthropology students than history. One history student I remember very well is Helen Gardner, now at Deakin University, who took History III IWP in its first year and did Honours in 1993, when I supervised her thesis on a topic inspired by Theme 2 of our subject. We had several terrific visiting lecturers, including Pat Grimshaw, Margaret Jolly, Klaus Neumann and Nick Thomas.

Teaching with Martha was a joy—endlessly stimulating and often surprising. I did not teach undergraduates after 1995, because I was on leave the following year and then left La Trobe for a research position at The Australian National University (ANU). At much the same time, Martha also moved from La Trobe to join Warwick Anderson's Centre for the Study of Health and Society at the University of Melbourne. However, the experience of creating and teaching our subject together set important directions for my future thinking and writing. My initial position at ANU was with the State, Society and Governance in Melanesia (SSGM) program, where I devised a project on Women and Christianity in Melanesia. Martha's inspiration and support strongly motivated the theme and the stream of publications that followed. At the same time, I was beginning to work on the history of human difference and race in Oceania. An important trigger for that interest is listed as Topic 8 in the subject proposal, on Polynesian and Melanesian women (see Figure 2). The first year we taught the subject, one workshop question asked 'what were the major criteria of racial classification used by Johann Reinhold Forster and Dumont d'Urville?' By the second year, I had refined it to 'compare and contrast the casual ethnocentrism of Forster's scientific empiricism with Dumont d'Urville's *a priori* racism', having realised that important differences existed in the language used in each text and the discourses informing them. I spent nearly 20 years determining the nature of that distinction and writing much about it (Douglas, 2008, 2014).

La Trobe University
MEMORANDUM

TO   History Department

SUBJECT   New Subject Proposal, 1992

DATE   11 March 1991.

HISTORY II 'WP'/III 'WP': Women in the Pacific
(hopefully a.k.a. Sociology II 'WP'/III 'WP', Women's Studies II 'WP'/III 'WP') (full unit):

Co-ordinators: Bronwen Douglas, Martha Macintyre

This subject will explore textual images of women in the Pacific, including, where available, female representations of themselves and other women. Its main methodological concern will be with ways of deconstructing the ethnocentric and gendered bias of most texts, with particular attention to the social, cultural and political contexts which they described and in which they were written. Theories of gender, representation and postmodernist cultural critique will be considered for their utility in explicating the texts consulted and will themselves be subject to critical scrutiny. There will be four main themes: images of paradise (early European contacts with Tahiti and Hawaii; the myth of 'paradise lost'); women and Christianity (especially in Vanuatu); ethnographic representations of Pacific women (Trobriands, Samoa); women in the colonial and contemporary Pacific (Papua New Guinea, Solomon Islands, Vanuatu).

Class requirements: One 1-hour lecture and one 2-hour workshop per week.

Assessment: two 3,000 word essays (one per semester, 30% each), one 3,000 word take-home final test (30%) and workshop participation (10%).

Recommended reading:
Dening, G. *The Bounty: an Ethnographic History*, History Dept., U. of Melbourne 1988.
Grimshaw, P. *Paths of Duty: American Missionary Wives in Nineteenth Century Hawaii*, U. Hawaii Press 1989.
Jolly, M. and Macintyre, M. (eds), *Family and Gender in the Pacific: Domestic Contradictions and the Colonial Impact*, CUP 1989
Strathern, M. (ed.) *Dealing with Inequality: Analysing Gender Relations in Melanesian and Beyond*, CUP 1987.

Proposed weekly timetable:
SEMESTER I
1. Introduction.

2. Understanding 'others': reading about 'natives' and women (Torgovnick).

Theme I: Images of paradise:

3. Early European representations of women in Tahiti (Robertson, Banks).

4. The *Bounty* mutineers and Tahitian women and men (Morrison, Dening).

Figure 2: Bronwen Douglas and Martha Macintyre, new subject proposal, La Trobe University (11 March 1991).
Source: Proposal formulated by Douglas and Macintyre.

Another great gift from Martha to my future research was learning to take visual materials seriously—as engaged modes of representing encounters and Indigenous people, rather than simply passive reflections or pretty illustrations. This stimulus soon bore fruit in my enduring commitment to critical interpretation of voyage artwork as ethno-historical texts, often saturated in Indigenous presence (Douglas, 1999). We also integrated numerous videos into the subject. Martha helped transform my public performances by introducing me to sociology's really cool new machine, which projected transparencies made on the photocopier on to a screen— otherwise called an overhead projector, but unknown at that time in the History Department. Before then, all my presentations were illustrated by slides, and these were of poor quality. I was much better at making transparencies than taking photos for slides and used an overhead projector in lectures and seminar or conference papers for more than 10 years, before graduating to PowerPoint.

In March 1993, Martha and I escaped from teaching for 10 days to attend the Association for Social Anthropology in Oceania (ASAO) conference in Kona, on the Big Island of Hawai'i. She had strongly encouraged me to submit an abstract, and it found a home on a panel for which it was quite unsuited. En route, we stayed in a hotel in Waikiki, where Martha demonstrated an amazing talent for colour coding her pyjamas with the hotel room decor (see Figure 3).

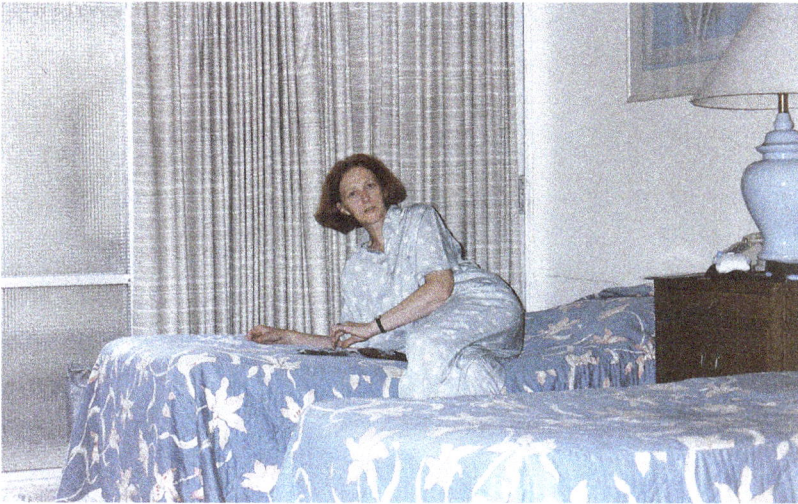

Figure 3: Martha Macintyre at the Outrigger Reef Towers Hotel, Waikiki, Hawai'i (20 March 1993).
Source: Photo by Douglas.

513

Figure 4: Epeli Hauʻofa and Mark Mosko, ASAO conference, Kona, Hawaiʻi (26 March 1993).
Source: Photo by Douglas.

I was enthralled by the conference. As a historian, I was out of my element and roamed about the dinner photographing anthropologists—the historical empire striking back. This annoyed some anthropologists, but not Epeli Hauʻofa (see Figure 4), who gave a keynote at the dinner on the democracy movement in Tonga. A few days later, he spoke at the University of Hawaiʻi in Hilo on 'Our sea of islands', having been inspired by the dramatic volcanic landscape on the drive between Kona and Hilo to rethink the notion of Pacific Islands smallness. This was the first iteration of a paper that quickly became a canonical text on Pacific Islander identity and connections (Hauʻofa, 1994). There was a Mt Hagen big man, disguised as Andrew Strathern, photographed chatting with another celebrated highlands anthropologist, the late Paula Brown Glick (see Figure 5). I snapped the late, much-lamented Dawn Ryan talking to Melbourne University's Mary Patterson (see Figure 6). I also took a sadly historic photo, the last ever of Roger Keesing, with his partner Christine Jourdan, approximately six weeks before his sudden death on a dance floor in Canada (see Figure 7).

Figure 5: Paula Brown Glick and Andrew Strathern, ASAO conference, Kona, Hawai'i (26 March 1993).
Source: Photo by Douglas.

Figure 6: Dawn Ryan and Mary Patterson, ASAO conference, Kona, Hawai'i (26 March 1993).
Source: Photo by Douglas.

Figure 7: Roger Keesing and Christine Jourdan, ASAO conference, Kona, Hawai'i, 26 March 1993.
Source: Photo by Douglas.

However, here are the important ones: She Who Must not Be Spoken Too Much of Today with Bob Tonkinson (see Figure 8) and the escapees from La Trobe with Margaret Jolly (see Figure 9). Puzzlingly, I am wearing a Kanak *robe mission* (mission dress), presumably in the spirit of the ASAO tradition of dressing up for the dinner. En route home, Martha slept most of the way while I read frantically for the class I had to travel to directly from the airport. The denouement of the trip occurred later down the track, when Martha contacted me, urgently seeking the receipts she knew I'd kept for my tax return. She couldn't be bothered claiming her share at the time, but the Australian Tax Office had unwisely decided to audit her. In retribution, she chased up all the deductions she could find. She must be one of the few people ever to make a profit from a tax audit.

Figure 8: Martha Macintyre and Robert Tonkinson, ASAO conference, Kona, Hawai'i (26 March 1993).
Source: Photo by Douglas.

Figure 9: Martha Macintyre, Bronwen Douglas and Margaret Jolly, ASAO conference, Kona, Hawai'i (26 March 1993).
Source: Photo by Douglas.

Figure 10: Participants in the 'Women, Christians, citizens: Being female in Melanesia today' workshop, Sorrento (November 1998).
Source: Photo by Douglas.

After leaving La Trobe, Martha and I worked together off and on for several years, particularly on Christian women's groups in Melanesia. She was a key contributor to a 1998 SSGM workshop I organised in Sorrento, Victoria, on 'Women, Christians, citizens: Being female in Melanesia today'. It was a remarkable event, at which 13 women from the region gave papers (see Figure 10). Martha was one of six non-Melanesian presenters, speaking on 'Women's organisations in Lihir', in place of her friend Jacklynne Membup from Lihir, who was unable to come at the last minute. Five years later, Martha published an important paper on an umbrella women's group in Lihir in an *Oceania* special issue I edited on 'Women's groups and everyday modernity in Melanesia' (Macintyre, 2003). Debra McDougall and Margaret Jolly were also contributors. Martha's paper was crucial—her unsentimental pragmatism regarding the immense difficulties facing women and their organisations in Papua New Guinea was both exemplary and salutary.

That collection was my swansong with SSGM; afterwards, our work went in different directions. We were rarely in touch until a happy serendipity five years ago brought us in electronic contact on the supervision panel for Michael Main's doctoral thesis (see Main's contribution to this section). This virtual reconnection was materialised in 2017, when we were co-participants in a workshop at the Melbourne Museum and resumed old conversations as if they had never stopped.

References

Douglas, B. (1999). Art as ethno-historical text: Science, representation and Indigenous presence in eighteenth and nineteenth century Oceanic voyage literature. In N. Thomas & D. Losche (Eds), *Double vision: Art histories and colonial histories in the Pacific* (pp. 65–99). Cambridge, England: Cambridge University Press.

Douglas, B. (2008). '*Novus orbis australis*': Oceania in the science of race, 1750–1850. In B. Douglas & C. Ballard (Eds), *Foreign bodies: Oceania and the science of race 1750–1940* (pp. 99–155). Canberra, ACT: ANU E Press, doi.org/10.22459/FB.11.2008

Douglas, B. (2014). *Science, voyages and encounters in Oceania 1511–1850*. Basingstoke, England; New York, NY: Palgrave Macmillan.

Hau'ofa, E. (1994). Our sea of islands. *Contemporary Pacific*, 6(1), 148–161.

Macintyre, M. (2003). Petztorme women: Responding to change in Lihir, Papua New Guinea. *Oceania*, 74(1–2), 120–133, doi.org/10.1002/j.1834-4461.2003.tb02839.x

Humour, Homes and Gardens: Martha, Feminism and Anthropology

Kalissa Alexeyeff

In 1991, while studying at La Trobe University, I first encountered Martha's writing. We read 'Reflections of an anthropologist who mistook her husband for a yam' and 'Better homes and gardens' in an Honours elective subject, and I still have the paper version of 'Reflections' in my possession all these years later—Martha's first draft from the 1989 Association for Social Anthropology in Oceania conference, held in San Antonio. Both texts transformed my ideas about what could be meaningfully written about in academia and changed the course of my life forever! These works are also indicative of the imprint Martha has made on feminist anthropology and, perhaps remarkably, given its hyper-masculinist tendencies, her influence and leadership in the field of Melanesian anthropology.

During the 1980s and 1990s, the academics in humanities and social sciences at La Trobe University included a heady mix of Marxists, both homegrown and European. We were taught by pot-smoking phenomenologists and a range of feminists, including eco-feminist (Janna Thompson in Philosophy), radical feminist (Adrian Hearn in Legal Studies) and feminist film critic (Barbara Creed, who introduced us to such alarming cultural tropes as *vagina dentata*). Psychoanalysis, via Freud and the Frankfurt school, was popular and postmodernism was also beginning to make its mark. Lecturers smoked during class and supported our activism over actions such as the introduction of university fees. Perhaps every undergraduate student feels like this, but it did seem to be a significant period in which we could still change 'the system', be this capitalism or patriarchy. Certainly, drinking cask red wine during an afternoon tutorial, while discussing Marshall Berman's wonderful interpretation of Marx in *All that is solid melts into air* (1982), made it seem so.

Martha's anthropology class was certainly cutting edge. We read many papers that were still in draft form—Martha's enthusiasm for these new and theoretically exciting works was infectious. One article that nearly drove me to drop out of the class because it seemed simply too difficult was the late Patrick Wolfe's 'On being woken up: The dreamtime in anthropology and Australian settler culture' (1991). In it, he demonstrated how anthropology and colonialism creates 'others' as non-contemporaneous. 'Authentic' Indigenous Australians are located in the 'dreamtime'—a time that is out of place. It is this displacement that served to legitimise colonial rule and its logic of elimination. Martha's careful and methodical elucidation of this argument helped to both blow my mind and encourage me to return for another week of class.

This was also the time of growing critique of the concept of 'culture' and the ethnographic method. We read *Writing culture* (Clifford & Marcus, 1986) and *Orientalism* (Said, 1978), which was also reaching peak popularity, in addition to many of the emerging anthropological and feminist critiques. It was both an exciting and challenging time. I remain grateful for Martha's solid commentary on both the promise and the pitfalls of these critiques of objectivity, the crisis of representation and reflexivity.

Martha's 'Reflections' is a perfect example of this balance, in the way it utilises a reflexive style to demonstrate the political purposes of humour. In this article, Martha discusses joking as a form of 'ritual clowning' that encompasses teasing, parody and burlesque and its function as 'gentle forms of castigation' and a style of social incorporation. On Tubetube, joking is 'a feminine social grace' (Macintyre, 1992, p. 142) that is connected to skills of hospitality. Here, I digress slightly to note that I like to think of Martha as 'Jane Austen of the Pacific'—a vigorous commentator on injustice, in possession of searing insight into oft-overlooked details of social interaction.

Martha is also a bit racier than Austen. This was evident, for example, when she recounted her attempt to explain her Freudian interpretation of some local myths to her key informants. She selected a story in which the protagonist is 'a small hairy yam with a voracious sexual appetite'—

an obvious phallic symbol, or so Martha thought. The old men thought this to be hilariously far-fetched, and an older female relative scoffed in ridicule. Martha recounted:

> I should have realised that her mischievous smile disguised a plot. She had me at last! My rigid celibacy, had (as she'd predicted) warped my mind. Deprived of sex for months on end, my disturbed mind could no longer distinguish between yams and penises. If I squatted while weeding in a garden she would make some comment about my hoping for my lover to emerge. If I was in a group peeling yams, I was most expressly *not* to be given the small elongated hairy yams—goodness knows what I might do with them!

> … the joking was a means of managing my alien status, of incorporating me with laughter at those points where my behaviour or ignorance revealed my relationship as fictive. No woman in their thirties would voluntarily remain chaste while her husband and his family were miles away. Well then, I must have secret lovers … even if they turned out to be yams! (Macintyre, 1992, p. 137)

As a relatively innocent 21-year-old, I recall being shocked that you could talk about sex, let alone joke about it at university. Several years later, during fieldwork in the Cook Islands, I again recalled the significance of this work as I explored the use of humour to articulate relationships. These commonly involved inverting forms of social power between chiefs and commoners, men and women and locals and outsiders (from colonial officials to present-day tourists). Highly sexualised forms of joking were also particularly popular in same-sex interactions. Although I honed my ability to appreciate sexual innuendo, a particular 'drinking song' still makes me blush, to this day. It was sung by older women sitting in a church hall, industriously weaving mats. The song's lyrics referenced the resident pastor and attributed to him some highly unorthodox sexual predilections. The women's mirth was amplified by his proximity in the adjoining building and presumably by the women's public status as village and church leaders.

'Better homes and gardens' appeared in *Family and gender in the Pacific*, edited by Martha and Margaret Jolly (1989). This book was a landmark publication that challenged representations of the domestic and the so-called 'private' sphere as unchanged by missionary and colonial intervention. In addition to showing how kinship, the gendered division of labour, patterns of marriage, eating, sleeping and child care were reconfigured during this period, the authors collectively make a case for the consideration of these changes as more than simply indicators of more fundamental economic and political shifts in the public sphere. It is a work that has assisted younger scholars in interrogating further the colonial impact on local understandings of intimacy, sexuality and gender relations.

Martha's chapter in the book examines changes in house style, gardens and trade in relation to missionary intervention on Tubetube. One striking aspect of the work is that it reveals how the contemporary architecture of villages—bush huts, tropical flowers, fruits and vegetables—while evoking untouched paradisical 'life lived off the soil' (Macintyre, 1989, p. 169), are in fact a recent construction. Prior to missionisation, houses on Tubetube were large communal structures and gardens were insignificant because most subsistence items were imported via the islands' vast trade networks.

The chapter also argues that the burning of local houses by Australian patrol officers and their replacement by homes that Wesleyan missionaries considered more familial did not simply mark the end of a specific architecture, but also ushered in new forms of consumerism: 'on Tubetube the items which people perceive as essential accoutrements of the civilised Christian household are those things they saw first in missionaries' houses; lamps, tables, chairs, crockery, cutlery and linen' (Macintyre, 1989, p. 169). We read precise and appealing Austen-esque detail about the linen too: 'linen (hand-embroidered or decorated with tatting)' (p. 169). For those like me, who were unfamiliar with this last term, tatting is a handcrafting technique used to make lace edging, doilies and collars.

As I re-read 'Better homes and gardens' for this festschrift, it also struck me how Martha attends to masculinity as a politicised identity. To my mind, this represents an early attempt in anthropology to understand men in feminist terms—that is, as a gendered construct produced by structures and relations of power. Martha shows how men's public roles in maritime trade were severely curtailed and, in some respects, women's economic standing increased. The promotion of horticultural activities by missionaries enhanced women's status as traditional landowners and gardeners, while white traders eroded the men's roles as traders and 'pacification' by colonial administrators meant that they could no longer be warriors.

These two works have had a huge impact on me, because they enabled me to consider the possibility of writing about things I valued, such as fashion, gardens and music, in relation to seemingly more serious concerns. Both works dealt with subjects such as domestic space, aesthetics and social repartee alongside the political economy. Thanks to feminism, these feminine arts and gendered politics came to be considered politically significant aspects of social life and as worthy of scholarly scrutiny as kava drinking or pig tusks in ceremonial exchange.

Martha's level-headedness, in addition to her curiosity about new ideas and fashions in anthropology and beyond, meant that she was always prepared to encourage people to 'move on' and expand their horizons. This helped when I asked at the end of my Honours year, 'who is this Derrida everyone is talking about?' Martha, always with her finger on the pulse, recommended I undertake a master's degree in comparative literature and critical theory with Elizabeth Grosz, which covered all manner of European philosophy from Derrida and Lacan to Irigaray and Kristeva. In the mid-1990s, it was the coolest degree in town. I went on to write a thesis on dance, femininity and globalisation, aiming in part to pay legitimate attention to the humour and philosophies of happiness that were so important to Cook Islands sociality. Martha was influential here too, suggesting that I undertake this PhD at the new Centre for Cross-Cultural Research at The Australian National University. This place too felt like the spot to be, as it was filled with so many inspiring people, whose ideas were at the forefront of postcolonial scholarship.

Finally, both 'Reflections' and 'Better homes and gardens' arc also emblematic of Martha's life outside academia. As those who have been to her home will know, she has the best garden ever. She is also a quilter and a bag maker, she has incredible jewellery, and she is an amazing cook. Martha even makes very realistic marzipan fruit every Christmas. She spreads her remarkable talents through her social graces, the fruits of her garden, her culinary delicacies and her sage advice, in addition to through her very important and inspiring scholarly work.

References

Berman, M. (1982). *All that is solid melts into air: The experience of modernity*. New York, NY: Penguin.

Clifford, J. & Marcus, G. E. (Eds). (1986). *Writing culture: The politics and poetics of ethnography*. Berkeley, CA: University of California Press.

Macintyre, M. (1989). Better homes and gardens. In M. Jolly & M. Macintyre (Eds), *Family and gender in the Pacific: Domestic contradictions and the colonial impact* (pp. 156–169). Cambridge, England: Cambridge University Press.

Macintyre, M. (1992). Reflections of an anthropologist who mistook her husband for a yam. In W. E. Mitchell (Ed.), *Clowning as critical practice: Performance humor in the South Pacific* (pp. 130–144). Pittsburgh, PA: University of Pittsburgh Press.

Said, E. (1978). *Orientalism*. New York, NY: Pantheon Books.

Wolfe, P. (1991). On being woken up: The dreamtime in anthropology and in Australian settler culture. *Comparative History and Society, 33*(2), 197–224.

I First Met Martha Macintyre Twice: Or How I Became an Anthropologist

John Cox

I first met Martha Macintyre twice. The first of my first meetings occurred in 2002 or 2003. I was then a program manager working at Australian Volunteers International (AVI), and we had invited Martha to give an address to the cohort of volunteers departing for placements in the Pacific. I think the venue was International House, one of the residential colleges of the University of Melbourne.

Martha was challenging and authoritative. We had invited her to give the volunteers a briefing in cultural sensitivity that would equip them for work in the Pacific. However, as so often happens, the development industry's assumptions about 'culture' did not quite map on to the anthropologist's ideas. I clearly remember Martha's injunction to volunteers to learn the local language well enough that they could articulate the theory of evolution to their new Pacific friends and explain why they were atheists. Having been a volunteer who learned the language (in Kiribati), but who had also internalised the volunteer agency's received wisdom—which involved skirting awkwardly around other people's religiosity and trying to fit in as best we could without rocking the boat—I found this advice a little disturbing. And, I must say, also refreshing.

However, I've never followed it, having been, in my time, on both sides of circular debates about the truth of religion. I'm also not sure that Martha has either, although in her apparently uncited (until now) article 'On equivocal ethnography', she does write movingly about the affinity she had with her close friend John Wesley, a Papua New Guinean of modernist leanings whom she described as 'the only self-confessed atheist on Tubetube' (Macintyre, 1997, p. 12). However, I have taken Martha's advice as an injunction not to allow a paternalistic respect for perceived cultural differences to presume an absence of curiosity and intellect among the people we work with in the Pacific.

The second time I first met Martha was the real first time. I say 'real first' because it was the beginning of the relationship that I now have with her. It was 2004. After severe cuts to the volunteer program, I had accepted a redundancy from the aforementioned position. On the day after this job had ended, I made an uncharacteristic visit to the Queen Victoria Market. There, by chance, I bumped into Simon Foale (another contributor to this volume) and began berating him for not having told me that he was coming to Melbourne (he was then working at The Australian National University in Canberra). Simon and I had met in 1999 in Gizo, Solomon Islands, where he had been a technical adviser to the environmental non-government organisation World Wildlife Fund (Foale, 2001). I had recruited an outstanding volunteer to work with him there—the late Vicki Kalgovas, a thoughtful, warm and generous woman who loved Solomon Islands. I learned much about Solomon Islands from her and Simon and their wonderful colleague and friend Jully Makini (whose poetry Martha quotes in a chapter on human rights [Macintyre, 2000]).

Simon was meeting Martha for lunch. He and I sat outside the Victoria Market food hall and talked through why I'd left AVI. 'Are you going to do a PhD?' he asked. I replied, 'I'd do one if I had a topic'. At this point, the tale turns apocalyptic—I remember the crowd stopping still and a ball of light approaching us. A voice spoke, as if from the heavens, 'I've got plenty of topics'. It was, of course, Martha and I was surprised that she recognised me after only one brief previous meeting.

She did, of course, have plenty of topics. This encounter shaped the next 15 years of my life as I snuck in the back door of anthropology. Martha and Mary Patterson had succeeded in applying for an Australian Research Council grant—'Managing modernity: Capitalism, globalisation and governance in Melanesia' (Patterson & Macintyre, 2011)—and they employed me as a research assistant with the role of looking into fast money schemes in Papua New Guinea (PNG) and Solomon Islands. Under this project, I made my first visit to PNG (in 2005), collecting court records and newspaper reports and following up leads that Martha had already teased out. I had been expecting this to be a somewhat sensitive and secretive topic (scams are, after all, illegal), but was astonished to find that fast money schemes were something that everyone wanted to talk about. I put this down to Martha's ability to find the everyday concerns of contemporary Melanesians intellectually interesting and her commitment to taking them seriously and seeing how they reflect broader structures of power.

For me, the rest is history. The fast money schemes aspect of the project became my PhD (supervised by Martha, Mary Patterson and Benedicta Rousseau), a book (Cox, 2018) and, altogether, a strange, rather 'scammy' induction to PNG and anthropology. Thank you, Martha, for these remarkable opportunities and for the great expansion of my mind that has occurred under your guidance and with your love and friendship.

References

Cox, J. (2018). *Fast money schemes: Hope and deception in Papua New Guinea*. Bloomington, IN: Indiana University Press.

Foale, S. (2001). Where's our development? Land-owner expectations and environmentalist agendas in Western Solomon Islands. *The Asia Pacific Journal of Anthropology*, *2*(2), 44–67.

Macintyre, M. (1997). On equivocal ethnography. *Canberra Anthropology*, *20*(1–2), 7–20.

Macintyre, M. (2000). 'Hear us, women of Papua New Guinea': Melanesian women and human rights. In A. Hilsdon, M. Macintyre, V. Mackie & M. Stivens (Eds), *Human rights and gender politics: Perspectives on the Asia-Pacific region* (pp. 147–71). London, England: Routledge.

Patterson, M. & M. Macintyre (Eds). (2011). *Managing modernity in the Western Pacific*. St Lucia, Qld: University of Queensland Press.

What Would Martha Do? Confessions of a Hypochondriac in the Field

Michael Main

Like many others in the profession, I came to anthropology mid-career and sideways. First came geology and the mining industry, followed by contaminated land and groundwater environmental consulting. At the University of Melbourne, I was assigned to Martha because the research that I wanted to do was about the anthropology of risk. Just to be clear, I was not interested in anthropology as risk, but in the ways that anthropology could reveal the ways in which people perceived risk. Anthropologists, as I at the time was blissfully unaware, tend to embody a perception of risk that was not within the realm of my own experience— to say the least. I was interested in the risk to human health of pollution from the Ok Tedi mine in the Middle Fly and the ways that risk was being perceived culturally by landowners along the river. Papua New Guinea (PNG), mining, pollution, ethnography and Martha Macintyre—my destiny was sealed.

I want to provide some background about my professional training in the corporate world at the time I met Martha because it related to risk. The corporate concept of risk had been profoundly shaped by the Exxon Valdez oil spill of 1989. This disaster resulted in ExxonMobil quickly becoming the most risk-averse corporation on the planet. Over the next decade or so, ExxonMobil's risk-aversion culture was adopted by corporations in many parts of the world. It certainly was in Australia— right now, as we speak, there are people sitting in corporate offices enduring the requisite pre-meeting safety tip and raising their hands to cite 'paper cuts' as a potential work-related risk for the office environment. Prior to meeting Martha, this was the perception of risk that I had had drummed into me during my career.

I had been to PNG only once, when assigned to manage a small team of archaeologists working on the collection of cultural heritage data for the nascent PNG Liquefied Natural Gas (PNG LNG) project at Komo. Prior to being sent to PNG, ExxonMobil's risk-aversion machine kicked into high gear. We were given training courses in how to prepare for every worst nightmare that could be encountered by an organisation that embodies such a deep fear of paper cuts. We had satellite phones and requirements to call in by a specific time every day, just so that the office would know that we were still alive. We were required to report every potential incident, every bug bite, every time we forgot to wear our cut-proof Kevlar gloves and received, horror of horrors, a cut that actually occurred ex-bureau. We were given a list of things to include in our first aid kits, which had to be compulsorily carried on our person during all our fieldwork activities. The list was so long that it tipped me over into excess luggage and included a special bag in which to place body parts. However, it was never explained to me if the bag was intended for my own body parts or those of someone else who forgot to wear their Kevlar gloves that day.

Above all else, we were trained and told never ever under any circumstances to ever contract malaria. For anyone who ever got malaria on that project, the entire global corporation knew about it within minutes. We were shown films that taught us what the female anopheles mosquito looked like, how it behaved, how it transmitted the parasite, what to wear and when (which amounted to wear everything at all times) and how to duck and cover when a female anopheles mosquito malaria threat emerged. We were given malaria test kits that required us to take a sample of our own blood—that is, deliberately cutting ourselves in the field. Not as bad as malaria! We learned of the options for treatment and preventative medication and the fact that Larium[1] could result in permanent damage to your mental health. There is a clear logic attached to the fact that Larium is still being manufactured and prescribed—that malaria is clearly

---

1   Mefloquine, an anti-malarial medication sold under the brand name Larium.

worse than permanent psychosis. If there is one good thing that emerged from the Exxon Valdez disaster (I thought), it is that fewer people in the world are going to contract malaria.

However, the PNG highlands had changed me forever—sometime later, I returned to the University of Melbourne to find Martha and change my career and life immeasurably for the better. Little did I know that, in my choice of the Middle Fly as a field site, still shit-scared of malaria, I was about to enter female anopheles mosquito ground zero. I had with me all my ExxonMobil-issued head-to-toe protective netting, repellent for your skin that melts plastic and my as-yet unused malaria self-test kit. However, this time, I had taken with me something that no doctor could prescribe because Martha had started telling me some of her stories of her time in the field. Martha's stories of her experiences in the field emerge quite naturally in conversation, gently and with ironic humour and a compelling narrative that slowly raises in levels of alarm such that you find yourself listening with mouth agape and wanting to rush home and tell all your friends. At least, this was the impact that Martha's stories had on her new and profoundly risk-averse student.

To this day, I am sure that I contracted malaria in Kiunga, although my test kit showed a negative result. But, for a while, hours even, I was convinced that I was slipping into its grasp. Martha had told me about an experience of hers with malaria. Feeling like I was slipping away, lying in my unbearably hot room in the Kiunga Guesthouse, the question 'what would Martha do?' at least made me come to my senses. Martha had come down with cerebral malaria in her unbearably hot room and was so sick that she was unable even to raise herself to the sink to swallow her medication. Martha had tumbled herself onto the floor, crawled across the room, grabbing some pills, dragged herself into the shower and, with a final spurt of whatever energy was left, reached to turn on the shower tap and lie face-up under the shower rose while her mouth filled with enough water to swallow the medicine. Lying in my room, I knew that this was not me … yet. However, even if it was, Martha had survived to tell the tale; therefore, I was at least in with a chance. And besides, I wanted to be like Martha and have my own set of stories to tell.

Martha guided me expertly through my Master's thesis, and I found myself with a scholarship to undertake a PhD and take another look at ExxonMobil, this time from the other side of the risk-averse, electrified, razor-wire fence. In Hela Province, I faced a different set of risk-aversion issues, one of which was food. I had with me a veritable rainbow of the antibiotic spectrum and every drop of water that I drank I blasted with ultraviolet (UV) light using my UV water-treatment probe that ran on enough batteries to treat 70 litres (and I had a spare set of batteries with me). But, what I hadn't expected were the times when I simply found it difficult to obtain enough food to eat or a balance of foods that would supply me with sufficient nutrients. I should probably come clean at this point and reveal that I have an aversion to illness. One small grace of the PNG LNG project was that the companies sourced locally grown produce to feed their staff—the last time I was in the PNG highlands, I experienced some of the best food I have ever eaten. Not only that, I had 24-hour access to a soft-serve ice cream machine. But, on the other side of the fence, I had no land and, before I could establish myself and become immersed, I had no *wantoks* to save me. I had also started my fieldwork at the tail end of the drought that eventually drew in support of the UN World Food Program. All I had for support and nourishment were Martha's stories. How on earth was I going to survive on tinned fish and noodles and what the hell are lamb flaps? What would Martha do? Martha also undertook her PhD fieldwork during a drought, but she managed to cop the whole drought. It was literally days before I figured out my situation. Martha had told me about how she was chronically short of food for months, losing a serious amount of weight—when she did return to the broader, market economy, she found herself eating an entire block of butter, which would normally make anyone ill, but her state was such that her body was able to take in maybe half a pound of butter. After that experience, Martha produced some of the most admired ethnographic writing of the discipline and continued to have a really successful career. These footsteps cannot be bad. In the end, I did lose weight (because I got giardia)—but, if I was lighter and more agile of mind, it was largely because there seemed to be a 'Martha did it tougher' story for every occasion and I knew that Martha believed in what I was doing and knew that I could do it.

To conclude my reflection, I want you to imagine a scenario in which you are the sole passenger in a small aircraft trying to land on an island in the Bismarck Sea. There is too much cloud cover and the pilot cannot land. You notice that the pilot is starting to sweat and become agitated and seems to be fiddling more than usual with the controls. Eventually, he turns and says those eight little words that few people have heard from a pilot and then lived to tell the tale: 'we are going to run out of fuel'.

So, the pilot says to tie this belt to you so you don't fall out, go to the back and start throwing out all the cargo. You do, and the pilot says that he will go back and land on a remote little airstrip inland and drop you off. He does, and you are left alone with absolutely no idea where you are, except that you are in PNG. So, you wait until dark and then you can see firelight about two kilometres away. You walk towards that light and come to a little village where nobody can speak your language, or you theirs— but they are kind to you and keep you fed. The only way out is to get back on that plane, when and if it comes to collect you. I can imagine myself thinking, maybe I could just live here, in this nice little village where people are kind, and everything is safe—and I will never have to get on a plane again. However, you have work to do and stories to tell, and your stories will contain little details that are important to people in ways that you do not realise, and you will inspire and be part of the makeup of your students in ways that you do not know. What would Martha do? Martha got back on that plane.

Martha, My Mentor

Sarah Richards-Hewat

Martha was my PhD supervisor from 2010 to 2016. However, her supervision actually predates this. In 2000, I was briefly enrolled as her student at the Centre for Health and Society but, after having one too many babies, I was compelled to give up.

I first met Martha in the 1990s. She was teaching gender and anthropology at the University of Melbourne. I was studying for a Bachelor of Letters in anthropology at Deakin University. She said I could attend her classes—just to listen. Martha's eyes lit up when she taught. She took us on journeys across the Pacific, through time and through the eyes of women.

At the time, I had already lived in Wamena (West Papua) for several years. I had a sense of what it was like to live in New Guinea. It seemed to attract tough types of white people. I found it hard to reconcile how Martha, so petite and beautiful and elegant, could live for so long, roughing it on a tiny Pacific island. Not only did she look urbane, but I also came to learn that she loves cosmopolitan food, cultivated gardens and the opera.

When I think of Martha, the word 'brave' comes to mind. She was brave to go to Tubetube as a young mum and brave to study at a patriarchal, snobby university like Cambridge, with two small children in tow. She has been brave to take on consultancies with mining companies and the Papua New Guinea (PNG) constabulary.

Her bravery appears in her writing as truthfulness. By 'truthful', I mean more than the ability to report accurately what people say, do and feel. To me, 'truthful' means conveying human experience and social situations in a way that is not curated for theoretical trends. It means having the courage to let the data speak—and not to filter to appease political sensibilities.

I will give a quick example of how Martha writes without concern for ideology or causing offence. In her essay, 'Police and thieves, gunmen and drunks: Problems with men and problems with society in Papua New Guinea', Martha explains that young men in New Ireland are often attracted to violence (Macintyre, 2008). She notes that for these men, violent activities may be experienced as 'exciting, even enjoyable' and valued as 'an expression of potent masculinity' (Macintyre, 2008, p. 180).

Martha points out that the problem of violence in PNG is historically grounded, rather than an outcome of cultural dislocation, in turn caused by social changes associated with the toxic influences of globalisation. While also relativising violence as something historically and culturally specific, she makes the singular point that violence hurts people, especially women and children.

Another example of Martha's truthful style comes from a lecture she gave last year. Martha describes a 'PNG native'—a word that Martha finds highly effective—expressing regret about an acid lake left by a mining company. His regret was for a lost opportunity to reap the rewards of development but not, as you might expect, for a now-toxic ecosystem.

The value of such ethnographic nuggets—that Indigenous people do not always live in harmony with their environment or that violence can be exciting—cannot be underestimated. The promise of anthropology to disrupt right-wing assumptions about race, gender and other absolutes is well recognised. Martha's work shows the power of being able to unsettle the 'truths' of the left. Running against the left-wing grain, after all, made Margaret Mead famous and, I believe, will justify the relevance of anthropology into the future.

I remember the pleasurable shock of having my left-wing assumptions unsettled when I took Martha's medical anthropology course. Martha helped push me beyond the 'beauty myth' paradigm—the theory that beauty is a myth created by companies to exploit female insecurities for profit. She pointed out that people, some more than others, are quite simply vain.

This is what I love about Martha's work—her ideas straddle binaries in social theory without trying to 'transcend them'. She illuminates cultural relativity while also advocating for human rights. Martha's work blends heart and head. This blend is also found in her supervision. She guided me as her PhD student with a perfect balance of razor-sharp intellect and profound compassion.

Martha's writing is solid, caring, classic and clear. She taught me that you do not have to speak academic to be sophisticated. Complexity comes from good data, rather than fancy prose. For example, in the paper I mentioned earlier, Martha uses her findings about the pain and destruction caused by individual acts of violence to expose the limits of 'partability'—a key trope in the dominant and relational theory of Melanesian personhood.

If the self is a research tool, Martha's truthful style communicates her character. Martha calls a spade a spade and people to account. Martha's radar for inequality and other injustices in Melanesia is not simply a sensibility specific to her fieldwork. She lives it in her daily life.

I'm sure everyone close to Martha has a story of when she went to bat for them, or for someone they know. Three memories stand out for me.

One occurred when the scholarships office refused me maternity leave, on the grounds that I had already taken maternity leave. Martha wrote them a letter stating it was against human rights to sanction a woman for her number of children.

Another time, Martha offered to write a letter to *The Age* in defence of my reputation. The director of *60 Minutes* had taken offence with an editorial I had written that exposed one of their episodes as a primitivist sham. The director wrote that I was a rubbish student and not worthy of my PhD candidature. Martha would not tolerate this.

Before I re-enrolled as her student in 2010, Martha gave me teaching and research assistant work. This helped me ease back into university. Above all, I am grateful to Martha for standing beside me for a good 16 years. Raising three kids without partner support, while doing a PhD, was not easy. One reason that I never gave up the dream to finish the thesis was because Martha herself didn't.

Thank you, Martha!

References

Macintyre, M. (2008). Police and thieves, gunmen and drunks: Problems with men and problems with society in Papua New Guinea. *The Australian Journal of Anthropology*, *19*(2), 179–193. doi.org/10.1111/j.1835-9310.2008.tb00121.x

Martha: My Friend, My Role Model

Dora Kuir-Ayius

Martha and I met in 1995 at La Trobe University in Melbourne. She asked if I was from Papua New Guinea (PNG) and if I knew how to speak Tok Pisin. When I answered 'yes', she asked if I could teach her Tok Pisin. This was when our friendship started—we have been friends ever since. Although we do not contact each other regularly, our friendship remains intact.

Our Tok Pisin lessons started the week after our initial meeting. Martha knew exactly what she needed to learn, and we straight away began meeting specific objectives she had set for herself. During the lessons, she would have her list of English words she wanted the Tok Pisin translations for, and we would take it from there. That method appeared to work for Martha. There were no tests of any sort.

Martha eventually met my family—my husband Albert and our three children: Annitha (four), Albertine (three) and Kingsbury (five months old). She met Daniel, the last of my children, several years later in Port Moresby. In 1995, on Christmas Day, my family and I met her family— her husband Stuart and their two daughters.

Since then, Martha has been one of my role models, influencing me through her positive attitude and many words of encouragement spoken softly but with authority. Her words have had a great impact on me as a professional Melanesian woman and, most importantly, as an academic, particularly in a developing country that experiences challenges related to low development indicators. She shared a lot of her experiences of the impacts of mining stretching across economic, political, environmental and social dimensions (as is also reflected in many of her published articles). Some of the experiences she shared with me were centred on inequalities in culture that undermined the ability of women to be equal partners in development. Women were, and still are in many ways, seen as less important by their male relatives, who sometimes make decisions on their behalf. Many of these decisions have had a negative impact on the lives of these women, including sometimes in their relationships with men on the mine sites who were away from their wives and children.

My career—especially as a Melanesian woman—is surrounded by cultural expectations and challenges influenced by norms and I value my friendship with this empowering academic who had the time to persist not only verbally, but also by her actions. By involving me in research activities, Martha created the interest in me to pursue a career in academia. Little did I realise that being friends with Martha would influence me in my career. Martha reminded me of a *bilum*, a traditional PNG bag, either knitted or woven by hand. I could say that she was the *bilum* full of things (including knowledge) that needed another *bilum* to unpack some stuff into, to share the load.

I remember Martha, through her actions, involving me in one of her research projects with the Royal PNG Constabulary in Port Moresby. She talked to the police personnel and I observed how she was conducting this research. Although I had completed a master's by coursework in social work, at that point, I had not been involved in any research or consulting work—this was an important learning experience.

In 2004, Martha and I caught up in Madang at a conference on 'Women and mining in Papua New Guinea', at which she presented a paper. During the conference, someone asked Martha who I was; she introduced me as Dora, who has completed a Master's in social work, and said 'I will make sure she goes further to do a PhD'. At that stage, I had hardly thought about embarking on a PhD; however, my role model was miles ahead and foreseeing me as a 'doctor'. During this conference, among other things, she also introduced me to her women group from Lihir Island—little did I know that I would one day choose Lihir as a case study site for my PhD studies. Almost six years after that introduction, I pursued my doctoral studies and chose Lihir, Misima and Hidden Valley as my case studies. I used Martha's network to connect with interviewees in Lihir.

When I was in Port Moresby preparing for my fieldwork, Martha gave me the name of her friend on Misima, who I then visited. I appreciated the fact that there was someone, at least, in the community where I was doing fieldwork that I could connect to. I used this link to begin familiarising myself with the people and culture of my research context.

Through my conversations with Martha, I understood the impact of mining, including issues that related to women and children in PNG communities. These conversations created my interest in mining, which later developed into me choosing the following PhD topic 'Building community resilience in mine impacted communities: A case study on the delivery of health services in Papua New Guinea' (Kuir-Ayius, 2016). I set out to explore the notion of community resilience in mine-affected communities in PNG. The research used the case of health, specifically the delivery of health services, as a lens for understanding resilience in three of these communities. The resilience and sustainability of these communities were explored through the concept of 'community capitals' (CCs). In this study, CCs were natural, human, financial, cultural, social, political and built capitals. In my thesis, the CCs were also viewed through a Melanesian lens—I proposed a '*Bilum* Framework' to better illustrate the ways in which strengthening these entwined capitals can build community resilience. It was chosen as a metaphor because the many strings used to weave it resemble the interactions of CCs that can build more resilient communities. An explicit aim of the research was to understand how the strengthening of the various capitals can improve resilience to achieve more sustainable communities.

The findings drew together three main themes that underpinned my study: 1) the lack of policy alignment between the different actors in terms of health service delivery, 2) the lack of access to health services in mine-affected communities and 3) the fluctuating levels of community resilience across stages of mining. The study discussed how these issues affected the building of resilience in mine-affected communities and how the interconnectedness that underpinned the *Bilum* Framework could provide new ways of approaching the building of resilience for these communities.

I also appreciate Martha's research and publications on other topics, besides mining, that relate to PNG culture. When I was writing a section in my thesis on 'traditional and informal approaches to healing', I came across her (and others') article on 'Medical pluralism and the maintenance of traditional healing techniques on Lihir, Papua New Guinea' (Macintyre et al., 2005). My discovery prompted a sigh of relief because I had searched for months for a relevant article to support what I had written.

Martha has a 'naispla lewa'—a good heart or passion to encourage others and bring out the potential of those she interacts with in one way or another. My friend and role model is like a *bilum*, full of knowledge, wisdom and love that has flowed and is still flowing far and wide to discover the unknown and make it known.

Martha apet! Ateu oa! Mi kaikai lewa blo yu!
Martha, thank you! My heart you! I love you!

References

Kuir-Ayius, D. (2016). Building community resilience in mine impacted communities: A study on delivery of health services in Papua New Guinea (Unpublished doctoral thesis). Massey University, Palmerston North, New Zealand.

Macintyre, M., Foale, S., Bainton, N. & Moktel, B. (2005). Medical pluralism and the maintenance of a traditional healing technique on Lihir, Papua New Guinea. *Pimatisiwin: A Journal of Aboriginal and Indigenous Community Health, 3*(1), 87–98.

The Work of Martha Macintyre, So Far

Theses

Macintyre, M. (1983). Changing paths: An historical ethnography of traders of Tubetube (Unpublished doctoral thesis). The Australian National University, Canberra, ACT.

Books

Macintyre, M. (1983). *The kula: A bibliography*. Cambridge, England: Cambridge University Press.

Macintyre, M. & Dennerstein, L. (1994). *Shifting latitudes: Changing attitudes. Immigrant women's health experiences, attitudes, knowledge and beliefs.* Melbourne, Vic.: Key Centre for Women's Health in Society.

Edited Books

Biersack, A. & Macintyre, M. (Eds). (2017). *Emergent masculinities in the Pacific.* London, England: Routledge.

Biersack, A., Jolly, M. & Macintyre, M. (Eds). (2016). *Gender violence and human rights: Seeking justice in Fiji, Papua New Guinea and Vanuatu.* Canberra, ACT: ANU Press, doi.org/10.22459/GVHR.12.2016

Hildson, A.-M., Macintyre, M., Mackie, V. & Stivens, M. (Eds). (2000). *Human rights and gender politics: Perspectives on the Asia Pacific Region.* London, England: Routledge.

Jolly, M. & Macintyre, M. (Eds). (1989). *Family and gender in the Pacific: Domestic contradictions and the colonial impact.* Cambridge, England: Cambridge University Press.

Lahiri-Dutt, K. & Macintyre, M. (Eds). (2006). *Women miners in developing countries: Pit women and others.* Aldershot, England: Ashgate Publishing Ltd.

Macintyre, M. & Spark, C. (Eds). (2017). *Transformations of gender in Melanesia.* Canberra, ACT: ANU Press, doi.org/10.22459/TGM.02.2017

Patterson, M. & Macintyre, M. (Eds). (2011). *Managing modernity in the Western Pacific.* St Lucia, Qld: University of Queensland Press.

Book Chapters

Bainton, N. A. & Macintyre, M. (2016). Mortuary ritual and mining riches in island Melanesia. In D. Lipset & E. K. Silverman (Eds), *Mortuary dialogues: Death ritual and the reproduction of moral community in Pacific modernities* (pp. 110–132). Berghahn, NY: Berghahn.

Biersack, A. & Macintyre, M. (2016). Introduction: Gender violence and human rights in the Western Pacific. In A. Biersack, M. Jolly & M, Macintyre (Eds), *Gender violence and human rights: Seeking justice in Fiji, Papua New Guinea and Vanuatu* (pp. 1–45). Canberra, ACT: ANU Press, doi.org/10.22459/GVHR.12.2016

Brown, P., Macintyre, M., Morpeth, R. & Prendergast, S. (1981). A daughter, a thing to be given away. In Cambridge Women's Studies Group (Ed.), *Women in society: Interdisciplinary essays* (pp. 127–147). London, England: Virago Press.

Lahiri-Dutt, K. & Macintyre, M. (2006). Introduction: Where life is in the pits (and elsewhere) and gendered. In. K. Lahiri-Dutt & M. Macintyre (Eds), *Women miners in developing countries: Pit women and others* (pp. 1–22). Aldershot, England: Ashgate.

Macintyre, M. (1983). Kune on Tubetube and in the Bwanabwana region of the Southern Massim. In E. R. Leach & J. W. Leach (Eds), *The kula: New perspectives on Massim exchange* (pp. 369–382). Cambridge, England: Cambridge University Press.

Macintyre, M. (1986). Female autonomy in a matrilineal society. In N. Grieve & A. Burns (Eds), *Australian women: New feminist perspectives* (pp. 248–58). Melbourne, Vic.: Oxford University Press.

Macintyre, M. (1987). Flying witches and leaping warriors: Supernatural origins of power and matrilineal authority in Tubetube society. In M. Strathern (Ed.), *Dealing with inequality: Analysing gender relations in Melanesia and beyond* (pp. 207–229). Cambridge, England: Cambridge University Press.

Macintyre, M. (1988). The unhappy wife and the dispensable husband: Myths of a matrilineal order. In D. Gewertz (Ed.), *The myth of matriarchy reconsidered* (pp. 185–195). Sydney, NSW: Oceania Monograph Series.

Macintyre, M. (1989). Better homes and gardens. In M. Jolly & M. Macintyre (Eds), *Family and gender in the Pacific: Domestic contradictions and the colonial impact* (pp. 156–69). Melbourne, Vic.: Cambridge University Press.

Macintyre, M. (1989). The triumph of the Susu. In F. H. Damon & R. Wagner (Eds), *Death rituals and life in the societies of the kula ring* (pp. 133–153). De Kalb, IL: Northern Illinios University Press.

Macintyre, M. (1990). Christianity, cargo cultism and the concept of the spirit of Misiman cosmology. In J. Barker & C. Forman (Eds), *Christianity in Oceania, ethnographic perspectives* (pp. 81–110). Lanham, MD: University Press of America, ASAO Monograph Series.

Macintyre, M. (1992). Reflections of an anthropologist who mistook her husband for a yam: Female comedy on Tubetube. In W. E. Mitchell (Ed.), *Clowning as critical practice: Performance humour in the South Pacific* (pp. 130–45). Pittsburgh, PA; London, England: University of Pittsburgh Press.

Macintyre, M. (1993). Fictive kinship or mistaken identity?: Fieldwork on Tubetube, Papua New Guinea. In P. Caplan & D. Bell (Eds), *Gendered fields* (pp. 44–62). London, England: Routledge.

Macintyre, M. (1993). Women and mining. In *Papua New Guinea and Australia: Towards 2000* (pp. 43–49). Fitzroy, Vic.: Community Aid Abroad/Freedom from Hunger, Fitzroy.

Macintyre, M. (1994). An anthropologist looks at postnatal depression. In J. Carter (Ed.), *Postnatal depression: Towards a research agenda for human services and health* (Issues for Research, Vol. 2) (pp. 11–16). Canberra, ACT: Commonwealth Department of Human Services and Health.

Macintyre, M. (1994). Migrant women from El Salvador and Vietnam in Australian hospitals. In C. Waddell & A. R. Peterson (Eds), *Just health: Inequality in illness, care and prevention* (pp. 159–68). Melbourne, Vic.: Churchill Livingstone.

Macintyre, M. (1998). The persistence of inequality: Women in Papua New Guinea since independence. In. L. Zimmer-Tamakoshi (Ed.), *Modern Papua New Guinea* (pp. 211–231). Kirkville, MO: Thomas Jefferson University Press.

Macintyre, M. (2000). Hear us, women of Papua New Guinea: Melanesian women and human rights. In A. Hilsdon, M. Macintyre, V. Mackie & M. Stivens (Eds), *Human rights and gender politics: Perspectives on the Asia-Pacific region* (pp. 147–171). London, England: Routledge.

Macintyre, M. (2002). Women and mining projects in Papua New Guinea: Problems of consultation, representation and women's rights. In I. Macdonald & C. Rowland (Eds), *Tunnel vision: Women mining and communities* (pp. 26–29). Melbourne, Vic.: Oxfam-Community Aid Abroad.

Macintyre, M. (2002). Women's health in Oceania. In C. Kramarae & D. Spender (Eds), *Routledge international encyclopedia of women: Global women's issues and knowledge*. London, England; New York, NY: Routledge.

Macintyre, M. (2003). Indigenous healing. In. T. Robson (Ed.), *An introduction to complementary medicine* (pp. 33–47). Sydney, NSW: Allen and Unwin.

Macintyre, M. (2005). Taking care of culture: Consultancy, anthropology and gender issues. In P. Stewart & A. Strathern (Eds), *Anthropology and consultancy: Issues and debates* (pp. 124–138). New York, NY: Berghahn.

Macintyre, M. (2006). Women working in the mining industry in Papua New Guinea: A case study from Lihir. In K. Lahiri-Dutt & M. Macintyre (Eds), *Women miners in developing countries: Pit women and others* (pp. 131–144). Aldershot, England: Ashgate.

Macintyre, M. (2011). Modernity, gender and mining: Experiences from Papua New Guinea. In K. Lahiri-Dutt (Ed.), *Gendering the field: Towards sustainable livelihoods for mining in mining communities* (pp. 21–32). Canberra, ACT: ANU E Press, doi.org/10.22459/GF.03.2011

Macintyre, M. (2011). Money changes everything: Papua New Guinean women in the modern economy. In M. Patterson & M. Macintyre (Eds), *Managing modernity in the Western Pacific* (pp. 90–120). St Lucia, Qld: University of Queensland Press.

Macintyre, M. (2012). Gender violence in Melanesia and the problem of Millennium Development Goal No. 3. In M. Jolly & C. Stewart (Eds), *Engendering violence in Papua New Guinea* (pp. 239–266). Canberra, ACT: ANU E Press, doi.org/10.22459/EVPNG.07.2012

Macintyre, M. (2013). Instant wealth: Visions of the future on Lihir, New Ireland, Papua New Guinea. In M. Tabani & M. Abong (Eds), *Kago, kastom and kalja: The study of indigenous movements in Melanesia today* (pp. 123–146). Marseilles, France: Pacific-Credo Publications.

Macintyre, M. (2013). Post-colonial societies: Melanesia. In J. Carrier & D. Gewertz (Eds), *A handbook of social anthropology* (pp. 403–420). New York, NY: Berghahn and Bloomsbury.

Macintyre, M. (2017). Flux and change in Melanesian gender relations. In M. Macintyre & C. Spark (Eds), *Transformations of gender in Melanesia* (pp. 1–22). Canberra, ACT: ANU Press, doi.org/10.22459/TGM.02.2017

Macintyre, M. (2019). Gender relations and human rights in Melanesia. In E. Hirsch & W. Rollason (Eds), *The Melanesian World* (pp. 285–299). London, England; New York, NY: Routledge.

Macintyre, M. (2019). Values in flux: Reflections on resilience and change in Melanesia (Afterword). In L. Dousset & M. Nayral (Eds), *Pacific realities: Changing perspectives on resilience and resistance* (pp. 151–165). New York, NY; Oxford, England: Berghahn.

Macintyre, M. & Allen, J. (1990). Trading for subsistence: The case for the Southern Massim. In D. Yen (Ed.), *Pacific production systems* (pp. 120–36). Canberra, ACT: The Australian National University.

Macintyre, M. & Foale, S. (2004). Global imperatives and local desires: Competing economic and environmental interests in Melanesian communities. In V. S. Lockwood (Ed.), *Pacific Island societies in a global world* (pp. 149–64). New York, NY: Prentice Hall.

Macintyre, M. & Gerritsen, R. (1991). Dilemmas of distribution: The case of the Misima gold mine in Papua New Guinea. In R. Howitt & J. Connell (Eds), *Mining and indigenous people in the Pacific Rim* (pp. 35–54). Sydney; Melbourne: Sydney University Press; Oxford University Press.

Macintyre, M. & MacKenzie, M. (1992). Focal length as an analogue of cultural distance. In E. Edwards (Ed.), *Anthropology and photography 1860–1920* (pp. 158–164). New Haven, CT: Yale University Press.

Macintyre, M. & Patterson, M. (2011). Capitalism, cosmology and globalisation in the Pacific. In Patterson, M. & M. Macintyre (Eds), *Managing modernity in the Western Pacific* (pp. 1–29). St Lucia, Qld: University of Queensland Press.

Macintyre, M. & Young, M. W. (1983). The persistence of traditional trade and ceremonial exchange in the Massim. In R. May (Ed.), *Beyond diversity: Changing Melanesia* (pp. 207–223). Canberra, ACT: Australian National University Press.

Macintyre, M., Yelland, J. & Gifford, S. (1994). Explanatory models about maternal and infant health and sudden infant death syndrome among Asian-born mothers. In P. L. Rice (Ed.), *Asian mothers, Australian birth: Pregnancy, childbirth and childrearing: The Asian experience in an English-speaking country* (pp. 175–191). Melbourne, Vic.: Ausmed Publications.

McLeod, A. & Macintyre, M. (2011). The Royal Papua New Guinea Constabulary. In V. Luker & S. Dinnen (Eds), *Civic insecurity: Law, order and HIV in Papua New Guinea* (Studies in State and Society in the Pacific, No. 6) (pp. 167–178). Canberra, ACT: ANU E Press, doi.org/10.22459/CI.12.2010

Articles

Bainton, N. A. & Macintyre, M. (2013). 'My land, my work': Business development and large-scale mining in Papua New Guinea. *Research in Economic Anthropology, 33*, 139–165. doi.org/10.1108/S0190-1281(2013)0000033008

Cox, J. & Macintyre, M. (2014). Christian marriage, money scams and Melanesian social imaginaries. *Oceania, 84*(2), 138–157. doi.org/10.1002/ocea.5048

Fabinyi, M., Foale, S. & Macintyre, M. (2015). Managing inequality or managing stocks? An ethnographic perspective on the governance of small-scale fisheries. *Fish and Fisheries, 16*, 471–485.

Filer, C. & Macintyre, M. (2006). Grass roots and deep holes: Community responses to mining in Melanesia. *The Contemporary Pacific, 18*(2), 215–232.

Foale, S. & Macintyre, M. (2000). Dynamic and flexible aspects of land and marine tenure at West Nggela: Implications for marine resource management. *Oceania, 71*(1), 30–45.

Foale, S. & Macintyre, M. (2004). *Fujichrome green: The photographic fetishisation of biodiversity by environmentalists* (Resource Management in Asia-Pacific Working Paper 54). Canberra, ACT: Research School of Pacific and Asian Studies, The Australian National University.

Foale, S. & Macintyre, M. (2005). Green fantasies: Photographic representations of biodiversity and ecotourism in the Western Pacific. *Journal of Political Ecology, 12*, 1–22.

Foale, S., Cohen, P. Januchowski-Hartley, S., Wenger, A. & Macintyre, M. (2011). Tenure and taboos: Origins and implications for fisheries in the Pacific. *Fish and Fisheries, 12*, 356–369.

Macintyre, M. (1978). '*Desperately wicked*': A study of Jane Cameron, female convict. *Women's Studies International Quarterly, 1*(1), 39–46.

Macintyre, M. (1978). Recent Australian feminist historiography. *History Workshop Journal*, *5*(1), 98–110.

Macintyre, M. (1982). Pottery manufacture on Tubetube. *Canberra Anthropology*, *5*(2), 34–57.

Macintyre, M. (1983). Warfare and the changing context of kune on Tubetube. *The Journal of Pacific History*, *18*(1–2), 11–34.

Macintyre, M. (1984). The problem of the semi-alienable pig. *Canberra Anthropology*, *7*(1–2), 109–123.

Macintyre, M. (1985). Women and local politics on Tubetube, Milne Bay Province (Working Paper 6). In *Women in Politics in Papua New Guinea* (pp. 19–25). Canberra, ACT: Department of Political and Social Change, Research School Pacific Studies, The Australian National University.

Macintyre, M. (1987). Nurturance and nutrition: Change and continuity in concepts of food and feasting in a southern Massim community. *Journal de la Société des Océanistes*, *84*, 51–59.

Macintyre, M. (1994). Anthropology's histories: Dealing with time and transformation in the Pacific (Review Essay). *Reviews in Anthropology*, *22*, 275–283.

Macintyre, M. (1994). Too many chiefs? Leadership in the Massim in the colonial era. *History and Anthropology*, *7*(1–4), 241–262.

Macintyre, M. (1995). Violent bodies and vicious exchanges: Objectification and personification in the Massim. *Social Analysis*, *37*, 29–43.

Macintyre, M. (1998). On equivocal ethnography. *Canberra Anthropology*, *21*(1–2), 7–31.

Macintyre, M. (2000). Violence and peacemaking in Papua New Guinea: A realistic assessment of the social and cultural issues at grassroots level. *Development Bulletin*, *53*, 34–38.

Macintyre, M. (2001). Taking care of culture: Consultancy, anthropology and gender issues. *Social Analysis*, *45*(2), 108–119.

Macintyre, M. (2002). *Politicised ecology: Local responses to mining in Papua New Guinea* (RMAP Working Paper No. 30). Canberra, ACT: Research School of Pacific and Asian Studies, The Australian National University.

Macintyre, M. (2003). Petztorme women: Responding to change in Lihir, Papua New Guinea. *Oceania*, *74*(1/2), 120–133.

Macintyre, M. (2004). Thoroughly modern mothers: Maternal aspirations and declining mortality on the Lihir Islands, Papua New Guinea. *Health Sociology Review: International Journal of Health Sociology: Policy, Promotion and Practice, 13*(1), 43–53.

Macintyre, M. (2006). Indicators of violence against women. Measuring gender equality: Indicators of change. *Development Bulletin, 71,* 61–62.

Macintyre, M. (2007). Informed consent and mining projects: A view from Papua New Guinea. *Pacific Affairs, 80*(1), 49–65.

Macintyre, M. (2008). Police and thieves, gunmen and drunks: Problems with men and problems with society in Papua New Guinea. *The Australian Journal of Anthropology, 19*(2), 179–193.

Macintyre, M. (2008). Public affairs: Responding to gender violence in Papua New Guinea. *Anthropology News, 49*(3), 28 & 30.

Macintyre, M. (2012). The value of open access publishing. *HAU Journal of Ethnographic Theory, 2*(1), 385–411.

Macintyre, M. (2018). Places, migration and sustainability: Anthropological reflections on mining and movement (Afterword). *Sustainable Development, 26*(5), 501–505.

Macintyre, M. & Foale, S. (2002). Environmental damage as a resource: Claims for compensation in the context of mining developments in Papua New Guinea. *Development Bulletin, 58,* 41–45.

Macintyre, M. & Foale, S. (2004). Politicised ecology: Local responses to mining in Papua New Guinea. *Oceania, 74*(3), 231–251.

Macintyre, M. & Foale, S. (2007). Land and marine tenure, ownership and new forms of entitlement on Lihir: Changing notions of property in the context of a goldmining project. *Human Organization, 66*(1), 49–59.

Macintyre, M. & Foale, S. (2013). Science, traditional ecological knowledge and anthropology: Managing the impacts of mining in Papua New Guinea. *Collaborative Anthropologies, 6,* 400–418.

Macintyre, M., Foale, S., Bainton, N. & Moktel, B. (2005). Medical pluralism and the maintenance of a traditional healing technique on Lihir, Papua New Guinea. *Pimatisiwin: A Journal of Aboriginal and Indigenous Community Health, 3*(1), 87–98.

Macintyre, M., Mee, W. & Solomon, F. (2008). Evaluating social performance in the context of an audit culture: A pilot social review of a gold mine in Papua New Guinea. *Corporate Social Responsibility and Environmental Management, 15*(2), 100–110.

Membup, J. & Macintyre, M. (2000). Petztorme: A woman's organisation in the context of a PNG mining project. *Development Bulletin, 51*, 55–57.

Morton, J. & Macintyre, M. (1995). Introduction: Bodies, selves, emotions. *Social Analysis, 37*, 5–14.

Consultancy Reports

Brewer, D. et al. (2003). *Assessment of mine impacts on Lihir Island fish communities with an estimation of the potential fisheries resources.* Brisbane, Qld: CSIRO.

Enright, N. et al. (2000). *Baseline study of Kirthar National Park, Pakistan.* Melbourne, Vic.: University of Melbourne.

Filer, C., Foale, S. & Macintyre, M. (2004). Sub-global Working Group State of the Assessment Report Lihir, Papua New Guinea. Sub-Global Assessment of Coastal, Small Island and Coral Reef Ecosystems in Papua New Guinea. Unpublished report for the Millennium Ecosystem Assessment. Canberra, ACT: The Australian National University.

Johnson, P. & Macintyre, M. (2004). *A study of local responses to tuberculosis from Lihir Island, New Ireland Province, Papua New Guinea.* Melbourne, Vic.: Centre for Health and Society, University of Melbourne.

Macintyre, M. (1996). *Interim report on social impact of the construction phase of Lihir Gold.* Papua New Guinea: Papua New Guinea Department of Environment and Conservation and Lihir Gold Pty Ltd.

Macintyre, M. (1997). *Report on baseline data for monitoring of social impact on Lihir 1996–1997.* Papua New Guinea: Department of Environment and Conservation.

Macintyre, M. (1997). *Report on the social and economic impact of the mining project on Lihir, 1996–1997.* Papua New Guinea: Lihir Gold Pty Ltd.

Macintyre, M. (2012). *Report on the social impact of flooding on communities along the Middle Fly River.* Papua New Guinea: Papua New Guinea Sustainable Development Program.

Macintyre, M. & Dennerstein, L. (1994). *Immigrant women's health report. A study of migrant women from seven ethnic groups in Melbourne. Attitudes, experience and culture: Access to hospital services.* Australia: Department of Ethnic Affairs and Immigration.

Macintyre, M. & Foale, S. (2000). *Social impact on Lihir report for 1998–1999*. Papua New Guinea: Lihir Gold and Department of Environment and Conservation; Australia: The Export Finance and Insurance Corporation.

Macintyre, M. & Foale, S. (2002). *Social impact on Lihir report for 2000–2001*. Papua New Guinea: Lihir Gold and Department of Environment and Conservation; Australia: The Export Finance and Insurance Corporation.

Macintyre, M. & Foale, S. (2003). *Social impact on Lihir report for 2001–2002*. Papua New Guinea: Lihir Gold and Department of Environment and Conservation; Australia: The Export Finance and Insurance Corporation.

Macintyre, M. & Foale, S. (2004). *Social impact on Lihir report for 2002–2003*. Papua New Guinea: Lihir Gold and Department of Environment and Conservation; Australia: The Export Finance and Insurance Corporation.

Macintyre, M. & Gerritsen, R. (1986). *Social impact study for a proposed goldmine on Misima, Milne Bay Province*. Papua New Guinea: Department of Minerals and Energy and Milne Bay Provincial Government.

Macintyre, M. & Gerritsen, R. (1995). *The Lihir Gold mining project, PNG: Risk assessment*. Australia: The Export Finance and Insurance Corporation.

Macintyre, M. & Parsons, S. (2000). *Evaluation of design of Bougainville Wharves Project*. Australia: AusAID.

Macintyre, M., Collett, G. & Glare, K. (1998). *Design of Australian aid to The Royal PNG Constabulary 1999–2004*. Australia: AusAID.

Macintyre, M., Collett, G. & Glare, K. (1998). *Review of Australian aid to the Royal PNG Constabulary 1988–1998*. Australia: AusAID.

Macintyre, M., Mee, W. & Solomon, F. (2005). *Design, pilot and evaluation of a social review for the Lihir Goldmine*. Melbourne, Vic.: CSIRO Minerals Division.

Macintyre, M. et. al. (1995). *Report on migrant women's access to hospitals in Melbourne*. Australia: Department of Immigration and Ethnic Affairs and The Mercy Hospital for Women.

Macintyre, M. et al. (1996). *Traditional land tenure in Papua New Guinea*. Australia: AusAID.

Macintyre, M. et al. (1997). *Gender, economic development and the status of women in Papua New Guinea*. The World Bank; SMEC International.

Contributors

John Aini is the founder and director of Ailan Awareness, a marine conservation and indigenous empowerment focused NGO in New Ireland, Papua New Guinea. He is a Maimai—a chief in the Malangan culture in northern New Ireland; a Ainpidik, in the Tumbuan Society from southern New Ireland; and a Merengen from his own Tungak culture from Lovongai, New Hanover. Trained in Fisheries Management, he has worked as a community-based resource management expert and Lecturer at the National Fisheries College of Papua New Guinea. He is the co-founder of The Ranguva Solwara Skul.

Kalissa Alexeyeff is a Senior Lecturer in Gender Studies at the University of Melbourne. She has a background in critical theory and social anthropology and conducts ongoing research in the Cook Islands and Sāmoa in the home islands and diaspora. Her main research interest is the intersection of gender, sexuality and culture in contemporary contexts. She is the author of *Dancing from the heart: Movement, gender and Cook Islands globalization* (2009) and co-editor of *Gender on the edge: Transgender, gay, and other Pacific Islanders* (2014) and *Touring Pacific cultures* (2016).

Nick Bainton is an Associate Professor and Principal Research Fellow in the Centre for Social Responsibility in Mining at the University of Queensland. He has been studying the social impacts of large-scale resource extraction in Papua New Guinea for nearly two decades. He has written widely on the social and political effects of extractive capitalism in Melanesia and is the author of *The Lihir destiny: Cultural responses to mining in Melanesia* (2010), also published by ANU Press.

John Barker is Professor of Anthropology at the University of British Columbia. He has written extensively on Christianity in Oceanic and First Nations communities in Canada as well as the history of

555

anthropology in Canada and the Pacific. His books include *Christianity in Oceania* (1990), *The anthropology of morality in Melanesia and beyond* (2007) and *Ancestral lines: The Maisin of Papua New Guinea and the fate of the rainforest* (2016).

John Cox has 25 years' experience in the Pacific, working as a volunteer, NGO program manager, development consultant and anthropologist. His core work on 'fast money schemes' explores the moral and developmental aspirations of the growing middle classes of the Pacific. John has published on gender, politics and developmental challenges in Papua New Guinea, the Solomon Islands and Fiji, including new communications technologies, sorcery accusations, disaster response and livelihoods. John is an Honorary Lecturer with the School of Culture History and Language at ANU and an Honorary Associate in the School of Humanities and Social Sciences at La Trobe University. He currently works at the University of Melbourne on the ARC Laureate Project 'Future Islands: Catalysing Solutions to Climate Change in Low-Lying Islands'.

Melissa Demian is a Senior Lecturer in Social Anthropology at the University of St Andrews in Scotland. She has conducted research in Papua New Guinea for over 20 years and publishes on the topics of law, kinship, gender and urbanisation.

Bronwen Douglas is Honorary Professor in the College of Arts & Social Sciences at ANU. She taught Pacific History at La Trobe University for 25 years before moving to a research position at ANU in 1997. In the early 1990s, she and Martha Macintyre taught an exciting transdisciplinary course on women in the Pacific. Bronwen's research and writing combine the ethnohistory of encounters in Oceania with the history of the human sciences and the sciences of place. She is the author of *Science, voyages, and encounters in Oceania 1511–1850* (2014) and *Across the great divide: Journeys in history and anthropology* (1998).

Frederick Errington is Distinguished Professor of Anthropology (Emeritus) at Trinity College, Hartford, Connecticut. Interested in the ways people make meaning, often under difficult and changing circumstances, he has written about 'cargo cultures', religious change, aesthetics, gender, class formation and global engagements in the Pacific and beyond. Collaborating with Deborah Gewertz, he co-authored *Cultural alternatives and a feminist anthropology* (1987), *Twisted histories, altered contexts* (1991), *Articulating change in the 'last unknown'* (1995),

Emerging class in Papua New Guinea (1999) and *Yali's question: Sugar, culture, and history* (2004). Most recently, they wrote about world food systems in *Cheap meat: Flap food nations in the Pacific Islands* (2010) and *The noodle narratives: The global rise of an industrial food into the twenty-first century* (2013). Their current research concerns environmental issues in Papua New Guinea and South Dakota, about which they have published several major articles.

Colin Filer is an Honorary Professor in the Crawford School of Public Policy at ANU. He has a PhD in Social Anthropology from the University of Cambridge. Between 1975 and 1994, he taught anthropology and sociology at the Universities of Glasgow (1975-82) and Papua New Guinea (1983–94). From 1991 to 1994 he also managed the University of Papua New Guinea business arm, Unisearch PNG. From 1995 to 2000, he was head of the Social and Environmental Studies Division at the PNG National Research Institute. From 2001 to 2012, he was Convenor of the Resource Management in Asia-Pacific Program in the ANU College of Asia and the Pacific. He is now a member of the Resources, Environment and Development group in the Crawford School.

Simon Foale is currently Academic Head of Social Sciences at James Cook University in North Queensland, Australia, where he teaches anthropology of development and political ecology, and has devoted considerable energy as a branch committee member of the NTEU to address pressing issues of inequality and the destructive impacts of neoliberal managerialism within Australian universities. After graduating as a marine scientist in the 1980s, he decided anthropology was more interesting and has been trying to reinvent himself as an anthropologist for around 30 years. He maintains a keen interest in coastal fishery management and marine conservation, but now with a critical political ecology focus.

Deborah Gewertz is G. Henry Whitcomb Professor of Anthropology at Amherst College, Amherst, Massachusetts. Having pursued anthropological research in Papua New Guinea, Fiji, New Zealand, Australia and the United States, she has written about ethnohistory, gender, sociocultural change, class formation and global engagements. With Frederick Errington, she co-authored *Cultural alternatives and a feminist anthropology* (1978), *Twisted histories, altered contexts* (1991), *Articulating change in the 'last unknown'* (1995), *Emerging class in Papua New Guinea* (1999), *Yali's question: Sugar, culture, and history* (2004), *Cheap meat: Flap food nations in the Pacific Islands* (2010) and *The noodle* *narratives: The global rise of an industrial food into the twenty-first century* (2013). Their work on environmental issues in Papua New Guinea and South Dakota has resulted in several major articles.

Alex Golub is an Associate Professor of Anthropology at the University of Hawai'i at Mānoa. He is a political anthropologist who studies mining in Papua New Guinea, especially the Porgera gold mine. His book on this topic, *Leviathans at the gold mine*, was published in 2014. He also has an interest in the history of anthropology and is the co-editor of the 2016 volume *A practice of anthropology: The thought and influence of Marshall Sahlins.*

Chris Gregory is Emeritus Professor of Anthropology at ANU. He has been engaged in ongoing fieldwork in central India since 1982 and has lived and worked for seven years in Papua New Guinea and Fiji. His research interests include the political economy and culture of rice growing in central India, kinship, gift exchange, money, the value question and morality.

Susan R. Hemer is a social anthropologist based at the University of Adelaide whose work focuses on medical and psychological wellbeing, as well as issues of development, particularly in the context of Papua New Guinea. With four years' ethnographic field research in Papua New Guinea since 1997, she has published articles on gender, health care, emotion, death and grief. She is the author of *Tracing the Melanesian person: Emotions and relationships in Lihir* (2013).

Margaret Jolly, AM, FASSA, is Professor Emerita in the School of Culture, History and Language, College of Asia and the Pacific, ANU. An Australian Research Council Laureate Fellow (2010–16), she has written on gender in the Pacific, exploratory voyages, Christianity, maternity and sexuality, cinema and art. Her current research focuses on gender and climate change. She has taught at ANU, Macquarie University, the University of Hawai'i at Mānoa and the University of California at Santa Cruz and supervised over 60 PhD students. She held a Poste Rouge (Visiting Professor) at CNRS and EHESS in France in 2009. Her publications can be found at researchers.anu.edu.au/researchers/jolly-ma.

Dan Jorgensen is a newly minted Professor Emeritus in the Department of Anthropology at Western University in London, Canada. Originally an anthropologist of religion, he has conducted fieldwork among Papua New Guinea's Telefolmin people since the 1970s and became a student of their historical experience along the way. Much of his work is on spirit-driven Christianity and the regional mining economy. More recently, he studied mobile phones, social media and the uses to which they are put in Papua New Guinea. His most recent fieldwork was devoted to reporting and understanding the consequences of the El Niño drought. He and Imke Jorgensen are happy parents of children living in North America and Europe.

Dora Kuir-Ayius is a Lecturer in Social Work in the School of Humanities and Social Sciences at the University of Papua New Guinea. She attained her PhD in Development Studies from Massey University, New Zealand, and a Master of Social Work from La Trobe University, Australia. Dora has conducted research on various issues including gender-based violence, biodiversity conservation, socioeconomic impact on road usage, child protection and family sexual violence and the impact of climate change on families. She specialises in building resilience through the development of community capitals to achieve sustainable communities.

Neil Maclean began research for his PhD (University of Adelaide) with the Maring of Papua New Guinea (Jiwaka Province) in 1979. He has written about the local relationship to the cash economy, the postcolonial nation state and the implications for anthropological method. Between 1985 and 2019, Neil taught anthropology at the University of Sydney and helped establish a Development Studies program. He also edited *Oceania*, a major journal in the anthropology of the Oceanic region. More recently, he has begun working on anthropological perspectives on autism and autistic adults, as well as enjoying retirement and dabbling in critical theory.

Debra McDougall is a Senior Lecturer in Anthropology at the University of Melbourne, author of *Engaging with strangers: Love and violence in the rural Solomon Islands* (2016) and co-editor of *Christian politics in Oceania* (2013). Her current research is focused on a remarkable vernacular language movement, the Kulu Language Institute of Ranongga, and she is interested in other grassroots challenges to socioeconomic, political and epistemological inequality in Oceania.

Michael Main completed his PhD in Anthropology at ANU in April 2020. Michael's research focused on the Huli population in the Papua New Guinea highlands and the impact of ExxonMobil's massive Papua New Guinea Liquefied Natural Gas project. In 2014, Michael completed a Master of Development Studies at the University of Melbourne, where he undertook field research on the environmental consequences of Papua New Guinea's Ok Tedi mine and the impact on West Papuan refugee communities living on the Fly River downstream from the mine. Michael has a professional background in geology and environmental science.

Sarah Richards-Hewat is a consulting anthropologist with a BA (Hons) in Psychology and a PhD in Anthropology. She is interested in sexuality, gender, morality and West Papua, where she has done extensive fieldwork. Sarah has published on topics including hip hop and HIV and has worked in the international development sector on various issues including female genital mutilation, post-disaster reconstruction, emergency management, mental health, waste management and post-conflict social restoration.

Paige West is the Claire Tow Professor of Anthropology at Barnard College and Columbia University. She has conducted ethnographic field research in Papua New Guinea since 1996 and is the co-founder of The Papua New Guinea Institute of Biological Research and The Ranguva Solwara Skul. She currently serves as the director of the Center for the Study of Social Difference at Columbia University. She is the author of three books about Papua New Guinea and her most recent book, *Dispossession and the environment: Rhetoric and inequality in Papua New Guinea* (2016), was the winner of the 2017 Columbia University Press Distinguished Book Award.

Laura Zimmer-Tamakoshi (PhD, Bryn Mawr College) has held positions at the University of Papua New Guinea and Truman State University. She has undertaken research in Papua New Guinea since 1982. Focusing on inequality and its intersections, her interests include historical ethnography, economic anthropology, gender, the social impacts of migration, mining and unequal development, and the politics of culture. Her publications include *First fieldwork: Pacific anthropology, 1960–1985* (editor, 2018) and 'Inequality and changing masculinities among the Gende in Papua New Guinea' in *Emergent Masculinities in the Contemporary Pacific* (special issue of *The Asia Pacific Journal of Anthropology*, edited by Aletta Biersack, Margaret Jolly and Martha Macintyre, 2016).